BRASSERIE
Abbaye du Val-Dieu
Brune
satan
ARTOIS
Brugs
ABBAYE · ABDIJ
Blond-Blonde
Affligem
BIERE DES TRAPPIST
10
ORVAL
SCOTCH
GORDON
Westvleteren
CHIMAY
Trappist
MAES
25cl
PRIMUS
VEDETT
CERVEZA-BIRRA

All Belgian Beers
Les Bières Belges
Alle Belgische Bieren

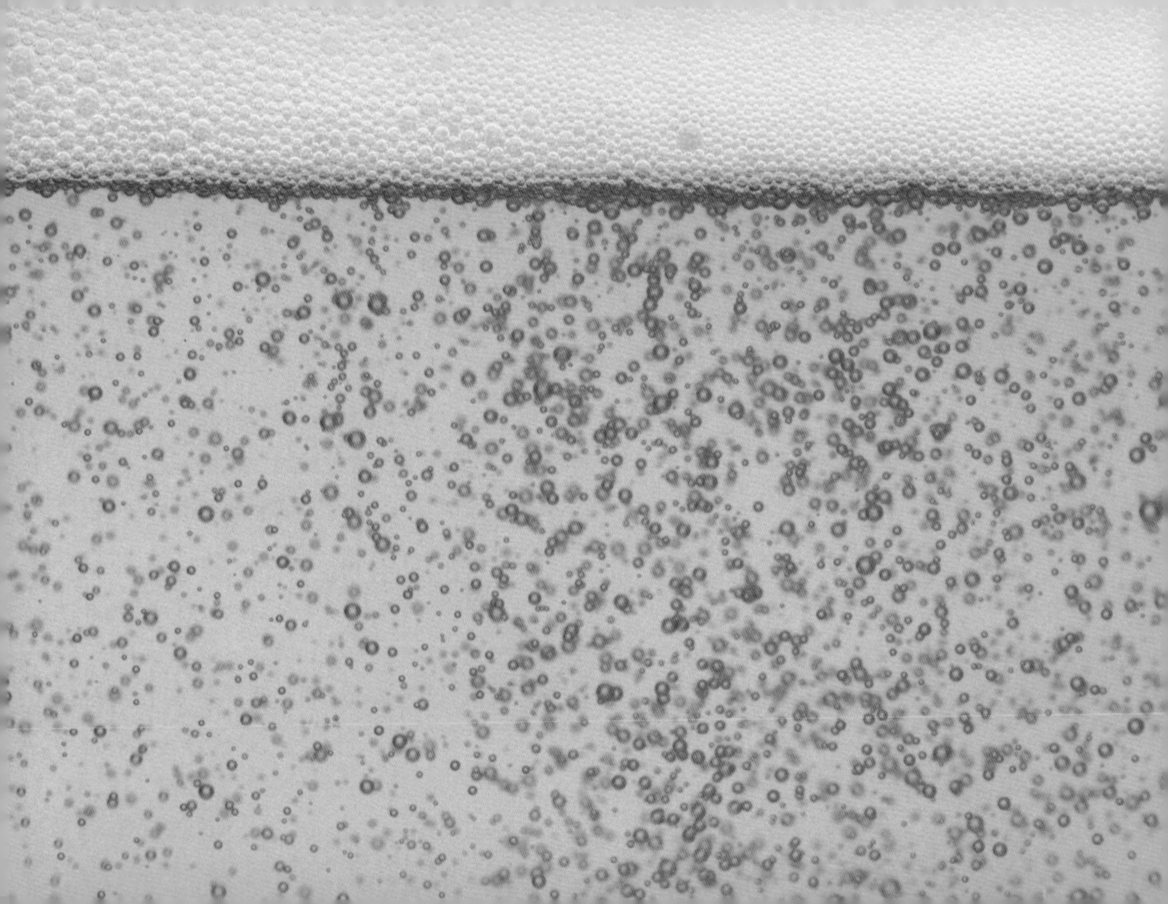

All Belgian Beers

Les Bières Belges

Alle Belgische Bieren

stichting kunstboek

Preface

Even though the Belgian beer culture needs no introduction when it comes to quality and diversity, we are a long way off the bottom of this incredible riches. In fact, this book is living proof of this: where the previous edition comprised more than 700 Belgian beers, we have now come to the rather gratifying conclusion that there are more than 1,000. What better proof is there to illustrate that Belgian beer is on the up?

This development has not come out of nowhere. Over the past decades, we have clearly noticed that the Belgians still enjoy a refreshing pint of amber or white beer, but that they increasingly venture out to the special beers that are enjoyed with a discriminating palate and knowledge. Moreover, considerably more smaller breweries have been set up, which is exactly what makes our country unique: very large and very small breweries, and anything in between, can cater for every individual.

Not just for the Belgian connoisseur, by the way. Only a few years ago, we witnessed a historic event in that we now export more beer than we drink. And it's not just our neighbouring countries that are familiar with our vast range of beers. The rest of the world has also caught on to this well-kept secret now, and with the publication of this unique beer encyclopaedia, this treasure trove is being uncovered further still.

There are countries where the consumption of beer is higher than ours, which boast more and larger breweries and which brew very good beers indeed, but there is no other beer country in the world that accommodates so many beers, breweries, beer styles and types and fermentation processes per square mile.

Welcome to Beerparadise Belgium, for which this book provides the perfect SatNav.

Sven Gatz
Belgian Brewers Director

➤ pg 10

Préface

Célébrer la culture de la bière belge pour sa qualité et sa diversité, c'est enfoncer des portes ouvertes. Et pourtant, nous sommes encore loin de voir la fin de cette richesse inimaginable. Ce livre en est la preuve vivante : si sa précédente édition comptait déjà plus de sept cents bières belges, nous sommes fiers de pouvoir dire ici que nous dépassons à présent très largement les mille. Qu'imaginer de mieux pour démontrer la bonne santé de la bière belge ?

Cette évolution ne s'est pas faite d'un coup de baguette magique. Ces dernières décennies, nous voyons très clairement que certes le Belge raffole toujours d'un demi bien rafraîchissant et d'une délicieuse ambrée ou d'une savoureuse bière blanche, mais également qu'il ou elle prend de plus en plus le chemin des bières spéciales, ces bières que l'on déguste avec goût et réflexion. L'on enregistre en outre l'apparition d'un nombre nettement plus important de microbrasseurs sur la scène de la bière, et cela a le don de rendre notre pays tout simplement unique : de fort grosses et de fort petites brasseries et tous les formats intermédiaires, il y en a pour tous les goûts.

Et pas uniquement d'ailleurs pour le fin connaisseur belge. Voici quelques années seulement, une inversion historique est intervenue : nous exportons désormais davantage de bière vers l'étranger que nous n'en buvons dans notre propre pays. Si jusqu'à il y a peu seuls nos pays voisins étaient familiarisés avec notre multiplicité de bières, c'est aujourd'hui le reste du monde qui a découvert ce secret bien gardé. Grâce à la publication de cet ouvrage encyclopédique unique, cette caverne d'Ali Baba de la bière se trouve encore mieux dévoilée.

Il existe des pays qui boivent plus de bière que nous, qui possèdent plus de brasseries et de plus grosses et qui brassent aussi de la fort bonne bière, mais il n'existe aucun autre pays de la bière où l'on rencontre autant de bières, de brasseries, de styles et de sortes de bière et de méthodes de fermentation par kilomètre carré.

Bienvenue donc dans le Beerparadise Belgium, pour lequel ce livre constitue le GPS idéal.

Sven Gatz
Directeur Brasseurs Belges

➤ pg 11

Voorwoord

De Belgische Biercultuur roemen om haar kwaliteit en diversiteit is een open deur intrappen. Toch zijn we nog lang niet aan het eind van deze onvoorstelbare rijkdom gekomen. Dit boek is daar het levende bewijs van: telde de vorige uitgave ervan al meer dan zevenhonderd Belgische bieren, dan komen we hier tot de prettige vaststelling dat we nu heel ruim boven de duizend uitkomen. Bestaat er een beter bewijs dat het goed gaat met het Belgisch Bier?

Deze evolutie kwam er niet zomaar. De laatste decennia zien we heel duidelijk dat de Belg nog altijd van een verfrissende pint en lekker amber of witbier houdt, maar ook dat hij of zij meer en meer de weg inslaat van de speciale bieren, die men met smaak en met verstand degusteert. Daarnaast zijn er ook beduidend meer microbrouwers op het biertoneel verschenen en dat maakt ons land net uniek: hele grote en hele kleine brouwerijen en alles wat daartussen zit, bieden voor elk wat wils.

En niet alleen voor de Belgische fijnproever overigens. Enkele jaren geleden nog maar vond een historische ommezwaai plaats: we exporteren nu meer bier naar het buitenland dan dat we er in eigen land drinken. Waren tot voor kort enkel onze buurlanden vertrouwd geraakt met onze veelheid aan bieren, dan heeft nu ook de rest van de wereld dit goed bewaard geheim ontdekt. Met de uitgave van dit unieke encyclopedische boek wordt deze biergrot van Ali Baba verder onthuld.

Er bestaan landen die meer bier drinken dan wij, die meer en grotere brouwerijen hebben en die ook zeer goed bier brouwen, maar er is geen enkel ander bierland waar zoveel bieren, brouwerijen, bierstijlen en -soorten en gistingswijzen per vierkante kilometer bestaan.

Welkom in Beerparadise Belgium, waarvoor dit boek de geschikte GPS is.

Sven Gatz
Directeur Belgische Brouwers

➤ pg 12

The *All Belgian Beers* book (updated version 2011) offers an alphabetical overview of the beers, brewed by the recognised Belgian (contract) brewers for their own assortment or for other beer companies.

The brewers are divided into four categories (see the overview on page 1185) according to Filip Geerts' website www.belgianbeerboard.com:

- Brewers who have their own brewery infrastructure.
- Belgian Brew Firms: "Brewery renters", as they are called in Belgium, who do not possess a (complete) brewing infrastructure and brew part or all of their beer at the facilities of fellow brewers.
- Belgian Beer Firms: Contract brewers, individuals or companies, who commercialise beers with an original recipe as their main product, without brewing the beers themselves. They hire a brewery to produce their beers – in part or all of it – according to their guidelines.
- Gueuze blenders who buy lambic from different brewers and blend it according to their own recipes.

This beer catalogue features both beers from big, industrial companies and from smaller craft breweries, microbreweries or home breweries, as long as they are bottled and sold.

Own-label beers brewed for supermarkets and private-label beers have deliberately not been included in this publication. Occasional beers are partially presented. The reason has nothing to do with their taste or quality, but rather with the almost infinite number of these beers that exist in the Belgian market. Many occasional beers are created to give a personal or festive touch to some regional event. Almost any association or village has its own beer, which is not really a surprise: after all, we are talking about Belgium...

Publications like these are only a snapshot of the country at a certain moment in time. Not all Christmas and summer beers were available during the production phase of this book. Therefore, the list of seasonal beers described here is certainly not exhaustive. Some small breweries did not have certain beers in stock because they were temporarily sold out. On the other hand, there are undoubtedly already new beers available today, while others may have disappeared all together.

The choise has been made to provide only objective information, leaving assessments and ratings to the beer lovers and experts. Only facts and figures, provided by the brewers themselves, have been included: fermenting and beer style, composition, alcohol content, colour, brightness, how to serve and temperatures. The brewers also give their personal description of the character and taste of their beers, but in the end it is up to the individual tasters to indicate their preferences.

We wish you a cheerful – or should we say: "beerful" – discovery!

Hilde Deweer
Compiler

Vous trouverez en effet dans *Toutes les bières belges* (version mise à jours 2011) un aperçu alphabétique des bières brassées par les brasseurs (ou brasseurs locataires) belges, qu'ils soient reconnus pour leur propre assortiment ou par les firmes brassicoles.

Selon le site internet www.belgianbeerboard.com de Filip Geerts, l'on y distingue quatre catégories (voir aperçu à la page 1185)

- Les brasseurs qui disposent de leur propre infrastructure brassicole.
- Les locataires de brasserie – à savoir les brasseurs qui ne disposent pas d'une installation de brassage (complète) et qui brassent partiellement ou totalement chez un collègue brasseur.
- Les sociétés brassicoles – en l'occurrence les personnes ou entreprises qui ont pour activité principale la commercialisation de bières de recette originale mais qu'ils ne brassent pas eux-mêmes. Ils les font produire (entièrement ou partiellement) 'à façon' par une brasserie.
- Les coupeurs de gueuze qui achètent du lambic à différents brasseurs et les mélangent selon leur goût.

Tant les bières de grands industriels que celles des brasseries familiales sont prises en compte dans ce catalogue. Et ce, pour autant qu'elles soient mises en bouteille et mises en vente.

Les bières brassées et distribuées sous des marques mandatées par des supermarchés et les bières à étiquette ne sont pas, et c'est un choix, prises en considération. Les bières de circonstance ou bières occasionnelles sont partiellement représentées. Ce parti pris n'est pas dicté par des critères de goût ou de qualité, mais par la quantité énorme de bières que cela représenterait. En effet, de nombreuses bières occasionnelles résultent d'une touche personnelle ou festive dans le cadre d'un événement ou happening régional. Chaque association et village possèdent sa propre bière. Comment pourrait-il en être autrement en Belgique !

Une publication dans ce domaine est par nature un instantané partiel. Ainsi, lors de l'élaboration de ce livre, toutes les bières de Noël et d'été n'étaient pas disponibles. Ce dernier ne présente donc pas la liste exhaustive de toutes les bières de saison. Des brasseries de plus petite taille ne possédaient parfois plus certaines bières en réserve car elles étaient temporairement épuisées. Par ailleurs, de nouvelles bières seront entre-temps apparues sur le marché alors que d'autres auront peut-être disparu.

Un autre parti pris pour cette édition a été de ne donner que des informations objectives. Les appréciations et les cotations sont laissées aux papilles gustatives des fans et experts de bières. Seules les fiches signalétiques fournies par les brasseurs eux-mêmes sont reprises ici: nature de la fermentation et style de bière, composition et pourcentage d'alcool, couleur et clarté, méthode de servir et température idéale. L'occasion a été donnée à chaque brasseur de décrire le caractère et le goût de ses bières. En fin de compte toutefois, il revient au goûteur individuel de pointer ses préférences dans sa 'bible de la bière'.

Nous vous souhaitons une belle ballade riche en saveurs et découvertes !

Hilde Deweer
Rédactrice

Alle Belgische Bieren (updated versie 2011) biedt een alfabetisch overzicht van de bieren die worden gebrouwen door de erkende Belgische (huur)brouwers voor het eigen assortiment of voor dat van de bierfirma's.

Er wordt hierbij een onderscheid gemaakt tussen vier categorieën (zie overzicht op pagina 1185) volgens de website www.belgianbeerboard.com van Filip Geerts:

- De brouwers met een eigen brouwerij-infrastructuur.
- De brouwerijhuurders: brouwers die niet zelf beschikken over een (volledige) brouwinstallatie en die gedeeltelijk of volledig gaan brouwen bij een collega-brouwer.
- De bierfirma's: personen of firma's die bieren met een origineel recept als hoofdactiviteit commercialiseren maar niet zelf brouwen. Zij laten hun bieren (volledig of gedeeltelijk) 'à façon' produceren door een brouwerij.
- De geuzestekers: kopen lambiek aan bij verschillende brouwers en gaan die mengen volgens eigen smaak.

Zowel de bieren van grote industriële concerns als die van artisanale micro- of huisbrouwerijen komen in deze biercatalogus aan bod, voor zover ze gebotteld zijn en te koop worden aangeboden.

Distributiemerken gebrouwen in opdracht van supermarkten en etiketbieren worden in deze publicatie bewust buiten beschouwing gelaten. Gelegenheidsbieren of occasionele bieren zijn beperkt vertegenwoordigd. Deze keuze is niet ingegeven door smaak- of kwaliteitsnormen, maar heeft veeleer te maken met de haast onoverzienbare hoeveelheid aan bieren die deze oefening zou opleveren. Veel gelegenheidsbieren zijn immers het resultaat van een persoonlijke of feestelijke toets die aan een evenement of regionale happening wordt gegeven. Bijna iedere vereniging, quasi elk dorp heeft – hoe kan het ook anders in België – zijn eigen biertje.

Elke publicatie is een momentopname. Niet alle kerst- en zomerbieren waren beschikbaar tijdens de productiefase van dit boek. Het totale geregistreerde aanbod aan seizoensbieren is dus zeker geen exhaustieve lijst. Enkele kleinere brouwerijen hadden ook hier of daar een bier niet op voorraad omdat het tijdelijk was uitverkocht. Daarnaast zullen er intussen ongetwijfeld ook al nieuwe bieren hun opwachting maken, terwijl andere misschien alweer verdwenen zijn.

Bij de samenstelling van deze uitgave werd bewust gekozen om enkel objectieve informatie te geven. Beoordelingen en quoteringen worden overgelaten aan de geoefende smaakpapillen van de bierfanaten en -experten. Enkel de beschikbare facts en figures, verschaft door de brouwers zelf, zijn hier aan de orde: gisting en bierstijl, samenstelling en alcoholpercentage, kleur en helderheid, schenkmethode en -temperatuur. De brouwer is ook zelf aan het woord bij de omschrijving van het karakter en de smaak van zijn bieren, maar uiteindelijk is het aan de individuele proever om zijn bevindingen en eventuele voorkeuren in 'zijn'of 'haar' bierbijbel aan te stippen.

We wensen u een geestrijke ontdekkingstocht!

Hilde Deweer
Samensteller

Alcohol by volume percentage / ° plato Pourcentage d'alcool / ° plato Alcoholgehalte / ° plato	%	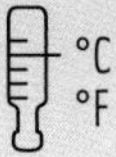	Temperature Température Schenktemperatuur

	Fermentation	Fermentation	Gisting
	Beer style	Style de bière	Bierstijl
	Ingredients	Ingrédients	Ingrediënten
	Colour and transparancy	Couleur et clarté	Kleur en helderheid
	Character, taste and flavour	Caractère, goût et saveur	Karakter, smaak en aroma
	How to serve	Méthode de servir	Schenkmethode
	Tips and facts	Conseils et détails intéressants	Tips en weetjes

Aardmonnik

De Struise Brouwers at Brouwerij Deca

8%

	mixed fermentation	fermentation mixte	gemengde gisting
	Flemish old brown	vieille brune flamande	Vlaams oud bruin
	pilsner, caramel malt, carafa, corn, wheat malt, candy sugar, yeast, water, hops (Bramling Cross, Hallertau Mittelfrueh), herbs (cinnamon, sweet orange rind, thyme, coriander), matures in oak barrels for 18 months.	malt de pils et de caramel, carafa, maïs, malt de froment, sucre candi, levure, eau, houblon (Bramling Cross, Hallertau Mittelfrueh), herbes (cannelle, écorce d'orange doux, thym, coriandre). Mûrit en fûts de chêne pendant 18 mois.	pilsmout, karamelmout, carafa, maïskorn, tarwemout, kandijsuiker, gist, water, hop (Bramling Cross, Hallertau Mittelfrueh), kruiden (kaneel, zoete sinaasschil, tijm, koriander). Rijpt 18 maanden op eikenhouten vaten.
	(91 EBC) dark brown unfiltered, not pasteurised creamy foam head	brun foncé (91 EBC) non filtrée, non pasteurisée faux col crémeux	donkerbruin (91 EBC) ongefilterd, niet gepasteuriseerd romige schuimkraag
	Complex, earthy aroma with a wine-like elegance.	Arôme terreux complexe avec une élégance de vin.	Complex aards aroma met een wijnachtige elegantie.
	The name of the beer refers to its earthy character. It is a blend of 2 top-fermenting beers with an identical method of preparation.	Le nom de la bière renvoie à son caractère terreux. La bière est un mélange de 2 bières à fermentation haute qui se préparent de la même façon.	De naam verwijst naar het aardachtig karakter. Het bier is een blend van 2 bovengistende bieren van identieke receptuur.

Abbaye de Forest

Brasserie de Silly — **6,50% (14° plato)** — 5 - 8 °C / 41 - 46 °F

	top-fermentation re-fermented in the bottle	fermentation haute refermentation en bouteille	hoge gisting hergisting in de fles
	tripel regional beer	triple bière régionale	tripel streekbier
	pale malt, sugar, yeast, Kent and Hallertau hops, water	malt pâle, sucre, levure, houblon Kent et Haller-tau, eau	bleke mout, suiker, gist, Kent en Hallertauhop, water
	(9,8 EBC) blonde	blonde (9,8 EBC)	blond (9,8 EBC)
	Slighty perfumed char-acter beer with a fine bitter taste, and a subtle fruitiness of dry grapes which provides a re-freshing bitter in the throat.	Bière de caractère légè-rement parfumée avec un goût amer raffiné. Laisse une saveur fruitée subtile de raisins secs aboutissant en un goût amer rafraîchissant dans la gorge.	Licht geparfumeerd ka-rakterbier met fijn-bit-tere smaak. Laat een subtiele fruitigheid van droge druiven na die uit-mondt in een opkikke-rend bitter in de keel.
	Provision beer brewed with respect for the ab-bey beer tradition.	Bière de conservation brassée en respectant la tradition des bières d'abbaye.	Bewaarbier gebrouwen met respect voor de tra-ditie van het abdijbier.

Abbaye de la Thure

Brasserie Brootcoorens

10% | 6 - 14 °C | 43 - 57 °F

	top-fermentation natural re-fermentation in the bottle	fermentation haute refermentation naturelle en bouteille	hoge gisting natuurlijke hergisting in de fles
	abbey beer double natural	bière d'abbaye double naturelle	abdijbier dubbel natuurbier
	barley malt, wheat, Erquelinnes hops (grown locally), yeast, herbs, water	malt d'orge, froment, houblon d'Erquelinnes (cultivée sur place) herbes, eau	gerstemout, tarwe, hop van Erquelinnes (ter plaatse geteeld), gist, kruiden, water
	dark, clear not filtered or pasteurised	fonceé, claire non filtrée, non pasteurisée	donker, helder ongefilterd, niet gepasteuriseerd
	Serve in a clean, degreased Pokal Harzer glass. Store the bottle upright.	Verser dans un verre Pokal Harzer dégraissé et rincé. Conserver la bouteille en position verticale.	Uitschenken in een ontvet en gespoeld Pokal Harzer-glas. De fles rechtop bewaren.
	Limited production. Beer dedicated to the Hainault abbey (13th - end 18th century) along the banks of the river Thure.	Production limitée. Bière dédiée à l'abbaye hainuyère (13e - fin du 18e siècle) sur les rives de la Thure.	Beperkte productie. Bier opgedragen aan de Henegouwse abij (13e - eind 18e eeuw) aan de oevers van de Thure.

Brasserie de Brunehaut

7% 6 °C 43 °F

Abbaye de Saint-Martin Blonde

	top-fermentation naturally re-fermented in the bottle	fermentation haute refermentation naturelle en bouteille	hoge gisting natuurlijke hergisting in de fles
	Recognised Belgian blond abbey beer	Bière d'abbaye belge reconnue, blonde	Erkend Belgisch Abdijbier blond
	malt, hops, yeast, herbs, water	malt, houblon, levure, herbes, eau	mout, kruiden, hop, gist, water
	gold-coloured, clear with creamy foam head	dorée, claire avec un faux col crémeux	goudkleurig, helder met romige schuimkraag
	Round, balanced and full onset. Then floral, elegant, almost feminine. Pleasant bitter aftertaste.	Approche initiale ronde, équilibrée et franche. Ensuite fleuri, élégant, presque féminin. Agréable amertume en arrière-bouche.	Ronde, evenwichtige en volle aanzet. Daarna bloemig, elegant, bijna vrouwelijk. Aangename bitterheid in de afdronk.
	Brewed for the first time in 1096 in the St. Martin's Abbey of Tournai. Perfect match for hard-rind cheeses.	Brassée pour la première fois en 1096 à l'abbaye de Saint-Martin à Tournai. Accompagne parfaitement les fromages à croûte dure.	Voor de eerste maal gebrouwen in 1096 in de abdij van St-Martin in Doornik. Perfecte match voor kazen met harde korst.

A

Abbaye de Saint-Martin Brune

Brasserie de Brunehaut 8% 7 °C 44 °F

	top-fermentation naturally re-fermented in the bottle	fermentation haute refermentation naturelle en bouteille	hoge gisting natuurlijke hergisting in de fles
	Recognised Belgian dark abbey beer	Bière d'abbaye belge reconnue, brune	Erkend Belgisch Abdijbier dubbel
	malt, hop, yeast, herbs, water	malt, houblon, levure, herbes, eau	mout, kruiden, hop, gist, water
	mahogany, clear with creamy foam head	acajoue, claire avec faux col crémeux	acajou, helder met romige schuimkraag
	Roasted and grilled aromas and flavours with dominant hint of caramel. A pleasant freshness that provides balance.	Touches rôties et grillées dans le bouquet et la bouche, caramel prononcé. Une agréable fraîcheur, source d'équilibre.	Geroosterde en gegrilde toetsen in neus en mond, uitgesproken karamel. Een aangename frisheid die voor evenwicht zorgt.
	Brewed for the first time in 1096 in the St.Martin's Abbey of Tournai. Voted the world's best brown Abbey beer in 2009 (WBA).	Brassée pour la première fois en 1096 à l'abbaye de Saint-Martin à Tournai. Élue meilleure bière d'abbaye brune au monde en 2009 (WBA).	Voor de eerste maal gebrouwen in 1096 in de abdij van St-Martin in Doornik. Verkozen tot beste bruin abdijbier ter wereld in 2009 (WBA).

Brasserie de Brunehaut 8,50% 7 °C 44 °F

Abbaye de Saint-Martin Cuvée de Noël

	top-fermentation natural re-fermentation in the bottle	fermentation haute refermentation naturelle en bouteille	hoge gisting natuurlijke hergisting in de fles
	Recognised Belgian tripel abbey beer winter beer	Triple d'abbaye belge reconnue bière hivernale	Erkend Belgisch Abdijbier tripel winterbier
	malt, herbs, hops, yeast, water	malt, herbes, houblon, levure, eau	mout, kruiden, hop, gist, water
	dark amber, clear with a creamy foam head filtered, not pasteurised	ambré foncé, claire avec un faux col crémeux filtrée, non pasteurisée	donkeramber, helder met een romige schuimkraag gefilterd, niet gepasteuriseerd
	Surprising, spicy nose and taste: cinnamon, clove, warm eastern herbs.	Bouquet et goût surprenants, épicés :cannelle, clou de girofle, épices orientales chaudes.	Verrassende, kruidige neus en smaak: kaneel, kruidnagel, warme oosterse kruiden.
	Serve in a tulip glass.	Verser dans un verre tulipe.	Uitschenken in een tulpglas.
i	Brewed for the first time in the abbey of St Martin in Tournai in 1096. Silver medal 'World Beer Championship' 2011 in Chicago.	Brassée pour la première fois en 1096 à l'abbaye de Saint-Martin à Tournai. Médaille d'argent 'World Beer Championship' 2011 à Chicago.	Voor de eerste maal gebrouwen in 1096 in de abdij van St-Martin in Doornik. Zilveren medaille 'World Beer Championship' 2011 in Chicago.

A

Abbaye de Saint-Martin Triple

Brasserie de Brunehaut

9% 7 °C 44 °F

	top-fermentation natural re-fermentation in the bottle	fermentation haute refermentation naturelle en bouteille	hoge gisting natuurlijke hergisting in de fles
	Recognised Belgian tripel abbey beer	Triple d'abbaye belge reconnue	Erkend Belgisch Abdijbier tripel
	malt, herbs, hops, yeast, water	malt, herbes, houblon, levure, eau	mout, kruiden, hop, gist, water
	Gold, clear with a creamy foam head filtered, not pasteurised	dorée, claire avec un faux col crémeux filtrée, non pasteurisée	Goud, helder met een romige schuimkraag gefilterd, niet gepasteuriseerd
	Nimble, smooth, full-bodied onset. Rich sipping beer.	Première approche souple, ronde, pleine. Riche bière de dégustation.	Soepele, ronde, volle aanzet. Rijk degustatiebier.
	Serve in a tulip glass.	Verser dans un verre tulipe.	Uitschenken in een tulpglas.
	Brewed for the first time in the abbey of St Martin in Tournai in 1096. Gold medal 'World Beer Championship' 2011 in Chicago.	Brassée pour la première fois en 1096 à l'abbaye de Saint-Martin à Tournai. Médaille d'or 'World Beer Championship' 2011 à Chicago.	Voor de eerste maal gebrouwen in 1096 in de abdij van St-Martin in Doornik. Gouden medaille 'World Beer Championship' 2011 in Chicago.

Abbaye des Rocs Blonde

Brasserie de l'Abbaye des Rocs 7,50% (16° plato) 6 °C 43 °F

top-fermentation	fermentation haute	hoge gisting
Belgian abbey beer blond	Bière d'abbaye belge blonde	Belgisch abdijbier blond
malt (pilsner), hops (Hallertau, Brewers Gold), well water from a rocky subsoil	malt (pils), houblon (Hallertau, Brewers Gold), eau de puits d'un sous-sol rocailleux	mout (pilsen), hop (Hallertau, Brewers Gold), boorputwater uit een rotsrijke ondergrond
blonde	blonde	blond
White flowers and vanilla aromas. No herbs added. Rich flavour palette with a pronounced bitter taste.	Arômes de fleurs blanches et de vanille. Sans adjonction d'herbes. Riche en saveurs avec une amertume prononcée.	Aroma's van witte bloemen en vanille. Zonder toevoeging van kruiden. Rijk smakenpalet met uitgesproken bitterheid.
Savour in a balloon glas.	A déguster dans un verre ballon.	Degusteren in een ballonvormig glas.
The abbey 'L'Abbaye des Rocs' dates back from the 12th century. The beer keeps for about a year in a dark room. Also known as 'Nounette triple blonde'.	'L'Abbaye des Rocs' date du 12ième siècle. La bière se conserve environ un an à l'abri de la lumière. Même bière que la 'Nounette triple blonde'.	De abdij 'L'Abbaye des Rocs' dateert uit de 12e eeuw. Het bier is ongeveer een jaar houdbaar in een donkere ruimte. In het buitenland wordt dit bier verkocht onder de naam 'Nounette triple blonde'.

A

Abbaye des Rocs Brune

Brasserie de l'Abbaye des Rocs **9% (18° plato)** 12 °C 54 °F

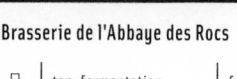

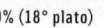

	top-fermentation	fermentation haute	hoge gisting
	Belgian abbey beer dark - ale	Bière d'abbaye belge foncée - ale	Belgisch abdijbier donker - ale
	malt (pale, Münich, biscuit, roasted, caramel, aromatic), hops (Hallertau, Styrie, Brewers Gold), well water from a rocky subsoil	malt (pâle, Münich, biscuit, brûlé, caramélisé, aromatique), houblon (Hallertau, Styrie, Brewers Gold), eau de puits d'un sous-sol rocailleux	mout (bleek, Münich, biscuit, gebrand, karamel, aromatisch), hop (Hallertau, Styrie, Brewers Gold), boorputwater uit een rotsrijke ondergrond
	Brown-red like the volcano stone from the region.	Brun rouge comme la pierre de volcan de la région.	Bruinrood zoals de vulkaansteen uit de regio.
	Full-bodied bitterness, balanced by a fruity flavour. Touches of roasty wood and a very long aftertaste.	Saveur amère corsée, équilibrée par un certain goût fruité. Touches de bois brûlé et arrière-bouche prolongée.	Gecorseerde bitterheid in evenwicht gebracht door een zekere fruitigheid. Toetsen van gebrand hout en zeer lange nasmaak.
	Savour in a balloon glass.	A déguster dans un verre ballon.	Degusteren uit een ballonvormig glas.
	The abbey 'L'Abbaye des Rocs' dates back from the 12th century. The beer keeps for about a year in a dark room.	'L'Abbaye des Rocs' date du 12ième siècle. La bière se conserve environ un an à l'abri de la lumière.	De abdij 'L'Abbaye des Rocs' dateert uit de 12e eeuw. Het bier bewaart ongeveer een jaar in een donkere ruimte.

Abbaye des Rocs Grand Cru

A

Brasserie de l'Abbaye des Rocs 10% (18° plato) 12 °C 54 °F

	top-fermentation	fermentation haute	hoge gisting
	Belgian abbey beer dark - ale	Bière d'abbaye belge foncée - ale	Belgisch abdijbier donker - ale
	malt (pale, (cara) Münich, biscuit, roasted, caramel, aromatic), hops (Hallertau, Styrie, Saaz, Brewers Gold), well water from a rocky subsoil	malt (pâle, (cara)Münich, biscuit, brûlé, caramélisé, aromatique), houblon (Hallertau, Styrie, Saaz, Brewers Gold), eau de puits d'un sous-sol rocailleux	mout (bleek, (cara) Münich, biscuit, gebrand, karamel, aromatisch), hop (Hallertau, Styrie, Saaz, Brewers Gold), boorputwater uit een rotsrijke ondergrond
	dark red	rouge foncé	donkerrood
	Complex but very powerful aroma, influenced by herbs and hops. Easy digestible in spite of its density.	Arôme complexe mais très corsé par les herbes et le houblon. Facilement digestible malgré sa densité.	Complex maar zeer krachtig aroma beïnvloed door kruiden en hop. Licht verteerbaar ondanks zijn densiteit.
	Savour in a balloon glass.	A déguster dans un verre ballon.	Degusteren uit een ballonvormig glas.
	The abbey 'L'Abbaye des Rocs' dates back from the 12th century. The beer keeps for about a year in a dark room. Originally created for the American market, now also available in Europe.	'L'Abbaye des Rocs' date du 12ième siècle. La bière se conserve environ un an à l'abri de la lumière. Fabriquée à l'origine pour le marché américain, maintenant également disponible en Europe.	De abdij 'L'Abbaye des Rocs' dateert uit de 12e eeuw. Het bier bewaart ongeveer een jaar in een donkere ruimte. Oorspronkelijk gemaakt voor de Amerikaanse markt, nu ook in Europa verkrijgbaar.

Abbaye des Rocs, Spéciale Noël

Brasserie de l'Abbaye des Rocs 9% 12 °C 54 °F

	top-fermentation centrifuged	fermentation haute centrifugée	hoge gisting gecentrifugeerd
	Christmas beer	bière de Noël	kerstbier
	well water, malt, hops and herbs. No sugar or chemical additives added.	eau de puits, malt, houblon et herbes. Aucune ajoute de sucre ou d'additifs chimiques.	putwater, mout, hop en kruiden. Geen suiker of chemische additieven toegevoegd.
	red-brown not filtered	brun rouge non filtrée	roodbruin ongefilterd
	Complex aroma, powerful thanks to the hops and herbs used. Easily digestible despite its density.	Arôme complexe, puissant dû au houblon et aux épices utilisés. Facilement digestible malgré sa densité.	Complex aroma, krachtig door de gebruikte hop en kruiden. Gemakkelijk verteerbaar ondanks zijn dichtheid.
	Serve in a balloon glass.	Verser dans un verre ballon.	Uitschenken in een ballonglas
i			

Brouwerij der Sint-Benedictusabdij De Achelse Kluis

8% — 8 °C / 46 °F

	top-fermentation	fermentation haute	hoge gisting
	trappist	trappiste	trappist
	malt, hops, yeast, water	malt, houblon, levure, eau	mout, hop, gist, water
	golden blond slightly cloudy by re-fermentation in the bottle	blond doré légèrement trouble par la refermentation en bouteille	goudblond lichttroebel door hergisting op de fles
	Intense character. Hop flavour with a slight touch of caramel, typical yeast flavour. Bitter and a little fruity with some green banana. Dry aftertaste with some hoppy bitter.	Caractère intense. Arôme houblonné avec touche légèrement caramélisée, arôme de levure typique. Amer et un peu fruité avec un peu de banane verte. Arrière-bouche sèche et un peu amère de houblon.	Intens karakter. Hoppig aroma met lichte karameltoets, typisch gistaroma. Bitter en beetje fruitig met wat groene banaan. Nasmaak droog en wat hopbitter.
	Pour slowly and leave approx. 1 cm of sediment in the bottle.	Verser doucement et laisser environ 1 cm de lie dans la bouteille.	Zachtjes uitschenken en ca. 1 cm in de fles laten.
	Brewed at Saint Benedict's Abbey.	Brassée dans l'Abbaye de Saint-Benoît.	Gebrouwen in de Sint-Benedictusabdij.

Achel Bruin

Brouwerij der Sint-Benedictusabdij De Achelse Kluis

8% | 8 °C 46 °F

	top-fermentation	fermentation haute	hoge gisting
	trappist	trappiste	trappist
	barley malt, hops, yeast, water	malt d'orge, houblon, levure, eau	gerstemout, hop, gist, water
	dark red-brown	brun rouge foncé	donker roodbruin
	Smooth but powerful. Flavour: candy, nuts, earth tones and some yeast. Taste: strong, full-bodied caramel taste. Aftertaste: hop and bitter.	Douce mais corsée, Arôme: candi, noix, tons terreux et un peu de levure. Saveur franche, caramélisée, prononcée. Arrière-bouche houblonnée et amère.	Zacht maar krachtig. Aroma: kandij, noten, aardse tonen en wat gist. Smaak: volmondig, flinke karamelsmaak. Nasmaak: hoppig en bitter.
	Pour slowly. Leave approx. 1 cm of sediment in the bottle and pour the yeast sediment if desired.	Verser doucement et laisser environ 1 cm de lie dans la bouteille. Le dépôt de levure peut éventuellement être versé.	Zachtjes uitschenken en ca. 1 cm in de fles laten. Het gistdepot mag desgewenst uitgeschonken worden.
i	Brewed at Saint Benedict's Abbey.	Brassée dans l'Abbaye de Saint-Benoît.	Gebrouwen in de Sint-Benedictusabdij.

Achel Bruin Extra

Brouwerij der Sint-Benedictusabdij De Achelse Kluis 10% 8 °C 46 °F

	top-fermentation re-fermented in the bottle	fermentation haute refermentation en bouteille	hoge gisting hergisting op de fles
	trappist	trappiste	trappist
	barley malt, hops, yeast, dark candy sugar, water	malt d'orge, houblon, levure, sucre candi brun, eau	gerstemout, hop, gist, donkere kandijsuiker, water
	red-brown	brun rouge	roodbruin
	Generous, frank character. Sweetish and full-bodied with a considerable alcohol taste. Slightly roasty with some chocolate touches. Strong and bitter with a caramel aftertaste.	Caractère royal et généreux. Douceâtre et franc avec un sérieux goût d'alcool. Un peu brûlé avec quelques touches de chocolat. Arrière-bouche fort amère et quelque peu caramélisée.	Royaal en gul karakter. Zoetig en volmondig met een serieuze streep alcohol. Beetje gebrand met wat chocoladetoetsen. Nadronk stevig bitter met karamelachtige nasmaak.
	Pour slowly and leave approx. 1 cm of sediment in the bottle.	Verser doucement et laisser environ 1 cm de lie dans la bouteille.	Zachtjes uitschenken en ca. 1 cm in de fles laten.
i	Brewed at Saint Benedict's Abbey.	Brassée dans l'Abbaye de Saint-Benoît.	Gebrouwen in de Sint-Benedictusabdij.

Ada Blonde des Pères 6°

Brasserie Val de Sambre — 6% (14° plato) — 8 °C / 46 °F

	top-fermentation	fermentation haute	hoge gisting
	abbey beer	bière d'abbaye	abdijbier
	first quality malts and hops	malts et houblons de premier choix	mouten en hoppen van eerste keuze
	gold-coloured	dorée	goudkleurig
	Subtle bitterness and pronounced round.	Goût amer subtil et rond prononcé.	Subtiele bitterheid en uitgesproken rond.
	Produced in the ruins of the Cistercian abbey of Aulne. ADA is short for Abbaye d'Aulne.	Fabriquée dans la ruine de l'abbaye des Cisterciennes d' Aulne. ADA est l'abrégé de Abbaye d'Aulne.	Wordt gefabriceerd in de ruïne van de Cisterciënzerinnenabdij van Aulne. ADA is de afkorting van Abbaye d'Aulne.

Ada Brune des Pères 6°

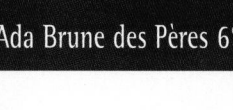

Brasserie Val de Sambre

6% (14° plato) — 10 °C / 50 °F

	top-fermentation	fermentation haute	hoge gisting
	abbey beer	bière d'abbaye	abdijbier
	first quality malts and hops	malts et houblons de premier choix	mouten en hoppen van eerste keuze
	deep copper	cuivre intense	diepkoper
	Rich, perfumed aroma and creamy mouthfeel.	Arôme riche, parfumé et sensation savoureuse dans la bouche.	Rijk, geparfumeerd aroma en smeuïg mondgevoel.
	Produced in the ruins of the Cistercian abbey of Aulne. ADA is short for Abbaye d'Aulne.	Fabriquée dans la ruine de l'abbaye des Cisterciennes d' Aulne. ADA est l'abrégé de Abbaye d'Aulne.	Wordt gefabriceerd in de ruïne van de Cisterciënzerinnenabdij van Aulne. ADA is de afkorting van Abbaye d'Aulne.

A

Ada Super Noël 9°

Brasserie Val de Sambre 9% (20° plato) 10 °C 50° F

	top-fermentation re-fermented in the bottle	fermentation haute refermentation en bouteille	hoge gisting hergisting in de fles
	abbey beer	bière d'abbaye	abdijbier
	first quality malts and hops	malts et houblons de premier choix	mouten en hoppen van eerste keuze
	Pour slowly.	Verser lentement.	Traag uitschenken.
	Produced in the ruins of the Cistercian abbey of Aulne. ADA is short for Abbaye d'Aulne.	Fabriquée dans la ruine de l'abbaye des Cisterciennes d' Aulne. ADA est l'abrégé de Abbaye d'Aulne.	Wordt gefabriceerd in de ruïne van de Cisterciënzerinnenabdij van Aulne. ADA is de afkorting van Abbaye d'Aulne.

Ada Triple Blonde 8°

Brasserie Val de Sambre 6,30% 8 °C 46 °F

	top-fermentation re-fermented in the bottle	fermentation haute refermentation en bouteille	hoge gisting hergisting in de fles
	abbey beer	bière d'abbaye	abdijbier
	first quality malts and hops	malts et houblons de premier choix	mouten en hoppen van eerste keuze
	golden warm colour	dorée chaude	gulden warme kleur
	Round, strong and subtle flavour.	Goût rond, fort et subtil.	Ronde, sterke en subtie-le smaak.
	Pour slowly.	Verser lentement.	Traag uitschenken.
	Produced in the ruins of the Cistercian abbey of Aulne. ADA is short for Abbaye d'Aulne.	Fabriquée dans la ruine de l'abbaye des Cister-ciennes d' Aulne. ADA est l'abrégé de Ab-baye d'Aulne.	Wordt gefabriceerd in de ruïne van de Cisterciën-zerinnenabdij van Aulne. ADA is de afkorting van Abbaye d'Aulne.

Ada Triple Brune 8°

Brasserie Val de Sambre 8% 8° C 46° F

	top-fermentation re-fermented in the bottle	fermentation haute refermentation en bouteille	hoge gisting hergisting in de fles
	abbey beer	bière d'abbaye	abdijbier
	first quality malts and hops	malts et houblons de premier choix	mouten en hoppen van eerste keuze
	Powerful aroma.	Arôme puissant.	Krachtig aroma.
	Pour slowly.	Verser lentement.	Traag uitschenken.
	Produced in the ruins of the Cistercian abbey of Aulne. ADA is short for Abbaye d'Aulne.	Fabriquée dans la ruine de l'abbaye des Cisterciennes d' Aulne. ADA est l'abrégé de Abbaye d'Aulne.	Wordt gefabriceerd in de ruïne van de Cisterciënzerinnenabdij van Aulne. ADA is de afkorting van Abbaye d'Aulne.

Ada Val de Sambre 6° Ambrée

Brasserie Val de Sambre 6,40% 8 °C 46 °F

	top-fermentation re-fermented in the bottle	fermentation haute refermentation en bouteille	hoge gisting hergisting in de fles
	abbey beer	bière d'abbaye	abdijbier
	first quality malts and hops	malts et houblons de premier choix	mouten en hoppen van eerste keuze
	amber	ambrée	amberrood
	Character beer in perfect harmony with the powerful and refined aromas.	Bière de caractère, en parfaite harmonie avec les arômes puissants et raffinés.	Karakterbier in perfecte harmonie met de krachtige en verfijnde aroma's.
	Produced in the ruins of the Cistercian abbey of Aulne. ADA is short for Abbaye d'Aulne.	Fabriquée dans la ruine de l'abbaye des Cisterciennes d' Aulne. ADA est l'abrégé de Abbaye d'Aulne.	Wordt gefabriceerd in de ruïne van de Cisterciënzerinnenabdij van Aulne. ADA is de afkorting van Abbaye d'Aulne.

Adelardus Trudoabdijbier

Brouwerij Kerkom by Brouwerij Sint-Jozef or Proefbrouwerij 7%

top-fermentation re-fermented in the bottle	fermentation haute refermentation en bouteille	hoge gisting nagisting op de fles
abbey beer dubbel	bière d'abbaye double	abdijbier dubbel
made with gruit (herbs), 5 malt varieties, 2 Belgian hop varieties, dark candy sugar, yeast, well water	fabriquée de gruit (herbes), 5 sortes de malt, 2 sortes de houblon belges, sucre candi foncé, levure, eau de source	gemaakt met gruut (kruiden), 5 moutsoorten, 2 Belgische hopsoorten, donkere kandijsuiker, gist, bronwater
dark, unfiltered	foncée, non filtrée	donker, ongefilterd
A full taste with a soft, slightly spicy nose and a light, bitter aftertaste.	Saveur pleine avec parfum moelleux légèrement relevé et une arrière-bouche légèrement amère.	Een volle smaak met zachte, licht kruidige neus en een licht bittere nasmaak.
Gently pour into a degreased, dry glass without sloshing and leave 1 cm yeast sediment in the bottle or add it at the end.	Verser tranquillement sans clapotage dans un verre dégraissé et sec. Laisser un dépôt de levure de 1 cm dans la bouteille ou ajouter par après.	Rustig inschenken zonder klokgeluid in een ontvet en droog glas. Een gistdepot van 1 cm in de fles laten of achteraf bijgieten.
In the past, gruits or groats were subject to taxes and the brewers had to buy it at the Gruuthuus, the groats house.	Le gruit était frappé d'impôts dans des siècles précédents et le brasseur devait se le procurer dans le 'Gruuthuus'.	Gruut werd in vroegere eeuwen belast en de brouwer moest het aankopen in het Gruuthuus.

Adelardus Trudoabdijbier Tripel

Brouwerij Kerkom by Brouwerij Sint-Jozef or Proefbrouwerij 9%

	top-fermentation re-fermented in the bottle	fermentation haute refermentation en bouteille	hoge gisting nagisting op de fles
	tripel	triple	tripel
	2 malt varieties, 2 Belgian hop varieties, white candy sugar, gruut, yeast, brewing water	2 sortes de malt, 2 sortes belges de houblon, sucre candi blanc, gruyt, levure, eau de brassage	2 moutsoorten, 2 Belgische hopsoorten, witte kandijsuiker, gruut, gist, brouwwater
	high blond to light orange unfiltered	blond doré à orange clair non filtrée	hoogblond tot licht oranje ongefilterd
	Complex and full with vanilla and honey flavour. Beer with high alcohol content with a very long, slightly bitter and full aftertaste.	Complexe et pleine avec un arôme de vanille et de miel. Bière de dégustation avec une arrière-bouche très longue légèrement amère et pleiné.	Complex en vol met aroma van vanille en honing. Degustatiebier met een zeer lange, licht bittere en volle nasmaak.
	Gently pour into a degreased, dry glass without sloshing and leave a 1 cm yeast sediment in the bottle or add it at the end.	Verser tranquillement sans clapotage dans un verre dégraissé et sec. Laisser un dépôt de levure de 1 cm dans la bouteille ou ajouter par après.	Rustig inschenken zonder klokgeluid in een ontvet en droog glas. Een gistdepot van 1 cm in de fles laten of achteraf bijgieten.
	Brewed for the opening of the abbey tower in Sint-Truiden on May 1st, 2005.	Brassée à l'occasion de l'ouverture de la tour de l'abbaye à Saint-Trond le 1 ier mai 2005.	Gebrouwen ter gelegenheid van de opening van de Abdijtoren in Sint-Truiden op 1 mei 2005.

Adler

Brouwerij Haacht

6,50% 3 °C 37 °F

bottom-fermentation centrifuged	fermentation basse centrifugée	lage gisting gecentrifugeerd
Dortmunder pilsner	pilsen Dortmunter	dortmunderpils
barley malt, maize, sugar, hops, water	malt d'orge, maïs, sucre, houblon, eau	gerstemout, mais, suiker, hop, water
gold-coloured, clear foam head with fine bubbles filtered	dorée claire avec un faux col à petites bulles filtrée	goudkleurig, helder met fijnbellige schuimkraag gefilterd
Lager beer with the full taste of special beer and the thirst-quenching character of pilsner. Fine aroma and a sweet palette with bitter undertones and a well-balanced dry aftertaste. Fine flavour with a well-balanced, dry aftertaste.	Bière blonde avec la saveur pleine d'une bière spéciale et le caractère désaltérant d'une pils. Arôme raffiné et une palette douceâtre avec un peu d'amertume dans le fond et une arrière-bouche sèche équilibrée.	Lagerbier met de volle smaak van speciaalbier en het dorstlessende karakter van pils. Fijn aroma en een zoetig palet met wat bitter op de achtergrond en een uitgebalanceerde droge afdronk.
Pour carefully into a rinsed, wet glass, avoiding contact with the glass or foam.	Verser prudemment dans un verre rincé, humide sans que la bouteille touche le verre ou l'écume	Voorzichtig uitschenken in een gespoeld, nat glas zonder dat de fles het glas of schuim raakt.

Brouwerij Roman 8,50% 6 °C 43 °F

Adriaen Brouwer

A

	top-fermentation re-fermented in the bottle	fermentation haute refermentation en bouteille	hoge gisting hergisting in de fles
	Belgian style strong ale	Belgian style strong ale	Belgian style strong ale
	barley malt, maize, hops, candy sugar, yeast, well water	malt d'orge, maïs, houblon, sucre candi, levure, eau de source	gerstemout, mais, hop, kandijsuiker, gist, bronwater
	red-brown clear creamy foam head	brun rouge claire faux col crémeux	roodbruin helder romige schuimkraag
	Sipping beer with a thirst-quenching character. Caramel malt aroma. Caramel sweet bitterish taste.	Bière de dégustation avec un caractère désaltérant. Arôme caramel malté. Saveur douce caramélisée et amère.	Degustatiebier met een dorstlessend karakter. Karamelmoutig aroma. Karamelzoete bitterige smaak.
	Slowly pour into a degreased, rinsed beer glass, forming a nice foam head.	Verser lentement dans un verre de bière dégraissé et rincé et former un faux col solide.	Langzaam uitschenken in een ontvet en gespoeld bierglas en een mooie schuimkraag vormen.
	Store in a dark, cool room. Adriaen Brouwer was a famous painter from Oudenaarde.	Conserver à l'abri de la lumière et de la chaleur. Adriaen Brouwer était un peintre fameux d'Audenarde.	Donker en koel bewaren. Adriaen Brouwer was een bekende Oudenaardse schilder.

Adriaen Brouwer Dark Gold

Brouwerij Roman 8,50% 6° 43°

	top-fermentation re-fermentation in the bottle	fermentation haute refermentation en bouteille	hoge gisting hergisting in de fles
	Flemish brown or old brown	Flamande brune ou vieille brune	Vlaams bruin of oud bruin
	malt, hops, sugar, yeast, brewing water	malt, houblon, sucre, levure, eau de brassage	mout, hop, suiker, gist, brouwwater
	brown (70 EBC)	brune (70 EBC)	bruin (70 EBC)
	Strong brown with hoppy aroma. Taste: touches of caramel, chocolate and dried fruit.	Brune forte à l'arôme houblonné. Goût :touches de caramel, de chocolat et de fruits secs.	Sterk bruin met hoppig aroma. Smaak: toetsen van karamel, chocolade en gedroogd fruit.
	Pour out with care and leave approx. 1/2 cm in the bottle.	Verser prudemment et laisser ca. 1/2 cm dans la bouteille.	Voorzichtig uitschenken en ca. 1/2 cm in de fles laten.
i	Adriaen Brouwer is a 17th century painter from Oudenaarde who could appreciate a nice beer. The Adriaen Brouwer Bier Festival takes place in Oudenaarde the last weekend of June.	Adriaen Brouwer est un peintre d'Audenarde du 17e siècle qui raffolait d'une bonne petite bière. Le dernier week-end de juin, les Adriaen Brouwer Bierfeesten se déroulent à Audenarde.	Adriaen Brouwer is een Oudenaardse schilder uit de 17e eeuw die hield van een lekker biertje. Het laatste weekend van juni vinden in Oudenaarde de Adriaen Brouwer Bierfeesten plaats.

Brouwerij Alken-Maes 6,80% 8 - 10 °C 46 - 50 °F

	top-fermentation re-fermented in the bottle	fermentation haute refermentation en bouteille	hoge gisting hergisting in de fles
	Recognised Belgian blond abbey beer	Bière d'abbeye belge reconnue, blonde	Erkend Belgisch abdijbier blond
	barley malt, hops, yeast, water	malt d'orge, houblon, levure, eau	gerstemout, hop, gist, water
	gold-coloured clear	dorée claire	goudkleurig helder
	Fresh, strong, aromatic smell. Malty, hoppy taste with pleasant, bitter aftertaste.	Parfum frais, très aromatisé. Saveur maltée, houblonnée avec fin de bouche amère agréable.	Frisse, sterk aromatische geur. Moutige, hoppige smaak met aangename bitterheid in de afdronk.
	Slowly pour, leaving the yeast in the bottle.	Verser lentement et laisser la levure dans la bouteille.	Langzaam uitschenken en de gist in de fles laten.
	The abbey of Affligem is located on the border of the provinces of Flemish-Brabant and East-Flanders. It was founded in 1074 as a Benedictine convent.	L'abbaye de Affligem est située à la frontière des provinces du Brabant flamand et de la Flandre orientale et a été fondée en 1074 comme monastère de bénédictins.	De abdij van Affligem ligt op de grens van de provincies Vlaams-Brabant en Oost-Vlaanderen en ontstond in 1074 als Benedictijnerklooster.

Affligem Dubbel

Brouwerij Alken-Maes 6,80% 8 - 10 °C 46 - 50 °F

	top-fermentation re-fermented in the bottle	fermentation haute refermentation en bouteille	hoge gisting hergisting in de fles
	Recognised Belgian dark abbey beer	Bière d'abbaye belge reconnue, brune	Erkend Belgisch abdijbier donker
	barley malt, hops, yeast, water	malt d'orge, houblon, levure, eau	gerstemout, hop, gist, water
	red-brown	brun rouge	roodbruin
	Mild, slightly spicy taste with slightly sweet and smooth aftertaste. Roasty candy flavour.	Saveur tendre, légèrement relevée avec une fin de bouche légèrement douce et moelleuse. Parfum de candi brûlé.	Milde, licht kruidige smaak met lichtzoete en zachte afdronk. Geur van gebrande kandij.
	Slowly pour, leaving the yeast in the bottle.	Verser lentement et laisser la levure dans la bouteille.	Langzaam uitschenken en de gist in de fles laten.
i	The abbey of Affligem is located on the border of the provinces of Flemish-Brabant and East-Flanders. It was founded in 1074 as a Benedictine convent.	L'abbaye de Affligem est située à la frontière des provinces du Brabant flamand et de la Flandre orientale et a été fondée en 1074 comme monastère de bénédictins.	De abdij van Affligem ligt op de grens van de provincies Vlaams-Brabant en Oost-Vlaanderen en ontstond in 1074 als Benedictijnerklooster.

Affligem Tripel

Brouwerij Alken-Maes 9,50% 8 - 10 °C / 46 - 50 °F

	top-fermentation re-fermented in the bottle	fermentation haute refermentation en bouteille	hoge gisting hergisting in de fles
	Recognised Belgian tripel abbey beer	Bière d'abbaye belge reconnue, triple	Erkend Belgisch abdijbier tripel
	barley malt, blond candy sugar, hops, yeast, water	malt d'orge, sucre candi blanc, houblon, levure, eau	gerstemout, blonde kandijsuiker, hop, gist, water
	deep golden very full foam head	doré intense faux col très solide	diepgoud zeer volle schuimkraag
	Spicy, bitter character. Full, complex taste with hop and malt flavour.	Corsée, caractère amer. Saveur pleine, complexe avec un arôme de houblon et de malt.	Pittig, bitter karakter. Volle, complexe smaak met aroma van hop en mout.
	Slowly pour, leaving the yeast in the bottle.	Verser lentement et laisser la levure dans la bouteille.	Langzaam uitschenken en de gist in de fles laten.
i	The abbey of Affligem is located on the border of the provinces of Flemish-Brabant and East-Flanders. It was founded in 1074 as a Benedictine convent.	L'abbaye de Affligem est située à la frontière des provinces du Brabant flamand et de la Flandre orientale et a été fondée en 1074 comme monastère de bénèdictins.	De abdij van Affligem ligt op de grens van de provincies Vlaams-Brabant en Oost-Vlaanderen en ontstond in 1074 als Benedictijnerklooster.

A Agrumbocq

Brasserie du Bocq

3,10% 4 - 6 °C 39 - 43 °F

	top-fermentation re-fermentation in the bottle	fermentation haute refermentation en bouteille	hoge gisting hergisting in de fles
	white beer with fruit (juice)	bière blanche fruitée	witbier met fruit(sap)
	barley malt, wheat, natural aromas of citrus fruits (8%), tangerine juice, sugar, sweeteners, hops, yeast, water	malt d'orge, froment, arômes naturels d'agrumes (8%), jus de mandarine, sucre, édulcorant, houblon, levure, eau	gerstemout, tarwe, natuurlijke aroma's van citrusvruchten (8%), mandarijnsap, suiker, zoetstof, hop, gist, water
	pink grapefruit colour, cloudy, fine pale-pink foam head	couleur de pamplemousse rose, trouble, faux col fin légèrement rose	kleur van roze pompelmoes, troebel, fijne lichtroze schuimkraag
	Fruity nose. Perfect balance between delicate flavours, acidified by the citrus and slight bitterness.	Bouquet fruité. Équilibre parfait d'un goût doux, acidifié par le citrus et une légère amertume.	Fruitige neus. Perfect evenwicht van een zachte smaak, aangezuurd door de citrus en een lichte bitterheid.

Brouwerij Nieuwhuys 10%

	top-fermentation	fermentation haute	hoge gisting
	dark tripel	triple foncée	donkere tripel
	barley malt, wheat, Poperinge hops, yeast, water	malt d'orge, froment, houblon de Poperinge, levure, eau	gerstemout, tarwe, Poperingse hop, gist, water
	Named after Countess Alpaïde who governed the County of Bruningrode. She founded the Huardis chapter which later became the beer village of Hoegaarden.	Elle doit son nom à la comtesse Alpaïde, qui a régné sur le comté de Bruningerode. Celle-ci fonda le chapitre d'Huardis, qui devint plus tard le village de la bière d'Hoegaarden.	Genoemd naar gravin Alpaïde die regeerde over het graafschap Bruningrode. Ze stichtte het kapittel Huardis dat later het bierdorp Hoegaarden werd.

Alpaïde Blond, Cuvée van de generaal

Brouwerij Nieuwhuys 8,50%

	top-fermentation	fermentation haute	hoge gisting
	blond tripel	triple blonde	blonde tripel
	barley malt, wheat, Poperinge hops, yeast, water	malt d'orge, froment, houblon de Poperinge, levure, eau	gerstemout, tarwe, Poperingse hop, gist, water

Altitude 6

Brasserie de l'Abbaye des Rocs **6% (12° plato)** 6 °C 43 °F

	top-fermentation	fermentation haute	hoge gisting
	ale	ale	ale
	pale malt, hops (Hallertau, Brewers Gold), well water from a rocky subsoil	malt pâle, houblon (Hallertau, Brewers Gold), eau de puits d'un sous-sol rocailleux	bleke mout, hop (Hallertau, Brewers Gold), boorputwater uit een rotsrijke ondergrond
	blond	blonde	blond
	Soft, refreshing flavour with a refined bitterness.	Rafraîchissante, arôme moelleux avec une amertume raffinée.	Verfrissend, zacht aroma met een geraffineerde bitterheid.
	Savour in a glass with a stem.	À déguster dans un verre à pied.	Degusteren uit een glas met voet.
	The abbey 'L'Abbaye des Rocs' dates back from the 12th century. The beer keeps for about a year in a dark room.	'L'Abbaye des Rocs' date du 12ième siècle. La bière se conserve environ un an à l'abri de la lumière.	De abdij 'L'Abbaye des Rocs' dateert uit de 12e eeuw. Het bier is ongeveer een jaar houdbaar in een donkere ruimte.

Alvino

Picobrouwerij Alvinne 5,50%

	top-fermentation natural re-fermentation in the bottle	fermentation haute refermentation naturelle en bouteille	hoge gisting natuurlijke hergisting in de fles
	beer containing fresh grapes which matures in Burgundy casks for a few months.	bière avec raisins frais qui mûrit pendant quelques mois en fûts Bourgogne.	bier met verse druiven dat enkele maanden rijpt op Bourgognevaten.
	Touches of grapes and red wine.	Touches de raisins et de vin rouge.	Toetsen van druiven en rode wijn.
	Limited availability of the beer.	La disponibilité de la bière est réduite.	Het bier is beperkt beschikbaar.

Het Alternatief at Picobrouwerij Alvinne

10% 12 °C 54 °F

	top-fermentation re-fermentation in the bottle not centrifuged	fermentation haute refermentation en bouteille non centrifugée	hoge gisting hergisting in de fles niet gecentrifugeerd
	heavy stout	stout forte	zware stout
	many roasted malt varieties, quite hoppy bitter for a stout	plusieurs malts torréfiés, houblon assez amer pour un stout	veel gebrande mouten, tamelijk hopbitter voor een stout
	almost black (144 EBC) with dark beige foam head not filtered	presque noir (144 EBC) avec faux col beige foncé non filtrée	bijna zwart (144 EBC) met donkerbeige schuimkraag ongefilterd
	Malty, strong body, slightly bitter, many roasted malt varieties and very long aftertaste. Touches of dark chocolate, coffee and chicory root. 43 EBU.	Maltée, corps puissant, légèrement amere, beaucoup de malt torréfié et une arrière-bouche très longue. Touches de chocolat noir, de café et de racine de chicorée. 43 EBU.	Moutig, sterke body, licht bitter, veel gebrande mout en zeer lange afdronk. Toetsen van donkere chocolade, koffie en cichoreiwortel. 43 EBU.
	Serve in a tulip glass.	Verser dans un verre tulipe.	Uitschenken in een tulpglas.
	The logo on the label has been designed especially for the beer by the Izegem artist Johan Herman.	La statuette sur l'étiquette a été créée spécialement pour la bière par l'artiste izegemois Johan Herman.	Het beeldje op het etiket werd speciaal voor het bier gemaakt door de Izegemse kunstenaar Johan Herman.

Ambetanterik

Angelus Blonde

Brasserie Brootcoorens **7%** 4 - 14 °C / 39 - 57 °F

	top-fermentation	fermentation haute	hoge gisting
	specialty beer blond	bière spéciale blonde	speciaalbier blond
	pilsner and amber malt, home-grown aromatic hops, yeast, water	malt de pils et d'ambre, houblon aromatique de propre culture, levure, eau	pils- en ambermout, aromatische hop van eigen teelt, gist, water
	light amber unfiltered	ambré clair non filtrée	licht amber niet gefilterd
	Lively, natural beer with hoppy taste and aroma.	Bière naturelle vive avec saveur et arôme houblonnés.	Levend natuurbier met hoppige smaak en aroma.
	Take care not to agitate the bottle and pour carefully.	Prendre soin que la bouteille n'a pas été secouée et verser prudemment.	Zorgen dat de fles niet geschud is en voorzichtig uitschenken.
i			

Brasserie Brootcoorens 7% 8 - 14 °C 46 - 57 °F

Angelus Brune

A

	top-fermentation	fermentation haute	hoge gisting
	dubbel	double	dubbel
	pilsner and amber malt, chocolate malt, aromatic hops, a touch of carafa, yeast, water	malt de pils et d'ambre, malt de chocolat, houblon aromatique, une pointe de carafa, levure, eau	pils- en ambermout, chocolademout, aromatische hop, een vleugje carafa, gist, water
	brown and transparent unfiltered	brune et transparente non filtrée	bruin en transparant niet gefilterd
	Pleasant, smooth and very accessible character. Subtle Carafa flavour and aromatic hop.	Caractère doux, agréable et très abordable. Saveur subtile de carafa et de houblon aromatique.	Aangenaam, zacht en zeer toegankelijk karakter. Subtiele smaak van carafa en aromatische hop.
	Take care not to agitate the bottle and pour carefully.	Prendre soin que la bouteille n'a pas été secouée et verser prudemment.	Zorgen dat de fles niet geschud is en voorzichtig uitschenken.

Angelus Spéciale Noël

Brasserie Brootcoorens 9% 4 - 10 °C / 39 - 50 °F

	top-fermentation	fermentation haute	hoge gisting
	Christmas beer	bière de Noël	kerstbier
	pilsner and amber malt, aromatic hops, yeast, water	malt de pils et d'ambre, houblon aromatique, levure, eau	pils- en ambermout, aromatische hop, gist, water
	copper-blond	blond cuivré	koperblond
	Pleasant, round and original but very accessible creamy beer with vanilla flavour. Prepared on a open fire with extra malt.	Agréable, ronde et originale mais très abordable. Bière onctueuse avec saveur de vanille, cuisson à feu nu avec adjonction accrûe de malt.	Aangenaam, rond en origineel maar toch zeer toegankelijk zacht bier met vanillesmaak. Gekookt op open vuur met extra mout.
	Take care not to agitate the bottle and pour carefully.	Prendre soin que la bouteille n'a pas été secouée et verser prudemment.	Zorgen dat de fles niet geschud is en voorzichtig uitschenken.
(i)			

Brouwerij Het Anker 3,50% 5 - 7 °C 41 - 45 °F

Anker Boscoulis

	top-fermentation	fermentation haute	hoge gisting
	fruity boutique beer based on blond	bière artisanale fruitée à base de bière blonde	artisanaal fruitbier op basis van blond
	barley malt, hops, sugar, yeast, fruit juice, water	malt d'orge, houblon, sucre, levure, jus de fruits, eau	gerstemout, hop, suiker, gist, vruchtensap, water
	burgundy brown	brun bordeaux	bordeauxbruin
	Smooth and well-balanced.	Douce et équilibrée.	Zacht en uitgebalanceerd.
	Refers to the culinary term 'coulis': a liquid substance of pureed fruits.	Renvoie au terme culinaire 'coulis' : une substance liquide de fruits en purée.	Verwijst naar de culinaire term 'coulis': een vloeibare substantie van gepureerde vruchten.

Anker Pils

Brouwerij Het Anker

5,20% — 4 - 5 °C / 39 - 41 °F

	bottom-fermentation	fermentation basse	lage gisting
	pilsner	pils	pils
	only Belgian hops	houblon exclusivement belge	uitsluitend Belgische hop
	gold-yellow	jaune doré	goudgeel
i	Only available in the region of Mechelen. Brewed in honour of the inhabitants of Mechelen who tried to extinguish the moon...	Seulement disponible dans la région de Malines et brassée en l'honneur des Malinois qui essayaient d'éteindre la lune...	Enkel verkrijgbaar in de regio Mechelen en gebrouwen ter ere van de Mechelaars die de maan probeerden te blussen...

Antiek Blond

Brouwerij Deca 8% 6 - 10 °C / 43 - 50 °F

	top-fermentation fermentation in the bottle	fermentation haute refermentation en bouteille	hoge gisting hergisting in de fles
	ale	ale	ale
	barley malt, hops, candy sugar, yeast, water	malt d'orge, houblon, sucre candi, levure, eau	gerstemout, hop, kandijsuiker, gist, water
	amber	ambrée	amber
	Full-bodied character. Slighty bitter.	Caractère franc, légèrement amere.	Volmondig karakter. Lichtbitter.
	Bottle can be emptied.	Peut être versée complètement.	Mag helemaal uitgeschonken worden.
	The brewery has existed since the 19th century.	La brasserie existe déjà depuis le 19 ième siècle.	De brouwerij bestaat al sinds de 19e eeuw.

Antiek Bruin

Brouwerij Deca

8% 6 - 10 °C 43 - 50 °F

	top-fermentation fermentation in the bottle	fermentation haute refermentation en bouteille	hoge gisting hergisting in de fles
	ale	ale	ale
	barley malt, hops, candy sugar, yeast, water	malt d'orge, houblon, sucre candi, levure, eau	gerstemout, hop, kandijsuiker, gist, water
	dark brown	brun foncé	donkerbruin
	Bottle can be emptied.	Peut être versée complètement.	Mag helemaal uitgeschonken worden.

Antiek Super 5 Blond

Brouwerij Deca 5% 6 - 10 °C / 43 - 50 °F

	top-fermentation fermentation in the bottle	fermentation haute refermentation en bouteille	hoge gisting hergisting in de fles
	ale	ale	ale
	barley malt, hops, candy sugar, yeast, water	malt d'orge, houblon, sucre candi, levure, eau	gerstemout, hop, kandijsuiker, gist, water
	blond	blonde	blond
	Bottle can be emptied.	Peut être versée complètement.	Mag helemaal uitgeschonken worden.

A

Antwerps Blond Bier

Brouwerij 't Pakhuis

5% 2 - 3 °C / 36 - 37 °F

	top-fermentation not centrifuged	fermentation haute non centrifugée	hoge gisting niet gecentrifugeerd
	blond	blonde	blond
	malt, barley, hops, water	malt, orge, houblon, eau	mout, gerst, hop, water
	light blond and cloudy; not filtered or pasteurised	blonde clair, très voilée; non filtrée ni pasteurisée	lichtblond met zeer duidelijke troebele schijn; ongefilterd, niet gepasteuriseerd
	Refreshing thirst-quenching session beer with a delicious aroma of malt and fine hops.	Bière rafraîchissante, facilement buvable. Caractère désaltérant. Arôme délicieux de malt et de houblon fin.	Frisse, vlotte doordrinker. Dorstlessend met een heerlijk aroma van mout en fijne hop.
	Pour into a bulb glass with long stem.	Verser dans un verre ballon à pied haut.	Uitschenken in een bol glas op hoge voet.
	Available at 't Pakhuis Brewery only.	Disponible seulement à la Brasserie 't Pakhuis.	Enkel verkrijgbaar in 't Pakhuis.

Antwerps Bruin Bier

A

Brouwerij 't Pakhuis 5,80% 2 - 3 °C / 36 - 37 °F

	top-fermentation not centrifuged	fermentation haute non centrifugée	hoge gisting niet gecentrifugeerd
	dubbel	double	dubbel
	coloured malt, barley, hops, water	malt coloré, orge, houblon, eau	gekleurde mout, gerst, hop, water
	light black, clear with a nice thin foam head; filtered, not pasteurised	presque noire, claire, avec joli faux col fin; filtrée, non pasteurisée	lichtzwart met heldere schijn en mooie, dunne schuimkraag; gefilterd, niet gepasteuriseerd
	More full-bodied and longer aftertaste than the blond beer owing to the coloured malt types. Typical brown-beer flavour.	Un goût un peu plus franc et une arrière-bouche plus longue que la bière blonde, dus aux variétés colorées de malt. Goût typique de la bière brune.	Iets volmondiger smaak en langere afdronk dan het blonde bier door de gekleurde moutsoorten. Typische smaak van bruin bier.
	Pour into a bulb glass with long stem.	Verser dans un verre ballon à pied haut.	Uitschenken in een bol glas op hoge voet.
	Available at 't Pakhuis Brewery only.	Disponible seulement à la Brasserie 't Pakhuis.	Enkel verkrijgbaar in 't Pakhuis.

Brouwerij Lindemans 3,50% 3 - 4 °C 37 - 39 °F

	spontaneous fermentation	fermentation spontanée	spontane gisting
	fruit beer based on Lambic	bière fruitée à base de lambic	fruitbier op basis van lambiek
	malt, wheat, hop, apple juice (25%), fructose, water	malt, froment, houblon, jus de pommes (25%), fructose, eau	mout, tarwe, hop, appelsap (25%), fructose, water
	yellow slightly hazy	jaune légèrement voilée	geel licht gesluierd
	Fruity character. Lively and strong onset turning into a balance of sweet (fruit) and smooth sour (lambic).	Caractère fruité. Début vif et corsé passant à un équilibre entre le caractère doux (fruits) et légèrement acidulé (lambic).	Fruitig karakter. Levendige en sterke aanzet die overgaat in een evenwicht van zoet (fruit) en zacht zuur (lambiek).
	Pour into a flute glass.	A verser dans une flûte.	In een fluitglas uitschenken.
i	Suitable as an aperitif and as a thirst-quencher.	Convient comme apéritif et comme boisson désaltérante.	Geschikt als aperitief en als dorstlesser.

Apple White Beer

Corsendonk by Brasserie du Bocq **3,10%** 4 - 6 °C / 39 - 43 °F

	top-fermentation	fermentation haute	hoge gisting
	white beer with fruit (juice)	bière blanche fruitée	witbier met fruit(sap)
	light straw blond	jaune paille clair	licht stroblond
	Fruity apple aromas.	Arômes de pomme fruités.	Fruitige appelaroma's.

Applebocq

Brasserie du Bocq 3,10% 2 - 4 °C / 36 - 39 °F

	top-fermentation	fermentation haute	hoge gisting
	fruit beer	bière fruitée	fruitbier
	barley malt, wheat, hop varieties, yeast, herbs, apple juice (30%), water, natural apple juicearo-mas	malt d'orge, froment, houblon, levure, herbes, jus de pommes (30%), eau, arômes naturels de jus de pommes	gerstemout, tarwe, hop, gist, kruiden, appelsap (30%), water, natuurlijke aroma's van appelsap
	straw-yellow (4 EBC) naturally cloudy	jaune paille (4 EBC) trouble naturelle	strogeel (4 EBC) natuurlijk troebel
	Nose that swings be-tween apple and cinna-mon, on a coriander and bitterorange base. Slightly sour apple, sweet with a touch of wheat.	Bouquet entre pomme et cannelle sur une base de coriandre et d'orange amère. Pomme légère-ment acidulée, douce avec une pointe de fro-ment.	Neus die schommelt tus-sen appel en kaneel, op een basis van koriander en bittere sinaasappel. Lichtzure appel, zoet met een tintje tarwe.
	Pour half of the bottle, then smoothly revolve it to loosen up the flavour palette and to enhance the cloudy effect. Pour the rest of the bottle.	Verser le verre à moitié plain, tourner la bou-teille pour dégager la palette aromatique et maximaliser l'effet trouble, puis verser le reste de la bière.	Het glas halfvol inschen-ken, de fles rondwalsen om het aromapalet los te maken en het troebel ef-fect te maximaliseren. De fles daarna uitschen-ken.
i			

Arabier

Brouwerij De Dolle Brouwers 8% 8 - 10 °C / 46 - 50 °F

	top-fermentation re-fermented in the bottle not centrifuged	fermentation haute refermentation en bouteille non centrifugée	hoge gisting nagisting op de fles niet gecentrifugeerd
	strong blond	blonde forte	sterk blond
	pale malt, nugget hops from Poperinge. Dry-hopping: part of the hops are submitted to lagering for a month.	malt pâle, cônes de houblon nugget de Poperinge. Dryhopping: une quantité de cônes de houblon est ajoutée pendant un mois.	bleke mout, nugget hopbellen uit Poperinge. Dryhopping: een hoeveelheid bellenhop gaat een maand in de lagering.
	blond unfiltered	blonde non filtrée	blond ongefilterd
	Bitter.	Amère.	Bitter.
	Connoisseurs prefer drinking it straight from the bottle.	Les connaisseurs préfèrent boire cette bière à la bouteille.	Kenners verkiezen dit bier uit de fles te drinken.
	Preferably drink one year before the best before date (see info on cap). The name refers to theArabic desert, where a fresh thirst-quencher like this one must be verywelcome.	Déguster de préférence 1 an avant la date de péremption (voir info capsule). Le nom se réfère au désert arabe où un désaltérant comme celui-ci doit être la bienvenue.	Bij voorkeur 1 jaar voor vervaldatum degusteren (zie info capsule). De naam refereert naar de Arabische woestijn waar een frisse dorstlesser als deze welkom moet zijn.

A

Arend Blond

Brouwerij De Ryck 6,50% 6 °C 43 °F

	top-fermentation re-fermented in the bottle	fermentation haute refermentation en bouteille	hoge gisting hergisting in de fles
	blond	blonde	blond
	malt, hops, yeast, sucrose, herbs, water	malt, houblon, levure, sucrose, herbes, eau	mout, hop, gist, sucrose, kruiden, water
	gold-coloured slightly hazy	dorée légèrement voilée	goud licht gesluierd
	Rich, spicy, warming. Smooth, slightly sweet and spicy taste with fresh yeast and hop aromas.	Riche, relevée, réchauffante. Saveur douce, légèrement sucrée et fruitée avec des parfums frais de levure et de houblon.	Rijk, kruidig, verwarmend. Zachte, licht zoete en kruidige smaak met frisse gist- en hopgeuren.
	Rinse the glass with cold water, take it by the stem and hold it slightly tilted. Pour slowly in a single movement, avoiding contact between bottle and glass or foam. Either leave the 1 cm yeast sediment in the bottle or pour it along with the beer.	Rincer le verre à l'eau froide, le tenir par le pied et légèrement en oblique. Verser la bière lentement et en un seul mouvement sans que la bouteille touche le verre ou l'écume. Laisser un dépôt de levure de 1 cm dans la bouteille ou la vider.	Het glas koud spoelen, bij de voet vastnemen en licht schuin houden. Het bier traag en in 1 beweging inschenken zonder dat de fles het glas of schuim raakt. Het gistdepot van 1 cm in de fles laten ofwel uitschenken.
	The draught version of this beer is clear (filtered).	La bière au fût est claire (filtrée).	Van het vat is het bier helder (gefilterd).

rouwerij De Ryck 6,50% 6 °C 43 °F

Arend Dubbel

	top-fermentation re-fermented in the bottle	fermentation haute refermentation en bouteille	hoge gisting hergisting in de fles
	dubbel	double	dubbel
	malt, hops, yeast, sucrose, herbs, water	malt, houblon, levure, sucrose, herbes, eau	mout, hop, gist, sucrose, kruiden, water
	brown slightly hazy	brune légèrement voilée	bruin licht gesluierd
	Rich and warming. Sweet caramel taste and flavour, combined with smooth hop bitterness.	Riche et réchauffante. Saveur caramélisée douce en combinaison avec le goût amer moelleux houblonné.	Rijk en verwarmend. Zoete karamelsmaak en -aroma in combinatie met zachte hopbitterheid.
	Rinse the glass with cold water, take it by the stem and hold it slightly tilted. Pour slowly in a single movement, avoiding contact between bottle and glass or foam. Either leave the 1 cm sediment in the bottle or pour it out along with the beer.	Rincer le verre à l'eau froide, le tenir par le pied et légèrement en oblique. Verser la bière lentement et en un seul mouvement sans que la bouteille touche le verre ou l'écume. Laisser un dépôt de levure de 1 cm dans la bouteille ou la vider.	Het glas koud spoelen, bij de voet vastnemen en licht schuin houden. Het bier traag en in 1 beweging inschenken zonder dat de fles het glas of schuim raakt. Het gistdepot van 1 cm in de fles laten ofwel uitschenken.
i	The draught version of this beer is clear (filtered).	La bière au fût est claire (filtrée).	Van het vat is het bier helder (gefilterd).

A Arend Tripel

Brouwerij De Ryck 8% 6° 43°

	top-fermentation re-fermentation in the bottle; centrifuged	fermentation haute refermentation en bouteille; centrifugée	hoge gisting hergisting in de fles; gecentrifugeerd
	tripel	triple	tripel
	barley malt, hops, sugar, sucrose, corn, herbs, yeast, water	malt d'orge, houblon, sucre, sucrose, maïs, herbes, levure, eau	gerstemout, hop, suiker, sucrose, maïs, kruiden, gist, water
	gold blond and slightly veiled filtered, not pasteurised	blond doré et légèrement voilée filtrée, non pasteurisée	goudblond en licht gesluierd gefilterd, niet gepasteuriseerd
	Sipping beer with hoppy nose and soft malt flavour. Soft bitter, heart-warming aftertaste.	Bière de dégustation au bouquet houblonné et au goût de malt doux. Arrière-bouche douce-amère, réchauffante.	Degustatiebier met hoppige neus en zachte moutsmaak. Zacht bittere, verwarmende afdronk.
	See Arend Blond	Voir Arend Blond	Zie Arend Blond
i	Arend [Eagle] refers to the brewery's original name (Brewery De Arend). This beer, a tribute to the founder Gustaaf De Ryck, has scooped different medals at international competitions (gold at the European beer star in Nuremberg and second at the tripel duel between Belgium and the Netherlands where Affligem tripel was the winner).	Arend fait référence au nom original de la brasserie (Brouwerij De Arend). Cette bière, un homm age au fondateur Gustaaf De Ryck, a obtenu à plusieurs reprises déjà des médailles à des concours internationaux (l'or à l'European Beer Star à Nuremberg, 2e au duel des tripel entre la Belgique et les Pays-Bas, où la gagnante a été l'Affligem Tripel).	Arend verwijst naar de originele naam van de brouwerij (Brouwerij De Arend). Dit bier, een eerbetoon aan de stichter Gustaaf De Ryck, kaapte al meermaals medailles op internationale wedstrijden (goud bij European beer star in Nürnberg, 2e op het tripelduel tussen België en Nederland waar Affligem tripel de winnnaar was).

Brouwerij De Ryck 6,30% 6 °C 43 °F

Arend Winter

A

top-fermentation re-fermentation in the bottle; centrifuged	fermentation haute refermentation en bouteille; centrifugée	hoge gisting hergisting in de fles; gecentrifugeerd
winter or Christmas beer ale	bière hivernale ou bière de Noël - ale	winter- of kerstbier ale
malt, hops, yeast, sugar, herbs, water	malt, houblon, sucre, levure, herbes, eau	mout, hop, gist, suiker, kruiden, water
dark amber, slightly veiled filtered, not pasteurised	ambré foncé, légèrement voilée filtrée, non pasteurisée	donker amber, licht gesluierd gefilterd, niet gepasteuriseerd
Typical winter beer with a heartwarming character, rich malt caramel taste, hoppy touches and a long aftertaste.	Bière hivernale typique au caractère réchauffant, un riche goût de caramel malt, des touches houblonnées et une longue arrière-bouche.	Typisch winterbier met verwarmend karakter, rijke mout-karamelsmaak, hoppige toetsen en een lange afdronk.
See Arend Blond	Voir Arend Blond	Zie Arend Blond
The earlier Christmas Pale Ale (recipe dating back to 1963) was given a makeover in 2007. Arend [Eagle] refers to the brewery's original name (Brouwerij De Arend) as a mark of honour to the founder Gustaaf De Ryck.	L'ancienne Christmas Pale Ale (recette de 1963) a reçu en 2007 une présentation rénovée. Arend fait référence au nom original de la brasserie (Brouwerij De Arend) et constitue un hommage au fondateur Gustaaf De Ryck.	De vroegere Christmas Pale Ale (recept uit 1963) in 2007 in een nieuw jasje gestoken. Arend verwijst naar de originele naam van de brouwerij (Brouwerij De Arend) en is een eerbetoon aan de stichter Gustaaf De Ryck.

A Armand'4 Herfst

Geuzestekerij 3 Fonteinen 6%

	spontaneous fermentation	fermentation spontanée	spontane gisting
	old gueuze	vieille gueuze	oude geuze
	mixture of lambic beer that is 1, 2 and 3 years old (60% barley malt, 40% wheat, more than one-year old hops, water) brewed, matured and bottled by Armand Debelder.	mélange de vieille lambic de 1,2, et 3 ans (60% de malt d'orge, 40% de froment, houblon âgé de plus d'un an,eau) brassé, mûri et mis en bouteille par Armand Debelder.	mengeling van 1, 2 en 3 jaar oude lambiek (60% gerstemout, 40% tarwe, overjaarse hop, water) gebrouwen, gerijpt en gebotteld door Armand Debelder.
	Limited and unique edition. The seasons refer to the four lambic elements (water, hops, wheat and air). The label displays Pajottenland and the Zenne as the original source of the wild yeasts. Armand'4 should be read as 'Armand's fier' [Armand's pride].	Tirage limité et unique. Les saisons font référence aux 4 éléments du lambic (eau, houblon, blé et air). Sur l'étiquette, l'on voit le Pajottenland et la Senne, en tant que source d'origine des levures sauvages. Armand'4 se lit 'Armand's fier'.	Beperkte en unieke oplage. De seizoenen verwijzen naar de 4 elementen van lambiek (water, hop, graan en lucht). Op het etiket staat het Pajottenland en de Zenne als oerbron van de wilde gisten. Armand'4 lees je als 'Armand's fier'.

	spontaneous fermentation	fermentation spontanée	spontane gisting
	old gueuze	vieille gueuze	oude geuze
	mixture of lambic beer that is 1, 2 and 3 years old (60% barley malt, 40% wheat, more than one-year old hops, water) brewed, matured and bottled by Armand Debelder.	mélange de vieille lambic de 1,2, et 3 ans (60% de malt d'orge, 40% de froment, houblon âgé de plus d'un an, eau) brassé, mûri et mis en bouteille par Armand Debelder.	mengeling van 1, 2 en 3 jaar oude lambiek (60% gerstemout, 40% tarwe, overjaarse hop, water) gebrouwen, gerijpt en gebotteld door Armand Debelder.
	Limited and unique edition. The seasons refer to the four lambic elements (water, hops, wheat and air). The label displays Pajottenland and the Zenne as the original source of the wild yeasts. Armand'4 should be read as 'Armand's fier' [Armand's pride].	Tirage limité et unique. Les saisons font référence aux 4 éléments du lambic (eau, houblon, blé et air). Sur l'étiquette, l'on voit le Pajottenland et la Senne, en tant que source d'origine des levures sauvages. Armand'4 se lit 'Armand's fier'.	Beperkte en unieke oplage. De seizoenen verwijzen naar de 4 elementen van lambiek (water, hop, graan en lucht). Op het etiket staat het Pajottenland en de Zenne als oerbron van de wilde gisten. Armand'4 lees je als 'Armand's fier'.

Armand'4 Winter

Geuzestekerij 3 Fonteinen

6%

	spontaneous fermentation	fermentation spontanée	spontane gisting
	old gueuze	vieille gueuze	oude geuze
	mixture of lambic beer that is 1, 2 and 3 years old (60% barley malt, 40% wheat, more than one-year old hops, water) brewed, matured and bottled by Armand Debelder.	mélange de vieille lambic de 1, 2, et 3 ans (60% de malt d'orge, 40% de froment, houblon âgé de plus d'un an, eau) brassé, mûri et mis en bouteille par Armand Debelder.	mengeling van 1, 2 en 3 jaar oude lambiek (60% gerstemout, 40% tarwe, overjaarse hop, water) gebrouwen, gerijpt en gebotteld door Armand Debelder.
	Limited and unique edition. The seasons refer to the four lambic elements (water, hops, wheat and air). The label displays Pajottenland and the Zenne as the original source of the wild yeasts. Armand'4 should be read as 'Armand's fier' [Armand's pride].	Tirage limité et unique. Les saisons font référence aux 4 éléments du lambic (eau, houblon, blé et air). Sur l'étiquette, l'on voit le Pajottenland et la Senne, en tant que source d'origine des levures sauvages. Armand'4 se lit 'Armand's fier'.	Beperkte en unieke oplage. De seizoenen verwijzen naar de 4 elementen van lambiek (water, hop, graan en lucht). Op het etiket staat het Pajottenland en de Zenne als oerbron van de wilde gisten. Armand'4 lees je als 'Armand's fier'.

Armand'4 Zomer

Geuzestekerij 3 Fonteinen 6%

	spontaneous fermentation	fermentation spontanée	spontane gisting
	old gueuze	vieille gueuze	oude geuze
	mixture of lambic beer that is 1, 2 and 3 years old (60% barley malt, 40% wheat, more than one-year old hops, water) brewed, matured and bottled by Armand Debelder.	mélange de vieille lambic de 1,2, et 3 ans (60% de malt d'orge, 40% de froment, houblon âgé de plus d'un an, eau) brassé, mûri et mis en bouteille par Armand Debelder.	mengeling van 1, 2 en 3 jaar oude lambiek (60% gerstemout, 40% tarwe, overjaarse hop, water) gebrouwen, gerijpt en gebotteld door Armand Debelder.
	Limited and unique edition. The seasons refer to the four lambic elements (water, hops, wheat and air). The label displays Pajottenland and the Zenne as the original source of the wild yeasts. Armand'4 should be read as 'Armand's fier' [Armand's pride].	Tirage limité et unique. Les saisons font référence aux 4 éléments du lambic (eau, houblon, blé et air). Sur l'étiquette, l'on voit le Pajottenland et la Senne, en tant que source d'origine des levures sauvages. Armand'4 se lit 'Armand's fier'.	Beperkte en unieke oplage. De seizoenen verwijzen naar de 4 elementen van lambiek (water, hop, graan en lucht). Op het etiket staat het Pajottenland en de Zenne als oerbron van de wilde gisten. Armand'4 lees je als 'Armand's fier'.

Artevelde

Brouwerij Huyghe 5,70% 5 ° 41 °

top-fermentation	fermentation haute	hoge gisting
amber or speciale belge	ambrée ou spéciale belge	amber of speciale belge
malt, hops, yeast, water	malt, houblon, levure, eau	mout, hop, gist, water
amber-coloured, clear with a slightly pearly and solid foam head filtered, pasteurised	ambrée, limpide avec pétillement léger et faux col solide collant au verre filtrée, pasteurisée	amberkleurig, helder met lichte pareling en stevige, wandklevende schuimkraag gefilterd, gepasteuriseerd
Thirst-quencher with a caramel touch. Relatively short aftertaste with soft bitterness.	Agréable, facilement buvable avec une touche de caramel. Assez courte arrière-bouche avec une douce amertume.	Vlot doordrinkbier met karameltoets. Vrij korte afdronk met zachte bitterheid.
Has been around since 1985.	Existe déjà depuis 1985.	Bestaat al sinds 1985.

rouwerij Huyghe 7,20% 5 °C 41 °F

Artevelde Grand Cru

	top-fermentation re-fermentation in the bottle	fermentation haute refermentation en bouteille	hoge gisting hergisting in de fles
	double	double	dubbel
	different malt varieties (including caramel malt), hops, yeast, water	diverses variétés de malt (e.a. malt caramélisé), houblon, levure, eau	diverse moutsoorten (o.a. karamelmout), hop, gist, water
	dark red-brown with solid, creamy, cream-coloured foam head not filtered or pasteurised	brun rouge foncé avec faux col solide crémeux crème non filtrée, non pasteurisée	donker roodbruin met stevige, romige, crèmekleurige schuimkraag ongefilterd, niet gepasteuriseerd
	Perfect aroma of roasted malt, caramel and the sweet fruitiness of the alcohol. Taste: caramel, sweet fruitiness and nice bitterness. Aftertaste with a strong toffee hint and a touch of date.	Arôme parfait de malt torréfié, caramel et fruité douceâtre de l'alcool. Goût :caramel, fruité doux et jolie amertume. Arrière-bouche avec une touche relevée de caramel mou et une pointe de datte.	Perfect aroma van gebrande mout, karamel en zoetige fruitigheid van de alcohol. Smaak: karamel, zoete fruitigheid en mooie bitterheid. Afdronk met een pittige toffeehint en een vleugje dadel.
	Pour carefully and leave the yeast sediment in the bottle if necessary.	Verser prudemment et laisser le dépôt de levure dans la bouteille selon les souhaits.	Voorzichtig uitschenken en het gistdepot desgewenst in de fles laten.
	Produced at the request of a German customer.	Réalisée à la demande d'un client allemand.	Gerealiseerd op aanvraag van een Duitse klant.

Augrenette

Brasserie Augrenoise

4,50% 4° 39°

top-fermentation re-fermentation in the bottle	fermentation haute refermentation en bouteille	hoge gisting hergisting in de fles
blond	blonde	blond
based on barley and wheat malt	à base de malt d'orge et de froment	op basis van gerste- en tarwemout
cloudy blond	blonde trouble	blond troebel
Thirst-quencher reminiscent of a white beer.	Boisson désaltérante qui fait penser à de la bière blanche.	Dorstlesser die doet denken aan witbier.
The boutique beers of Augrenoise are produced in the context of an integration project for adults with a disability.	Les bières artisanales de l'Augrenoise sont produites dans le cadre d'un projet d'intégration pour personnes moins valides adultes.	De artisanale bieren van Augrenoise worden geproduceerd in het kader van een integratieproject voor volwassen andersvaliden.

Brasserie Augrenoise

6,50% — 4 °C / 39 °F

	top-fermentation	fermentation haute	hoge gisting
	cloudy blond	trouble blonde	troebel blond
	barley malt, wheat malt, unmalted wheat, oat,Styrian Golding hops. Brewed following the infusion method with yeast from the Orval brewery.	malt d'orge, malt de froment, froment non malté, avoine, houblon Styrian Golding. Brassée selon la méthode d'infusion avec levure de la brasserie d'Orval.	gerstemout, tarwemout, niet gemoute tarwe, haver, Styrian Golding hop. Gebrouwen volgens infusiemethode met gist van brouwerij Orval.
	blond and cloudy (13,4 EBC)	blonde trouble (13,4 EBC)	blond troebel (13,4 EBC)
	Slightly sour and very refreshing. Flavours of sweetwood and lime with a touch of honey. Lowbitterness: 9,7 EBU.	Légèrement acidulée et très rafraîchissante. Arômes de réglisse et de tilleul avec une touche de miel. Goût amer limité de 9,7 EBU.	Lichtzuur en zeer verfrissend. Aroma's van zoethout en linde met een toets honing. Beperkte bitterheid: 9,7 EBU.
	Brewed under the supervision of the Orval engineer-brewer. Brewed in the framework of an educational integration project for handicapped people.	Brassée sous la supervision de l'ingénieur de brassage d'Orval. Brassée dans le cadre d'un projet pédagogique d'intégration pour handicapés.	Gebrouwen onder supervisie van de ingenieur-brouwer van Orval. Gebrouwen in het kader van een pedagogisch integratieproject voor gehandicapten.

Augrenoise Blonde de Noël

Brasserie Augrenoise

10% 4° 39°

	top-fermentation	fermentation haute	hoge gisting
	cloudy blond	blonde trouble	troebel blond
	barley malt, wheat malt, unmalted wheat, oat, Styrian Golding hop. An extra portion of barley malt is added to increase the alcohol volume.	malt d'orge, malt de froment, froment non malté, avoine, houblon Styrian Golding. Une portion supplémentaire de malt d'orge est ajoutée pour une teneur d'alcool plus élevée.	gerstemout, tarwemout, niet gemoute tarwe, haver, Styrian Golding hop. Een extra portie gerstemout wordt toegevoegd voor een hoger alcoholvolume.
	blond and cloudy (13,4 EBC)	blonde trouble (13,4 EBC)	blond troebel (13,4 EBC)
	Refreshing. Aroma of lime and liquorice with a honey taste. Bitterness: 8,8 EBU.	Rafraîchissante. Arôme de tilleul et de réglisse avec une saveur de miel. Goût amer de 8,8 EBU.	Verfrissend. Aroma van linde en zoethout met een honingsmaak. Bitterheid 8,8 EBU.
i	Brewed under the supervision of the Orval engineer-brewer. Brewed in the framework of an educational integration project for handicapped people.	Brassée sous la supervision de l'ingénieur de brassage d'Orval. Brassée dans le cadre d'un projet pédagogique d'intégration pour handicapés.	Gebrouwen onder supervisie van de ingenieur-brouwer van Orval. Gebrouwen in het kader van een pedagogisch integratieproject voor gehandicapten.

Augustijn Blond

Brouwerij Van Steenberge 7,50% (16 °plato) 8 °C 46 °F

	top-fermentation re-fermentation in the bottle	fermentation haute refermentation en bouteille	hoge gisting hergisting in de fles
	blond abbey beer	bière d'abbaye blonde	blond abdijbier
	barley malt, hops, yeast, water	malt d'orge, houblon, levure, eau	gerstemout, hop, gist, water
	amber-coloured with a white foam head	ambrée avec faux col blanc	amberkleur met wittte schuimkraag
	Malty, fruity and hoppy aroma. Full-bodied and mild malty, hoppy flavour with a slight vanilla touch. Slightly bitter, soft aftertaste.	Arôme malté, fruité et houblonné. Goût franc et généreux avec une saveur maltée, du houblon et une légère touche de vanille. Arrière-bouche douce, légèrement amère.	Moutig, fruitig en hoppig aroma. Volmondig en milde smaak met moutigheid, hop en een lichte vanilletoets. Lichtbittere, zachte afdronk.
	see Augustijn Grand Cru.	voir Augustijn Grand Cru.	zie Augustijn Grand Cru.
	Authentic abbey beer that has been brewed by Augustinians in Ghent since 1925. In the Middle Ages, it used to be safer to drink beer (which is boiled during brewing process) because the water was often contaminated.	Authentique bière d'abbaye qui a été brassée depuis 1925 par les Pères Augustins à Gand. Au Moyen Âge, il était plus sûr de boire de la bière (on la fait bouillir pendant le processus de brassage), parce que l'eau était souvent polluée.	Authentiek kloosterbier dat sinds 1925 wordt gebrouwen door de Paters Augustijnen in Gent. In de Middeleeuwen was het veiliger om bier te drinken (wordt gekookt tijdens het brouwproces) omdat het water vaak verontreinigd was.

A

Augustijn Donker

Brouwerij Van Steenberge 7% (16 °plato) 8° 46°

	top-fermentation re-fermentation in the bottle	fermentation haute refermentation en bouteille	hoge gisting hergisting in de fles
	brown abbey beer dark specialty beer	bière d'abbaye brune bière spéciale foncée	bruin abdijbier donker speciaalbier
	barley malt, hops, yeast, water	malt d'orge, houblon, levure, eau	gerstemout, hop, gist, water
	red-brown hazelnut colour with rich foam head	brun rouge noisette avec faux col riche	roodbruine hazelnootkleur met rijke schuimkraag
	Aroma of red fruit, slightly smoked. Full-bodied, balanced and mild flavour with hints of raisins and chocolate. Not sweet, but rather caramelly and nutty. Slightly bitter, mellow dry aftertaste.	Arôme de fruits rouges, légèrement fumé. Goût franc, équilibré et généreux, avec des touches de raisins secs et de chocolat. Pas sucrée, plutôt caramel et noix. Arrière-bouche doucement sèche, légèrement amère.	Aroma van rood fruit, lichtjes gerookt. Volmondig, evenwichtige en milde smaak met toetsen van rozijnen en chocolade. Niet zoet, eerder karamel en noten. Licht bittere, zachtdroge afdronk.
	see Augustijn Grand Cru.	voir Augustijn Grand Cru.	zie Augustijn Grand Cru.
i	In 1982, the blond Augustinian beer was relaunched by brewer Jozef Van Steenbergen. The double was launched in 2009.	C'est en 1982 que le brasseur Jozef Van Steenbergen relança la bière Augustijn blonde. La double fut lancée en 2009.	In 1982 werd het blonde Augustijnbier opnieuw gelanceerd door brouwer Jozef Van Steenbergen. De dubbele werd gelanceerd in 2009.

Augustijn Grand Cru

Brouwerij Van Steenberge — 9% (18,5 ° plato) — 8 °C / 46 °F

	top-fermentation re-fermentation in the bottle	fermentation haute refermentation en bouteille	hoge gisting hergisting in de fles
	tripel abbey beer	bière d'abbaye triple	tripel abdijbier
	barley malt, hops, yeast, water	malt d'orge, houblon, levure, eau	gerstemout, hop, gist, water
	straw-yellow with a white foam head	jaune paille avec faux col blanc	strogeel met witte schuimkraag
	Strikingly dry with the fruity quality of tripel. Decidedly full-bodied with touches of malt. Dry, bitter aftertaste.	Étonnamment seche, avec le fruité de la triple. Sensation très franche en bouche, avec des touches de malt. Arrière-bouche sèche, amère.	Opvallend droog met de fruitigheid van tripel. Zeer vol mondgevoel met toetsen van mout. Droge, bittere afdronk.
	Pour slowly into a tilted glass, avoiding contact between the bottle and the glass. Lift the bottle and leave approx. 1 cm of the yeast sediment in the bottle or pour along.	Verser lentement dans un verre incliné sans que la bouteille ne touche le verre. Lever la bouteille plus haut et laisser un dépôt de levure de ca. 1 cm dans la bouteille ou le verser également.	Traag uitschenken in een schuingehouden glas zonder dat de fles het glas raakt. De fles hoger brengen en het gistdepot van ca. 1 cm in de fles laten of uitschenken.
i			

Authentique 621

Authentique Brasserie

7,50% 6,5 ° 44 °

top-fermentation	fermentation haute	hoge gisting
traditionally brewed beer dubbel	bière artisanale double	artisanaal dubbel
yeast, sugar, six malt varieties, hops, corn, wheat, water	levure, sucre, 6 sortes de malt, houblon, maïs, froment, eau	gist, suiker, 6 moutsoorten, hop, maïs, tarwe, water
brown	brune	bruin
Slightly sugared and easily digestible beer with a pleasant bitterness.	Bière peu sucrée et facilement digestible avec un goût amer agréable.	Weinig gesuikerd en licht verteerbaar bier met een aangename bitterheid.
Serve in a thoroughly rinsed and dried glass.	Verser dans un verre suffisamment rincé et séché.	Uitschenken in voldoende gespoeld en gedroogd glas.
Boutique beer. Store the bottles upright.	Bière brassée de façon artisanale. Conserver les bouteilles en position verticale.	Artisanaal gebrouwen bier. Flesjes rechtopstaand bewaren.

Authentique Brasserie

5% — 6,5 °C / 44 °F

	top-fermentation	fermentation haute	hoge gisting
	amber	ambrée	amber
	yeast, malt, hops, brown sugar, water	levure, malt, houblon, sucre cassonade, eau	gist, mout, hop, bruine suiker, water
	transparent copper	cuivre transparente	transparant koper
	Accessible and refreshing taste with noble bitterness. Varied flavours of nuts and brown sugar.	Saveur accessible et rafraîchissante avec un goût amer noble. Arômes variés de noix et de cassonade.	Toegankelijke en verfrissende smaak met nobele bitterheid. Gevarieerde aroma's van nootjes en bruine suiker.
	Serve in a thoroughly rinsed and dried glass.	Verser dans un verre suffisamment rincé et séché.	Uitschenken in voldoende gespoeld en gedroogd glas.
	Boutique beer. Store the bottles upright.	Bière brassée de façon artisanale. Conserver les bouteilles en position verticale.	Artisanaal gebrouwen bier. Flesjes rechtopstaand bewaren.

Authentique Blonde

Authentique Brasserie

6,50% 6,5 °C 44 °F

top-fermentation	fermentation haute	hoge gisting
blond	blonde	blond
yeast, malt, sugar, hops, white pepper, coriander, water	levure, malt, sucre, houblon, poivre blanc, coriandre, eau	gist, mout, suiker, hop, witte peper, koriander, water
transparent blonde	blonde transparente	transparant blond
Luxury beer with a lively, powerful character. Touches of white pepper and coriander.	Bière de luxe avec un caractère vif et corsé. Touches de poivre blanc et de coriandre.	Luxebier met een levendig en krachtig karakter. Toetsen van witte peper en koriander.
Serve in a thoroughly rinsed and dried glass.	Verser dans un verre suffisamment rincé et séché.	Uitschenken in voldoende gespoeld en gedroogd glas.
Boutique beer. Store the bottles upright.	Bière brassée de façon artisanale. Conserver les bouteilles en position verticale.	Artisanaal gebrouwen bier. Flesjes rechtopstaand bewaren.

Authentique Brasserie

9% 6,5 °C 44 °F

	top-fermentation	fermentation haute	hoge gisting
	winter beer	bière hivernale	winterbier
	yeast, sugar, malt, hops, star anise, juniper berry, water	levure, sucre, malt, houblon, anis, baie de genièvre, eau	gist, suiker, mout, hop, steranijs, jeneverbes, water
	transparent blond	blonde transparente	transparant blond
	Dessert beer with light sour taste.	Bière de dessert avec un goût légèrement acidulé.	Dessertbier met lichtzure smaak.
	Serve in a thoroughly rinsed and dried glass.	Verser dans un verre suffisamment rincé et séché.	Uitschenken in voldoende gespoeld en gedroogd glas.
	Boutique beer. Store the bottles upright.	Bière brassée de façon artisanale. Conserver les bouteilles en position verticale.	Artisanaal gebrouwen bier. Flesjes rechtopstaand bewaren.

Authentique Blonde de Noël

A Authentique Triple

Authentique Brasserie 9,50% 6,5 °C 44 °F

	top-fermentation	fermentation haute	hoge gisting
	tripel	triple	tripel
	yeast, sugar, hops, malt, water	levure, sucre, houblon, malt, eau	gist, suiker, hop, mout, water
	transparent amber	ambre transparente	transparant amber
	Sipping beer that excels with cheese. Smooth and bitter taste, sugared and naturally alcoholised.	Bière de dégustation qui s'accorde parfaitement avec le fromage. Saveur moelleuse et amère, sucrée et alcoolisée par voie naturelle.	Degustatiebier dat uitstekend past bij kaas. Zachte en bittere smaak, gesuikerd en natuurlijk gealcoholiseerd.
	Serve in a thoroughly rinsed and dried glass.	Verser dans un verre suffisamment rincé et séché.	Uitschenken in voldoende gespoeld en gedroogd glas.
	Boutique beer. Store the bottles upright.	Bière brassée de façon artisanale. Conserver les bouteilles en position verticale.	Artisanaal gebrouwen bier. Flesjes rechtopstaand bewaren.

Autruche Bière des Gilles

Brasserie de Silenrieux 7% 7 - 10 °C / 45 - 50 °F

	top-fermentation re-fermented in the bottle	fermentation haute refermentation en bouteille	hoge gisting hergisting in de fles
	specialty beer	bière spéciale	speciaalbier
	malt, hops, herbs, water	malt, houblon, herbes, eau	mout, hop, kruiden, water
	blond cloudy (unfiltered)	blonde trouble (non filtrée)	blond troebel (niet gefilterd)
	Malty taste. Refreshing.	Saveur maltée. Rafraîchissante.	Moutsmaak. Verfrissend.
	Gently revolve or shake the bottle before opening to obtain a cloudy beer.	Tourner légèrement ou secouer la bouteille avant de l'ouvrir pour obtenir une bière trouble.	De fles licht draaien of schudden voor het openen om een troebel bier te bekomen.
i			

B Bacchus

Brouwerij Van Honsebrouck 4,50% 5 °C 41 °F

	mixed fermentation	fermentation mixte	gemengde gisting
	Flemish red	Rouge flamande	Vlaams rood
	malt, sugar, hops, water	malt, sucre, houblon, eau	mout, suiker, hop, water
	red-brown clear	brun rouge claire	roodbruin helder
	Refreshing. Smoothly sourish with a fruity aftertaste. The taste is influenced by the temporary storage in oak-wood barrels.	Rafraîchissante. Acidulé moelleux avec une fin de bouche fruitée. La saveur est influencée par une conservation partielle en fûts de chêne.	Verfrissend. Zachtzurig met een fruitige afdronk. De smaak wordt beïnvloed door gedeeltelijke bewaring in eikenhouten vaten.
	Pour into a newly rinsed glass keeping it upright near the end.	Verser dans un verre récemment rincé d'abord tenu en oblique et à la fin en position verticale.	Uitschenken in een vers gespoeld glas dat eerst schuin gehouden wordt en op het einde verticaal gehouden wordt.
	The brewery classifies this beer as old-brown.	La brasserie classe cette bière parmi les vieilles brunes.	De brouwerij catalogeert het bier als oud bruin.

Brouwerij Van Honsebrouck 5% 5 °C 41 °F

	mixed fermentation centrifuged	fermentation mixte centrifugée	gemengde gisting gecentrifugeerd
	fruit beer	bière fruitée	fruitbier
	malt, unprocessed wheat, sugar, hops, natural simple juice, water	malt, froment brut, sucre, houblon, jus naturel simple, eau	mout, ruwe tarwe, suiker, hop, natuurlijk enkelvoudig sap, water
	clear red-brown with solid foam head filtered, pasteurised	brun rouge clair avec faux col solide filtrée, pasteurisée	helder roodbruin met stevige schuimkraag gefilterd, gepasteuriseerd
	Soft raspberry aroma and flavour.	Douce, avec arôme et goût de framboises.	Zacht met frambozenaroma en -smaak.
	Pour carefully into a Bacchus glass.	Verser prudemment dans un verre bacchus.	Voorzichtig uitschenken in een bacchusglas.

Bacchus Kriek

Brouwerij Van Honsebrouck

5,80% 5 °C 41 °F

	mixed fermentation centrifuged	fermentation mixte centrifugée	gemengde gisting gecentrifugeerd
	fruit beer	bière fruitée	fruitbier
	malt, unprocessed wheat, sugar, hops, natural simple juice, vitamin C, water	malt, froment brut, sucre, houblon, jus naturel simple, vitamine C, eau	mout, ruwe tarwe, suiker, hop, natuurlijk enkelvoudig sap, vitamine C, water
	clear red-brown with solid foam head filtered, pasteurised	brun rouge clair avec faux col solide filtrée, pasteurisée	helder roodbruin met stevige schuimkraag gefilterd, gepasteuriseerd
	Soft cherry aroma and flavour.	Douce, avec arôme et goût de cerises.	Zacht met kersenaroma en -smaak.
	Pour carefully into a Bacchus glass.	Verser prudemment dans un verre bacchus.	Voorzichtig uitschenken in een bacchusglas.
i			

Balthazar

Picobrouwerij Alvinne 8,90% 10 - 12 °C / 50 - 54 °F

	top-fermentation	fermentation haute	hoge gisting
	regional beer winter beer	bière régionale bière hivernale	streekbier winterbier
	5 different malts, 2 different hops (Magnum and EK Goldings), yeast, coriander, ginger, cardamom, water	5 variétés de malt, 2 variétés de houblon (Magnum et EK Goldings), levure, coriandre, gingembre, cardemon, eau	5 moutsoorten, 2 hopsoorten (Magnum en EK Goldings), gist, koriander, gember, kardemom, water
	black 125 EBC	noire 125 EBC	zwart 125 EBC
	Spicy aroma and taste. Full bodied. 35 EBU.	Arôme et saveur relevés. Goût franc. 35 EBU.	Kruidig aroma en smaak. Volmondig. 35 EBU.
	Pour into a tulip-shaped glass or goblet. Leave the yeast (approx. 1 cm) at the bottom of the bottle. Pour slowly to obtain a nice foam head.	Verser dans un verrre tulipe ou calice. Laisser la levure (environ 1 cm) au fond de la bouteille. Verser lentement de sorte qu'un faux col solide se forme.	Uitschenken in een tulp- of kelkvormig glas. De gist (ca. 1 cm) op de bodem van de fles laten. Langzaam schenken zodat er een mooie schuimkraag ontstaat.
i			

Brasserie Lefebvre 8% 5 °
41 °

	top-fermentation naturally re-fermented in the bottle centrifuged	fermentation haute refermentation naturelle en bouteille centrifugée	hoge gisting natuurlijke hergisting in de fles gecentrifugeerd
	amber or speciale belge honey beer	ambrée ou spéciale belge bière de miel	amber of speciaal belge honingbier
	barley malt, wheat, honey, hops, sugar, curaçao orange, yeast, water	malt d'orge, froment, miel, houblon, sucre, orange curaçao, levure, eau	gerstemout, tarwe, honing, hop, suiker, curaçaosinaasappel, gist, water
	amber-blond thick foam head that lingers not pasteurised	blond ambré avec un faux col gras solide non pasteurisée	amberblond vettige schuimkraag die lang blijft niet gepasteuriseerd
	Fruity and spicy strong blond beer. The honey provides for subtle aromas and does not take away from the refreshing character.	Bière blonde forte fruitée et épicée. Le miel produit de subtils arômes et ne rompt pas le caractère rafraîchissant.	Fruitig en kruidig sterk blond bier. De honing zorgt voor subtiele aroma's en doet geen afbreuk aan het verfrissende karakter.
	Pour into a pint-pot.	Verser dans une chope.	Uitschenken in een pintglas.
i			

Barbãr Bok

rasserie Lefebvre

8% 5 °C 41 °F

top-fermentation centrifuged	fermentation haute centrifugée	hoge gisting gecentrifugeerd
amber or speciale belge honey beer	ambrée ou spéciale belge bière de miel	amber of speciale belge honingbier
barley malt, wheat, honey, hops, sugar, curaçao orange, yeast, coriander, water	malt d'orge, froment, miel, houblon, sucre, orange curaçao, levure, coriandre, eau	gerstemout, tarwe, honing, hop, suiker, curaçaosinaasappel, gist, water, koriander
dark brown with red glow not pasteurised	brun foncé avec reflet rouge non pasteurisée	donkerbruin met rode schijn niet gepasteuriseerd
Pour into a pint-pot.	Verser dans une chope.	Uitschenken in een pintglas.

B

Barbe d'Or - Goudbaard

Brouwerij Verhaeghe 7,50% (16 °plato)

	top-fermentation centrifuged	fermentation haute centrifugée	hoge gisting gecentrifugeerd
	strong blond	blonde forte	sterk blond
	slightly roasted malt varieties, yeast, hops, water	variétés de malt légèrement torréfié, levure, houblon, eau	licht gebrande moutsoorten, gist, hop, water
	gold blond filtered, pasteurised	blond doré filtrée, pasteurisée	goudblond gefilterd, gepasteuriseerd
	Nice, extended bitterness with fruity aftertaste.	Jolie amertume s'écoulant longuement, avec une arrière-bouche fruitée.	Mooie, lang uitvloeiende bitterheid met fruitige afdronk.
	Name of a Liège brewery (16th century) which belonged to Mrs De Romsée, spouse of Jacques Verhaege (brewer of the 3rd generation). The family crest depicting the man with the gold beard is on the label.	Nom d'une brasserie liégeoise (16e siècle) qui appartenait à Madame De Romsée, épouse de Jacques Verhaege. Les armoires de la famille, où l'homme à la barbe d'or est bien en vue, ornent l'étiquette.	Naam van een Luikse brouwerij (16e eeuw) die toebehoorde aan mevr. De Romsée, echtgenote van Jacques Verhaeghe (brouwer van de 3e generatie). Het familiewapen waar de man met de gouden baard prominent aanwezig is, siert het etiket.

Barbe Rouge - Roodbaard

rouwerij Verhaeghe 8% (17 °plato)

top-fermentation centrifuged	fermentation haute centrifugée	hoge gisting gecentrifugeerd
strong amber	ambrée forte	sterk amber
dried malt varieties, yeast, hops, water. Dry-hopping before lagering.	variétés de malt touraillé, levure, houblon, eau. Dry-hopping avant conditionnement.	geëeste moutsoorten, gist, hop, water. Dry-hopping voor de lagering.
copper red due to the malt	rouge cuivre par le malt	koperrood door de mout
Caramel malty and bitter taste.	Goût malté caramel et amer.	Karamelmoutige en bittere smaak.
Copper red counterpart of the Barbe d'Or. The third beer of the series, Barbe noire - Blackbeard is due end 2011.	Frère cuivre rouge de la Barbe d'Or. La 3e bière dans la série, Barbe noire - Zwartbaard, est prévue pour la fin de 2011.	Koperrode broer van de Barbe d'Or. Het 3e bier in de reeks, Barbe noire - Zwartbaard, is voorzien voor eind 2011.

t Brugs Bierinstituut by De Proefbrouwerij

7% 13 - 15 ° / 55 - 59 °

top-fermentation re-fermentation in the bottle not centrifuged	fermentation haute refermentation en bouteille non centrifugée	hoge gisting hergisting op de fles niet gecentrifugeerd
amber	ambrée	amber
5 malt types, 2 different hops (Saaz and Amarillo)	5 variétés de malt, 2 variétés de houblon (Saaz et Amarillo)	5 moutsoorten, 2 hopsoorten (Saaz en Amarillo)
clear, dark copper (57 EBC) with creamy foam head not pasteurised	limpide, cuivre foncé (57 EBC) avec faux col crémeux non pasteurisée	helder, donker koper (57 EBC) met romige schuimkraag niet gepasteuriseerd
Thirst-quenching with soft caramel aromas thanks to malt. Subtle fruit (orange) and spicy aroma with refined bitterness thanks to the hops.	Désaltérante avec de doux arômes de caramel grâce au malt. Fruit subtil (orange) et arôme épicé avec une amertume raffinée engendrée par le houblon.	Dorstlessend met zachte karamelaroma's door de mout. Subtiel fruit (sinaasappel) en kruidig aroma met verfijnde bitterheid door de hop.
Serve with a foam head of approx. 2.5 cm.	Servir avec un faux col de ca. 2,5 cm.	Serveren met een schuimkraag van ca. 2,5 cm.
St Basil lived in Cappadocia in the fourth century. In the 12th century, Count of Flanders Diederik van de Elzas commissioned the Basil Church in Bruges. That is where a dorsal vertebra is said to be kept as a relic.	Le saint Basile a vécu en Cappadoce au 4e siècle. Au 12e siècle, le comte Diederik van de Elzas fit bâtir l'église de Basile à Bruges. C'est là qu'une prétendue vertèbre dorsale se trouve conservée comme relique.	De heilige Basilius leefde in Cappadocië in de 4e eeuw. In de 12e eeuw liet graaf Diederik van de Elzas de Basiliuskerk bouwen in Brugge. Daar wordt een vermeende ruggenwervel als relikwie bewaard.

5,20% 4 - 6 °C 39 - 43 °F

Bavik pony-stout

	top-fermentation centrifuged	fermentation haute centrifugée	hoge gisting gecentrifugeerd
	stout	stout	stout
	barley malt, corn, hops, yeast, pure spring water	malt d'orge, maïs, houblon, levure, eau minérale pure	gerstemout, mais, hop, gist, zuiver bronwater
	dark with brown-creamy foam head filtered, pasteurised	foncée avec faux col crémeux brun filtrée, pasteurisée	donker met bruinromige schuimkraag gefilterd, gepasteuriseerd
	Pleasantly sweet with typical bitter taste and pleasantly roasted caramel aroma.	Agréablement sucrée, avec un goût amer typique du caramel et un arôme de caramel agréablement brûlé.	Aangenaam zoet met typische karamelbittere smaak en aangenaam gebrand karamelaroma.
	Pour into a clean, degreased, wet glass, avoiding contact with the foam.	Verser dans un verre humide dégraissé rincé sans que la bouteille touche l'écume.	Uitschenken in een ontvet, gespoeld nat glas zonder dat de fles het schuim raakt.

Bavik Premium Pils

Brouwerij Bavik 5,20% 2 - 4° 36 - 39°

	bottom-fermentation	fermentation basse	lage gisting
	pils or lager	pils ou lager	pils of lagerbier
	barley malt, hops, yeast, pure spring water	malt d'orge, houblon, levure, eau de source pure	gerstemout, hop, gist, zuiver bronwater
	pale yellow, clear filtered, not pasteurised	jaune clair, limpide filtrée, non pasteurisée	lichtgeel, helder gefilterd, niet gepasteuriseerd
	Crispy, pleasant and smooth taste, created by the fine hop species. Full-bodied character with a fresh bitterness.	Picotante et agréablement douce par les variétés délicates de houblon. Caractère franc avec un goût amer frais.	Knisperig en aangenaam zacht (hop). Volmondig karakter met een frisse bitterheid.
	Pour into a degreased, rinsed and wet glass, avoiding contact between bottle and foam.	Verser dans un verre dégraissé, rincé et mouillé sans que la bouteille touche le faux col.	Uitschenken in een ontvet, gespoeld nat glas zonder dat de fles het schuim raakt.
	Crowned Belgium's best pilsner beer on different occasions (2005 Testaankoop, 2009 Nieuwsblad, 2011 Pilstest Waregem beer fans).	Couronnée à plusieurs reprises meilleure pils de Belgique (2005 Test-Achats, 2009 Nieuwsblad, 2011 Pilstest Waregemse Bierfanaten).	Meermaals bekroond als beste pils van België (2005 Testaankoop, 2009 Nieuwsblad, 2011 Pilstest Waregemse Bierfanaten).

rouwerij Bavik 3% 2 - 4 °C 36 - 39 °F

Bavik Triple Bock

	Combination of a bottom- and top-fermentation beer. centrifuged	Coupage d'une bière de fermentation basse avec une bière de fermentation haute. centrifugée	Versnijding van een bier van lage gisting met een bier van hoge gisting. gecentrifugeerd
	bock	bock	bock
	barley malt, corn, hops, yeast, pure spring water	malt d'orge, maïs, houblon, levure, eau minérale pure	gerstemout, mais, hop, gist, zuiver bronwater
	pale yellow, clear filtered, pasteurised	jaune clair, limpide filtrée, pasteurisée	lichtgeel, helder gefilterd, gepasteuriseerd
	Soft, refreshing taste with a light, pleasant bitterness. Ideal refreshing session beer thanks to is lower alcohol content.	Goût doux, rafraîchissant avec une agréable légère amertume. Bière facilement buvable idéale pour se désaltérer, du fait de sa teneur assez faible en alcool.	Zachte, verfrissende smaak met een lichte, aangename bitterheid. Ideale verfrissende doordrinker door zijn lager alcoholgehalte.
	Pour into a clean, degreased, wet glass, avoiding contact with the foam.	Verser dans un verre humide dégraissé rincé sans que la bouteille touche l'écume.	Uitschenken in een ontvet, gespoeld nat glas zonder dat de fles het schuim raakt.
i			

Beersel Blond

Geuzestekerij 3 Fonteinen 7%

	top-fermentation re-fermented in the bottle	fermentation haute refermentation en bouteille	hoge gisting hergisting in de fles
	blond	blonde	blond
	lager malt, 10% wheat, hops, water	malt de conservation, 10% froment, houblon, eau	lagermout, 10% tarwe, hop, water
	blond	blonde	blond
	Slightly sweetish taste, fine bitter thrist-quencher.	Saveur légèrement douce, désaltérante amère raffinée.	Lichtzoetige smaak, fijn-bittere dorstlesser.

euzestekerij 3 Fonteinen

5,20%

	bottom-fermentation re-fermented in the bottle	fermentation basse refermentation en bouteille	lage gisting hergisting op de fles
	full-malt Lager	lager maltée complète	lager volmout
	barley malt, Saaz hops, lager yeast, sugar, water	malt d'orge, houblon Saaz, levure de conservation, sucre, eau	gerstemout, Saaz hop, lagergist, suiker, water
	blond unfiltered	blonde non filtrée	blond ongefilterd
	Finely hopped with a pleasant bitterness.	Houblonnée raffinée avec un goût amer agréable	Fijn gehopt met een aangename bitterheid.

Bel Pils

Duvel Moortgat Corporation

5% 3 - 4 37 - 39

	bottom-fermentation	fermentation basse	lage gisting
	typically Belgian pilsner Belgian strong golden ale	pils typiquement belge Belgian strong golden ale	typisch Belgische pils Belgian strong golden ale
	barley malt, sugar, fine hop varieties, yeast, water	malt d'orge, sucre, variétés fines de houblon, levure, eau	gerstemout, suiker, fijne hopsoorten, gist, water
	blond	blonde	blond
	Pure, dry and well-hopped pilsner with a slightly bitter touch. Typical taste of Saaz hop and lager yeast.	Pils pure, sèche et bien houblonnée avec une touche légèrement amère. Goût typique de houblon Saaz et de levure de conservation.	Zuivere, droge en welgehopte pils met een lichtbittere toets. Typische smaak van Saazhop en lagergist.
	Pour in a single movement into a cool glass, previously rinsed with pure, cold water. Let the foam run over the rim of the glass and skim off the excess foam and big bubbles with a spatula or knife (big carbon dioxide bubbles cause the foam head to disappear more quickly).	Verser d'un seul trait dans un verre rincé à l'eau froide et propre. Laisser dépasser l'écume et enlever l'écume débordante ainsi que les grosses bulles avec une spatule ou un couteau du bord du verre (de grandes bulles d'oxyde carbonique font disparaître l'écume).	In 1 keer uitschenken in een koel glas dat vooraf gespoeld is met koud,zuiver water. Laten overschuimen en het overtollige schuim en grove bellen met een spatel of mes van de rand van het glas afhalen (grote koolzuurbellen doen het schuim verdwijnen).

Belgian Angel Stout

rasserie Brootcoorens

5,20% — 3 - 8 °C / 37 - 46 °F

	top-fermentation	fermentation haute	hoge gisting
	stout	stout	stout
	pilsner, roasted and amber malt, home-grown hops, yeast, water	malt de pils, malt brûlé et malt ambré, houblon aromatique de propre culture, levure, eau	pils-, gebrande en ambermout, aromatische hop van eigen teelt, gist, water
	dark brown	brun foncé	donkerbruin
	Creamy, pronounced although not aggressive malt taste. Prepared on a open fire, with extra malt added.	Onctueuse avec bonne présence de malt torréfié mais sans agressivité. Cuisson à feu nu et adjonction accrûe de malt.	Zacht met uitgesproken gebrande mout zonder agressief te zijn. Gekookt op open vuur met extra toevoeging van mout.
	Pour slowly.	Verser lentement.	Langzaam uitschenken.
i	This beer is brewed for the hop feast, every second weekend of September.	Brassée à l'occasion de la fête du houblon chaque deuxième weekend de septembre.	Wordt gebrouwen naar aanleiding van het hoppefeest elk tweede weekend van september.

B Belgian Framboises

Brasserie Lefebvre **3,50%** 2 - 4 / 36 - 39

top-fermentation centrifuged	fermentation haute centrifuged	hoge gisting gecentrifugeerd
witbier with fruit	bière blanche fruitée	witbier met fruit
barley malt, wheat, hops, raspberry juice (10%), sugar, yeast, flavouring, acesulfame K, water	malt d'orge, froment, houblon, jus de framboise (10%), sucre, levure, arômes, acesulfam. K, eau	gerstemout, tarwe, hop, frambozensap (10%), suiker, gist, aroma's, acesulfam. K, water
ruby red, transparent or cloudy if very cold pasteurised	rouge rubis , transparente ou trouble si très froide pasteurisée	robijnrood, transparant of troebel indien zeer koud gepasteuriseerd
Fine balance between sweet raspberry flavour and refreshing white beer.	Joli équilibre entre le goût de framboises sucré et la bière blanche rafraîchissante.	Mooi evenwicht tussen de gesuikerde frambozensmaak en het verfrissende witbier.
Pour into a glass with a stem.	Verser dans un verre à pied.	Uitschenken in een glas met voet.

top-fermentation centrifuged	fermentation haute centrifugée	hoge gisting gecentrifugeerd
witbier with fruit	bière blanche fruitée	witbier met fruit
malt, wheat, hop varieties, cherry juice (20%), sugar, yeast, flavourings, acesulfame K, water	malt, froment, houblon, jus de cerises (20%), sucre, levure, arômes, acesulfam. K, eau.	mout, tarwe, hop, kersensap (20%), suiker, gist,aroma's, acesulfam.K, water
cherry red clear pasteurised	rouge cerise claire pasteurisée	kersenrood helder gepasteuriseerd
Sugared and very fruity beer. Cherry and almond taste and aroma.	Bière sucrée et très fruitée. Saveur et arôme de cerise et d'amande.	Gesuikerd en zeer fruitig bier. Smaak en aroma van kers en amandel.

Belgian Pêches

Brasserie Lefebvre 3,50% 2 - 4 / 36 - 39

top-fermentation centrifuged	fermentation haute centrifugée	hoge gisting gecentrifugeerd
witbier with fruit	bière blanche fruitée	witbier met fruit
barley malt, wheat, hop varieties, peach juice (15%), sugar, yeast,flavourings, acesulfame.K, water.	malt d'orge, froment, houblon, jus de pêches (15%), sucre, levure, arômes, acesulfam. K, eau.	gerstemout, tarwe, hop, perzikensap (15%), suiker, gist, aroma's, acesulfam.K, water.
yellow peach cloudy if served very cold pasteurised	pêche jaune trouble si très froide pasteurisée	gele perzik troebel indien zeer koud gepasteuriseerd
Flavour and aroma of peaches, apricots and mango. Subtle blend of white beer and peach juice.	Saveur et arôme de pêches, abricots et mangue. Subtile mélange de bière blanche et de jus de pêches.	Smaak en aroma van perziken, abrikozen en mango. Subtiele mengeling van witbier en perzikensap.
Pour into a glass with a stem.	Verser dans un verre à pied.	Uitschenken in een glas met voet.

 8,10% 6 °C 43 °F

 B

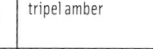

top-fermentation re-fermentation in the bottle	fermentation haute refermentation en bouteille	hoge gisting hergisting in de fles
tripel amber	triple ambrée	tripel amber
barley malt, 4 different hops (East Kent Golding, Northern Brewer, Cascade, Hallertau Hersbrucker), yeast, sugar, water. Dry hopping.	malt d'orge, 4 variétés de houblon, (East Kent Golding, Northern Brewer, Cascade, Hallertau Hersbrucker), levure, sucre, eau. Dry hopping.	gerstemout, 4 hopsoorten (East Kent Golding, Northern Brewer, Cascade, Hallertau Hersbrucker), gist, suiker, water. Dry hopping.
amber-coloured not filtered	ambrée non filtrée	amberkleurig ongefilterd
Pour gently into a tilted glass. Remove the bottle from the glass and hold the glass upright to obtain a fine foam head (approx. 2 cm). Leave the yeast sediment in the bottle.	Verser lentement dans un verre tenu incliné. Eloigner la bouteille du verre et tenir le verre en position verticale pour former un faux col solide (ca 2 cm). Laisser le dépôt de levure dans la bouteille.	Langzaam uitschenken in een schuingehouden glas. De fles van het glas verwijderen en het glas rechthouden voor een mooie schuimkraag (ca. 2 cm). Het gistdepot in de fles laten.

Belgoo Luppoo

Belgoobeer at Brasserie La Binchoise 6,50% 6 43

	top-fermentation re-fermentation in the bottle	fermentation haute refermentation en bouteille	hoge gisting hergisting in de fles
	blond	blonde	blond
	barley malt, oat, hops, yeast, water. Dry-hopped.	malt d'orge, avoine, houblon, levure, eau. Dry hopped.	gerstemout, haver, hop, gist, water. Dry-hopped.
	blond not filtered	blonde non filtrée	blond ongefilterd
	Pour gently into a tilted glass. Remove the bottle from the glass and hold the glass upright to obtain a fine foam head (approx. 2 cm). Leave the yeast sediment in the bottle.	Verser lentement dans un verre tenu incliné. Eloigner la bouteille du verre et tenir le verre tout droit pour former un faux col solide (ca 2 cm). Laisser le dépôt de levure dans la bouteille.	Langzaam uitschenken in een schuingehouden glas. De fles van het glas verwijderen en het glas rechthouden voor een mooie schuimkraag (ca. 2 cm). Het gistdepot in de fles laten.
i			

elgoobeer at Brasserie La Binchoise 6,60% 6 - 8 °C 43 - 46 °F

top-fermentation re-fermentation in the bottle	fermentation haute refermentation en bouteille	hoge gisting hergisting in de fles
blond multigrain beer	bière blonde quatre céréales	blond viergranenbier
barley malt, wheat malt, oat, spelt or German wheat (triticum spelta), hops (Saaz), yeast, water	malt d'orge, malt de froment, avoine, épeautre ou froment Allemand (triticum spelta), houblon (Saaz), levure, eau	gerstemout, tarwemout, haver, spelt of Duitse tarwe (triticum spelta), hop (Saaz), gist, water
cloudy white not filtered	trouble blanc non filtrée	troebel wit ongefilterd
Hoppy aftertaste with pleasant, lingering bitterness.	Arrière-bouche houblonnée avec une agréable amertume persistante.	Hoppige afdronk met aangename, blijvende bitterheid.
Pour gently into a tilted glass. Remove the bottle from the glass and hold the glass upright to obtain a fine foam head (approx. 2 cm). Leave the yeast sediment in the bottle.	Verser lentement dans un verre tenu incliné. Eloigner la bouteille du verre et tenir le verre en position verticale pour former un faux col joli (ca 2 cm). Laisser le dépôt de levure dans la bouteille.	Langzaam uitschenken in een schuingehouden glas. De fles van het glas verwijderen en het glas rechthouden voor een mooie schuimkraag (ca. 2 cm). Het gistdepot in de fles laten.

Bella Mère

Brasserie Artisanale Millevertus

6,50% 7 45

	top-fermentation	fermentation haute	hoge gisting
	ale	ale	ale
	different malt, hop and yeast varieties, water	différentes sortes de malt, de houblon et de levure, eau	verschillende mout-, hop- en gistsoorten, water
	amber blond	blond ambré	amberblond
	Overall bitterness.	Amère sur toute la ligne.	Bitter over de hele lijn.

Belle Cies

rouwerij den Tseut 10% 2 - 3 °C / 36 - 37 °F

top-fermentation re-fermentation in the bottle not centrifuged	fermentation haute refermentation en bouteille non centrifugée	hoge gisting hergisting in de fles niet gecentrifugeerd
blond specialty beer	blonde bière spéciale	blond speciaalbier
mixture of barley malt (pilsner malt), yeast, Poperinge hops (Challenger, Magnum), water. Re-fermented with champagne yeast.	mélange de malt d'orge (malt de pils), levure, houblon de Poperinge (Challenger, Magnum), eau. Refermenté avec levure Champagne.	mengeling van gerstemout (pilsmout), gist, Poperingse hop (Challenger, Magnum), water. Hergegist met champagnegist.
light blond, slightly cloudy with a big, white foam head not filtered or pasteurised	blond clair, légèrement trouble, avec faux col gras, blanc non filtrée, non pasteurisée	lichtblond, licht troebel, met een vette, witte schuimkraag ongefilterd, niet gepasteuriseerd
Fruity and slightly bitter with soft aftertaste. Scent of pure hops.	Fruité et légèrement amere avec une arrière-bouche douce. Parfum de houblon pur.	Fruitig en lichtbitter met zachte afdronk. Geur van pure hop.
Leave the bottles upright to chill. Serve in a flute glass.	Laisser refroidir les bouteilles en position verticale. Verser dans une flûte.	De flessen rechtop laten koelen. Uitschenken in een fluitglas.
Specialty beer suitable as an aperitif. Each bottle contains a hop bubble ('Belle' means bubble). Cies refers to the old Cistercienser cloister in Oosteeklo.	Bière spéciale qui convient comme bière d'apéritif. Dans chaque bouteille, il y a un cône de houblon ('Belle' veut dire cône). Cies fait référence à l'ancien couvent des Cisterciennes à Oosteeklo.	Speciaalbier dat geschikt is als aperitiefbier. In elke fles zit een hoppebel (Belle). Cies verwijst naar het oude Cisterciënzerinnenklooster in Oosteeklo.

B Bellebier Amber

Paeleman by Brouwerij Van Steenberge 5,20%

	top-fermentation	fermentation haute	hoge gisting
	amber	ambre	amber

aeleman by Brouwerij Van Steenberge 6,20%

	top-fermentation	fermentation haute	hoge gisting
	double	double	dubbel

Bellebier Dubbel

Bellebier Trippel

Paeleman by Brouwerij Van Steenberge

8%

	top-fermentation	fermentation haute	hoge gisting
	tripel	triple	tripel

Brouwerij Bockor (Vander Ghinste) 5,50% 5 - 8 °C 41 - 46 °F

	lage gisting	fermentation basse	lage gisting
	(West-Flemish) red-brown	brune-rouge de la Flandre Occidentale	(Westvlaams) roodbruin
	barley malt, wheat, hops, yeast, water	malt d'orge, froment, houblon, levure, eau	gerstemout, tarwe, hop, gist, water
	burgundy colour	couleur bourgogne	bourgognekleur
	Sharp and thirst-quenching with a pleasant sourness. Well-balanced sweet-and-sour taste with a slightly fruity aroma.	Âpre et désaltérante avec une agréable acidité. Saveur aigre-douce équilibrée et arôme fruité léger.	Scherp en dorstlessend met een aangename wrangheid. Evenwichtige, zoetzure smaak en licht fruitig aroma.
	Rinse the glass with cold water, tilt it a little, pour carefully half of the bottle then keep the glass upright and pour the rest of the bottle in a single movement.	Rincer le verre à l'eau froide, le tenir légèrement incliné et verser la bière prudemment à moitié. Puis relever le verre et vider la bouteille d'un seul trait.	Het glas koud spoelen, licht schuin houden en voorzichtig half inschenken. Daarna het glas rechthouden en de rest in 1 beweging uitschenken.
i	Bockor's very first beer. Called 'Ouden Tripel' at the beginning in 1892.	La toute première bière de Bockor. Au départ, en 1892, elle s'appelait 'Ouden Tripel'.	Het allereerste bier van Bockor. Bij de start in 1892 heette het 'Ouden Tripel'.

Bellegems Witbier

Brouwerij Bockor (Vander Ghinste) 5% 4 - 6 ° / 39 - 43 °

	top-fermentation	fermentation haute	hoge gisting
	witbier	bière blanche	witbier
	barley malt, wheat, hops, yeast, herbs, water	malt d'orge, froment, houblon, levure, herbes, eau	gerstemout, tarwe, hop, gist, kruiden, water
	white-yellow	jaune blanc	witgeel
	Fresh and thirst-quenching owing to the fruitiness and herby aromas.	Caractère frais et désaltérant dû au fruité et aux arômes épicés.	Fris en dorstlessend karakter door de fruitigheid en de kruidige aroma's.
	Rinse the glass cold, tilt slightly and gently pour half of the bottle. Then hold the glass upright and pour the rest in a single movement.	Rincer le verre à l'eau froide, le tenir légèrement incliné et remplir prudemment à moitié. Puis tenir le verre en position verticale et verser le reste d'un seul mouvement.	Het glas koud spoelen, licht schuin houden en voorzichtig half inschenken. Daarna het glas rechthouden en de rest in 1 beweging uitschenken.
i			

Belle-Vue Extra Kriek

Brasserie Belle-Vue (Inbev)

4,10% 3 °C 37 °F

	spontaneous fermentation	fermentation spontanée	spontane gisting
	fruit beer based on lambic	bière fruitée à base de lambic	frutbier op basis van lambiek
	wheat, barley malt, hops, coriander, orange peel, cherry juice, griotte cherries, elderberry juice	froment, malt d'orge, houblon, coriandre, écorce d'orange, jus de cerises, cerises griottes, jus de baies de sureau	tarwe, gerstemout, hop, koriander, sinaasschil, kriekensap, griottes krieken, vlierbessensap
	ruby red, clear with a fine, white foam head filtered pasteurised	rouge rubis, clair avec un faux col fin, blanc filtrée, pasteurisée	robijnrood, helder met een fijne, witte schuimkraag gefilterd, gepasteuriseerd
	Pronounced aromas of cherry and almond with typical touches of Lambic. A distinct tartness that is brought into balance by the soft fruit. More intense and softer than the regular Kriek owing to the larger griotte cherry content.	Arômes prononcés de cerise et d'amande, avec des touches typiques de lambic. Une acidité nette, qui est équilibrée par la douceur du fruit. Un goût plus intense et plus doux que pour la kriek habituelle, du fait de la plus grande teneur en griottes.	Uitgesproken aroma's van kers en amandel met typische toetsen van lambiek. Een duidelijke zurigheid die in evenwicht wordt gebracht door het zachte fruit. Intenser en zachter dan de gewone kriek door het grotere gehalte aan griottes.
	Pour into a degreased, rinsed glass in a single, smooth movement. Skim off in a 45° angle. A 3 cm foam head is perfect.	Verser d'un seul mouvement dans un verre dégraissé, rincé. Écumer sous un angle de 45°. Un faux col de 3 cm est parfait.	In 1 beweging vlot uitschenken in een vetvrij, gespoeld tulpglas. Afschuimen onder een hoek van 45°. Een schuimkraag van 3 cm is perfect.

Belle-Vue Framboise

Brasserie Belle-Vue (Inbev) **5,70%** 3° 37°

	spontaneous fermentation	fermentation spontanée	spontane gisting
	lambic-based fruit beer	bière fruitée à base de lambic	frutbier op basis van lambiek
	barley malt, wheat, hops, coriander, orange peel, juice of raspberry and red fruits, sugar	malt d'orge, froment, houblon, coriandre, écorce d'orange, jus de framboises et de fruits rouges, sucre	gerstemout, tarwe, hop, koriander, sinaasschil, sap van frambozen en rode vruchten, suiker
	orange-red, clear with a fine, white foam head filtered, pasteurised	rouge orange, limpide avec un faux col fin, blanc filtrée, pasteurisée	oranjerood, helder met een fijne, witte schuimkraag gefilterd, gepasteuriseerd
	Aromas of lambic with clear hints of raspberry and strawberry. Full-bodied. Fine sweet and sour balance.	Arômes de lambic avec des touches claires de framboise et de fraise. Beaucoup de corps. Joli équilibre entre acide et sucre.	Aroma's van lambiek met duidelijke hints van framboos en aardbei. Veel body. Mooi evenwicht tussen zuur en suiker.
	Serve in a goblet.	Verser dans un verre calice.	Uitschenken in een kelkglas.
i	Brewed for exports.	Brassée pour l'exportation.	Gebrouwen voor export.

rasserie Belle-Vue (Inbev) 5,50% 3 °C 37 °F

spontaneous fermentation	fermentation spontanée	spontane gisting
gueuze	gueuze	geuze
barley malt, wheat, hops, coriander, orange peel, sugar	malt d'orge, froment, houblon, coriandre, écorce d'orange, sucre	gerstemout, tarwe, hop, koriander, sinaasschil, suiker
amber, clear with a fine, white foam head filtered, pasteurised	ambrée, limpide avec un faux col fin, blanc filtrée, pasteurisée	amber, helder met een fijne, witte schuimkraag gefilterd, gepasteuriseerd
Typical lambic aromas with hints of apricot. Fine sweet and sour balance.	Arômes de lambic typiques avec des touches d'abricot. Joli équilibre entre acide et sucre.	Typische lambiekaroma's met toetsen van abrikoos. Mooi evenwicht tussen zuur en suiker.
Serve in a tumbler.	Verser dans un verre tumbler.	Uitschenken in een tumblerglas
Lambic, the basic beer of gueuze, is made in 600 l casks or 40,000 l barrels, where the wort ferments spontaneously from September to March and changes into lambic.	Le lambic, la bière de base de la gueuze, est fabriqué en tonneaux de 600 l ou en foudres de 40.000 l. Le moût de malt y fermente spontanément de septembre à mars et se transforme en lambic.	Lambiek, het basisbier van geuze, wordt gemaakt in tonnen van 600 l of foeders van 40,000 l. Het wort gist er spontaan van september tot maart en transformeert in lambiek.

Belle-Vue Kriek

Brasserie Belle-Vue (Inbev)

5,10% 3° 37°

	spontaneous fermentation	fermentation spontanée	spontane gisting
	fruit beer based on lambic	bière fruitée à base de lambic	frutbier op basis van lambiek
	wheat, barley malt, hops, coriander, orange peel, cherry juice, griotte cherries, elderberry juice	froment, malt d'orge, houblon, coriandre, écorce d'orange, jus de cerises, cerises griottes, jus de baies de sureau	tarwe, gerstemout, hop, koriander, sinaasschil, kriekensap, griottes krieken, vlierbessensap
	ruby red, clear with a fine, white foam head filtered pasteurised	rouge rubis, claire avec un faux col fin, blanc filtrée, pasteurisée	robijnrood, helder met een fijne, witte schuimkraag gefilterd, gepasteuriseerd
	Pronounced aromas of cherry and almond with typical touches of lambic. A distinct tartness that is brought into balance by the soft fruit.	Arômes prononcés de cerise et d'amande, avec des touches typiques de lambic. Une acidité nette, qui est équilibrée par la douceur du fruit.	Uitgesproken aroma's van kers en amandel met typische toetsen van lambiek. Een duidelijke zurigheid die in evenwicht wordt gebracht door het zachte fruit.
	Pour into a degreased, rinsed glass in a single, smooth movement. Skim off in a 45° angle. A 3 cm foam head is perfect.	Verser d'un seul mouvement dans un verre dégraissé, rincé. Ecumer sous un angle de 45°. Un faux col de 3 cm est parfait.	In 1 beweging vlot uitschenken in een vetvrij, gespoeld ballonglas. Afschuimen onder een hoek van 45°. Een schuimkraag van 3 cm is perfect.
i	Brewed annually during the cherry harvest (end of June). Kriek lambic is used as a basis for this beer.	Elle est brassée chaque année pendant la récolte des griottes (fin juin). La kriek lambic sert de base à cette bière...	Wordt jaarlijks gebrouwen tijdens de kriekenoogst (eind juni). Kriek lambic dient als basis voor dit bier.

Brouwerij Maenhout

7% 10 °C 50 °F

Berentemmer

B

	top-fermentation re-fermentation in the bottle not centrifuged	fermentation haute refermentation en bouteille non centrifugée	hoge gisting hergisting op de fles niet gecentrifugeerd
	double	double	dubbel
	pale ale, chocolate and Special B malt, Tettnanger hops	malt pale ale, malt chocolat et malt Spécial B, houblon Tettnanger	pale ale, chocolade- en Special B mout, Tettnanger hop
	dark brown with dark foam head not filtered or pasteurised	brun foncé avec faux col foncé non filtrée, non pasteurisée	donkerbruin met donkere schuimkraag ongefilterd, niet gepasteuriseerd
	Smoked accents, touches of raisins and a slightly bitter aftertaste.	Accents fumés, touches de raisins secs et une arrière-bouche légèrement amère.	Gerookte accenten, toetsen van rozijnen en een licht bittere afdronk.
	Pour slowly into a chalice.	Verser lentement dans un verre calice.	Traag uitschenken in een kelkglas.
	Brewed for the inhabitants of Meulebeke, also known as the 'bear municipality'. A beer, therefore, to tame bears...	Brassée pour les habitants de Meulebeke, aussi appelée commune des ours. Une petite bière donc pour dompter les ours...	Gebrouwen voor de inwoners van Meulebeke, ook wel berengemeente genoemd. Een biertje dus om beren te temmen...

Oud Beersel at/by Brouwerij Huyghe

4,50% 8 - 12 ° 46 - 54 °

	top-fermentation re-fermentation in the bottle	fermentation haute refermentation en bouteille	hoge gisting hergisting op de fles
	barley malt, hops, yeast, water	malt d'orge, houblon, levure, eau	gerstemout, hop, gist, water
	golden-yellow not pasteurised	jaune doré non pasteurisée	goudgeel niet gepasteuriseerd
	Hoppy aroma with a fruity nose.	Arôme houblonné, avec un bouquet fruité.	Hoppig aroma met een fruitige neus.
	Bersalis Kadet helps protect the traditional lambic beers of Oud Beersel. Thanks to the sale of Bersalis, it was possible to relaunch the traditional production of the Lambic beers and the beers are accessible to a larger public.	La Bersalis Kadet contribue à défendre les traditionnelles bières de lambic d'Oud Beersel. C'est grâce aux ventes de Bersalis que la production traditionnelle des bières de lambic a pu être relancée et qu'un plus large public a l'occasion de faire la connaissance de ces bières.	Bersalis Kadet helpt om de traditionele lambiekbieren van Oud Beersel te beschermen. Dankzij de verkoop van Bersalis kon de traditionele productie van de lambiekbieren heropgestart worden en kan een ruimer publiek met die bieren kennis maken.

Bersalis Tripel

B

ud Beersel at/by Brouwerij Huyghe 9,50% 8 - 12 °C / 46 - 54 °F

	top-fermentation re-fermented in the bottle	fermentation haute refermentation en bouteille	hoge gisting nagisting op de fles
	tripel	triple	tripel
	wheat malt, barley malt, hops, yeast, herbs, water	malt de froment et d'orge, houblon, levure, herbes, eau	tarwemout, gerstemout, hop, gist, kruiden, water
	gold-yellow	jaune doré	goudgeel
	Rich, spicy, full round and intriguing. Refreshing aroma of citrus and malt. Full taste of wheat mout, first fruity bitter, then roundish and sweet. Pleasant, spicy aftertaste.	Riche, corsée, plein ronde et intrigante. Arôme rafraîchissant d'agrumes de malt. Saveur pleine de froment malté, d'abord amer fruité, par la suite rond et doux. Arrière-bouche agréable d'herbes.	Rijk, pittig, volrond en intrigerend. Verfrissend aroma van citrus en mout. Volle smaak van tarwemout, eerst fruitig bitter, daarna rondig en zoet. Aangename nasmaak van kruiden.
	Pour swiftly to make the beer swirl in a degreased, dry glass. Avoid contact between bottle and foam. Leave the yeast in the bottle.	Verser agilement de sorte que la bière tourne dans le verre dégraissé et séché sans que la bouteille touche l'écume. Laisser la levure dans la bouteille.	Gezwind uitschenken zodat het bier ronddraait in het ontvette, droge glas zonder dat de fles het schuim raakt. De gist in de fles laten.
i	see Bersalis Kadet	voir Bersalis Kadet	zie Bersalis Kadet

Betchard Blonde

Brasserie de Tubize

5,50% 5° 41°

	top-fermentation re-fermented in the bottle	fermentation haute refermentation en bouteille	hoge gisting nagisting op de fles
	regional beer	bière régionale	streekbier
	based on pale malt, hops and house yeasts	à base de malt blond, houblons et levures maison	op basis van bleke mout, hopsoorten en huisgist
	blond, slightly cloudy with a nice foam head; not filtered	blonde, très légèrement trouble avec un grand faux col; non filtrée	blond, lichttroebel met royale schuimkraag; niet gefilterd
	Natural thirst-quenching beer with a distinct hops taste and a slight fruitiness.	Bière naturelle, très désaltérante avec goût de houblon prononcé et une saveur légèrement fruitée.	Dorstlessend licht fruitig natuurbier met een uitgesproken hopsmaak.
	Pour out in a large tulip glass.	Verser dans un grand verre type tulipe.	Uitschenken in een groot tulpglas.
i			

7% 6 °C 43 °F

	top-fermentation	fermentation haute	hoge gisting
	dubbel	double	dubbel
	brown with a nice foam head not filtered	brune avec grand faux col non filtrée	bruin met ruime schuimkraag ongefilterd
	Character beer with distinct chocolate flavour and sweetwood flavour.	Bière de caractère au goût chocolat prononcé et goût de réglisse.	Karakterbier met uitgesproken chocoladesmaak en smaak van zoethout.
	Pour out in a large tulip glass to enjoy all the perfumes.	Verser dans un grand verre type tulipe pour permettre à la bière de dégager tout son parfum.	Uitschenken in een groot tulpglas zodat het bier al zijn aroma's kan vrijgeven.
i			

Betchard Brune

Bieken

Brouwerij Boelens

8,50% 8° 46°

	top-fermentation re-fermented in the bottle	fermentation haute refermentation en bouteille	hoge gisting hergisting op de fles
	tripel blond	triple blonde	tripel blond
	water, malt, honey	eau, malt, miel	water, mout, honing
	blond clear	blonde claire	blond helder
	Very malty and full flavour with flowery aftertaste.	Très maltée et pleine avec une fin de bouche fleurie.	Zeer moutig en vol met een bloemige afdronk.
	Pour carefully so that the yeast sediment stays at the bottom of the bottle.	Verser prudemment pour laisser le dépôt de levure dans la bouteille.	Voorzichtig uitschenken om het gistbezinksel op de bodem te laten.
i	The name refers to the spice cake factory the Biekens in Sint-Niklaas. In this region, Bieke is also a popular woman's pet name.	Le nom de cette bière renvoie à l'usine de pain d'épices Biekens à Sint-Niklaas. Bieke est dans cette région aussi une appellation affectueuse pour une femme.	De naam verwijst naar de peperkoekfabriek De Biekens in Sint-Niklaas. Bieke is in deze streek ook de koosnaam voor een vrouw.

5,80% 6 - 8 °C / 43 - 46 °F

	top-fermentation re-fermented in the bottle	fermentation haute refermentation en bouteille	hoge gisting hergisting op de fles
	specialty beer	bière spéciale	speciaalbier
	malt, wheat, hops, fig juice, yeast, water. Boutique beer without herbs or additives.	malt, froment, houblon, jus de figues, levure, eau. Produit artisanal sans herbes ou additifs.	mout, tarwe, hop, vijgensap, gist, water. Artisanaal product zonder kruiden of additieven.
	unfiltered	non filtrée	niet gefilterd
	Digestive and refreshing. Fine bitterness, fruity but not sugared.	Digestive et rafraîchissante. Saveur amère raffinée, fruitée mais non sucrée.	Digestief en verfrissend. Fijne bitterheid, fruitig maar niet gesuikerd.
	The name refers to an ancient, typical dish of the region. The Darbystes are the disciples of priest Darby, who gather in the region of Mons-Borinage.	Le nom de cette bière renvoie à un plat ancien régional. Les Darbystes sont les adeptes du Curé Darby qui se réunissent dans la région de Mons-Borinage.	De naam verwijst naar een oud streekgerecht. De Darbystes zijn de leerlingen van Pastoor Darby die samenkomen in de streek van Mons-Borinage.

Bière Darbyste

Bière de Brabant Blanche

Groep John Martin by various breweries 5%

	top-fermentation	fermentation haute	hoge gisting
	witbier (white beer)	bière blanche	witbier
	Subtly tart owing to the coriander.	Acide subtil dû à la coriandre.	Subtiel zuur door de koriander.
	Serve with a slice of lemon, if possible.	Servir de préférence avec une rondelle de citron.	Bij voorkeur serveren met een schijfje citroen.

roep John Martin by various breweries 6%

Bière de Brabant Blonde

B

	top-fermentation	fermentation haute	hoge gisting
	strong blond	blonde forte	sterk blond
	Fresh with a discrete aroma and dry bitterness. Thirst-quenching, balanced, without any bitterness in the aftertaste.	Fraîche, avec un arôme discret et une amertume sèche. Bière désaltérante, équilibrée, sans amertume dans l'arrière-bouche.	Fris met een discreet aroma en droge bitterheid. Dorstlessend, evenwichtig, zonder bitterheid in de afdronk.

Bière de Brabant Rousse

Groep John Martin by various breweries **5,20%** 4 - 5° 39 - 41°

top-fermentation	fermentation haute	hoge gisting
special ale	ale spéciale	speciale ale
copper, amber-coloured	cuivre, ambrée	koper, amberkleurig
Delicate aroma of roasted malt and subtly sweet. Taste: subtle mixture of malt, slightly bitter caramel and sweet undertones. Bitter aftertaste.	Arôme délicat de malt torréfié et subtilement sucré. Goût :subtile mélange de malt, de caramel légèrement amer et d'un accent sucré. Arrière-bouche amère.	Delicaat aroma van gebrande mout en subtiel zoet. Smaak: subtiele mengeling van mout, licht bittere karamel en een zoete ondertoon. Bittere afdronk.

ssenhofke by De Proefbrouwerij

10% 9 - 11 °C / 48 - 52 °F

	top-fermentation re-fermentation in the bottle centrifuged	fermentation haute refermentation en bouteille centrifugée	hoge gisting hergisting in de fles gecentrifugeerd
	strong dark	double forte	sterk donker
	barley malt, wheat malt, roasted malts, candy sugar, bitter hops (Challenger), aroma hops (Goldings and Fuggles), garlic, water	malt d'orge, malt de froment, malts torréfiés, sucre candi, houblon amer (Challenger), houblon aromatique (Goldings et Fuggles), ail, eau	gerstemout, tarwemout, gebrande mouten, kandijsuiker, bitterhop (Challenger), aromahop (Goldings en Fuggles), knoflook, water
	red-brown with solid foam head not filtered or pasteurised	brun rouge avec faux col solide non filtrée, non pasteurisée	roodbruin met stevige schuimkraag ongefilterd, niet gepasteuriseerd
	Somewhere inbetween sweet and bitter with a heartwarming aftertaste.	Entre sucrée et amère avec une chaude arrière-bouche.	Tussen zoet en bitter met een warme afdronk.
	Serve in a sipping glass and leave the yeast sediment in the bottle, if necessary. Provide a generous foam head.	Verser dans un verre de dégustation et laisser éventuellement le dépôt de levure dans la bouteille. Former un faux col généreux.	In een degustieglas uitschenken en het gistdepot eventueel in de fles laten. Een royale schuimkraag voorzien.
	Originally brewed to mark 750 years' anniversary of Grendel Gate in Valkenburg, but now permanently included in the range.	Brassée à l'origine à l'occasion des 750 ans de la Grendelpoort à Valkenburg, mais à présent reprise de façon permanente dans l'assortiment.	Origineel gebrouwen ter gelegenheid van 750 jaar Grendelpoort in Valkenburg maar nu permanent in het assortiment opgenomen.

B

Bière de Miel Bio

Brasserie Dupont 8% 12 54

	top-fermentation re-fermented in the bottle	fermentation haute refermentation en bouteille	hoge gisting hergisting op de fles
	honey beer	bière de miel	honingbier
	Based on organic honey, with a very particular taste.	À base de miel biologique avec un goût particulier.	Op basis van biologische honing, met aparte smaak.
	amber-coloured	ambrée	amberkleurig
	Prominent honey taste and aroma but not sweet due to the re-fermentation of the honey. Complex beer because of the secondary fermentation in the cellar.	Saveur et arôme de miel dominants mais pas sucrés par la fermentation secondaire du miel. Bière complexe par la refermentation évoluant encore dans la cave.	Dominerende honingsmaak en -aroma maar niet zoet door de hergisting van de honing. Complex bier door de nagisting dat verder evolueert in de kelder.
	Has a "Biogarantie label". The label on the bottle is a reproduction of the original one from 1880, when the honey beer was a specialty of the farm brewery Rimaux-Deridder.	Avec le label Biogarantie®. L'étiquette est une reproduction de l'étiquette originale de 1880 au moment où la bière de miel était une spécialité de la brasserie de ferme Rimaux-Deridder.	Met label Biogarantie®. Het etiket is een reproductie van het oorspronkelijke etiket uit 1880 toen het honingbier een specialiteit was van hoevebrouwerij Rimaux-Deridder.

asserie Artisanale La Binchoise 8,50%

	top-fermentation re-fermented in the bottle	fermentation haute refermentation en bouteille	hoge gisting hergisting in de fles
	honey beer	bière de miel	honingbier
	before the main fermentation, honey is added	ajout de miel avant la fermentation principale	vóór de hoofdgisting wordt honing toegevoegd
	blond	blonde	blond
	Smooth and aromatic sipping or aperitif beer.	Bière de dégustation ou d'apéritif douce et aromatisée.	Zacht en aromatisch degustatie- of aperitiefbier.
i	The high alcohol content is the result of the yeast sugars in the honey.	La teneur élevée en alcool est le résultat des sucres de levure dans le miel.	Het hoge alcoholgehalte is het resultaat van de gistsuikers in de honing.

Bière du Corsaire Cuvée Spéciale

Brouwerij Huyghe 9,40%

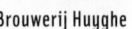

	top-fermentation re-fermented in the bottle	fermentation haute refermentation en bouteille	hoge gisting hergisting op de fles
	Belgian Ale double malt strong blond	Belgian ale malt double blonde forte	Belgian ale dubbelmoutig sterk blond
	barley malt, hops, yeast, candy sugar, water	malt d'orge, houblon, levure, eau, sucre candi	gerstemout, hop, gist, kandijsuiker, water
	blond	blonde	blond
	Sipping beer with a light roasted bitter aftertaste and a touch of roasted caramel.	Bière de dégustation avec une fin de bouche fumée légèrement amère et une touche de caramélisé brûlé.	Degustatiebier met lichtgerookte bittere afdronk, toets van gebrande karamel.
	Heavy brother of Delirium, pirate beer.	Le frère plus fort de delirium, bière pirate.	Zwaardere broer van delirium, piratenbier.

asserie de Brunehaut

8% 6 - 10 °C / 43 - 50 °F

Bière du Mont Saint-Aubert

B

	top-fermentation re-fermented in the bottle	fermentation haute refermentation en bouteille	hoge gisting hergisting op de fles
	blond	blonde	blond
	malt, hops, yeast, water	malt, houblon, levure, eau	mout, hop, gist, water
	blond	blonde	blond
	Strong and full-bodied.	Forte et corsée.	Sterk en krachtig.

Brasserie Artisanale La Binchoise

5%

	top-fermentation re-fermented in the bottle	fermentation haute refermentation en bouteille	hoge gisting hergisting in de fles
	spéciale belge	spéciale belge	speciale belge
	amber not pasteurised	ambrée non pasteurisée	amber niet gepasteuriseerd
	Fine bitterness.	Saveur amère raffinée.	Fijne bitterheid.

ouwerij Bavik 5% 2 - 4 °C 36 - 39 °F

Big Bavik

	bottom-fermentation	fermentation basse	lage gisting
	pilsner	pils	pilsbier
	barley malt, hops, yeast, pure spring water	malt d'orge, houblon, levure, eau de source pure	gerstemout, hop, gist, zuiver bronwater
	clear gold-yellow	jaune doré vif	helder goudgeel
	Slightly spicy with sweet malt. Fresh, light, crispy and hoppy character.	Légèrement relevée avec un goût sucré malté. Caractère frais, léger, picotant et houblonné.	Licht kruidig met een moutige zoetheid. Fris, licht, knisperig en hoppig karakter.
	Pour into a degreased, rinsed and wet glass,avoiding contact between bottle and foam.	Verser dans un verre dégraissé, rincé et mouillé sans que la bouteille touche le faux col.	Uitschenken in een ontvet, gespoeld en nat glas zonder dat de fles het schuim raakt.
i			

Bink Bloesem

Brouwerij Kerkom by Brouwerij Sint-Jozef or Proefbrouwerij 7,10%

	top-fermentation re-fermented in the bottle	fermentation haute refermentation en bouteille	hoge gisting hergisting in de fles
	blond	blonde	blond
	5 malt varieties, 1 hop-variety, yeast, honey-from Sint-Truiden, pear syrup from Vrolingen, brewing water	5 sortes de malt, 1 variété de houblon, levure, miel de Saint-Trond, sirop de poire de Vrolingen, eau de brassage	5 moutsoorten, 1 hop-soort, gist, honing van Sint-Truiden, perenstroop van Vrolingen, brouwwater
	dark amber with red hues unfiltered, unpasteurised	ambre foncé avec des teintes rouges non filtrée ni pasteurisée	donker amber met rode tint ongefilterd, niet gepasteuriseerd
	Fruity with a light sweet tone and a long, fruity, smoothly bitter aftertaste.	Fruitée avec un teint légèrement doux et une fin de bouche longue, fruitée et douce-amère.	Fruitig met een lichtzoete tint en een lange fruitige, zacht bittere afdronk.
	Gently pour into a degreased, dry glass without sloshing. Leave 1 cm yeast sediment in the bottle or add it at the end.	Verser tranquillement sans clapotage dans un verre dégraissé et sec. Laisser un dépôt de levure de 1 cm dans la bouteille ou l'ajouter par après.	Rustig inschenken zonder klokgeluid in een ontvet en droog glas. Een gistdepot van 1 cm in de fles laten of achteraf bijgieten.
i			

top-fermentation re-fermented in the bottle	fermentation haute refermentation en bouteille	hoge gisting hergisting op de fles
blond	blonde	blond
2 malt varieties, 3 Belgian hop varieties (Challenger, Saaz, East-Kent Goldings), yeast, brewing water	2 sortes de malt, 3 variétés belges de houblon (Challenger, Saaz, East-Kent Goldings), levure, eau de brassage	2 moutsoorten, 3 Belgische hopsoorten (Challenger, Saaz, East-Kent Goldings), gist, brouwwater
copper-coloured unfiltered	cuivrée non filtrée	koperkleurig ongefilterd
Exceptional character beer: bitter, hoppy thirst-quencher with a low alcohol content, not taking part in the sweetening trend of Belgian beers. Fresh and easily digestible, fruity taste, hoppy nose, bitterish aftertaste.	Bière de caractère rare :désaltérante amère et houblonnée avec une teneur basse en alcool, par laquelle elle s'écarte de la tendance de l'adoucissement des bières belges. Fraîche et facilement digestible, goût fruité, parfum houblonné, arrière-goût amer.	Zeldzaam karakterbier: bittere, hoppige dorstlesser met laag alcoholgehalte, waarmee het afwijkt van de trend van de verzoeting van de Belgische bieren. Fris en licht verteerbaar, fruitige smaak, hoppige neus, bitterige nasmaak.
Gently pour into a degreased, dry glass without sloshing. Leave 1 cm yeast sediment in the bottle or add it at the end.	Verser tranquillement sans clapotage dans un verre dégraissé et sec. Laisser un dépôt de levure de 1 cm dans la bouteille ou l'ajouter par après.	Rustig inschenken zonder klokgeluid in een ontvet en droog glas. Een gistdepot van 1 cm in de fles laten of achteraf bijgieten.

Bink Bruin

Brouwerij Kerkom by Brouwerij Sint-Jozef or Proefbrouwerij 5,50%

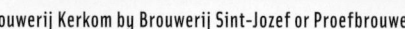

	top-fermentation re-fermented in the bottle	fermentation haute refermentation en bouteille	hoge gisting hergisting in de fles
	Scottish style type	type scotch	scotchtype
	4 malt varieties, 1 Belgian hop variety, yeast, brewing water	4 sortes de malt, 1 variété belge de houblon, levure, eau de brassage	4 moutsoorten, 1 Belgische hopsoort, gist, brouwwater
	dark brown unfiltered, unpasteurised	brun foncé non filtrée ni pasteurisée	donkerbruin ongefilterd, niet gepasteuriseerd
	Full-bodied and smoothly bitter with a sweetish malt aftertaste.	Franche et légèrement amère avec une fin de bouche douce maltée.	Volmondig en zacht bitter met een zoetig moutige afdronk.
	Gently pour into a degreased, dry glass without sloshing. Leave 1 cm yeast sediment in the bottle or add it at the end.	Verser tranquillement sans clapotage dans un verre dégraissé et sec. Laisser un dépôt de levure de 1 cm dans la bouteille ou l'ajouter par après.	Rustig inschenken zonder klokgeluid in een ontvet en droog glas. Een gistdepot van 1 cm in de fles laten of achteraf bijgieten.
i			

asserie Dupont 3,50% Slightly cooled

	top-fermentation re-fermented in the bottle	fermentation haute refermentation en bouteille	hoge gisting hergisting op de fles
	saisons	bière de saison	saison
	blond	blonde	blond
	Light and refreshing, well-balanced and relatively complex, distinctive despite the low alcohol content. Taste and aromas of malt and citrus fruits.	Légère et rafraîchissante, équilibrée et relativement complexe, pleine de caractère malgré la basse teneur d'alcool. Saveur et arômes de malt et de fruits de citron.	Licht en verfrissend, evenwichtig en relatief complex, karaktervol ondanks het laag alcoholgehalte. Smaak en aroma's van mout en citrusvruchten.
	The production is supervised by Ecocert®, with a 'Biogarantie' -label.	La production est contrôlée par Ecocert®. Avec le label Biogarantie®.	De productie wordt gecontroleerd door Ecocert®. Met label Biogarantie®.

Bitter Sweet Symphony

Brouwerij 't Gaverhopke

7,80%

	top-fermentation	fermentation haute	hoge gisting
	Belgian ale double IPA	Belgian ale double IPA	Belgian ale double IPA
	barley malt, 4 different hops (mainly from USA), yeast, water	malt d'orge, 4 variétés de houblon (principalement des États-Unis) levure, eau	gerstemout, 4 hopsoorten (vooral uit USA), gist, water
	amber with a thick white foam head that lingers on the glass.	ambrée avec faux col épais blanc collant parfaitement au verre.	amber met dikke witte schuimkraag die mooi aan het glas kleeft.
	Hoppy aroma with hints of lychee and grapefruit. Fresh and balanced flavour with the same accents. Dry, extended aftertaste. Bitter (78 EBU) and sweet in perfect harmony. (Description by William Roelens).	Arôme houblonné avec des touches de litchi et de pamplemousse. Goût fleuri et équilibré avec les mêmes accents. Arrière-bouche sèche, s'écoulant longuement. Amer (78 EBU) et sucré en parfaite harmonie. (Description par William Roelens).	Hoppig aroma met toetsen van lychee en pompelmoes. Fleurige en evenwichtige smaak met dezelfde accenten. Droge, lang uitvloeiende afdronk. Bitter (78 EBU) en zoet in perfecte harmonie. (Beschrijving door William Roelens).
	Brewed in tandem with brewer Jean Brouillet (USA).	Brassée en collaboration avec le brasseur Jean Brouillet (États-Unis).	Gebrouwen in samenwerking met brouwer Jean Brouillet (USA).

t Alternatief by Brouwerij De Graal

11% 8 °C 46 °F

top-fermentation re-fermentation in the bottle	fermentation haute refermentation en bouteille	hoge gisting hergisting op de fles
Belgian IPA	Belgian IPA	Belgian IPA
4 types of hops (Poperinge and American bitter hops), light cara malts	4 variétés de houblon (de Poperinge et houblon amer Américain), malts cara légers	4 soorten hop (Poperingse en Amerikaanse bitterhop), lichte caramouten
blond (11 EBC) clear with solid white foam head filtered	blonde (11 EBC) limpide avec faux col solide blanc filtrée	blond (11 EBC), helder met stevige witte schuimkraag gefilterd
Very bitter and hoppy (100 EBU) but accessible. Malty, strong body. Very long bitter aftertaste.	Fort amère et houblonnée (100 EBU) mais accessible. Maltée, corps puissant. Arrière-bouche amère très longue.	Zeer bitter en hoppig (100 EBU) maar toegankelijk. Moutig, sterke body. Zeer lange bittere afdronk.
Serve in a tulip glass.	Verser dans un verre tulipe.	Uitschenken in een tulpglas.
The logo on the label has been designed especially for the beer by the Izegem artist Johan Herman.	La statuette sur l'étiquette a été créée spécialement pour la bière par l'artiste izegemois Johan Herman.	Het beeldje op het etiket werd speciaal voor het bier gemaakt door de Izegemse kunstenaar Johan Herman.

Black Albert

De Struise Brouwers at Brouwerij Deca

13% 8 - 10 46 - 50

	top-fermentation re-fermentation in the bottle not centrifuged	fermentation haute refermentation en bouteille non centrifugée	hoge gisting hergisting op de fles niet gecentrifugeerd
	Belgian royal stout	Belgian royal stout	Belgian royal stout
	turbid, intense black with a dense beige foam head not filtered or pasteurised	noir intense opaque avec un faux col épais beige non filtrée, non pasteurisée	ondoorzichtig, intens zwart met een dichte beige schuimkraag ongefilterd, niet gepasteuriseerd
	Roasted touches (coffee and chocolate) and a hint of candied fruit (cherries, raisins). Rich, yet elegant flavour with hints of coffee, dark chocolate, toast and a hint of candied fruit. Long aftertaste with a slightly sweet accent of residual sugar, alcohol and refreshing hops.	Arôme: des touches grillées (café et chocolat) et un peu de fruits confits (cerises, raisins secs). Goût riche mais élégant, avec des touches de café, de chocolat noir, de pain grillé et un peu de fruits secs. Longue arrière-bouche avec un accent légèrement sucré de sucre résiduel, d'alcool et de houblon rafraîchissant.	Geur: geroosterde toetsen (koffie en chocolade) en wat gekonfijt frui (kersen, rozijnen). Rijke maar elegante smaak met hints van koffie, zwarte chocolade, geroosterd brood en ietwa gedroogd fruit. Lange afdronk met een licht zoet accent van restsuiker, alcohol en verfrissende hop.
	Stout is black and Royal refers to the Belgian King Albert. This beer has been developed by Ebenezer's Pub in Lovell (Maine), one of America's most renowned beer pubs.	La stout est noire (black) et la Royal est complétée par le nom du roi des Belges (Albert). Cette bière a été développée pour l'Ebenezer's Pub à Lovell (Maine), l'un des plus fameux pubs à bière d'Amérique.	Stout is zwart (black) en Royal wordt ingevuld door de naam van de Bel gische koning (Albert). Dit bier werd ontwikkeld voor Ebenezer's Pub in Lovell (Maine) een van Amerika's befaamste bierpubs.

Black Damnation 1

Struise Brouwers at Brouwerij Deca 13% 8 - 10 °C / 46 - 50 °F

top-fermentation re-fermentation in the bottle not centrifuged	fermentation haute refermentation en bouteille non centrifugée	hoge gisting hergisting op de fles niet gecentrifugeerd
Russian Imperial Stout	Russian Imperial Stout	Russian Imperial Stout
see Black Albert	voir Black Albert	zie Black Albert
Rich aroma with intensely roasted touches (bread crust, espresso, dark chocolate, port, dried fruit). Robust, fleshy and very complex flavour with hints of black coffee, roasted malts and dark chocolate. Very long, intense aftertaste with slightly sweet accent and crispy hops.	Riche arôme avec des touches intensément grillées (croûte de pain, espresso, chocolat amer, porto, fruits secs). Goût robuste, charnu et fort complexe, avec des touches de café noir, de malts grillés et de chocolat noir. Arrière-bouche épicée fort longue, avec un accent légèrement sucré et du houblon croquant.	Rijk aroma met intens geroosterde toetsen (broodkorst, espresso, bittere chocolade, port, gedroogd fruit). Robuuste, vlezige en erg complexe smaak met toetsen van zwarte koffie, geroosterde mouten en donkere chocolade. Zeer lange, pittige afdronk met lichtzoet accent en crispy hop.
Pour gently into a Struise or cognac glass. Lift bottle up slightly towards the end to obtain a fine foam head.	Verser lentement dans un verre Struise ou un verre cognac. Vers la fin tenir la bouteille un peu plus haut pour former un faux col joli.	Traag uitschenken in een Struise- of cognacglas. De fles naar het einde toe iets hoger houden voor een mooie schuimkraag.
Mixed beer of Black Albert and Hel & Verdoemenis (beer from De Molen brewery, Nl).	Bière de mélange de Black Albert et Hel & Verdoemenis (bière de Brouwerij De Molen, Pays-Bas).	Mengbier van Black Albert en Hel & Verdoemenis (bier van Brouwerij De Molen, Nl).

Black Damnation II (Mocha Bomb)

De Struise Brouwers at Brouwerij Deca 12% 8 - 10 46 - 50

	top-fermentation re-fermentation in the bottle not centrifuged	fermentation haute refermentation en bouteille non centrifugée	hoge gisting hergisting op de fles niet gecentrifugeerd
	Russian Imperial Stout	Russian Imperial Stout	Russian Imperial Stout
	see Black Albert	voir Black Albert	zie Black Albert
	Coffee aroma with hints of caramel, bourbon, oak, dark chocolate and candied plums. Rich taste with hints of liquorice, coffee, dried fruit and American oak. Very long aftertaste with roasted touches and refined hops.	Arôme de café avec des notes de caramel, de bourbon, de chêne, de chocolat noir et de prunes confites. Riche goût, avec des touches de réglisse, de café, de fruits secs et un peu de chêne américain. Fort longue arrière-bouche avec des touches grillées et du houblon raffiné.	Koffiearoma met tonen van karamel, bourbon, eik, zwarte chocolade en gekonfijte pruimen. Rijke smaak met hints van zoethout, koffie, gedroogd fruit en ietwat Amerikaanse eik. Zeer lange afdronk met geroosterde toetsen en verfijnde hop.
	see Black Damnation I	voir Black Damnation I	zie Black Damnation I
	Combination of 50% Black Albert, matured in Columbian coffee beans, 25% Cuvée Delphine, matured in Four Roses casks and 25% Hel & Verdoemenis, matured inn Jack Daniels casks.	Assemblage de 50% de Black Albert mûrie sur des grains de café colombiens, 25% de Cuvée Delphine mûrie en fûts de Four Roses et 25% de Hel & Verdoemenis mûrie en fûts de Jack Daniels.	Samenstelling van 50% Black Albert gerijpt op Columbiaanse koffiebonen, 25% Cuvée Delphine gerijpt op vaten van Four Roses en 25% Hel & Verdoemenis gerijpt op vaten van Jack Daniels.

Black Damnation III (Black Mes)

Struise Brouwers at Brouwerij Deca — 13% — 8 - 10 °C / 46 - 50 °F

top-fermentation re-fermentation in the bottle not centrifuged	fermentation haute refermentation en bouteille non centrifugée	hoge gisting hergisting op de fles niet gecentrifugeerd
Russian Imperial Stout	Russian Imperial Stout	Russian Imperial Stout
Matured in Coal Ila whisky casks (distillers' version 1995).	Mûri en fûts de Coal Ila whisky (distillers version 1995).	Gerijpt op vaten van Coal Ila whisky (distillers versie 1995).
intense black with a compact brown-beige foam head not filtered or pasteurised	noir intense opaque avec un faux col compact brun beige non filtrée, non pasteurisée	intens zwart met een compacte bruinbeige schuimkraag ongefilterd, niet gepasteuriseerd
Strong roasted aroma with complex touches of peat, caramel, currant loaf, coffee, roasted grains and a hint of stone fruit. Solid and very complex flavour with touches of roasted grains, caramel, fruit, currant loaf, oak and Isly whisky.	Puissant arôme brûlé, avec des touches complexes de tourbe, de caramel, de pain aux raisins, de café, de céréales grillées et un peu de fruits à noyau. Goût massif et fort complexe, avec des touches de céréales grillées, du caramel, des fruits, du pain aux raisins, du chêne et de l'Islay whisky.	Sterk gebrand aroma met complexe toetsen van turf, karamel, krentenbrood, koffie, geroosterde granen en ietwat steenfruit. Massieve en zeer complexe smaak met toetsen van geroosterde granen, karamel, fruit, krentenbrood, eik en Isly whisky.
see Black Damnation I	voir Black Damnation I	zie Black Damnation I
The name refers to Paul Mellia, aka Mes, who introduced the Isly casks.	Le nom fait référence à Paul Mellia, alias Mes, qui s'est occupé des fûts d'Islay.	De naam verwijst naar Paul Mellia, alias Mes, die zorgde voor de Isly-vaten.

B Black Damnation IV (Coffée Club)

De Struise Brouwers at Brouwerij Deca 13% 8 - 10 / 46 - 50

top-fermentation re-fermentation in the bottle not centrifuged	fermentation haute refermentation en bouteille non centrifugée	hoge gisting hergisting op de fles niet gecentrifugeerd
Russian Imperial Stout	Russian Imperial Stout	Russian Imperial Stout
Black Albert matured in very old rum casks for some six months.	Black Albert mûri pendant environ six mois en très vieux fûts de rum.	Black Albert die een 6-tal maanden gerijpt is op zeer oude rumvaten.
turbid jet black wit compact brown-beige foam head not filtered or pasteurised	noir comme jais avec un faux col compact brun beige non filtrée, non pasteurisée	ondoorzichtig gitzwart met compacte bruinbeige schuimkraag ongefilterd, niet gepasteuriseerd
Mild aroma with hints of roasted coffee, cane sugar, soft chocolate, nuts, roast chestnuts and raisins. Rich, yet soft and complex, luxuriant roast flavour. Touches of coffee, roasted grains, maple syrup and a hint of apricot. Rich aftertaste with refreshing hint of refined hops.	Arôme généreux, avec des touches de café torréfié, de sucre de canne, de chocolat doux, de noix, de châtaignes grillées et de petits raisins secs. Goût brûlé abondant, riche mais doux et complexe. Touches de café, de céréales grillées, de sirop d'érable et un peu d'abricot sec. Riche arrière-bouche, avec une touche de houblon raffinée, rafraîchissante.	Mild aroma met toetsen van gebrande koffie, rietsuiker, zachte chocolade, noten, gepofte kastanjes en rozijntjes. Rijke maar zachte en complexe, weelderige gebrande smaak. Toetsen van koffie, geroosterde granen, esdoornsiroop en ietwat gedroogde abrikoos. Rijke afdronk met verfrissende, verfijnde hoptoets.
see Black Damnation I	voir Black Damnation I	zie Black Damnation I

e Struise Brouwers at Brouwerij Deca 26% 8 - 10 °C 46 - 50 °F

Black Damnation V (Double Black)

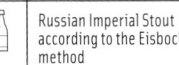

top-fermentation re-fermentation in the bottle not centrifuged	fermentation haute refermentation en bouteille non centrifugée	hoge gisting hergisting op de fles niet gecentrifugeerd
Russian Imperial Stout according to the Eisbock method	Russian Imperial Stout suivant la méthode Eisbock	Russian Imperial Stout volgens de Eisbock methode
Black Albert/Cuvée Delphine matured in bourbon casks.	Black Albert/Cuvée Delphine mûri en fûts de bourbon.	Black Albert/Cuvée Delphine gerijpt op bourbonvaten.
jet black with extra thick dark-brown foam head	noir comme jais avec faux col super épais brun foncé	pikzwart met superdikke donkerbruine schuimkraag
Decadent aroma and complex, overwhelming flavour. Touches of fruit, roasted espresso, tar, pitch, liquorice, caramel, toast, bourbon, oak, caramelised nuts...	Arôme décadent et goût complexe. Touches de fruits, d'espresso torréfié, de goudron, de poix, de bois de réglisse, de caramel, de pain grillé, de réglisse, de bourbon, de bois de chêne, de noix caramélisées...	Decadent aroma en complexe, verpletterende smaak. Toetsen van fruit, gebrande espresso, teer, pek, zoethout, karamel, geroosterd brood, drop, bourbon, eikenhout, gekaramelliseerde noten...
Pour very slowly. Lift the bottle up slightly towards the end to obtain a fine foam head.	Verser très lentement. Vers la fin tenir la bouteille un peu plus haut pour former un faux col joli.	Zeer traag uitschenken. De fles naar het einde toe iets hoger houden voor een mooie schuimkraag.
Goes really well with a nice Havana cigar after a meal. Cuvée Delphine that was raised from 13% to 26%.	Accompagne à la perfection un délicieux havane après le repas. Cuvée Delphine qui a été élevée de 13% à 26%.	Perfect bij een lekkere havana na de maaltijd. Cuvée Delphine die van 13% naar 26% werd opgetrokken.

Black Hole

Brouwerij Roman 5,60% 3° 37°

	bottom-fermentation	fermentation basse	lage gisting
	premium Lager	premium lager	premium lager
	barley malt, hops, corn, yeast, well water	malt d'orge, houblon, maïs, levure, eau de source	gerstemout, hop, mais, gist, bronwater
	light-yellow clear	jaune clair claire	lichtgeel helder
	Distinctive thirst-quencher. Fruity hop taste of Czech aroma hop and dry bitter aftertaste.	Désaltérant de caractère. Saveur houblonnée fruitée de houblon aromatique Tchèque et fin de bouche amère sèche.	Karaktervolle dorstlesser. Fruitige hopsmaak van Tsjechische aromahop en droge bittere afdronk.
	Pour slowly into a degreased, rinsed beer glass.	Verser lentement dans un verre de bière dégraissé et rincé.	Langzaam uitschenken in een ontvet en gespoeld bierglas.
	Store in a dark, cool room.	Conserver à l'abri de la lumière et de la chaleur.	Donker en koel bewaren.

Black Jack

e Struise Brouwers at Brouwerij Deca 7%

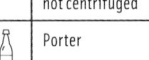

	top-fermentation re-fermentation in the bottle not centrifuged	fermentation haute refermentation en bouteille non centrifugée	hoge gisting hergisting op de fles niet gecentrifugeerd
	Porter	Porter	Porter
	almost black with attractive beige foam head not filtered or pasteurised	presque noir avec faux col séduisant beige non filtrée, non pasteurisée	bijna zwart met aantrekkelijke beige schuimkraag ongefilterd, niet gepasteuriseerd
	Fruity, slightly roasted porter with a soft, refined aroma of blossoms, coffee, cocoa and a hint of fruit. Silky smooth flavour with hints of nuts, coffee, maple syrup, liquorice and candied fruit. Medium mouth sense.	Porter fruité, légèrement brûlé, d'un arôme doux, raffiné de fleurs, de café, de cacao et d'un peu de fruits. Le goût est soyeux, avec des touches de noix, de café, de sirop d'érable, de réglisse et de fruits confits. Sensation de demi-sec en bouche.	Fruitige, licht gebrande porter met een zacht, verfijnd aroma van bloesems, koffie, cacao en wat fruit. De smaak is zijdezacht met toetsen van noten, koffie, esdoornsiroop, drop en gekonfijt fruit. Medium mondgevoel.
	Brewed at the request of a Swedish customer.	Brassée pour le compte d'un client suédois.	Gebrouwen in opdracht van een Zweedse klant.

Blanche d'Ardenne

Corsendonk by Brasserie du Bocq

4,30% 4 - 6 ° 39 - 43 °

	top-fermentation	fermentation haute	hoge gisting
	witbier (white beer)	bière blanche	witbier

Blanche de Bouillon

Brasserie de Bouillon

5,50%

	top-fermentation re-fermentation in the bottle	fermentation haute refermentation en bouteille	hoge gisting hergisting in de fles
	witbier (white beer)	bière blanche	witbier
	wheat malt, hops, yeast, water	froment, malt, houblon, levure, eau	tarwe, mout, hop, gist, water
	not filtered	non filtrée	ongefilterd

Blanche de Bruxelles

Brasserie Lefebvre — 4,50% — 2 - 5° / 36 - 41°

	top-fermentation centrifuged	fermentation haute centrifugée	hoge gisting gecentrifugeerd
	witbier	bière blanche	witbier
	barley malt, wheat (40%), hop varieties, sugar, yeast, coriander, curaçao, water	malt d'orge, froment (40%), sortes de houblon, sucre, levure, coriandre, curaçao, eau	gerstemout, tarwe (40%), hopsoorten, suiker, gist, koriander, curaçao, water
	very pale cloudy unpasteurised	très pâle trouble non pasteurisée	zeer bleek troebel niet gepasteuriseerd
	Fresh and light beer with a strong fruity (citrus) and spicy taste.	Bière fraîche, légère, d'un goût fort fruité (citrus) et épicé.	Fris, licht bier met een heel fruitige (citrus) en kruidige smaak.
	Pour into a yard glass.	Verser dans un verre conique.	Uitschenken in een konisch glas.
i			

rasserie Val de Sambre

5%

	top-fermentation re-fermentation in the bottle	fermentation haute refermentation en bouteille	hoge gisting hergisting op de fles
	witbier (white beer) on yeast	bière blanche sur levure	witbier op gist
	based on barley and wheat malt	à base de malt de froment et d'orge	op basis van tarwe- en gerstemout
	turbid	trouble	troebel
	Soft bitter, mellow flavour, yet fruity and refreshing.	Goût rond, doucement amer, avec un caractère fruité et rafraîchissant.	Zacht bittere, ronde smaak met fruitig en verfrissend karakter.

Blanche de Namur

Brasserie du Bocq

4,50% 2 - 4° 36 - 39°

	top-fermentation re-fermented in the bottle	fermentation haute refermentation en bouteille	hoge gisting hergisting op de fles
	witbier	bière blanche	witbier
	barley malt, wheat, hop varieties, yeast, herbs, water	malt d'orge, froment, sortes de houblon, levure, herbes, eau	gerstemout, tarwe, hopsoorten, gist, kruiden, water
	blonde (5 EBC) cloudy and milky	blond (5 EBC) trouble et laiteuse	blond (5 EBC) troebel en melkachtig
	Coriander and bitter orange rind flavours (12EBU). Smooth, fine and thirst-quenching beer, slightly sour, not bitter (12 EBU).	Arômes de coriandre et de zeste d'orange amer. Bière moelleuse raffinée et désaltérante, légèrement acidulée et non amère (12EBU).	Aroma's van koriander en bittere sinaasappelschil. Zacht, fijn en dorstlessend bier, lichtjes zuur, niet bitter (12EBU).
	see Applebocq	voir Applebocq	zie Applebocq
	Voted the world's best white beer/wheat beer in 2009 by www.tastingsbeers.com. This prestigious prize is awarded by a international jury of specialists from the brewing world. Blanche de Namur was the daughter of Count Jan de Namur (14th century).	Élue en 2009 meilleure bière blanche/bière de froment au monde par www.tastingsbeers.com. Ce prestigieux prix est attribué par un jury international de spécialistes du monde des brasseurs. Blanche de Namur était la fille du Duc Jean de Namur (14e siècle).	In 2009 verkozen tot beste witbier/tarwbier ter wereld door www.tastingsbeers.com. Deze prestigieuze prijs wordt toegekend door een internationale jury van specialisten uit de brouwerswereld. Blanche de Namur was de dochter van Hertog Jan van Namur (14e eeuw).

·asserie de Tubize

4,80% 3 °C 37 °F

	top-fermentation	fermentation haute	hoge gisting
	fruit beer based on wit-bier	bière fruitée à base de bière blanche	fruitbier op basis van witbier
	Refreshing wheat beer with distinct citrus fla-vours.	Blanche rafraîchissante avec goût et parfum d'agrumes prononcés.	Zeer verfrissend witbier met uitgesproken ci-trusaroma en -smaak.

Blanche de Tubize

B Blanche des Honnelles

Brasserie de l'Abbaye des Rocs 6% (16° plato) 6 43

	top-fermentation	fermentation haute	hoge gisting
	witbier	bière blanche	witbier
	malt (of wheat, oat, barley), hops (Hallertau, Brewers Gold), well water from a rocky subsoil	malt (de froment, avoine, orge), houblon (Hallertau, Brewers Gold), eau de puits d'un sous-sol rocailleux	mout (van tarwe, haver, gerst), hop (Hallertau, Brewers Gold), boorputwater uit een rotsrijke ondergrond
	cloudy blond beer	bière blonde trouble	troebel blond bier
	Smooth and refreshing.	Douce et rafraîchissante.	Zacht en verfrissend.
	Savour in a flute-glass.	À déguster dans une flûte.	Degusteren uit een fluitglas.
	The abbey 'L'Abbaye des Rocs' dates back from the 12th century. The beer keeps for about a year in a dark room.	'L'Abbaye des Rocs' date du 12ième siècle. La bière se conserve environ un an à l'abri de la lumière.	De abdij 'L'Abbaye des Rocs' dateert uit de 12e eeuw. Het bier bewaart ongeveer een jaar in een donkere ruimte.

ouwerij Huyghe

5% 4 °C 39 °F

Blanche des Neiges

top-fermentation natural re-fermentation	fermentation haute refermentation naturelle	hoge gisting natuurlijke hergisting
witbier	bière blanche	witbier
60% barley malt, 40% wheat, re-fermentation sugar, hops, yeast, aroma, water, coriander, orange rind	60% malt d'orge, 40% froment, sucre de refermentation, houblon, levure, arômes, eau, coriandre, écorce d'orange	60% gerstemout, 40% tarwe, hergistingssuiker, hop, gist, aroma, water, koriander, sinaasschil
light-yellow cloudy	jaune clair trouble	lichtgeel troebel
Fruity witbier.	Bière blanche fruitée	Fruitig witbier.
This is the same beer as Floris Witbier, but for the Belgian market.	Bière identique à la blanche Floris; destinée au marché belge.	Is hetzelfde bier als Floris witbier; bestemd voor de Belgische markt.

Blanche du Hainaut Bio

Brasserie Dupont 5,50% sligh[t] cool

	top-fermentation re-fermented in the bottle	fermentation haute refermentation en bouteille	hoge gisting nagisting in de fles
	witbier	bière blanche	witbier
	Based on organic barley and wheat malt, organic hops, coriander and orange rind.	À base de malt d'orge et de froment biologique, houblon biologique, coriandre et zeste d'orange.	Op basis van biologische gerst- en tarwemout, biologische hop, koriander en sinaasschil.
	yellow	jaune	geel
	Light and smooth with a touch of bitterness. Refreshing owing to the combination of sour, coriander and orange.	Légère et douce avec une pointe d'amertume. Désaltérante par une combinaison d'acidité et d'une touche de coriandre et d'orange.	Licht en zacht met een vleugje bitterheid. Verfrissend door de combinatie van zuurheid met een snuifje koriander en sinaas.
	The production is supervised by Ecocert® and has the 'Biogarantie label'.	La production est contrôlée par Ecocert®. Avec le label Biogarantie®.	De productie wordt gecontroleerd door Ecocert®. Met label Biogarantie®.

asserie Artisanale Millevertus 5% 4 °C 39 °F

Blanchette de Lorraine

	top-fermentation re-fermented in the bottle	fermentation haute refermentation en bouteille	hoge gisting hergisting op de fles
	fruit beer based on wit-bier	bière fruitée à base de bière blanche	fruitbier op basis van witbier
	different malt and hop varieties, wheat, yeast, mashed mirabelles, co-riander, orange rind, water	différentes sortes de malt et de houblon, fro-ment, levure, purée de mirabelles, coriandre, écorce d'orange, eau	verschillende mout- en hopsoorten, tarwe, gist, mirabellenpuree, kori-ander, sinaasschil, water
	orange cloudy	orange trouble	oranje troebel
	Fresh and fruity.	Fraîche et fruitée.	Fris en fruitig.
	Serve in a frozen glass.	Verser dans un verre ge-lé.	Uitschenken in een be-vroren glas.
	Brewed in Belgian Lor-raine with Lorraine mi-rabelles, which are French mirabelles with 'appellation contrôlée'.	Brassée en Lorraine Belge avec des mira-belles françaises 'appel-lation contrôlée' mirabelle de Lorraine'.	Gebrouwen in Belgisch Lotharingen met mira-belles de Lorraine, Fran-se mirabellen met 'appellation contrôlée'.

Blauwersbier

Brouwerij Van Eecke 6,50% 6 43

	top-fermentation re-fermentation in the bottle	fermentation haute refermentation en bouteille	hoge gisting hergisting op de fles
	mixed beer	bière de coupage	versnijbier
	barley hops, sugar, coriander, wheat, dried orange peel, yeast, water	orge, houblon, sucre, coriandre, froment, écorce d'orange séchée, levure, eau	gerst, hop, suiker, koriander, tarwe, gedroogde sinaasschil, gist, water
	blond-grey, cloudy with tufty foam not filtered or pasteurised	gris blond, trouble avec écume rocailleuse non filtrée, non pasteurisée	blondgrijs, troebel met rotsachtig schuim ongefilterd, niet gepasteuriseerd
	Malty and spicy. The fullness of a tripel and the spiciness of a white beer.	Maltée et épicée. La plénitude de la triple et le caractère épicé de la bière blanche.	Moutig en kruidig. De volheid van de tripel en het kruidige van het witbier.
	Pour in a single movement (to get the yeast moving) into a bulb glass.	Verser agilement (mettre la levure en mouvement) dans un verre ballon.	Vlot uitschenken (de gis in beweging brengen) in een bolglas.
i	Mix of Kapittel Tripel Abt and Watou's white beer produced for Taverne Blauwershof in Godewaersvelde (Fr).	Bière de mélange de Kapittel Tripel Abt et de bière blanche de Watou, réalisée pour la Taverne Blauwershof à Godewaersvelde (France).	Mengbier van Kapittel Tripel Abt en Watou's witbier gemaakt voor Taverne Blauwershof in Godewaersvelde (Fr).

Bloemenbier

Proefbrouwerij 7%

	top-fermentation re-fermented in the bottle	fermentation haute refermentation en bouteille	hoge gisting hergisting op de fles
	Belgian strong ale	Belgian strong ale	Belgian strong ale
	Malt, hops, yeast, flowers, spring water. Fortified with flowers and plants.	Malt, houblon, levure, eau de source. Enrichie de fleurs et plantes.	mout, hop, gist, bronwater. Verrijkt met bloemen en planten.
	amber	ambrée	amber

Blonde Bie

Brouwerij De Bie

8%

	top-fermentation	fermentation haute	hoge gisting
	blond	blonde	blond
	malt, hops, sugar, yeast, herbs, water	malt, houblon, sucre, levure, herbes, eau	mout, hop, suiker, gist, kruiden, water
	blond clear	blonde claire	blond helder

uwerij Het Sas 1,80% 3 °C 37 °F

	bottom-fermentation	fermentation basse	lage gisting
	table beer	bière de table	tafelbier
	malt, rice, hops, water	malt, riz, houblon, eau	mout, rijst, hop, water
	blond clear	blonde claire	blond helder
	Sweet and slightly alcoholic thirst-quencher. Sweet and fruity.	Désaltérant douce et légèrement alcoolisée. Douce et fruitée.	Zoete en licht alcoholische dorstlesser. Zoet en fruitig.
	Pour slowly in a single, smooth movement in a degreased glass. Keep the glass tilted and avoid sloshing the beer. Skim off the foam.	Verser lentement en un seul mouvement fluide dans un verre dégraissé tenu en oblique. Ne pas laisser la bière clapoter. Ecumer le verre.	Traag en in 1 vloeiende beweging uitschenken in een vetvrij glas dat wordt schuin gehouden. Het bier niet laten klotsen. Het glas afschuimen.
i			

Bock Leroy

Bock Pils

Palm Breweries 5,20%

	bottom-fermentation	fermentation basse	lage gisting
	pilsner	pils	pils
	pilsner malts, 100% Czech Saaz hop, yeast, water	malts de pils, houblon 100% Saaz tchèque, levure, eau	pilsmouten, 100% Saaz hop uit Tsjechië, gist, water
	blond	blonde	blond
	Pleasantly bitter with a dry aftertaste. Hoppy and slightly spiced.	Goût amer agréable avec une fin de bouche sèche. Houblonné et légèrement aromatisé.	Aangenaam bitter met droge afdronk. Hoppig en licht gekrui
	Can be emptied in a pilsner glass.	Peut être complètement versé dans un verre pils.	Mag helemaal uitgeschonken worden in ee pilsglas.
i			

uwerij Bockor (Vander Ghinste)

5,20% 4 - 6 °C 39 - 43 °F

	bottom-fermentation	fermentation basse	lage gisting
	pilsner or lager dortmunder or export	pils ou lager dortmunder ou export	pils- of lagerbier dortmunder of export
	barley malt, corn, hops, yeast, water	malt d'orge, maïs, houblon, levure, eau	gerstemout, mais, hop, gist, water
	blond, clear filtered	blonde, claire filtrée	blond, helder gefilterd
	Smooth texture. Pure and light in the mouth.	Texture douce. Pure et légère dans la bouche.	Zachte textuur, zuiver en licht in de mond.
	Preferably drink from the bottle	Peut être bue de préférence à la bouteille.	Bij voorkeur uit de fles drinken.
	The export variety was very popular in the 50s. It was rebranded a few years back as contemporary export variety.	Le type export était fort populaire dans les années '50. Il a été repositionné il y a quelques années comme un type export contemporain.	Het type export was heel populair in de jaren '50. Het werd enkele jaren terug geherpositioneerd als een hedendaags type export.

Bockor Pils

Brouwerij Bockor (Vander Ghinste) 5,20% 4 - 39 - 4

	bottom-fermentation	fermentation basse	lage gisting
	pilsner or lager	pils ou lager	pils- of lagerbier
	barley malt, corn, hops, yeast, water	malt d'orge, maïs, houblon, levure, eau	gerstemout, mais, hop, gist, water
	blond, clear filtered	blonde, claire filtrée	blond, helder gefilterd
	Session beer with modest bitterness. Dry, neutral taste with a bitter aftertaste.	Pils facilement buvable avec un goût amer restreint. Saveur sèche et neutre, puis amère.	Vlot drinkbare pils met ingetoomde bitterheid. Droge, neutrale smaak die bitterig uitvloeit.
	Rinse the glass with cold water, tilt it a little and pour half of the bottle carefully. Then keep the glass upright and pour the rest of the bottle in a single movement.	Rincer le verre à l'eau froide, le tenir légèrement incliné et le remplir prudemment à moitié. Relever le verre et vider la bouteille en un seul mouvement.	Het glas koud spoelen, licht schuin houden en voorzichtig half inscher ken. Daarna het glas rechthouden en de rest in 1 beweging uitschen-ken.
i			

Boerke Blond

uwerij Angerik 6,80%

top-fermentation re-fermented in the bottle	fermentation haute refermentation en bouteille	hoge gisting hergisting op fles
blond	blonde	blond
malt, hops, herbs (coriander), yeast, water	malt, houblon, herbes (coriandre), levure, eau	mout, hop, kruiden (koriander), gist, water
blond-amber unfiltered, cloudy	blond-ambré non filtrée, trouble	blond-amber ongefilterd, troebel
Robust beer with a rich flavour palette, aftertaste with hop touch.	Bière forte avec une palette de saveurs riche, fin de bouche avec touche de houblon.	Robuust bier met een rijk smakenpalet, afdronk met hoppetoets.
The name Angerik is a contraction of Angelo and Erik, the founders' names. This beer is only brewed with Belgian hop and malt.	Le nom Angerik provient de la contraction d'Angelo et d'Erik, les prénoms des fondateurs. Cette bière est brassée uniquement avec des houblons et malts belges.	De naam Angerik is een samenvoeging van Angelo en Erik, de namen van de stichters. Dit bier wordt enkel met Belgische hop en mout gebrouwen.

B Boerke Bruin

Brouwerij Angerik

6,80%

	top-fermentation re-fermented in the bottle	fermentation haute refermentation en bouteille	hoge gisting hergisting op de fles
	double	double	donker
	roasted malt, hops, herbs, yeast, water	malt brûlé, houblon, herbes, levure, eau	gebrande mout, hop, kruiden, gist, water
	dark red	rouge foncé	donkerrood
	Smooth with powerful aftertaste.	Douce avec fin de bouche corsée.	Zacht met krachtige afdronk.
	The name Angerik is a contraction of Angelo and Erik, the founders' names. This beer is only brewed with Belgian hop and malt.	Le nom Angerik provient de la contraction d'Angelo et d'Erik, les prénoms des fondateurs. Cette bière est brassée uniquement avec des houblons et malts belges.	De naam Angerik is een samenvoeging van Angelo en Erik, de namen van de stichters. Dit bie wordt enkel met Belgische hop en mout gebrouwen.

top-fermentation	fermentation haute	hoge gisting
fruit beer	bière fruitée	fruitbier
malt, hop, Schaarbeek cherries (8 kg/50 l), yeast, water	malt, houblon, cérises de Schaarbeek (8 kg/50 l), levure, eau	mout, hop, kruiden, Schaarbeekse krieken (8 kg/50 l), gist, water
The name Angerik is a contraction of Angelo and Erik, the founders' names. This beer is only brewed with Belgian hop and malt.	Le nom Angerik provient de la contraction d'Angelo et d'Erik, les prénoms des fondateurs. Cette bière est brassée uniquement avec des houblons et malts belges.	De naam Angerik is een samenvoeging van Angelo en Erik, de namen van de stichters. Dit bier wordt enkel met Belgische hop en mout gebrouwen.

Bokkereyer

Brouwerij Sint-Jozef **6%** 2 - 4 36 - 39

	top-fermentation	fermentation haute	hoge gisting
	amber	ambrée	amber
	malt, hops, sugar, herbs, starch, caramel sugar, water	malt, houblon, sucre, herbes, fécule, sucre caramel, eau	mout, hop, suiker, kruiden, zetmeel, karamelsuiker, water
	light brownish	brun clair	lichtbruinig
	Rich beer with soft aromas and a gentle aftertaste.	Biere riche avec des arômes moelleux et une fin de bouche moelleuse.	Rijk bier met zachte aroma's en zachte afdronk.
	Pour into a clean, degreased glass, avoiding contact between the bottle and the foam.	Verser dans un verre propre, dégraissé sans que la bouteille touche l'écume.	Uitschenken in een zuiver, ontvet glas zonder dat de fles het schuim raakt.
i			

erkens by Brasserie du Bocq

7,20% 6 - 10 °C 43 - 50 °F

top-fermentation re-fermented in the bottle	fermentation haute refermentation en bouteille	hoge gisting hergisting op de fles
blond abbey beer	bière d'abbaye blonde	blond abdijbier
malt, hops, yeast, water	malt, houblon, levure, eau	mout, hop, gist, water
light blond filtered	blond clair filtrée	lichtblond gefilterd
Solid and heavy. Citrus and honey flavours. Powerful taste of alcohol and herbs. Mild bitterness.	Solide et lourde. Arôme d'agrumes et de miel. Saveur forte d'alcool et d'herbes, goût amer moelleux.	Stevig en zwaar. Aroma van citrus en honing. Krachtige smaak van alcohol, kruiden en milde bitterheid.
Carefully serve in the sipping glass, with a generous foam head.	Verser prudemment dans le verre de dégustation avec faux col solide.	Voorzichtig uitschenken in het degustatieglas met een ruime schuimkraag.
Over 90% of the production is exported.	Plus de 90% est destiné à l'exportation.	Meer dan 90% is bestemd voor export.

B Bon Homme

Brouwerij De Leite 6,50% 4 - 10 / 39 - 50

	top-fermentation re-fermentation in the bottle not centrifuged	fermentation haute refermentation en bouteille non centrifugée	hoge gisting hergisting in de fles niet gecentrifugeerd
	double	double	dubbel
	5 malt types, hops, 4 different spices, yeast, water	5 variétés de malt, houblon, 4 variétés d'herbes, levure, eau	5 moutsoorten, hop, 4 soorten kruiden, gist, water
	robust brown-red with a fine foam head not filtered, pasteurised	brun rouge fort avec un faux col joli non filtrée, pasteurisée	robuust bruinrood met een mooie schuimkraag ongefilterd, gepasteuriseerd
	Aroma of caramel with a slight hoppy touch. The malty flavour ends in fine lingering bitterness.	Arôme de caramel, avec une légère touche de houblon. Le goût malté se transforme en fine amertume, qui reste en suspension.	Aroma van karamel met een lichte hoptoets. De moutige smaak gaat over in fijne bitterheid die blijft hangen.
	Serve in a Münich glass.	Verser dans un verre Münich.	Uitschenken in een Münichglas
	The label designed by Tinus Vermeersch: caricature of brewer Luc's father and depiction of Flemish sayings about inebriety. 'Bon Homme' an 'incredibly' nice beer and the brewery's second beer is the husband of 'Femme Fatale'.	L'étiquette a été dessinée par Tinus Vermeersch :caricature du père du brasseur Luc et évocation de dictons flamands au sujet de l'ivresse. 'Bon Homme', une ravissante bière 'incroyable' et la 2e bière de la brasserie, est l'homme de 'Femme Fatale'.	Het etiket werd ontworpen door Tinus Vermeersch: het is een karikatuur van de vader van brouwer Luc en uitbeelding van Vlaamse spreuken over dronkenschap. 'Bon Homme', een 'onvoorstelbaar' lief bier en het 2e bier van de brouwerij, is de man van 'Femme Fatale'.

Bon Secours Ambrée

asserie Caulier

8% 6 - 10 °C 43 - 50 °F

top-fermentation	fermentation haute	hoge gisting
amber	ambrée	amber
malt, hops, yeast, candy sugar, water	malt, houblon, levure, sucre candi, eau	mout, hop, gist, kandij-suiker, water
amber	ambrée	amber
Round, malty and hoppy with a bitter aftertaste.	Ronde, maltée et hou-blonnée avec une ar-rière-bouche amère.	Rond, moutig en hoppig met een bittere na-smaak.
Slowly pour half of the bottle in order to obtain a nice foam head.	Verser doucement la moitié de la bouteille de sorte qu'un faux col so-lide se forme.	De helft van de fles zachtjes uitschenken zo-dat er zich een mooie schuimkraag vormt.

Bon Secours Blonde

Brasserie Caulier

8% 6 - 10 / 43 - 50

top-fermentation	fermentation haute	hoge gisting
blond	blonde	blond
malt, hops, yeast, candy sugar, water	malt, houblon, levure, sucre candi, eau	mout, hop, gist, kandijsuiker, water
blond	blonde	blond
Round and well-balanced, light bitterness and malt taste, hoppy.	Ronde et équilibrée, saveur légèrement amère et maltée, houblonnée.	Rond en evenwichtig, lichte bitterheid en moutsmaak, hoppig.
Slowly pour half of the bottle in order to obtain a nice foam head.	Verser doucement la moitié de la bouteille de sorte qu'un faux col solide se forme.	De helft van de fles zachtjes uitschenken zodat er zich een mooie schuimkraag vormt.

asserie Caulier 10% 6 - 10 °C 43 - 50 °F

Bon Secours Blonde de Noël

	top-fermentation	fermentation haute	hoge gisting
	winter beer	bière hivernale	winterbier
	malt, hops, yeast, candy sugar, water	malt, houblon, levure, sucre candi, eau	mout, hop, gist, kandij-suiker, water
	blond	blonde	blond
	Powerful with a strong taste, caramel.	Corsé avec une saveur prononcée, caramélisée.	Krachtig met sterke smaak, karamel.
	Slowly pour half of the bottle in order to obtain a nice foam head.	Verser doucement la moitié de la bouteille de sorte qu'un faux col so-lide se forme	De helft van de fles zachtjes uitschenken zo-dat er zich een mooie schuimkraag vormt.
i			

Bon Secours Brune

Brasserie Caulier 8% 6 - 10 / 43 - 50

	top-fermentation	fermentation haute	hoge gisting
	dubbel	double	dubbel
	malt, hops, yeast, candy sugar, water	malt, houblon, levure, sucre candi, eau	mout, hop, gist, kandij-suiker, water
	brown	brune	bruin
	Smooth and perfumed character. Flavour of mocca, anise and roasty touch. Bitter aftertaste.	Caractère doux et parfumé. Arôme de moka, d'anis et de brûlé. Arrière-bouche amère.	Zacht en geparfumeerd karakter. Aroma van moka, anijs en gebrand. Bittere nasmaak.
	Slowly pour half of the bottle in order to obtain a nice foam head.	Verser doucement la moitié de la bouteille de sorte qu'un faux col solide se forme.	De helft van de fles zachtjes uitschenken zodat er zich een mooie schuimkraag vormt.
i			

top-fermentation	fermentation haute	hoge gisting
fruit beer	bière fruitée	fruitbier
malt, hops, yeast, raspberry juice, water	malt, houblon, levure, jus de framboises, eau	mout, hop, gist, frambozensap, water
red	rouge	rood
Forest fruit.	Fruits des bois.	Bosvruchten.
Slowly pour half of the bottle in order to obtain a nice foam head.	Verser doucement la moitié de la bouteille de sorte qu'un faux col solide se forme.	De helft van de fles zachtjes uitschenken zodat er zich een mooie schuimkraag vormt.
Sugar-free.	Sans sucres.	Suikervrij.

Bon Secours Myrtille

Brasserie Caulier

7% 6 - 10 43 - 50

	top-fermentation	fermentation haute	hoge gisting
	fruit beer	bière fruitée	fruitbier
	malt, hops, yeast, myrtil juice, water	malt, houblon, levure, jus de myrtilles, eau	mout, hop, gist, myrtillensap, water
	dark red	rouge foncé	donkerrood
	Forest fruit.	Fruits des bois.	Bosvruchten.
	Slowly pour half of the bottle in order to obtain a nice foam head.	Verser doucement la moitié de la bouteille de sorte qu'un faux col solide se forme.	De helft van de fles zachtjes uitschenken zodat er zich een mooie schuimkraag vormt.
	Sugar-free.	Sans sucres.	Suikervrij.

rasserie de Tubize 9% 8 - 10 °C 46 - 50 °F

	top-fermentation	fermentation haute	hoge gisting
	abbey beer dubbel	bière d'abbaye double	abdijbier dubbel
	red brown with a large, beige good lacing foam head.	brun rouge avec faux col beige et solide collant au verre	roodbruin met een ruime wandklevende beige schuimkraag
	Quite malty aroma, quite sweet, bitter and spicy in taste.	Un arôme assez malté, un goût plutôt sucré, amer, épicé.	Vrij moutig aroma, vrij zoete, bittere, kruidige smaak.

B Bons Vœux

Brasserie Dupont 9,50% 12° 54°

	top-fermentation re-fermented in the bottle	fermentation haute refermentation enbouteille	hoge gisting nagisting in de fles
	blond	blonde	blond
	Long maturation phase. With dry-hopping.	Longue période de mûrissement. Avec dry hopping.	Lange rijpingsfase. Met dry hopping.
	copper-blond	blond cuivre	koperblond
	Complex aroma and flavour owing to the fine hop and yeast types used. Smooth, bitter and fruity.	Arôme et saveur complexes par le houblon fin et les sortes de levure. Douce, amère et fruitée.	Complex aroma en smaak door de fijne hop en gistsoorten. Zacht, bitter en fruitig.
	Offered to the customers as a New Year's present from 1970 onwards, it was also introduced to the market because of its great success. Store at cellar temperature for an optimal taste evolution.	Offerte aux clients à partir de 1970 comme cadeau de fin d'année et suite au grand intérêt commercialisée par la suite. Conserver à température de cave pour une évolution optimale du goût.	Werd vanaf 1970 aangeboden als nieuwjaarsgeschenk voor de klanten en door de grote belangstelling later ook gecommercialiseerd. Bewaren op keldertemperatuur voor een optimale smaakevolutie.

8% (16° plato) 10 - 12 °C 50 - 54 °F

Bornem Dubbel

top-fermentation re-fermented in the bottle	fermentation haute refermentation en bouteille	hoge gisting hergisting in de fles
Recognised Belgian abbey beer	Bière d'abbaye belge reconnue	Erkend Belgisch abdijbier
barley malt, hops, yeast, water	malt d'orge, houblon, levure, eau	gerstemout, hop, gist, water
Dark brown with burgundy-red undertone. Creamy, rich foam head.	Brun foncé avec une nuance rouge bordeaux. Faux col crémeux et riche.	Donkerbruin met bordeauxrode ondertoon. Romige, rijke schuimkraag.
Fruity taste with a light touch of grain.	Saveur fruitée avec une légère touche de céréales.	Fruitige smaak met lichte toets van graan.
Pour in a single, fluent and smooth movement, leaving 1 cm of yeast sediment in the bottle.	Verser en un seul mouvement fluide et doux et laisser 1 cm de dépôt de levure dans la bouteille.	Uitschenken in 1 vloeiende, zachte beweging en 1 cm gistdepot in de fles laten.
A living abbey beer brewed by order of the Saint Bernard abbey in Bornem.	Une bière d'abbaye vive brassée à la demande de l'abbaye de Saint-Bernard à Bornem.	Een levend abdijbier gebrouwen in opdracht van de Sint-Bernardusabdij in Bornem.

Bornem Tripel

Brouwerij Van Steenberge **9% (18,5° plato)** 10 - 12 / 50 - 54

	top-fermentation re-fermented in the bottle	fermentation haute refermentation en bouteille	hoge gisting hergisting in de fles
	Recognised Belgian abbey beer	Bière d'abbaye belge reconnue	Erkend Belgisch abdijbier
	barley malt, hops, yeast, water	malt d'orge, houblon, levure, eau	gerstemout, hop, gist, water
	blond nice foam head	blonde faux col solide	blond mooie schuimkraag
	Smooth mouthfeel, hoppy and full of taste, excellent sweet bitter balance, pleasant aroma and long-lasting aftertaste.	Douce dans la bouche, goût houblonnée et pleine, équilibre doux-amer excellent, parfum agréable et arrière-bouche longue.	Zacht in de mond, hoppig en vol van smaak, uitstekende zoetbitter balans, aangename geur en lange nasmaak.
	Pour in a single, fluent and smooth movement, leaving 1 cm of yeast sediment in the bottle. The sediment can be poured, for a cloudy beer.	Verser en un seul mouvement fluide et doux et laisser 1 cm de dépôt de levure dans la bouteille. Le depôt peut être versé et rend la bière trouble.	Uitschenken in 1 vloeiende, zachte beweging en 1 cm gistdepot in de fles laten. De gistfond kan worden uitgeschonken en maakt het bier troebel.
i	A living abbey beer brewed by order of the Saint Bernard abbey in Bornem.	Une bière d'abbaye vivante brassée à la demande de l'abbaye de Saint-Bernard à Bornem.	Een levend abdijbier gebrouwen in opdracht van de Sint-Bernardusabdij in Bornem.

Bos Bier

rouwerij DijkWaert

9% | 10 - 12 °C | 50 - 54 °F

top-fermentation natural re-fermentation in the bottle	fermentation haute refermentation naturelle en bouteille	hoge gisting natuurlijke hergisting in de fles
fruit beer, not sweet	bière fruitée non sucrée	niet zoet fruitbier
malts, hops, spices, yeasts, blackberries, raspberries, blackcurrants, water	malts, houblons, herbes, levures, mûres, framboises, groseilles, eau	mouten, hoppen, kruiden, gisten, bramen, frambozen, zwarte bessen, water
brown (40 EBC)	brune (40 EBC)	bruin (40 EBC)
Slightly sweet and spicy with a touch of forest fruits (blackberries, bilberries, raspberries) in both aroma and flavour. Soft bitter (28 EBU).	Légèrement sucrée et épicée, avec une touche de fruits des bois (mûres, myrtilles, framboises) dans l'arôme et le goût. Doucement amère (28 EBU).	Lichtzoet en kruidig met een toets van bosvruchten (bramen, bosbessen, frambozen) in aroma en smaak. Zacht bitter (28 EBU).

Bos Bier
licht zoet, kruidig bier
een toets van bosvruchten.
Bier Van Hoge Goesting.

B Bosbier

Brouwerij Sint-Jozef

4% 2 - 4 / 36 - 39

	bottom-fermentation	fermentation basse	lage gisting
	regional beer pilsner with fruit	bière régionale pils avec jus de fruits	streekbier pils met vruchtensap
	malt, hops, starch, bil-berry juice, water	malt, houblon, amidon, jus de myrtilles, eau	mout, hop, zetmeel, bosbessensap, water
	bilberry	myrtilles	bosbessen
	Fruity and refreshing. Full-bodied bilberry taste and aroma.	Fruitée et rafraîchis-sante. Goût et parfum francs de groseilles.	Fruitig en verfrissend. Volmondige bosbes-sensmaak en -geur.
	Pour into a clean, de-greased glass, avoiding contact between bottle and foam.	Verser dans un verre propre et dégraissé sans que la bouteille touche l'écume.	Uitschenken in een zui-ver, ontvet glas zonder dat de fles het schuim raakt.
i			

10% 10 - 12 °C / 50 - 54 °F

	top-fermentation re-fermented in the bottle uncentrifuged	fermentation haute refermentation en bouteille non centrifugée	hoge gisting nagisting op de fles niet gecentrifugeerd
	tripel Easter beer	triple Bière de Pâques	tripel Paasbier
	With cane sugar and Golding hops.	On utilise le sucre de canne et le houblon Golding.	Er wordt gebruik gemaakt van rietsuiker en Golding hop.
	pale to amber unfiltered	blanche touchant l'ambrée non filtrée	bleek tot amber ongefilterd
	Smooth.	Douce.	Zacht.
	Serve in an Oerbeer glass or wine glass.	À verser dans un verre oerbier ou un verre de vin.	Serveren in een oerbierglas of wijnglas.
	Easter beer. The name refers to the nickname of one of the 'Dolle Brouwers' (mad brewers).	Bière de Pâques dont le nom se réfère au sobriquet d'un des 'Dolle Brouwers'.	Paasbier waarvan de naam refereert aan de spotnaam van een van de 'Dolle Brouwers'.

Bosprotter

t Hofbrouwerijke 8,50% 10 - 12 / 50 - 54

	top-fermentation	fermentation haute	hoge gisting
	tripel	triple	tripel
	malt, hops, yeast, herbs, water	malt, houblon, levure, herbes, eau	mout, hop, gist, kruiden, water
	corn-gold blond slightly cloudy, unfiltered	jaune blé doré légèrement trouble (non filtrée)	korengoudblond licht troebel, ongefilterd
	Full-bodied malt taste with a light caramel touch and a refreshing, bitter aftertaste.	Saveur maltée franche avec une légère touche de caramel et une fin de bouche rafraîchissante, amère.	Volmondige moutsmaak met lichte karameltoets en een verfrissende bittere afdronk.
	Pour carefully, leaving 1 cm in the bottle.	Verser prudemment et laisser 1 cm dans la bouteille.	Voorzichtig uitschenken en 1 cm in het flesje laten.
	Can be stored for a very long time.	Peut se conserver longtemps.	Kan lang bewaard worden.

oep John Martin

6%

	top-fermentation	fermentation haute	hoge gisting
	strong blond	blonde forte	sterk blond
	blond	blonde	blond
	Rich bitter from the onset with strong, dry, bitter aftertaste. The tart bitterness slightly conceals the alcohol content.	Richement amère dès l'approche initiale, avec une arrière-bouche puissante, sèche, amère. L'amertume aigre masque un peu le volume d'alcool.	Rijkbiter van bij de aanzet met sterke, droge, bittere afdronk. De wrange bitterheid verhult het alcoholvolume een beetje.

Bourgogne des Flandres Blonde

Bourgogne des Flandres Brune

Groep John Martin 5%

	mixed fermentation	fermentation mixte	gemengde gisting
	specialty beer	bière spéciale	speciaalbier
	brown	brune	bruin
	Similar to the red-brown ale but without the acidity. Sweet accents, bitter but dry with a sharp aftertaste.	S'appuie sur la bière brune-rouge, mais sans caractère acidulé. Accents sucrés, goût amer mais sec, avec une arrière-bouche piquante.	Leunt aan bij de donkere roodbruine Vlaamse maar dan zonder zurig karakter. Zoete accenten, bitter maar droog met een scherpe afdronk.

asserie de Bellevaux

6,50% 8 - 12 °C 46 - 54 °F

	top-fermentation	fermentation haute	hoge gisting
	dark ale	ale foncée	donkere ale
	barley malt, hops, water	malt d'orge, houblon, eau	gerstemout, hop, water
	almost black solid, cream-coloured foam head unfiltered, unpasteur-ised	presque noir faux col de couleur crème prononcée non filtrée ni pasteuri-sée	bijna zwart stevige crèmekleurige schuimkraag niet gefilterd, niet ge-pasteuriseerd
	Strong and full-bodied character. Taste and aroma of but-terscotch, roasted malt Bitter aftertaste.	Caractère corsé et plein. Saveur et arôme de but-terscotch, malt grillé Fin de bouche amère.	Krachtig en vol karakter. Smaak en aroma van but-terscotch, geroosterde mout Bittere afdronk.
	Pour into a tall glass that has been rinsed with cold water.	Verser dans un verre haut rincé à l'eau froide.	Uitschenken in een met koud water gespoeld hoog glas.

Brasserie de Bellevaux Black

Brasserie de Bellevaux Blanche

Brasserie de Bellevaux 4,80% 5 - 8 / 41 - 46

	top-fermentation	fermentation haute	hoge gisting
	witbier	bière blanche	witbier
	barley malt, wheat malt, hops, herbs, well water	malt d'orge, malt de froment, houblon, herbes, eau de source	gerstemout, tarwemout, hop, kruiden, bronwater
	pale yellow fine white foam unfiltered, unpasteurised	jaune pâle écume blanche fine non filtrée ni pasteurisée	bleekgeel fijn wit schuim ongefilterd, niet gepasteuriseerd
	Refreshing and thirst-quenching character. Taste and aroma of citrus fruit, sourish with light bitter aftertaste.	Rafraîchissante et de caractère désaltérante. Saveur et arôme d'agrumes, rance avec fin de bouche légèrement amère.	Verfrissend en dorstlessend karakter. Smaak en aroma van citrusfruit, ranzig met licht bittere afdronk.
	Pour into a tall glass, rinsed with cold water.	Verser dans un verre haut rincé à l'eau froide.	Uitschenken in een met koud water gespoeld hoog glas.
i	Suitable as an aperitif.	Convient comme apéritif.	Geschikt als aperitief.

Brasserie de Bellevaux Blonde

7% 6 - 10 °C / 43 - 50 °F

top-fermentation	fermentation haute	hoge gisting
abbey beer	bière d'abbaye	abdijbier
barley malt, hops, candy sugar, well water	malt d'orge, houblon, sucre candi, eau de source	gerstemout, hop, kandijsuiker, bronwater
Dark blond with white foam head. Clear to slightly cloudy. Unfiltered, unpasteurised	Blond foncé avec faux col blanc. Claire à légèrement trouble. Non filtrée ni pasteurisée	Donkerblond met witte schuimkraag. Helder tot licht troebel. Ongefilterd, niet gepasteuriseerd
Rich and spicy character. Fruity and slightly sweet with a bitter aftertaste.	Caractère riche et relevé. Fruitée et légèrement douce avec fin de bouche amère.	Rijk en kruidig karakter. Fruitig en licht zoet met bittere afdronk.
Pour into a degreased goblet. Leave the yeast sediment in the bottle.	Verser tranquillement dans un verre calice dégraissé et laisser le dépôt de levure dans la bouteille.	Rustig uitschenken in een vetvrij kelkglas en het gistdepot in de fles laten.

Brasserie de Bellevaux Brune

Brasserie de Bellevaux

6,80% 8 - 12 / 46 - 54

	top-fermentation	fermentation haute	hoge gisting
	abbey beer	bière d'abbaye	abdijbier
	barley malt, hops, candy sugar, well water	malt d'orge, houblon, sucre candi, eau de source	gerstemout, hop, kandijsuiker, bronwater
	hazelnut unfiltered, unpasteurised	noisette non filtrée ni pasteurisée	hazelnoot niet gefilterd, niet gepasteuriseerd
	Full and smooth character. Full-bodied, slightly malty sweet, smooth aftertaste.	Caractère plein et doux. Franche, légèrement maltée-douce, fin de bouche douce.	Vol en zacht karakter. Volmondig, licht moutig zoet, zachte nasmaak.
	Pour slowly in a degreased goblet, leaving the yeast sediment in the bottle.	Verser tranquillement dans un verre calice dégraissé et laisser le dépôt de levure dans la bouteille.	Rustig uitschenken in een vetvrij kelkglas en het gistdepot in de fles laten.
i			

dochter van de Korenaar

6,50% — 7 °C / 45 °F

	top-fermentation re-fermentation in the bottle not centrifuged	fermentation haute refermentation en bouteille non centrifugée	hoge gisting hergisting in de fles niet gecentrifugeerd
	top-fermenting Rauch beer	rauchbier à fermentation haute	bovengistend rauchbier
	barley malt, wheat malt, yeast, hops, water	malt d'orge, malt de froment, levure, houblon, eau	gerstemout, tarwemout, gist, hop, water
	not filtered or pasteurised	non filtrée, non pasteurisée	ongefilterd, niet gepasteuriseerd
	Beer with a slight smoked flavour.	Bière avec un léger goût de fumé.	Bier met een lichte rooksmaak.
i			

Brasserie Grain d'Orge

7,50% 4 - 6 39 - 43

	top-fermentation re-fermented in the bottle	fermentation haute refermentation en bouteille	hoge gisting hergisting in de fles
	regional beer	bière régionale	streekbier
	malt, hops, yeast, sugar, herbs, water	malt, houblon, sucre, levure, herbes, eau	mout, hop, gist, suiker, kruiden, water
	deep blond transparent	blond soutenu transparente	krachtig blond transparant
	Fresh, fruity session beer. Fresh nose with touches of spices and smooth hop.	Bière fraîche, facilement buvable. Parfum frais avec des touches d'herbes et de houblon moelleux.	Fris, fruitig doordrinkbier. Frisse neus met toetsen van kruiden en zachte hop.
	Pour in a single movement, leaving the yeast sediment (ca. 5 mm) in the bottle.	Verser en un seul mouvement et laisser le dépôt de levure (environ 5 mm) dans la bouteille.	In 1 beweging uitschenken en het gistdepot (ca 5 mm) in de fles laten.
i			

9% 8 °C 46 °F

top-fermentation re-fermented in the bottle	fermentation haute refermentation en bouteille	hoge gisting hergisting in de fles
regional beer blond	bière régionale blonde	streekbier blond
barley malt, wheat malt, hops, yeast, sugar, water	malt d'orge, malt de froment, houblon, levure, sucre, eau	gerstemout, tarwemout, hop, gist, suiker, water
dark blond clear	blond foncé claire	donkerblond helder
Hoppy and spicy. Full taste with wheat malt influences. Bitter aftertaste.	Houblonnée et aromatisée. Saveur pleine avec influence de froment malté. Fin de bouche amère.	Hoppig en kruidig. Volle smaak met invloed van tarwemout. Bittere afdronk.
Pour into a newly rinsed glass. Tilt it first, then straighten. Yeast can be poured, according to taste.	Verser dans un verre récemment rincé d'abord tenu en oblique et à la fin en position verticale. La levure est versée selon le goût.	Uitschenken in een vers gespoeld glas dat eerst schuin gehouden wordt en op het einde verticaal gehouden wordt. De gist wordt volgens eigen smaak al dan niet uitgeschonken.

Broeder Jacob by Brasserie du Bocq

7,50% 4 - 1
39 - 5

top-fermentation re-fermentation in the bottle centrifuged	fermentation haute refermentation en bouteille centrifugée	hoge gisting hergisting in de fles gecentrifugeerd
very dark	double forte	sterk donker
barley malt, hops, yeast, sugar, natural herbs water	malt d'orge, houblon, levure, sucre, herbes naturelles, eau	gerstemout, hop, gist, suiker, natuurlijke kruiden, water
filtered, pasteurised	filtrée, pasteurisée	gefilterd, gepasteuriseerd
Fruity aroma of banana, with a malty, slightly bitter touch of chocolate.	Arôme fruité de banane, avec une touche de chocolat malté, légèrement amer.	Fruitig aroma van banaan, met een moutige, lichtbittere chocoladetoets.
Tilt glass slightly and carefully pour the beer in a single movement. A G clef has been etched on the bottom of this glass to make the beer effervesce.	Tenir le verre légèrement incliné et verser la bière prudemment d'un seul mouvement fluide. Au fond de la bouteille se trouve un scratch en forme de la clé sol pour faire pétiller la bière.	Het glas licht schuin houden en het bier voor zichtig uitschenken in 1 vloeiende beweging. Op de bodem van dit glas zi een scratch in de vorm van een solsleutel om het bier te laten borrelen.
Produced in tandem with Pierre Celis.	Réalisée avec la collaboration de Pierre Celis.	Tot stand gekomen met de medewerking van Pierre Celis.

oeder Jacob by Brasserie du Bocq

7,50% 4 - 12 °C 39 - 54 °F

	top-fermentation re-fermentation in the bottle centrifuged	fermentation haute refermentation en bouteille centrifugée	hoge gisting hergisting in de fles gecentrifugeerd
	tripel	triple	tripel
	barley malt, hops, yeast, sugar, natural herbs water	malt d'orge, houblon, levure, sucre, herbes naturelles, eau	gerstemout, hop, gist, suiker, natuurlijke kruiden, water
	golden-yellow and sparkling clear, with a full, solid foam head filtered, pasteurised	jaune doré et pétillant limpide, avec faux col plein, solide filtrée, pasteurisée	goudgeel en sprankelend helder, met een volle, stevige schuimkraag gefilterd, gepasteuriseerd
	Complex taste pallet with a soft bitterness of fine hops and herbs. Despite its high % a very drinkable and harmonious tripel.	Palette de goûts complexe avec une douce amertume de houblon noble et d'épices. Malgré son % élevé, une triple facile à boire et harmonieuse.	Complex smaakpalet met een zachte bitterheid van edele hop en kruiden. Ondanks zijn hoge % een vlot drinkbare en harmonieuze tripel.
	see Broeder Jacob bruin	voir Broeder Jacob bruin	zie Broeder Jacob bruin
	Innovative beer that has come about in tandem with Pierre Celis.	Bière innovante qui a été réalisée avec la collaboration de Pierre Celis.	Vernieuwend bier dat tot stand is gekomen met de medewerking van Pierre Celis.

B Brugge Tripel

Palm Breweries **8,70%**

	top-fermentation re-fermented in the bottle	fermentation haute refermentation en bouteille	hoge gisting hergisting in de fles
	city beer heavy blond	bière citadine blonde forte	stadsbier zwaar blond
	special malts, fine aromatic hops, yeast, water	malts spéciaux, houblons aromatiques fins, levure, eau	speciale mouten, fijne aromahoppen, gist, water
	blond	blonde	blond
	Spicy and roasty bouquet. Very full taste and malty character. Dry fruitiness in the aftertaste.	Bouquet aromatisé et fumé. Saveur très pleine et caractère malté. Goût fruité sec en fin de bouche.	Kruidig en gerookt boeket. Zeer volle smaak en moutkarakter. Droge fruitigheid in de afdronk.
	Serve in a very tall glass.	Servir dans un verre très haut.	Serveren in een heel hoog glas.

ouwerij Alken-Maes

4,80% 2 - 4 °C 36 - 39 °F

top-fermentation	fermentation haute	hoge gisting
witbier	bière blanche	witbier
light-yellow naturally cloudy	jaune clair aspect trouble naturel	lichtgeel natuurlijke troebelheid
Well-balanced sweet-and-sour, fresh and fruity with a rich character. Touches of wheat, hop, orange, apple peel and coriander.	Aigre-doux équilibré, fraîche et fruitée avec un caractère riche. Saveur de froment, houblon, zeste d'orange et peau de pomme, coriandre.	Evenwichtig zuurzoet, fris en fruitig met een rijk karakter. Smaak van tarwe, hop, sinaas- en appelschil, koriander.
Empty in a degreased, rinsed and wet glass. Let overflow and skim off the foam.	Verser complètement dans un verre dégraissé, rincé et mouillé. Laisser déborder et écumer.	Helemaal uitschenken in een ontvet, gespoeld en nat glas. Laten overlopen en afschuimen.

B

Brugse Zot Blond

Brouwerij De Halve Maan

6% 7 45

	top-fermentation re-fermented in the bottle	fermentation haute refermentation en bouteille	hoge gisting hergisting in de fles
	ale	ale	ale
	4 malt varieties and 2 aromatic hop varieties, candy sugar, yeast, water	4 sortes de malt et 2 variétés de houblon aromatique, sucre candi, levure, eau	4 moutsoorten en 2 aromatische hopvariëteiten, kandijsuiker, gist, water
	golden blond rich foam head clear	blond doré faux col riche claire	goudblond rijke schuimkraag helder
	Dry, light bitter, fruity aroma with citrus touches. Hoppy character ending in a tasteful dryness with a fruity effect.	Arôme fruité, sec, légèrement amer avec des touches d'agrumes. Caractère houblonné aboutissant en un goût sec savoureux se présentant fruité.	Fruitig, droog, licht bitter aroma met toetsen van citrus. Hoppig karakter eindigend in een smakelijke droogheid di fruitig overkomt.
	Pour carefully, leaving 1 cm of yeast sediment in the bottle.	Verser prudemment et laisser un dépôt de levure de 1 cm dans la bouteille.	Voorzichtig uitschenken en 1 cm gistdepot in de fles laten.
	The name of the beer refers to the nickname of the inhabitants of Bruges (a legend from the times of Maximilian of Austria).	Le nom de la bière renvoie au sobriquet des Brugeois (légende qui date du temps de Maximilien d'Autriche).	De naam van het bier refereert aan de bijnaam van de Bruggelingen (legende uit de tijd van Maximiliaan van Oostenrijk).

7,50% 8 °C 46 °F

Brugse Zot Dubbel

	top-fermentation re-fermented in the bottle	fermentation haute refermentation en bouteille	hoge gisting hergisting in de fles
	dubbel ale	ale double	ale dubbel
	6 special malt varieties and Saaz hops, candy sugar, yeast, water	6 sortes de malt et houblon Saaz, sucre candi, levure, eau	6 speciale moutsoorten en Saaz hop, kandijsuiker, gist, water
	ruby red	rouge rubis	robijnrood
	Rich aroma and bitter hop touch. Taste of roasted malt with a bitter touch of Czech Saaz hop.	Arôme riche et touche houblonnée amère. Saveur de malt grillé avec une touche amère du houblon Saaz tchèque.	Rijk aroma en bittere hoptoets. Smaak van geroosterde mout met een bittere toets van de Tjechische Saaz hop.
	Pour carefully, leaving 1 cm of yeast sediment in the bottle.	Verser prudemment et laisser un dépôt de levure de 1 cm dans la bouteille.	Traag uitschenken en 1 cm gistdepot in de fles laten.
i	The name of the beer refers to the nickname of the inhabitants of Bruges (a legend from the times of Maximilian of Austria).	Le nom de la bière renvoie au sobriquet des Brugeois (légende qui date du temps de Maximilien d'Autriche).	De naam van het bier refereert aan de bijnaam van de Bruggelingen (legende uit de tijd van Maximiliaan van Oostenrijk).

B

Bruin Leroy

Brouwerij Het Sas 1,80% 3 37

	bottom-fermentation	fermentation basse	lage gisting
	table beer	bière de table	tafelbier
	malt, rice, hops, caramel, artificial sweetener, water	malt, riz, houblon, caramel, édulcorant artificiel, eau	mout, rijst, hop, karamel, kunstmatige zoetstof, water
	dark brown	brun foncé	donkerbruin
	Sweet and slightly alcoholic thirst-quencher. Sweet and fruity.	Désaltérant doux et légèrement alcoolisé. Doux et fruité.	Zoete en licht alcoholische dorstlesser. Zoet en fruitig.
	Pour slowly in a single, smooth movement in a degreased glass. Keep the glass tilted and avoid sloshing the beer. Skim off the foam.	Verser lentement en un seul mouvement fluide dans un verre dégraissé tenu en oblique. Ne pas laisser la bière clapoter. Ecumer le verre.	Traag en in 1 vloeiende beweging uitschenken in een vetvrij glas dat wordt schuingehouden. Het bier niet laten klotsen. Het glas afschuimen.

rasserie de Brunehaut

6,50% 6 °C 41 - 46 °F

Brunehaut Bio Amber

B

top-fermentation re-fermented in the bottle	fermentation haute refermentation en bouteille	hoge gisting natuurlijke hergisting in de fles
amber	ambrée	amber
malt, hops, yeast, water	malt, houblon, levure, eau	mout, hop, gist, water
amber, shiny, with a creamy foam head filtered, not pasteurised	ambrée, brillante, avec un faux col crémeux filtrée, non pasteurisée	amber, glanzend, met een romige schuimkraag gefilterd, niet gepasteuriseerd
Round and perfumed. Intense, manly and not too sugary.	Ronde et parfumée. Corsée, virile et pas trop sucrée.	Rond en geparfumeerd. Gecorseerd, mannelijk en niet al te suikerig.
Gluten-free organic beer. Gold medal at the 'US Open Beer Championship' 2011.	Une bière biologique sans gluten. Médaille d'or à l''US Open Beer Championship' 2011.	Glutenvrij biologisch bier. Gouden medaille 'US Open Beer Championship' 2011.

Brunehaut Bio Blanche

Brasserie de Brunehaut

5% 5 - 6 / 41 - 43

top-fermentation re-fermented in the bottle	fermentation haute refermentation en bouteille	hoge gisting natuurlijke hergisting in de fles
witbier organic	bière blanche biologique	witbier biologisch
malt, wheat, hops, yeast, herbs, water	malt, froment, houblon, levure, herbes, eau	mout, tarwe, hop, gist, kruiden, water
pale yellow and shiny with a creamy foam head not filtered, not pasteurised	brillante et jaune clair avec un faux col crémeux non filtrée, non pasteurisée	lichtgeel en glanzend met een romige schuimkraag ongefilterd, niet gepasteuriseerd
Refreshing and perfumed. Smooth onset, not too bitter, almost round with a fresh aftertaste. Fruity with a touch of bitterness.	Rafraîchissante et parfumée. Fruitée et un peu amère. Approche initiale souple, goût pas trop amer, presque rond ensuite et une fraîche arrière-bouche.	Verfrissend en geparfumeerd. Fruitig en een vleugje bitter. Soepele aanzet, niet te bitter, bijna rond daarna en frisse afdronk.
Bronze medal at the 'World Beer Championship' in Chicago in 2009.	Médaille de bronze au 'World Beer Championship' 2009 à Chicago.	Bronzen medaille 'World Beer Championship' 2009 in Chicago.

rasserie de Brunehaut

6,50% — 6 °C / 41 - 46 °F

	top-fermentation re-fermented in the bottle	fermentation haute refermentation en bouteille	hoge gisting natuurlijke hergisting in de fles
	blond	blonde	blond
	malt, hops, yeast, water	malt, houblon, levure, eau	mout, hop, gist, water
	pale yellow and shiny with a creamy foam head not filtered, not pasteurised	brillante et jaune clair avec un faux col crémeux non filtrée, non pasteurisée	lichtgeel en glanzend met een romige schuimkraag ongefilterd, niet gepasteuriseerd
	Light and refreshing. Smooth, balanced, almost round onset with earhtly hint. Slightly spicy yeast aroma.	Légère et rafraîchissante. Une approche initiale souplement équilibrée, presque ronde, avec une touche de terre. Arôme de levure légèrement épicé.	Licht en verfrissend. Soepel evenwichtige, bijna ronde aanzet met aardse toets. Licht kruidig gistaroma.
	Gluten-free organic beer. Silver medal at the 'US Open Beer Championship' 2011.	Une bière biologique sans gluten. Médaille d'argent à l''US Open Beer Championship' 2011.	Glutenvrij biologisch bier. Zilveren medaille 'US Open Beer Championship' 2011.

Brussels Fruit Beer Peaches

Brasserie du Bocq 3,20% 3 37

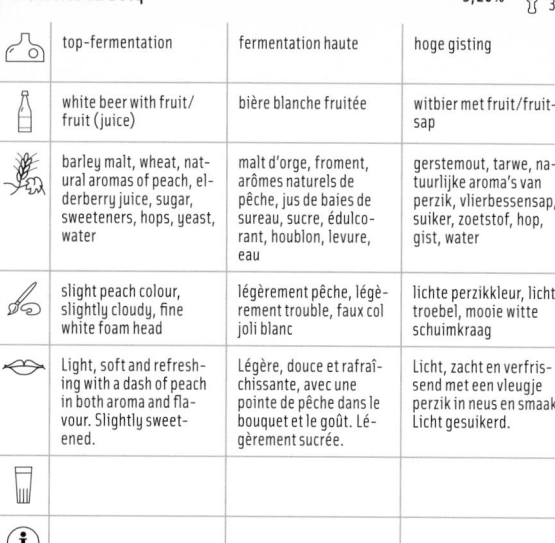

top-fermentation	fermentation haute	hoge gisting
white beer with fruit/ fruit (juice)	bière blanche fruitée	witbier met fruit/fruit-sap
barley malt, wheat, natural aromas of peach, elderberry juice, sugar, sweeteners, hops, yeast, water	malt d'orge, froment, arômes naturels de pêche, jus de baies de sureau, sucre, édulcorant, houblon, levure, eau	gerstemout, tarwe, natuurlijke aroma's van perzik, vlierbessensap, suiker, zoetstof, hop, gist, water
slight peach colour, slightly cloudy, fine white foam head	légèrement pêche, légèrement trouble, faux col joli blanc	lichte perzikkleur, licht troebel, mooie witte schuimkraag
Light, soft and refreshing with a dash of peach in both aroma and flavour. Slightly sweetened.	Légère, douce et rafraîchissante, avec une pointe de pêche dans le bouquet et le goût. Légèrement sucrée.	Licht, zacht en verfrissend met een vleugje perzik in neus en smaak. Licht gesuikerd.

Brussels Fruit Beer Pommes

rasserie du Bocq 3,20% 3 °C 37 °F

	top-fermentation	fermentation haute	hoge gisting
	white beer with fruit/fruit (juice)	bière blanche fruitée	witbier met fruit/fruit-sap
	barley malt, wheat, apple juice (30%), hops, yeast, water	malt d'orge, froment, jus de pommes (30%), houblon, levure, eau	gerstemout, tarwe, appelsap (30%), hop, gist, water
	Refreshing with a slight taste of apple and cider.	Rafraîchissante, avec un léger goût de pomme et de cidre.	Verfrissend met een lichte smaak van appel en cider.

Brussels Fruit Beer Red Fruit

Brasserie du Bocq 3,20% 3 37

top-fermentation	fermentation haute	hoge gisting
white beer with fruit/ fruit (juice)	bière blanche fruitée	witbier met fruit/fruit-sap
aromatised with red fruits	aromatisé avec fruits rouges	gearomatiseerd met rode vruchten
pink-red, cloudy and milky, fine pink foam head	rouge rose, trouble et laiteuse, faux col joli rose	rozerood, troebel en melkachtig, mooie roze schuimkraag
Light, soft and refreshing with red fruits (raspberry, blackcurrant and blueberry) in aroma and flavour. Slightly sweetened.	Légère, douce et rafraîchissante, avec des fruits rouges (framboise, cassis et myrtille) dans le bouquet et le goût. Légèrement sucrée.	Licht, zacht en verfrissend met rode vruchten (framboos, cassis en myrtille) in neus en smaak. Licht gesuikerd.

rouwerij Van den Bossche

6,50% 6 - 8 °C / 43 - 46 °F

top-fermentation re-fermented in the bottle	fermentation haute refermentation en bouteille	hoge gisting hergisting in de fles
regional beer	bière régionale	streekbier
hops, yeast, fermentable sugar, water. Malt varieties: pilsner, Pale Ale, caramel, roast	houblon, levure, sucre de fermentation, eau Sortes de malt: pils, pale ale, caramélisé, grillé	hop, gist, vergistbare suiker, water. Moutsoorten: pils, pale ale, karamel, roast
dark	foncée	donker
Pour slowly for a nice foam head with hat. Leave a small amount in the bottle (it can be served afterwards) and present the bottle with the glass.	Verser lentement pour obtenir un faux col solide avec chapeau. Laisser un peu de biére dans la bouteille (peut être versé par la suite) et offrir aussi la bouteille.	Langzaam inschenken voor een mooie schuimkraag en schuimhoed. Een restje in de fles laten (kan achteraf bijgeschonken worden) en de fles mee aanbieden.
Has existed since 1907 and is the brewery's oldest beer. The name refers to the Buffalo Bill circus.	Existe depuis 1907 et est la bière la plus ancienne de la brasserie. Le nom se réfère au cirque Buffalo Bill.	Bestaat sedert 1907 en is het oudste bier van de brouwerij. De naam verwijst naar het circus Buffalo Bill.

Buffalo 1907

Buffalo Belgian Stout

Brouwerij Van den Bossche 9% 6 - 8 / 43 - 46

top-fermentation re-fermented in the bottle	fermentation haute refermentation en bouteille	hoge gisting hergisting in de fles
stout regional beer	stout bière régionale	stout stads- of streekbier
hops, yeast, fermentable sugar, water Malt varieties: pilsner, Pale Ale, caramel, roast	malt, houblon, sucre de fermentation, eau Sortes de malt: pils, pale ale, caramélisé, grillé	hop, gist, vergistbare suiker, water Moutsoorten: pils, pale ale, karamel, roast
dark brown to black, beige creamy foam head	brun foncé-noire, faux col beige, crémeux	donkerbruin tot zwart beige, romige schuimkraag
Nose of roasted malt with alcohol and chocolate touches. Taste: first sweet with a chocolate and roasted coffee flavour. Dry and bitter aftertaste.	Parfum de malt brûlé avec des touches d'alcool et de chocolat. Goût :début doux avec des arômes de chocolat et de café brûlé. Fin de bouche sèche et amère.	Neus van gebrande mout met toetsen van alcohol en chocolade. Smaak: zoete aanhef met chocolade en gebrande koffie. Droge en bittere afdronk.
Pour slowly for a nice foam head. Leave a small amount in the bottle and present the bottle with the glass.	Verser lentement pour obtenir un faux col solide. Laisser un peu de bière dans la bouteille et offrir aussi la bouteille.	Langzaam inschenken voor een mooie schuimkraag. Een restje in de fles laten en de fles mee aanbieden.
Beer created to mark the 100th anniversary of the Buffalo beer (now 'Buffalo 1907'), initially at the US importer's request.	Brassée à l'occasion du centenaire de la bière 'Buffalo' (maintenant 'Buffalo 1907'), à l'origine à la demande de l'importateur pour les États-Unis.	Gebrouwen t.g.v. het 100-jarig bestaan van het bier 'Buffalo' (nu 'Buffalo 1907'), aanvankelijk op verzoek van de importeur voor USA.

ouwerij Van den Bossche

8% 6 - 8 °C / 43 - 46 °F

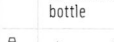

	top-fermentation re-fermentation in the bottle	fermentation haute refermentation en bouteille	hoge gisting hergisting in de fles
	city or regional beer	bière citadine ou régionale	stads- of streekbier
	pilsner malt, 3 different hops (Styrian Gold, First Gold, Cascade), fermentable sugar, yeast, water	malt de pils, 3 variétés de houblon (Styrian Gold, First Gold, Cascade), sucre fermentable, levure, eau	pilsmout, 3 hopsoorten (Styrian Gold, First Gold, Cascade), vergistbare suiker, gist, water
	blond with a creamy white foam head filtered, not pasteurised	blonde avec un faux col crémeux blanc filtrée, non pasteurisée	blond met een romige witte schuimkraag gefilterd, niet gepasteuriseerd
	Hoppy nose. Strong hoppy taste. Very long and bitter aftertaste.	Bouquet houblonné. Fort goût de houblon. Arrière-bouche fort longue et amère.	Hoppige neus. Sterke hopsmaak. Zeer lange en bittere afdronk.
	Pour slowly, and avoid sloshing the beer, to achieve a nice foam head. Leave the yeast sediment in the bottle and add later, if necessary.	Verser lentement sans clapotage pour former un faux col solide. Laisser le dépôt de levure dans la bouteille et le verser éventuellement par après.	Langzaam uitschenken zonder dat het bier klokt en een mooie schuimkraag vormen. Het gistdepot in de fles laten en eventueel achteraf bijschenken.
	Initially brewed at the request of an Italian importer.	Brassée à l'origine à la demande de l'importateur italien.	Aanvankelijk gebrouwen op vraag van de Italiaanse importeur.

Buffalo Bitter - Belgian Ale

Buitenlust Dubbel Blond

Buitenlust by Proefbrouwerij 8,50% 8 - 10 °C / 14 - 15 46 - 50 °F / 57 - 59

	top-fermentation re-fermented in the bottle	fermentation haute refermentation en bouteille	hoge gisting hergisting in de fles
	strong blond	blonde forte	sterk blond
	barley malt, hops, yeast, water	malt d'orge, houblon, levure, eau	gerstemout, hop, gist, water
	Dark blond because of the concentration of the ingredients (18 °plato).	Blond foncé par la concentration des matières premières (18 ° plato).	Donkerblond door de concentratie van de grondstoffen (18 ° plato).
	Provision beer with taste evolution. Alcohol, malt and hop are well-balanced and blur each other. The bitternes (30 EBU) is compensated by the malt sugar.	Bière de conservation avec saveur évolutive. L'alcool, le malt et le houblon sont bien équilibrés et se cachent l'un l'autre : le goût amer (30 EBU) est compensé par le sucre malté.	Bewaarbier met smaakevolutie. Alcohol, mout en hop zijn mooi in balans en verdoezelen elkaar: bitter (30 EBU) wordt gecompenseerd door de moutsuiker.
	Pour smoothly in a single movement, leaving the sediment in the bottle. Do not serve too cold so as to fully appreciate the aroma.	Verser doucement en un seul mouvement et laisser le dépôt dans la bouteille. Ne pas servir trop froide, sinon l'odeur disparaît.	Zacht uitschenken in 1 beweging en het bezinksel in de fles laten. Niet te koud schenken, anders is de geur weg.
i	The label is an old, original family picture.	L'étiquette est une vieille photo de la famille.	Het etiket is een oude, originele familiefoto.

asserie Dubuisson 12% 10 °C 50 °F

Bush Ambrée

	top-fermentation	fermentation haute	hoge gisting
	strong blond	blonde forte	sterk blond
	malt, hops, natural sugar, yeast, water	malt, houblon, sucre naturel, levure, eau	mout, hop, natuurlijke suiker, gist, water
	red-copper 100% filtered	cuivre rouge 100 % filtrée	roodkoper 100 % gefilterd
	Digestive, typical bittersweet taste, powerful aroma of roasty nuts.	Digestive, saveur typiquement amère-douce, arôme corsé de noix brûlés.	Digestief, typische bitterzoete smaak, krachtig aroma van gebrande noten.

Bush Ambrée Triple

Brasserie Dubuisson 12% 8 - 10 46 - 50

top-fermentation natural re-fermentation in the bottle	fermentation haute refermentation naturelle en bouteille	hoge gisting natuurlijke hergisting in de fles
amber tripel Belgian ale	triple ambrée Belgian ale	amber tripel Belgian ale
3 types of barley malt, 2 types of aromatic hops, sugar, yeast, well water	3 variétés de malt d'orge, 2 variétés de houblon aromatique, sucre, levure, eau de puits	3 soorten gerstemout, 2 soorten aromatische hop, suiker, gist, putwater
amber, naturally cloudy not filtered	ambrée, trouble naturel non filtrée	amber, natuurlijk troebel ongefilterd
The re-fermentation does not only turn the sweet-bitter flavour and powerful aromas smoother but also more intense. Exceptionally smooth and soft.	Le goût doux-amer et les puissants arômes prennent plus de rondeur du fait de la refermentation, mais aussi plus d'intensité. Exceptionnellement rond et doux.	De zoetbittere smaak en de krachtige aroma's worden door de hergisting ronder maar ook intenser. Uitzonderlijk rond en zacht.
Created in 2008 to mark the 75th anniversary of Bush Ambrée. Bottled in a bottle with silk-screen printing and champagne cork.	Créée en 2008, à l'occasion des 75 ans de la Bush Ambrée. Embouteillée dans une bouteille portant une sérigraphie et avec un bouchon de champagne.	Gecreëerd in 2008 n.a.v. 75 jaar Bush Ambrée. Gebotteld in een geserigrafeerde fles met champagnekurk.

Bush Blonde

asserie Dubuisson 10,50% 10 °C 50 °F

	top-fermentation	fermentation haute	hoge gisting
	strong blond	blonde forte	sterk blond
	malt, hops (Saaz), sugar, yeast, water	malt, houblon (Saaz), sucre, levure, eau	mout, hop (Saaz), suiker, gist, water
	amber blond 100% filtered	blond ambré 100% filtrée	amberblond 100% gefilterd
	Very easily digestible beer with well-balanced flavours, smooth and round.	Bière facile à digérer avec des arômes équilibrés, doux et ronds.	Zeer licht verteerbaar bier met evenwichtige aroma's, zacht en rond.

Bush Blonde Triple

Brasserie Dubuisson 10,50% 8 - 1 / 46 - 5

	top-fermentation natural re-fermentation in the bottle	fermentation haute refermentation naturelle en bouteille	hoge gisting natuurlijke hergisting in de fles
	strong blond tripel Belgian ale	blonde forte triple Belgian ale	sterk blond tripel Belgian ale
	2 different barley malts, 2 different aromatic hops, sugar, yeast, well water	2 variétés de malt d'orge, 2 variétés de houblon aromatique, sucre, levure, eau de puits	2 soorten gerstemout, 2 soorten aromatische hop, suiker, gist, putwater
	blond, naturally cloudy not filtered	blonde, trouble naturel non filtrée	blond, natuurlijk troebel ongefilterd
	Subtle but very distinct aromas. Exceptionally smooth and soft.	Arômes subtils mais clairement présents. Exceptionnellement rond et doux.	Subtiele maar duidelijk aanwezige aroma's. Uitzonderlijk rond en zacht.
i	Created in 2008 to mark the 10th anniversary of the Bush blond and bottled in a bottle with silk-screen printing and champagne cork.	Créée en 2008, à l'occasion des 10 ans d'existence de la Bush Blonde, et embouteillée dans une bouteille portant une sérigraphie et avec un bouchon de champagne.	Gecreëerd in 2008 t.g.v. het 10-jarig bestaan van de Bush blond en gebotteld in een geserigrafeerde fles met champagnekurk.

12% 10 °C 50 °F

	top-fermentation	fermentation haute	hoge gisting
	strong blond winter beer	blonde forte bière hivernale	sterk blond winterbier
	malt, caramel malt, yeast, sugar, hops, water	malt, malt caramélisé, levure, sucre, houblon, eau	mout, karamelmout, gist, suiker, hop, water
	red-copper 100% filtered	cuivre rouge 100 % filtrée	roodkoper 100 % gefilterd
	Well-balanced fruit taste with a slightly hop- py flavour.	Saveur fruitée équilibrée avec un arôme légère- ment houblonné.	Evenwichtige fruitsmaak met een licht hoppig aroma.

Bush de Noël Premium

Brasserie Dubuisson 13%

	top-fermentation re-fermented in the bottle (75 cl)	fermentation haute refermentation en bouteille (75 cl)	hoge gisting nagisting op de fles (75 cl)
	strong blond winter beer	blonde forte bière hivernale	sterk blond winterbier
	malt, caramel malt, hops, sugar, yeast, water	malt, malt caramélisé, houblon, sucre, levure, eau	mout, karamelmout, hop, suiker, gist, water
	copper slightly cloudy	cuivre légèrement trouble	koper licht troebel

Bush de Nuits Cuvée 2010

top-fermentation natural re-fermentation in the bottle	fermentation haute refermentation naturelle en bouteille	hoge gisting natuurlijke hergisting in de fles
amber cuvée speciale tripel Belgian ale	ambrée cuvée spéciale triple Belgian ale	amber tripel, cuvée speciale Belgian ale
3 different barley malts, 2 different aromatic hops, sugar, yeast, well water	3 variétés de malt d'orge, 2 variétés de houblon aromatique, sucre, levure, eau de puits	3 soorten gerstemout, 2 soorten aromatische hop, suiker, gist, putwater
amber not filtered	ambrée non filtrée	amber ongefilterd
Very rich taste pallet, scented with wine aromas of red fruits. Surprising harmonious balance in the mouth.	Très riche palette de goûts, parfumé avec des arômes de vin de fruits rouges. Équilibre étonnamment harmonieux en bouche.	Zeer rijk smakenpalet, geparfumeerd met wijnaroma's van rode vruchten. Verrassend harmonisch evenwicht in de mond.
Inspired by a visit to Nuits Saint Georges in 2007, Hugues Dubuisson struck upon the idea to mature the Bush de Noël for 6 months in a cask of Côte de Nuits.	Inspiré par une visite à Nuits-Saint-Georges en 2007, Hugues Dubuisson a conçu l'idée de faire mûrir la Bush de Noël pendant 6 mois dans un fût de Côte de Nuits.	Geïnspireerd door een bezoek aan Nuits-Saint-Georges in 2007 kreeg Hugues Dubuisson het idee om de Bush de Noël 6 maanden te laten rijpen in een vat van Côte de Nuits.

Bush Pêche Mel

Brasserie Dubuisson 8,50% 6 -
43 - 4

	top-fermentation	fermentation haute	hoge gisting
	fruit beer Belgian ale	bière fruitée Belgian ale	fruitbier Belgian ale
	3 types of barley malt, 2 types of aromatic hops, sugar, fruit juice (peach), natural peach aromas, yeast, well water	3 variétés de malt d'orge, 2 variétés de houblon aromatique, sucre, jus de fruits (pêches), arôme naturel de pêches, levure, eau de puits	3 soorten gerstemout, 2 soorten aromatische hop, suiker, fruitsap (perzik), natuurlijke perzikaroma's, gist, putwater
	amber filtered, not pasteurised	ambrée filtrée, non pasteurisée	amber gefilterd, niet gepasteuriseerd
	Natural peach aromas. The fruit aromas and extracts blend in perfectly with the original bitterness of the bush ambrée. Full-bodied.	Arômes naturels de pêche. Les arômes de fruits et les essences s'harmonisent parfaitement avec l'amertume originelle de la Bush ambrée. Goût franc en bouche.	Natuurlijke perzikaroma's. De fruitaroma's en extracten harmoniëren perfect met de originele bitterheid van de bush ambrée. Vol in de mond.
	Created years ago by students as a cocktail by mixing equal parts of Bush and Gueuze peach. In 2009, the brewery decided to brew it according to the original recipe based on peach extracts.	Créée il y a des années par des étudiants comme cocktail en mélangeant de la Bush à de la gueuze pêche en parts égales. En 2009, la brasserie décide de la brasser selon une recette originale à base d'extraits de pêche.	Jaren terug door studenten gecreëerd als cocktail door Bush met geuze perzik in gelijke delen te mengen. In 2009 besliste de brouwerij om het te brouwen volgens een origineel recept op basis van perzikextracten.

asserie Dubuisson

13% 10 °C 50 °F

	top-fermentation in oak barrels re-fermented in the bottle (75 cl)	fermentation haute en fûts de chêne refermentation en bouteille (75 cl)	hoge gisting op eikenhouten vaten nagisting op de fles (75 cl)
	strong blond	blonde forte	sterk blond
	malt, sugar, hops, yeast, water	malt, sucre, houblon, levure, eau	mout, suiker, hop, gist, water
	amber naturally cloudy by the re-fermentation in the bottle	ambrée trouble naturel par refermentation en bouteille	amber natuurlijk troebel door hergisting in de fles
	Typical character owing to the tannin of the oakwood barrels. Forest flavours and a powerful, round taste.	Caractère typique par les tannins des fûts de chêne. Arômes boisés, saveur corsée et ronde.	Typisch karakter door de tannine van de eikenhouten vaten. Bosaroma's, krachtige en ronde smaak.
	Store in the drawer of the refrigerator at 43 to 45 °F.	Conserver dans le tiroir du réfrigérateur à 6 à 7 °C.	Bewaren in de frigolade op 6 à 7 °C.

Cambrinus

Brouwerij Verhaeghe 5,10%

top-fermentation	fermentation haute	hoge gisting
Belgian ale	ale belge	Belgische ale
malt, hops, yeast, water	malt, houblon, levure, eau	mout, hop, gist, water
amber filtered	ambrée filtrée	amber gefilterd
Malty with a fruity yeast touch.	Maltée avec une touche fruitée de levure.	Moutig met een fruitige gisttoets.
Pour in a dry bulb jar with stem.	Verser dans un verre ballon sec à pied.	Uitschenken in een droog bolglas met voet.

Campus

ouwerij Huyghe 7%

	top-fermentation re-fermented in the bottle	fermentation haute refermentation en bouteille	hoge gisting hergisting in de fles
	strong dark	foncée forte	sterk donker
	roasted malt varieties, hops, yeast, herbs, water	variétes de malt brûlé, houblon, levure, herbes, eau	gebrande moutsoorten, hop, gist, kruiden, water
	red-brown	brun rouge	roodbruin
	Rich amber beer with a honey touch in harmony with a discrete fruity flavour and pronounced maltiness. Aftertaste: dry and bitter caramel.	Bière ambrée riche avec des touches de miel en harmonie avec un goût fruité discret et un goût malté prononcé. Fin de bouche sèche et amère caramélisée.	Rijk amberbier met honingtoets in harmonie met een discrete fruitigheid en een duidelijke moutigheid. Afdronk droog en bitter karamel.
	Serve in a bulb jar.	Verser dans un verre ballon.	Uitschenken in een bolglas.
i			

Campus Gold

Brouwerij Huyghe

6,20%

	top-fermentation re-fermented in the bottle	fermentation haute refermentation en bouteille	hoge gisting hergisting in de fles
	blond	blonde	blond
	roasted malt varieties, hops, yeast, herbs, water	variétés de malt brûlé, houblon, levure, herbes, eau	gebrande moutsoorten, hop, gist, kruiden, wate
	blond	blonde	blond
	Fresh taste, less bitter than Campus.	Goût frais, moins amer que la Campus.	Frisse smaak, minder bitter dan de Campus.
	Serve in a bulb jar.	Verser dans un verre ballon.	Uitschenken in een bolglas.
	Originally brewed by the former Brabant brewery De Biertoren.	A l'origine brassée par l'ancienne brasserie du Brabant De Biertoren.	Oorspronkelijk gebrouwen door de toenmalige Brabantse brouwerij De Biertoren.

uwerij Huyghe | 5% | 4 °C 39 °F

Campus Premium

	bottom-fermentation	fermentation basse	lage gisting
	pilsner or lager beer	pils ou lager	pils of lagerbier
	barley malt, hops, yeast, water	malt d'orge, houblon, levure, eau	gerstemout, hop, gist, water
	crystal-clear with fine, white foam head filtered, pasteurised	cristal clair avec faux col joli blanc filtrée, pasteurisée	kristalhelder met mooie, witte schuimkraag gefilterd, gepasteuriseerd
	Nice clean pilsner nose with pleasant hop aromas. Slightly malt sweet with a good, bitter, balanced and rich flavour.	Joli parfum pur de pils avec des arômes agréables de houblon. Légèrement doux malté avec un bon goût amer, équilibré et riche.	Mooi zuivere pilsneus met aangename hoparoma's. Licht moutzoet met een goede bitterige, evenwichtige en rijke smaak.

Canaille

Brasserie Grain-d'Orge

5,20% 4.

	top-fermentation natural re-fermentation in the bottle	fermentation haute refermentation naturelle en bouteille	hoge gisting natuurlijke hergisting i de fles
	boutique white beer	bière blanche artisanale	artisanaal witbier
	malt, multigrain (including wheat), hops, orange peel, coriander, cinnamon, yeast, water	malt, 3 céréales (e.a. froment), houblon, écorce d'orange, coriandre, cannelle, levure, eau	mout, 3 granen (o.a. tar we), hop, sinaasschil, koriander, kaneel, gist, water
	white and cloudy (wheat) with a big foam head not filtered or pasteurised	blanc et trouble (froment) avec un faux col gras non filtrée, non pasteurisée	wit en troebel (tarwe) met een vettige schuim kraag ongefilterd, niet gepasteuriseerd
	Fragrant and distinctive thirst-quencher with low hops levels.	Bière désaltérante parfumée et très caractéristique, avec peu de houblon.	Geurige en karaktervoll dorstlesser met weinig hop.
	Pour out in a single movement.	Verser complètement d'un seul mouvement.	In 1 beweging helemaal uitschenken.

uwerij De Glazen Toren 8,70% 7 - 8 °C 45 - 46 °F

Canaster

	top-fermentation re-fermented in the bottle	fermentation haute refermentation en bouteille	hoge gisting nagisting op de fles
	winter scotch	scotch hivernal	winterscotch
	barley malt, wheat malt, caramel malts, dark candy sugar, hops, yeast, water	malt d'orge, malt de froment, malts caramélisés, sucre candi brun, houblon, levure, eau	gerstemout, tarwemout, karamelmouten, donkere kandijsuiker, hop, gist, water
	Dark red to brown, with fine bubbles. Clear with solid foam head.	Rouge foncé à brun, finement pétillante. Claire avec faux col solide.	Donkerrood tot bruin, fijnparelend. Helder met stevige schuimkraag.
	Dry character. Flavour of roasty malt, fruity esters, light caramel and candy and a little liquorice.	Caractère sec. Arôme de malt brûlé, esters fruités, caramel léger, candi et un peu de réglisse.	Droog karakter. Aroma van gebrande mout, fruitige esters, lichte karamel, kandij en drop.
	Pour carefully into a dry, long glass (e.g. tulip glass).	Verser prudemment dans un verre sec, oblong (p. ex. tulipe).	Voorzichtig uitschenken in een droog, langwerpig (bv. tulpvormig) glas.
i			

Caper Fumatis

Picobrouwerij Alvinne

6,30% 8 - 1 46 - 5

top-fermentation natural re-fermentation in the bottle	fermentation haute refermentation naturelle en bouteille	hoge gisting natuurlijke hergisting i de fles
5 different malts, 3 different hops (Magnum, Chinook and EK Goldings), Morpheus yeast, water	5 variétés de malt, 3 variétés de houblon (Magnum, Chinook, EK Goldings), levure Morpheus, eau	5 moutsoorten, 3 hopsoorten (Magnum, Chinook, EK Goldings), Morpheusgist, water
123 EBC	123 EBC	123 EBC
43 EBU	43 EBU	43 EBU

tain Cooker by De Proefbrouwerij

5,70% 5 - 8 °C 41 - 46 °F

top-fermentation re-fermentation in the bottle	fermentation haute refermentation en bouteille	hoge gisting hergisting in de fles
amber	ambrée	amber
malt, hops, manuka leaves of the tea tree from New Zealand, yeast, water	malt, houblon, feuilles manuka du 'tea tree' de la Nouvelle-Zélande, levure, eau	mout, hop, manukabladeren van de 'tea tree' uit Nieuw-Zeeland, gist, water
Unique character owing to the use of manuka which also has a healing quality (see www.captaincooker.com/manuka).	Caractère unique grâce à l'utilisation de manuka, qui a en outre une action très bénéfique (voir www.captaincooker.com/manuka).	Uniek karakter door het gebruik van manuka dat tevens een zeer heilzame werking heeft (zie www.captaincooker.com/manuka).
Captain Cooker is the world's first 'open brewery': under certain conditions, you as (amateur) brewer can make the manuka beer in accordance with the brewery's recipe and launch it under that name.	Captain Cooker est la première 'brasserie ouverte' au monde :à certaines conditions, vous pouvez réaliser, dans le rôle du brasseur (amateur), la bière de manuka selon la recette de la brasserie et la lancer sous ce nom.	Captain Cooker is de eerste 'open brouwerij' ter wereld: onder bepaalde voorwaarden kun je als (amateur)brouwer het manukabier maken volgens het recept van de brouwerij en het onder die naam lanceren.

Captain Cooker Manuka Beer

Captain Cooker's White Manuka Beer

Captain Cooker by De Proefbrouwerij 4,50% 5 - 41 - 4

	top-fermentation re-fermentation in the bottle	fermentation haute refermentation en bouteille	hoge gisting hergisting in de fles
	white beer	bière blanche	witbier
	malt, hops, manuka leaves from New Zealand, yeast, water	malt, houblon, feuilles manuka de la Nouvelle-Zélande, levure, eau	mout, hop, manukabladeren uit Nieuw-Zeeland, gist, water

sserie Caracole

7,50% — 12 °C / 54 °F

	top-fermentation	fermentation haute	hoge gisting
	amber	ambrée	amber
	5 malt varieties, 2 hop varieties, yeast, orange rind, water	5 variétés de malt, 2 sortes de houblon, levure, écorce d'orange, eau	5 moutsoorten, 2 hopsoorten, gist, sinaasschil, water
	amber	ambrée	amber
	Round (cara malt and orange rind) and fruity with rich aroma's and a very distinctive taste.	Ronde (malt cara et zeste d'orange) et fruitée avec arômes riches et saveur très spécifique.	Rond (caramout en sinaasschil) en fruitig met rijke aroma's en een zeer specifieke smaak.

Du Lion à Plume at Brasserie de Bastogne

4,80% 10 - 1 50 - 5

	top-fermentation natural re-fermentation in the bottle not centrifuged	fermentation haute refermentation naturelle en bouteille non centrifugée	hoge gisting natuurlijke hergisting i de fles niet gecentrifugeerd
	white beer	bière blanche	witbier
	barley and wheat malt, wheat, hops (Amarillo and Cascade), yeast, water	malt d'orge et de froment, froment, houblon (Amarillo et Cascade), levure, eau	gerste- en tarwemout, tarwe, hop (Amarillo en Cascade), gist, water
	pale blond, slightly cloudy not filtered or pasteurised	blond clair, légèrement trouble non filtrée, non pasteurisée	lichtblond, licht troebe ongefilterd, niet gepasteuriseerd
	Dry beer with slight citrus flavour (lemon, grapefruit) and slight bitterness owing to hops. Unlike traditional wheat beer, it does not contain coriander. Slightly acidulous owing to wheat. Light and subtle thirst-quencher.	Bière sèche avec un léger goût de citrus (citron, pamplemousse) et une légère amertume due au houblon. À l'opposé d'une bière de froment classique, elle ne renferme pas de coriandre. Légèrement acidulé du fait du froment. Bière rafraîchissante d'un goût léger et subtil.	Droog bier met lichte ci trussmaak (citroen, pompelmoes) en lichte bitterheid door de hop. In tegenstelling tot een klassiek tarwebier beva het geen koriander. Lichtzurig door de tarw Dorstlesser met een lichte en subtiele smaa
	Pour out carefully in a slightly tilted glass at eye level. Then lift the bottle for a nice foam head.	Verser prudemment dans un verre légèrement tenu incliné à hauteur des yeux. Puis lever la bouteille plus haut pour former un faux col solide.	Voorzichtig uitschenke in een licht schuingehouden glas op ooghoogte. De fles daarna hoger tillen voor een mooie schuimkraag.
i			

as at Brouwerij De Graal

6,11% 6 °C 43 °F

top-fermentation re-fermentation in the bottle	fermentation haute refermentation en bouteille	hoge gisting hergisting in de fles
blond	blonde	blond
barley malt, hops, yeast, herbs, water	malt d'orge, houblon, levure, herbes, eau	gerstemout, hop, gist, kruiden, water
Pour slowly into a degreased glass without sloshing the beer.	Verser lentement dans un verre dégraissé sans clapotage de la bière.	Traag inschenken in een ontvet glas zonder dat het bier klokt.
Only available from De Bierloods during the carnival season.	Seulement en vente chez De Bierloods pendant la période du carnaval.	Enkel verkrijgbaar bij De Bierloods tijdens de carnavalsperiode.

Carnavalsbier

Carrousel

Brouwerij De Vlier

6% 4 - 39 - 4

	bottom-fermentation re-fermentation in the bottle not centrifuged	fermentation basse refermentation en bouteille non centrifugée	lage gisting hergisting in de fles niet gecentrifugeerd
	blond with spelt malt and citrus hops	blonde avec blé épeautre et houblon citronné	blond met speltmout en citrushop
	pilsner and spelt malt, hops (Citra and Saaz), yeast, water	malt de pils et d'épeautre, houblon (Citra et Saaz), levure, eau	pils- en speltmout, hop (Citra en Saaz), gist, water
	straw-yellow, cloudy blond with thick white foam head not filtered or pasteurised	jaune paille blond trouble avec faux col blanc collant au verre non filtrée, non pasteurisée	strogeel troebel blond met witte wandklevende schuimkraag ongefilterd, niet gepasteuriseerd
	Pleasant hoppy citrus aroma, refreshing taste, full and slightly acidulous, slightly bitter aftertaste.	Agréable arôme de citrus houblonné, goût rafraîchissant, franc et légèrement acide, arrière-bouche légèrement amère.	Aangenaam hoppig citrusaroma, verfrissende smaak, vol en lichtzuur, licht bittere afdronk.
	Pour into a tulip glass and leave the yeast sediment in the bottle or pour along.	Verser dans un verre tulipe et laisser le dépôt de levure dans la bouteille ou le verser également.	Uitschenken in een tulpvormig glas en de gistbodem in de fles laten o meeschenken.
i	Brewed for the first time to mark the Carrousel Festival in Kessel-Lo, organised by 30 CC (Cultural association from Louvain).	Brassée pour la première fois en l'honneur des Carrouselfeesten à Kessel-Lo, qui sont organisées par 30 CC (association culturelle de Louvain).	Voor de eerste maal gebrouwen ter ere van de Carrouselfeesten in Kessel-Lo die georganiseerd worden door 30 CC (Cultuurvereniging uit Leuven).

uwerij Lindemans 3,50% 3 - 4 °C 37 - 39 °F

Cassis Lindemans

spontaneous fermentation	fermentation spontanée	spontane gisting
fruit beer based on Lambic	bière fruitée à base de lambic	fruitbier op basis van lambiek
malt, wheat, hops, blackberry juice (25%), fructose, water	malt, froment, houblon, jus de baies noires (25%), fructose, eau	mout, tarwe, hop, zwartebessensap (25%), fructose, water
dark red slightly hazy	rouge foncé légèrement voilée	donkerrood licht gesluierd
Fruity character. Lively and strong onset turning into a balance of sweet (fruit) and slightly sour (lambic).	Caractère fruité. Début vif et corsé passant à un équilibre de douceur (fruits) et d'acidité légère (lambic).	Fruitig karakter. Levendige en sterke aanzet die overgaat in een evenwicht van zoet (fruit) en zacht zuur (lambiek).
Pour into a flute glass.	Verser dans une flûte.	In een fluitglas uitschenken.
Suitable as an aperitif and as a thirst-quencher.	Convient comme apéritif et comme boisson désaltérante.	Geschikt als aperitief en als dorstlesser.

C

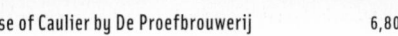

Caulier Blonde

The House of Caulier by De Proefbrouwerij

6,80% 6 -
43 - 4

	top-fermentation natural re-fermentation in the bottle	fermentation haute refermentation naturelle en bouteille	hoge gisting natuurlijke hergisting i de fles
	blond	blonde	blond
	100% malt, hops (East Kent Golding flowers or pellets) coriander, orange, yeast, spring water	100% malt, houblon (fleurs ou pellets East Kent Golding) coriandre, oranges, levure, eau de source	100% mout, hop (East Kent Golding bloemen o pellets) koriander, sinaas, gist, bronwater
	gold-blond with abundant foam head not filtered or pasteurised	blond doré avec faux col abondant non filtrée, non pasteurisée	goudblond met overvloedige schuimkraag ongefilterd, niet gepasteuriseerd
	A wealth of aromatic and citrus aromas followed up by soft herbs. A pleasant flavour hat creates a fresh impression owing to the natural carbon dioxide and the absence of sugar. A soft and dry sipping or aperitif beer.	Un bienfait d'arômes aromatiques et de citrus, suivis d'épices douces. Un goût agréable qui crée une impression vive, fraîche grâce au gaz carbonique naturel et à l'absence de sucre. Une bière de dégustation ou d'apéritif douce et sèche.	Een weldaad van aromatische en citrusaroma's gevolgd door zachte kruiden. Een aangenam smaak die een levendige, frisse indruk creëer door het natuurlijke koolzuurgas en de afwezigheid van suiker. Een zacht en droog degustatie- of aperitiefbier.
	see Caulier brune	voir Caulier brune	zie Caulier brune
	Exceptionally low calorie and carbon-dioxide content.	Teneur en calories et en glucides exceptionnellement faible.	Uitzonderlijk laag calorie- en koolhydrategehalte.

House of Caulier by De Proefbrouwerij 6,80% 8 - 10 °C 46 - 50 °F

top-fermentation natural re-fermentation in the bottle	fermentation haute refermentation naturelle en bouteille	hoge gisting natuurlijke hergisting in de fles
amber brown	ambrée foncée	amber bruin
100% malt, hops (flowers or pellets), wild herbs	100% malt, houblon (fleurs ou pellets), herbes sauvages	100% mout, hop (bloemen of pellets), wilde kruiden
burgundy-brown in colour not filtered	bourgogne à brun non filtrée	bourgognekleur tot bruin ongefilterd
Overwhelming wealth of aromas, starting off with chocolate and cara malt, followed by wild herbs, and finishing on an aromatic, bitter note that leaves the palate refreshed. Thirst-quenching owing to the natural carbon dioxide and absence of sugar.	Richesse d'arômes étourdissante. Malt de chocolat et Caramalt, puis des herbes sauvages et finalement une touche aromatique, amère qui rafraîchit le palais. Bière désaltérante grâce au gaz carbonique naturel et à l'absence de sucre.	Overweldigende rijkdom van aroma's. Chocolade- en caramout, daarna wilde kruiden en finaal een aromatische, bittere toets die het gehemelte verfrist. Dorstlessend door het natuurlijke koolzuurgas en de afwezigheid van suiker.
Serve in a cold rinsed (and not dried) balloon glass. Use a large wine glass so as to be able to do justice to the aromas.	Verser dans un verre ballon rincé à l'eau froide (et non séché). Employer un grand verre de vin pour permettre aux arômes de bien se manifester.	Uitschenken in een koud gespoeld (en niet gedroogd) ballonglas. Gebruik een groot wijnglas zodat de aroma's goed tot hun recht komen.
Exceptionally low calorie and carbon-dioxide content.	Teneur en calories et en glucides exceptionnellement faible.	Uitzonderlijk laag calorie- en koolhydrategehalte.

Caulier Brune

Caulier Special Extra

The House of Caulier by De Proefbrouwerij

4,30% 4 - 6 39 - 43

	top-fermentation natural re-fermentation in the bottle	fermentation haute refermentation naturelle en bouteille	hoge gisting natuurlijke hergisting in de fles
	special lager	lager spéciale	special lager
	100% malt, hops (Simcoe), yeast, water. Simcoe is a very aromatic American bitter hop.	100% malt, houblon (Simcoe), levure, eau. Simcoe est une variété très aromatique de houblon très amer Américain.	100% mout, hop (Simcoe), gist, water. Simcoe is een zeer aromatische Amerikaanse bitterhop.
	gold blond not filtered, pasteurised	blond doré non filtrée, pasteurisée	goudblond ongefilterd, gepasteuriseerd
	Citrus aromas owing to the cold hopping with Simcoe. Fizzy light bubbles that are refreshing owing to the natural carbon dioxide and the absence of sugar. Rich and intense thirst-quencher.	Arômes de citrus dûs au houblonnage à froid avec du Simcoe. Légères bulles piquantes qui rafraîchissent grâce au gaz carbonique naturel et à l'absence de sucre. Bière désaltérante au goût riche et intense.	Citrusaroma's door het koud hoppen met Simcoe. Prikkelende lichte bubbels die verfrissen door het natuurlijke koolzuurgas en de afwezigheid van suiker. Dorstlesser met rijke en intense smaak.
	Cool in an ice bucket and pour into a white wine glass. Serve with a slice of lemon.	Refroidir dans un seau à glaçons et verser dans un verre de vin blanc. Servir avec un morceau de citron.	In een ijsemmer koelen en uitschenken in een wittewijnglas. Serveren met een partje citroen.
i	Exceptionally low calorie and carbon-dioxide content (only 30 kcal per 100 ml).	Teneur en calories et en glucides exceptionnellement faible (seulement 30 kcal pour 100 ml).	Uitzonderlijk laag calorie- en koolhydrategehalte (slechts 30 kcal voor 100 ml).

5% (12° plato) 6 °C 43 °F

top-fermentation	fermentation haute	hoge gisting
witbier	bière blanche	witbier
barley malt, hops, yeast, wheat flour, water	malt d'orge, houblon, levure, farine de froment, eau	gerstemout, hop, gist, tarwemeel, water
blond cloudy, misty white veil	blonde trouble, voile blanc fade	blond troebel, wazigwitte sluier
Touch of fruit and spices. Refreshing and light.	Touches de fruits et d'herbes. Rafraîchissante et légère.	Toets van fruit en kruiden. Verfrissend en licht.
Pour till there is 4 cm beer left in the bottle. Revolve the bottle and pour the rest for a nice glass of cloudy beer.	Verser jusqu'à ce qu'il reste 4 cm de bière dans la bouteille. Secouer la bouteille et la vider pour avoir un joli verre de bière bien trouble.	Uitschenken tot er nog 4 cm bier in de fles is. De fles even rondwalsen en de rest van het bier uitschenken tot het mooi troebel het glas vult.
Brewed under licence following the original recipe of Pierre Celis (brewer of the Hoegaarden witbier). Sales are allowed in all countries except the USA.	Fabriquée sous licence d'après la recette originale de Pierre Celis (brasseur de la Bière Blanche de Hoegaarden) acceptée pour commercialisation dans tous les pays, sauf aux Etats-Unis.	Wordt gemaakt onder licentie volgens het originele recept van Pierre Celis (brouwer van het Witbier van Hoegaarden) en mag in alle landen, behalve USA, worden gecommercialiseerd.

Celis White

Celtic Angel Serafijn

Microbrouwerij Achilles

6,20%

	top-fermentation re-fermented in the bottle	fermentation haute refermentation en bouteille	hoge gisting met hergisting op de fles
	amber	ambrée	amber
	coloured malt, aromatic hops, yeast, water	malt coloré, houblon aromatique, levure, eau	kleurmout, aromatische hop, gist, water
	deep warm amber	ambré intense chaud	diepwarm amber
	Distinctive, round and spicy flavour, created by the malt. Slight touch of natural bitterness.	Goût relevé arrondi et de caractère par l'utilisation de malts. Touche légère d'amertume naturelle.	Karaktervolle en afgeronde kruidigheid door de mouten. Lichte toets van natuurlijke bitterheid.

asserie Dupont

8% — Slightly cooled.

	top-fermentation re-fermented in the bottle	fermentation haute refermentation en bouteille	hoge gisting nagisting op de fles
	blond	blonde	blond
	barley and wheat malt, hops, herbs and spices	malt d'orge et de froment, houblon, herbes et condiments	gerst- en tarwemout, hop, kruiden en specerijen
	blond	blonde	blond
	Unusual taste and aroma of flowers and herbs. Refreshing and thirst-quenching.	Saveur inhabituelle, arômes de fleurs et d'herbes. Fraîche et désaltérante.	Ongewone smaak en aroma's van bloemen en kruiden. Fris en dorstlessend.
i	Brewed since 1983 upon the initiative of the Archéosite d'Aubechies, an archeological site near the brewery.	Brassée depuis 1983 à l'initiative de l'Archéosite d'Aubechies, un site archéologique dans les alentours de la brasserie.	Gebrouwen sinds 1983 op initiatief van de Archéosite d'Aubechies, een archeologische site in de omgeving van de brouwerij.

Chapeau Abricot

Brouwerij De Troch

3,50% 6 43

	spontaneous fermentation	fermentation spontanée	spontane gisting
	fruit beer based on lambic	bière fruitée à base de lambic	fruitbier op basis van lambiek
	lambic mixed with apricot juice	mélange de lambic et de jus d'abricots	lambiek gemengd met abrikozensap
	blond	blonde	blond
	Refreshingly sweet.	Douce, rafraîchissante.	Verfrissend zoet.

Chapeau Banana

rouwerij De Troch

3,50% 6 °C 43 °F

	spontaneous fermentation	fermentation spontanée	spontane gisting
	fruit beer based on lambic	bière fruitée à base de lambic	fruitbier op basis van lambiek
	lambic mixed with banana juice	mélange de lambic et de jus de bananes	lambiek gemengd met bananensap
	blond cloudy	blonde trouble	blond troebel
	Refreshingly sweet with banana flavour.	Douce, rafraîchissante avec un arôme de banane.	Verfrissend zoet met aroma van banaan.
	First banana beer in Europe. Originally brewed under the name Leopard de Troch.	Première bière de banane en Europe, commercialisée à l'origine sous le nom de Leopard De Troch.	Eerste bananenbier in Europa. Oorspronkelijk gecommercialiseerd onder de naam Leopard De Troch.

Chapeau Cuvee Oude Gueuze

Brouwerij De Troch 5,50% 7 45

	spontaneous fermentation	fermentation spontanée	spontane gisting
	gueuze lambic	gueuze lambic	geuze lambiek
	lambic, hops, barley malt, wheat, water	lambic, houblon, malt d'orge, froment, eau	lambiek, hop, gerste-mout, tarwe, water
	Refreshing and spontaneous. Sour taste and aroma.	Rafraîchissante et spontanée. Saveur et arôme acidulés.	Verfrissend en spontaan. Zure smaak en aroma.
	Pour gently while revolving the glass.	Verser doucement en tournant le verre.	Zacht inschenken en ondertussen het glas draaien.
i	Recognised regional product.	Produit régional reconnu.	Erkend streekproduct.

3,50% | 6 °C 43 °F

	spontaneous fermentation	fermentation spontanée	spontane gisting
	fruit beer based on lambic	bière fruitée à base de lambic	fruitbier op basis van lambiek
	lambic mixed with pineapple juice	mélange de lambic et de jus d'ananas	lambiek gemengd met ananassap
	blond	blonde	blond
	Refreshingly sweet.	Douce, rafraîchissante.	Verfrissend zoet.
	Particularly appreciated in Ghana.	Surtout apprécié sur le marché ghanéen.	Vooral in trek op de Ghanese markt.

Chapeau Faro

Brouwerij De Troch 4,75% 6 43

	spontaneous fermentation	fermentation spontanée	spontane gisting
	sweetened gueuze	gueuze adoucie	aangezoete geuze
	Sweetened with candy sugar	Edulcoré au sucre candi	Aangezoet met kandij-suiker
	very dark amber	ambré très foncé	zeer donker amber
	Refreshingly sweet.	Douce, rafraîchissante.	Verfrissend zoet.

rouwerij De Troch 3,50% 6 °C 43 °F

Chapeau Fraises

	spontaneous fermentation	fermentation spontanée	spontane gisting
	fruit beer based on lambic	bière fruitée à base de lambic	fruitbier op basis van lambiek
	lambic mixed with strawberry juice	mélange de lambic et de jus de fraises	lambiek gemengd met aardbeiensap
	red	rouge	rood
	Refreshingly sweet.	Douce, rafraîchissante.	Verfrissend zoet.

Chapeau Framboise

Brouwerij De Troch 3,50% 6° 43°

	spontaneous fermentation	fermentation spontanée	spontane gisting
	fruit beer based on lambic	bière fruitée à base de lambic	fruitbier op basis van lambiek
	lambic mixed with raspberry juice	Mélange de lambic et de jus de framboises	lambiek gemengd met frambozensap
	red	rouge	rood
	Refreshingly sweet.	Douce, rafraîchissante.	Verfrissend zoet.

rouwerij De Troch

5,50%

	spontaneous fermentation	fermentation spontanée	spontane gisting
	gueuze	gueuze	geuze
	yeast, hops, malt, wheat, sugar, water	levure, houblon, malt, froment, sucre, eau	gist, hop, mout, tarwe, suiker, water
	dark amber	ambré foncé	donker amber
	Sweet-and-sour.	Aigre-douce.	Zoetzurig.

Chapeau Kriek

Brouwerij De Troch 3,50% 6 43

	spontaneous fermentation	fermentation spontanée	spontane gisting
	fruit beer based on lambic	bière fruitée à base de lambic	fruitbier op basis van lambiek
	lambic mixed with cherries	mélange de lambic et de cerises	lambiek gemengd met krieken
	red	rouge	rood
	Refreshingly sweet.	Douce, rafraîchissante.	Verfrissend zoet.

ouwerij De Troch

3,50% 6 °C 43 °F

Chapeau Lemon

	spontaneous fermentation	fermentation spontanée	spontane gisting
	fruit beer based on lambic	bière fruitée à base de lambic	fruitbier op basis van lambiek
	lambic mixed with lemon juice	mélange de lambic et de jus de citron	lambiek gemengd met citroensap
	blond	blonde	blond
	Very refreshing. Sweet-and-sour.	Très rafraîchissante. Aigre-douxe.	Zeer verfrissend. Zuur-zoet.
	Particularly appreciated in Thailand.	Surtout appréciée sur le marché thailandais.	Vooral in trek op de Thaise markt.

Chapeau Mirabelle

Brouwerij De Troch 3,50% 6 43

	spontaneous fermentation	fermentation spontanée	spontane gisting
	fruit beer based on lambic	bière fruitée à base de lambic	fruitbier op basis van lambiek
	lambic mixed with pressed mirabelle juice	mélange de lambic et de jus pressé de mirabelles	lambiek gemengd met geperst mirabellensap
	blond cloudy	blonde trouble	blond troebel
	Refreshingly sweet.	Douce, rafraîchissante.	Verfrissend zoet.
	Particularly appreciated in France.	Surtout en faveur sur le marché français.	Vooral in trek op de Franse markt.

rouwerij De Troch 3,50% 6 °C 43 °F

Chapeau Pêche

	spontaneous fermentation	fermentation spontanée	spontane gisting
	fruit beer based on lambic	bière fruitée à base de lambic	fruitbier op basis van lambiek
	lambic mixed with peach juice	mélange de lambic et de jus de pêche	lambiek gemengd met perzikensap
	blond cloudy	blonde trouble	blond troebel
	Refreshingly sweet.	Douce, rafraîchissante.	Verfrissend zoet.

Chapeau Winter Gueuze

Brouwerij De Troch 5,60% 7 45

	spontaneous fermentation	fermentation spontanée	spontane gisting
	gueuze Christmas beer	gueuze bière de Noël	geuze kerstbier
	yeast, hops, malt, wheat, sugar, aroma, water	levure, houblon, malt, froment, sucre, arôme, eau	gist, hop, mout, tarwe, suiker, aroma, water
	Pour gently, revolving the glass whilst pouring.	Verser doucement en tournant le verre.	Zacht inschenken en ondertussen het glas draaien.

Chimay Bleue

asserie de l'Abbaye N.D. de Scourmont 9% 10 - 12 °C 50 - 54 °F

top-fermentation re-fermented in the bottle	fermentation haute refermentation en bouteille	hoge gisting hergisting op de fles
trappist	trappiste	trappist
barley malt, wheat, sugar, yeast, hops, water	malt d'orge, froment, sucre, levure, houblon, eau	gerstemout, tarwe, suiker, gist, hop, water
dark brown, unfiltered. Thick, brown creamy foam head.	brun foncé, non filtrée. Faux col épais, brun crémeux.	donkerbruin, niet gefilterd. Dikke, bruincrèmige schuimkraag.
Powerful and complex. Bouquet of fine spices with a shade of caramel.	Corsée et complexe. Bouquet d'herbes fines, pointe de caramel.	Krachtig en complex. Boeket van fijne kruiden, vleugje karamel.
Degrease the glass and avoid fingerprints. Hold the glass by its stem, slightly tilted, and slowly pour the beer, avoiding contact between bottle and glass or foam.	Dégraisser le verre complètement et éviter des empreintes de doigts. Tenir le verre légèrement incliné par le pied et verser lentement la bière sans que la bouteille touche le verre ou l'écume.	Het glas helemaal ontvetten en vingerafdrukken vermijden. Het glas bij de voet licht schuin houden en het bier langzaam inschenken zonder dat de fles het glas of het schuim raakt.
Becomes more complex with age. Keep upright.	Devient plus complexe en mûrissant. Se conserve en position verticale.	Wordt complexer met verouderen. Verticaal bewaren.

Chimay Rouge

Brasserie de l'Abbaye N.D. de Scourmont

7% 8 46

top-fermentation re-fermented in the bottle	fermentation haute refermentation en bouteille	hoge gisting hergisting op de fles
trappist	trappiste	trappist
barley malt, wheat, sugar, yeast, hops, water	malt d'orge, froment, sucre, levure, houblon, eau	gerstemout, tarwe, suiker, gist, hop, water
red-copper, unfiltered. Compact, creamy foam head.	cuivre rouge, non filtrée. Faux col compact et crémeux.	roodkoper, niet gefilterd. Dichte en romige schuimkraag.
Smooth but solid aroma. Apricot-like fruit, matured by fermentation. Silky smoothness with a slightly bitter touch.	Douce mais solide. Parfum fruité d'abricot par la fermentation. Soyeuse en bouche avec une touche légèrement amère.	Zacht maar stevig. Abrikoosachtige fruitgeur gerijpt door de gisting. Zijdezacht met een lichte bittere toets.
Degrease the glass and avoid fingerprints. Hold the glass by its stem, slightly tilted, and slowly pour the beer, avoiding contact between bottle and glass or foam.	Dégraisser le verre complètement et éviter des empreintes de doigts. Tenir le verre légèrement incliné par le pied et verser lentement la bière sans que la bouteille touche le verre ou l'écume.	Het glas helemaal ontvetten en vingerafdrukken vermijden. Het glas bij de voet licht schuin houden en het bier langzaam inschenken zonder dat de fles het glas of het schuim raakt.
Store upright at cellar temperature.	Conserver en position verticale à température de cave.	Verticaal bewaren op keldertemperatuur.

asserie de l'Abbaye N.D. de Scourmont

8% 6 - 8 °C 43 - 46 °F

top-fermentation re-fermented in the bottle	fermentation haute refermentation en bouteille	hoge gisting hergisting op de fles
trappist	trappiste	trappist
barley malt, wheat, sugar, yeast, hops, water	malt d'orge, froment, sucre, levure, houblon, eau	gerstemout, tarwe, suiker, gist, hop, water
Blond amber, slightly hazy, unfiltered	Blond ambré, légèrement voilée, non filtrée	Blond amber, licht gesluierd, niet gefilterd
Silky smoothness with a fine, bitter aftertaste. Hoppy flavour with a dominating touch of fruity muscat and dry grapes.	Soyeuse avec une fin de bouche amère raffinée. Arôme houblonné avec une dominance de touches fruitées de muscadet et de raisin séché.	Zijdezacht met fijne bitterheid in de afdronk. Hoppig aroma met dominantie van fruitige muscattoets en droge-druiftoets.
Degrease the glass and avoid fingerprints. Hold the glass by its stem, slightly tilted, and slowly pour the beer, avoiding contact between bottle and glass or foam.	Dégraisser le verre complètement et éviter des empreintes de doigts. Tenir le verre légèrement incliné par le pied et verser lentement la bière sans que la bouteille touche le verre ou l'écume.	Het glas helemaal ontvetten en vingerafdrukken vermijden. Het glas bij de voet licht schuin houden en het bier langzaam inschenken zonder dat de fles het glas of het schuim raakt.
Drink the beer when it is young and fresh. In 75 cl, it is referred to as 'Cinq Cents'.	Déguster la bière jeune et fraîche. En 75 cl, on l'appelle 'Cinq Cents'.	Het bier jong en fris degusteren. In 75 cl wordt hij 'Cinq Cents' genoemd.

Christmas Leroy

Brouwerij Het Sas 7,50% 8 - 1 / 46 - 5

	top-fermentation re-fermented in the bottle	fermentation haute refermentation en bouteille	hoge gisting nagisting op de fles
	specialty beer winter beer	bière spéciale bière hivernale	speciaalbier winterbier
	malt, sugar, spices, sweetener, yeast, water	malt, sucre, condiments, édulcorant, levure, eau	mout, suiker, specerijen, zoetstof, gist, water
	dark red-brown	brun rouge foncé	donker roodbruin
	Spicy and wintry. Pronounced spicy touch (cherry, curaçao).	Relevée et hivernale. Touche d'herbes prononcée (réglise, cerises, curaçao).	Kruidig en winters. Uitgesproken kruidige toet (zoethout, kers, curaçao).
	Pour slowly in a single, smooth movement in a degreased glass. Keep the glass tilted and avoid sloshing. Skim off the foam.	Verser lentement en un seul mouvement fluide dans un verre dégraissé tenu en oblique. Ne pas laisser la bière clapoter. Ecumer le verre.	Traag en in 1 vloeiende beweging uitschenken in een vetvrij glas dat wordt schuingehouden. Het bier niet laten klotsen. Het glas afschuimen.
i			

uwerij Verhaeghe

7,20% 3 °C 37 °F

top-fermentation	fermentation haute	hoge gisting
winter beer	bière hivernale	winterbier
malt, hops, yeast, water	malt, houblon, levure, eau	mout, hop, gist, water
blond filtered	blonde filtrée	blond gefilterd
Hoppy and bitter, which is quite unique for a winter beer.	Houblonnée et amère, ce qui est plutôt unique pour une bière hivernale.	Hoppig en bitter wat vrij uniek is voor een winterbier.
Serve in a dry beer snifter with foot.	Verser dans un verre ballon sec à pied.	Uitschenken in een droog bolglas met voet.

Ciney Blond

Brouwerij Alken-Maes 7% 4

	top-fermentation	fermentation haute	hoge gisting
	specialty beer	bière spéciale	speciaalbier
	gold blond clear	dorée claire	goudblond helder
	Soft, fruity taste with a well-balanced, pleasant bitterness.	Saveur douce, fruitée avec un goût amer équilibré et agréable.	Zacht. Fruitige smaak met evenwichtige, aangename bitterheid.
	Pour carefully into a degreased, dry glass. Pour slowly to obtain a nice foam head.	Verser soigneusement dans un verre dégraissé et sec. Verser lentement de sorte qu'un faux col solide se forme.	Zorgvuldig uitschenken in een ontvet, droog glas. Langzaam schenken zo dat er een mooie schuimkraag ontstaat.
i			

uwerij Alken-Maes

7% · 6 °C / 43 °F

	top-fermentation	fermentation haute	hoge gisting
	specialty beer	bière spéciale	speciaalbier
	dark brown with red shades	brun foncé avec des teintes rouges	donkerbruin met rode tinten
	Distinctive, fruity taste. Full-bodied with a smooth aftertaste.	Saveur fruitée de caractère. Fin de bouche franche et douce.	Karaktervolle, fruitige smaak. Volmondig en zacht in de afdronk.
	Pour carefully into a degreased, dry glass. Pour slowly to obtain a nice foam head.	Verser soigneusement dans un verre dégraissé et sec. Verser lentement de sorte qu'un faux col solide se forme.	Zorgvuldig uitschenken in een ontvet, droog glas. Langzaam schenken zodat er een mooie schuimkraag ontstaat.

Ciney Bruin

Cluysenaer by De Proefbrouwerij

7% 6 - 1 43 - 5

	top-fermentation re-fermentation in the bottle centrifuged	fermentation haute refermentation en bouteille centrifugée	hoge gisting hergisting in de fles gecentrifugeerd
	light amber Belgian ale	légèrement ambrée Belgian ale	licht amber Belgian ale
	pilsner and aroma malt, bitter hops and aroma hops, 2 yeast stems, water	malt de pils et malt aromatique, houblon amer et houblon aromatique, 2 variétés de levure, eau	pils- en aromamout, bi terhop en aromahop, 2 giststammen, water
	light amber, slightly cloudy with a creamy, white foam head not filtered or pasteurised	ambré clair, légèrement trouble avec faux col blanc crémeux non filtrée, non pasteurisée	licht amber, licht troeb met een romige, witte schuimkraag ongefilterd, niet gepas teuriseerd
	Slightly fruity citrus aroma (aromatic hops), full-bodied, slightly sweet flavour that is followed by an intense, hop-bitter aftertaste.	Arôme de citrus (houblon aromatique) légèrement fruité, goût franc légèrement sucré qui s'écoule dans une arrière-bouche piquante, avec l'amertume du houblon.	Licht fruitig citrusarom (aromatische hop), vol mondige lichtzoete smaak die uitvloeit in een pittige, hopbittere afdronk.
i	Launched in 2002 to mark the first arts and crafts market in Kluizen (old spelling Cluysen). The name also refers to the 'long and lonely' search for an original and pure beer concept.	Lancée en 2002 à l'occasion du premier marché des artisans à Kluizen (ancienne graphie :Cluysen). Le nom est en outre une allusion à la recherche acharnée, 'solitaire et silencieuse', de plusieurs années, d'une recette de bière originale et pure.	Gelanceerd in 2002 t.g. de eerste ambachtenmarkt in Kluizen (oude schrijfwijze Cluysen). D naam is tevens een zinspeling op de jarenlang 'eenzame en stille' zoek tocht naar een originee en zuiver bierrecept.

uwerij Cnudde

5% 4 - 5 °C 39 - 41 °F

	top-fermentation	fermentation haute	hoge gisting
	Oudenaards brown	brune d'Audenarde	Oudenaards bruin
	barley malt, sugar, hops, yeast, water.	malt d'orge, sucre, houblon, épices, levure, eau	gerstemout, suiker, hop, gist, water
	amber brown clear	brun ambré claire	amberbruin helder
	Also called 'graveyard beer' because the wells from which the water is pumped, are located near the graveyard of Eine.	Est aussi appelée bière de cimetière parce que les puits dont l'eau est tirée sont situés près du cimetière de Eine.	Ook kerkhofbier genoemd omdat de boorputten waaruit het water wordt gehaald in de buurt van het kerkhof van Eine gesitueerd zijn.

Cnudde Bizon Bier

Brouwerij Cnudde 5,50% 4 - 39 -

top-fermentation	fermentation haute	hoge gisting
fruit beer	bière fruitée	fruitbier
barley malt, Morello cherries, hops, yeast, water	malt d'orge, cerises, houblon, levure, eau	gerstemout, krieken, hop, gist, water
red clear	rouge claire	rood helder
Bizon [buffalo] refers to the Ohio bridge across the Scheldt which is a reminder of the First World War. Buffalo statues are located at regular intervals on the bridge.	Bizon fait référence au pont de l'Ohio sur l'Escaut, qui est un souvenir de la Première Guerre mondiale. À chacune des têtes de pont, il y a un bison.	Bizon verwijst naar de Ohiobrug over de Schelde die een herinnering aan WO I. Op elk van de bruggenhoofden staat een bizon.

5% 8 - 12 °C 46 - 54 °F

Colère Rouge

	top-fermentation	fermentation haute	hoge gisting
	Belgian dark ale	Belgian dark ale	Belgian dark ale
	malt, hops, yeast, water	malt, houblon, levure, eau	mout, hop, gist, water
	orange-amber with small foam head not pasteurised	ambré orange avec petit faux col non pasteurisée	oranjeamber met kleine schuimkraag niet gepasteuriseerd
	Aroma of peach and berries. Fruity taste with orange peel and aromatic hops.	Arôme de pêche et de groseilles. Goût fruité avec de l'écorce d'orange et du houblon aromatique.	Aroma van perzik en bessen. Fruitige smaak met sinaasschil en aromatische hop.
	Bière de Longwy brewed in tandem with Feller Associés.	Bière de Longwy brassée en collaboration avec Feller Associés.	Bière de Longwy gebrouwen in samenwerking met Feller Associés.

Contra Pils

Brouwerij Contreras

5% 2 - 4 36 - 39

	bottom-fermentation	fermentation basse	lage gisting
	pilsner	pils	pilsbier
	barley malt, hop (Saaz), bottom-fermenting yeast, water	malt d'orge, houblon (Saaz), levure de fermentation basse, eau	gerstemout, hop (Saaz), lagegistingsgist, water
	gold-yellow crystal-clear	jaune doré claire comme du cristal	goudgeel kristalhelder
	Fresh and distinctive. Smooth bitterness, hoppy aroma.	Fraîche et pleien de caractère. Goût amer moelleux, arôme houblonné.	Fris en karaktervol. Zachte bitterheid, hoppig aroma.
	Empty in a degreased, rinsed and wet glass. Tilt the glass about 45° and pour the beer, avoiding contact between bottle and foam. Provide a foam head of approx. 2 cm.	Verser complètement dans un verre dégraissé, rincé et mouillé. Tenir le verre incliné à 45°, verser la bière sans que la bouteille touche l'écume. Prévoir un faux col de 2 cm environ.	Helemaal uitschenken in een ontvet, gespoeld en nat glas. Het glas 45° schuin houden, het bier uitschenken zonder dat de fles het schuim raakt. Een schuimkraag van ca 2 cm voorzien.
i	Since 1954	Depuis 1954	Sinds 1954

Contreras' Especial Mars

C

uwerij Contreras

6,50% | 7 °C 45 °F

top-fermentation re-fermented in the bottle	fermentation haute refermentation en bouteille	hoge gisting hergisting op de fles
season beer	bière de saison	seizoensbier
barley malt, hop (Hallertau, Styrian, Brewers gold), sugar (for re-fermentation), top-fermenting yeast, water	malt d'orge, houblon (Hallertau, Styrian, Brewers gold), sucre (pour refermentation), levure de fermentation haute, eau	gerstemout, hop (Hallertau, Styrian, Brewers gold), suiker (voor hergisting), hogegistingsgist, water
amber blond clear	blond ambré claire	amberblond helder
Malty, slightly sour.	Maltée, légèrement acidulée.	Moutig, licht zurig.
Empty in a degreased, rinsed and dry glass. Tilt the glass about 45° and gently pour the beer, avoiding contact between bottle and foam. Provide a foam head of approx. 5 cm.	Verser complètement dans un verre dégraissé, rincé et sec. Tenir le verre incliné à 45°, verser la bière sans que la bouteille touche l'écume. Prévoir un faux col de 5 cm environ.	Helemaal uitschenken in een ontvet, gespoeld en droog glas. Het glas 45° schuin houden, uitschenken zonder dat de fles het schuim raakt. Een schuimkraag van ca. 5 cm voorzien.
Store upright. Most breweries used to make a spring beer. Contreras is one of the few that holds on to this tradition. Since 1898.	Conserver en position verticale. La plupart des brasseries fabriquaient autrefois une bière de printemps. Contreras fait honneur à cette tradition. Depuis 1898.	Verticaal bewaren. De meeste brouwerijen maakten vroeger een lentebier. Contreras is een van weinige brouwerijen die deze traditie in ere houdt. Sinds 1898.

Cookie Beer

Brasserie d'Ecaussinnes 8%

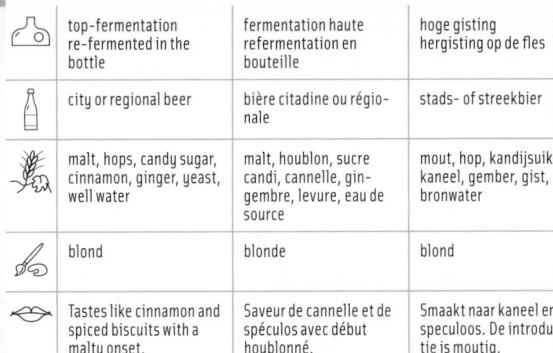

	top-fermentation re-fermented in the bottle	fermentation haute refermentation en bouteille	hoge gisting hergisting op de fles
	city or regional beer	bière citadine ou régio-nale	stads- of streekbier
	malt, hops, candy sugar, cinnamon, ginger, yeast, well water	malt, houblon, sucre candi, cannelle, gin-gembre, levure, eau de source	mout, hop, kandijsuiker, kaneel, gember, gist, bronwater
	blond	blonde	blond
	Tastes like cinnamon and spiced biscuits with a malty onset.	Saveur de cannelle et de spéculos avec début houblonné.	Smaakt naar kaneel en speculoos. De introductie is moutig.

	top-fermentation re-fermented in the bottle	fermentation haute refermentation en bouteille	hoge gisting hergisting op de fles
	tripel	triple	tripel
	golden-yellow, clear	jaune doré, claire	goudgeel, helder
	A fresh and lively beer with a spicy taste that evolves into a hoppy af-tertaste.	Bière fraîche et vive avec une saveur corsée abou-tissant en une fin de bouche houblonnée.	Een fris en levendig bier met een pittige smaak die evolueert in een ge-hopte afdronk.
	Pour carefully, avoid the beer sloshing. Leave 1 cm yeast in the bottle. Never store in the fridge. Serve the bottle in an icebucket if you want to drink it chilled.	Verser lentement dans un verre incliné sans que la bière clapote. Laisser 1 cm de levure dans la bouteille. À ne jamais conserver au réfrigéra-teur :servir la bière dans un seau à glaces si on veut la boire ra-fraîchie.	Traag uitschenken in een schuingehouden glas zonder dat het bier klokt. 1 cm gist op de bodem van de fles laten. Nooit in de frigo bewaren: het bier in een ijsemmer ser-veren als je het gekoeld wilt drinken.
i	Store the bottles upright in a cool, dark cellar (10 to 14 °C).	Bouteilles à conserver en position verticale dans une cave fraîche et à l'abri de la lumière (10 à 14 °C).	Flessen verticaal bewa-ren in een koele, donke-re kelder (10 à 14 °C).

Corsendonk Agnus Tripel

Corsendonk Christmas Ale

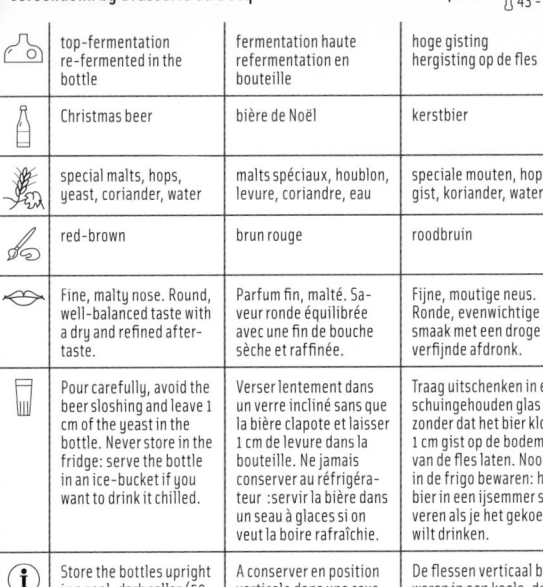

Corsendonk by Brasserie du Bocq 8,50% 6 - 8 43 - 46

	top-fermentation re-fermented in the bottle	fermentation haute refermentation en bouteille	hoge gisting hergisting op de fles
	Christmas beer	bière de Noël	kerstbier
	special malts, hops, yeast, coriander, water	malts spéciaux, houblon, levure, coriandre, eau	speciale mouten, hop, gist, koriander, water
	red-brown	brun rouge	roodbruin
	Fine, malty nose. Round, well-balanced taste with a dry and refined after-taste.	Parfum fin, malté. Saveur ronde équilibrée avec une fin de bouche sèche et raffinée.	Fijne, moutige neus. Ronde, evenwichtige smaak met een droge en verfijnde afdronk.
	Pour carefully, avoid the beer sloshing and leave 1 cm of the yeast in the bottle. Never store in the fridge: serve the bottle in an ice-bucket if you want to drink it chilled.	Verser lentement dans un verre incliné sans que la bière clapote et laisser 1 cm de levure dans la bouteille. Ne jamais conserver au réfrigérateur :servir la bière dans un seau à glaces si on veut la boire rafraîchie.	Traag uitschenken in een schuingehouden glas zonder dat het bier klokt 1 cm gist op de bodem van de fles laten. Nooit in de frigo bewaren: het bier in een ijsemmer serveren als je het gekoeld wilt drinken.
i	Store the bottles upright in a cool, dark cellar (50 to 57 °F).	A conserver en position verticale dans une cave fraîche et à l'abri de la lumière (10 à 14 °C).	De flessen verticaal bewaren in een koele, donkere kelder (10 à 14 °C).

rsendonk by Brasserie du Bocq

7,50% 6 - 8 °C 43 - 46 °F

top-fermentation re-fermented in the bottle	fermentation haute refermentation en bouteille	hoge gisting hergisting op de fles
dubbel	double	dubbel
malt, hops, yeast, water	malt, houblon, levure, eau	mout, hop, gist, water
deep brown-red	brun rouge intense	diepbruin rood
A fresh and lively beer with a smooth and round taste.	Bière fraîche et vive avec une saveur douce et ronde.	Een fris en levendig bier met een zachte en ronde smaak.
Pour carefully, avoid the beer sloshing. Leave 1 cm yeast in the bottle. Never store in the fridge. Serve the bottle in an ice-bucket if you want to drink it chilled.	Verser lentement dans un verre incliné sans que la bière clapote. Laisser 1 cm de levure au fond de la bouteille. À ne jamais conserver au réfrigérateur :servir la bière dans un seau à glaces si on veut la boire rafraîchie.	Traag uitschenken in een schuingehouden glas zonder dat het bier klokt. 1 cm gist op de bodem van de fles laten. Nooit in de frigo bewaren: het bier op ijs serveren in een ijsemmer als je het gekoeld wil drinken.
Store the bottles upright in a cool, dark cellar (50 to 57 °F).	Bouteilles à conserver en position verticale dans une cave fraîche et à l'abri de la lumière (10 à 14 °C).	De flessen verticaal bewaren in een koele, donkere kelder (10 à 14 °C).

Corsendonk Pater Dubbel

Corsendonk Rousse

Corsendonk by Brasserie du Bocq

8%

	top-fermentation re-fermentation in the bottle	fermentation haute refermentation en bouteille	hoge gisting hergisting in de fles
	amber	ambrée	amber

ouwerij Strubbe

6,50%

top-fermentation re-fermentation in the bottle	fermentation haute refermentation en bouteille	hoge gisting hergisting in de fles
different herbs and hops	différentes herbes et variétés de houblon	verschillende kruiden en hopsoorten
amber-coloured	ambrée	amberkleurig
Mellow aftertaste owing to the tertiary post-fermentation in the bottle.	Arrière-bouche souple du fait de la fermentation tertiaire dans la bouteille.	Soepele afdronk door de tertiaire nagisting in de fles.

Couckelaerschen Doedel

De Dochter van de Korenaar

8%

top-fermentation re-fermentation in the bottle not centrifuged	fermentation haute refermentation en bouteille non centrifugée	hoge gisting hergisting in de fles niet gecentrifugeerd
herbal beer winter or Christmas beer	bière aromatisée bière hivernale ou bière de Noël	kruidenbier winter- of kerstbier
barley malt, wheat malt, yeast, hops, herbs (star anise, liquorice, elderberry, rooibos) water	malt d'orge, malt de froment, levure, houblon, herbes (anis étoilé, réglisse, baie de sureau, rooibos), eau	gerstemout, tarwemout, gist, hop, kruiden (steranijs, zoethout, vlierbes, rooibos), water
not filtered or pasteurised	non filtrée, non pasteurisée	ongefilterd, niet gepasteuriseerd
Spicy and malty chocolate aroma with a touch of almond. Quite sweet, roasted flavour mix of chocolate, cinnamon and herbs.	Arôme de chocolat épicé et malté, avec une pointe d'amande. Plutôt sucré, mélange de goûts grillés de chocolat, cannelle et épices.	Kruidig en moutig chocoladearoma met een vleugje amandel. Tamelijk zoet, geroosterde smakenmix van chocolade, kaneel en kruiden.

rouwerij Het Sas

5% | 4 °C / 39 °F

	bottom-fermentation	fermentation basse	lage gisting
	pilsner or lager beer	pils ou lager	pils- of lagerbier
	barley, hops, yeast, water	malt, houblon, levure, eau	gerst, hop, gist, water
	blond, clear with a white foam head filtered, not pasteurised	blonde, limpide avec un faux col blanc filtrée, non pasteurisée	blond, helder met een witte schuimkraag gefilterd, niet gepasteuriseerd
	Malty and hoppy.	Maltée et houblonnée.	Moutig en hoppig.
	Pour in a single movement and skim off the excess.	Verser agilement et écumer.	Doorschenken en afschuimen.

Crackpils

Crianza

Brasserie de la Senne

7% 5 41

top-fermentation naturally re-fermented in the bottle not centrifuged	fermentation haute refermentation naturelle en bouteille non centrifugée	hoge gisting natuurlijke hergisting in de fles niet gecentrifugeerd
Blended beer with Lambic. Matured in oak barrels for nine months.	Bière mixte avec lambic. Mûrie en fûts de chêne pendant 9 mois.	Mengbier met lambiek. 9 maanden gerijpt op eikenhout.
malt, hops, barley, yeast, water	malt, houblon, orge, levure, eau	mout, hop, gerst, gist, water
A touch of sherry on a pleasant sourish undertone.	Pointe de xéres sur un arrière-fond acidulé agréable.	Een vleugje sherry op een aangenaam zurige ondertoon.
Serve in the corresponding glass.	Verser dans le verre approprié.	Uitschenken in het bijpassende glas.

Cristal

rouwerij Alken-Maes 4,80% 3 °C 37 °F

	bottom-fermentation	fermentation basse	lage gisting
	pilsner	pils	pils- of lagerbier
	pure, blond pilsner	pils pure, blonde	zuivere, blonde pils
	Distinctive taste. Refreshingly bitter aftertaste.	Saveur de caractère. Fin de bouche rafraîchissante et amère.	Karaktervolle smaak. Verfrissende bitterheid in de afdronk.
	Empty in a degreased, rinsed and wet glass. Let overflow and skim off the foam.	Verser complètement dans un verre dégraissé, rincé et mouillé. Laisser déborder et écumer.	Helemaal uitschenken in een ontvet, gespoeld en nat glas. Laten overlopen en afschuimen.
	Belgium's very first pilsner (1928)	La toute première pils belge (1928).	De allereerste Belgische pils (1928)

Cristal 1928

Brouwerij Alken-Maes

5,80% 3 37

bottom-fermentation	fermentation basse	lage gisting
premium pilsner	premium pils	premium pils
barley, wheat, hops, yeast, water	orge, froment, houblon, levure, eau	gerst, tarwe, hop, gist, water
pure, blond pilsner	pils pure, blonde	zuivere, blonde pils
Very intense and full-bodied flavour with a distinct, but pleasant bitterness.	Goût fort intense et franc, avec une amertume claire, mais agréable.	Zeer intense en volmondige smaak met een duidelijke, maar aangename bitterheid.
Pour in a single movement into a degreased, rinsed and wet glass. Let the beer run over and skim off excess.	Verser complètement dans un verre dégraissé, rincé et humide. Laisser déborder et écumer.	Helemaal uitschenken in een ontvet, gespoeld en nat glas. Laten overlopen en afschuimen.
Launched to mark the 80th anniversary of Cristal and brewed using the original pilsner recipe in the early 20th century.	Lancée à l'occasion des 80 ans d'existence de la Cristal et brassée dans le style de la pilsner d'origine au début du 20e siècle.	Gelanceerd n.a.v. het 80-jarig bestaan van Cristal en gebrouwen in de stijl van de originele pilsner begin 20e eeuw.

Cuvée Angélique

ouwerij De Glazen Toren 8,30% 6 - 10 °C / 43 - 50 °F

	top-fermentation	fermentation haute	hoge gisting
	double special belge	double spéciale belge	dobbel special belge
	barley malt, sugar, hops, yeast, water hopped twice	malt d'orge, sucre, houblon, levure, eau doublement houblonné	gerstemout, suiker, hop, gist, water tweemaal gehopt
	Slowly pour into a dry, chalice-shaped glass. Hold the bottle horizontally and do not remove the wrapper.	Verser prudemment dans un verre calice sec. Tenir la bouteille horizontalement et ne pas enlever l'emballage.	Voorzichtig uitschenken in een droog kelkvormig glas. De fles horizontaal houden en de wikkel niet verwijderen.
	The name refers to Angelique and Domien, 2 buskers from the beginning of the 20th century who used to frequent the Aalst cafés and the market square. They became an Aalst legend.	Le nom fait référence à Angélique et Domien, 2 musiciens de rue du début du 20e siècle, qui demandaient l'aumône dans les cafés d'Alost et sur le marché. Ils sont devenus une légende alostoise.	De naam verwijst naar Angelique en Domien, 2 straatmuzikanten van begin 20e eeuw die bedelden in de Aalsterse cafés en op de markt. Ze werden een Aalsterse legende.

Cuvée de Bouillon

Brasserie de Bouillon 6,50% 8 - 12 / 46 - 54

	top-fermentation re-fermented in the bottle	fermentation haute refermentation en bouteille	hoge gisting hergisting op de fles
	abbey beer blond	bière d'abbaye blonde	abdijbier blond
	barley malt, hops, Orval yeast, nut extract, citrus and orange rind, water	malt d'orge, houblon, levure d'Orval, extrait de noix, écorce d'oranges et d'agrumes, eau	gerstemout, hop, Orvalgist, notenextract, citrus- en sinaasschil, water
	blond unfiltered, unpasteurised	blonde non filtrée ni pasteurisée	blond niet gefilterd of gepasteuriseerd
	Slightly soury, traditionally brewed sipping beer. Refreshing, lively beer with taste evolution.	Bière de dégustation légèrement acidulée. Bière rafraîchissante et vive avec saveur évolutive.	Licht zurig ambachtelijk degustatiebier. Verfrissend en levend bier met smaakevolutie.
	Hold the glass slightly tilted while pouring the beer.	Tenir le verre légèrement incliné et verser.	Het glas licht schuin houden en inschenken.
i			

	mixed fermentation natural re-fermentation in the bottle not centrifuged	fermentation mixte refermentation naturelle en bouteille non centrifugée	gemengde gisting natuurlijke hergisting in de fles niet gecentrifugeerd
	strong double mixed beer	double forte bière de coupage	sterk donker versnijbier
	70% own Western Flemish acidified with 30% Lambic Girardin	70% d'origine Flandre Occidentale acidifié avec 30% Lambic Girardin	70% eigen Westvlaams verzuurd met 30% Lambiek Girardin
	amber, veiled not filtered or pasteurised	ambrée, voilée non filtrée, non pasteurisée	amber, gesluierd ongefilterd, niet gepasteuriseerd
	Wine-like, a great deal of lambic in the nose, medium tart.	Vineuse, beaucoup de lambic dans le bouquet, moyennement acide.	Vineus, veel lambiek in de neus, medium zuur.
i			

Cuvée Delphine

De Struise Brouwers at Brouwerij Deca

13% 8 - 10 / 46 - 50

	top-fermentation re-fermentation in the bottle not centrifuged	fermentation haute refermentation en bouteille non centrifugée	hoge gisting hergisting in de fles niet gecentrifugeerd
	Belgian Royal Stout	Belgian Royal Stout	Belgian Royal Stout
	matured in bourbon casks	mûri en fûts bourbon	gerijpt op bourbonvaten
	jet black with nice brown-beige foam head	noir comme jais avec faux col joli brun beige	gitzwart met mooie bruinbeige schuimkraag
	Elegant and refined stout. Touches of caramel, espresso, roasted nuts, chocolate, roasted malt, candied fruits, tar, liquorice and fresh floral hops in the nose.	Une stout élégante et raffinée. Touches de caramel, espresso, noix brûlées, chocolat, malt grillé, fruits confits, goudron, réglisse et houblon floral frais dans le bouquet.	Elegante en verfijnde stou Toetsen van karamel, espresso, gebrande noten, chocolade, geroosterde mout, gekonfijte vruchten teer, drop en frisse florale hop in de neus.
	see Black Damnation I	voir Black Damnation I	zie Black Damnation I
	When Jim O'Hare, the man from Delphine Boël, found out that De Struise Brouwers were about to introduce a beer onto the market that referred to his wife, he suggested to use one of her works of art for the label, a suggestion which was gratefully accepted. It was decided to use 'Truth can set you free'.	Jim O'Hare, le compagnon de Delphine Boël, avait appris que De Struise Brouwers allaient lancer sur le marché une bière qui ferait référence à sa femme. Il proposa d'utiliser une des œuvres d'art de Delphine Boël pour l'étiquette, ce qui fut accepté avec gratitude. Le choix s'est porté sur 'Truth can set you free'.	Jim O'Hare, de man van Delphine Boël, vernam dat De Struise Brouwers een bier op de markt zouden brengen dat naar zijn vrouw refereerde. Hij stelde voor om een van haar kunstwerken voor het label te gebruiken, wat in dank werd aangenomen. De keuze ging naar 'Truth can set you free'.

Cuvee d'Erpigny - Oak Collection

:cobrouwerij Alvinne 15%

	top-fermentation natural re-fermentation in the bottle	fermentation haute refermentation naturelle en bouteille	hoge gisting natuurlijke hergisting in de fles
	strong dark blond barley wine quadrupel	blonde fonceé forte vin d'orge quadruple	zwaar donkerblond gerstewijn quadrupel
	matured in Monbazillac casks	mûri en fûts Monbazillac	gerijpt op Monbazillac-vaten
	ruby-red	rouge rubis	robijnrood
	Desert beer	Bière de dessert	Dessertbier
	Serve in a Trappist glass.	Verser dans un verre trappiste.	Uitschenken in een trap-pistglas.

Cuvée des Trolls Refermentée

Brasserie Dubuisson 7% 8 - 10 / 46 - 50

	top-fermentation naturally re-fermented in the bottle	fermentation haute refermentation naturelle en bouteille	hoge gisting natuurlijke hergisting in de fles
	strong blond tripel, cuvée speciale Belgian ale	blonde forte triple, cuvée spéciale Belgian ale	sterk blond tripel, cuvée speciale Belgian ale
	2 different barley malts, 2 different aromatic hops, sugar, yeast, well water. Dried orange peel is added during the boiling process.	2 variétés de malt d'orge, 2 variétés de houblon aromatique, sucre, levure, eau de puits. A la cuisson de l'écorce d'orange séchée est ajoutée.	2 soorten gerstemout, 2 soorten aromatische hop, suiker, gist, putwater. Tijdens het koken wordt gedroogde sinaasschil toegevoegd.
	blond unfiltered	blonde non filtrée	blond ongefilterd
	Fine fruit taste. Round flavour with finesse	Un fin goût de fruit. Goût rond avec de la finesse.	Fijne fruitsmaak. Ronde smaak met finesse.
	Created in 2010 to mark the 10th anniversary of Cuvée des Trolls.	Créée en 2010, à l'occasion des 10 ans de la Cuvée des Trolls.	Gecreëerd in 2010 n.a.v. 10 jaar Cuvée des Trolls.

Cuvée du Château

	top-fermentation centrifuged	fermentation haute centrifugée	hoge gisting gecentrifugeerd
	strong double	foncée forte	sterk donker
	malt, sugar, hops, vitamin C, water	malt, sucre, houblon, vitamine C, eau	mout, suiker, hop, vitamine C, water
	clear dark-brown to black in colour with a creamy foam head filtered, pasteurised	limpide, brun foncé-noir, avec faux col crémeux filtrée, pasteurisée	helder donkerbruin-zwart met een romige schuimkraag gefilterd, gepasteuriseerd
	Roasted malt with madeira.	Malt torréfié avec du madère.	Gebrande mout met madeira.
	Pour in a single movement into a burgundy glass.	Verser agilement dans un verre bourgogne.	Goed doorschenken in een bourgogneglas.
i			

C

Cuvée du Flo Ambrée

Brasserie artisanale du Flo 8,50% 8 46

	top-fermentation	fermentation haute	hoge gisting
	amber or speciale belge	ambrée ou belge spé-ciale	amber of speciale belge
	pale ale malt, hops (Goldings), yeast, water	malt de pale ale, houblon (Goldings), levure, eau	pale ale mout, hop (Gol-dings), gist, water
	pale brown not filtered	brun léger non filtrée	lichtbruin ongefilterd
	Fruity, apricots	Fruitée, abricots	Fruitig, abrikozen

sserie artisanale du Flo

8% 7 °C 45 °F

	top-fermentation	fermentation haute	hoge gisting
	strong blond	blonde forte	sterk blond
	pilsner malt, hops (Goldings), herbs, yeast, water	malt de pils, houblon (Goldings), herbes, levure, eau	pilsmout, hop (Goldings), kruiden, gist, water
	blond not filtered	blonde non filtrée	blond ongefilterd
	Aroma of flowers	Arôme de fleurs	Aroma van bloemen

Cuvée du Flo Blonde

Cuvée du Flo Brune

Brasserie artisanale du Flo 9%

	top-fermentation	fermentation haute	hoge gisting
	strong double	double forte	sterk bruin
	black not filtered	noir non filtrée	zwart ongefilterd
	Aromas of coffee and pepper.	Arômes de café et de poivre.	Aroma's van koffie en peper.

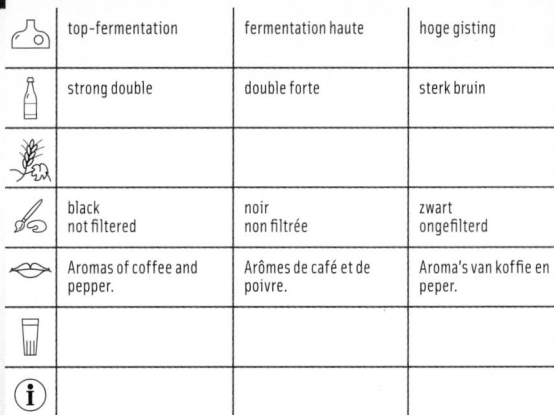

Cuvée du Flo Fruit

sserie artisanale du Flo 6,50% 5 °C 41 °F

	top-fermentation	fermentation haute	hoge gisting
	fruit beer	bière fruitée	fruitbier
	pilsner malt, hops (Goldings), apple juice, yeast, water	malt de pils, houblon (Goldings), jus de pommes, levure, eau	pilsmout, hop (Goldings), appelsap, gist, water
	pasteurised	pasteurisée	gepasteuriseerd
	Apple and flowers.	Pomme et fleurs.	Appel en bloemen.

Cuvée du Flo Miel

Brasserie artisanale du Flo

8,50% 4

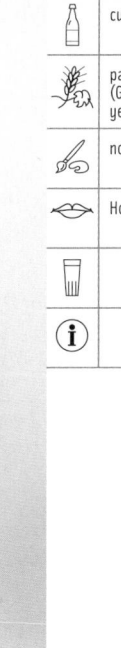

	top-fermentation	fermentation haute	hoge gisting
	cuvée spéciale	cuvée spéciale	cuvée spéciale
	pale ale malt, hops (Goldings), honey, yeast, water	malt de pale ale, houblon (Goldings), miel, levure, eau	pale ale mout, hop (Goldings), honing, gist, water
	not filtered	non filtrée	ongefilterd
	Honey and flowers.	Miel et fleurs.	Honing en bloemen.

sserie Saint-Monon 7,80% 8 °C 46 °F

	top-fermentation	fermentation haute	hoge gisting
	specialty beer boutique beer	bière spéciale artisanale	speciaalbier artisanaal
	malt varieties, hop varieties, honey, herbs, yeast, water	variétés de malt, variétés de houblon, miel, herbes, levure, eau	moutsoorten, hopsoorten, honing, kruiden, gist, water
	amber slightly cloudy	ambrée légèrement trouble	amber licht troebel
	Flowery character. Liquorice, fig and honey flavours. Aroma of ripe fruits with some flowery touches.	Caractère fleuri. Saveur de réglisse, figue et miel. Arôme de fruits mûrs avec quelques touches fleuries.	Bloemig karakter. Smaak van zoethout, vijg en honing. Aroma van rijpe vruchten met enkele bloemige toetsen.
	Serve in a 38 cl Cervoise glass.	Dans un verre type Cervoise de 38 cl.	In een glas type Cervoise van 38 cl.

C Cuvée Jolie Môme

Brasserie artisanale du Flo 4,50%

	top-fermentation	fermentation haute	hoge gisting
	witbier (white beer)	bière blanche	witbier
	pilsner malt, wheat, oat, hops (Goldings, Amarillo), herbs, yeast, water	malt de pils, froment, avoine, houblon (Goldings, Amarillo), herbes, levure, eau	pilsmout, tarwe, haver hop (Goldings, Amaril- lo), kruiden, gist, wate
	Bitter and fruity (citrus).	Amère et fruitée (citrus).	Bitter en fruitig (citrus
	The beer is brewed in tandem with the Italian winegrower Mathieu Ferré (son of Léo Ferré).	La bière est brassée en collaboration avec le vigneron italien Mathieu Ferré (fils de Léo Ferré).	Het bier wordt gebrouwen in samenwerking met de Italiaanse wijnbouwer Mathieu Ferré (zoon van Léo Ferré).

uwerij Lindemans

5,50% 5 °C 41 °F

spontaneous fermentation	fermentation spontanée	spontane gisting
gueuze lambic	gueuze lambic	geuze lambiek
malt, wheat, hops, water	malt, froment, houblon, eau	mout, tarwe, hop, water
golden blond clear	blond doré claire	goudblond helder
Smoothly sourish. Sparkling, slightly sourish and well-balanced taste with a dry, refreshingly sourish aftertaste.	Moelleuse, acidulée. Saveur pétillante, douce, acidulée et équilibrée avec une fin de bouche sèche, fraîche et acidulée.	Zacht zurig. Sprankelende, zachtzurige en uitgebalanceerde smaak met een droge, fris zurige afdronk.
Pour into an gueuze or champagne glass.	Verser dans un verre de gueuze ou de champagne.	In een geuze- of champagneglas uitschenken.
This beer can be kept for many years due to the refermentation in the bottle. Like wine, it experiences a taste evolution.	Par la refermentation en bouteille, cette bière peut se conserver pendant des années; tout comme le vin, elle subit une évolution de la saveur.	Dit bier is jaren houdbaar door hergisting op de fles. Het ondergaat een smaak-evolutie net als wijn.

Cuvée René Oude Geuze

C

C

Cuvée René Oude Kriek

Brouwerij Lindemans 6% 4

	spontaneous fermentation	fermentation spontanée	spontane gisting
	fruit beer lambic	bière fruitée lambic	fruitbier lambiek
	malt, wheat, hops, Belgian cherries, water	malt, froment, houblon, cerises belges, eau	mout, tarwe, hop, Belg sche krieken, water
	red clear	rouge claire	rood helder
	Smoothly sourish. Sparkling, smoothly sourish and well-balanced taste with a fruity cherry touch and a dry, refreshingly sourish aftertaste.	Moelleuse, acidulée. Saveur pétillante, douce, acidulée et équilibrée avec une touche fruitée de cerises et une fin de bouche sèche, fraîche et acidulée.	Zacht zurig. Sprankelen de, zachtzurige en uitgebalanceerde smaak met een fruitige toets van krieken en een dro fris zurige afdronk.
	Pour into a gueuze or champagne glass. Open carefully and leave the yeast sediment in the bottle.	Verser dans un verre de gueuze ou de champagne. Ouvrir prudemment et laisser le dépôt de levure dans la bouteille.	In een geuze- of champagneglas uitschenken Voorzichtig openen en het gistdepot in de fles laten.
	This beer can be kept for many years due to the refermentation in the bottle. Like wine, it experiences a taste evolution.	Cette bière peut se conserver pendant des années par sa refermentation en bouteille; tout comme le vin, elle subit une évolution de la saveur.	Dit bier is jaren houdba door hergisting op de fles. Het ondergaat een smaak-evolutie net als wijn.

asserie artisanale du Flo 7,50% 7 - 8 °C 45 - 46 °F

Cuvée St Antoine Blonde

	top-fermentation re-fermented in the bottle	fermentation haute refermentation en bouteille	hoge gisting hergisting op de fles
	abbey beer	bière d'abbaye	abdijbier
	pilsener malt, sugar, hop varieties, herbs, yeast, water	malt de pils, sucre, sortes de houblon, herbes, levure, eau	pilsmout, suiker, hop-soorten, kruiden, gist, water
	blond to rusty unpasteurised	blond rouille non pasteurisée	blond tot roest niet gepasteuriseerd
	Slightly fruity character. Flowery taste with pronounced bitterness.	Caractère légèrement fruité. Saveur fleurie avec goût amer prononcé.	Licht fruitig karakter. Bloemensmaak met uitgesproken bitterheid.
	Pour carefully tilting the rinsed, dry glass.	Verser prudemment dans un verre rincé et séché tenu en oblique.	Voorzichtig uitschenken in een gespoeld en gedroogd glas dat schuingehouden wordt.
i			

Cuvée St Antoine Brune

Brasserie artisanale du Flo 9% 7 - 8 45 - 46

	top-fermentation re-fermented in the bottle	fermentation haute refermentation en bouteille	hoge gisting hergisting op de fles
	scotch	scotch	scotch
	pilsener malt, crystal malt, sugar, hops, herbs, yeast, water	malt de pils, malt de cristal, sucre, houblon, herbes, levure, eau	pilsmout, cristalmout, suiker, hop, kruiden, gist, water
	brown to black unpasteurised	brune à noire non pasteurisée	bruin tot zwart niet gepasteuriseerd
	Light fruity character. Flowery taste with pronounced bitterness.	Caractère légèrement fruité. Saveur fleurie avec un goût amer prononcé.	Licht fruitig karakter. Bloemensmaak met uitgesproken bitterheid.
	Pour carefully into a rinsed, dry glass, holding the glass tilted.	Verser prudemment dans un verre rincé et séché tenu en oblique.	Voorzichtig uitschenken in een gespoeld en gedroogd glas dat schuin gehouden wordt.
i			

D

ouwerij De Graal

6,50% 8 - 10 °C / 46 - 50 °F

	top-fermentation re-fermented in the bottle	fermentation haute refermentation en bouteille	hoge of bovengisting nagisting op de fles
	specialty beer, blond	bière spéciale, blonde	speciaalbier, blond
	Malt, yeast, sugar, hops, water. Dry-hopping for natural hop flavours.	Malt, levure, sucre, houblon, eau. Dryhopping pour les arômes naturels.	Mout, gist, suiker, hop, water. Dryhopping voor natuurlijke hoparoma's.
	gold blond, clear	blond doré, claire	goudblond, helder
	Soft, not bitter beer. Malty, citrus-like aroma. Spicy, flowery taste, nuts and vanilla. Touch of alcohol in the aftertaste.	Bière douce et pas amère. Arôme malté et d'agrumes. Saveur relevée, fleurie, de noix et de vanille. Touche d'alcool en fin de bouche	Zacht, niet bitter bier. Moutig en citrusachtig aroma. Kruidige, bloemige smaak, noten en vanille. Milde alcoholtoets in de afdronk.
	Pour carefully in a single, smooth movement and leave the yeast sediment in the bottle.	Verser prudemment en un seul mouvement fluide et laisser le dépôt de levure dans la bouteille.	In 1 vloeiende beweging voorzichtig uitschenken en het gistdepot in de fles laten.
	Store the bottle upright in a dark, cool room.	Conserver la bouteille en position verticale, à l'abri de la lumière et de la chaleur.	Fles verticaal bewaren op een donkere, koele plaats.

De Graal Dubbel

Brouwerij De Graal 6,50% 8 - 10 / 46 - 50

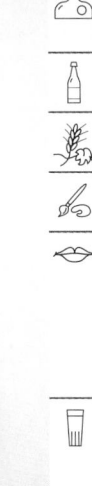

	top-fermentation re-fermented in the bottle	fermentation haute refermentation en bouteille	hoge of bovengisting nagisting op de fles
	specialty beer, dubbel	bière spéciale, double	speciaalbier, dubbel
	malt, yeast, brown candy sugar, hops, water	malt, houblon, sucre de candi brun, levure, eau	mout, gist, bruine kandijsuiker, hop, water
	red-brown clear	brun rouge claire	roodbruin helder
	Smooth beer with a spicy undertone. Aroma of malt and spices. Slightly sweet taste of sweet chocolate, caramel and raisin with a touch of bitterness.	Bière douce avec un arrière-fond relevé. Arômes de malt et d'herbes. Saveur légèrement douce de chocolat, de caramel et de raisins avec un goût légèrement amer.	Zacht bier met een kruidige ondertoon. Aroma van mout en kruiden. Lichtzoete chocolade-, karamel- en rozijnensmaak met lichte bitterheid.
	Pour carefully in a single, smooth movement and leave the yeast sediment in the bottle.	Verser prudemment en un seul mouvement fluide et laisser le dépôt de levure dans la bouteille.	In 1 vloeiende beweging voorzichtig uitschenken en het gistdepot in de fles laten.
i	Store the bottle upright in a dark, cool room.	Conserver la bouteille en position verticale, à l'abri de la lumière et de la chaleur.	Fles verticaal bewaren op een donkere, koele plaats.

De Graal Gember

ouwerij De Graal

8% 8 - 10 °C / 46 - 50 °F

top-fermentation re-fermented in the bottle	fermentation haute refermentation en bouteille	hoge of bovengisting nagisting op de fles
specialty beer blond	bière spéciale blonde	speciaalbier blond
malt, yeast, ginger, hops, water	malt, levure, gingembre, houblon, eau	mout, gist, gember, hop, water
blond clear	blonde claire	blond helder
Fresh thirst-quencher. Sweet, bitter and spicy beer with pronounced though not dominating ginger touch.	Désaltérant fraîche. Bière douce, amère et relevée avec un goût de gingembre prononcé, non dominant.	Frisse dorstlesser. Zoet, bitter en kruidig bier met geprononceerde gember die niet overheerst.
Pour carefully in a single, smooth movement and leave the yeast sediment in the bottle.	Verser prudemment en un seul mouvement fluide et laisser le dépôt de levure dans la bouteille.	In 1 vloeiende beweging voorzichtig uitschenken en het gistdepot in de fles laten.
Store the bottle upright in a dark, cool room.	Conserver la bouteille en position verticale, à l'abri de la lumière et de la chaleur.	Fles verticaal bewaren op een donkere, koele plaats.

De Graal Quest

Brouwerij De Graal 9% 8 - 1 46 - 5

	top-fermentation re-fermentation in the bottle centrifuged	fermentation haute refermentation en bouteille centrifugée	hoge gisting hergisting in de fles gecentrifugeerd
	tripel city or regional beer	triple bière régionale	tripel stads- of streekbier
	intense blond brewed with pilsner malt and 3 different hops (Hallertau, East Kent Golding, Saaz). Fermented using trappist yeast. Fully fermented beer, brewed using dry-hopping method.	blonde forte brassée avec malt de pils et 3 variétés de houblon (Hallertau, East Kent Golding, Saaz). Fermentée avec levure de trappiste. Bière complètement fermentée, brassée avec dry hopping.	zwaar blond gebrouwen met pilsmout en 3 hopsoorten (Hallertau, Eas Kent Golding, Saaz). Vergist met trappistengist. Volledig uitgegist bier, met dry hopping.
	clear blond with solid foam head not filtered or pasteurised	blond clair avec faux col solide non filtrée, non pasteurisée	helder blond met stevig schuimkraag ongefilterd, niet gepasteuriseerd
	Hoppy aroma owing to the dry-hopping. Hints of orange. No sugar added, yet a nice bitter and rich taste.	Parfum de houblon aromatique dû au houblonnage à cru, avec des touches d'orange. Sans sucre, mais tout de même une jolie amertume et un goût riche.	Aromatische hopgeur door de dryhopping. Toetsen van sinaasappe Suikervrij maar toch eer mooie bitterheid en rijk smaak.
	Pour out gently (for a clear beer) and leave the yeast in the bottle.	Verser prudemment (pour bière limpide) et laisser la levure dans la bouteille.	Voorzichtig uitschenker (voor helder bier) en de gist in de fles laten.
i	Suitable for diabetics (sugar-free).	Convient aux diabétiques (absence de sucre).	Geschikt voor diabetici (suikervrij).

ouwerij De Graal | 9% | 8 - 10 °C / 46 - 50 °F

	top-fermentation re-fermented in the bottle	fermentation haute refermentation en bouteille	hoge of bovengisting nagisting op de fles
	specialty beer tripel	bière spéciale triple	speciaalbier tripel
	malt, German hops, yeast, water	malt, houblon allemand, levure, eau	mout, Duitse hop, gist, water
	blond clear	blonde claire	blond helder
	Bitter and richly hopped heavy beer. Powerfully sweet, spicy, fruity and alcoholic aroma. The sweet taste is at the same time fruity (peaches) and spicy.	Bière forte amère et richement houblonnée. Arôme corsé doux, relevé, fruité et alcoolisé. Saveur douce et en même temps fruitée (pêches) et aromatisée.	Bitter en rijkelijk gehopt zwaar bier. Krachtig zoet, kruidig, fruitig en alcoholisch aroma. Zoete smaak die tegelijk fruitig (perziken) en kruidig is.
	Pour carefully in a single, smooth movement and leave the yeast sediment in the bottle.	Verser prudemment en un seul mouvement fluide et laisser le dépôt de levure dans la bouteille.	In 1 vloeiende beweging voorzichtig uitschenken en het gistdepot in de fles laten.
i	Store the bottle upright in a dark, cool room.	Conserver la bouteille en position verticale, à l'abri de la lumière et de la chaleur.	Fles verticaal bewaren op een donkere, koele plaats.

De Graal Tripel

De Graal Triverius

Brouwerij De Graal 6,80% 8 - 10 / 46 - 50

	top-fermentation re-fermented in the bottle	fermentation haute refermentation en bouteille	hoge gisting hergisting in de fles
	specialty beer wheat double white	bière spéciale froment double white	speciaalbier tarwe double white
	malt, wheat, hops, coriander, orange, powerful yeast. 40% more malt and wheat than common Witbier.	malt, froment, houblon, coriandre, orange, levure forte. 40% plus de malt et de froment que dans la bière blanche ordinaire.	mout, tarwe, hop, koriander, sinaas, krachtige gist. 40% meer mout en tarwe dan gewoon witbier.
	blond, clear	blonde, claire	blond, helder
	Refreshing, smooth and slightly bitter wheat beer. Non-sweet, dry flavours of special yeast and wheat with coriander. Spicy lime and a dry, citrus-like aftertaste.	Bière de froment rafraîchissante, douce légèrement amère. Goût non sucré, sec, arômes de levure spéciale et froment au coriandre. Citron vert relevé, fin de bouche sèche avec goût d'agrumes.	Verfrissend, zacht en lichtbitter tarwebier. Niet zoet, droog, aroma' van speciale gist en tarwe met koriander. Kruidige limoen en een droge, citrusachtige afdronk.
	Pour carefully in a single, smooth movement and leave the yeast sediment in the bottle.	Verser prudemment en un seul mouvement fluide et laisser le dépôt de levure dans la bouteille.	In 1 vloeiende beweging voorzichtig uitschenken en het gistdepot in de fles laten.
i	Store the bottle upright in a dark, cool room.	Conserver la bouteille verticalement, à l'abri de la lumière et de la chaleur.	Fles verticaal bewaren op een donkere, koele plaats.

top-fermentation	fermentation haute	hoge gisting
amber	ambrée	amber
malt, hops, yeast, water	malt, houblon, levure, eau	mout, hop, gist, water
amber clear	ambrée claire	amber helder
Malty taste. Fresh flavour with aromatic, hop-bitter finish.	Caractère malté. Goût frais, amertume due au houblon, avec une fin aromatique, amère houblonnée.	Moutig karakter. Frisse, hopbittere smaak met aromatische, hop-bittere finish.
Hold the bottle up high at the start and empty in a single movement.	Tenir la bouteille élevée au départ et verser agilement jusqu'à ce que la bouteille soit vide.	De fles hoog houden bij de start en doorschenken tot de fles leeg is.

De Koninck Triple d'Anvers

Duvel Moortgat Corporation

8% 8 - 10
43 - 46

top-fermentation	fermentation haute	hoge gisting
tripel	triple	tripel
malt, hops, yeast, organic cane sugar, water	malt, houblon, levure, sucre de canne biologique, eau	mout, hop, gist, biologische rietsuiker, water
gold-yellow clear	jaune doré claire	brons helder
Warm alcoholic nature, yet also refreshing session beer. Soft, sweet onset, changing into fruity esters at the very peak. Aftertaste: aromatic Saaz hop (bitter).	Bière facilement buvable désaltérante au caractère alcoolisé chaleureux. Approche initiale douce, sucrée, avec un sommet franc d'esters fruités. Arrière-bouche : lupuline aromatique (Saaz).	Warm alcoholisch karakter en tegelijk verfrissende doordrinker. Zachte, zoete start met een volmondig hoogtepunt van fruitige esters. Afdronk: aromatisch hopbitter (Saaz).
Hold the bottle high to start with and pour in one movement until the bottle is empty.	Tenir la bouteille haut au début et continuer à verser jusqu'à ce qu'elle soit vide.	De fles hoog houden bij de start, en langzaam zakken tot een mooie schuimkraag is gevormd

vel Moortgat Corporation 6,50% 6 - 10 °C 43 - 50 °F

De Koninck Winter

	top-fermentation	fermentation haute	hoge gisting
	winter beer	bière hivernale	winterbier
	malt, hops, yeast, organic cane sugar, water	malt, houblon, levure, sucre de canne biologique, eau	mout, hop, gist, biologische rietsuiker, water
	dark red clear creamy foam head	rouge foncé claire faux col couleur crème	donkerrood helder crème-achtige schuimkraag
	Perfect balance between sweet, bitter and roasty. Soft, warm start. Full-bodied with touches of roasted malt. Bitter aftertaste because of the Saaz hops.	Equilibre parfait entre doux, amer et brûlé. Goût initial doux, chaleureux. Franc avec des touches de malt brûlé. Fin de bouche amère par le houblon Saaz.	Perfecte balans tussen zoet, bitter en gebrand. Zachte, warme start. Volmondig met toetsen van gebrande mout. Afdronk bitter door de Saaz hop.
	Lift the bottle high when pouring starts, then lower it slowly, until a nice foam head is formed.	Tenir la bouteille haut au début et la baisser lentement jusqu'à la formation d'un beau faux col.	De fles hoog houden bij de start, en langzaam laten zakken tot er een mooie schuimkraag is gevormd.
i			

De Nacht

Brouwerij Vissenaken

5,20%

	top-fermentation re-fermentation in the bottle	fermentation haute refermentation en bouteille	hoge gisting hergisting in de fles
	winter beer	bière hivernale	winterbier
	wheat, 4 different barley malts, hops, herbs, sugar, yeast, brewing water	froment, 4 variétés de malt d'orge, houblon, herbes, sucre, levure, eau de brassage	tarwe, 4 soorten gerstemout, hop, kruiden, suiker, gist, brouwwater
	black with pale brown foam head not filtered	noire avec faux col brun clair non filtrée	zwart met lichtbruine schuimkraag ongefilterd
	Fruity and slightly floral aroma with pleasant scent. Roasted malt and slightly bitter.	Arôme fruité et légèrement floral, avec un parfum agréable. Malt grillé et légèrement amer.	Fruitig en licht floraal aroma met aangenaam parfum. Geroosterde mout en licht bitter.

De Vlier X-mas

rouwerij De Vlier 8,50% 4 - 6 °C 39 - 43 °F

	top-fermentation re-fermentation in the bottle not centrifuged	fermentation haute refermentation en bouteille non centrifugée	hoge gisting hergisting in de fles niet gecentrifugeerd
	scotch ale stout winter or Christmas beer	scotch ale stout bière hivernale ou bière de Noël	scotch ale stout winter- of kerstbier
	pilsner, chocolate and wheat malts, oats, Saaz hops	malt de pils, de chocolat et de froment, flocons d'avoine, houblon Saaz	pils-, chocoalade- en tarwemout, havervlokken, Saazhop
	dark with thick white foam head not filtered or pasteurised	foncée avec faux col collant blanc non filtrée, non pasteurisée	donker met wandklevende witte schuimkraag ongefilterd, niet gepasteuriseerd
	Hoppy coffee aroma, full flavour with complex bitterness of the malt and hops, bitter yet refreshing aftertaste.	Arôme de café houblonné, goût franc, avec l'amertume complexe du malt et du houblon, arrière-bouche rafraîchissante amère.	Hoppig koffiearoma, volle smaak met complexe bitterheid van de mout en de hop, bittere verfrissende afdronk.
	Pour into a tulip glass and leave yeast sediment in bottle or pour along.	Verser dans un verre tulipe et laisser le dépôt de levure dans la bouteille ou le verser également.	Uitschenken in een tulpvormig glas en de gistbodem in de fles laten of meeschenken.
i			

Delirium Christmas

Brouwerij Huyghe 10% 7 45

	top-fermentation	fermentation haute	hoge gisting
	winter beer	bière hivernale	winterbier
	barley malt, hops, yeast, water fermented three times	malt d'orge, houblon, levure, eau triple fermentation	gerstemout, hop, gist, water 3x gegist
	chestnut amber with a fine, creamy, thick white foam head not filtered or pasteurised	ambré marron avec un faux col fin, crémeux, blanc collant au verre non filtrée, non pasteurisée	kastanjeamber met een fijne, romige, wandklevende witte schuimkraag ongefilterd, niet gepasteuriseerd
	Very complex with caramel malt, fruit, herbs and deriving its sweetness mainly from the alcohol. Very spicy flavour with a bitter touch. Sweet, spicy and slightly bitter aftertaste.	Fort complexe, avec du malt de caramel, des fruits, des épices et surtout le sucre de l'alcool. Goût fortement épicé, avec une touche d'amertume. Arrière-bouche sucrée, épicée et légèrement amère.	Zeer complex met karamelmout, fruit, kruiden en vooral zoet van de alcohol. Sterk kruidige smaak met bittertoets. Zoete, kruidige en licht bittere afdronk.
	Pour carefully and leave the yeast sediment in the bottle if necessary.	Verser prudemment et laisser le dépôt de levure dans la bouteille suivant les souhaits.	Voorzichtig uitschenken en het gistdepot desgewenst in de fles laten.
i	The pink elephant in a Christmassy mood ...	L'éléphant rose dans une ambiance de Noël...	De roze olifant in kerststemming...

Delirium Nocturnum

ouwerij Huyghe

8,50%

top-fermentation re-fermented in the bottle	fermentation haute refermentation en bouteille	hoge gisting hergisting in de fles
strong dark	foncée forte	sterk donker
malt (including roasted malt varieties), hops, yeast, herbs, water	malt (e.a. des variétés de malt brûlées), houblon, levure, herbes, eau	mout (o.a. gebrande moutsoorten), hop, gist, kruiden, water
deep brown	brun intense	diepbruin
More robust and harder than the Delirium tremens. Warm, velvety soft character beer with a very strong taste: tones of alcohol, hops and bitter rind. Long-lasting, bitter after-taste.	Plus corsé et fort que le Delirium tremens. Bière de caractère chaude, moelleuse et veloutée avec un goût corsé : touches d'alcool, houblon et zeste amer. Fin de bouche amère longue.	Meer gecorseerd en harder dan de Delirium tremens. Warm en fluweelzacht karakterbier met een zeer sterke smaak: tonen van alcohol, hop en bittere schil. Lange bittere afdronk.
Serve in a goblet.	Verser dans un verre ballon.	Uitschenken in een bolglas.

Delirium Red

Brouwerij Huyghe

8,50% 5 41

	top-fermentation	fermentation haute	hoge gisting
	fruit beer	bière fruitée	fruitbier
	barley malt, Morello cherries, Morello cherry juice, elderberry juice, sugar, hops, yeast, aroma, sweetener	malt d'orge, cerises, jus de cerises, jus de baies de sureau, sucre, houblon, levure, arômes, édulcorant	gerstemout, krieken, kriekensap, vlierbessensap, suiker, hop, gist, aroma, zoetstof
	deep dark red with compact and thick pale pink foam head not filtered or pasteurised	rouge profond foncé avec faux col rose clair compact et collant au verre non filtrée, non pasteurisée	diepdonkerrood met compacte en wandklevende lichtroze schuimkraag ongefilterd, niet gepasteuriseerd
	Soft, fruity aroma with hints of almond, tart cherries and cherries in the nose. Soft, mild fruity onset. Fine sweet-and-sour balance, ideal as a desert beer.	Arôme doucement fruité, avec des touches d'amande, de griottes doucement acides et de cerises dans le bouquet. Approche initiale sucrée, doucement fruitée. Joli équilibre de sucré et d'acidulé, parfaite comme bière de dessert.	Zacht fruitig aroma met hints van amandel, mildzure krieken en kersen in de neus. Zoete, zacht fruitige aanzet. Mooie balans van zoet en zurig, perfect als dessertbier.
	The Delirium glass with dancing elephants is known the world over.	Verre délirium avec de petits éléphants dansants mondialement connu.	Het deliriumglas met dansende olifantjes is wereldberoemd.
	Delirium Tremens enriched with a variation of red-fruit juices.	Delirium Tremens enrichie d'une variété de jus de fruits rouges.	Delirium Tremens verrijkt met een variatie van rodevruchtensappen.

Delirium Tremens

ouwerij Huyghe 8,50%

	top-fermentation re-fermented in the bottle	fermentation haute refermentation en bouteille	hoge gisting hergisting in de fles
	tripel	triple	tripel
	malt, hops, yeast, herbs, water	malt, houblon, levure, herbes, eau	mout, hop, gist, kruiden, water
	blond clear	blonde claire	blond helder
	Malty nose with bitter tones. Aftertaste: peppery and bitter, but never aggressive.	Parfum malté avec des touches amères. Fin de bouche poivrée et amère sans agressivité.	Moutige neus met bittere tonen. Afdronk: peper en bitter zonder agressiviteit.
	Serve in a goblet.	Verser dans un verre ballon.	Uitschenken in een bolglas.
i			

Het Alternatief at Brouwerij Alvinne

5% 5 41

	top-fermentation re-fermentation in the bottle	fermentation haute refermentation en bouteille	hoge gisting hergisting in de fles
	pilsner or lager beer	pils ou lager	pils of lagerbier
	pilsner and pale ale malt, hops (EKG and Challeng-er)	malt de pils et de pale ale, houblon (EKG et Challenger)	pils- en pale ale-mout, hop (EKG en Challenger)
	pale blond and clear with solid, intensely white foam head not filtered or pasteur-ised	blond clair et limpide avec faux col solide blanc comme neige non filtrée en non pas-teurisée	lichtblond en helder met stevige spierwitte schuimkraag ongefilterd en niet ge-pasteuriseerd
	Full malt taste, tart la-ger.	Bière blonde pleinement maltée, un peu amère.	Volmoutige, bitterige la-ger.
	Slowly pour into a tulip glass. Leave yeast sedi-ment in the bottle.	Verser prudemment dans un verre tulipe. Laisser le dépôt de levure dans la bouteille.	Voorzichtig uitschenken in een tulpglas. De gist-bodem in de fles laten.
i			

Den Bi3r

D

uwerij den Tseut 9,50% 4 °C 39 °F

top-fermentation re-fermentation in the bottle not centrifuged	fermentation haute refermentation en bouteille non centrifugée	hoge gisting hergisting in de fles niet gecentrifugeerd
tripel city or regional beer	triple bière citadine ou régionale	tripel stads- of streekbier
pilsner malt, rye malt, Poperinge hops (Magnum and Challenger), yeast, water. Dry-hopping	malt de pils, malt d'orge, houblon de Poperinge (Magnum et Challenger), levure, eau. Dry-hopping	pilsmout, roggemout, Poperingse hop (Magnum en Challenger), gist, water. Dry-hopping
blond, slightly cloudy with a white foam head not filtered or pasteurised	blonde, légèrement trouble avec un faux col fin non filtrée, non pasteurisée	blond, lichttroebel met een fijne schuimkraag ongefilterd, niet gepasteuriseerd
Full malt taste, spicy touch of rye, tart aftertaste.	Pleinement malté, touche épicée de seigle, arrière-bouche amère.	Volmoutig, kruidige toets van rogge, bittere afdronk.
Pour out in a single movement and leave the yeast sediment (approx. 1 cm) in the bottle.	Verser d'un mouvement fluide et laisser le dépôt de levure (ca 1 cm) dans la bouteille.	In een vlotte beweging uitschenken en het gistbezinksel (ca. 1 cm) in de fles laten.
'Tseut' means pig in the local dialect. 'Bi3r' is the dialect word for a male pig (boar), also the heaviest, therefore…	'Tseut' signifie 'cochon' dans le dialecte local. 'Bi3r' est le mot dialectal pour un cochon mâle, donc aussi le plus lourd.	'Tseut' betekent varken in het lokale dialect. 'Bi3r' is het dialectwoord voor een mannelijk varken, wat meteen het zwaarste is…

Den Bras

Brouwerij den Tseut

7,50%

	top-fermentation re-fermentation in the bottle not centrifuged	fermentation haute refermentation en bouteille non centrifugée	hoge gisting hergisting in de fles niet gecentrifugeerd
	double city or regional beer	double bière citadine ou régionale	dubbel stads- of streekbier
	pilsner, Münich and caramel malt, Poperinge hops (Saaz, East Kent Goldings), yeast, water	malt de pils, malt Münich et malt caramélisé, houblon de Poperinge (Saaz, East Kent Goldings), levure, eau	pils-, Münich- en karamelmout, Poperingse hop (Saaz, East Kent Goldings), gist, water
	dark brown with a nice, firm foam head not filtered or pasteurised	brun foncé avec un faux col joli solide non filtrée, non pasteurisée	donkerbruin met een mooie, stevige schuimkraag ongefilterd, niet gepasteuriseerd
	Full malt taste, flavour and aroma of natural caramel.	Pleinement malté, goût et parfum de caramel naturel.	Volmoutig, smaak en geur van natuurlijke karamel.
	Pour out in a single movement and leave the yeast sediment (approx. 1 cm) in the bottle.	Verser d'un mouvement fluide et laisser le dépôt de levure (ca 1 cm) dans la bouteille.	In een vlotte beweging uitschenken en het gist bezinksel (ca. 1 cm) in d fles laten.
	'Tseut' means pig in the local dialect. 'Bras' refers to the pig feed.	'Tseut' signifie 'cochon' dans le dialecte local. 'Bras' fait référence à la nourriture des cochons.	'Tseut' betekent varken in het lokale dialect. 'Bras' verwijst naar het varkensvoeder.

uwerij den Tseut

8,50% — 4 °C / 39 °F

top-fermentation re-fermentation in the bottle not centrifuged	fermentation haute refermentation en bouteille non centrifugée	hoge gisting hergisting in de fles niet gecentrifugeerd
amber or speciale belge city or regional beer winter beer	ambrée ou spéciale belge bière citadine ou régionale bière hivernale	amber of speciale belge stads- of streekbier winterbier
pilsner malt, pale ale malt, Münich malt, Poperinge hops (Challenger), candy sugar, yeast and water.	malt de pils, malt de pale ale, malt de Münich, houblon de Poperinge (Challenger), candi, levure et eau.	pilsmout, pale ale mout, Münichmout, Poperingse hop (Challenger), kandij, gist en water.
amber, slightly cloudy with a thick foam head not filtered or pasteurised	ambrée, légèrement trouble avec un faux col plein non filtrée, non pasteurisée	amber, licht troebel met een volle schuimkraag ongefilterd, niet gepasteuriseerd
Full malt taste with a slightly tart touch owing to the candy sugar. Slightly bitter aftertaste.	Pleinement malté, avec une touche légèrement acidulée du sucre candi. Arrière-bouche légèrement amère.	Volmoutig met een lichtzurige toets van de kandij. Licht bittere afdronk.
Pour out in a single movement and leave the yeast sediment (approx. 1 cm) in the bottle.	Verser d'un mouvement fluide et laisser le dépôt de levure (ca. 1 cm) dans la bouteille.	In een vlotte beweging uitschenken en het gistbezinksel (ca. 1 cm) in de fles laten.
Winter beer brewed from November to February.	Bière hivernale qui est brassée de novembre à février.	Winterbier dat wordt gebrouwen van november tot februari.

D Den Herberg Amber

Brouwerij Den Herberg 5,50%

	top-fermentation re-fermentation in the bottle	fermentation haute refermentation en bouteille	hoge gisting hergisting op de fles
	amber	ambrée	amber
	wheat malt, malt, hops, yeast, water	malt de froment, malt, houblon, levure, eau	tarwemout, mout, hop, gist, water
	amber-coloured not pasteurised	ambrée non pasteurisée	amberkleurig niet gepasteuriseerd
	Soft bitter.	Doucement amère.	Zacht bitter.
i			

ouwerij Den Herberg 5,50%

	top-fermentation re-fermentation in the bottle	fermentation haute refermentation en bouteille	hoge gisting hergisting op de fles
	blond	blonde	blond
	wheat malt, malt, hops, yeast, water	malt de froment, malt, houblon, levure, eau	tarwemout, mout, hop, gist, water
	gold-blond with thick foam head not pasteurised	blond doré avec faux col solide non pasteurisée	goudblond met forse schuimkraag niet gepasteuriseerd
	Intense and slightly hoppy taste.	Vive et finement houblonnée.	Pittig en fijn gehopt.

Den Herberg Blond

Den Herberg Bruin

Brouwerij Den Herberg 5,50%

	top-fermentation re-fermentation in the bottle	fermentation haute refermentation en bouteille	hoge gisting hergisting op de fles
	double	double	dubbel
	wheat malt, 6 different malts, hops, yeast, water	malt de froment, 6 variétés de malt, houblon, levure, eau	tarwemout, 6 moutsoorten, hop, gist, water
	dark red-brown not pasteurised	brun rouge foncé non pasteurisée	donkerroodbruin niet gepasteuriseerd

ouwerij Den Herberg 5%

Den Herberg Tarwe

D

	top-fermentation re-fermentation in the bottle	fermentation haute refermentation en bouteille	hoge gisting hergisting op de fles
	witbier (white beer)	bière blanche	witbier
	wheat malt, malt, hops, coriander, yeast, water	malt de froment, malt, houblon, coriandre, levure, eau	tarwemout, mout, hop, koriander, gist, water
	blond with solid foam head not pasteurised	blond doré avec faux col solide non pasteurisée	hoogblond met stevige schuimkraag niet gepasteuriseerd

Den Mulder

Brouwerij den Tseut

8%

	top-fermentation re-fermentation in the bottle not centrifuged	fermentation haute refermentation en bouteille non centrifugée	hoge gisting hergisting in de fles niet gecentrifugeerd
	blond city or regional beer	blonde bière citadine ou régionale	blond stads- of streekbier
	pilsner malt, spelt malt, spelt, rye, oat, Poperinge hops (East Kent Goldings), yeast, water.	malt de pils, malt d'épeautre, épeautre, seigle, avoine, houblon de Poperinge (East Kent Goldings), levure, eau	pilsmout, speltmout, spelt, rogge, haver, Poperingse hop (East Kent Goldings), gist, water
	blond, slightly cloudy and a nice, white foam head. not filtered or pasteurised	blonde, légèrement trouble et un faux col joli blanc. non filtrée, non pasteurisée	blond, lichttroebel en een mooie, witte schuimkraag ongefilterd, niet gepasteuriseerd
	Full malt taste, soft, refreshing and slightly bitter with typical spelt taste.	Pleinement maltée, douce, rafraîchissante et légèrement amère, avec un goût d'épeautre typique.	Volmoutig, zacht, verfrissend en licht bitter met typische speltsmaak.
	Pour out in a single movement and leave the yeast sediment (approx. 1 cm) in the bottle.	Verser d'un mouvement fluide et laisser le dépôt de levure (ca 1 cm) dans la bouteille.	In een vlotte beweging uitschenken en het gistbezinksel (ca. 1 cm) in de fles laten.
	A real miller's beer brewed at the request of the miller of the Stenen Molen (spelt mill) in Ertvelde.	Une véritable bière de moulin, qui a été brassée à la demande du meunier du Stenen Molen (moulin à épeautre) à Ertvelde.	Een echt molenbier dat gebrouwen werd op aanvraag van de molenaar van de Stenen Molen (speltmolen) in Ertvelde.

ouwerij Den Toetëlèr 5,20%

	top-fermentation re-fermentation in the bottle	fermentation haute refermentation en bouteille	hoge gisting hergisting in de fles
	white beer with fruit	bière blanche fruitée	witbier met fruit
	malt, barley, wheat, oat, hops, elderberry flowers, yeast, water	malt, orge, froment, avoine, houblon, fleur de sureau, levure, eau	mout, gerst, tarwe, haver, hop, vlierbloesem, gist, water
	not filtered	non filtrée	ongefilterd
	'Toëtelèr' means elder bush in the Limburg dialect. Old wood from the elder bush is hollow and that is why it was used as a whistle (toeter).	'Toëtelèr' signifie buisson de sureau en dialecte limbourgeois. Le vieux bois du buisson de sureau est creux et il a pour cette raison été utilisé comme flûte ou corne (toeter).	'Toëtelèr' betekent vlierstruik in het Limburgs dialect. Oud hout van de vlierstruik is hol en het werd daarom als fluitje of toeter gebruikt.

Brouwerij den Tseut

6,50%

top-fermentation re-fermentation in the bottle not centrifuged	fermentation haute refermentation en bouteille non centrifugée	hoge gisting hergisting in de fles niet gecentrifugeerd
blond regional beer Belgian ale	bière blonde régionale Belgian ale	blond streekbier Belgian ale
pilsner malt, wheat malt, Münich malt, Poperinge hops (Saaz, East Kent Goldings, Challenger), yeast, water	malt de pils, malt de froment, malt de Münich, houblon de Poperinge (Saaz, East Kent Goldings, Challenger), levure, eau	pilsmout, tarwemout, Münichmout, Poperingse hop (Saaz, East Kent Goldings, Challenger), gist, water
dark blond, slightly cloudy with a creamy foam head not filtered or pasteurised	blond foncé, légèrement trouble avec un faux col crémeux non filtrée, non pasteurisée	donkerblond, licht troebel met een crèmige schuimkraag ongefilterd, niet gepasteuriseerd
Full malt taste, slightly bitter, with somewhat sweet aftertaste. Aroma of an old granary.	Pleinement maltée, légèrement amère, avec une arrière-bouche un peu douceâtre. Arôme d'un vieux grenier à blé.	Volmoutig, licht bitter, met iets zoetige afdronk. Aroma van een oude graanschuur.
see Den Mulder	voir Den Mulder	zie Den Mulder
'Tseut' means pig in the local dialect. Varken [pig] is also a nickname for the people from Oosteeklo. House beer from the brewery with the same name.	'Tseut' signifie 'cochon' dans le dialecte local. Varken ('cochon') est aussi un sobriquet des habitants d'Oosteeklo. Bière maison de la brasserie du même nom.	'Tseut' betekent varken in het lokale dialect. Varken is ook een spotnaam voor de Oosteeklonaren. Huisbier van de gelijknamige brouwerij.

as at Brouwerij De Graal

6,60% — 6 °C / 43 °F

	top-fermentation re-fermentation in the bottle	fermentation haute refermentation en bouteille	hoge gisting hergisting in de fles
	barley malt, hops, yeast, herbs, water	malt d'orge, houblon, levure, herbes, eau	gerstemout, hop, gist, kruiden, water
	Pour slowly into a degreased glass without sloshing the beer.	Verser lentement dans un verre dégraissé sans clapotage de la bière.	Traag inschenken in een ontvet glas zonder dat het bier klokt.
	Only available from De Bierloods.	Seulement en vente chez De Bierloods.	Enkel verkrijgbaar bij De Bierloods.

Dendermonde Tripel Abdijbier

Brouwerij De Block 8% 6 - 43 - 4

	top-fermentation re-fermented in the bottle	fermentation haute refermentation en bouteille	hoge gisting hergisting op de fles
	Recognised Belgian abbey beer tripel	Triple d'abbaye belge reconnue	Erkend Belgisch Abdijbier tripel
	wheat, malt, hops, yeast, water	froment, malt, houblon, levure, eau	tarwe, mout, hop, gist, water
	copper, amber full, creamy foam head	cuivre, ambreé faux col crémeux et plein	koper, amber volle, romige schuimkraag
	Full-bodied and fruity. Rich with a slightly caramelized taste.	Franche et fruitée. Goût riche, légèrement caramélisé.	Volmondig en fruitig. Rijke, licht gekaramelliseerde smaak.
	cfr. Chimay	cfr. Chimay	cfr. Chimay
i			

Dentergems Witbier

uwerij Het Anker 5% 4 - 6 °C / 39 - 43 °F

top-fermentation re-fermentation in the bottle centrifuged	fermentation haute refermentation en bouteille centrifugée	hoge gisting hergisting in de fles gecentrifugeerd
witbier (white beer)	bière blanche	witbier
barley malt, hops, yeast, herbs, water	malt d'orge, houblon, levure, herbes, eau	gerstemout, hop, gist, kruiden, water
white beer, slightly cloudy, steady foam head not filtered, pasteurised	bière blanche, légèrement trouble, faux col stable non filtrée, pasteurisée	witbier, licht troebel, stabiele schuimkraag ongefilterd, gepasteuriseerd
Summery with a slight citrus aroma.	D'été, avec un léger arôme de citrus.	Zomers met een licht citrusaroma.
Tilt glass slightly and pour out beer gently.	Tenir le verre légèrement incliné et verser prudemment la bière.	Het glas licht schuin houden en het bier voorzichtig uitschenken.
Only brewed for exports (USA). Launched in the 80s by the then Riva brewery. When Liefmans went into receivership, was taken over by Duvel-Moortgat and since 2011 by Het Anker.	Uniquement brassée pour l'exportation (États-Unis). Lancée dans les années '80 par la brasserie Riva de l'époque. Lors de la faillite de Liefmans, reprise par Duvel-Moortgat et, depuis 2011, par Het Anker.	Enkel voor export gebrouwen (USA). In de jaren '80 door de toenmailge brouwerij Riva gelanceerd. Bij het faillissement van Liefmans overgenomen door Duvel-Moortgat en sinds 2011 door Het Anker.

Brasserie du Bocq

7,30%

	top-fermentation re-fermented in the bottle	fermentation haute refermentation en bouteille	hoge gisting hergisting op de fles
	strong blond	bière blonde forte	sterk blond
	slightly cloudy	légèrement trouble	licht troebel
i	From November 2011 onwards available in 33 cl.	A partir de Novembre 2011 disponible en 33 cl seulement.	Vanaf november 2011 in 33cl fles.

uwerij Bosteels

11,50% 2 - 4 °C 36 - 39 °F

	first top-fermentation bottom re-fermented in the bottle	fermentation haute refermentation basse en bouteille	hoge eerste gisting lage hergisting op de fles
	brut beer	bière brute	brut bier
	barley malts, hops, water	malt d'orge, houblon, eau	gerstemouten, hop, water
	Light blond, pale golden, clear saturation with extremely small bubbles. Fine, very white, merengue-like foam head.	Blond clair, saturation claire légèrement dorée avec des bulles minuscules. Faux col fin, blanc, comme de la meringue.	Lichtblond, bleekgouden, heldere saturatie met uiterst minuscule belletjes. Fijne, spierwitte, merengueachtige schuimkraag.
	Delicate and complex: aromas of fresh apples, enhanced by mint, thyme, ginger, lemon skin, malt, pear, hops, allspice and cloves. Creamy and sparkling, light and airy, sweet and fruity, with dry finishing touch.	Délicate et complexe :arômes de pomme, menthe, thym, gingembre, zeste de citron, malt, poire, houblon, poivre de la Jamaïque et girofle. Crémeux et pétillant, léger, doux et fruité avec finition sèche.	Delicaat en complex: aroma's van verse appels versterkt door munt, tijm, gember, citroenschil, mout, peer, hop, allspice en kruidnagel. Romig en sprankelend, licht en luchtig, zoet en fruitig, met droge afwerking.
	Chill in the refrigerator for 6 to 12 hours and lay in an ice bucket before serving.Gently pour into a cooled flute-glass.	Mettre au réfrigérateur pendant 6 à 12 heures et ensuite dans un seau à glace. Verser doucement dans des flûtes rafraîchies.	6 à 12 uur op temperatuur brengen in de koelkast en voor het uitschenken in een ijsemmer leggen. Zacht uitschenken in gekoelde fluitglazen.
i			

Deus, Brut des Flandres

Diabolici

Groep John Martin by various breweries

8%

	top-fermentation re-fermentation in the bottle	fermentation haute refermentation en bouteille	hoge gisting hergisting in de fles
	blond tripel	triple blonde	blonde tripel

6,50% | 6 °C 43 °F

	top-fermentation	fermentation haute	hoge gisting
	amber	ambrée	amber
	Ambrée malt, cara Münich, hops, herbs, yeast, water	malt ambré, cara Münich, houblon, herbes, levure, eau	ambermout, caramünich, hop, kruiden, gist, water
	amber by the malt varieties used filtered	ambrée par les variétés de malt utilisées filtrée	amber door de gebruikte moutsoorten gefilterd
	Malty, hoppy.	Maltée, houblonnée.	Moutig, hoppig.
i	Originally brewed by order of a group of Ostend beer lovers. The name refers to the popular name of a statue in Ostend. The label features this sculpture by Constant Permeke's grandson.	A l'origine brassée à la demande d'un groupe d'amateurs de bière d'Ostende. Le nom de la bière renvoie à la dénomination populaire d'une statue à Ostende. L'étiquette représente cette statue de la main du petit-fils de Constant Permeke.	Oorspronkelijk gebrouwen in opdracht van een groep Oostendse bierliefhebbers. De naam verwijst naar de volkse benaming van een standbeeld uit Oostende. Dit beeld van de kleinzoon van Constant Permeke staat op het etiket.

Dominus Double

Groep John Martin by various breweries **6,50%** 6 -
43 - 4

	top-fermentation	fermentation haute	hoge gisting
	abbey beer	bière d'abbaye	abdijbier
	barley malt, sugar, hops, water	malt d'orge, sucre, houblon, eau	gerstemout, suiker, hop water
	brown	brune	bruin
	Dry bitterness from the first moment, obtained by the typical Pale Ale malts and the aromatised hop.	Saveur amère sèche dès la première gorgée par les malts pale ale typiques et le houblon aromatisé.	Droge bitterheid vanaf de eerste slok door de typische pale-ale-mouten en de gearomatiseerde hop.

ep John Martin by various breweries 8% 6 - 8 °C 43 - 46 °F

top-fermentation	fermentation haute	hoge gisting
abbey beer	bière d'abbaye	abdijbier
barley malt, sugar, hops, water	malt d'orge, sucre, houblon, eau	gerstemout, suiker, hop, water
blond/amber	blonde/ambrée	blond/amber
Bitter with exotic smoothness (white raisin sugar). Dry bitter but at the same time fruity aftertaste.	Goût amer avec une douceur exotique (sucre de raisins secs blancs). Arrière-bouche sèche, amère mais aussi fruitée.	Bitter met exotische zachtheid (suiker van witte rozijnen). Droogbittere maar ook fruitige nasmaak.

D Donkere Stoere

Donkere Stoere
Een aromatisch, bruin bier van
hoge gisting
Alc 8,2%
Bier Van Hoge Goesting

Brouwerij DijkWaert

8,20% 10 - 1 / 50 - 5

	top-fermentation natural re-fermentation in the bottle	fermentation haute refermentation naturelle en bouteille	hoge gisting natuurlijke hergisting i de fles
	strong double	foncée forte	sterk donker
	malt, hops, herbs, yeasts, water	malt, houblons, herbes, levures, eau	mout, hoppen, kruiden, gisten, water
	dark brown (80 EBC)	brun foncé (80 EBC)	donkerbruin (80 EBC)
	Rich, soft, creamy aroma and taste pallet with long aftertaste.	Riche, douce, arôme crémeux et palette de goûts avec une longue fin de bouche.	Rijk, zacht, romig aroma en smakenpallet met lange nasmaak.
i	This brewery will soon launch a new beer: Mc Thals (refers to Herentals and the use of whisky malt).	Une nouvelle bière de cette brasserie sortira d'ici peu :la Mc Thals (fait référence à Herentals et à l'utilisation de malt de whisky).	Binnenkort komt er een nieuw bier van deze brouwerij: Mc Thals (ver wijst naar Herentals en het gebruik van whisky-mout).

uwerij De Bie

6%

top-fermentation	fermentation haute	hoge gisting
dubbel	double	dubbel
dark brown	brun foncé	donkerbruin
Sweet and fairly bitter.	Douce et assez amère.	Zoet en vrij bitter.

Double Enghien Blonde

Brasserie de Silly 7,50% (16,5° plato) 4 - 8 39 - 46

	top-fermentation	fermentation haute	hoge gisting
	regional beer	bière régionale	streekbier
	pale malt, sugar, Kent and Hallertau hops, yeast, water	malt pâle, sucre, houblon Kent et Hallertau, levure, eau	bleke mout, suiker, Kent en Hallertau hop, gist, water
	blond (9,5 EBC)	blonde (9,5 EBC)	blond (9,5 EBC)
	Well-balanced bitter in the middle and round in the aftertaste.	Goût central amer équilibré, rond en fin de bouche.	Evenwichtig bitter in het midden en rond in de afdronk.
	Pour carefully into a narrow goblet.	Verser tranquillement dans un verre calice large.	Rustig uitschenken in een breed kelkglas.
	Boutique beer. Brewed by Tennstedt Decroes in Enghien till 1975.	Brassée de façon artisanale. Brassée jusqu'à 1975 par la Brasserie Tennstedt Decroes à Enghien.	Artisanaal gebrouwen. Werd tot 1975 gebrouwen door Brouwerij Tennstedt Decroes in Enghien.

Double Enghien Brune

asserie de Silly — 8% (17,5° plato) — 5 - 9 °C / 41 - 48 °F

top-fermentation	fermentation haute	hoge gisting
regional beer	bière régionale	streekbier
pale malt, caramelised malt, aromatic malt, sugar, Kent and Hallertau hops, yeast, water	malt pâle, malt caramélisé, malt aromatisé, sucre, houblon Kent et Hallertau, levure, eau	bleke mout, gekaramelliseerde mout, aromatische mout, suiker, Kent en Hallertau hop, gist, water
amber (24 EBC)	ambrée (24 EBC)	amber (24 EBC)
Unique flavour obtained by the different malt types used.	Arôme unique par les variétés de malt utilisées.	Uniek aroma door de gebruikte moutsoorten.
Pour carefully into a goblet.	Verser tranquillement dans un verre calice large.	Rustig uitschenken in een breed kelkglas.
Boutique beer. Until 1975 brewed by Brouwerij Tennstedt Decroes in Enghien.	Brassée de façon artisanale. Brassée jusqu'à 1975 par la Brasserie Tennstedt Decroes à Enghien.	Artisanaal gebrouwen. Werd tot 1975 gebrouwen door Brouwerij Tennstedt Decroes in Enghien.

Druïde Blond

Druïde by De Proefbrouwerij

6,50% 8 - 1 / 46 - 5

	top-fermentation re-fermented in the bottle	fermentation haute refermentation en bouteille	hoge gisting hergisting op de fles
	blond specialty beer	bière spéciale blonde	blond speciaalbier
	4 malt varieties, sugar, 2 hop varieties, yeast, water	4 variétés de malt, sucre, 2 sortes de houblon, levure, eau	4 moutsoorten, suiker, 2 hopsoorten, gist, water
	golden blond brilliantly clear, filtered; fine carbon dioxide bubbles and big, white foam head.	blond doré claire, brillante, filtrée, pétillement léger de gaz carbonique et grand faux col blanc.	goudblond briljant helder, gefilterd fijne koolzuurpareling e grote, witte schuimkraag.
	Full taste with pleasant bitterness and a slightly fruity aftertaste. Fresh with a hoppy character, obtained by the dry-hopping.	Saveur pleine avec un goût amer agréable et une fin de bouche légèrement fruitée. Fraîche avec caractère houblonné par le dryhopping.	Volle smaak met aangename bitterheid en licht fruitige afdronk. Fris met een hoppig karakter door dryhopping.
	Serve in the appropriate glass, with a solid foam head. The ideal thirst-quencher when served cold. At room temperature, a pleasant hop flavour with a light, spicy touch.	Verser dans le verre approprié avec un faux col solide. Rafraîchie, cette bière est un désaltérant idéal. A température de chambre, elle a un arôme houblonné agréable avec une touche légère, relevée.	Uitschenken in het bijhorende glas en voorzie van een stevige schuimkraag. Koud geschonken: ideale dorstlesser. Kamertemperatuur: aan genaam hoparoma met lichte, kruidige toets.
i	Store vertically in a cool, dark room (54 °F).	Conserver en position verticale à l'abri de la chaleur et de la lumière.	Verticaal bewaren op ee koele en donkere plaats (12 °C).

uïde by De Proefbrouwerij 6,50% 10 - 13 °C 50 - 55 °F

Druïde Bruin

D

top-fermentation re-fermented in the bottle	fermentation haute refermentation en bouteille	hoge gisting hergisting op de fles
dubbel specialty beer	bière spéciale double	dubbel speciaalbier
4 malt varieties, sugar, 2 hop varieties, yeast, water	4 variétés de malt, sucre, 2 sortes de houblon, levure, eau	4 moutsoorten, suiker, 2 hopsoorten, gist, water
clear ruby red filtered creamy foam head	rouge rubis clair filtrée faux col crémeux	helder robijnrood gefilterd romige schuimkraag
Full-bodied with a bitter aftertaste. Slightly sweet with roasted malt, bitter and dry near the end. Malt and caramel aroma.	Franche avec une fin de bouche amère. Goût légèrement doux, malt brûlé, amer et sec en fin de bouche. Arômes de malt et de caramel.	Volmondig met een bittere afdronk. Een lichte zoetigheid, gebrande mout, bitter en droog op het einde. Aroma van mout en karamel.
Serve in the corresponding glass, with a solid foam head.	Verser dans le verre approprié avec un faux col solide.	Uitschenken in het bijhorende glas en voorzien van een stevige schuimkraag.
Store vertically in a cool, dark room (54 °F).	Conserver en position verticale à l'abri de la chaleur et de la lumière.	Verticaal bewaren op een koele en donkere plaats (12 °C).

Druïde by De Proefbrouwerij

8,50% 6 - 10 / 43 - 50

top-fermentation re-fermentation in the bottle	fermentation haute refermentation en bouteille	hoge gisting hergisting op de fles
blond tripel	triple blonde	blonde tripel
malt, sugar, hops, yeast, water	malt, sucre, houblon, levure, eau	mout, suiker, hop, gist, water
gold-blond crystal-clear not filtered or pasteurised	blond doré brillant clair non filtrée, non pasteurisée	goudblond briljant helder ongefilterd, niet gepasteuriseerd
Bitter taste with a slightly fruity aftertaste.	Goût amer, avec une arrière-bouche légèrement fruitée.	Bittere smaak met een lichtfruitige afdronk.
Serve in the special glass and provide a generous foam head. Serve chilled: perfect thirst-quencher. Room temperature: pleasant hoppy aroma with slightly spicy touch.	Verser dans le verre approprié et former un faux col solide. Versée froide : altérant idéal. A température ambiante : arôme de houblon agréable avec touche légèrement relevée.	Uitschenken in het bijhorende glas en voorzien van een stevige schuimkraag. Koud geschonken: ideale dorstlesser. Kamertemperatuur: aangenaam hoparoma met lichte, kruidige toets.
Q refers to the French word 'queue' (which means cask but also butt)	Q est un clin d'œil au mot français 'queue' (dans le sens de futaille, tonneau).	Q is een knipoog naar het Franse woord 'queue' (betekent ton, fust, maar ook achterwerk)

3% 5 - 8 °C 41 - 46 °F

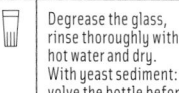

top-fermentation re-fermented in the bottle	fermentation haute refermentation en bouteille	hoge gisting nagisting in de fles
fruit beer	bière fruitée	fruitbier
with 30% blackcurrant, malt, hops, yeast, fructose, water	adjonction de 30 % de baies de cassis, malt, houblon, levure, fructose, eau	met toevoeging van 30 % zwarte cassisbessen, mout, hop, gist, fructose, water
ruby red	rouge rubis	robijnrood
Smooth, refreshing, sourish. Pronounced aroma of blackcurrant and red fruits.	Douce, rafraîchissante, acidulée. Arômes prononcés de cassis et de fruits rouges.	Zacht, verfrissend, lichtzurig. Uitgesproken aroma van cassis en rode vruchten.
Degrease the glass, rinse thoroughly with hot water and dry. With yeast sediment: revolve the bottle before serving the last third. Without yeast sediment: pour carefully and leave the sediment in the bottle.	Dégraisser les verres, bien les rincer à l'eau chaude et sécher. Avec dépôt de levure : tourner le dernier tiers de la bière avant de verser. Sans dépôt : laisser le fond dans la bouteille.	Het glas ontvetten, spoelen met warm water en drogen. Met gistbezinkel: het laatste derde van de fles walsen voor het uitschenken. Zonder gistbezinksel: voorzichtig uitschenken en de fond in de fles laten.
First top-fermenting beer with real blackcurrant. Made in collaboration with 2 farmers from Nuits Saint-Georges.	Première bière de haute fermentation avec du vrai cassis en collaboration avec 2 cultivateurs de Nuits-Saint-Georges.	Eerste bier van hoge gisting met echte cassis, in samenwerking met 2 telers uit Nuits Saint-Georges.

D

Duchesse de Bourgogne

Brouwerij Verhaeghe 6,20% 4 °C / 8 - 12 39 °F / 46 - 54

	mixed fermentation	fermentation mixte	gemengde gisting
	West-Flanders red-brown	brune-rouge de la Flandre Occidentale	Westvlaams roodbruin
	Different malt varieties, wheat, more than one year old hops, water. Lagered in oak barrels.	Différentes variétés de malt, froment, houblon suranné, eau. Conservée en fûts de chêne.	Verschillende moutsoorten, tarwe, overjaarse hop, water. Gelagerd op eikenhouten vaten.
	red-brown filtered	brun rouge filtrée	roodbruin gefilterd
	Sweet and fresh sipping beer. Fruity character, obtained by the tannins in the oak-wood barrels.	Bière de dégustation douce et fraîche. Caractère fruité par les tannins des fûts de chêne.	Zoet en fris degustatiebier. Fruitig karakter door de looistoffen van de eikenhouten vaten.
	Pour in one movement in a dry bulb jar with stem.	Verser en un seul mouvement dans un verre ballon sec sur pied.	Uitschenken in 1 beweging in een droog bolglas op voet.
i			

ouwerij Boon

5% max. 14 °C max. 57 °F

Duivels Bier

	top-fermentation re-fermented in the bottle	fermentation haute refermentation en bouteille	hoge gisting hergisting op de fles
	dark specialty beer	bière spéciale foncée	donker speciaalbier
	3 varieties of barley malt, candy sugar, leaf hops, yeast, water	3 variétés de malt d'orge, sucre candi, feuilles de houblon, levure, eau	3 soorten gerstemout, kandijsuiker, bladhop, gist, water
	dark brown	brun foncé	donkerbruin
	Specialty beer from the city of Halle since 1833.	Bière spéciale de la ville de Halle depuis 1833.	Speciaalbier van de stad Halle sinds 1833.

Dulle Griet

De Scheldebrouwerij 6,50% 7 - 9 / 45 - 48

	top-fermentation re-fermentation in the bottle	fermentation haute refermentation en bouteille	hoge gisting hergisting op de fles
	double	double	dubbel
	barley malt, aroma 150, cara 120, hops, yeast, water	malt d'orge, arôme 150, cara 120, houblon, le-vure, eau	gerstemout, aroma 150, cara 120, hop, gist, water
	dark red-brown (81 EBC) with a beige full foam head. not filtered or pasteur-ised	brun rouge foncé (81 EBC) avec un faux col plein beige non filtrée, non pasteu-risée	donker roodbruin (81 EBC) met een beige volle schuimkraag. ongefilterd, niet gepas-teuriseerd
	Modest fruity nose. Sweet liquorice taste with a bitter aftertaste. Quite fizzy on the tongue. Bitter, dry af-tertaste. 20 EBU.	Bouquet fruité discret. Goût douceâtre (ré-glisse), avec une petite amertume après coup. Un peu de picotement raisonnable sur la lan-gue. Fin de bouche un peu amère, arrière-bouche sèche. 20 EBU.	Bescheiden fruitige neus. Zoetige smaak (drop) met een bittertje achteraf. Redelijk wat prikkeling op de tong. Bitterige nasmaak, dro-ge afdronk. 20 EBU.
	'Dulle Griet' is the monu-mental, cast-iron can-non (12.250 kg) which the people from Ghent used against the Spanish back in the 16th century and from which missiles up to 295 kg were fired.	'Dulle Griet' est le canon monumental en fonte (12.250 kilos) que les Gantois utilisaient au 16e siècle contre les Es-pagnols. Il pouvait tirer des projectiles allant jusqu'à 295 kilos.	'Dulle Griet' is het monu-mentale, gietijzeren ka-non (12.250 kg) dat de Gentenaren in de 16e eeuw gebruikten tegen de Spanjaarden. Projec-tielen tot 295 kg konden ermee afgevuurd wor-den.

ouwerij De Dolle Brouwers

10% 10 - 12 °C / 50 - 54 °F

	top-fermentation re-fermented in the bottle centrifuged	fermentation haute refermentation en bouteille non centrifugée	hoge gisting nagisting op de fles niet gecentrifugeerd
	tripel	triple	tripel
	malt, white candy sugar, Golding hops	malt, sucre candi blanc, houblon Golding	mout, witte kandijsuiker, Golding hop
	light amber unfiltered	légèrement ambrée non filtrée	licht amber ongefilterd
	Stubborn, a little smoother than Arabier but fairly treacherous.	Capiteuse, un peu plus moelleux que la bière 'arabier' mais très traître!	Koppig, iets zachter dan arabier maar vrij verraderlijk!
	Serve in an Oerbeer glass or wine glass.	Dans un verre oerbier ou un verre de vin.	In een oerbierglas of wijnglas.
	The original English translation 'mad bitch' was rejected by the US FDA. In that country, it is sold under the name 'triple'. The label was designed by the Bruges artist Peter Six and redesigned by Kris Herteleer.	La traduction anglaise originale 'mad bitch' a été refusée par l'Agence Fédérale Alimentaire des Etats-Unis. La bière y est vendue sous le nom 'triple'. L'étiquette a été conçue par l'artiste brugeois Peter Six et redessinée par Kris Herteleer.	De oorspronkelijke Engelse vertaling 'mad bitch' werd geweigerd door het US Federaal Voedselagentschap. Het bier wordt in USA verkocht onder de naam tripel. Het etiket werd ontworpen door de Brugse kunstenaar Peter Six en hertekend door Kris Herteleer.

Dulle Teve

Duvel Moortgat Corporation

8,50% 6 - 10 43 - 50

top-fermentation re-fermented in the bottle	fermentation haute refermentation en bouteille	hoge gisting hergisting op de fles
specialty beer	bière spéciale	speciaalbier
barley malt, sugar, fine hop varieties, yeast, water, hops (Saaz-Saaz from the Czech Republic and Styrian Golding from Slovenia)	malt d'orge, sucre, variétés fines de houblon, levure, eau, houblon (Saaz-Saaz Tchèque et Styrian Golding de Slovénie)	gerstemout, suiker, fijne hopsoorten, gist, water, hop (Saaz-Saaz uit Tsjechië en Styrian Golding uit Slovenië)
golden blond	blond doré	goudblond
Slightly malt-sweet flavour onset that becomes hoppy and turns tart at the end. Decidely hoppy, fruity and extremely aromatic.	Saveur initiale légèrement douce-maltée, puis houblonnée et amère en fin de bouche. Bière fortement houblonnée, fruitée et extrêmement aromatique.	Licht moutzoetige smaakaanzet die hoppig wordt en uitvloeit in bitterheid. Stevig gehopt bier, fruitig en uiterst aromatisch.
The yeasts are still cultivated on the original Scottish source yeast which Albert Moortgat brought with him from Scotland in 1918. The beer boasts a unique bottling process which is responsible for the sophisticated flavour: it re-ferments for 2 weeks in hot cells and rests in cold cells for 6 weeks after that.	Les levures sont toujours cultivées à partir de la levure souche écossaise d'origine qu'Albert Moortgat ramena d'Écosse en 1918. La bière a un processus d'embouteillage unique, qui est déterminant pour le goût sophistiqué :elle refermente 2 semaines en cellules chaudes et reste ensuite au repos 6 semaines en cellules froides.	De gisten worden nog steeds gecultiveerd op de originele Schotse brongist die Albert Moortgat in 1918 meebracht uit Schotland. Het bier heeft een uniek bottelingsproces dat bepalend is voor de gesofisticeerde smaak: het hergist 2 weken in warme cellen en blijft daarna 6 weken rusten in koude cellen.

Duvel gefilterd

uvel Moortgat Corporation 7,50% 6 - 10 °C 43 - 50 °F

	top-fermentation	fermentation haute	hoge gisting
	specialty beer	bière spéciale	speciaalbier
	barley malt, sugar, fine hop varieties, yeast, water	malt d'orge, sucre, variétés fines de houblon, levure, eau	gerstemout, suiker, fijne hopsoorten, gist, water
	golden blond	blond doré	goudblond
	Light, fruity and dry aroma. Slightly alcoholic-sweet taste, thirst-quencher with a pronounced hoppy character.	Arôme léger, fruité, sec. Saveur légèrement alcoolisée, douce, désaltérante avec un caractère de houblon prononcé.	Licht, fruitig, droog aroma. Licht alcoholzoete smaak, dorstlesser met een uitgesproken hopkarakter.
	Pour into a dry glass.	Verser dans un verre sec.	Uitschenken in een droog glas.

Duvel Tripel Hop (new edition)

Duvel Moortgat Corporation 9,50%

	top-fermentation re-fermentation in the bottle	fermentation haute refermentation en bouteille	hoge gisting hergisting op de fles
	specialty beer special edition ale	bière spéciale special edition ale	speciaalbier special edition ale
	barley malt, 3 different hops (Saaz-Saaz, Styrian Golding, Amarillo), yeast, water dry-hopping with Styrian Golding	malt d'orge, 3 variétés de houblon (Saaz-Saaz, Styrian Golding, Amarillo),levure, eau dry-hopping avec Styrian Golding	gerstemout, 3 soorten hop (Saaz-Saaz, Styrian Golding, Amarillo), gist, water dry-hopping met Styrian Golding
	Rich taste pallet (mellow taste of aroma hops S. Golding, floral herbs of the Amarillo), extra hop scents with a velvety bitterness (aroma hops Saaz-Saaz) and bitter aftertaste because of the hops (especially Amarillo).	Riche palette de goûts (goût doux du houblon aromatique S. Golding, goût épicé floral de l'Amarillo), arômes houblonnés supplémentaires, avec une amertume de velours (houblon aromatique Saaz-Saaz) et une fin de bouche amère due au houblon (surtout Amarillo).	Rijk smakenpallet (milde smaak van de aromahop S. Golding, florale kruidensmaak van de Amarillo), extra hoparoma's met een fluwelen bitterheid (aromahop Saaz-Saaz) en bittere nasmaak door de hop (vooral Amarillo).
i	Inspiration for this beer was an old advertising board for Hopbier by Moortgat. The first beer from 2007 was received with such enthusiasm that the beer was brewed again.	L'inspiration pour cette bière a été un vieux panneau publicitaire pour la Hopbier de Moortgat. Le premier brassin de 2007 a reçu un tel accueil enthousiaste que la bière a connu un nouveau brassage.	De inspiratie voor dit bier was een oud reclamebord voor Hopbier van Moortgat. Het eerste brouwsel uit 2007 werd zo enthousiast onthaald dat het bier nog eens werd gebrouwen.

6,80% 6 °C 43 °F

Echt Kriekenbier

mixed fermentation	fermentation mixte	gemengde gisting
fruit beer based on red-brown	bière fruitée à base de brune rouge	fruitbier op basis van roodbruin
malt, wheat, hops, full Limburg cherries, water. Brewed with red-brown Ale. Matured in oak barrels for approximately 8 months.	Malt, froment, houblon, cerises limbourgeoises, eau. Brassée à base de ale brune-rouge. Mûrie en moyenne 8 mois en fûts de chêne.	mout, tarwe, hop, volle Limburgse krieken, water. Gebrouwen op basis van roodbruine ale. Gemiddeld 8 maanden gerijpt op eikenhouten vaten.
red filtered	rouge filtrée	rood gefilterd
Sweet, refreshing and fruity thirst-quencher.	Désaltérant doux-fraîche et fruitée.	Zoetfrisse en fruitige dorstlesser.
A tall glass with foot is recommended. Pour slowly into a tilted glass in one smooth movement, avoiding contact between bottle and glass or foam head.	Verser prudemment et en oblique en un seul mouvement fluide sans que la bouteille touche le verre ou le faux col. Un verre haut à pied est recommandé.	Voorzichtig en schuin uitschenken in 1 vlotte beweging zonder dat de fles het glas of de schuimkraag raakt. Een hoog glas op voet is aangewezen.

Eerwaarde Pater

Het Alternatief by Brouwerij De Graal

9% 10 50

	top-fermentation natural re-fermentation in the bottle not centrifuged	fermentation haute refermentation naturelle en bouteille non centrifugée	hoge gisting natuurlijke hergisting in de fles niet gecentrifugeerd
	(Western Flemish) red-brown	brune-rouge de la Flandre Occidentale	(Westvlaams) roodbruin
	cara, pilsner and chocolate malt	malt de cara, de pils et de chocolat	cara-, pils- en chocolademout
	dark-brown not pasteurised	brun foncé non pasteurisée	donkerbruin niet gepasteuriseerd
	Roasted malt, slightly tart, hints of wood, wine and port.	Malt torréfié, légèrement acidulée, impressions de bois, vin et porto.	Gebrande mout, lichtzurig, indrukken van hout, wijn en porto.
	Slowly pour into a tulip glass. Leave yeast sediment in the bottle or pour along.	Verser prudemment dans un verre tulipe. Laisser le dépôt de levure dans la bouteille ou le boire également.	Voorzichtig schenken in een tulpglas. Gistbodem in de fles laten of uitdrinken.
i	Goes really well with game, cheese and square meals. Only brewed for exports	Accompagne excellemment le gibier, le fromage et les mets forts. Uniquement brassée pour l'exportation.	Past uitstekend bij wild, kaas en stevige kost. Enkel voor export gebrouwen

	top-fermentation natural re-fermentation in the bottle	fermentation haute refermentation naturelle en bouteille	hoge gisting natuurlijke hergisting in de fles
	strong double	foncée forte	sterk donker
	malt, hops, herbs, yeasts, water	malt, houblon, herbes, levures, eau	mout, hop, kruiden, gis- ten, water
	Very aromatic.	Fort aromatique.	Zeer aromatisch.
	Brewed to mark the brewer's wedding.	'Donkere Stoere' brassée à l'occasion du mariage du brasseur.	'Donkere Stoere' ge- brouwen naar aanleiding van het huwelijk van de brouwer.

Dijk Waert
Eeuwige Liefde
Een aromatisch, bruin bier van hoge gisting, voor het eerst gebrouwen ter gelegenheid van het huwelijk van brouwmeester.
Bier Van Hoge Goesting.

Crombé by Brouwerij Strubbe

7%

	top-fermentation	fermentation haute	hoge gisting
	blond tripel	triple blonde	blonde tripel
	amber	ambrée	amber
	Zottegem triple, beer with taste evolution.	Bière triple de Zottegem avec saveur évolutive.	Zottegemse tripel, bier met smaakevolutie.
	Brewed by Brouwerij Strubbe in Ichtegem following an ancient, original recipe of Crombé.	Brassée par la Brasserie Strubbe de Ichtegem d'auprès une recette originale de Crombé.	Gebrouwen door Brouwerij Strubbe uit Ichtegem naar een oud, origineel recept van Crombé.

Elliot Brew

Struise Brouwers at Brouwerij Deca 9% 6 - 8 °C / 43 - 46 °F

top-fermentation re-fermentation in the bottle not centrifuged	fermentation haute refermentation en bouteille non centrifugée	hoge gisting hergisting in de fles niet gecentrifugeerd
Imperial IPA	Imperial IPA	Imperial IPA
slightly cloudy, intense amber with highlights of red copper, compact yellow-beige foam head not filtered or pasteurised	légèrement flou, ambré intense avec des accents de cuivre rouge, faux col compact beige jaune non filtrée, non pasteurisée	licht wazig, intens amber met highlights van rood koper, compacte geel-beige schuimkraag ongefilterd, niet gepasteuriseerd
Intense floral hoppy aroma with touches of grass, fern, flowers and pine needles. Dry malt taste, slightly fruity, very complex and full of bitter hops. Very long aftertaste that ends in a lingering freshness. 163 - 216 EBU.	Intense arôme de houblon floral, avec des touches d'herbe, de fougères, de fleurs et d'aiguilles de pin. Le goût est malté sec, légèrement fruité, fort complexe et plein de lupulines délicieuses. Très longue arrière-bouche, qui se termine par une fraîcheur brûlante. 163 - 216 EBU.	Intens floraal hoparoma met toetsen van gras, varens, bloemen en dennennaalden. De smaak is droogmoutig, licht fruitig, zeer complex en vol smakelijke hopbitters. Zeer lange afdronk die eindigt met een zinderende fraicheur. 163 - 216 EBU.
Pour out in a single movement.	Verser agilement.	Vlot uitschenken.
Probably the Belgian beer with the largest hop content.	Probablement la bière belge la plus fortement houblonnée.	Waarschijnlijk het zwaarst gehopte Belgische bier.

Embrasse

De dochter van de Korenaar

9% 10 50

	top-fermentation re-fermentation in the bottle not centrifuged	fermentation haute refermentation en bouteille non centrifugée	hoge gisting hergisting in de fles niet gecentrifugeerd
	strong double	foncée forte	sterk donker
	9 different barley and wheat malts, yeast, hops, water	9 variétés de malt d'orge et de froment, levure, houblon, eau	9 soorten gerste- en tar wemout, gist, hop, wate
	not filtered or pasteur-ised	non filtrée, non pasteu-risée	ongefilterd, niet gepas-teuriseerd
	Full malt taste, heavy beer that is situated be-tween a stout and a trap-pist.	Bière lourde pleinement maltée, qui se situe entre une stout et une trappiste.	Volmout zwaar bier dat zich situeert tussen een stout en een trappist.

Embrasse Special Edition

dochter van de Korenaar 9% 10 °C 50 °F

	top-fermentation re-fermentation in the bottle not centrifuged	fermentation haute refermentation en bouteille non centrifugée	hoge gisting hergisting in de fles niet gecentrifugeerd
	strong dubbel	foncée forte	sterk donker
	100% malt of 20°plato	malt plein à 20° platon	volmout van 20 °plato
	not filtered or pasteur-ised	non filtrée, non pasteu-risée	ongefilterd, niet gepas-teuriseerd
	Embrasse matured on wooden cask. There are 2 types: Embrasse Oak Aged and Embrasse Peated Oak Aged (winner Zythos Beer Festival 2011).	Embrasse mûrie en fût de bois. Il existe 2 va-riantes :Embrasse Oak Aged et Embrasse Pea-ted Oak Aged (gagnante du Zythos Festival de la bière 2011).	Embrasse gerijpt op houten vat. Er zijn 2 vari-anten: Embrasse Oak Aged en Embrasse Pea-ted Oak Aged (winnaar Zythos Bierfestival 2011).

Ename Blond

Brouwerij Roman 6,50% 4

	top-fermentation re-fermented in the bottle	fermentation haute refermentation en bouteille	hoge gisting nagisting op de fles
	Recognised Belgian abbey beer	Bière d'abbaye belge reconnue	Erkend Belgisch abdijbier
	barley malt, hops, sugars, yeast, well water	malt d'orge, houblon, sucres, levure, eau de source	gerstemout, hop, suikers, gist, bronwater
	blond	blonde	blond
	Strong alcoholic yet thirst-quenching. Malt-sweetish, fruity and slightly hoppy aroma. Well-balanced taste with pronounced, pleasant hoppy bitterness.	Très alcoolisée mais rafraîchissante. Doux-maltée, fruitée et arôme légèrement houblonné. Saveur équilibrée avec un accent sur l'amertume houblonnée agréable.	Sterk alcoholisch maar toch dorstlessend. Moutzoetig, fruitig en licht hoppig aroma. Uitgebalanceerde smaak met nadruk op aangena me hopbitterheid.
	Pour carefully in a single, smooth movement and leave the yeast sediment in the bottle.	Verser prudemment en un mouvement fluide et laisser le dépôt de levure dans la bouteille.	Voorzichtig uitschenke in 1 vlotte beweging en de gistfond in de fles la ten.
	Store in a dark, cool room.	Conserver à l'abri de la lumière et de la chaleur.	Donker en koel bewarer

Ename Cuvée 974

uwerij Roman

7% | 6 °C / 43 °F

top-fermentation re-fermented in the bottle	fermentation haute refermentation en bouteille	hoge gisting nagisting op de fles
Recognised Belgian abbey beer	Bière d'abbaye belge reconnue	Erkend Belgisch abdijbier
barley malt, hops, sugars, yeast, herbs, well water	malt d'orge, houblon, sucres, levure, eau de source	gerstemout, hop, suikers, gist, kruiden, bronwater
amber-red	rouge ambré	amberrood
Winter beer with an aroma of malt, vanilla and berries. Fruity taste of sweetish caramel and smooth bitterness.	Bière hivernale avec un arôme de malt, de vanille et de groseilles. Saveur fruitée de caramel doux, amertume douce.	Winterbier met een aroma van mout, vanille en bessen. Fruitige smaak van zoetig karamel en zachte bitterheid.
Pour carefully in a single, smooth movement and leave the yeast sediment in the bottle.	Verser prudemment en un mouvement fluide et laisser le dépôt de levure dans la bouteille.	Voorzichtig uitschenken in 1 vlotte beweging en de gistfond in de fles laten.
Store in a dark, cool room.	Conserver à l'abri de la lumière et de la chaleur.	Donker en koel bewaren.

Ename Dubbel

Brouwerij Roman 6,50% 4

	top-fermentation re-fermented in the bottle	fermentation haute refermentation en bouteille	hoge gisting nagisting op de fles
	Recognised Belgian abbey beer	Bière d'abbaye belge reconnue	Erkend Belgisch abdijbier
	barley malt, hops, candy sugar, yeast, well water	malt d'orge, houblon, sucre candi, levure, eau de source	gerstemout, hop, kandijsuiker, gist, bronwater
	dark red-brown	brun rouge foncé	donkerrood bruin
	Aroma of caramelized malt and sweetened fruit. Caramel taste of roasted malt and smooth, hoppy bitterness	Arôme de malt caramélisé et de fruit sucré. Goût caramélisé de malt grillé et goût amer doux, houblonné.	Aroma van gekaramelli seerde mout en gezoet fruit. Karamelsmaak va geroosterde mout en zachte, hoppige bitterheid.
	Pour carefully, avoiding contact between bottle and foam head. Leave the yeast sediment in the bottle.	Verser prudemment sans que la bouteille touche le faux col et laisser le dépôt de levure dans la bouteille.	Voorzichtig uitschenke zonder dat de fles de schuimkraag raakt en d gistfond in de fles late
	Store in a dark, cool room.	Conserver à l'abri de la lumière et de la chaleur.	Donker en koel beware

uwerij Roman

8,50% 6 °C 43 °F

Ename Tripel

top-fermentation re-fermented in the bottle	fermentation haute refermentation en bouteille	hoge gisting nagisting op de fles
Recognised Belgian abbey beer	Bière belge d'abbaye reconnue	Erkend Belgisch abdijbier
barley malt, hops, sugars, yeast, well water	malt d'orge, houblon, sucres, levure, eau de source	gerstemout, hop, suikers, gist, bronwater
blond	blonde	blond
Smoothly malty, slightly spicy, fruity and alcoholic flavour. Spicy, malty taste with smoothly bitter, alcoholic aftertaste.	Houblonné-douce, légèrement relevée, arôme fruité et alcoolisé. Goût relevé, malté avec une fin de bouche moelleuse-amère alcoolisée.	Zacht moutig, licht kruidig, fruitig en alcoholisch aroma. Pittige, moutige smaak met zachtbittere alcoholische afdronk.
Pour carefully in one, smooth movement and leave the yeast sediment in the bottle.	Verser prudemment en un mouvement fluide et laisser le dépôt de levure dans la bouteille.	Voorzichtig uitschenken in 1 vlotte beweging en de gistfond in de fles laten.
Store in a dark, cool room.	Conserver à l'abri de la lumière et de la chaleur.	Donker en koel bewaren.

Enfant Terriple

Brouwerij De Leite

8,20% 4 - 39 -

	top-fermentation re-fermentation in the bottle not centrifuged	fermentation haute refermentation en bouteille non centrifugée	hoge gisting hergisting in de fles niet gecentrifugeerd
	tripel	triple	tripel
	not filtered, pasteurised	non filtrée, pasteurisée	ongefilterd, gepasteu-seerd
	'Devilishly' sunny and fresh with a playful nose. Fine bitterness with subtle citrus touch enveloped by a simple spicy malt taste. Pleasant bitterness that lingers.	'Diablement' ensoleillée et fraîche, avec un bouquet plein de fantaisie. Une fine amertume, avec une touche de citrus d'une finesse légère couronnée par un goût malté sobrement épicé. Agréable amertume qui persiste longtemps.	'Duivels' zonnig en fris met een speelse neus. Fijne bitterheid met lichtfijne citrustoets omkranst door een sob kruidige moutsmaak. Aangename bitterheid die lang blijft.
	Serve in a Münich glass.	Verser dans un verre Münich.	Uitschenken in een Münichglas.
	'Femme Fatale' and 'Bonne Homme' have their first baby 'Enfant Terriple' (play on words 'enfant terrible'). 'Unpredictably' playful beer. The label was designed by Robin Vermeersch.	'Femme Fatale' et 'Bon Homme' reçoivent un 1er enfant, 'Enfant Terriple' (jeu de mots sur tripel et terrible). Une bière pleine de fantaisie 'imprévisible'. L'étiquette a été créée par Robin Vermeersch.	'Femme Fatale' en 'Bonne Homme' krijgen een 1e kindje 'Enfant Terriple' (woordspeling van tripel en terrible). Een 'onvoorspelbaar' speels bier. Het etiket werd ontworpen door Robin Vermeersch.

Enghien Noël

asserie de Silly

9% (20° plato) | 5 - 8 °C 41 - 46 °F

	top-fermentation re-fermented in the bottle	fermentation haute refermentation en bouteille	hoge gisting hergisting op de fles
	tripel regional beer Christmas beer	bière régionale triple bière de Noël	tripel streekbier kerstbier
	pale malt, sugar, yeast, Kent and Hallertau hops, water	malt pâle, sucre, levure, houblon Kent et Haller-tau, eau	bleke mout, suiker, gist, Kent en Hallertauhop, water
	blond (10,2 EBC)	blonde (10,2 EBC)	blond (10,2 EBC)
	A combination of fresh-ness, warmth and pleas-ant bitterness. Covers the palate from the first sip, developing a re-freshing vanilla flavour with a touch of pepper.	Une combinaison de fraîcheur et de chaleur avec une amertume agréable. Recouvre le palais dès la première gorgée et déploie un goût de vanille rafraî-chissant avec une pointe de poivre.	Een combinatie van fris-heid en warmte met aan-gename bitterheid. Bedekt het gehemelte vanaf de eerste slok en ontplooit een verfris-sende vanillesmaak met een vleugje peper.
	Provision beer.	Bière à conserver.	Bewaarbier.

E Equinox

Brasserie de la Senne

8% 12 54

	top-fermentation natural re-fermentation in the bottle not centrifuged	fermentation haute refermentation en bouteille non centrifugée	hoge gisting natuurlijke hergisting in de fles niet gecentrifugeerd
	strong dubbel	fonceé forte	sterk bruin
	malt, yeast, hops, sugar (during boiling), water	malt, levure, houblon, sucre (en chaudière), eau	mout, gist, hop, suiker (tijdens koken), water
	dark brown with dense and fine foam head not filtered or pasteurised	brun foncé avec faux col dense et fin non filtrée, non pasteurisée	donkerbruin met dichte en fijne schuimkraag ongefilterd, niet gepasteuriseerd
	Punchy and complex beer, distinctly malty with light chocolate touch and roast flavour. First smooth but then rather dry. Develops a pleasant bitterness.	Bière forte et complexe, caractère malté prononcé, avec une légère touche de chocolat et un rien de brûlé. D'abord rond mais ensuite assez sec. Développe une agréable amertume.	Krachtig en complex bier, uitgesproken moutkarakter met lichte chocoladetoets en ietsje gebrand. Eerst rond maar daarna vrij droog. Ontwikkelt een aangename bitterheid.
	Pour carefully and leave 1 cm (yeast) in the bottle. Finish yeast separately, if you prefer.	Verser prudemment et laisser 1 cm (de levure) dans la bouteille. Boire éventuellement la levure séparément.	Voorzichtig uitschenken en 1 cm (gist) in de fles laten. Gist eventueel afzonderlijk uitdrinken.
i			

5,20% 3 °C 37 °F

Estaminet Premium Pils

	top-fermentation re-fermentation in the bottle centrifuged	fermentation haute refermentation en bouteille centrifugée	hoge gisting hergisting in de fles gecentrifugeerd
	Premium pilsner	Premium pils	Premium pils
	100% summer barley, yeast, Saaz hops, water	100% orge d'été, levure, houblon Saaz, eau	100% zomergerst, gist, Saaz-hop, water
	filtered, pasteurised	filtrée, pasteurisée	gefilterd, gepasteuriseerd
	Serve in a luxury flute glass.	Verser dans une flûte de luxe.	Uitschenken in een luxe fluitglas.
	Gold medal in the Lager category at 'Brewing Industry International Awards 2011' in UK. The beer matures for six weeks following slow and traditional bottom-fermentation.	Médaille d'or en catégorie Lager aux 'Brewing Industry International Awards 2011' au Royaume-Uni. La bière mûrit 6 semaines après une lente et traditionnelle fermentation basse.	Gouden medaille categorie Lager bij 'Brewing Industry International Awards 2011' in UK. Het bier rijpt 6 weken na een trage en traditionele lage gisting.

Eupener

Brouwerij Haacht 5%

	bottom-fermentation	fermentation basse	lage gisting
	premium pilsner	pils premium	premium pils
	barley malt, hops, water	malt d'orge, houblon, eau	gerstemout, hop, water
	clear and light blond foam head with fine bubbles filtered	blond clair, limpide faux col avec des bulles fines filtrée	helder en lichtblond; schuimkraag met fijne bellen gefilterd
	Pour carefully into a rinsed, wet bulb jar avoiding contact between bottle and foam head.	Verser prudemment dans un verre mouillé sans que la bouteille touche l'écume.	Voorzichtig uitschenken in een gespoeld, nat kogelglas zonder dat de fles het schuim raakt.
	Typical Eupener Bier brewed following the German Reinheitsgebot. This is a regulation from 1516 stating that only pure malt, noble hops, yeast and water must be used in the brewing process.	Bière typique d'Eupen brassée selon le 'Reinheitsgebot' allemand (ordonnance de 1516) prévoyant que seulement du malt pur, du houblon sélectionné, de la levure et de l'eau peuvent être utilisés pendant le brassage.	Typisch Eupener Bier gebrouwen volgens het Duitse Reinheitsgebot (verordening uit 1516) waarbij alleen zuivere mout, edele hop, gist en water mogen worden gebruikt tijdens het brouwproces.

4,70% 3 °C 37 °F

Export 8

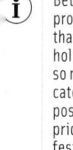

bottom-fermentation centrifuged	fermentation basse centrifugée	lage gisting gecentrifugeerd
Dortmunder	Dortmunder	Dortmunder
barley malt, corn, hops, water	malt d'orge, maïs, houblon, eau	gerstemout, mais, hop, water
clear pale blond with foam head with fine bubbles; filtered	limpide blond clair avec faux col à bulles fines ; filtrée	helder lichtblond met een fijnbellige schuimkraag; gefilterd
More mellow onset than the traditional pilsner. Real session beer owing to the dry, very thirst-quenching aftertaste, combined with a relatively low alcohol content.	Approche initiale plus douce que pour une pils classique. Facilement buvable grâce à l'arrière-bouche sèche, fort désaltérante, combinée avec une teneur en alcool relativement faible.	Zachtere aanzet dan een klassieke pils. Echt doordrinkbier door de droge, zeer dorstlessende afdronk gecombineerd met een relatief laag alcoholgehalte.
See Adler	voir Adler	zie Adler
Between 1925 and approx. '75 very popular thanks to its lower alcohol content. Lower % also means lower excise category, which impacts positively on the selling price. Is often served at festivals and fairs. Typically bottled in 33 cl.	Très populaire , des années 1925 à ca '75, du fait de sa teneur en alcool assez faible. Un % assez faible voulait aussi dire une catégorie d'accises plus basse, avec une influence positive sur le prix de vente. Cette bière était fréquemment servie lors de fêtes populaires et de kermesses. Typiquement embouteillée en 33 cl.	Van 1925 tot ca. '75 zeer populair door zijn lager alcoholgehalte. Lager % betekende ook lagere accijnscategorie wat de verkoopprijs positief beïnvloedde. Werd vaak geschonken op volksfeesten en kermissen. Typisch gebotteld in 33 cl.

Ezel Bruin

Brouwerij Bavik 6,50% 6 - 8 / 43 - 46

	top-fermentation	fermentation haute	hoge gisting
	dark amber	ambreé foncé	donker amber
	barley malt, hops, yeast, fine herbs, pure well water	malt d'orge, houblon, levure, fines herbes, eau de source pure	gerstemout, hop, gist, fijne kruiden, zuiver bronwater
	light brown slightly cloudy	brun clair légèrement trouble	lichtbruin licht troebel
	Solid with a pronounced fruity aroma. Full-bodied and fruity character.	Solide avec un arôme fruité prononcé. Caractère franc et fruité.	Stevig met een uitgesproken fruitig aroma. Volmondig en fruitig karakter.
	Pour into a degreased, rinsed and wet glass, avoiding any contact between bottle and foam.	Verser dans un verre dégraissé, rincé et mouillé sans que la bouteille touche le faux col.	Uitschenken in een ontvet, gespoeld en nat glas zonder dat de fles het schuim raakt.

Ezel Wit

rouwerij Bavik

5,80% 4 - 6 °C 39 - 43 °F

top-fermentation	fermentation haute	hoge gisting
witbier amber-coloured	bière blanche ambrée	witbier amberkleurig
barley malt, hops, yeast, wheat, pure well water	malt d'orge, houblon, levure, froment, eau de source pure	gerstemout, hop, gist, tarwe, zuiver bronwater
pale-yellow amber slightly cloudy	ambré jaune pâle légèrement trouble	bleekgeel amber licht troebel
Creamy and smooth, but with a spicy aftertaste. Full and solid character.	Crémeuse et douce mais corsée en fin de bouche. Caractère plein et solide.	Romig en zacht maar toch pittig in de afdronk. Vol en stevig karakter.
Pour into a degreased, rinsed and wet glass avoiding contact between bottle and foam.	Verser dans un verre dégraissé, rincé et mouillé sans que la bouteille touche le faux col.	Uitschenken in een ontvet, gespoeld en nat glas zonder dat de fles het schuim raakt.

Fancy Low Alcohol

Brouwerij Bavik 1% 2 - 4 / 36 - 39

	bottom-fermentation centrifuged	fermentation basse centrifugée	lage gisting gecentrifugeerd
	low-alcohol	bière pauvre en alcool	alcoholarm
	barley malt, corn, hops, yeast, pure spring water	malt d'orge, maïs, houblon, levure, eau minérale	gerstemout, mais, hop, gist, zuiver bronwater
	pale yellow, clear filtered, pasteurised	jaune clair, limpide filtrée, pasteurisée	lichtgeel, helder gefilterd, gepasteuriseerd
	Soft, refreshing taste with a light, pleasant bitterness. Ideal refreshing, low-alcohol session beer.	Goût doux, rafraîchissant, avec une légère amertume agréable. Bière facilement buvable idéale, rafraîchissante, pauvre en alcool.	Zachte, verfrissende smaak met een lichte aangename bitterheid. Ideale verfrissende, alcoholarme doordrinker.
	Pour into a clean, degreased glass, avoiding contact with the foam.	Verser dans un verre dégraissé rincé sans que la bouteille touche l'écume.	Uitschenken in een ontvet gespoeld glas zonder dat de fles het schuim raakt.
i			

asserie Fantôme

8%

	top-fermentation	fermentation haute	hoge gisting
	malt, hops, yeast, sugar, herbs, water	malt, houblon, levure, sucre, herbes, eau	mout, hop, gist, suiker, kruiden, water

Fantôme BBB Dark White

Brasserie Fantôme 4,50%

	top-fermentation	fermentation haute	hoge gisting
	Belgian Ale	ale belge	Belgian ale
	with herbs (including black pepper)	contient des herbes (e.a. du poivre noir)	bevat kruiden (o.a. zwarte peper)
	Serve in a Trappist or tulip-shaped glass.	Verser dans un verre trappiste ou tulipe.	Uitschenken in een trappist- of tulpglas.
	BBB refers to the website www.babblebelt.com, of The Burgundian Babble Belt, an international community of Belgian beer lovers.	BBB fait référence au site web www.babblebelt.com du Burgundian Babble Belt, une communauté internationale d'amateurs de bières belges.	BBB verwijst naar de website www.babblebelt.com van The Burgundian Babble Belt, een internationale community van Belgisch-bierfanaten.

8%

Fantôme Black Ghost

	top-fermentation	fermentation haute	hoge gisting
	Belgian strong Ale	Belgian strong Ale	Belgian strong ale
	barley malt, hops, yeast, water	malt d'orge, houblon, levure, eau	gerstemout, hop, gist, water
	Serve in a Trappist or tulip-shaped glass.	Verser dans un verre trappiste ou tulipe.	Uitschenken in een trappist- of tulpglas.
	The Fantôme beers are hard to come by in Belguim. Even the brewer heardly has them in stock.	Les bières de la brasserie Fantôme sont difficiles à trouver en Belgique, même le brasseur a peu de stock.	De bieren van Fantôme zijn in België heel moeilijk te vinden, zelfs de brouwer heeft weinig op voorraad.

Fantôme Eté

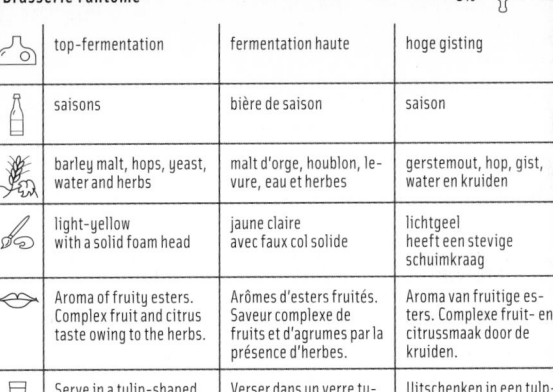

Brasserie Fantôme 8%

	top-fermentation	fermentation haute	hoge gisting
	saisons	bière de saison	saison
	barley malt, hops, yeast, water and herbs	malt d'orge, houblon, levure, eau et herbes	gerstemout, hop, gist, water en kruiden
	light-yellow with a solid foam head	jaune claire avec faux col solide	lichtgeel heeft een stevige schuimkraag
	Aroma of fruity esters. Complex fruit and citrus taste owing to the herbs.	Arômes d'esters fruités. Saveur complexe de fruits et d'agrumes par la présence d'herbes.	Aroma van fruitige esters. Complexe fruit- en citrussmaak door de kruiden.
	Serve in a tulip-shaped glass (cfr. Duvel).	Verser dans un verre tulipe (voir Duvel).	Uitschenken in een tulpglas (cfr. Duvel).

ouwerij Boon

4% 8 °C 46 °F

	spontaneous fermentation	fermentation spontanée	spontane gisting
	faro	faro	faro
	barley malt, wheat, candy sugar, sweeteners. Mixture of old Lambic and Meerts beer.	malt d'orge, froment, sucre candi, édulcorant. Mélange de vieille lambic et de bière Meerts.	gerstemout, tarwe, kandijsuiker, zoetstof. Mengeling van oude lambiek en Meerts bier.
	pale brown (owing to the candy sugar)	brun clair (par le sucre candi)	lichtbruin (door de kandijsuiker)
	Sweet-and-sour.	Doux-acide.	Zoetzuur.
	In a Gueuze or Faro glass.	Dans un verre gueuze ou faro.	In een geuze- of faro-glas.
i			

Faro Boon

Faro Girardin

Brouwerij Girardin 5% 4 - 6 / 39 - 43

	spontaneous fermentation centrifuged	fermentation spontanée centrifugée	spontane gisting gecentrifugeerd
	faro	faro	faro
	barley malt, wheat, hops, caramel, sucralose, water	malt d'orge, froment, houblon, caramel, sucralose, eau	gerstemout, tarwe, hop, caramel, sucralose, water
	clear amber-coloured with light foam head filtered, not pasteurised	limpide ambré avec faux col léger filtrée, non pasteurisée	helder amberkleurig met lichte schuimkraag gefilterd, niet gepasteuriseerd
	Slightly tart (lambic) with a slightly fruity soft-sweet touch. Thirst-quenching.	Quelque peu acidulé (lambic), avec une touche doucement sucrée légèrement fruitée. Désaltérante.	Ietwat zurig (lambiek) met een licht fruitige zachtzoete toets. Dorstlessend.
	In a Gueuze or Faro glass.	Dans un verre gueuze ou faro.	In een geuze- of faroglas.
	Ideal with stew dishes.	Accompagne excellemment les plats de viande en daube.	Past uitstekend bij stoofvleesgerechten.

Faro Lambic Lindemans

uwerij Lindemans | 4,50% | 3 - 4 °C / 37 - 39 °F

spontaneous fermentation	fermentation spontanée	spontane gisting
faro lambic	faro lambic	faro lambiek
malt, wheat, hops, candy sugar, water	malt, froment, houblon, sucre candi, eau	mout, tarwe, hop, kandijsuiker, water
pearl-brown clear	brun perlé claire	parelbruin helder
Sweet-and-sour and thirst-quenching. Sweet taste of candy with slightly sourish aftertaste.	Aigre-douce et désaltérante. Saveur douce de candi avec une fin de bouche douce, acidulée.	Zoetzuur en dorstlessend. Zoete smaak van kandij met zachtzurige afdronk.
Pour into a pint jug.	Verser dans une chope.	In een pintglas uitschenken.
Goes nicely with many desserts.	Convient avec beaucoup de desserts.	Past bij vele desserts.

Fasso Blond

Brouwerij Vissenaken 6,50% 8 - 12 / 46 - 54

top-fermentation re-fermented in the bottle	fermentation haute refermentation en bouteille	hoge gisting hergisting op de fles
blond	blonde	blond
barley malt, wheat malt, hops, sugar, yeast, brewing water. Boutique beer.	malt d'orge et de froment, houblon, sucre, levure, eau de brassage. Brassage artisanal.	gerstemout, tarwemout, hop, suiker, gist, brouwwater. Ambachtelijk gebrouwen.
blond cloudy (unfiltered)	blonde trouble (non filtrée)	blond troebel (ongefilterd)
Savoury thirst-quencher. Bitter beer with a full malt taste and an exotic, fruity aroma.	Désaltérant savoureuse. Bière plutôt amère avec un goût malté plein et un arôme fruité exotique.	Smaakvolle dorstlesser. Bitterig bier met een volle moutsmaak en een exotisch-fruitig aroma.
Pour slowly into a bulb jar, with or without yeast sediment.	Verser lentement dans un verre ballon, avec ou sans dépôt de levure.	Langzaam inschenken in een bolvormig glas, met of zonder gist.
Store upright at cellar temperature. The taste is at its best three months after the bottling date.	Conserver en position verticale à température de cave. Ce n'est que 3 mois après la mise en bouteilles que la saveur arrive à son sommet.	Rechtop bewaren op keldertemperatuur. Pas 3 maanden na botteldatum is de smaak geëvolueerd tot op zijn best.

rysse by Brouwerij Verhaeghe

4,80% | 4 °C 39 °F

	top-fermentation centrifuged	fermentation haute centrifugée	hoge gisting gecentrifugeerd
	Oudenaarde brown	bière brune d'Oude-naarde	Oudenaards bruin
	pilsner and roasted malt, hops (Golding and Saaz), house yeast, water. Combination of young and mature beers.	malt de pils et malt torréfié, houblon (Golding et Saaz), levure maison, eau. Coupage de jeunes et de vieilles bières.	pilsner en geroosterde mout, hop (Golding en Saaz), huisgist, water. Versnijding van jonge en oude bieren.
	brown with a dense foam head filtered	brun avec faux col compact filtrée	bruin met hechte schuimkraag gefilterd
	Soft bitter beer. Mellow in the mouth in combination with a complex caramel flavour and a wine-like touch.	Bière doucement acide. Sensation douce en bouche, en combinaison avec un goût de caramel complexe et une touche vineuse.	Zacht zuur bier. Zacht mondgevoel in combinatie met een complexe karamelsmaak en een vineuze toets.
	Serve chilled.	La mettre un peu au réfrigérateur avant de la servir.	Voor het serveren even in de koelkast plaatsen.

Felix Speciaal

Femme Fatale

Brouwerij De Leite 6,50% 4 - 1 / 39 - 5

	top-fermentation re-fermentation in the bottle not centrifuged	fermentation haute refermentation en bouteille non centrifugée	hoge gisting hergisting in de fles niet gecentrifugeerd
	amber or speciale belge	ambrée ou spéciale belge	amber of speciale belge
	2 malt types, 2 different hops, spices, yeast, water	2 variétés de malt, 2 variétés de houblon, herbes, levure, eau	2 moutsoorten, 2 hopsoorten, kruiden, gist, water
	pale amber-coloured with a nice white foam head not filtered, pasteurised	limpide ambré avec un faux col joli blanc non filtrée, pasteurisée	licht amberkleurig met een mooie witte schuimkraag ongefilterd, gepasteuriseerd
	Mellow, malt taste and full-bodied. The bitter hop taste is balanced out by a soft, fine slightly tart citrus touch. Malty aroma with fruity touches that turn slightly bitter.	Douce, maltée et franche. Le goût amer houblonné est arrondi par une douce touche fine de citrus légèrement acidulée. Arôme malté, avec des touches fruitées qui deviennent légèrement amères.	Zacht, moutig en vol. De hopbittere smaak wordt afgerond met een zachte, fijne lichtzurige citrustoets. Moutig aroma met fruitige toetsen die licht bitter worden.
	Serve in a Münich glass.	Verser dans un verre Münich.	Uitschenken in een Münichglas.
	Name and label designed by artist Rik Vermeersch. Brewery's first beer	Le nom et l'étiquette ont été conçus par l'artiste Rik Vermeersch. Première bière de la brasserie.	Naam en etiket zijn bedacht door kunstenaar Rik Vermeersch. Eerste bier van de brouwerij

Dochter van de Korenaar

8,50% — 8 °C / 46 °F

top-fermentation re-fermentation in the bottle not centrifuged	fermentation haute refermentation en bouteille non centrifugée	hoge gisting hergisting in de fles niet gecentrifugeerd
multigrain tripel	triple trois céréales	driegranentripel
barley malt, wheat malt, rye malt, yeast, hops water	malt d'orge, malt de froment, malt de seigle, levure, houblon, eau	gerstemout, tarwemout, roggemout, gist, hop, water
not filtered or pasteurised	non filtrée, non pasteurisée	ongefilterd, niet gepasteuriseerd
Slightly hoppy aroma. Malty flavour. Quite sweet, spicy with a hint of caramel.	Arôme légèrement houblonné. Goût malté. Plutôt sucrée, épicée, un peu de caramel.	Licht hoppig aroma. Moutige smaak. Tamelijk zoet, kruidig, wat karamel.
Matured on pinetree resin.	Mûrie dans de la résine de pin.	Gerijpt op pijnboomhars.

Floreffe Blonde

Brasserie Lefebvre 6,30% 2- 39-4

	top-fermentation centrifuged	fermentation haute centrifugée	hoge gisting gecentrifugeerd
	Recognised Belgian abbey beer blond	Bière d'abbaye belge reconnue blonde	Erkend Belgisch Abdijbier blond
	barley malt, hops, candy sugar, yeast, water	malt d'orge, sucre candi, houblon, levure, eau	gerstemout, hop, kandijsuiker, gist, water
	clear unpasteurised	claire non pasteurisée	helder niet gepasteuriseerd
	Malty beer with a subtle balance between bitter (hops) and fruity scents owing to fermentation.	Bière maltée avec un subtil équilibre entre une amertume houblonnée et les parfums fruités de la fermentation.	Moutig bier met een subtiel evenwicht tusse hopbitter en fruitige parfums van de gisting.
	Pour into a goblet.	Verser dans un verre ballon.	Uitschenken in een ballonglas.

sserie Lefebvre 6,30% 4 - 7 °C 39 - 45 °F

Floreffe Double

top-fermentation centrifuged	fermentation haute centrifugée	hoge gisting gecentrifugeerd
recognised Belgian abbey beer brown	Bière d'abbaye belge reconnue brune	Erkend Belgisch Abdijbier bruin
barley malt, hops, candy sugar, yeast, water	malt d'orge, houblon, sucre candi, levure, eau	gerstemout, hop, kandijsuiker, gist, water
brown unpasteurised	brune non pasteurisée	bruin niet gepasteuriseerd
Aromatic malt flavours owing to the considered dosage of the malt varieties.	Goût malté aromatique grâce au dosage bien étudié des variétés de malt.	Aromatische moutsmaak door de uitgekiende dosering van de moutsoorten.
Pour into a goblet.	Verser dans un verre ballon.	Uitschenken in een ballonglas.

Floreffe Prima Melior

Brasserie Lefebvre 8% 4 - / 39 - 4

	top-fermentation naturally re-fermented in the bottle centrifuged	fermentation haute refermenation naturelle en bouteille centrifugée	hoge gisting natuurlijke hergisting i de fles gecentrifugeerd
	recognised Belgian abbey beer brown	Bière d'abbaye belge reconnue brune	Erkend Belgisch Abdijbier bruin
	barley malt, roasted malt, hops, candy sugar, yeast, herbs, water	malt d'orge, malt torréfié, houblon, sucre candi, levure, herbes, eau	gerstemout, gebrande mout, hop, kandijsuiker, gist, kruiden, water
	very dark brown unpasteurised	brun très foncé non pasteurisée	zeer donkerbruin niet gepasteuriseerd
	Smooth and slightly bitter. Changing, deep taste influenced by the special malt types and spices. Flavour of anise and spices.	Moelleuse et légèrement amère. Saveur évolutive et profonde renvoyant aux variétés spéciales de malt et d'herbes. Arôme d'anis et d'herbes.	Zacht en licht bitter. Evoluerende, diepe sma die refereert naar de speciale moutsoorten e de kruiden. Aroma van anijs en kruide
	Place the bottle upright 48 hours before serving. Pour into a glass with a stem.	Mettre la bouteille en position verticale 48 heures avant la dégustation. Verser dans un verre à pied.	De fles 48 uren voor het degusteren verticaal zetten. Uitschenken in een glas met voet.
i			

sserie Lefebvre

8% 4 - 8 °C 39 - 46 °F

Floreffe Triple

top-fermentation naturally re-fermented in the bottle centrifuged	fermentation haute refermenation naturelle en bouteille centrifugée	hoge gisting natuurlijke hergisting in de fles gecentrifugeerd
Recognised Belgian abbey beer tripel	Bière d'abbaye belge reconnue triple	Erkend Belgisch Abdijbier tripel
barley malt, hops, candy sugar, yeast, water	malt d'orge, houblon, sucre candi, levure, eau	gerstemout, hop, kandijsuiker, gist, water
slightly hazy if served cold amber	légèrement voilé si servie froide ambrée	licht gesluierd indien koud geserveerd amber
Smouth, lemony tartness with a slight touch of caramel owing to the candy sugar.	Amertume souple, citronnée, avec une légère touche de caramel due au sucre candi.	Soepele, citroenachtige bitterheid met een lichte karameltoets door de kandijsuiker.
Pour into a glass with a stem and leave the yeast sediment in the bottle.	Verser dans un verre à pied et laisser le dépôt de levure dans la bouteille.	Uitschenken in een glas met voet en het gistdepot in de fles laten.
Store the bottles upright.	Conserver les bouteilles en position verticale.	De flessen verticaal bewaren.

Florilège de Pensée

Brasserie d'Ecaussinnes

9% 4 - 39 - 4

	top-fermentation natural re-fermentation in the bottle	fermentation haute refermentation naturelle en bouteille	hoge gisting natuurlijke hergisting i de fles
	fruit and flower beer	bière fruitée et de fleurs	fruit- en bloemenbier
	malt, hops, yeast, spring water, fruits, flowers, herbs	malt, houblon, levure, eau minérale, fruits, fleurs, herbes	mout, hop, gist, bronw ter, vruchten, bloemen kruiden
	blond-orange not filtered	blond orange non filtrée	blond-oranje ongefilterd
	Brewed in tandem with 'Les Vignerons des Fleurs' in Soignies.	Brassée en collaboration avec 'Les Vignerons des Fleurs' à Soignies.	Gebrouwen in samen-werking met 'Les Vigne rons des Fleurs' in Soignies.

9% 4 - 6 °C 39 - 43 °F

Florilège de Rose

	top-fermentation natural re-fermentation in the bottle	fermentation haute refermentation naturelle en bouteille	hoge gisting natuurlijke hergisting in de fles
	fruit and flower beer	bière fruitée et de fleurs	fruit- en bloemenbier
	malt, hops, yeast, spring water, fruits, flowers, herbs	malt, houblon, levure, eau minérale, fruits, fleurs, herbes	mout, hop, gist, bronwater, vruchten, bloemen, kruiden
	not filtered	non filtrée	ongefilterd
	Brewed in tandem with 'Les Vignerons des Fleurs' in Soignies.	Brassée en collaboration avec 'Les Vignerons des Fleurs' à Soignies.	Gebrouwen in samenwerking met 'Les Vignerons des Fleurs' in Soignies.

Florilège de Sureau

Brasserie d'Ecaussinnes

9% 4 - 6 39 - 43

	top-fermentation re-fermentation in the bottle	fermentation haute refermentation en bouteille	hoge gisting hergisting in de fles
	fruit and flower beer	bière fruitée et de fleurs	fruit- en bloemenbier
	malt, hops, yeast, spring water, fruits, flowers, herbs	malt d'orge, houblon, levure, fruits, fleurs, herbes	mout, hop, gist, bronwater, vruchten, bloemen, kruiden

sserie d'Ecaussinnes

9% — 4 - 6 °C / 39 - 43 °F

Florilège d'Hibiscus

top-fermentation natural re-fermentation in the bottle	fermentation haute refermentation naturelle en bouteille	hoge gisting natuurlijke hergisting in de fles
fruit and flower beer	bière fruitée et de fleurs	fruit- en bloemenbier
malt, hops, yeast, spring water, fruits, flowers, herbs	malt, houblon, levure, eau minérale, fruits, fleurs, herbes	mout, hop, gist, bronwater, vruchten, bloemen, kruiden
burgundy not filtered	rouge bordeaux non filtrée	bordeauxrood ongefilterd
Brewed in tandem with 'Les Vignerons des Fleurs' in Soignies.	Brassée en collaboration avec 'Les Vignerons des Fleurs' à Soignies.	Gebrouwen in samenwerking met 'Les Vignerons des Fleurs' in Soignies.

Floris Apple

Brouwerij Huyghe 3,60% 3

	top-fermentation	fermentation haute	hoge gisting
	witbier with fruit	bière blanche fruitée	witbier met fruit
	60% barley malt, 40% wheat, apple juice (30%), hops, yeast, natural fruit flavouring, water,coriander, orange rind.	60% malt d'orge, 40% froment, jus de pommes (30%), houblon, levure, arôme naturel de fruits, eau, coriandre, écorce d'orange	60 % gerstemout, 40 % tarwe, appelsap (30%), hop, gist, natuurlijk fruitaroma, water, koriander, sinaasschil.
	yellow	jaune	geel
	Serve in a fluteglass.	Verser dans une flûte.	Uitschenken in een fluit glas.

uwerij Huyghe 4,20% 4 °C 39 °F

Floris Chocolat

top-fermentation	fermentation haute	hoge gisting
witbier with chocolate	bière blanche au chocolat	witbier met chocolade
60% barley malt, 40% wheat, chocolate, hops, yeast, aroma, water, coriander, orange rind	60% malt d'orge, 40% froment, chocolat, houblon, levure, arômes, eau, coriandre, écorce d'orange	60 % gerstemout, 40 % tarwe, chocolade, hop, gist, aroma, water, koriander, sinaasschil
chestnut cloudy	marron trouble	kastanjebruin troebel
Bitter with a pronounced fondant flavour. Slightly dry aftertaste, rounded off by the chocolate.	Amère avec goût fondant prononcé. Fin de bouche légèrement amère arrondie par le chocolat.	Bitter met uitgesproken fondantsmaak. Lichtdroge afdronk die wordt afgerond door de chocolade.
Serve in a flute-glass.	Verser dans une flûte.	Uitschenken in een fluitglas.

Floris Fraise

Brouwerij Huyghe 3,60%

	top-fermentation	fermentation haute	hoge gisting
	witbier with fruit	bière blanche fruitée	witbier met fruit
	60% barley malt, 40% wheat, strawberry juice (30%), hops, yeast, natural fruit aroma, water, coriander, orange rind	60% malt d'orge, 40% froment, jus de fraises (30%), houblon, levure, arôme naturel de fruits, eau, coriandre, écorce d'orange	60 % gerstemout, 40 tarwe, aardbeiensap (30%), hop, gist, natuurlijk fruitaroma, w ter, koriander, sinaasschil
	dark pink cloudy	rose foncé trouble	donkerroze troebel
	Strawberry flavour and aroma. Sweet with a slightly bitter touch.	Arôme et saveur de fraise. Douce avec une touche légèrement amère.	Aroma en smaak van aardbei. Zoet met lich bittere toets.
	Serve in a flute-glass.	Verser dans une flûte.	Uitschenken in een fl glas.

uwerij Huyghe

3,70% 4 °C 39 °F

Floris Framboos

top-fermentation	fermentation haute	hoge gisting
white beer with fruit	bière blanche fruitée	witbier met fruit
60 % barley malt, 40 % wheat, raspberry juice (30%), hops, yeast, natural fruit aroma, water, coriander, orange peel	60% de malt d'orge, 40% de froment, jus de framboise (30%), houblon, levure, arôme fruité naturel, eau, coriandre, écorce d'orange	60 % gerstemout, 40 % tarwe, frambozensap (30%), hop, gist, natuurlijk fruitaroma, water, koriander, sinaasschil
deep wine-red, cloudy with an ultrafine, compact, thick pink foam head not filtered, pasteurised	rouge vin profond, trouble avec un faux col rose ultrafin, compact, collant au verre non filtrée, pasteurisée	diep wijnrood, troebel met een ultrafijne, compacte, wandklevende rozige schuimkraag ongefilterd, gepasteuriseerd
The raspberry aroma in combination with the coriander and orange peel forms a perfect balance. Sweet raspberry in the mouth and aftertaste. Pleasant session beer with sweet-and-sour balance.	L'arôme de framboise forme un équilibre parfait avec la coriandre et de l'écorce d'orange. Sensation en bouche et arrière-bouche de framboise sucrée. Bière facilement buvable agréable, avec une balance acide-sucré équilibrée.	Het framboosaroma vormt een perfect evenwicht met de koriander en sinaasschil. Zoetframboos mondgevoel en afdronk. Aangename doordrinker met evenwichtige zuur-zoet-balans.
Serve in a flute glass.	Verser dans une flûte.	Uitschenken in een fluitglas.

Floris Honey

Brouwerij Huyghe 4,50%

	top-fermentation	fermentation haute	hoge gisting
	witbier with honey	bière blanche au miel	witbier met honing
	60% barley malt, 40% wheat, honey (15%), hops, yeast, aroma, water,coriander, orange rind	60% malt d'orge, 40% froment, miel (15%), houblon, levure, arômes, eau, coriandre, écorce d'orange	60 % gerstemout, 40 % tarwe, honing (15%), hop, gist, aroma, wate koriander, sinaasschil
	yellow cloudy	jaune trouble	geel troebel
	First sweet and slightly bitter, then honey. Honey aroma. Atertaste: honey and dry, bitter orange rind.	Douce et légèrement amère cédant au miel. Arôme de miel. Fin de bouche :miel et zeste d'orange sec et amer.	Zoet en lichtbitter die plaatsmaken voor honing. Honingaroma. Afdronk: honing en drc ge, bittere sinaasschil
	Serve in a flute-glass.	Verser dans une flûte.	Uitschenken in een flu glas.

Floris Kriek

uwerij Huyghe 3,60% 4 °C 39 °F

	top-fermentation	fermentation haute	hoge gisting
	witbier with fruit	bière blanche fruitée	witbier met fruit
	60% barley malt, 40% wheat, sour cherry juice (30%), hops, yeast, natural fruit flavouring, water, coriander, orange rind.	60% malt d'orge, 40% froment, jus de cerises griottes (30%), houblon, levure, arôme naturel de fruits, eau, coriandre, écorce d'orange.	60 % gerstemout, 40 % tarwe, kriekensap van griottes (30%), hop, gist, natuurlijk fruitaroma, water, koriander, sinaasschil.
	cherry red	rouge cerise	kersenrood
	Sweet cherry taste with a bitter touch in the middle of the palate.	Saveur douce de cerises avec une touche amère au milieu du palais.	Zoete kersensmaak met een bittere toets in het midden van het gehemelte.
	Serve in a flute-glass.	Verser dans une flûte.	Uitschenken in een fluitglas.

Floris Mango

Brouwerij Huyghe 3,60%

	top-fermentation	fermentation haute	hoge gisting
	white beer with fruit	bière blanche fruitée	witbier met fruit
	60 % barley malt, 40 % wheat, mango juice (30%), hops, yeast, natural fruit aroma, water, coriander, orange peel	60% de malt d'orge, 40% de froment, jus de mangue (30%), houblon, levure, arôme fruité naturel, eau, coriandre, écorce d'orange	60 % gerstemout, 40 % tarwe, mangosap (30 hop, gist, natuurlijk fruitaroma, water, kor ander, sinaasschil
	golden-yellow, veiled with a thick, cream-coloured foam head not filtered, pasteurised	jaune doré, voilée avec un faux col stable crème, collant au verre non filtrée, pasteurisée	goudgeel, gesluierd m een vaste, wandkleve de crèmekleurige schuimkraag ongefilterd, gepasteu seerd
	Nose with aromas of mango, papaya, pepper and a dash of lemon. Excellent taste thanks to the use of 100% fresh mango juice. Sweet, fruity aftertaste.	Bouquet avec des arômes de mangue, de papaye, de poivre et une pointe de citron. Excellente sensation en bouche grâce à l'utilisation de 100% de jus de mangue frais. Arrière-bouche sucrée, fruitée.	Neus met aroma's van mango, papaya, pepe en een zweempje citroen. Uitstekend mo gevoel door het gebru van 100% vers mango sap. Zoete, fruitige a dronk.
	Serve in a flute glass.	Verser dans une flûte.	Uitschenken in een fl glas.
i			

top-fermentation	fermentation haute	hoge gisting
witbier with fruit	bière blanche fruitée	witbier met fruit
60% barley malt, 40% wheat, hops, yeast, natural fruit aroma, coriander, orange rind, water, fruit juices (mango, apricot, passion fruits, peach)	60% malt d'orge, 40% froment, houblon, levure, arôme naturel de fruits, coriandre, écorce d'orange, eau, jus de fruits (mangue, abricot, pêche, fruit de la passion)	60 % gerstemout, 40 % tarwe, hop, gist, natuurlijk fruitaroma, koriander, sinaasschil, water, fruitsappen (mango, abrikoos, passievruchten, perzik)
yellow, cloudy	jaune, trouble	geel, troebel
Special, deep aroma, less perfumed than other Floris beers. Progressive freshness of exotic fruits with in the middle the bitterness of nuts. Overall fruity flavour.	Arôme spécial et profond moins parfumé que celui des autres bières Floris. Fraîcheur progressive de fruits exotiques avec au milieu un goût amer de noix. Fruitée sur toute la ligne.	Speciaal en diep aroma dat minder geparfumeerd is dan dat van de andere Florisbieren. Progressieve frisheid van exotische vruchten met in het midden een bitterheid van noten. Fruitig over de hele lijn.
Serve in a flute-glass.	Verser dans une flûte.	Schenken in een fluitglas.
Floris and Ninke are the children of one of the key people involved in the development of Floris beers.	Floris et Ninke sont les prénoms des enfants d'un des promoteurs du développement des bières Floris.	Floris en Ninke zijn de namen van de kinderen van een van de drijvende krachten bij de ontwikkeling van de Florisbieren.

Floris Passion

Brouwerij Huyghe 3,60% 3

	top-fermentation	fermentation haute	hoge gisting
	witbier with fruit	bière blanche fruitée	witbier met fruit
	60% barley malt, 40% wheat, passion fruit juice (30%), hops, yeast, natural fruit flavouring, water, coriander, orange rind	60% malt d'orge, 40% froment, jus de fruits de la passion (30%), houblon, levure, arôme naturel de fruits, eau, coriandre, écorce d'orange	60 % gerstemout, 40 % tarwe, passievruchtensap (30%), hop, gist, na tuurlijk fruitaroma, water, koriander, sinaasschil
	dark-yellow	jaune foncée	donkergeel
	Warm, rich beer with a perfect harmony between aroma and taste.	Bière chaude et riche avec une harmonie parfaite d'arôme et de saveur.	Een warm en rijk bier waar aroma en smaak perfect harmoniëren.
	Serve in a flute-glass.	Verser dans une flûte.	Schenken in een fluitglas.

Floris Wit

ouwerij Huyghe **5%** 4 °C 39 °F

	top-fermentation	fermentation haute	hoge gisting
	witbier	bière blanche	witbier
	60% barley malt, 40% wheat, re-fermentation sugar, hops, yeast, aroma, water, coriander, orange rind	60% malt d'orge, 40% froment, sucre de refermentation, houblon, levure, arômes, eau, coriandre, écorce d'orange	60 % gerstemout, 40 % tarwe, hergistingssuiker, hop, gist, aroma, water, koriander, sinaasschil
	light-yellow cloudy	jaune clair trouble	lichtgeel troebel
	Fruity Witbier.	Bière blanche fruitée.	Fruitig witbier.
	Serve in a flute glass.	Verser dans une flûte.	Schenken in een fluitglas.
	This beer is equal to Blanche des Neiges and is intended for export.	La même bière que Blanche des Neiges; destinée au marché étranger.	Is hetzelfde bier als Blanche des Neiges; bestemd voor de buitenlandse markt.

Forestinne Ambrosia

B.G.V. at Brasserie Caracole 7,50% 10 - 1 / 50 - 5

	top-fermentation	fermentation haute	hoge gisting
	amber special	ambrée spéciale	amber special
	malt varieties, aroma malt, different hops, yeast, water	variétés de malt, malt aromatique, variétés de houblon, levure, eau	moutsoorten, aroma-mout, hopsoorten, gist, water
	amber	ambrée	amber
	Fruit and malt aromas. Tastes slightly sweetened with touches of sponge cake.	Arômes de fruits et de malt. A un goût légèrement sucré, avec des touches de biscuit.	Aroma's van fruit en mout. Smaakt licht gesuikerd met toetsen van biscuit.
	Pour out 3/4 of the bottle, leave the yeast sediment in the bottle.	Verser la bouteille pour 3/4, laisser le dépôt de levure dans la bouteille.	De fles voor 3/4 uitschenken, het gistdepo in de fles laten.
i			

.V. at Brasserie Caracole | 7,50% | 10 - 12 °C 50 - 54 °F

	top-fermentation	fermentation haute	hoge gisting
	scotch	scotch	scotch
	malt varieties, roasted malt, different hops, yeast, aromatic plants, water	variétés de malt, malt torréfié, variétés de houblon, levure, plantes aromatiques, eau	moutsoorten, gebrande mout, hopsoorten, gist, aromatische planten, water
	brown	brune	bruin
	Fruit and malt aromas. Mellow and slightly bitter taste.	Arômes de fruits et de malt. A un goût doux et légèrement amer.	Aroma's van fruit en mout. Smaakt zacht en licht bitter.
	Pour out 3/4 of the bottle, leave the yeast sediment in the bottle.	Verser la bouteille pour 3/4, laisser le dépôt de levure dans la bouteille.	De fles voor 3/4 uitschenken, het gistdepot in de fles laten.
i			

Forestinne Gothika

Forestinne Mysteria

B.G.V. at Brasserie Caracole 7,50% 10 - 1
50 - 5

	top-fermentation	fermentation haute	hoge gisting
	special blond	blonde spéciale	speciaal blond
	different malts, different hops, yeast, water	variétés de malt, variétés de houblon, levure, eau	moutsoorten, hopsoorten, gist, water
	blond	blonde	blond
	Fruity and flowery aromas. Soft, slightly bitter flavour.	Arômes fruités et fleuris. Goût doux, légèrement amer.	Fruitige en bloemige aroma's. Zachte, licht bittere smaak.
	Pour out 3/4 of the bottle, leave the yeast sediment in the bottle.	Verser la bouteille pour 3/4, laisser le dépôt de levure dans la bouteille.	De fles voor 3/4 uitschenken, het gistdepo in de fles laten.
i			

7,50% 10 - 12 °C 50 - 54 °F

	top-fermentation	fermentation haute	hoge gisting
	Christmas beer	bière de Noël	kerstbier
	different malts, different hops, yeast, herbs, water	variétés de malt, variétés de houblon, levures, herbes, eau	moutsoorten, hopsoorten, gisten, kruiden, water
	Spicy, slightly hoppy aroma. Slightly sugary flavour initially, ending in tart touches.	Arôme épicé, légèrement houblonné. Goût légèrement sucré lors de l'approche initiale, puis des touches amères.	Kruidig, licht hoppig aroma. Licht gesuikerde smaak bij de aanzet, daarna bittere toetsen.
	Pour out 3/4 of the bottle, leave the yeast sediment in the bottle.	Verser la bouteille pour 3/4, laisser le dépôt de levure dans la bouteille.	De fles voor 3/4 uitschenken, het gistdepot in de fles laten.
i			

Forestinne Nordika

Forestinne Primoria

B.G.V. at Brasserie Caracole 7,50% 10 - 12 / 50 - 54

	top-fermentation	fermentation haute	hoge gisting
	tripel special	triple spéciale	tripel special
	different malts, different hops, yeast, pine buds, water	variétés de malt, variétés de houblon, boutons de pin, levure, eau	moutsoorten, hopsoorten, gist, pijnknoppen, water
	copper-blond	blond cuivre	koperblond
	Aromas of wood with touches of malt. Not too sweet and not too bitter.	Arômes de bois, avec des touches de malt. Pas trop sucrée, ni trop amère.	Aroma's van hout met toetsen van mout. Niet te zoet en niet te bitter.
	Pour out 3/4 of the bottle, leave the yeast sediment in the bottle.	Verser la bouteille pour 3/4, laisser le dépôt de levure dans la bouteille.	De fles voor 3/4 uitschenken, het gistdepot in de fles laten.
i			

5%

	spontaneous fermentation	fermentation spontanée	spontane gisting
	fruit beer	bière fruitée	fruitbier
	Blend of young and old lambic, matured in oak barrels. With real raspberries (25%).	Mélange de lambic jeune et vieux mûri en fûts de chêne. Contient de vraies framboises (25%).	Versnijding van jonge en oude lambiek gerijpt op eikenhouten vaten. Met echte frambozen (25%).
	raspberry red	rouge framboise	frambozenrood
	Sweet-and-sour raspberry taste.	Saveur de framboise aigre-douce.	Zuurzoete frambozensmaak.
i	Kriek has existed since the 19th century, raspberry lambic was created in the early 20th century and has known a revival since the 1970's.	La kriek existe déjà depuis le 19ième siècle, le lambic de framboise est apparu au début du 20 ème siècle et connaît un renouveau depuis les années 1970.	Kriek bestaat al sinds de 19e eeuw, frambozenlambiek is ontstaan in het begin van de 20e eeuw en kent een revival sedert de jaren 1970.

F

Framboise Girardin

Brouwerij Girardin 5% Sligh cool

	spontaneous fermentation (no yeast added)	fermentation spontanée (sans adjonction de levure)	spontane gisting (geen toevoeging van gist)
	fruit beer lambic beer	bière fruitée bière lambic	fruitbier lambiekbier
	wheat, barley malt, more than one year old hops, raspberries, water	froment, malt d'orge, houblon suranné, framboises, eau	tarwe, gerstemout, overjaarse hop, frambozen, water
	raspberry colour clear	couleur framboise claire	frambozenkleur helder
	Fresh beer, great aperitif. Sweet-sour raspberry taste. The bitter substances are reduced by the fully-fermented hops.	Bière fraîche, convient comme apéritif. Saveur de framboise moelleuse, aigre-douce. Les substances amères sont réduites par les cônes de houblon séchés.	Fris, geschikt als aperitiefbier. Malse, zoetzure frambozensmaak. Door de belegen gedroogde hopbellen zijn de bitterstoffen gereduceerd.
	In a bulb jar or in a flute-glass like champagne.	Comme le champagne. Dans des flûtes.	In een bol glas of, zoals champagne, in fluitglazen.
	Made with real raspberries, which is fairly unique. Store horizontally in a dark, cool room (max. 59 °F).	Fabriquée avec de vraies framboises, ce qui est assez unique. Conserver en position horizontale, à l'abri de la lumière et de la chaleur (max. 15 °C).	Gemaakt met echte frambozen, wat vrij uniek is. Horizontaal, donker en koel (max. 15 °C) bewaren.

'ouwerij Lindemans 2,50% 3 - 4 °C 37 - 39 °F

	spontaneous fermentation	fermentation spontanée	spontane gisting
	fruit beer based on lambic	bière fruitée à base de lambic	fruitbier op basis van lambiek
	malt, wheat, hops, raspberry juice (25%), fructose, water	malt, froment, houblon, jus de framboises (25%), fructose, eau	mout, tarwe, hop, frambozensap (25%), fructose, water
	red slightly hazy	rouge légèrement voilée	rood licht gesluierd
	Fruity character. Lively and strong onset turning into a balance of sweet (fruit) and slightly sour (lambic).	Caractère fruité. Début vive et corsée passant à un équilibre de douceur (fruits) et de légère acidulité (lambic).	Fruitig karakter. Levendige en sterke aanzet die overgaat in een evenwicht van zoet (fruit) en zacht zuur (lambiek).
	Pour into a flute-glass.	Verser dans une flûte.	In een fluitglas uitschenken.
	Suitable as an aperitif and as a thirst-quencher.	Convient comme apéritif et comme désaltérant.	Geschikt als aperitief en als dorstlesser.

Framboise Max Jacobins

Brouwerij Bockor (Vander Ghinste)

3% | 5 - 8 | 41 - 46

fermentation	spontaneous fermentation	fermentation spontanée	spontane gisting
type	fruit beer	bière fruitée	fruitbier
ingredients	barley malt, wheat, hops, yeast, nature-identical aromas, water	malt d'orge, froment, houblon, arômes naturels, eau	gerstemout, tarwe, hop, gist, natuuridentische aroma's, water
colour	glowing red	rouge intense	gloedrood
taste	Fruity and fresh. Sweet-and-sour with a clear raspberry aroma.	Fruitée et fraîche. Aigre-douce avec un arôme prononcé de framboises.	Fruitig en fris. Zoetzurig met een duidelijk frambozenaroma.
glass	Rinse the glass cold, slightly tilt it and pour out half carefully. Then keep the glass upright and pour out the remainder in a single movement.	Rincer le verre à l'eau froide, le tenir légèrement incliné et le remplir prudemment à moitié. Puis relever le verre et vider la bouteille d'un seul trait.	Het glas koud spoelen, licht schuin houden en voorzichtig half inschenken. Daarna het glas rechthouden en de rest in 1 beweging uitschenken.
i			

ouwerij Oud Beersel

5% 2 - 8 °C / 36 - 46 °F

	spontaneous fermentation	fermentation spontanée	spontane gisting
	fruit beer	bière fruitée	fruitbier
	raspberries (220 g/l), Morello cherries (50 g/l), barley malt, wheat, hops, water	framboises (220 g/l), cerises (50 g/l), malt d'orge, froment, houblon, eau	frambozen (220 g/l), krieken (50 g/l), gerstemout, tarwe, hop, water
	red-pink	rouge rose	rozerood
	Balance between the authentic lambic flavour matured in old casks and the fruitiness of freshly ripened raspberries. A mellow natural beer, subtle and refreshing.	Harmonie entre le goût authentique du vieux lambic mûri en fûts de bois et le fruité de framboises mûres fraîches. Une bière naturelle douce, subtile et désaltérante.	Harmonie tussen de authentieke smaak van oude lambiek gerijpt op houten vaten en het fruitige van verse rijpe frambozen. Een zacht natuurlijk bier, subtiel en verfrissend.

Framboise Oud Beersel

Frasnoise Givrée

Brasserie Artisanale la Frasnoise **6,30%** 5 - 7 / 41 - 45

	top-fermentation re-fermented in the bottle	fermentation haute refermentation en bouteille	hoge gisting hergisting in de fles
	amber	ambrée	amber
	barley malt, yeasts, hop varieties, sugars, herbs, water	malt d'orge, levures, variétés de houblon, sucres, herbes, eau	gerstemout, gisten, hopsoorten, suikers, kruiden, water
	copper-coloured clear and transparent unfiltered	couleur cuivre claire et transparente non filtrée	koperkleurig helder en transparant niet gefilterd
	Complex taste, noticeable bitterness in the back of the mouth. Mixture of roundness and spices with a long-lasting effect. Wide range of generous, perfumed aromas, rich in essences.	Goût complexe, amertume en fin de bouche, avec un mélange de rondeur et d'épices qui se libèrent lentement. Arômes nombreux, riches et parfumés.	Complexe smaak, bitterheid in de afdronk, met een mengeling van rondheid en kruiden die zich langzaam manifesteren. Talrijke, rijke, geparfumeerde aroma's.
	Pour in a single movement to obtain a nice foam head.	Verser en un seul mouvement de sorte qu'un faux col solide se forme.	In 1 beweging uitschenken zodat er een mooie schuimkraag ontstaat.
	Natural, lively beer brewed following an ancient recipe.	Bière naturelle et vive basée sur une vieille recette.	Natuurlijk en levend bier op basis van een oud recept.

cobrouwerij Alvinne

3,80% 8 - 10 °C / 46 - 50 °F

top-fermentation re-fermentation in the bottle	fermentation haute refermentation en bouteille	hoge gisting hergisting in de fles
bitter English brown ale	bitter English brown ale	bitter English brown ale
4 malt types, 5 different hops (Pioneer, EK Goldings, Chinook, Colombus and Amarillo)	4 variétés de malt, 5 variétés de houblon (Pioneer, EK Goldings, Chinook, Colombus et Amarillo)	4 moutsoorten, 5 hopsoorten (Pioneer, EK Goldings, Chinook, Colombus en Amarillo)
18 EBC	18 EBC	18 EBC
42 EBU	42 EBU	42 EBU

Freaky Dark

Picobrouwerij Alvinne 3,80% 8 - 10 / 46 - 50

	top-fermentation re-fermentation in the bottle	fermentation haute refermentation en bouteille	hoge gisting hergisting in de fles
	5 different malts, hops (Pioneer and Hallertau mittelfrüh), Morpheus yeast, water	5 variétés de malt, houblon (Pioneer et Hallertau mittelfrüh), levure Morpheus, eau	5 moutsoorten, hop (Pioneer en Hallertau mittelfrüh), Morpheusgist, water
	196 EBC	196 EBC	196 EBC
	30 EBU	30 EBU	30 EBU

Fruitig Bierreke

ouwerij DijkWaert — 8,20% — 6 - 8 °C / 43 - 46 °F

	top-fermentation natural re-fermentation in the bottle	fermentation haute refermentation naturelle en bouteille	hoge gisting natuurlijke hergisting in de fles
	fruit beer, not sweet	bière fruitée non sucrée	niet zoet fruitbier
	malt, hops, herbs, yeasts, Morello cherries, water	malt, houblon, herbes, levures, cerises, eau	mout, hop, kruiden, gis-ten, krieken, water
	red-brown (30 EBC)	brun rouge (30 EBC)	roodbruin (30 EBC)
	Fresh tart touch of More-llo cherries and subtle bitterness (25 EBU).	Une touche acide fraîche de griottes et une amer-tume subtile (25 EBU).	Friszure toets van krie-ken en subtiele bitter-heid (25 EBU).
i			

Gaspar

Picobrouwerij Alvinne 7,90% 8 - 10 46 - 50

	top-fermentation	fermentation haute	hoge gisting
	regional beer winter beer	bière régionale bière hivernale	streekbier winterbier
	malt (pilsner, wheat, amber), granulated sugar, hops, yeast, water	malt (pils, froment, ambre), sucre cristallisé, houblon, levure, eau.	mout (pils, tarwe, amber), kristalsuiker, hop, gist, water.
	dark blond 20 EBC	blond foncé 20 EBC	donkerblond 20 EBC
	Dominating hoppy taste and aroma, bitter. 115 EBU	Saveur et arômes houblonnés dominants, goût amer. 115 EBU	Een en al hoppigheid in smaak en aroma. Bitter. 115 EBU
	Pour into a tulip-glass or goblet. Leave the yeast (approx. 1 cm) at the bottom of the bottle. Pour slowly to obtain a nice foam head.	Verser dans un verre tulipe ou calice. Laisser la levure (environ 1 cm) au fond de la bouteille. Verser lentement de sorte qu'un faux col solide se forme.	Uitschenken in een tulp- of kelkvormig glas. De gist (ca. 1 cm) op de bodem van de fles laten. Langzaam schenken zodat er een mooie schuimkraag ontstaat.
i			

	top-fermentation re-fermented in the bottle	fermentation haute refermentation en bouteille	hoge gisting met hergisting in de fles
	specialty beer amber	bière spéciale ambrée	speciaalbier amber
	4 different malts, 4 different hops (Magnum, Chinook, Colombus and Hall. Mittelfrüh), yeast, water	4 variétés de malt, 4 variétés de houblon (Magnum, Chinook, Colombus et Hall. Mittelfrüh), levure, eau	4 moutsoorten, 4 hopsoorten (Magnum, Chinook, Colombus en Hall. Mittelfrüh), gist, water
	amber-coloured (30 EBC) clear and gently sparkling; fine, generous foam head	couleur ambrée (30 EBC), claire et finement pétillante; faux col fin, ample	amberkleurig (30 EBC), helder, fijn sprankelend; fijne, gulle schuimkraag
	Pleasant mixture of hop flavours and a light touch of liquorice. Clear bitterness (30 EBU), smooth and thirst-quenching beer.	Mélange agréable d'arômes de houblon et touche légère de réglisse. Saveur amère prononcée (30 EBU), bière douce et désaltérante.	Aangename mengeling van hoparoma's en lichte toets van zoethout. Duidelijke bitterheid (30 EBU), zacht en dorstlessend bier.
	Gently pour into a perfectly degreased glass. Leave the yeast sediment (due to natural refermenting) in the bottle.	Verser doucement dans un verre parfaitement dégraissé. Laisser le dépôt de levure (refermentation naturelle) dans la bouteille.	Zacht uitschenken in een perfect ontvet glas. Het gistbezinksel (natuurlijke hergisting) in de fles laten.
i	Gauloise was the brewery's first beer (1858) inspired by many Gallic-Roman sites from the region.	La Gauloise fut la première bière de la brasserie (1858), avec pour inspiration les nombreux sites gallo-romains de la région.	Gauloise was het eerste bier van de brouwerij (1858) geïnspireerd op de talrijke gallo-romeinse sites uit de regio.

G

Gauloise Blonde

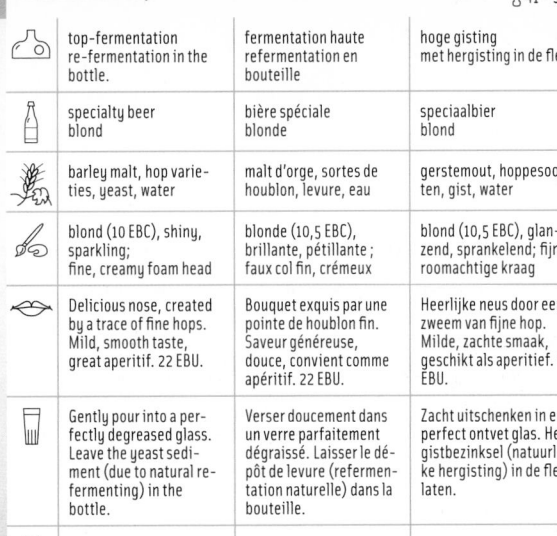

Brasserie du Bocq

6,30% 5 - 12 / 41 - 54

	top-fermentation re-fermentation in the bottle.	fermentation haute refermentation en bouteille	hoge gisting met hergisting in de fles
	specialty beer blond	bière spéciale blonde	speciaalbier blond
	barley malt, hop varieties, yeast, water	malt d'orge, sortes de houblon, levure, eau	gerstemout, hoppesoorten, gist, water
	blond (10 EBC), shiny, sparkling; fine, creamy foam head	blonde (10,5 EBC), brillante, pétillante ; faux col fin, crémeux	blond (10,5 EBC), glanzend, sprankelend; fijne, roomachtige kraag
	Delicious nose, created by a trace of fine hops. Mild, smooth taste, great aperitif. 22 EBU.	Bouquet exquis par une pointe de houblon fin. Saveur généreuse, douce, convient comme apéritif. 22 EBU.	Heerlijke neus door een zweem van fijne hop. Milde, zachte smaak, geschikt als aperitief. 22 EBU.
	Gently pour into a perfectly degreased glass. Leave the yeast sediment (due to natural refermenting) in the bottle.	Verser doucement dans un verre parfaitement dégraissé. Laisser le dépôt de levure (refermentation naturelle) dans la bouteille.	Zacht uitschenken in een perfect ontvet glas. Het gistbezinksel (natuurlijke hergisting) in de fles laten.
i			

8,10% | 8 - 12 °C / 46 - 54 °F

Gauloise Brune

	top-fermentation re-fermentation in the bottle.	fermentation haute refermentation en bouteille	hoge gisting hergisting in de fles
	specialty beer strong dubbel	bière spéciale double forte	speciaalbier sterk bruin
	barley malt, hop varieties, yeast, herbs, water	malt d'orge, sortes de houblon, levure, herbes, eau	gerstemout, hoppesoorten, gist, kruiden, water
	dark ruby red (70 EBC) clear and lively fine, full, white foam head	rouge rubis foncé (70 EBC) claire et vive faux col fin, ample, blanc	donker robijnrood (70 EBC) helder en levendig fijne, volle, witte kraag
	The nose is typical, rich, well-balanced and with a light coriander smell. Taste of special malts, full-bodied, well-balanced, with a slightly bitter aftertaste (32 EBU).	Bouquet typique, riche, équilibré avec un parfum léger de coriandre. Saveur de malts spéciaux, franche, équilibrée, avec une arrière-bouche légèrement amère (32 EBU).	De neus is typisch, rijk, evenwichtig met een lichte koriandergeur. Smaak van speciale mouten, volmondig, evenwichtig, met licht bittere nasmaak (32 EBU).
	Gently pour into a perfectly degreased glass. Leave the yeast sediment (natural re-fermenting) in the bottle.	Verser doucement dans un verre parfaitement dégraissé. Laisser le dépôt de levure (refermentation naturelle) dans la bouteille.	Zacht uitschenken in een perfect ontvet glas. Het gistbezinksel (natuurlijke hergisting) in de fles laten.
i			

G

Gauloise Fruits Rouges

Brasserie du Bocq

8,20% 7 45

	top-fermentation	fermentation haute	hoge gisting
	fruit beer based on strong blond	bière fruitée à base de blonde forte	fruitbier op basis van sterk blond
	tripel with 4 fruit juices (cherry, strawberry, plum, blackcurrant)	triple avec 4 jus de fruits (cerises, fraises, prunes, cassis)	tripel met 4 vruchten-sappen (kers, aardbei, pruim, zwarte bes)
	shining red with a creamy, pink foam head and fine carbon dioxide bubbles	rouge brillant avec un faux col crémeux, rose et pétillement carbonique fin	glanzend rood met een romige, roze schuim-kraag en fijne koolzuur-pareling
	Treacherous, mellow and sweet with a distinct fruity aroma and flavour.	Perfide, douce et légère-ment douceâtre, avec un arôme et un goût fruités prononcés.	Verraderlijk, zacht en lichtzoetig met een uit-sproken fruitig aroma en smaak.

asserie du Bocq 8,10% 8 - 12 °C 46 - 54 °F

Gauloise Kerstbier

G

	top-fermentation re-fermentation in the bottle.	fermentation haute refermentation en bouteille	hoge gisting nagisting in de fles
	specialty beer strong dubbel	bière spéciale double forte	speciaalbier sterk bruin
	barley malt, hop varieties, yeast, herbs, water	malt d'orge, sortes de houblon, levure, herbes, eau	gerstemout, hoppesoorten, gist, kruiden, water
	dark coloured (70 EBC), clear, with fine, generous white foam head	foncée (70 EBC), claire, avec faux col blanc, fin et abondant	donkerkleurig (70 EBC), helder, met fijne, overvloedige, witte schuimkraag
	Rich nose with a touch of coriander and liquorice. Full-bodied, delicious aroma of typical, special malts. Bitterness: 32 EBU.	Bouquet riche avec une touche de coriandre et de réglisse. Franc, arôme exquis de malts spéciaux typiques. Amertume 32 EBU.	Rijke neus met een toets van koriander en zoethout. Volmondig, heerlijk aroma van typische, speciale mouten. Bitterheid 32 EBU.
	Gently pour into a perfectly degreased glass. Leave the yeast sediment (due to natural refermenting) in the bottle.	Verser doucement dans un verre parfaitement dégraissé. Laisser le dépôt de levure (refermentation naturelle) dans la bouteille.	Zacht uitschenken in een perfect ontvet glas. Het gistbezinksel (natuurlijke hergisting) in de fles laten.
i	Typical New Year's beer, Season's beer.	Bière typique de fin d'année, bière de saison.	Typisch eindejaarsbier, seizoensbier.

Gentse Strop - Fier Gents bier

Brouwerij Roman 6,90% 6 43

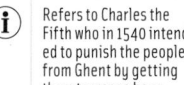

	top-fermentation re-fermentation in the bottle	fermentation haute refermentation en bouteille	hoge gisting hergisting in de fles
	strong blond	blonde forte	sterk blond
	malt, hops, sugar, yeast, brewing water	malt, houblon, sucre, levure, eau de brassage	mout, hop, suiker, gist, brouwwater
	clear blond with solid foam head	limpide blond avec un faux col solide	helder blond met een stevige schuimkraag
	Fruity, hoppy aroma with a pleasant bitter aftertaste.	Fruitée, arôme houblonné, avec une agréable arrière-bouche amère.	Fruitig, hoppig aroma met een aangename bittere afdronk.
	Pour carefully into a chalice and keep the yeast sediment in the bottle.	Verser prudemment dans un verre calice et garder le dépôt de levure dans la bouteille.	Voorzichtig uitschenken in een kelkglas en de gistbodem in de fles houden.
	Refers to Charles the Fifth who in 1540 intended to punish the people from Ghent by getting them to wear a hangman's rope.	Fait référence à l'Empereur Charles Quint, qui voulut punir en 1540 les Gantois en leur faisant porter une corde.	Verwijst naar Keizer Karel die in 1540 de Gentenaars wilde straffen doo ze een strop te laten dragen.

asserie Cantillon

5% — 12 - 16 °C / 54 - 61 °F

	spontaneous fermentation naturally re-fermented in the bottle	fermentation spontanée refermentation naturelle en bouteille	spontane gisting natuurlijke hergisting op de fles
	gueuze lambic	gueuze lambic	geuze lambiek
	barley malt, wheat, more than one year old hops	malt d'orge, froment, houblon suranné	gerstemout, tarwe, overjaarse hop
	gold-coloured	dorée	goudkleurig
	Strong-bodied, pronounced sour but smooth taste. Aroma: a touch of natural cider	Saveur corsée, acidulée prononcée mais moelleuse. Arôme :une pointe de cidre naturel.	Gecorseerd, uitgesproken zure maar zachte smaak. Aroma: een vleugje natuurcider.
	The use of a wine basket is recommended if the bottle was stored horizontally. Place the bottle in an upright position 48 hours before serving, so as to decant the sediment.	Un panier verseur est recommandé si la bouteille a été conservée en position horizontale. Mettre la bouteille 48 heures avant de servir en position verticale pour faire descendre le dépôt.	Een schenkmandje is aangewezen wanneer de fles horizontaal bewaard werd. De fles 48 uur voor het uitschenken verticaal plaasten om het bezinksel te decanteren.
i			

Geuze Cantillon 100% Lambic

G Geuze Fond Girardin

Brouwerij Girardin 5% 10 - 1 / 50 - 5

	spontaneous fermentation re-fermentation in the bottle	fermentation spontanée refermentation en bouteille	spontane gisting hergisting op de fles
	gueuze, lambic beer	gueuze, bière lambic	geuze lambiekbier
	wheat, barley malt, more than 1 year old hops, water	froment, malt d'orge, houblon suranné, eau	tarwe, gerstemout, overjaarse hop, water
	Gold-yellow. Clarity depends on way of serving. The yeast sits at the bottom and makes the beer cloudy.	Jaune doré. La limpidité dépend de la méthode de verser. La levure se trouve dans le fond et rend la bière trouble.	Goudgeel. De helderheid hangt af van de schenkmethode: de biergist zit in de fond en maakt het bier troebel.
	Excellent aperitif. Fresh, sour, solid, fruity and dry.	Apéritif excellent. Fraîche, acidulée, solide, fruitée, sèche.	Geschikt als aperitief. Fris, zuur, stevig, fruitig, droog.
	Rinse the glass with pure, tepid water. Tilt the bottle, stop the cork and pour the glass in one movement. Leave the sediment in the bottle for a clear beer.	Rincer le verre à l'eau tiède propre, tenir la bouteille bien en oblique, retenir le bouchon et verser d'un seul mouvement. Ne pas verser la levure pour avoir une bière claire.	Het glas spoelen met lauw zuiver water. Drogen naar wens. De fles goed schuin houden, he kurk tegenhouden en in beweging schenken. De fond niet meegieten voor een heldere pint.
	Store horizontally in a dark, cool place.	Conserver en position horizontale à l'abri de la lumière et de la chaleur.	Donker, koel en horizontaal bewaren.

uwerij Van Honsebrouck

5% 5 °C 41 °F

spontaneous fermentation re-fermented in the bottle	fermentation spontanée refermentation en bouteille	spontane gisting nagisting op de fles
gueuze lambic	gueuze lambic	geuze lambiek
malt, hops, wheat, water, 100% old lambic	malt, houblon, froment, eau, 100% vieux lambic	mout, hop, tarwe, water, 100% oude lambiek
blond slightly cloudy, unfiltered	blonde légèrement trouble, non filtrée	blond licht troebel, niet gefilterd
Very fresh. Sourish with strong noticeable influence of wheat, wild yeast and the storage in oakwood barrels.	Très fraîche. Acidulée avec une influence perceptible de froment, levures sauvages. Conservation en fûts de chêne.	Zeer fris. Zurig met sterk waarneembare invloed van tarwe, wildgisten en bewaring op eikenhouten vaten.
Slowly pour into a newly rinsed glass. Tilt the glass first, then put it in a vertical position. Leave the yeast sediment in the bottle.	Verser lentement dans un verre rincé tenu d'abord en oblique et à la fin en position verticale. Laisser le dépôt de levure dans la bouteille.	Langzaam uitschenken in een vers gespoeld glas dat eerst schuin en op het einde verticaal gehouden wordt. Het gistdepot in de fles laten.
This is the gueuze for connoisseurs.	C'est la gueuze des vrais amateurs.	Dit is de geuze voor de echte liefhebbers.

Geuze Fond Tradition

G Geuze Gefilterd Girardin

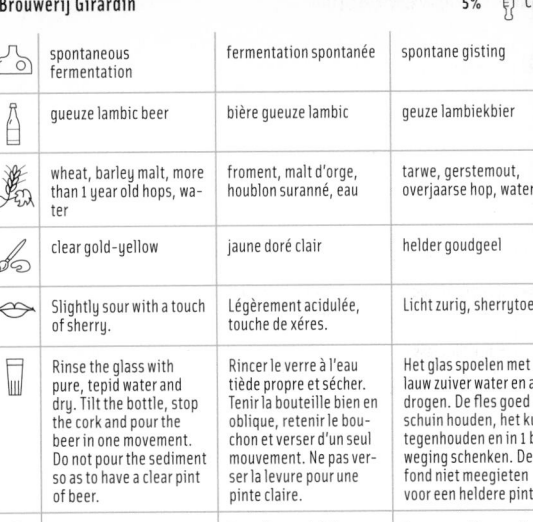

Brouwerij Girardin 5% Co

	spontaneous fermentation	fermentation spontanée	spontane gisting
	gueuze lambic beer	bière gueuze lambic	geuze lambiekbier
	wheat, barley malt, more than 1 year old hops, water	froment, malt d'orge, houblon suranné, eau	tarwe, gerstemout, overjaarse hop, water
	clear gold-yellow	jaune doré clair	helder goudgeel
	Slightly sour with a touch of sherry.	Légèrement acidulée, touche de xéres.	Licht zurig, sherrytoets
	Rinse the glass with pure, tepid water and dry. Tilt the bottle, stop the cork and pour the beer in one movement. Do not pour the sediment so as to have a clear pint of beer.	Rincer le verre à l'eau tiède propre et sécher. Tenir la bouteille bien en oblique, retenir le bouchon et verser d'un seul mouvement. Ne pas verser la levure pour une pinte claire.	Het glas spoelen met lauw zuiver water en afdrogen. De fles goed schuin houden, het kur tegenhouden en in 1 be weging schenken. De fond niet meegieten voor een heldere pint.
	A mix of Lambic beers of different ages. Re-fermentation happens in a reservoir and the beer is filtered before bottling.	Un mélange de bières lambics de différents âges. La refermentation se produit dans un réservoir et la bière est filtrée avant d'être mise en bouteille.	Een mengeling van lambiek van verschillende leeftijden. De hergistir gebeurt op een tank en het bier is gefilterd voc het op de fles komt.

uwerij Bockor (Vander Ghinste)

5,50% 5 - 8 °C 41 - 46 °F

spontaneous fermentation	fermentation spontanée	spontane gisting
gueuze	gueuze	geuze
wheat, barley malt, hops, water	froment, malt d'orge, houblon, eau	gerstemout, tarwe, hop, water
amber	ambrée	amber
Basic taste sweet-and-sour.	Saveur de base aigre-douce.	Zoetzurig.
Rinse the glass with cold water, tilt it a little and pour carefully half of the bottle. Next, keep the glass upright and pour the rest of the bottle in one single movement.	Rincer le verre à l'eau froide, le tenir légèrement incliné et le remplir prudemment à moitié. Puis relever le verre et verser la bière qui reste d'un seul trait.	Het glas koud spoelen, licht schuin houden en voorzichtig half inschenken. Daarna het glas rechthouden en de rest in 1 beweging uitschenken.

Geuze Lambic St Louis

Brouwerij Van Honsebrouck 4,50%

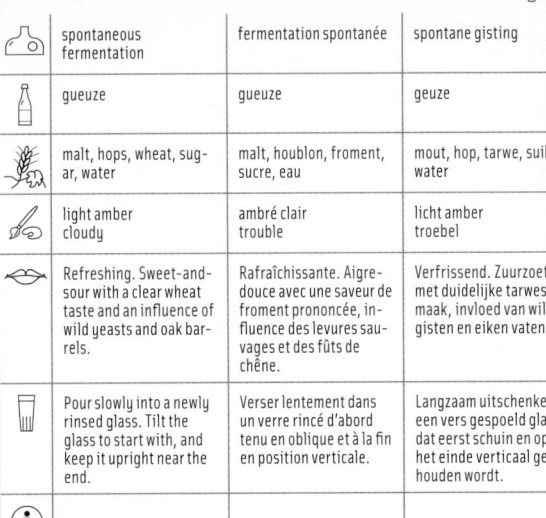

	spontaneous fermentation	fermentation spontanée	spontane gisting
	gueuze	gueuze	geuze
	malt, hops, wheat, sugar, water	malt, houblon, froment, sucre, eau	mout, hop, tarwe, suiker, water
	light amber cloudy	ambré clair trouble	licht amber troebel
	Refreshing. Sweet-and-sour with a clear wheat taste and an influence of wild yeasts and oak barrels.	Rafraîchissante. Aigre-douce avec une saveur de froment prononcée, influence des levures sauvages et des fûts de chêne.	Verfrissend. Zuurzoet met duidelijke tarwesmaak, invloed van wilde gisten en eiken vaten.
	Pour slowly into a newly rinsed glass. Tilt the glass to start with, and keep it upright near the end.	Verser lentement dans un verre rincé d'abord tenu en oblique et à la fin en position verticale.	Langzaam uitschenken in een vers gespoeld glas dat eerst schuin en op het einde verticaal gehouden wordt.
i			

5,50% 3 - 4 °C 37 - 39 °F

	spontaneous fermentation	fermentation spontanée	spontane gisting
	gueuze lambic	gueuze lambic	geuze lambiek
	malt, wheat, hops, fructose, water	malt, froment, houblon, fructose, eau	mout, tarwe, hop, fructose, water
	gold blond clear filtered	blonde doré claire filtrée	goudblond helder gefilterd
	Slightly sourish. Smooth gueuze with a slightly sweet onset and fresh sourish aftertaste.	Moelleux acidulée. Gueuze douce avec un début légèrement sucré et une fin de bouche fraîche, acidulée.	Zacht zurig. Zachte geuze met een lichtzoete aanzet en fris zurige afdronk.
	Pour into a Gueuze glass.	Verser dans un verre gueuze.	In een geuzeglas uitschenken.

Geuze Mariage Parfait

Brouwerij Boon 8%

	spontaneous fermentation. Re-fermented in the bottle by the young lambic which contains fermentable sugars.	fermentation spontanée. Refermentation en bouteille par le lambic jeune contentant des sucres commutables en levure.	spontane gisting. Nagisting op de fles do de jonge lambiek die vergistbare suikers bevat.
	Old Gueuze	Vieille gueuze	Oude geuze
	a selected blend of 90% mellow Lambic (at least 18 months), 5% distinctive 3 year-old beer and 5% very young Lambic	mélange sélectionné de 90% de lambic doux (au moins 18 mois), 5% de bière de caractère de 3 ans et 5% de lambic très jeune	geselecteerde mengeling van 90% malse lam biek (minstens 18 maa oud), 5% karaktervol bier van 3 jaar en 5% he jonge lambiek
	Only champagne bottles are suitable for gueuze because of the high pressure.	Seules les bouteilles de champagne résistent à la haute pression de la gueuze.	Enkel champagnefless kunnen weerstaan aan de hoge druk van de ge ze.

sserie Gigi

2,50% 12 °C 54 °F

bottom-fermentation	fermentation basse	lage gisting
table beer/pilsner	bière de table/pils	tafelbier/pils
pilsner malt, yeast, hops, sugar, sweetener, water	malt de pils, levure, houblon, sucre, édulcorant, eau	pilsmout, gist, hop, suiker, zoetstof, water
dark blond	blond foncé	donkerblond
Light thirst-quencher.	Désaltérant légère.	Lichte dorstlesser.
Pour like a pilsner.	Verser comme une pils.	Uitschenken als een pilsbier.
Boutique beer from the region Gaume.	Bière de la région de la Gaume brassée de façon artisanale.	Streekbier uit de Gaumeregio dat artisanaal gebrouwen wordt.

Brouwerij Haacht

7% 8 - 1 46 - 5

	top-fermentation centrifuged	fermentation haute centrifugée	hoge gisting gecentrifugeerd
	dubbel	double	dubbel
	barley malt, maize, sugar, hops, water	malt d'orge, maïs, sucre, houblon, eau	gerstemout, mais, suiker, hop, water
	dark creamy foam filtered, pasteurised	foncée faux col crémeux filtrée, pasteurisée	donker romig schuim gefilterd, gepasteuriseerd
	First mild and sweet. Aftertaste fairly strong but soft and sweet with a slightly bitter aftertaste.	Initialement mi-douce, arrière-bouche plutôt corsée mais douce, fin de bouche légèrement amère.	Eerst mildzoet. Afdron behoorlijk fors maar zachtzoet met een lich bittere nasmaak.
	Pour carefully into a rinsed, wet mug, avoiding contact between bottle and foam head.	Verser prudemment dans un verre mouillé sans que la bouteille touche l'écume.	Voorzichtig uitschenk in een gespoeld, nat g zonder dat de fles het schuim raakt.
i	Perfect to accompany a chocolate dessert. Forever linked with the guild's ball of the Diest archers' guild. At midnight, candidate members had to drink a litre of beer, standing on one leg, to become a member.	Accompagne parfaitement un dessert au chocolat. Depuis longtemps liée au bal de la guilde des tireurs de Diest, où les candidats-membres devaient boire à minuit un litre de bière en s'appuyant sur une jambe pour devenir membre.	Past uitstekend bij eer chocoladedessert. Van oudsher verbonde met het gildenbal van Diestse schuttersgild Vroeger moesten kand daat-leden om 12 u op één been 1 liter bier ui drinken om lid te worden.

uwerij DijkWaert

9,50% 8 - 10 °C / 46 - 50 °F

Goeie Koffe

G

	top-fermentation natural re-fermentation in the bottle	fermentation haute refermentation naturelle en bouteille	hoge gisting natuurlijke hergisting in de fles
	stout	stout	stout
	malt, different hops, herbs, coffee, yeasts, water	malt, houblons, herbes, café, levures, eau	mout, hopsoorten, kruiden, koffie, gisten, water
	black (150 EBC)	noire (150 EBC)	zwart (150 EBC)
	Rich aroma and taste, spicy with a dash of coffee. Long aftertaste.	Riches arôme et goût, épicé avec une pointe de café. Longue fin de bouche.	Rijk aroma en smaak, kruidig met een vleugje koffie. Lange nasmaak.

Goliath Blonde

Brasserie des Légendes 5,50% 6 - 43 - 4

	top-fermentation natural re-fermentation in the bottle not centrifuged	fermentation haute refermentation en bouteille non centrifugée	hoge gisting natuurlijke hergisting i de fles niet gecentrifugeerd
	regional beer	bière régionale	streekbier
	pale malt, hops, yeast, water	malt pâle,houblon, levure, eau	bleke mout, hop, gist, water
	blond with sparkling foam not filtered or pasteurised	blonde avec écume pétillante non filtrée, non pasteurisée	blond met parelend schuim ongefilterd, niet gepasteuriseerd
	Dry and thirst-quenching. Very fruity, yet distinctly hoppy. Dry and refreshing aftertaste.	Seche et désaltérante. Fort fruitée, avec un caractère houblonné prononcé. Arrière-bouche sèche et vive.	Droog en dorstlessend. Zeer fruitig met een uitgesproken hoppig karakter. Droge en levendige afdronk.
	Goliath is one of the famous Ath giants.	Goliath est l'un des fameux géants d'Ath.	Goliath is een van de fameuze reuzen van Ath.

sserie des Légendes

9% 8 - 12 °C / 46 - 54 °F

	top-fermentation re-fermented in the bottle	fermentation haute refermentation en bouteille	hoge gisting nagisting in de fles
	tripel special	triple spéciale	tripel speciaal
	malt, hops, yeast, water	malt, houblon, levure, eau	mout, hop, gist, water
	golden blond	blond doré	goudblond
	Fruity and spicy, round in the mouth. Well-balanced taste of hop and long-lasting bitterness.	Fruitée et relevée, ronde dans la bouche. Saveur équilibrée de houblon et goût amer prolongé.	Fruitig en kruidig, rond in de mond. Evenwichtige smaak van hop en lange bitterheid.
	Degrease the glass, rinse thoroughly with hot water and dry. With yeast sediment: smoothly revolve the bottle before serving the last third. Without yeast sediment: pour carefully and leave sediment in the bottle.	Dégraisser le verre, bien rincer à l'eau chaude et sécher. Avec dépôt de levure : tourner le dernier tiers de bière avant de le verser. Sans dépôt de levure : verser prudemment et laisser la levure dans la bouteille.	Het glas ontvetten, goed spoelen met warm water en drogen. Met gistbezinkel: het laatste derde van het bier walsen voor het uitschenken. Zonder gistbezinksel: voorzichtig schenken en de fond in de fles laten.
i			

Goliath Triple

Gordon Finest Chrome

Groep John Martin by various breweries 10,50%

	top-fermentation	fermentation haute	hoge gisting
	barley malt, sugar, hops, water	malt d'orge, sucre, houblon, eau	gerstemout, suiker, hop water
	The Gordon label displays the thistle (Scotland's emblem), tartan and blazon of the Gordon clan.	Sur les étiquettes de Gordon, se trouvent représentés le chardon (emblème de l'Écosse), le tartan et le blason du Clan Gordon.	Op de Gordon etiketten staan de distel (embleem van Schotland), tartan en blazoen van de Gordon-clan afgebeeld.

Gordon Finest Copper

oep John Martin by various breweries 6,60%

	top-fermentation	fermentation haute	hoge gisting
	strong blond	blonde forte	sterk blond
	intense gold with hints of copper	doré intense avec teints cuivre	intens goud met kopertinten
	Powerful and masculine.	Forte et virile.	Krachtig en mannelijk.
	John Martin and subsequently Anthony Martin have been developing the Gordon Finest Beers since the early 20th century.	Depuis le début du 20e siècle, John Martin et ensuite Anthony Martin développent les bières de Gordon Finest Beers.	Sinds het begin van de 20e eeuw ontwikkelen John Martin en daarna Anthony Martin de bieren van Gordon Finest Beers.

Gordon Finest Five

Groep John Martin by various breweries 5% 3 - 5 / 37 - 41

top-fermentation	fermentation haute	hoge gisting
Premium pilsner	Premium pils	Premium pils
blond, pale gold	blonde, blond doré	blond, licht goud
Elegant with a gradually developing, delicate bitterness. Mellow aftertaste.	Élégante, avec une délicate amertume qui apparaît petit à petit. Arrière-bouche douce.	Elegant met een delicate bitterheid die geleidelijk ontstaat. Zachte afdronk.
The brand refers to the Anglo-Normandy Gordon clan which enjoyed fame especially in the 13th century.	La marque déposée fait référence au Clan Gordon anglo-normand, qui se fit un nom surtout au 13e siècle.	De merknaam verwijst naar de Anglo-Normandische Gordon-clan die vooral in de 13e eeuw naam maakte.

oep John Martin by various breweries

10% 3 - 6 °C 37 - 43 °F

	bottom-fermentation	fermentation basse	lage gisting
	blond	blonde	blond
	barley malt, sugar, hops, water	malt d'orge, sucre, houblon, eau	gerstemout, suiker, hop, water
	blond	blonde	blond
	Strong and silky. Round taste, obtained by the high alcohol volume, which is toned down by the pale malts.	Forte et soyeuse. Saveur arrondie par la haute teneur en alcool adoucie par les malts pâles.	Sterk en zijdeachtig. Afgeronde smaak door het hoge alcoholvolume die verzacht wordt door de bleke mouten.

Gordon Finest Gold

Gordon Finest Platinum

Groep John Martin by various breweries 12% 3 - 6 / 37 - 43

	bottom-fermentation	fermentation basse	lage gisting
	strong blond	blonde forte	sterk blond
	barley malt, sugar, hops, water	malt d'orge, sucre, houblon, eau	gerstemout, suiker, hop, water
	blond	blonde	blond
	Soft, silky texture with a bitter touch. Full and slightly prickly on the tongue.	Veloutée avec une touche amère. Pleine et légèrement pétillante sur la langue.	Fluweelzacht met bittere toets. Vol en licht prikkelend op de tong.

·oep John Martin by various breweries 8,40% 6 - 8 °C 43 - 46 °F

Gordon Finest Red

	bottom-fermentation	fermentation basse	lage gisting
	strong red	rouge forte	sterk rood
	barley malt, sugar, hops, water	malt d'orge, sucre, houblon, eau	gerstemout, suiker, hop, water
	dark amber	ambré foncé	donker amber
	Dry, spicy touches. Smooth bitterness turning into an alcohol and peppery aftertaste.	Touches sèches, relevées. Goût amer moelleux aboutissant en une fin de bouche d'alcool et de poivre.	Droge, kruidige toetsen. Zachte bitterheid die overgaat in een nasmaak van alcohol en peper.
i			

Gordon Finest Scotch

Groep John Martin by various breweries

8,60% 6 - 8 / 43 - 46

	top-fermentation	fermentation haute	hoge gisting
	scottish Ale	scottish ale	scottish ale
	barley malt, sugar, corn, roasted barley, hops, malt, water	malt d'orge, sucre, maïs, orge brûlé, houblon, malt, eau	gerstemout, suiker, mais, gebrande gerst, hop, mout, water
	dark ruby red	rouge rubis foncé	donker robijnrood
	Smooth and full-bodied. Bitterness (aromatic hop) combined with sweet and roasty malt.	Douce et corsée. Saveur amère (houblon aromatisé) avec des touches de malt doux et brûlé.	Zacht en gecorseerd. Bitterheid (aromatische hop) gecombineerd met zoet en gebrande mout.

7,70% | 3 - 6 °C / 37 - 43 °F

	bottom-fermentation	fermentation basse	lage gisting
	strong blond	blonde forte	sterk blond
	barley malt, sugar, hops, water	malt d'orge, houblon, sucre, eau	gerstemout, suiker, hop, water
	blond	blonde	blond
	Round with a refined hop taste.	Ronde avec une saveur houblonnée raffinée.	Rond met verfijnde hopsmaak.
i			

Gordon Finest Zero

Groep John Martin by various breweries

0%

	bottom-fermentation	fermentation basse	lage gisting
	non-alcoholic version	version sans alcohol	alcoholvrij
	barley malt, sugar, hops, water	malt d'orge, houblon, sucre, eau	gerstemout, suiker, hop, water

ɔep John Martin by various breweries

8,80% — 6 - 8 °C / 43 - 46 °F

	top-fermentation	fermentation haute	hoge gisting
	scottish style ale Christmas beer	scotch ale bière de Noël	scotch ale kerstbier
	barley malt, corn, malt, roasted barley, sugar, hops, water	malt d'orge, maïs, malt, orge brûlé, sucre, houblon, eau	gerstemout, mais, mout, gebrande gerst, suiker, hop, water
	dark ruby red	rouge rubis foncé	donker robijnrood

Gordon Xmas

	top-fermentation natural re-fermentation in the bottle	fermentation haute refermentation naturelle en bouteille	hoge gisting natuurlijke hergisting in de fles
	amber	ambrée	amber
	malt, hops, herbs, yeasts, water	malt, houblon, herbes, levures, eau	mout, hop, kruiden, gisten, water
	pale brown (130 EBC)	brun clair (130 EBC)	lichtbruin (130 EBC)
	Touch of caramel, citrus fruits and veiled bitterness (27 EBU).	Touche de caramel, d'agrumes et une amertume ronde (27 EBU).	Toets van karamel, citrusvruchten en afgeronde bitterheid (27 EBU).

ouwerij Het Anker

8% 6 - 9 °C 43 - 48 °F

top-fermentation re-fermented in the bottle	fermentation haute refermentation en bouteille	hoge gisting hergisting op de fles
amber	ambrée	amber
different malt varieties, Belgian hop varieties and herbs	diférentes sortes de malt, sortes de houblon belge et herbes	verscheidene moutsoorten, Belgische hopsoorten en kruiden
light amber	ambré clair	licht amber
Combines the full-bodied character of brown beer with the freshness of blond beer. Aromatised and spicy.	Combine le goût franc de la bière brune avec la fraîcheur de la bière blonde. Aromatisé et corsé.	Combineert de volmondigheid van bruin bier met de frisheid van blond bier. Gearomatiseerd en pittig.
Hold a degreased goblet by the stem and tilt it a little. Pour the beer in one single movement avoiding contact with glass or foam.	Prendre un verre calice dégraissé par le pied et le tenir incliné. Verser la bière lentement en un seul mouvement sans toucher le verre ni l'écume.	Een vetvrij kelkglas bij de voet vastnemen en licht schuin houden. Het bier traag en in 1 beweging uitschenken zonder het glas of schuim te raken.
Brewed following the old recipe of Mechelsen Bruynen, a beer Charles Quint sent by ship to Spain. The original recipe goes back to 1421.	Brassée selon la recette séculaire de la Mechelsen Bruynen (la recette de base date de 1421), une bière exportée en Espagne par Charles Quint.	Gebrouwen volgens het recept van Mechelsen Bruynen (het basisrecept dateert van 1421), bier dat door Keizer Karel naar Spanje werd verscheept.

Gouden Carolus Ambrio

Gouden Carolus Christmas

Brouwerij Het Anker 10,50% 9 - 12 / 48 - 54

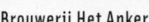

	top-fermentation re-fermented in the bottle	fermentation haute refermentation en bouteille	hoge gisting hergisting op de fles
	specialty beer heavy Christmas beer	bière spéciale bière de Noël forte	speciaalbier zwaar kerstbier
	specific seasoning (six species) in three phases of the brewing process, 3 varieties of Belgian hop	assaisonnement spécifique (6 sortes) en 3 phases du brassage, 3 sortes de houblon belge	specifieke kruiding (6 soorten) bij 3 fasen van het brouwproces, 3 soorten Belgische hop
	brown-red	rouge brun	bruinrood
	Spicy sipping beer with a very refined flavour that gives a warm feeling on cold winter evenings.	Bière de dégustation relevée avec un arôme très raffiné donnant un sentiment chaleureux lors des soirées hivernales froides.	Kruidig degustatiebier met een zeer geraffineerd aroma dat een warm gevoel geeft tijdens koude winteravonden.
i	Is brewed at the end of August and then matures for a few months in order to obtain the best possible flavour balance.	Est brassée fin août et mûrit par la suite quelques mois pour obtenir un équilibre de saveur optimal.	Wordt eind augustus gebrouwen en rijpt daarna een paar maanden voor een optimaal smaakevenwicht.

ouwerij Het Anker

8,50% 6 - 9 °C 43 - 48 °F

Gouden Carolus Classic

	top-fermentation re-fermented in the bottle	fermentation haute refermentation en bouteille	hoge gisting hergisting op de fles
	dark specialty beer	bière spéciale foncée	donker speciaalbier
	Brewed following the classical infusion method with Belgian hops, dark and aromatic malt varieties and caramel.	Brassée selon la méthode classique d'infusion avec du houblon belge, des variétés foncées et aromatisées de malt et du caramel.	Gebrouwen volgens de klassieke infusiemethode met Belgische hop, donkere en aromatische moutsoorten en karamel.
	ruby red	rouge rubis	robijnrood
	Beer with a high density that combines the warmth of wine with the freshness of beer.	Bière de haute densité englobant la chaleur du vin et la fraîcheur de la bière.	Bier met een hoge densiteit dat de warmte van wijn en de frisheid van bier verenigt.
	Hold a degreased goblet by the stem and tilt it a little. Pour the beer in a single movement avoiding contact with the glass or the foam.	Prendre un verre calice dégraissé par le pied et le tenir légèrement incliné. Verser la bière lentement en un seul mouvement sans toucher le verre ni l'écume.	Een vetvrij kelkglas bij de voet vastnemen en licht schuin houden. Het bier traag en in 1 beweging uitschenken zonder het glas of schuim te raken.
	Mechels Keizersbier is named after the gold coins in the time of Charlemagne.	Mechels Keizersbier dont le nom provient des pièces de monnaie d'or au temps de Charles Quint.	Mechels Keizersbier genoemd naar de gouden muntstukken ten tijde van Keizer Karel.

Gouden Carolus Cuvée van de Keizer Blauw

Brouwerij Het Anker 11% 6 - 9 43 - 48

	top-fermentation re-fermented in the bottle centrifuged	fermentation haute refermentation en bouteille centrifugée	hoge gisting hergisting in de fles gecentrifugeerd
	specialty beer	bière spéciale	speciaalbier
	barley malt, corn, sugar, hops, yeast, water	malt d'orge, maïs, sucre, houblon, levure, eau	gerstemout, mais, suiker, hop, gist, water
	ruby red	rouge rubis	robijnrood
	Perfect harmony between the soft warmth of wine and the freshness of beer. Sipping beer with a very refined taste and mysterious aromas.	Harmonie parfaite entre la chaleur moelleuse de vin et la fraîcheur de bière. Bière de dégustation avec un goût très raffiné et des arômes mystérieux.	Perfecte harmonie tussen de zachte warmte van wijn en de frisheid van bier. Degustatiebier met een zeer geraffineerde smaak en mysterieuze aroma's.
	Take a degreased goblet by the stem and hold it slightly tilted. Pour the beer slowly and in a single movement, avoiding contact with the glass or the foam.	Prendre un verre calice dégraissé par le pied et le tenir légèrement incliné. Verser la bière en un seul mouvement sans toucher le verre ou l'écume.	Een vetvrij kelkglas bij de voet vastnemen en licht schuin houden. Het bier traag en in 1 beweging uitschenken zonder het glas of schuim te raken.
i	Ideal storage beer. Charlemagne's Cuvée is brewed every year from 24 February, his birthday, in a limited quantity only.	Une bière de conservation idéale. La Cuvée van de keizer est chaque année brassée à partir du 24 février, anniversaire de l'Empereur Charles Quint, en quantité limitée.	Ideaal bewaarbier. Cuvée van de keizer wordt elk jaar vanaf 24 februari, verjaardag van Keizer Karel, gebrouwen in een gelimiteerde hoeveelheid.

Gouden Carolus Cuvée van de Keizer Rood

ouwerij Het Anker

10% (20 °plato) 7 °C 45 °F

	top-fermentation re-fermentation in the bottle centrifuged	fermentation haute refermentation en bouteille centrifugée	hoge gisting hergisting op de fles gecentrifugeerd
	strong blond specialty beer	blonde forte bière spéciale	sterk blond speciaalbier
	different malt varieties, herbs, Belgian hops	plusieurs variétés de malt, herbes, houblon Belge	verschillende moutsoorten, kruiden, Belgische hop
	gold-blond with fine foam head filtered, pasteurised	blond doré avec faux col fin filtrée, pasteurisée	goudblond met fijne schuimkraag gefilterd, gepasteuriseerd
	Heavier, spicy, yet refreshing beer. Full and balanced in taste.	Bière assez lourde, un peu épicée, mais tout de même désaltérante. Goût franc et équilibré.	Zwaarder, ietwat kruidig, maar toch verfrissend bier. Volle en evenwichtige smaak.
	Tilt the glass slightly and carefully pour the beer in a single movement.	Tenir le verre légèrement incliné et verser prudemment la bière d'un seul mouvement.	Het glas licht schuin houden en het bier in 1 beweging voorzichtig uitschenken.
	Launched in 2008 to mark the 10th anniversary of 'Cuvée van de Keizer Blauw'.	Lancée en 2008, à l'occasion des 10 ans de la 'Cuvée van de Keizer Blauw'.	Gelanceerd in 2008 ter gelegenheid van 10 jaar 'Cuvée van de Keizer Blauw'.

G

Gouden Carolus Easter Beer

Brouwerij Het Anker

10% 9 - 12 / 48 - 54

	top-fermentation re-fermented in the bottle centrifuged	fermentation haute refermentation en bouteille centrifugée	hoge gisting hergisting in de fles gecentrifugeerd
	specialty beer dark	bière spéciale foncée	speciaalbier donker
	barley malt, Belgian hops, yeast, herbs, water	malt d'orge, houblon belge, levure, herbes, eau	gerstemout, Belgische hop, gist, kruiden, water
	ruby red	rouge rubis	robijnrood
	Spicy spring beer, full-bodied and at the same time thirst-quenching. Smooth taste in spite of the high alcohol content.	Bière de printemps relevée à la fois franche et désaltérante. Malgré sa haute teneur en alcool, elle a une saveur moelleuse.	Kruidig voorjaarsbier dat tegelijk volmondig en dorstlessend is. Ondanks het hoge alcoholvolume heeft het toch een zachte smaak.

Gouden Carolus Hopsinjoor

ouwerij Het Anker

8% (18,5 °plato) 5 - 7 °C / 41 - 45 °F

top-fermentation re-fermentation in the bottle centrifuged	fermentation haute refermentation en bouteille centrifugée	hoge gisting hergisting op de fles gecentrifugeerd
strong blond	blonde forte	sterk blond
5 hop varieties fractionated at different times for the best possible aroma, barley malt, yeast, water	5 variétés de houblon d'une période différente fractionnées pour un arôme optimal, malt d'orge, levure, eau	5 hopsoorten op een verschillend tijdstip gefractioneerd voor een optimaal aroma, gerstemout, gist, water
blond, slightly cloudy, creamy foam head not filtered, pasteurised	blonde, légèrement trouble, faux col crémeux non filtrée, pasteurisée	blond, licht troebel, crèmige schuimkraag ongefilterd, gepasteuriseerd
Predominantly mellow with a distinctly bitter aftertaste.	Essentiellement douce, avec une arrière-bouche amère prononcée.	Overwegend zacht met een uitgesproken bittere afdronk.
Tilt the glass slightly and pour out the beer gently. Pour the sediment into the glass afterwards.	Tenir le verre légèrement incliné et verser prudemment la bière. Verser par la suite le dépôt de levure dans le verre.	Het glas licht schuin houden en het bier voorzichtig uitschenken. Het gistbezinksel achteraf in het glas gieten.
The name refers to the 5 different hops used and to 'Opsinjoor', a character from the history of Malines.	Le nom fait référence aux 5 variétés de houblon utilisées et à 'Opsinjoor', une figure de l'histoire malinoise.	De naam verwijst naar de 5 gebruikte hopsoorten en naar 'Opsinjoor' een figuur uit de Mechelse geschiedenis.

Gouden Carolus Tripel

Brouwerij Het Anker 9% 9 - 12 / 48 - 54

	top-fermentation re-fermented in the bottle	fermentation haute refermentation en bouteille	hoge gisting hergisting op de fles
	specialty beer tripel	bière spéciale triple	speciaalbier tripel
	barley malt, 5 different hops, sugar, yeast, water	malt d'orge, 5 variétés de houblon, sucre, levure, eau	gerstemout, 5 hopsoorten, suiker, gist, water
	gold-yellow	jaune doré	goudgeel
	Tender with a pure taste, full-bodied yet thirst-quenching. Heavy, refreshing and a little spicy.	Tendre avec une saveur pure, franche et néanmoins désaltérante. Forte, rafraîchissante et quelque peu relevée.	Teder met een zuivere smaak, volmondig en toch dorstlessend. Zwaar, verfrissend en ietwat kruidig.
	Hold a degreased goblet by the stem and tilt it a little. Pour the beer in a single movement, avoiding contact with glass or foam.	Prendre un verre calice dégraissé par le pied et le tenir légèrement incliné. Verser la bière lentement en un seul mouvement sans toucher le verre ni l'écume.	Een vetvrij kelkglas bij de voet vastnemen en licht schuin houden. Het bier traag en in 1 beweging uitschenken zonder het glas of schuim te raken.
i			

top-fermentation re-fermentation in the bottle	fermentation haute refermentation en bouteille	hoge gisting hergisting in de fles
tripel	triple	tripel
pilsner malt, Münich malt, 2 aromatic hop varieties, yeast, water	malt de pils, malt de Münich, 2 variétés de houblon aromatique, levure, eau	pilsmout, Münichmout, 2 aromatische hopvariëteiten, gist, water
gold-coloured with fine carbon dioxide bubbles and compact, thick foam head filtered, not pasteurised	dorée avec pétillement carbonique fin et faux col compact solide collant parfaitement au verre filtrée, non pasteurisée	goudkleurig met fijne koolzuurpareling en compacte wandklevende schuimkraag gefilterd, niet gepasteuriseerd
Malty aftertaste. Very fine hop aroma with light citrus touches.	Arrière-bouche maltée. Arôme houblonné fort fin, avec de légères touches de citrus.	Moutige afdronk. Zeer fijn hoparoma met lichte citrustoetsen.
Pour out in a single movement and avoid sloshing the beer. Leave yeast sediment (approx. 2 cm) in the bottle and add later, if necessary.	Verser d'un seul mouvement fluide sans clapotage de la bière. Laisser le dépôt de levure (ca. 2 cm) dans la bouteille et le verser éventuellement par après.	In 1 vlotte beweging uitschenken zonder dat het bier klokt. Het gistdepot (ca. 2 cm) in de fles laten en eventueel achteraf bijschenken.
Brewed traditionally according to the original recipe of 'De Orde van Pier Kloeffe' which holds the rich fishing history in esteem.	Brassée de manière artisanale selon une recette originale de 'De Orde van Pier Kloeffe', qui commémore le riche passé du pêcheur.	Ambachtelijk gebrouwen volgens een origineel recept van 'De Orde van Pier Kloeffe' die het rijke vissersverleden in ere houdt.

Gouyasse Tradition

Brasserie des Légendes

6% 5 - 8 41 - 46

	top-fermentation re-fermented in the bottle	fermentation haute refermentation en bouteille	hoge gisting nagisting in de fles
	specialty beer	bière spéciale	speciaalbier
	malt, hop, yeast, pure water	malt, houblon, levure, eau pure	mout, hop, gist, zuiver water
	light-yellow, pearly foam	jaune clair, écume perlée	lichtgeel, gepareld schuim
	Aroma of malt and fruit with some lemon. Perfect balance between dry bitterness and malt, weakening the hop taste.	Arôme de malt et de fruits avec une touche d'agrumes légère. Equilibre parfait entre le goût amer sec et le malt qui réduit l'effet du houblon.	Aroma van mout en fruit met lichte toets van citroen. Perfect evenwicht tussen droge bitterheid en mout die de hoptoets verzwakt.
	Degrease the glass, rinse thoroughly with hot water and dry. With yeast sediment: revolve the bottle before serving the last third. Without yeast sediment: pour carefully and leave sediment in the bottle.	Dégraisser le verre, le rincer bien à l'eau chaude et le sécher. Avec dépôt de levure : tourner le dernier tiers de bière avant de le verser. Sans dépôt de levure : verser prudemment et laisser la levure dans la bouteille.	Het glas ontvetten, goed spoelen met warm water en drogen. Met gistbezinkel: het laatste derde van het bier walsen voor het uitschenken. Zonder gistbezinksel: voorzichtig schenken en de fond in de fles laten.
	Store upright in the cellar or in the refrigerator.	Conserver en position verticale tant dans la cave qu'au réfrigérateur.	Verticaal bewaren zowel in de kelder als in de frigo.

5% 12 - 16 °C 54 - 61 °F

Grand Cru Bruocsella

spontaneous fermentation with re-fermentation in the bottle by adding a liqueur	fermentation spontanée refermentation en bouteille par ajoute de liqueur	spontane gisting met hergisting op de fles door toevoeging van likeur
lambic (3 years)	lambic (3 ans)	lambiek (3 jaar)
barley malt, wheat, more than one year old hops	malt d'orge, froment, houblon suranné	gerstemout, tarwe, overjaarse hop
gold-coloured	dorée	goudkleurig
Very powerful. Fine sourish taste, aromas of great oxidized wines (yellow wine, sherry...).	Très corsée. Saveur raffinée acidulée, arômes de grands vins oxydés (vin jaune, xérès...).	Zeer krachtig. Fijnzurige smaak, aroma's van grote geoxideerde wijnen (gele wijn, sherry...).
The use of a wine basket is recommended if the bottle was stored horizontally. Place the bottle in upright position 48 hours before serving.	Un panier verseur est recommandé si la bouteille a été conservée en position horizontale. Mettre la bouteille 48 heures avant de servir en position verticale pour faire descendre la levure.	Een schenkmandje is aangewezen wanneer de fles horizontaal bewaard werd. De fles 48 uur voor het uitschenken verticaal plaasten om het bezinksel te decanteren.

G Grand Cru St-Feuillien

Brasserie St-Feuillien 9,50% 8 - 1 46 - 5

	top-fermentation natural re-fermentation in the bottle	fermentation haute refermentation naturelle en bouteille	hoge gisting natuurlijke hergisting i de fles
	strong blond	blonde forte	sterk blond
	barley malt, sugar, hops, vitamin C, yeast, brewing water	malt d'orge, sucre, houblon, vitamine C, levure, eau de brassage	gerstemout, suiker, hop vitamine C, gist, brouw water
	pale blond filtered	blond clair filtrée	lichtblond gefilterd
	Sipping beer. The hoppy aftertaste has an intensely bitter twist.	Bière de dégustation. Dans l'arrière-bouche, domine le caractère houblonné, qui est encore accentué par une amertume intense.	Degustatiebier. Bij de afdronk overheerst het hoppig karakter dat nog wordt geaccentueerd door een intense bitterheid.
	Serve in a sipping glass.	Verser dans un verre de dégustation.	Uitschenken in een degustatieglas.
i			

Green Buzz (Bière Bio)

sserie Artisanale Millevertus — 6% — 6 - 12 °C / 43 - 54 °F

top-fermentation	fermentation haute	hoge gisting
blond spelt beer	bière blonde blé épeautre	blond speltbier
organic malt, hops, yeast, water	malt biologique, houblon, levure, eau	biologische mout, hop, gist, water
not filtered	non filtrée	ongefilterd
Lemon aroma.	Arôme de citron.	Citroenaroma.

Grelotte

Brasserie Grain-d'Orge

9%

	top-fermentation natural re-fermentation in the bottle	fermentation haute refermentation naturelle en bouteille	hoge gisting natuurlijke hergisting in de fles
	Christmas beer	bière de Noël	kerstbier
	4 different malts, hops, yeast, herbs, water	4 variétés de malt, houblon, levure, herbes, eau	4 moutsoorten, hop, gist, kruiden, water
	dark brown (malt) not filtered or pasteurised	brun foncé (malt) non filtrée, non pasteurisée	donkerbruin (mout) ongefilterd, niet gepasteuriseerd
	Very smooth and spicy winter beer. Nimble with aromas of winter chocolates.	Bière hivernale fort ronde et épicée. Souple avec des arômes de bonbons d'hiver.	Zeer rond en kruidig winterbier. Soepel met aroma's van winterse bonbons.
	Pour out slowly to form a fine foam head. Leave the yeast sediment in the bottle.	Verser lentement et former un faux col joli. Laisser le dépôt de levure dans la bouteille.	Langzaam uitschenken en een mooie schuimkraag vormen. Het gistdepot in de fles laten.
i			

Gribousine Blonde

serie de Malonne 8,50% 7 - 10 °C 45 - 50 °F

top-fermentation	fermentation haute	hoge gisting
strong blond	blonde forte	sterk blond

G

Gribousine Brune

Brasserie de Malonne 8,00% 7 - 1 45 - 5

	top-fermentation	fermentation haute	hoge gisting
	strong dubbel	double forte	sterk bruin

sserie de Malonne

8,50% 7 - 10 °C / 45 - 50 °F

	top-fermentation	fermentation haute	hoge gisting
	amber winter beer	ambrée bière hivernale	amber winterbier

G Grimbergen Blond

Brouwerij Alken-Maes 6,70% 4

	top-fermentation	fermentation haute	hoge gisting
	Recognised Belgian abbey beer	Bière d'abbaye belge reconnue	Erkend Belgisch abdijbier
	ochre-blond	blond ocre	okerblond
	Slightly fruity, bitter-sweet and full beer with caramel touches.	Bière légèrement fruitée, douce-amère et pleine aux touches caramélisées.	Lichtfruitig, zoetbitter vol bier met toetsen var karamel.
	Pour carefully into a degreased, dry glass. Pour slowly to obtain a nice foam head.	Verser soigneusement dans un verre dégraissé sec. Verser lentement de sorte qu'un faux col solide se forme.	Zorgvuldig uitschenken in een ontvet, droog glas. Langzaam schenken zodat er een mooie schuimkraag ontstaat.
	Authentic abbey beer, excellent to accompany a meal.	Cette authentique bière d'abbaye convient parfaitement aux repas.	Authentiek abdijbier ui stekend geschikt voor b de maaltijd.

uwerij Alken-Maes

6,50% 6 °C 43 °F

Grimbergen Dubbel

	top-fermentation	fermentation haute	hoge gisting
	Recognised Belgian abbey beer	Bière d'abbaye belge reconnue	Erkend Belgisch abdijbier
	deep red burgundy colour	couleur bourgogne rouge intense	dieprode bourgognekleur
	Bittersweet, full beer with caramel touches.	Doux-amère avec beaucoup de plénitude et des touches caramélisées.	Zoetbitter, vol bier met toetsen van karamel.
	Pour carefully into a degreased, dry glass. Pour slowly to obtain a nice foam head.	Verser soigneusement dans un verre dégraissé sec. Verser lentement de sorte qu'un faux col solide se forme.	Zorgvuldig uitschenken in een ontvet, droog glas. Langzaam schenken zodat er een mooie schuimkraag ontstaat.
i	Authentic abbey beer, excellent to accompany a meal.	Cette authentique bière d'abbaye convient parfaitement aux repas.	Authentiek abdijbier uitstekend geschikt voor bij de maaltijd.

Grimbergen Goud 8°

Brouwerij Alken-Maes 8%

	top-fermentation re-fermentation in the bottle	fermentation haute refermentation en bouteille	hoge gisting hergisting in de fles
	Recognised Belgian abbey beer strong blond	Bière d'abbaye belge reconnue blonde forte	Erkend Belgisch abdijbier sterk blond
	recipe with aromatic hops	recette avec houblon aromatique	recept met aromatisch[e] hop
	Refined bitterness, intense and aromatic, hoppy taste. Velvety hoppy aftertaste.	Amertume raffinée, caractère houblonné intense et aromatique. Arrière-bouche houblonnée veloutée.	Verfijnde bitterheid, in[-]tens en aromatisch, hop[-]pig karakter. Fluweelhoppige afdro[nk].
	Ardet nec consumitur (fire does not fade)' is the motto of the Grimbergen abbey (since 1128). Just like the phoenix - the abbey's emblem - is rising from the ashes, the abbey, too, has been rebuilt after having been destroyed on several occasions.	Ardet nec consumitur (elle brûle, mais ne se consume pas), voilà la devise de l'abbaye de Grimbergen (depuis 1128). Telle le phénix - l'emblème de l'abbaye - qui renaît de ses cendres, l'abbaye a aussi été rebâtie après avoir été détruite à plusieurs reprises.	Ardet nec consumitur (brandt maar vergaat niet) is de leuze van de abdij van Grimbergen (sinds 1128). Net zoals de feniks - het emblee[m] van de abdij - uit zijn as verrijst, is ook de abdij na herhaalde verwoestingen heropgebouwd.

…uwerij Alken-Maes

10% 6 °C 43 °F

Grimbergen Optimo Bruno

top-fermentation	fermentation haute	hoge gisting
Recognised Belgian abbey beer	Bière d'abbaye belge reconnue	Erkend Belgisch abdijbier
dark amber-coloured	ambré foncé	donker amberkleurig
Bittersweet with a pronounced, powerful alcoholic aftertaste. Good balance between hop and malt owing to the double fermentation.	Doux-amère avec une fin de bouche prononcée, alcoolisée corsée. La double fermentation assure un équilibre entre le houblon et le malt.	Zoetbitter met uitgesproken en krachtige alcoholische afdronk. De dubbele gisting zorgt voor balans tussen hop en mout.
Pour carefully into a degreased, dry glass. Pour slowly to obtain a nice foam head.	Verser soigneusement dans un verre dégraissé et sec. Verser lentement de sorte qu'un faux col solide se forme.	Zorgvuldig uitschenken in een ontvet, droog glas. Langzaam schenken zodat er een mooie schuimkraag ontstaat.
Authentic abbey beer.	Authentique bière d'abbaye.	Authentiek abdijbier.

Grimbergen Tripel

Brouwerij Alken-Maes 9% 6 - 1 / 43 - 5

	top-fermentation re-fermented in the bottle	fermentation haute refermentation en bouteille	hoge gisting hergisting op fles
	Recognised Belgian abbey beer	Bière belge d'abbaye reconnue	Erkend Belgisch abdijbier
	amber-blond	blond ambré	amberblond
	Bittersweet, spicy, full-bodied with a warm aftertaste.	Amer-douce, corsée, plein ronde avec fin de bouche chaleureuse.	Bitterzoet, pittig, volrond met warme afdronk
	Pour carefully into a degreased, dry glass. Pour slowly for a nice foam head.	Verser soigneusement dans un verre dégraissé et sec. Laisser la levure au fond de la bouteille.	Zorgvuldig uitschenken in een ontvet, droog glas. Langzaam schenken zodat er een mooie schuimkraag ontstaat.
i	Authentic abbey beer.	Authentique bière d'abbaye.	Authentiek abdijbier.

asserie Saint-Feuillien

5% 4 °C 39 °F

top-fermentation naturally re-fermented in the bottle	fermentation haute refermentation naturelle en bouteille	hoge gisting natuurlijke hergisting in de fles
witbier	bière blanche	witbier
barley malt, sugar, hops, yeast, vitamine C, brewing water	malt d'orge, sucre, houblon, levure, vitamine C, eau de brassage	gerstemout, suiker, hop, gist, vitamine C, brouwwater
blond and pearly veiled, unfiltered	blonde et perlante voilée, non filtrée	blond en parelend gesluierd, niet gefilterd
Light character beer with smooth taste and aroma.	Bière de caractère légère, saveur et arôme moelleux.	Licht karakterbier, zachte smaak en aroma.

Grisette Blanche

Grisette Blonde

Brasserie Saint-Feuillien 5% 4 39

	top-fermentation naturally re-fermented in the bottle	fermentation haute refermentation naturelle en bouteille	hoge gisting natuurlijke hergisting in de fles
	Belgian ale	Belgian ale	Belgian ale
	barley malt, wheat, sugar, hops, yeast, vitamine C, brewing water	malt d'orge, froment, sucre, houblon, levure, vitamine C, eau de brassage	gerstemout, tarwe, suiker, hop, gist, vitamine C, brouwwater
	straw-yellow filtered	jaune paille filtrée	strogeel gefilterd
	Refreshing summer beer. Rich perfumes when served at room temperature.	Bière d'été rafraîchissante. Parfums riches lors de la dégustation à température de chambre.	Verfrissend zomerbier. Rijke parfums bij degustatie op kamertemperatuur.

3,50% 4 °C 39 °F

top-fermentation	fermentation haute	hoge gisting
white beer with fruit	bière blanche fruitée	witbier met fruit
barley malt, wheat, hops, fructose syrup, natural fruit juice, cherry aroma, vitamin C, brewing water	malt d'orge, froment, houblon, sirop fructose, jus de fruits naturel, arôme de cerises, vitamine C, eau de brassage	gerstemout, tarwe, hop, fructosesiroop, natuurlijk fruitsap, kersenaroma, vitamine C, brouwwater
vermillion-red not filtered	rouge vermillon non filtrée	vermiljoenrood ongefilterd
A fine balance between beer and cherry, mellow and tart, fruity.	Un ensemble équilibré de bière et de cerise, doux et acidulé, fruité.	Een evenwichtig samenspel van bier en kers, zacht en zurig, fruitig.

Grisette Fruits des Bois

Brasserie Saint-Feuillien 3,50% 4 3

	top-fermentation naturally re-fermented in the bottle	fermentation haute refermentation naturelle en bouteille	hoge gisting natuurlijke hergisting i de fles
	white beer with fruit	bière blanche fruitée	witbier met fruit
	barley malt, wheat malt, fructose/glucose syrup, hops, natural juice of forest fruits, natural flavouring of red fruits, sweetener, vitamine C, ascorbine acid, brewing water	malt d'orge, malt de froment, sirop de fructose/glucose, houblon, jus naturel de fruits des bois, arôme naturel de fruits rouges, édulcorant, vitamine C, acide ascorbine, eau de brassage	gerstemout, tarwemout fructose/glucosesiroop, hop, natuurlijk bosvruchtensap, natuurlijk aroma van rode vruchten, zoetstof, vitamine C, ascorbinezuur, brouw water
	purple-red, like a young burgundy wine	rouge violet, fait penser à un Bourgogne jeune	purperrood, doet denke aan een jonge Bourgogne
	Contrast of sweet and sourish flavours, like a delicious fruit cocktail. Red fruit flavours.	Contraste de goûts doux et acidulés comme une coupe de fruits délicieuse. Arômes de fruits rouges.	Contrast van zoete en zurige smaken zoals een schitterende fruitcoupe Aroma's van rood fruit.
i			

Grotten Flemish Ale

rouwerij Sint-Bernardus 7,70%

	top-fermentation	fermentation haute	hoge gisting
	Belgian strong ale	Belgian strong ale	Belgian strong ale
	apricot-coloured firm foam head	couleur abricot faux col solide	abrikozenkleur stevige schuimkraag
	Mild flavour of yeast, with touches of citrus and coriander. Taste: sweet evolving in coriander, lemon rind and pepper. Aftertase: pepper, hops and a warm alcohol touch.	Arôme doux de houblon avec des touches d'agrumes et de coriandre. Goût : doux évoluant vers le coriandre, l'écorce de citron et le poivre. Fin de bouche : poivre, houblon et touche d'alcool.	Mild aroma van gist met toetsen van citrus en koriander. Smaak: zoet dat evolueert naar koriander, citroenschil en peper. Afdronk: peper, hop en warme alcoholtoets.
	Product for the USA.	Brassée pour les Etats-Unis.	Gebrouwen voor de USA.

Grottenbier/Grotten Brown

Brouwerij Sint-Bernardus 6,50% 6 - 10 43 - 50

	top-fermentation re-fermented in the bottle	fermentation haute refermentation en bouteille	hoge gisting hergisting op de fles
	regional beer	bière régionale	streekbier
	different malt varieties, hops, sugar, yeast, water The beer matures in the marl caves of Kanne and Valkenburg, where air humidity is very high.	différentes variétés de malt, houblon, sucre, levure, eau La bière mûrit dans les cavernes calcaires de Kanne et Valkenburg, où l'air est très humide.	verschillende moutsoorten, hop, suiker, gist, water Het bier rijpt in de mergelgrotten van Kanne en Valkenburg waar de lucht zeer vochtig is.
	dark brown unfiltered	brun foncé non filtrée	donkerbruin ongefilterd
	Pleasant fruity aroma, balanced between bitter and sweet.	Arôme fruité agréable avec un équilibre entre amertume et douceur.	Aangenaam fruitig aroma met een evenwicht tussen bitter en zoet.
	Pour into a glass, rinsed with cold water. Leave the glass upright and pour the beer carefully in one single, fluent movement. The yeast sediment is left in the bottle.	Verser dans un verre rincé à l'eau froide. Laisser le verre en position verticale et verser la bière prudemment en un seul mouvement fluide. Laisser le dépôt de levure dans la bouteille.	Uitschenken in een met koud water gespoeld glas. Het glas rechtop laten staan en het bier in 1 vloeiende beweging voorzichtig schenken. Het gistdepot in de fles laten.
	Created by the masterbrewer Pierre Celis.	Créée par maître brasseur Pierre Celis.	Gecreëerd door Meesterbrouwer Pierre Celis.

adsbrouwerij Gruut 6,60% 4 °C 39 °F

top-fermentation not centrifuged	fermentation haute non centrifugée	hoge gisting niet gecentrifugeerd
Belgian ale amber or speciale belge	Belgian ale ambrée ou spéciale belge	Belgian ale amber of speciale belge
4 different malts, gruit (herbal) mix, yeast, water	4 variétés de malt, gruit (herbes), levure, eau	4 moutsoorten, gruutkruiden, gist, water
amber-brown, clear with a white foam head filtered	ambré brun, limpide avec un faux col blanc filtrée	amberbruin, helder met een witte schuimkraag gefilterd
Balanced, peppery dryness with a hint of tart orange in the aftertaste.	Sécheresse équilibrée, poivrée, avec un soupçon d'orange acide dans l'arrière-bouche.	Gebalanceerde, peperachtige droogheid met een vermoeden van zure sinaas in de afdronk.
Pour out quite vigorously to obtain a fine foam head.	Verser bien agilement pour former un faux col solide.	Goed doorschenken voor een flinke schuimkraag.
An English pale ale brewed in accordance with the old English method without added sugars.	Une pale ale anglaise brassée selon l'ancienne méthode anglaise, sans recours à des sucres supplémentaires.	Een Engelse pale ale gebrouwen volgens de oude Engelse methode zonder gebruik te maken van extra suikers.

Gruut Blond

Stadsbrouwerij Gruut

5,50% 4 39

	top-fermentation not centrifuged	fermentation haute non centrifugée	hoge gisting niet gecentrifugeerd
	Belgian ale	Belgian ale	Belgian ale
	malt, herbs, yeast, water	malt, herbes, levure, eau	mout, kruiden, gist, water
	blond, cloudy with a white foam head not filtered or pasteurised	blonde, trouble avec faux col blanc non filtrée, non pasteurisée	blond, troebel met witte schuimkraag ongefilterd, niet gepasteuriseerd
	Neutral mellow taste with a tart aftertaste owing to the special mix of herbs (gruit).	Goût légèrement doux neutre, avec une arrière-bouche amère, grâce au mélange d'épices spécial du gruit.	Neutrale lichtzachte smaak met een bittere afdronk dank zij de speciale gruutkruiden.
	Pour out quite vigorously to obtain a fine foam head.	Verser bien agilement pour former un faux col solide.	Goed doorschenken voor een flinke schuimkraag.
i			

Gruut Bruin

adsbrouwerij Gruut

8% 6 °C 43 °F

	top-fermentation not centrifuged	fermentation haute non centrifugée	hoge gisting niet gecentrifugeerd
	Belgian ale	Belgian ale	Belgian ale
	different malts, herbs, yeast, water	variétés de malt, herbes, levure, eau	moutsoorten, kruiden, gist, water
	brown, slightly cloudy with a white, thick foam head not filtered or pasteurised	brune, légèrement trouble avec un faux col épais, blanc non filtrée, non pasteurisée	bruin, licht troebel met een witte, dikke schuimkraag ongefilterd, niet gepasteuriseerd
	Cuvee with a smooth and mellow onset and a unique lingering aftertaste owing to the variety of different nuts used.	Cuvée d'un début facile et doux, et avec une arrière-bouche persistante unique grâce à la variété des sortes de malt utilisées.	Cuvee met een vlot en zacht begin en een unieke blijvende afdronk door de variatie van gebruikte nootsoorten.
	Pour out vigorously so that foam develops from the start.	Verser bien agilement pour former pas mal d'écume dès le départ.	Goed doorschenken zodat er zich al van bij het begin veel schuim vormt.
	Brewed to mark the first anniversary of the Ghent City Brewery Gruut.	Brassée à l'occasion du 1er anniversaire de la Stadsbrouwerij Gruut de Gand.	Gebrouwen n.a.v. het 1-jarig bestaan van de Gentse Stadsbrouwerij Gruut.

Gruut Inferno

Stadsbrouwerij Gruut 9% 8 - 9 / 46 - 48

	top-fermentation re-fermentation in the bottle not centrifuged	fermentation haute refermentation en bouteille non centrifugée	hoge gisting hergisting in de fles niet gecentrifugeerd
	Belgian ale	Belgian ale	Belgian ale
	malt, hops, yeast, water	malt, houblon, levure, eau	mout, hop, gist, water
	gold-coloured filtered, not pasteurised	dorée filtrée, non pasteurisée	goudkleurig gefilterd, niet gepasteuriseerd
	Strong, full-bodied, intense and delicate flavour and aroma, lingering hoppy aftertaste.	Caractère fort, goût et arôme intenses et délicats francs, arrière-bouche houblonnée persistante.	Sterk karakter, volmondig intense en delicate smaak en aroma, blijvend hoppige afdronk.
	Pour out gently owing to the abundant and delicate foam formation.	Verser prudemment à cause de la forte et délicate formation d'écume.	Voorzichtig uitschenken wegens de hevige en delicate schuimvorming.
	Loose canon of the range because it has been brewed using hops. Produced in tandem with the 'Sosseteit van de Gensche Mannekes Pies Twielink' (see label). The Manneke Pis twin is Ghent's emblem.	Rebelle dans l'assortiment parce qu'elle est brassée avec du houblon. Réalisée en collaboration avec la 'Sosseteit van de Gensche Mannekes Pies Twielink' (voir étiquette). Les jumeaux Manneke Pis symbolisent la ville de Gand.	Rebel in het assortiment omdat hij met hop is gebrouwen. Gemaakt in samenwerking met de 'Sosseteit van de Gensche Mannekes Pies Twielink' (zie etiket). De Manneke Pis tweeling staat symbool voor de stad Gent.

adsbrouwerij Gruut

5% 4 °C 39 °F

top-fermentation centrifuged	fermentation haute centrifugée	hoge gisting gecentrifugeerd
Belgian ale white beer	Belgian ale bière blanche	Belgian ale witbier
malt, wheat, herbs, coriander, curaçao, yeast, water	malt, froment, herbes, coriandre, curaçao, levure, eau	mout, tarwe, kruiden, koriander, curaçao, gist, water
white not filtered or pasteurised	blanche non filtrée, non pasteurisée	wit ongefilterd, niet gepasteuriseerd
Very aromatic with a fragrant fruitiness and a light, spicy flavour. The herbs provide a smooth, subtle, yet complex taste.	Très aromatique, avec un fruité parfumé et un goût léger, épicé. Les épices donnent un goût rond, subtil et complexe.	Zeer aromatisch met een geurige fruitigheid en een lichte, kruidige smaak. De kruiden zorgen voor een ronde, subtiele en complexe smaak.
Pour out quite vigorously to obtain a fine foam head.	Verser bien agilement pour former un faux col solide.	Goed doorschenken voor een flinke schuimkraag.

Gruut Wit

Gulden Delle

Brouwerij De Vlier 8,50% 2 - 4 / 36 - 39

	mixed fermentation re-fermentation in the bottle not centrifuged	fermentation mixte refermentation en bouteille non centrifugée	gemengde gisting hergisting in de fles niet gecentrifugeerd
	mixed culture of yeast and lactic acid bacteria	mélange de levure et de bactéries d'acide lactique	mengcultuur van gist en melkzuurbacteriën
	pilsner and wheat malt, hops (Saaz), home-made elderflower syrup, yeast, water	malt de pils et de froment, houblon Saaz, sirop de baies de sureau fabriqué de façon artisanale, levure, eau	pils- en tarwemout, Saazhop, zelfgemaakte vlierbloesemsiroop, gist, water
	straw-yellow blond with minimal foam head not filtered or pasteurised	jaune paille blond avec faux col minime non filtrée, non pasteurisée	strogeel blond met minimale schuimkraag ongefilterd, niet gepasteuriseerd
	Pleasant fruity aroma, complex fruity flavour. Sweet-and-sour aperitif beer with touches of nutmeg. Very refreshing.	Arôme fruité agréable, goût fruité complexe, bière d'apéritif aigre-douce, avec des touches de muscat, très désaltérante.	Aangenaam fruitig aroma, complex fruitige smaak. Zuurzoet aperitiefbier met toetsen van muscat. Heel verfrissend.
i	Gulden Delle is a bog area (or 'delle') in Sint-Pieters-Rode with many yellow flowers (hence Golden) and elder bushes. Brewery De Vlier produces nothing but elder ('vlier') beer ...	Gulden Delle est une zone marécageuse (ou 'delle') à Sint-Pieters-Rode, avec beaucoup de fleurs jaunes (d'où Gulden) et de buissons de sureau. Brouwerij De Vlier ne se concevrait pas sans une bière au sureau ('vlier...').	Gulden Delle is een moerasgebied (of delle) in Sint-Pieters-Rode met veel gele bloemen (vandaar Gulden) en vlierstruiken. Brouwerij De Vlier kan niet zonder een bier met vlier...

top-fermentation re-fermented in the bottle	fermentation haute refermentation en bouteille	hoge gisting hergisting in de fles
strong dark	foncée forte	sterk donker
barley malt, hops, yeast, water	malt d'orge, houblon, levure, eau	gerstemout, hop, gist, water
dark red	rouge foncé	donkerrood
Typical, rich, glowing taste with a coffee or chocolate touch.	Saveur typique, riche, ardente qui fait penser au café ou au chocolat.	Typische, rijke, gloeiende smaak die doet denken aan koffie, of aan chocolade.
Pour in a single, fluent and smooth movement, leaving 1 cm of yeast sediment in the bottle. The sediment can be poured, making the beer cloudy.	Verser en un seul mouvement fluide et doux et laisser 1 cm de dépôt de levure dans la bouteille. Le depôt peut être versé et rend la bière trouble.	Uitschenken in 1 vloeiende, zachte beweging en 1 cm gistdepot in de fles laten. De gistfond kan worden uitgeschonken en maakt het bier troebel.
Named after the gold statue on top of the Ghent belfry.	Son nom renvoie à la statue en or au sommet du Beffroi de Gand.	Genoemd naar het gouden beeld bovenop het Gentse Belfort.

Guldenberg

Brouwerij De Ranke 8,50% Moderate coole

top-fermentation	fermentation haute	hoge gisting
tripel	triple	tripel
pale malt, hop flowers, industrial yeast With dry-hopping.	malt pâle, fleurs de houblon, levure de culture Avec dry hopping.	bleekmout, hopbloemen, cultuurgist Met dry hopping.
dark blond slightly cloudy	blond foncé légèrement trouble	donkerblond licht troebel
Hoppy and bittersweet.	Houblonnée et amer-douce.	Hoppig en zoetbitter.

rasserie Sainte-Hélène

9% 8 - 10 °C 46 - 50 °F

top-fermentation re-fermented in the bottle	fermentation haute refermentation en bouteille	hoge gisting hergisting op de fles
amber	ambrée	amber
pale ale malt, Elzas hops, yeast, sugar, water	malt pale ale, houblon d'Alsace, levure, sucre, eau	pale ale mout, Elzas hop, gist, suiker, water
unfiltered	non filtrée	ongefilterd
Powerful with pure malt and hop flavours.	Corsé avec des arômes purs maltés et houblonnés.	Krachtig met pure mout- en hoparoma's.
Boutique beer. The label was designed by the artist Palix.	Brassée de façon artisanale. L'étiquette est conçue par le dessinateur Palix.	Artisanaal gebrouwen. Het etiket is ontworpen door tekenaar Palix.

Haanse Witte

den Haene by Brouwerij Strubbe

5,50% — 4 - 5 / 39 - 41

	top-fermentation re-fermentation in the bottle	fermentation haute refermentation en bouteille	hoge gisting hergisting op de fles
	white beer brewed traditionally	bière blanche brassée de façon artisanale	witbier ambachtelijk gebrouwen
	barley, wheat, oat, hops (Poperinge, Saaz), sugar, yeast, water	orge, froment, avoine, houblon (Poperinge, Saaz), sucre, levure, eau	gerst, tarwe, haver, hop (Poperinge en Saaz), suiker, gist, water
	not filtered	non filtrée	ongefilterd
	Refreshing thirst-quencher, slightly spicy, pleasant bitterness.	Bière rafraîchissante, désaltérante, légèrement épicée, acidité agréable.	Verfrissende dorstlesser, licht gekruid, aangename zurigheid.
i			

…uzestekerij Hanssens Artisanaal 4%

	spontaneous fermentation	fermentation spontanée	spontane gisting
	lambic	lambic	lambiek
	Lambic (70%) and blue berries (30%)	lambic (70%) et cassis (30%)	lambiek (70%) en blauwe bessen (30%)
	Only brewed for exports.	Brassée uniquement pour l'exportation.	Enkel voor export gebrouwen.

Hanssens Lambic Experimental Cassis

Hanssens Lambic Experimental Raspberry

Geuzestekerij Hanssens Artisanaal 4%

	spontaneous fermentation	fermentation spontanée	spontane gisting
	lambic	lambic	lambiek
	Lambic (70%) and raspberries (30%)	lambic (70%) et framboises (30%)	lambiek (70%) en frambozen (30%)
	not filtered or pasteurised	non filtrée, non pasteurisée	ongefilterd, niet gepasteuriseerd

uwerij Alken-Maes 8,50% 8 °C 46 °F

Hapkin

	top-fermentation re-fermented in the bottle	fermentation haute refermentation en bouteille	hoge gisting hergisting op de fles
	strong blond	blonde forte	sterk blond
	blond unique, imposing, creamy foam head	blonde faux col unique, imposant et crémeux	blond unieke, imposante en romige kraag
	Flowery Saaz hop flavour. Smooth malty character. Sparkling, perfumed fruit flavour.	Arôme fleuri de houblon Saaz. Caractère houblonné moelleux. Goût fruité, parfumé, pétillant.	Bloemrijk aroma van Saazhop. Zacht moutig karakter. Sprankelende, geparfumeerde fruitigheid.
	Pour carefully into a degreased, dry glass. Fill the glass in one smooth movement for a nice, big foam head.	Verser soigneusement dans un verre dégraissé et sec. Remplir le verre doucement d'un seul trait pour obtenir un faux col solide.	Zorgvuldig uitschenken in een ontvet, droog glas. Het glas in 1 beweging zachtjes vullen voor een grote schuimkraag.

Hector tripel

Traagwater by Brouwerij De Graal 8,20% 6 - 1 43 - 5

	top-fermentation re-fermented in the bottle centrifuged	fermentation haute refermentation en bouteille centrifugée	hoge gisting hergisting op de fles gecentrifugeerd
	tripel	triple	tripel
	malt, hops, yeast, water	malt, houblon, levure, eau	mout, hop, gist, water
	blond with white foam head unfiltered, not pasteurised	blonde avec faux col blanc non filtrée, non pasteurisée	blond met witte schuimkraag ongefilterd, niet gepasteuriseerd
	Full-malty with a hefty dose of bitterness (hops) and a fruity touch. Long, dry and pleasant bitter aftertaste. Malty and somewhat spicy aroma.	Franchement maltée, avec une solide dose d'amertume houblonnée et une touche de fruité. Arrière-bouche longue, sèche et agréablement amère. Arôme malté et quelque peu épicé.	Volmoutig met een flink dosis hopbitter en een toets fruitigheid. Lange droge en aangenaam bittere afdronk. Moutig en enigszins kruidig aroma.
	Pour into a tulip-shaped glass. The yeast sediment can be poured out or left in the bottle.	Verser dans un verre tulipe. Laisser le dépôt de levure dans la bouteille selon les souhaits .	Uitschenken in een tulpvormig glas. Het bezinksel desgewenst in de fle laten.
i			

	top-fermentation re-fermentation in the bottle	fermentation haute refermentation en bouteille	hoge gisting hergisting op de fles
	specialty beer	bière spéciale	speciaalbier
	2 different malts, different hops, different granulated yeasts	2 variétés de malt, diverses variétés de houblon, diverses levures granuleuses	2 moutsoorten, diverse hopsoorten, diverse korrelgisten
	clear gold-blond	limpide blond doré	helder goudblond
	Particularly spicy owing to the American hops.	Particulièrement épicée à cause du houblon américain.	Bijzonder kruidig door de Amerikaanse hop.

Hellekapelle

Brouwerij De Bie 5%

	top-fermentation re-fermented in the bottle	fermentation haute refermentation en bouteille	hoge gisting hergisting in de fles
	blond	blonde	blond
	hops, yeast, malt, water	malt, houblon, levure, eau	hop, gist, mout, water
	blond slightly cloudy draught beer	blonde un peu trouble au fût	blond iets troebel van het va
	Spicy hop taste.	Saveur houblonnée corsée.	Pittige hopsmaak.

uwerij De Bie 7% 6 °C 43 °F

top-fermentation	fermentation haute	hoge gisting
amber	ambrée	amber
malt, hops, wheat, candy sugar, yeast, herbs, water	malt, houblon, froment, sucre candi, levure, herbes, eau	mout, hop, tarwe, kandijsuiker, gist, kruiden, water
amber	ambrée	amber
Spicy.	Epicée.	Kruidig.

Hercule Stout

Brasserie des Légendes

9% 8 - 1
46 - 5

	top-fermentation re-fermented in the bottle	fermentation haute refermentation en bouteille	hoge gisting nagisting in de fles
	stout	stout	stout
	pale malt, roasted malt, hops, yeast, water	malt pâle, malt brûlé, houblon, levure, eau	bleke mout, gebrande mout, hop, gist, water
	black	noire	zwart
	Robust and smooth. Creamy, mocca, spicy touch.	Solide et douce. Crémeuse, goût de moka, touche aromatique.	Robuust en zacht. Romig, mokka, kruidige toets.

7% 5 - 6 °C 41 - 43 °F

top-fermentation re-fermentation in the bottle	fermentation haute refermentation en bouteille	hoge gisting hergisting op de fles
Recognised Belgian brown abbey beer	Bière d'abbaye belge reconnue brune	Erkend Belgisch Abdijbier bruin
malt, hops, water	malt, houblon, eau	mout, hop, water
orange-amber, clear	ambré orange, limpide	oranje-amber, helder
Full of character with a hint of vanilla.	Bière très caractéristique, avec une touche de vanille.	Karaktervol bier met vanilletoets.
Pour into a clean, degreased glass, avoiding contact with the foam.	Verser dans un verre dégraissé et propre sans que la bouteille touche l'écume.	Uitschenken in een ontvet en zuiver glas zonder dat de fles het schuim raakt.

Herkenrode Bruin

Herkenrode Tripel

Brouwerij Sint-Jozef

7% 5 - 41 -

	top-fermentation re-fermentation in the bottle	fermentation haute refermentation en bouteille	hoge gisting hergisting op de fles
	Recognised Belgian tripel abbey beer	Triple d'abbaye belge re-connue	Erkend Belgisch Abdij bier tripel
	malt, hops, herbs, water with dry-hopping	malt, houblon, herbes, eau avec dry hopping	mout, hop, kruiden, w ter met dry-hopping
	gold-blond, clear	blond doré, limpide	goudblond,helder
	Bitter with a sweet touch and dry aftertaste.	Amère, avec une touche sucrée et une fin de bouche sèche.	Bitter met een zoete toets en droge nasma
	Pour into a clean, de-greased glass, avoiding contact with the foam.	Verser dans un verre dé-graissé et propre sans que la bouteille touche l'écume.	Uitschenken in een or vet en zuiver glas zon dat de fles het schuim raakt.
i			

Nest by De Scheldebrouwerij

6,50% 6 °C 43 °F

top-fermentation re-fermentation in the bottle not centrifuged	fermentation haute refermentation en bouteille non centrifugée	hoge gisting hergisting in de fles niet gecentrifugeerd
city or regional beer blond	bière citadine ou régionale blonde	stads- of streekbier blond
malt, hops, yeast, sugar, water	malt, houblon, levure, sucre, eau	mout, hop, gist, suiker, water
hazy red-blond with a firm fine pearly foam head not filtered or pasteurised	blond rouge fade avec un faux col solide à bulles fines non filtrée, non pasteurisée	wazig roodblond met een stevige fijncellige schuimkraag ongefilterd, niet gepasteuriseerd
Hoppy aroma owing to the different continental hops. A spicy flavour with a bitter aftertaste.	Arôme houblonné dû aux variétés continentales de houblon. Un goût épicé qui s'écoule avec une forte amertume.	Hoppig aroma door de continentale hopsoorten. Een kruidige smaak die sterk bitter uitvloeit.
Serve in a goblet with or without yeast sediment.	Verser avec ou sans levure dans un verre calice.	Met of zonder gist uitschenken in een kelkglas.
The name refers to Turnhout, capital of the game card, where the brewery is based.	Le nom fait référence à Turnhout, capitale du jeu de cartes, où la brasserie est aussi installée.	De naam verwijst naar Turnhout, hoofdstad van de speelkaart, waar ook de brouwerij is gevestigd.

Hertenheer

Hervoise

Brasserie Grain d'Orge

8,20% 6 - 43 - 4

	top-fermentation re-fermented in the bottle	fermentation haute refermentation en bouteille	hoge gisting hergisting in de fles
	regional beer	bière régionale	streekbier
	malt varieties, yeast, hops, sugar, pure sugar-free apple and pear syrup (14 kg/800 l), herbs, water	variétés de malt, levure, houblon, sucre, sirop pur sans sucre de pommes et de poires (14 kg/800 l), herbes, eau	moutsoorten, gist, ho suiker, pure suikervrij siroop van appels en p ren (14 kg/800 l), krui den, water
	red-brown	brun rouge	roodbruin
	Fresh, fruity (apple and pear), spicy and above all sourish.	Fraîche, fruitée (pommes et poires), relevée et surtout acidulée.	Fris, fruitig (appel en peer), kruidig en voor zurig.
	Leave the yeast sediment in the bottle.	Laisser le dépôt de levure dans la bouteille.	Het gistdepot in de fle laten.

t Alternatief by Brouwerij De Graal

6,50% — 6 - 8 °C / 43 - 46 °F

top-fermentation re-fermented in the bottle	fermentation haute refermentation en bouteille	hoge gisting hergisting op de fles
ale unpasteurised	ale non pasteurisée	ale niet gepasteuriseerd
three malt varieties (pilsener, Münich, wheat), three hop varieties, yeast, herbs, brewing water. No additives.	3 variétés de malt (pils, Münich, froment), 3 sortes de houblon, levure, herbes, eau de brassage. Pas d'additifs.	3 soorten mout (pils, Münich, tarwe), 3 hopsoorten, gist, kruiden, brouwwater. Geen additieven.
blond (11 EBC) unfiltered	blonde (11 EBC) non filtrée	blond (11 EBC) niet gefilterd
A lively full-malt beer with a full-bodied, fruity and bitter character. Taste and aroma: citrus, fruity, bitterness.	Une bière vive pleinement maltée avec un caractère franc fruité et amer. Saveur et arôme :agrumes, fruits, amertume.	Een levend volmoutbier met een volmondig fruitig en bitter karakter. Smaak en aroma: citrus, fruitig, bitterheid.
Pour carefully in the Alternatief glass.	Verser prudemment dans le verre Alternatief.	Voorzichtig uitschenken in het Alternatiefglas.

Hik Blond

Hik Bruin

Het Alternatief by Brouwerij De Graal

6,50% 8 -
46 -

	top-fermentation re-fermented in the bottle	fermentation haute refermentation en bouteille	hoge gisting hergisting op de fles
	between dubbel and stout unpasteurised	entre double et stout non pasteurisée	tussen dubbel en stou niet gepasteuriseerd
	6 malt varieties (including pilsner and chocolate malt), 3 hop varieties, yeast, candy sugar, brewing water, no additives	6 variétés de malt (e.a. malt de pils et de chocolat), 3 sortes de houblon, levure, sucre candi, eau de brassage, pas d'additifs	6 soorten mout (o.a. pils- en chocolademout), 3 hopsoorten, gist, kandijsuiker, brouwwater, geen add tieven
	dark brown (165 EBC) unfiltered	brun foncé (165 EBC) non filtrée	donkerbruin (165 EBC) niet gefilterd
	A lively, unsweetened beer, full-bodied and dry. Many flavour nuances, including hop bitter and chocolate bitter.	Une bière vive non sucrée franche et sèche. Beaucoup de nuances de saveur dont amer-houblon et amer-chocolat.	Een levend, niet zoet bier dat volmondig en droog is. Veel smaakn ances waaronder hopb ter en chocoladebitter
	Pour carefully in the Alternatief glass.	Verser prudemment dans le verre Alternatief.	Voorzichtig uitschenk in het Alternatiefglas.
i			

uwerij Vissenaken

6% 8 - 12 °C 46 - 54 °F

top-fermentation re-fermented in the bottle	fermentation haute refermentation en bouteille	hoge gisting hergisting op de fles
dark	foncée	donker
barley malt, hops, sugar, yeast, brewing water. Boutique beer.	malt d'orge, houblon, sucre, levure, eau de brassage. Brassage artisanal.	gerstemout, hop, suiker, gist, brouwwater. Ambachtelijk gebrouwen.
dark brown unfiltered	brun foncé non filtrée	donkerbruin ongefilterd
Savoury thirst-quencher. Sweet but not sticky, full malt taste with a bitter nuance and a fruity touch.	Désaltérant savoureuse. Douce mais pas collante, goût malté plein avec une nuance amère et une touche fruitée.	Smaakvolle dorstlesser. Zoet maar niet plakkerig, volle moutsmaak met een bittere nuance en fruitige toets.
Slowly pour into a bulb jar, with or without yeast.	Verser lentement dans un verre ballon, avec ou sans levure.	Langzaam inschenken in een bolvormig glas, met of zonder gist.
Store upright at cellar temperature. The taste evolution is at its best from three months after the bottling date onwards.	Conserver en position verticale à température de cave. Ce n'est que 3 mois après la date de la mise en bouteilles que la saveur arrive à son sommet.	Rechtop bewaren op keldertemperatuur. Pas 3 maanden na botteldatum is de smaak geëvolueerd tot op zijn best.

Hoegaarden Citron

AB-Inbev Leuven 3%

top-fermentation	fermentation haute	hoge gisting
white beer with fruit	bière blanche fruitée	witbier met fruit
aromatised with herbs and natural lemon and lime aromas.	aromatisée avec herbes et arômes naturels de citron et de limon	gearomatiseerd met kruiden en natuurlijke aroma's van citroen en limoen.
cloudy white not filtered	trouble blanc non filtrée	troebel wit ongefilterd
Fruity aromas are punctuated with distinctly hoppy touches.	Les arômes fruités sont truffés de touches houblonnées marquées.	Fruitige aroma's worden doorspekt met uitgesproken hoppige toetsen.

-Inbev Leuven 8,70% 5 °C 41 °F

Hoegaarden Grand Cru

	top-fermentation re-fermented in the bottle	fermentation haute refermentation en bouteille	hoge gisting hergisting op de fles
	strong blond	blonde forte	sterk blond
	wheat, malt, hops, yeast, coriander, orange rind, water	froment, malt, houblon, levure, coriandre, écorce d'orange, eau	tarwe, mout, hop, gist, koriander, sinaasappel-schil, water
	peach-yellow cloudy yeast veil	jaune pêche voile de levure trouble	perzikgeel troebele gistsluier
	Fruity aroma and taste bouquet, warm after-taste. Subtle and com-plex beer with a high alcohol content.	Arômes et bouquet de saveurs fruités, fin de bouche chaleureuse. Bière de dégustation subtile et complexe.	Fruitig aroma en smaak-boeket, warme afdronk. Subtiel en complex de-gustatiebier.
	Rinse the glass in cold water, tilt it and smooth-ly pour the beer. Skim off if desired	Rincer le verre à l'eau froide, le tenir incliné et verser la bière douce-ment. Ecumer selon le goût.	Het glas onder koud wa-ter spoelen, schuin hou-den en het bier zacht uitschenken. Desge-wenst afschuimen.
i			

Hoegaarden Rosée

AB-Inbev Leuven 4,50% 2 - 3 36 - 37

	top-fermentation re-fermented in the bottle	fermentation haute refermentation en bouteille	hoge gisting hergisting op de fles
	witbier aromatised	bière blanche aromatisée	witbier gearomatiseerd
	wheat, pale malt, corn, hops, yeast, coriander, orange rind, water, seasoned with herbs and natural raspberry flavour, sugar, minimum 10% fruit.	froment, malt pâle, maïs, houblon, levure, coriandre, écorce d'orange, eau, aromatisé aux herbes et à l'arôme naturel de framboises, sucre, 10% fruits minimum	tarwe, bleekmout, mais, hop, gist, koriander, sinaasschil, water, gearomatiseerd met kruiden en natuurlijk frambozenaroma, suiker, 10% frui minimum
	light pink, cloudy	rose clair trouble	lichtroze troebel
	Rinse the glass with cold water. Tilt it and pour half of the beer with sufficient foam. Loosen the yeast sediment from the bottom by firmly spinning the bottle and continue pouring until the creamy foam head reaches the edge of the glass. Skim off if desired.	Rincer le verre à l'eau froide, le tenir en oblique et verser la moitié de la bière avec suffisamment d'écume. Dégager le dépôt de levure en tournant fort et continuer à verser jusqu'à ce que le faux col crémeux arrive au bord du verre. Ecumer selon le goût.	Het glas onder koud water spoelen, schuin houden en het bier half uitschenken met voldoende schuim. De gistbodem losmaken door de fles krachtig rond te walsen en verder uitschenken tot de romige kraag aan de glasrand komt. Desgewenst afschuimen
i			

Hoegaarden Speciale

B-Inbev Leuven 5,50% 2 - 3 °C 36 - 37 °F

	top-fermentation re-fermented in the bottle	fermentation haute refermentation en bouteille	hoge gisting hergisting op de fles
	strong blond beer	bière blonde forte	sterk blond bier
	wheat, light roasted malts, hops, yeast, coriander, orange rind, water	froment, malt légèrement brûlé, houblon, levure, coriandre, écorce d'orange, eau	tarwe, licht gebrande mouten, hop, gist, koriander, sinaasappelschil, water
	golden blond cloudy yeast veil	blond doré voile de levure trouble	goudblond troebele gistsluier
	Sweeter and warmer than the common Hoegaarden witbier. Ample and deep nose with malt and fine hops. Bitter, long-lasting taste that covers the spiciness.	Plus douce et chaleureuse que la Hoegaarden Blanche ordinaire. Parfum large et profond de malt et de houblon raffiné. Saveur amère qui reste longtemps en bouche et qui couvre le goût relevé.	Zoeter en warmer dan het gewone Hoegaarden Witbier. Ruime en diepe neus met mout en fijne hop. Bittere smaak die lang in de mond blijft en de kruidigheid toedekt.
	Rinse the glass in cold water, tilt it and smoothly pour the beer. Skim off if desired.	Rincer le verre à l'eau froide, le tenir incliné et verser la bière doucement. Ecumer selon le goût.	Het glas onder koud water spoelen, schuin houden en het bier zacht uitschenken. Desgewenst afschuimen.
i			

Hoegaarden Verboden Vrucht

AB-Inbev Leuven

8,80% 5 41

	top-fermentation re-fermented in the bottle	fermentation haute refermentation en bouteille	hoge gisting hergisting op de fles
	strong dark	foncée forte	sterk donker
	dark malt, hops, yeast, coriander, water	malt foncé, houblon, levure, coriandre, eau	donkere mout, hop, gist, koriander, water
	brown-red very compact foam head	brun rouge faux col très épais	bruinrood zeer dichte schuimkraag
	Assertive onset with a very smooth, gratifying end. Spicy plant flavour, sweet but especially dry with a coriander accent, full in the mouth.	Début assertif, fin très douce et caressante. Arôme de plantes relevé, doux mais surtout sec avec un accent de coriandre plein dans la bouche.	Assertieve start maar zeer zacht en strelend einde. Kruidig plantenaroma, zoet maar vooral droog met korianderaccent, vol in de mond.
	Rinse the glass in cold water, tilt it and smoothly pour the beer. Skim off if desired.	Rincer le verre à l'eau froide, le tenir incliné et verser la bière doucement. Ecumer selon le goût.	Het glas onder koud water spoelen, schuin houden en het bier zacht uitschenken. Desgewenst afschuimen.
i			

B-Inbev Leuven 4,90% 2 - 3 °C / 36 - 37 °F

Hoegaarden Wit

top-fermentation re-fermented in the bottle	fermentation haute refermentation en bouteille	hoge gisting hergisting op de fles
witbier	bière blanche	witbier
wheat, pale malt, corn, hops, yeast, coriander, orange rind, water	froment, malt pâle, maïs, houblon, levure, coriandre, écorce d'orange, eau	tarwe, bleekmout, maïs, hop, gist, koriander, sinaasappelschil, water
white-yellow with cloudy yeast veil	blanc jaune avec une voile de levure trouble	witgeel met troebele gistsluier
Spicy, fresh aroma and taste with a strong coriander accent.	Arôme relevé et frais avec accent de coriandre prononcé.	Kruidig en fris aroma met sterk koriander-accent.
Rinse the glass in cold water, tilt it and pour half of the bottle creating sufficient foam. Loosen the yeast sediment by firmly revolving the bottle and continue filling the glass until the creamy head reaches the rim of the glass. Skim off if desired	Rincer le verre à l'eau froide, le tenir incliné et verser la moitié de la bière avec suffisamment d'écume. Dégager le dépôt de levure en secouant fort la bouteille et continuer à verser jusqu'à ce que le col crémeux atteigne le bord du verre. Ecumer selon le goût.	Het glas onder koud water spoelen, schuin houden en het bier half uitschenken met voldoende schuim. De gistbodem losmaken door de fles krachtig rond te walsen en verder uitschenken tot de romige kraag aan de glasrand komt. Desgewenst afschuimen.

H

Hof Korvatunturi

t Hofbrouwerijke

11%

	top-fermentation	fermentation haute	hoge gisting
	abbey beer double	bière d'abbaye double	abdijbier dubbel

evebrouwerij Hof ten Dormaal 7,50%

	top-fermentation	fermentation haute	hoge gisting
	amber	ambrée	amber
	barley malt, sugar, hops, yeast, water	malt de froment, sucre, houblon, levure, eau	gerstemout, suiker, hop, gist, water
	amber	ambrée	amber

Hof ten Dormaal Amber

H

Hof ten Dormaal Blond

Hoevebrouwerij Hof ten Dormaal 8%

	top-fermentation	fermentation haute	hoge gisting
	strong blond	blonde forte	sterk blond
	barley malt, sugar, hops, yeast, water	malt de froment, sucre, houblon, levure, eau	gerstemout, suiker, hop, gist, water
	blond	blonde	blond

[…]evebrouwerij Hof ten Dormaal 7,50%

top-fermentation	fermentation haute	hoge gisting
double	double	dubbel
barley malt, sugar, hops, yeast, water	malt de froment, sucre, houblon, levure, eau	gerstemout, suiker, hop, gist, water

Hof ten Dormaal Donker

Hof ten Dormaal Wit Goud, Witloofbier

Hoevebrouwerij Hof ten Dormaal 8%

	top-fermentation	fermentation haute	hoge gisting
	barley malt, sugar, hops, yeast, chicory root, water	malt d'orge, sucre, houblon, levure, racine de chicons, eau	gerstemout, suiker, hop, gist, witloofwortel, water
	Chicory, aka 'white gold', brought wealth to the region. All that remains now are the memories of smoking stoves and undulating sheets … (quote by brewer Andre Janssens)	La witloof (endives ou chicons), aussi appelée 'Or blanc', a apporté la prospérité dans la région. Aujourd'hui, seuls subsistent les souvenirs des petites cuisinières à charbon fumantes et des plaques ondulantes… (citation du brasseur André Janssens)	Witloof, ook 'Wit goud' genoemd, bracht welstand in de streek. Nu resten enkel de herinneringen aan walmende kacheltjes en golvende platen… (citaat van brouwer Andre Janssens)

Hofblues

Hofbrouwerijke

5,50% — 10 °C / 50 °F

	top-fermentation	fermentation haute	hoge gisting
	stout	stout	stout
	malt, hops, yeast, water	malt, houblon, levure, eau	mout, hop, gist, water
	dark to black dark foam head	foncée à noire faux col foncé	donker tot zwart donkere schuimkraag
	Spicy and hoppy. Nose of mocca, a well-balanced bitterness and a slightly roasty taste.	Corsée et houblonnée. Parfum de moka, saveur amère équilibrée et touche de goût légère-ment brûlée.	Pittig en hoppig. Neus van mokka, een even-wichtige bitterheid en een lichtgebrande smaaktoets.
	Pour carefully, leaving 1 cm in the bottle.	Verser prudemment et laisser 1 cm de bière dans la bouteille.	Voorzichtig uitschenken en 1 cm in het flesje la-ten.
i			

Hofdraak

t Hofbrouwerijke

6,20% 10 - 12 50 - 54

	top-fermentation	fermentation haute	hoge gisting
	dubbel	double	dubbel
	malt, hops, yeast, herbs, water	malt, houblon, levure, herbes, eau	mout, hop, gist, kruiden water
	dark clear	foncée, claire	donker helder
	Full and spicy. Full-bodied with a malty touch and a slightly bitter finish with a spicy aftertaste.	Pleine et relevée. Franche avec une touche maltée et une note finale légèrement amère, fin de bouche relevée.	Vol kruidig. Volmondig met een moutige toets en een licht bittere eindnoot die kruidig uitvloeit.
	Pour carefully, leaving 1 cm in the bottle.	Verser prudemment et laisser 1 cm de bière dans la bouteille.	Voorzichtig uitschenken en 1 cm in het flesje laten.
i			

Hofelf

Hofbrouwerijke 7,50% 10 - 12 °C / 50 - 54 °F

top-fermentation	fermentation haute	hoge gisting
wheat tripel	triple de froment	tarwetripel
malt, hops, yeast, herbs, water	malt, houblon, levure, herbes, eau	mout, hop, gist, kruiden, water
blond cloudy witbier creamy foam head	blonde bière blanche trouble faux col crémeux	blond troebel witbier romige schuimkraag
Slightly sourish but with a sweet touch of wheat malt. Full-bodied.	Légèrement acidulée avec une touche douce de froment malté. Franche.	Zachtzurig maar met zoete toets van tarwe-mout. Volmondig.
Pour carefully, leaving 1 cm in the bottle.	Verser prudemment et laisser 1 cm de bière dans la bouteille.	Voorzichtig uitschenken en 1 cm in het flesje la-ten.

Hofnar

t Hofbrouwerijke

5%

	top-fermentation re-fermentation in the bottle	fermentation haute refermentation en bouteille	hoge gisting hergisting op de fles
	amber Belgian ale	ambrée Belgian ale	amber Belgian ale
	brewed on the basis of whisky malt	brassée à base de malt de whisky	gebrouwen op basis van whiskymout
	pale amber with white tufty foam head not filtered	légèrement ambré avec faux col écume rocailleuse non filtrée	licht amber met wit rotsachtige schuimkraag ongefilterd
	Dry and slightly bitter. A fruity onset that turns into a bitter aftertaste. Subtle sharpness that lingers because of the whisky malt.	Seche et légèrement amère. Tout de même une approche initiale fruitée, qui passe lentement à l'amer. Une fine aigreur, qui reste longtemps en suspension du fait du malt de whisky.	Droog en lichtbitter. Toch een fruitige aanzet die langzaam naar bitter gaat. Fijne scherpte die lang blijft hangen door de whiskymout.

6,50% 6 - 12 °C 43 - 54 °F

	top-fermentation	fermentation haute	hoge gisting
	ale	ale	ale
	malt, hops, yeast, herbs, water	malt, houblon, levure, herbes, eau	mout, hop, gist, kruiden, water
	amber slightly cloudy, unfiltered	ambrée légèrement trouble, non filtrée	amber licht troebel, ongefilterd
	Bitter and hoppy character. Dry beer with a fresh slightly sourish flavour (owing to the special yeast stem). Wood flavour and a refreshing, bitter aftertaste.	Caractère amer et houblonné. Bière sèche avec un goût frais légèrement acidulé (type de levure spéciale). Arôme boisé et fin de bouche amère et rafraîchissante.	Bitter en hoppig karakter. Droog biertje met een frisse lichtzurigheid (speciale giststam). Houtaroma en verfrissend bittere afdronk.
	Pour carefully, leaving 1 cm in the bottle.	Verser prudemment et laisser 1 cm de bière dans la bouteille.	Voorzichtig uitschenken en 1 cm in het flesje laten.
i			

Holsbeek Lente Tripel

Brouwerij De Vlier — 8,50% — 4 - 6 / 39 - 43

	top-fermentation re-fermentation in the bottle not centrifuged	fermentation haute refermentation en bouteille non centrifugée	hoge gisting hergisting in de fles niet gecentrifugeerd
	tripel	triple	tripel
	pilsner and wheat malt, oat, hops (Saaz), yeast, water	malt de pils et de froment, flocons d'avoine, houblon Saaz, levure, eau	pils- en tarwermout, havervlokken, Saazhop, gist, water
	gold-coloured blond with thick, white foam head not filtered or pasteurised	doré blond avec faux col blanc collant au verre non filtrée, non pasteurisée	goudkleurig blond met wandklevende, witte schuimkraag ongefilterd, niet gepasteuriseerd
	Pleasant hoppy and fruity aroma. Full-bodied with a pleasant bitterness owing to the hops. Refreshing aftertaste.	Arôme houblonné et fruité agréable, goût franc, avec une agréable amertume due au houblon, arrière-bouche rafraîchissante.	Aangenaam hoppig en fruitig aroma. Volle smaak met een aangename bitterheid van de hop. Verfrissende afdronk.
	Pour into a tulip glass and leave yeast sediment in bottle or pour along.	Verser dans un verre tulipe et laisser le dépôt de levure dans la bouteille ou le verser également.	Uitschenken in een tulpvormig glas en de gistbodem in de fles laten of meeschenken.
	Spring beer brewed to mark the brewery's move from Kessel-Lo to Holsbeek.	Bière de printemps brassée à l'occasion du déménagement de la brasserie de Kessel-Lo à Holsbeek.	Lentebier gebrouwen naar aanleiding van de verhuizing van de brouwerij van Kessel-Lo naar Holsbeek.

ouwerij De Ranke 8%

Hop Harvest 2010

	top-fermentation not centrifuged	fermentation haute non centrifugée	hoge gisting niet gecentrifugeerd
	very dark wet-hop beer	foncée forte bière wet-hop	sterk donker wet-hop bier
	2010 edition: pilsner malt, candy sugar, hops (Hallertau)	édition 2010: malt de pils, candi, houblon (Hallertau)	editie 2010: pilsmout, kandij, hop (Hallertau)
	clear blond not filtered or pasteur-ised	limpide blond non filtrée, non pasteu-risée	helder blond ongefilterd, niet gepas-teuriseerd
	Wine-like, a great deal of lambic in the nose, medium tart.	Vineuse, beaucoup de lambic dans le bouquet, moyennement acide.	Vineus, veel lambiek in de neus, medium zuur.
i	Wet-hop beer is brewed with undried hops, straight from the field into the beer!	La bière au houblon hu-mide est brassée avec du houblon non séché, di-rectement du champ dans la bière !	Wet-hop bier wordt ge-brouwen met onge-droogde hop, van het veld rechtstreeks in het bier!

Hop-ruiter

De Scheldebrouwerij

8%

top-fermentation re-fermentation in the bottle	fermentation haute refermentation en bouteille	hoge gisting hergisting op de fles
blond tripel	triple blonde	blonde tripel
barley malt, American hops, coriander, yeast, water with dry-hopping	malt d'orge, houblon Américain, coriandre, levure, eau avec dry hopping	gerstemout, Amerikaanse hop, koriander, gist, water met dry-hopping
blond gold-yellow (21 EBC) with fine, white foam head.	blond jaune doré (21 EBC) avec faux col solide blanc.	blond goudgeel (21 EBC) met mooie, witte schuimkraag.
Fine, fruity and somewhat spicy nose. Light dry aftertaste with distinct hop aroma.	Bouquet fin, fruité et un peu épicé. Arrière-bouche légèrement sèche, avec un arôme de houblon particulier.	Fijne, fruitige en iets kruidige neus. Licht droge afdronk met bijzonder hoparoma.
Brewed at the request of an American customer.	Brassée pour le compte d'un client américain.	Gebrouwen in opdracht van een Amerikaanse klant.

Hopus

asserie Lefebvre 8,30%

	top-fermentation centrifuged	fermentation haute centrifugée	hoge gisting gecentrifugeerd
	amber or speciale belge	ambrée ou spéciale belge	amber of speciale belge
	barley malt, sugar, 5 different hops, yeast, water beer with dry-hopping	malt d'orge, sucre, 5 variétés de houblon, levure, eau bière avec dry-hopping	gerstemout, suiker, 5 hopsoorten, gist, water bier met dry-hopping
	filtered, not pasteurised	filtrée, non pasteurisée	gefilterd, niet gepasteuriseerd
	Perfectly balanced with a taste pallet of refined malts. Unique scent and bitterness owing to the different hop varieties used.	Parfait en équilibre, avec une palette de goûts de malts raffinés. Parfum unique et amertume du fait des variétés de houblon.	Perfect in evenwicht met een smakepalet van geraffineerde mouten. Uniek parfum en bitterheid door de hopvariëteiten.
	Serve in a stemmed beer glass. Leave the yeast sediment in the bottle or sample from a small glass.	Verser dans un verre avec pied. Laisser le dépôt de levure dans la bouteille ou le déguster dans un petit verre.	Uitschenken in een glas met voet. Het gistdepot in de fles laten of uit een klein glaasje degusteren.
i			

Houblon Chouffe Dobbelen IPA Tripel

Duvel Moortgat Corporation 9%

	top-fermentation re-fermentation in the bottle	fermentation haute refermentation en bouteille	hoge gisting hergisting op de fles
	double IPA tripel	double IPA triple	dubbele IPA tripel
	barley malt, sugar, 3 different hops, yeast, brewing water	malt d'orge, sucre, 3 variétés de houblon, levure, eau de brassage	gerstemout, suiker, 3 hopsoorten, gist, brouwwater
	pale-blond, not filtered	blond clair, non filtrée	lichtblond, niet gefilterd
	Aroma of citruslike hops sweetened with honey. Fruit and ester flavours brought into balance by the distinctive hops.	Arôme de houblon citrusé avec du miel. L'équilibre du goût de fruits et des esters est assuré par le caractère marqué du houblon.	Aroma van citrusachtige hop met honingzoet. Smaak van fruit en esters in evenwicht gebracht door uitgesproken hop.
	Brasserie Achouffe was founded in 1982 by Pierre Gobron and Christian Bauweraerts. In 2006, the brewery was taken over by Duvel-Moortgat.	La Brasserie Achouffe a été fondée en 1982 par Pierre Gobron et Christian Bauweraerts. En 2006, la brasserie a été reprise par Duvel-Moortgat.	Brasserie Achouffe werd in 1982 opgericht door Pierre Gobron en Christian Bauweraerts. In 2006 werd de brouwerij door Duvel-Moortgat overgenomen.

6,50% 4 - 6 °C 39 - 43 °F

Houten Kop

top-fermentation re-fermentation in the bottle	fermentation haute refermentation en bouteille	hoge gisting hergisting in de fles
grain varieties, different malts (incl. roasted barley malt), Poperinge hops, some 12 natural herbs	variétés de céréales, variétés de malt (e.a. malt d'orge torréfié), houblon de Poperinge, 12 herbes naturelles	graansoorten, moutsoorten (o.a. gebrande gerstemout), Poperingse hop, 12-tal natuurlijke kruiden
amber-coloured	ambrée brun rouge, filtrée	amberkleurig
Pour out vigorously to obtain a fine foam head and clear beer. The yeast can be poured.	Verser agilement pour obtenir un faux col joli et une bière limpide. Verser également le depôt de levure selon les souhaits.	Krachtig inschenken voor een mooie schuimkraag en helder bier. Het gistdepot desgewenst meeschenken.
Brewed according to a Zele recipe.	Brassée selon une recette de Zele.	Gebrouwen volgens een recept van Zele.

Ichtegem's Grand Cru

Brouwerij Strubbe

6,50% (15° plato) 4

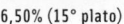

	mixed top-fermentation centrifuged	fermentation haute mixte centrifugée	gemengde hoge gistinc gecentrifugeerd
	West-Flanders red-brown	brune-rouge de la Flandre Occidentale	Westvlaams roodbruin
	80% pilsner malt, 10% caramel malt, 10% Münich malt, corn, sugar, yeast, water, more than one year old Poperinge hops, English Kent Golding, Styrian, Saaz Zatec. After two years' lagering the beer is blended with a young, sweet beer (40%).	80% malt de pils, 10% malt caramélisé, 10% malt Münich, maïs, sucre, levure, eau, houblon suranné de Poperinge, Kent Golding anglais, Styrian, Saaz Zatec. Après 2 ans de conservation, la bière est mélangée à une bière jeune et douce (40%).	80% pilsmout, 10% kar melmout, 10% Münich-mout, mais, suiker, gis water, hop (overjaarse Poperingse hop, Engels Kent Golding, Styrian, Saaz Zatec). Na 2 jaar lagering word het bier gemengd met een jong en zoet bier (40%).
	red-brown, filtered	brun rouge, filtrée	roodbruin, gefilterd
	Refreshing wood taste (18 months' lagering in oak barrels).	Goût boisé et rafraîchissant (conservée 18 mois en fûts de chêne).	Verfrissend, houtsmaa (18 maand gelagerd op eikenhout).
	The oak barrels come from the Bordeaux region, where they were used once to store wine.	Les fûts en bois de chêne proviennent de la région de Bordeaux et ont été utilisés une fois pour le vin.	De eikenhouten vaten komen uit de regio van Bordeaux en werden 1 maal voor wijn gebruik

ouwerij Strubbe 5,50% 6 °C 43 °F

Ichtegem's Oud Bruin

mixed and top-fermentation	fermentation haute et mixte	gemengde en hoge gisting
West-Flanders red-brown	brune-rouge de la Flandre Occidentale	Westvlaams roodbruin
75% pilsner malt, 20% amber malt, 5% caramel malt, corn, yeast, water. More than one year old hops from Poperinge. Matured in oak barrels for 12 months	75% malt de pils, 20% malt ambré, 5% malt caramélisé, maïs, levure, eau. Houblon suranné de Poperinge. Mûrie en fûts de chêne pendant 12 mois.	75% pilsmout, 20% ambermout, 5% karamelmout, mais, gist, water. Overjaarse hop uit Poperinge. 12 maanden gerijpt op eiken vaten.
red-brown filtered	brun rouge filtrée	roodbruin gefilterd
Sweet-and-sour, refreshing.	Aigre-douce, rafraîchissante.	Zoetzuur, verfrissend.
After the primary fermentation, 80% of the beer is stored for lagering for about two months. The rest undergoes a spontaneous lactic acid fermentation. This process can last up to 18 months.	Après la fermentation principale, 80% de la bière est stocké pour environ 2 mois. Le reste subit une fermentation spontanée d'acide lactique dans des réservoirs. Ce processus peut durer 18 mois.	Na de hoofdgisting gaat 80% in lagering voor ca. 2 maanden. De rest ondergaat een spontane melkzure gisting in de bewaartanks. Dit proces kan tot 18 maanden duren.

De Struise Brouwers at Brouwerij Deca

7% 4 - 39 - 4

	top-fermentation re-fermentation in the bottle not centrifuged	fermentation haute refermentation en bouteille non centrifugée	hoge gisting hergisting in de fles niet gecentrifugeerd
	IPA	IPA	IPA
	hopped with Chinook, Galena, Simcoe, Cascade and Amarillo	houblonné avec Chinook, Galena, Simcoe, Cascade et Amarillo	gehopt met Chinook, Ga-lena, Simcoe, Cascade e Amarillo
	copper-coloured amber, slightly hazy with a nice ivory-coloured foam head not filtered or pasteur-ised	cuivre ambré, légère-ment fade avec faux col joli ivoire non filtrée, non pasteu-risée	koperkleurig amber, licht wazig met een mooie ivoorkleurige schuimkraag ongefilterd, niet gepas-teuriseerd
	Very aromatic due to the hops. Medium-dry taste with touches of cereals and the shells of wal-nuts. Refined, mild bit-terness. Thirst-quencher with character.	Superaromatique grâce au houblon. Goût demi-sec, avec des touches de céréales et de coquille de noix. Amertume raffi-née, généreuse. Bière désaltérante.	Superaromatisch door d hop. Medium droge smaak met toetsen van granen en schil van ok-kernoten. Verfijnde, mil de bitterheid. Dorstlesser met karakte
	Pour out in a single movement to obtain a fine foam head.	Verser agilement pour former un faux col so-lide.	Vlot uitschenken zodat er een mooie schuim-kraag ontstaat.
	Was produced to mark the second Borefts Fes-tival in De Molen Brew-ery (NL). It is an interpretation of the beer 'Vuur en vlam' [Fire and Flame] brewed by De Molen.	Réalisée à l'occasion du 2e Borefts Festival à la Brouwerij De Molen (Pays-Bas). Il s'agit d'une interprétation de la bière 'Vuur en vlam', qui est brassée par De Molen.	Kwam tot stand t.g.v. he 2e Borefts Festival in Brouwerij De Molen (NL Het is een interpretatie van het bier 'Vuur en vlam' dat door De Moler wordt gebrouwen.

uwerij Strubbe 7,90%

IPA

top-fermentation re-fermentation in the bottle	fermentation haute refermentation en bouteille	hoge gisting hergisting in de fles
IPA	IPA	IPA
Brewed for the American market.	Brassée pour le marché américain.	Gebrouwen voor de Amerikaanse markt.

Iris

Brasserie Cantillon 6% 12 - 1 / 54 - 6

spontaneous fermentation re-fermented in the bottle by adding liqueur.	fermentation spontanée refermentation en bouteille par adjonction de liqueur	spontane gisting hergisting op de fles door toevoeging van likeur
pure malt beer (no gueuze or lambic)	bière maltée pure (pas de gueuze ou lambic)	puur moutbier (geen geuze of lambiek)
barley malt, pale ale type, 50% more than one year old hops, 50% fresh hops, water	malt d'orge type pale ale, 50% houblon suranné, 50% houblon frais, eau	gerstemout type pale ale, overjaarse hop (50%), verse hop (50% water
dark gold-coloured	doré foncé	donker goudkleurig
Dry and tart but also bitter and hoppy.	Seche et acidulée mais aussi amer et houblonné.	Droog en zurig maar oo bitter en hoppig.
Stand bottle upright 48 hours prior to pouring for sediment. Use wine basket when the bottle was stored horizontally.	Avant de verser dresser la bouteille 48 heures en position verticale pour le dépôt. Utiliser le panier verseur quand la bouteille est conservée en position horizontale	De fles 48 uur voor het uitschenken verticaal plaatsen voor bezinkse Schenkmand gebruiker wanneer de fles horizo taal bewaard werd.
The iris is the symbol of the City of Brussels. Spontaneous fermentation happens following the brewing process. Matures for an average of 2 years on wooden casks. Saaz hops is added two weeks prior to bottling.	L'iris est le symbole de la ville de Bruxelles. Une fermentation spontanée se produit après le processus de brassage. La bière mûrit en moyenne 2 ans en fûts de bois. 2 semaines avant l'embouteillage, du houblon Saaz est ajouté.	De iris is het symbool van de stad Brussel. Spontane gisting gebeurt na het brouwproces. Rijpt gemiddeld 2 jaar op houten vaten. 2 weken voor de bottelin wordt Saaz hop toegevoegd.

as at a brewery

5,50% 6 °C 43 °F

Irma

	top-fermentation re-fermentation in the bottle	fermentation haute refermentation en bouteille	hoge gisting hergisting in de fles
	boutique fruit beer	bière fruitée artisanale	ambachtelijk fruitbier
	barley malt, hops, yeast, herbs, fruits, strawberry extract, water	malt d'orge, houblon, levure, herbes, fruits, essence de fraises, eau	gerstemout, hop, gist, kruiden, vruchten, aardbeienextract, water
	Pour slowly into a degreased glass without sloshing the beer.	Verser lentement dans un verre dégraissé sans clapotage de la bière.	Traag inschenken in een ontvet glas zonder dat het bier klokt.
	Dedicated to Irma Van Canneyt (born in Adegem in 2008), brewer's daughter, and Irma Notteboom (Adegem, 1897-2007) Belgium's most senior citizen.	Dédiée à Irma Van Canneyt (née à Adegem en 2008), fille du brasseur, et à Irma Notteboom (Adegem, 1897-2007), la doyenne des Belges.	Opgedragen aan Irma Van Canneyt (geboren in Adegem in 2008), dochter van de brouwer, en aan Irma Notteboom (Adegem, 1897-2007) oudste Belg.

Itters Bruin Tafelbier

Brouwerij Sint-Jozef 1,25% 3 - 5 37 - 41

	bottom-fermentation	fermentation basse	lage gisting
	table beer	bière de table	tafelbier
	malt, hops, caramel, sugar	malt, houblon, caramel, sucre, eau	mout, hop, karamel, sui ker
	dark-brown	brun foncé	donkerbruin
	Sweet flavour with caramel touch.	Goût sucré, avec une touche de caramel.	Zoete smaak met karameltoets.
	Pour into a clean, degreased glass, avoiding contact with the foam.	Verser dans un verre dégraissé et propre sans que la bouteille touche l'écume.	Uitschenken in een ontvet en zuiver glas zonde dat de fles het schuim raakt.
i			

Jack'Ouille

[Br]asserie de Bouillon **5,50%**

	top-fermentation	fermentation haute	hoge gisting
	blond	blonde	blond
	barley malt, wheat, hops, yeast, herbs, water	malt d'orge, froment, houblon, levure, herbes, eau	gerstemout, tarwe, hop, gist, kruiden, water

Jaded - Stillwater Artisanal

De Struise Brouwers at Brouwerij Deca

10% 10 - 1 50 - 5

	top-fermentation re-fermentation in the bottle not centrifuged	fermentation haute refermentation en bouteille non centrifugée	hoge gisting hergisting in de fles niet gecentrifugeerd
	strong dark Belgian/American ale	double forte Belgo/American ale	sterk donker Belgo/American ale
	very hazy, chestnut-colour with warm-brown glow, firm yellow-beige foam head not filtered or pasteurised	très fade, marron à éclat brun chaud avec faux col solide beige jaune non filtrée, non pasteurisée	zeer wazig, kastanjekleur met warmbruine gloed, stevige geelbeig schuimkraag ongefilterd, niet gepasteuriseerd
	Delicate aroma of grains, wheat, citrus peel, milk bread, chocolate, berries, infusion tea and flowers. Mild taste full of character with hints of grains, wheat, caramel, coconut, rye bread, flowers and mellow hops.	Délicat arôme de céréales, de froment, de zeste de citrus, de pain au lait, de chocolat, de groseilles, de thé à infuser et de fleurs. Goût généreux et très caractéristique, avec des touches de céréales, de froment, de caramel, de coco, de pain de seigle, de fleurs et de houblon doux.	Delicaat aroma van granen, tarwe, citrusschil, melkbrood, chocolade, bessen, infusiethee en bloemen. Milde en karaktervolle smaak met toetsen van granen, tarwe, karamel, kokos, rog gebrood, bloemen en milde hop.
	Pour out in a single movement.	Verser agilement.	Vlot uitschenken.
	Realised in tandem with Brian Strumke, brewer at the Stillwater Brewing Company in USA.	Réalisée en collaboration avec Brian Strumke, brasseur chez Stillwater Brewing Company aux États-Unis,	Gerealiseerd in samenwerking met Brian Strumke, brouwer bij Stillwater Brewing Company in USA.

asserie de la Senne 8% 8 - 10 °C / 46 - 50 °F

Jambe-de-Bois

top-fermentation natural re-fermentation in the bottle not centrifuged	fermentation haute refermentation naturelle en bouteille non centrifugée	hoge gisting natuurlijke hergisting in de fles niet gecentrifugeerd
tripel	triple	tripel
different malts, sugar (during boiling), different hops, yeast, water	variétés de malt, sucre (en chaudière) variétés de houblon, levure, eau	moutsoorten, suiker (tijdens het koken), hopsoorten, gist, water
copper-blond, slightly veiled with dense and fine foam head not filtered or pasteurised	blond cuivre, légèrement voilée avec faux col compact fin non filtrée, non pasteurisée	koperblond, licht gesluierd met dichte en fijne schuimkraag ongefilterd, niet gepasteuriseerd
Powerful and punchy beer, a dry and bitter tripel. Aromas of ripe bananas and subtle old aromatic hops. Malt and fine fermentation esters dominate in the mouth, supported by a long, fine bitter taste.	Bière forte et corsée, une triple sèche et amère. Arômes de banane mûre et subtil vieil houblon aromatique. En bouche, dominent le malt et les fins esters de fermentation, soutenus par une amertume longue et fine.	Krachtig en pittig bier, een droge en bittere tripel. Aroma's van rijpe banaan en subtiele oude aromatische hop. In de mond domineren de mout en de fijne gistingsesters, ondersteund door een lange, fijne bitterheid.
Pour carefully and leave 1 cm (yeast) in the bottle. The yeast can be drunk separately.	Verser prudemment et laisser 1 cm (levure) dans la bouteille. Boire éventuellement la levure séparément.	Voorzichtig uitschenken en 1 cm (gist) in de fles laten. De gist eventueel afzonderlijk uitdrinken.
Belated tribute to the renowned leader of the Belgian revolution in 1830.	Hommage tardif au fameux leader de la Révolution belge de 1830.	Laat eerbetoon aan de fameuze leider van de Belgische revolutie in 1830.

Jan De Lichte 4-granen Dubbel Wit

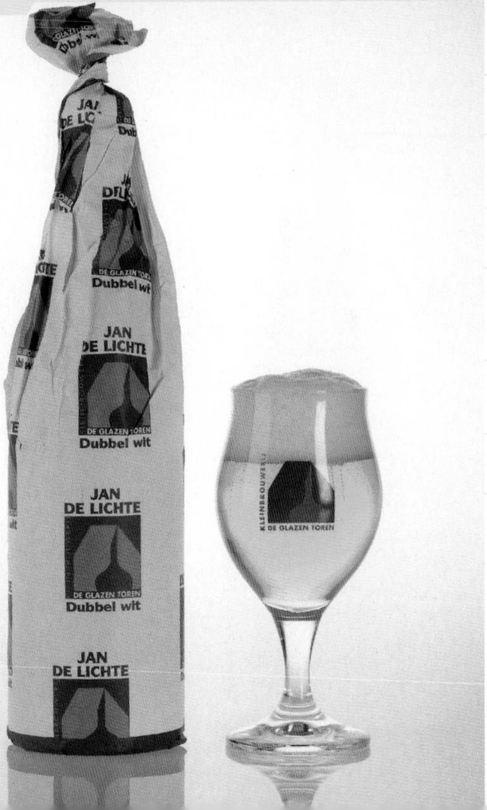

Brouwerij De Glazen Toren

7% 5 - 6 41 - 43

	top-fermentation re-fermented in the bottle	fermentation haute refermentation en bouteille	hoge gisting nagisting op de fles
	witbier	bière blanche	witbier
	barley malt, wheat malt, oat, buckwheat, water	malt d'orge, malt de froment, avoine, sarrasin, eau	gerstemout, tarwemout, haver, boekweit, water
	hazy straw-yellow very sparkling	jaune paille voilé très pétillante	strogeel gesluierd sterk parelend
	Spicy and slightly bitter. Grapefruit flavour and a velvety, dry aftertaste.	Aromatisée et légèrement amère. Arôme de pamplemousse et fin de bouche veloutée, sèche.	Kruidig en licht bitter. Aroma van pompelmoes en fluwelige, droge afdronk.
	Pour carefully into a dry, long glass (e.g. a tulip-shaped glass)	Verser prudemment dans un verre sec, oblong (par exemple tulipe).	Voorzichtig uitschenken in een droog, langwerpig (bijv. tulpvormig) glas.
i			

ssenhofke by De Proefbrouwerij

7% 9 - 11 °C / 48 - 52 °F

Jessenhofke Bruin

	top-fermentation re-fermentation in the bottle centrifuged	fermentation haute refermentation en bouteille centrifugée	hoge gisting hergisting in de fles gecentrifugeerd
	double	double	dubbel
	different roasted special malts, organic bitter hops (Challenger) and aromatic hops (Goldings and Fuggles), garlic, water	diverses variétés spéciales de malt torréfié, houblon amer biologique (Challenger) et houblon aromatique (Golding et Fuggles), ail, eau	diverse gebrande speciaalmouten, biologische bitterhop (Challenger) en aromahop (Goldings en Fuggles), knoflook, water
	brown with creamy, pale brown foam head not filtered or pasteurised	brune avec faux col crémeux brun clair non filtrée, non pasteurisée	bruin met romige, lichtbruine schuimkraag ongefilterd, niet gepasteuriseerd
	Aroma of coffee and chocolate (roasted malt), full malt taste, sweet-bitter aftertaste.	Arôme de café et de choco (malt torréfié), pleinement malté, arrière-bouche douce-amère.	Aroma van koffie en choco (gebrande mout), volmoutig, zoetbittere afdronk.
	see Jessenhofke Maya	voir Jessenhofke Maya	zie Jessenhofke Maya
	One of the few Belgian organic brown beers based entirely on special malts (pilsner malt not used) as Belgian roasted malts are hard to come by.	Une des peu nombreuses bières brunes biologiques belges entièrement à base de malts spéciaux (pas d'utilisation de malt de pils). Les malts torréfiés belges sont en effet difficiles à obtenir.	Een van de weinige Belgische biologische bruine bieren helemaal op basis van speciaalmouten (geen pilsmout gebruikt) . Belgische gebrande mouten zijn namelijk moeilijk verkrijgbaar.

Jessenhofke Maya

Jessenhofke by De Proefbrouwerij

6% 8 - 11 / 46 - 52

	top-fermentation re-fermentation in the bottle centrifuged	fermentation haute refermentation en bouteille centrifugée	hoge gisting hergisting in de fles gecentrifugeerd
	herbal beer	bière aromatisée	kruidenbier
	bitter hops (Challenger), 2 different aromatic hops (Goldings & Fuggles), garlic, water containing wheat (from seitan production)	houblon amer (Challenger), 2 variétés de houblon aromatique (Goldings et Fuggles), ail, eau contenant froment (provenant de la production de seitan)	bitterhop (Challenger), 2 aromatische hopsoorten (Goldings & Fuggles), look, tarwehoudend water (afkomstig van seitanproductie)
	very blond (14 EBC) with dense, long lingering foam head	très blonde (14 EBC) avec faux col compact, stable	zeer blond (14 EBC) met dichte, lang blijvende schuimkraag
	The organic Poperinge hops provide a spicy aroma, hint of wheat. Distinctly bitter. 33 EBU.	Le houblon biologique de Poperingue assure un arôme épicé, touche de froment. Amertume prononcée. 33 EBU.	De biologische Poperingse hop zorgt voor een kruidig aroma, toets van tarwe. Uitgesproken bitter. 33 EBU.
	Serve in a sipping glass and leave yeast sediment in the bottle, if necessary. Provide a generous foam head.	Verser dans un verre de dégustation et laisser le dépôt de levure éventuellement dans la bouteille. Former un faux col généreux.	In een degustieglas uitschenken en het gistdepot eventueel in de fles laten. Een royale schuimkraag voorzien.
	Jessenhofke uses garlic in its beers, which is quite unique and adds a special touch.	Jessenhofke utilise de l'ail dans ses bières, ce qui est assez unique et donne un caractère spécial.	Jessenhofke gebruikt look in zijn bieren, wat vrij uniek is en voor een speciaal karakter zorgt.

essenhofke by De Proefbrouwerij

8% 9 - 11 °C 48 - 52 °F

	top-fermentation re-fermentation in the bottle centrifuged	fermentation haute refermentation en bouteille centrifugée	hoge gisting hergisting in de fles gecentrifugeerd
	tripel	triple	tripel
	barley and wheat malt, unrefined cane sugar, bitter hops (Challenger), aromatic hops (Goldings & Fuggles), garlic	malt d'orge et de froment, sucre de cane non raffiné, houblon amer (Challenger), houblon aromatique (Goldings et Fuggles), ail	gerste- en tarwemout, ongeraffineerde rietsuiker, bitterhop (Challenger), aromahop (Goldings & Fuggles), knoflook
	blond with solid foam head not filtered or pasteurised	blonde avec faux col solide non filtrée, non pasteurisée	blond met stevige schuimkraag ongefilterd, niet gepasteuriseerd
	Typical spiciness of the Belgian organic hops. Perfect balance between dry, bitter, sweet and full-bodied flavours.	Goût épicé typique du houblon biologique belge. Équilibre parfait entre sécheresse, amertume, caractère sucré et plénitude.	Typische kruidigheid van de Belgische biologische hop. Perfecte balans tussen droogheid, bitterheid, zoet en volheid.
	see Jessenhofke Maya	voir Jessenhofke Maya	zie Jessenhofke Maya
	Served as label beer under the name of 'Dagelyckx bier' at the Benigna beguinage in Tongeren. The brewery's slogan is 'drink moderately yet regularly'.	Elle est servie comme bière étiquette sous le nom 'Dagelyckx bier' au béguinage Benigna à Tongres. Le slogan de la brasserie est 'drink matig doch regelmatig' ('buvez modérément, mais régulièrement').	Wordt als etiketbier onder de naam 'Dagelyckx bier' geserveerd in het begijnhof Benigna in Tongeren. De leuze van de brouwerij is 'drink matig doch regelmatig'.

Jessenhofke Tripel

Jezuwiet

Brouwerij Boelens 8,50%

	top-fermentation re-fermentation in the bottle	fermentation haute refermentation en bouteille	hoge gisting hergisting in de fles
	tripel special beer	triple spéciale	tripel speciaalbier
	barley malt, hops, aniseed, yeast, water	malt d'orge, houblon, anis, levure, eau	gerstemout, hop, anijs, gist, water

rasserie de Silenrieux 5,40% 7 - 10 °C / 45 - 50 °F

Joseph

	top-fermentation re-fermented in the bottle	fermentation haute refermentation en bouteille	hoge gisting nagisting op de fles
	specialty beer spelt beer	bière spéciale bière d'épeautre	speciaalbier speltbier
	barley, spelt, hops, herbs, water	orge, épeautre, houblon, herbes, eau	gerst, spelt, hop, kruiden, water
	blond cloudy (unfiltered) white, shiny foam head	blonde trouble (non filtrée) faux col blanc, brillant	blond troebel (niet gefilterd) witte, blinkende schuimkraag
	Slightly fruity and smooth. Refreshing session beer.	Légèrement fruitée et douce. Bière rafraîchissante qui se boit facilement.	Licht fruitig en zacht. Verfrissend doordrinkbier.
	Softly revolve or shake the bottle before opening to obtain a cloudy beer.	Tourner légèrement ou secouer la bouteille avant de l'ouvrir pour obtenir une bière trouble.	De fles licht draaien of schudden voor het openen om een troebel bier te bekomen.
	Also has an organic version. Spelt is an ancient grain and a predecessor of wheat. It is easy to grow.	Existe également en version BIO. L'épeautre est une vieille culture, prédécesseur du froment, dont la culture demande peu d'attention.	Bestaat ook in BIO-versie. Spelt is een oud gewas, de voorganger van tarwe. De teelt ervan vraagt weinig zorg.

Joup

Brasserie Grain d'Orge

7,50% 6 - 8 ° 43 - 46 °

	top-fermentation re-fermented in the bottle	fermentation haute refermentation en bouteille	hoge gisting hergisting in de fles
	regional beer	bière régionale	streekbier
	malt varieties, hop varieties, yeast, sugar, herbs, water	variétés de malt et de houblon, levure, sucre, herbes, eau	moutsoorten, hopsoorten, gist, suiker, kruiden, water
	brown with red hues	brune avec tintes rouges	bruin met rode tinten
	Smooth and round. Well-balanced hop taste with a variety of spices and caramel touches.	Douce et ronde. Saveur houblonnée équilibrée avec une variété d'herbes et de touches caramélisées.	Zacht en rond. Evenwichtige hopsmaak met een variëteit aan kruiden en toetsen van karamel.
	Leave the yeast sediment in the bottle.	Laisser le dépôt de levure dans la bouteille.	Het gistdepot in de fles laten.
i			

ouwerij Alken-Maes 8,50% 6 - 10 °C 43 - 50 °F

	top-fermentation re-fermented in the bottle	fermentation haute refermentation en bouteille	hoge gisting hergisting op de fles
	strong blond	blonde forte	sterk blond
	ochre-blond	blond ocre	okerblond
	Bittersweet, smooth and full-bodied.	Amer-douce, moelleuse et franche.	Bitterzoet, zacht en volmondig.
	Pour carefully into a degreased, dry glass. Fill the glass in one smooth movement for a nice, big foam head. Leave the yeast at the bottom of the bottle.	Verser soigneusement dans un verre dégraissé, sec. Remplir doucement le verre d'un seul trait pour obtenir un faux col solide. Laisser la levure au fond de la bouteille.	Zorgvuldig uitschenken in een ontvet, droog glas. Het glas in 1 beweging zachtjes vullen voor een grote schuimkraag. De gist op de bodem van de fles laten.

Jules de Bananes

Brouwerij De Ryck 4,90% 3 - 4 / 37 - 39

	top-fermentation re-fermented in the bottle	fermentation haute refermentation en bouteille	hoge gisting nagisting op de fles
	fruit beer	bière fruitée	fruitbier
	malt, hops, yeast, sucrose, natural banana flavours, milk base, sweeteners, water	malt, houblon, levure, sucrose, saveurs naturelles de banane, base de lait, édulcorants, eau	mout, hop, gist, sucrose, natuurlijke bananenflavors, melkbasis, zoetstoffen, water
	white banana colour	couleur banane blanche	witte bananenkleur
	Refreshing and summery. Overwhelmingly sweet fruity banana flavour, with a clear and beer-like aftertaste.	Rafraîchissante et estivale. Arôme dominant, fruitée et douce de bananes, fin de bouche avec saveur de bière.	Verfrissend en zomers. Overweldigend zoetfruitig bananenaroma, duidelijke en bierige afdronk.
	Rinse the glass with cold water, take it by the stem and tilt it slightly. Pour slowly in a single movement, avoiding contact between bottle and glass or foam. Empty the bottle.	Rincer le verre à l'eau froide et le tenir légèrement en oblique par le pied. Verser la bière lentement et complètement, en un seul mouvement sans que la bouteille touche le verre ou l'écume.	Het glas koud spoelen, bij de voet vastnemen en licht schuin houden. Het bier traag en in 1 beweging inschenken zonder dat de fles het glas of schuim raakt. Het flesje volledig uitschenken.
i			

ouwerij De Ryck 4,90% 3 - 4 °C 37 - 39 °F

Jules de Kriek

	top-fermentation re-fermented in the bottle	fermentation haute refermentation en bouteille	hoge gisting nagisting op de fles
	fruit beer	bière fruitée	fruitbier
	malt, hops, yeast, sucrose, natural cherry flavours, milk base, sweeteners, water	malt, houblon, levure, sucrose, goûts naturels de cerises, lait, édulcorants, eau	mout, hop, gist, sucrose, natuurlijke kriekenflavors, melkbasis, zoetstoffen, water
	pink-red	rouge rose	rozerood
	Refreshing and summery. Pronounced cherry aroma and taste, sweet and full-bodied. The fruity character does not take away the taste of beer.	Rafraîchissante et estivale. Parfum et saveur prononcés de cerise avec un goût franc doux. La saveur de bière reste malgré le caractère fruité.	Verfrissend en zomers. Geprononceerde kriekengeur en -smaak met zoete volmondigheid. De biersmaak blijft ondanks het fruitige karakter.
	Rinse the glass with cold water, take it by the stem and tilt it slightly. Pour slowly in a single movement, avoiding contact between bottle and glass or foam. Either leave the 1 cm yeast sediment in the bottle or pour it out along with the beer.	Rincer le verre à l'eau froide et le tenir légèrement en oblique par le pied. Verser la bière lentement et en un seul mouvement sans que la bouteille touche le verre ou l'écume. Laisser un dépôt de levure de 1 cm dans la bouteille ou la vider.	Het glas koud spoelen, bij de voet vastnemen en licht schuin houden. Het bier traag en in 1 beweging inschenken zonder dat de fles het glas of schuim raakt. Het gistdepot van 1 cm in de fles laten ofwel uitschenken.
i			

Jupiler

AB-Inbev Leuven 5,20% 3 37

	bottom-fermentation	fermentation basse	lage gisting
	pilsner	pils	pilsbier
	pale malt, corn, hops, yeast, water	malt pâle, maïs, houblon, levure, eau	bleekmout, maïs, hop, gist, water
	gold-coloured	dorée	goudkleurig
	Light taste but with a full malt mouthfeel. Fresh and slightly fruity (a touch of cherry and nut), with a smooth aftertaste.	Saveur légère avec une sensation maltée pleine dans la bouche. Fraîche et légèrement fruitée (un peu de cerise et de noix), fin de bouche douce.	Licht van smaak maar met een vol moutig mondgevoel. Fris en licht fruitig (tikkeltje kers en noot), zachte afdronk.
	Rinse the glass in cold water, tilt it and smoothly pour the beer. Skim off if desired.	Rincer le verre à l'eau froide, le tenir incliné et verser la bière doucement. Ecumer selon le goût.	Het glas onder koud water spoelen, schuin houden en het bier zacht uitschenken. Desgewenst afschuimen.
i			

B-Inbev Leuven

3,30% 3 °C / 37 °F

Jupiler Blue

	bottom-fermentation	fermentation basse	lage gisting
	pilsner	pils	pilsbier
	malt, corn, hops, brewing water	malt, maïs, houblon, eau de brassage	mout, maïs, hop, brouwwater
	gold-coloured	dorée	goudkleurig
	Light taste but with a full malt mouthfeel. Refreshing, smooth and slightly fruity.	Saveur légère avec une sensation maltée pleine dans la bouche. Rafraîchissante, douce et légèrement fruitée.	Licht van smaak maar met een vol moutig mondgevoel. Verfrissend, zacht en licht gefruit.
	Rinse the glass in cold water, tilt it and smoothly pour the beer. Skim off if desired.	Rincer le verre à l'eau froide, le tenir incliné et verser la bière doucement. Ecumer selon le goût.	Het glas onder koud water spoelen, schuin houden en het bier zacht uitschenken. Desgewenst afschuimen.
i			

Jupiler Tauro

AB-Inbev Leuven 8,30% 3 37

	bottom-fermentation centrifuged	fermentation basse centrifugée	lage gisting gecentrifugeerd
	strong lager	lager forte	strong lager
	barley malt, corn, hops, yeast, water	malt d'orge, maïs, houblon, levure, eau	gerstemout, mais, hop, gist, water
	blond filtered, pasteurised	blonde filtrée, pasteurisée	blond gefilterd, gepasteuriseerd
	Powerful pilsner beer with a high alcohol content and punchy bitterness that provides a balance in taste. Fruity aromas are punctuated with distinctly hoppy touches.	Pils forte, avec un pourcentage élevé d'alcool et une solide amertume, qui assure un équilibre des goûts. Arômes fruités, avec des touches houblonnées marquées.	Krachtig pilsbier met hoog alcoholpercentage en stevige bitterheid die zorgt voor een smaakevenwicht. Fruitige aroma's met uitgesproken hoppige toetsen.
	Serve in a robust pilsner 33 cl glass.	Verser dans un verre de pils robuste de 33 cl.	Uitschenken in een robuust pilsglas van 33 cl.
i			

Kalle

ouwerij Gulden Spoor

8% — 8 - 10 °C / 46 - 50 °F

	top-fermentation re-fermentation in the bottle not centrifuged	fermentation haute refermentation en bouteille non centrifugée	hoge gisting hergisting in de fles niet gecentrifugeerd
	tripel	triple	tripel
	barley malt, wheat flakes, hops, coriander, yeast, water	malt d'orge, flocons de froment, houblon, coriandre, levure, eau	gerstemout, tarwevlokken, hop, koriander, gist, water
	blond, slightly cloudy not filtered or pasteurised	blonde et légèrement trouble non filtrée, non pasteurisée	blond en licht troebel ongefilterd, niet gepasteuriseerd
	Intense and well-considered. Fruity with taste evolution.	Piquante et raisonnée. Fruitée, avec une évolution du goût.	Pittig en doordacht. Fruitig met smaakevolutie.
	Degrease the glass, tilt it slightly and carefully pour the beer in a single movement.	Dégraisser le verre, le tenir légèrement incliné et verser la bière prudemment d'un seul mouvement.	Het glas vetvrij maken, licht schuin houden en het bier voorzichtig in 1 beweging uitschenken.
i	Manten and his wife Kalle are the bell ringers or 'jacquemarts' of the Courtrai Belfry.	Manten et sa femme Kalle sont les frappeurs de cloche ou 'jacquemarts' du Beffroi de Courtrai.	Manten en zijn vrouw Kalle zijn de uurslagers of 'jacquemarts' van het Belfort in Kortrijk.

Kameleon Amber

Brouwerij Den Hopperd 6,50%

	top-fermentation re-fermented in the bottle	fermentation haute refermentation en bouteille	hoge gisting hergisting op de fles
	amber	ambrée	amber
	malt, hops, yeast, sugar, water	malt, houblon, levure, sucre, eau	mout, hop, gist, suiker, water
	amber slightly cloudy	ambrée légèrement troublée	amber lichttroebel
	Fruity, slightly bitter.	Fruitée, légèrement amère.	Fruitig, licht bitter
	Organic beer.	Bière biologique.	Biologisch bier.

ouwerij Den Hopperd

6%

Kameleon Donker

	top-fermentation	fermentation haute	hoge gisting
	organic double	double biologique	biologisch dubbel
	red-brown, cloudy	brun rouge, trouble	roodbruin, troebel
	Malty, spicy, refreshing and balanced. Roasted aromas and flavours.	Maltée, épicée, rafraîchissante et équilibrée. Arômes et goûts brûlés.	Moutig, kruidig, verfrissend en evenwichtig. Gebrande aroma's en smaken.

Kameleon Ginseng

Brouwerij Den Hopperd 6,50%

	top-fermentation re-fermented in the bottle	fermentation haute refermentation en bouteille	hoge gisting hergisting op de fles
	herbal beer	bière aux épices	kruidenbier
	barley malt, hops, yeast, sugar, ginseng root, water	malt d'orge, houblon, levure, sucre, racine de ginseng, eau	gerstemout, hop, gist, suiker, ginsengwortel, water
	blond cloudy	blonde légèrement trouble	blond lichttroebel
	Fruity, slightly bitter, ginseng flavour.	Fruité, légèrement amer, arôme de ginseng.	Fruitig, licht bitter, ginsengaroma.
	Organic boutique bier.	Bière biologique brassée de façon artisanale.	Ambachtelijk gebrouwen biologisch bier.

ouwerij Den Hopperd 8,50% 5° C 41°F

	top-fermentation re-fermented in the bottle	fermentation haute refermentation en bouteille	hoge gisting hergisting op de fles
	tripel	triple	tripel
	malt, hops, yeast, sugar, water	malt, houblon, levure, sucre, eau	mout, hop, gist, suiker, water
	blond slightly cloudy	blonde légèrement trouble	blond lichttroebel
	Fruity with bitter after-taste.	Fruité avec une fin de bouche amère.	Fruitig met bittere na-smaak.
	Organic beer.	Bière biologique.	Biologisch bier.

Kapittel Blond

Brouwerij Van Eecke

6,50% 8 - 1 / 46 - 5

	top-fermentation re-fermented in the bottle	fermentation haute refermentation en bouteille	hoge gisting nagisting op de fles
	abbey beer	bière d'abbaye	abdijbier
	malt, spices, yeast, sweetener, water	malt, condiments, levure, édulcorant, eau	mout, specerijen, gist, zoetstof, water
	blond	blonde	blond
	Session beer. Sweet, slightly malty flavour.	Bière qui se boit facilement. Arôme doux, légèrement malté.	Doordrinkbier. Zoet, licht moutaroma.
	Hold the glass by the stem and tilt it slightly. Slowly pour in a single movement. Leave 1 cm of beer (sediment) in the bottle.	Tenir le verre en oblique par le pied et verser lentement en un seul mouvement. Laisser 1 cm de bière (levure) dans la bouteille.	Het glas bij de voet schuin houden en het bier traag in 1 beweging uitschenken. 1 cm bier (depot) in het flesje laten.
i			

ouwerij Van Eecke   7,50%   8 - 13 °C / 46 - 55 °F

Kapittel Dubbel

top-fermentation re-fermented in the bottle	fermentation haute refermentation en bouteille	hoge gisting nagisting op de fles
abbey beer	bière d'abbaye	abdijbier
malt, caramel, spices, yeast, sweetener, water	malt, caramel, condiments, levure, édulcorant, eau	mout, karamel, specerijen, gist, zoetstof, water
dark brown	brun foncé	donkerbruin
Sweet and fruity. Light malt flavour with hoppy aftertaste.	Doux et fruité. Arôme légèrement malté avec une fin de bouche houblonnée.	Zoet en fruitig. Licht moutaroma met hoppige afdronk.
Hold the glass by the stem and tilt it slightly. Slowly pour in a single movement. Leave 1 cm of beer (sediment) in the bottle.	Tenir le verre en oblique par le pied et verser la bière lentement en un seul mouvement. Laisser 1 cm de bière (levure) dans la bouteille.	Het glas bij de voet schuin houden en het bier traag in 1 beweging uitschenken. 1 cm bier (depot) in het flesje laten.
Originally a blended beer. Today it is brewed as a separate topfermenting beer.	A l'origine une bière coupée, actuellement brassée comme bière séparée de fermentation haute.	Oorspronkelijk een versnijbier dat vandaag als een apart hogegistingsbier wordt gebrouwen.

K Kapittel Pater

Brouwerij Van Eecke 6% 8 - 1 / 46 - 5

	top-fermentation re-fermented in the bottle	fermentation haute refermentation en bouteille	hoge gisting nagisting op de fles
	abbey beer	bière d'abbaye	abdijbier
	malt, caramel, spices, yeast, sweetener, water	malt, caramel, condiments, levure, édulcorant, eau	mout, karamel, specerij en, gist, zoetstof, water
	dark brown	brun foncé	donkerbruin
	Session beer. Light sweet malt flavour, slightly bitter, caramel and liquorice.	Bière qui se boit facilement. Arôme malté légèrement doux, légèrement amer, caramel et réglisse.	Doordrinkbier. Licht zoet moutaroma, lichtjes bitter, karamel en zoethout.
	Hold the glass by the stem and tilt it slightly. Slowly pour in a single movement. Leave 1 cm of beer (sediment) in the bottle.	Tenir le verre en oblique par le pied et verser la bière lentement en un seul mouvement. Laisser 1 cm de bière (levure) dans la bouteille.	Het glas bij de voet schuin houden en het bier traag in 1 beweging uitschenken. 1 cm bier (depot) in het flesje laten.
	The term "kapittel" (chapter) refers to a hierarchic structure in an abbey or convent.	Le terme 'kapittel' renvoie à la hiérarchie au sein d'une abbaye ou d'une monastère.	De term kapittel staat voor de hiërarchie binnen een abdij of klooster.

9% 8 - 13 °C 46 - 55 °F

Kapittel Prior

top-fermentation re-fermented in the bottle	fermentation haute refermentation en bouteille	hoge gisting nagisting op de fles
abbey beer	bière d'abbaye	abdijbier
malt, caramel, spices, yeast, sweetener, water	malt, caramel, condiments, levure, édulcorant, eau	mout, karamel, specerijen, gist, zoetstof, water
dark brown	brun foncé	donkerbruin
Full-bodied and solid with an impressive aromatic palette. Alcohol, chocolate, spices, slightly roasted malts. Light bitter aftertaste with a sweet touch near the end.	Franche et corsée avec une palette de parfums impressionnante. Alcool, chocolat, épices, malts légèrement brûlés. Fin de bouche légèrement amère avec une touche finale douce.	Volmondig en stevig met een indrukwekkend geurenpalet. Alcohol, chocolade, specerijen, licht gebrande mouten. Licht bittere afdronk met zoete toets op het einde.
Hold the glass by its stem and tilt slightly. Slowly pour in a single movement. Leave 1 cm of beer (sediment) in the bottle.	Tenir le verre légèrement en oblique par le pied et verser la bière lentement en un seul mouvement. Laisser 1 cm de bière (levure) dans la bouteille.	Het glas bij de voet schuin houden en het bier traag in 1 beweging uitschenken. 1 cm bier (depot) in het flesje laten.

Kapittel Tripel Abt

Brouwerij Van Eecke 10% 8 - 1 46 - 5

top-fermentation re-fermented in the bottle	fermentation haute refermentation en bouteille	hoge gisting nagisting op de fles
abbey beer	bière d'abbaye	abdijbier
malt, spices, yeast, sweetener, water	malt, condiments, levure, édulcorant, eau	mout, specerijen, gist, zoetstof, water
light amber - ochre	ambré clair - ocre	licht amber - oker
Tripel with spicy, full round taste with warm chocolate touch.	Triple avec saveur corsée, pleine et ronde et une touche chaude de chocolat.	Tripel met pittige, volronde smaak met warm chocoladetoets.
Hold the glass by the stem and tilt it slightly. Slowly pour in a single movement. Leave 1 cm of beer (sediment) in the bottle.	Tenir le verre en oblique par le pied et verser lentement en un seul mouvement. Laisser 1 cm de bière (levure) dans la bouteille.	Het glas bij de voet schuin houden en het bier traag in 1 bewegin uitschenken. 1 cm bier (depot) in het flesje laten.

ouwerij De Block 6% 6 - 8 °C / 43 - 46 °F

	top-fermentation unpasteurised	fermentation haute non pasteurisée	hoge gisting niet gepasteuriseerd
	blond	blonde	blond
	wheat, malt, hops, yeast, sugar, water	froment, malt, houblon, levure, sucre, eau	tarwe, mout, hop, gist, suiker, water
	blond to copper clear with a full, round, creamy foam head	blonde à cuivre claire avec un faux col solide, rond et crémeux	blond tot koper helder met volle, ronde, romige schuimkraag
	Refreshing, deeply malty character. Pleasant touch of fresh yeast.	Caractère frais et malté profond. Touche agréable de levure fraîche.	Fris en diepmoutig karakter. Aangename toets van verse gist.
	cfr. Chimay	voir Chimay	cfr. Chimay

Kasteel(bier) Blond

Brouwerij Van Honsebrouck 7% 4

	top-fermentation centrifuged	fermentation haute centrifugée	hoge gisting gecentrifugeerd
	blond	blonde	blond
	malt, hops, water, vitamin C	malt, houblon, eau, vitamine C	mout, hop, water, vitamine C
	clear blond with solid foam head filtered, pasteurised	limpide blond avec faux col solide filtrée, pasteurisée	helder blond met stevig schuimkraag gefilterd, gepasteuriseerd
	Fresh with light malt taste and mellow bitterness.	Fraîche, avec un léger goût de malt et une douce amertume.	Fris met lichte moutsmaak en zachte bitterheid.
	Pour carefully.	Verser prudemment.	Voorzichtig uitschenke
(i)			

rouwerij Van Honsebrouck 11% 12 °C 54 °F

Kasteel(bier) Bruin

	top-fermentation	fermentation haute	hoge gisting
	regional brown beer	bière régionale brune	bruin streekbier
	malt, sugar, hops, yeast, water	malt, houblon, sucre, levure, eau	mout, suiker, hop, gist, water
	dark brown clear	brun foncé claire	donkerbruin helder
	Smooth and fully round. Strong influence of special malts and dark sugars.	Douce, pleine et ronde. Forte influence des malts spéciaux et des sucres foncés.	Zacht en volrond. Sterke invloed van speciale mouten en donkere suikers.
	Pour into a degreased, dry glass. Hold the glass vertically and fill in a single, fast movement.	Verser dans un verre dégraissé et sec. Tenir le verre en position verticale et verser rapidement d'un seul trait.	Uitschenken in een ontvet droog glas. Het glas verticaal houden en in 1 beweging snel inschenken.
i			

Kasteel(bier) Rouge

Brouwerij Van Honsebrouck 8% 12 54

	top-fermentation centrifuged	fermentation haute centrifugée	hoge gisting gecentrifugeerd
	fruit beer	bière fruitée	fruitbier
	malt, unprocessed wheat, sugar, hops, water, vitamin C, natural simple juice	malt, froment brut, sucre, houblon, eau, vitamine C, jus simple naturel	mout, ruwe tarwe, suiker, hop, water, vitamine C, natuurlijk enkelvoudig sap
	deep red with creamy foam head filtered, pasteurised	rouge profond avec faux col crémeux filtrée, pasteurisée	dieprood met romige schuimkraag gefilterd, gepasteuriseerd
	Strong cherry flavour.	Fort goût de cerises.	Sterke kersensmaak.
	Pour out vigorously.	Verser bien agilement.	Goed doorschenken.
i			

rouwerij Van Honsebrouck

11% 9 °C 48 °F

	top-fermentation re-fermented in the bottle	fermentation haute refermentation en bouteille	hoge gisting nagisting op de fles
	regional beer tripel	bière régionale triple	streekbier tripel
	malt, corn, sugar, hops, yeast, water	malt, maïs, sucre, houblon, levure, eau	mout, mais, suiker, hop, gist, water
	blond clear	blonde claire	blond helder
	Powerful and fully round. Full taste, fruity with smooth aftertaste.	Corsée, pleine et ronde. Goût plein, fruité avec une fin de bouche douce.	Krachtig en volrond. Volle smaak, fruitig met zachte afdronk.
	Pour into a degreased, dry glass. Hold the glass vertically and fill in a single, fast movement. The yeast is either poured in the glass or left in the bottle.	Verser dans un verre dégraissé et sec. Tenir le verre dans une position verticale et verser rapidement d'un seul trait. La levure est versée selon le goût.	Uitschenken in een ontvet droog glas. Het glas verticaal houden en in 1 beweging snel inschenken. De gist wordt volgens eigen smaak al dan niet uitgeschonken.
i			

Katje Special

Brouwerij Het Sas

6% 5 - 6 / 41 - 43

	bottom-fermentation	fermentation basse	lage gisting
	dark ale	ale foncée	donker ale
	malt, spices, sweetener, caramel, hops, water	malt, condiments, édulcorant, caramel, houblon, eau	mout, specerijen, zoetstof, karamel, hop, water
	clear	claire	helder
	Well-rounded but powerful. Slightly sweet with prominent malt flavour.	Arrondie mais corsée. Légèrement doux avec arôme de malt prononcé.	Afgerond maar krachtig. Licht zoet met prominent moutaroma.
	Pour slowly in a single, smooth movement, into a degreased glass. Keep the glass tilted and avoid sloshing the beer. Skim off the foam.	Verser lentement en un seul mouvement fluide dans un verre dégraissé tenu en oblique. Ne pas laisser la bière clapoter. Ecumer le verre.	Traag en in 1 vloeiende beweging uitschenken in een vetvrij glas dat wordt schuingehouden. Het bier niet laten klotsen. Het glas afschuimen.
i	Launched in May 1954 for the Ypres Kattenfeesten, which still take place every year.	Lancée en mai 1954 à l'occasion des fêtes du chat à Ypres qui ont toujours lieu chaque année.	Gelanceerd in mei 1954 ter gelegenheid van de Ieperse Kattenfeesten die jaarlijks nog plaatsvinden.

8,50% 7 °C 45 °F

Keizer Karel Goud Blond

	top-fermentation centrifuged	fermentation haute centrifugée	hoge gisting gecentrifugeerd
	specialty beer strong blond	bière spéciale blonde forte	speciaalbier sterk blond
	barley malt, corn, sugar, hops, water	malt d'orge, mais, sucre, houblon, eau	gerstemout, mais, suiker, hop, water
	golden blond filtered, pasteurised	blond doré filtrée, pasteurisée	goudblond gefilterd, gepasteuriseerd
	Spicy hop aroma, sweet taste and a pleasant, dry bitter aftertaste.	Arôme de houblon relevé, saveur douce et fin de bouche sèche, amère.	Kruidig hoparoma, zoete smaak en een aangenaam droge bittere afdronk.
	Pour carefully into a rinsed, wet Keizer Karel glass, avoiding contact with the foam, or else into the authentic 3-handled earthenware mug.	Verser prudemment dans un verre Charles Quint rincé, humide sans que la bouteille touche l'écume ou dans un pot de grés authentique à 3 oreilles .	Voorzichtig uitschenken in een gespoeld, nat Keizer-Karelglas zonder dat de fles het schuim raakt of in de authentieke aarden pot met 3 oren.
	Refers to the legend of Charles Quint in Olen. To allow the emperor to enjoy sunrise and sunset in summer, two beers were brewed. One was golden blond like the pure morning light, the other ruby red like the warm twilight.	Renvoie à la légende de Charles Quint à Olen. Pour permettre à l'empereur de profiter de la montée et de la descente du soleil de l'été, 2 bières ont été fabriquées :l'une blonde comme de l'or représentant la lumière pure du matin, l'autre rouge rubis représentant le crépuscule chaud.	Verwijst naar de legende van Keizer Karel in Olen. Om de keizer te laten genieten van het rijzen en dalen van de zomerzon, werden 2 bieren gebrouwen: 'het ene goudblond als het zuivere ochtendlicht, het andere robijnrood als de warme avondschemering'.

Keizer Karel Robijn Rood

Brouwerij Haacht 8,50% 7 45

	top-fermentation centrifuged	fermentation haute centrifugée	hoge gisting gecentrifugeerd
	specialty beer strong brown	bière spéciale brune forte	speciaalbier sterk bruin
	barley malt, herbs (orange peel), sugar, hops, water, antioxidant (ascorbic acid)	malt d'orge, herbes (écorce d'orange), sucre, houblon, eau, antioxydant (acide ascorbine)	gerstemout, kruiden (sinaasappelschil), suiker, hop, water, antioxidant (ascorbinezuur)
	dark filtered, pasteurised	foncée filtrée, pasteurisée	donker gefilterd, gepasteuriseerd
	Sweetish and fruity aroma, a smooth, full taste and a sweet hoppy aftertaste.	Arôme doux et fruité, goût doux plein et fin de bouche douce, houblonnée.	Zoetig en fruitig aroma, een zachte volle smaak en een zoethoppige afdronk.
	see Keizer Karel Gold Blond.	voir Charles Quint Blond Doré.	zie Keizer Karel Goud Blond.
i	Charlemagne (1500-1558) was born in Ghent and spent many of his formative years in Belgium. He is often considered the precursor of Europe. His kingdom was so vast it was said that the sun never set there. He was also an ardent beer enthousiast.	L'Empereur Charles Quint (1500-1558) était né à Gand et il passa une grande partie de sa jeunesse en Belgique. Il est souvent regardé comme le précurseur de l'Europe. Son empire était si vaste que l'on disait que le soleil ne s'y couchait jamais. Il était aussi un fervent amateur de bière.	Keizer Karel (1500-1558) werd geboren in Gent en bracht een groot deel van zijn jeugd door in België. Hij wordt vaak aanschouwd als de voorloper van Europa. Zijn rijk was zo groot dat men zei dat de zon er nooit onderging. Hij was ook een fervent bierliefhebber.

ieren Pirlot by De Proefbrouwerij (soon at own brewery) 7,50% 8 - 10 °C 46 - 50 °F

Kempisch Vuur 3-Dubbel

top-fermentation re-fermented in the bottle not centrifuged	fermentation haute refermentation en bouteille non centrifugée	hoge gisting hergisting in de fles niet gecentrifugeerd
double city or local beer scotch ale	double bière citadine ou régionale scotch ale	dubbel stads- of streekbier scotch ale
malt (pilsner, Münich, cara, roast), hops (Tomahawk), herbs, yeast, well water	malt (pils, Münich, cara, roast), houblon (Tomahawk), herbes, levure, eau de source	mout (pils, Münich, cara, roast), hop (Tomahawk), kruiden, gist, bronwater
The proteins of the wheat malt create a solid, stable foam head. Not filtered or pasteurised 55 EBC.	Les protéines du malt de froment assurent un faux col solide stable. Non filtreé, ni pasteuriseé 55 EBC.	Stevige schuimkraag (door de tarwemout). Ongefilterd, niet gepasteuriseerd. 55 EBC
Pleasantly full-bodied by the large quantity of Cara malt. Fruity, full taste, followed by a complex aftertaste which becomes well-rounded with a pleasant roasty touch. Bitterness: 26 EBU.	Agréable et franche par la grande quantité de malt cara. Saveur fruitée, pleine suivie d'une fin de bouche complexe arrondie par une touche brûlée agréable. Amertume de 26 EBU.	Aangenaam volmondig (caramout), fruitige volle smaak onmiddellijk gevolgd door een complexe afdronk met een aangename gebrande toets. 26 EBU
Pour in a single, slow movement in degreased, dry glasses. The yeast can be poured.	Verser lentement en un seul mouvement dans des verres dégraissés secs. Verser la levure selon le goût.	Traag en in 1 beweging schenken in ontvette, droge glazen. De gist naar keuze mee uitschenken.
Store in a dark, cool room.	Conserver à l'abri de la chaleur et de la lumière.	Donker en koel bewaren.

Kempisch Vuur Tripel

Bieren Pirlot by De Proefbrouwerij (soon at own brewery) 7,50% 8 - 10 46 - 50

top-fermentation re-fermented in the bottle not centrifuged	fermentation haute refermentation en bouteille non centrifugée	hoge gisting hergisting in de fles niet gecentrifugeerd
tripel city or local beer abbey beer	triple bière citadine ou régionale bière d'abbaye	tripel stads- of streekbier abdijbier
malt (pilsner, wheat, oat, maize), hops (Brewers Gold, Styrian), herbs, yeast, well water	malt (pils, froment, avoine, maïs), houblon (Brewers Gold, Styrian), herbes, levure, eau de source	mout (pils, tarwe, haver, mais), hop (Brewers Gold, Styrian), kruiden, gist, water
The proteins of the wheat malt create a solid, stable foam head. 11 EBC. Not filtered or pasteurised	Les protéines du malt de froment assurent un faux col solide stable. 11 EBC. Non filtreé ni pasteuriseé	11 EBC, stevige schuimkraag (tarwemout). Ongefilterd, niet gepasteuriseerd
Pleasantly full-bodied, fruity, full taste followed by a complex, harmonious and spicy aftertaste. Bitterness: 32 EBU.	Franche, agréable. Saveur fruitée et pleine suivie d'une fin de bouche complexe, harmonieuse et relevée. Amertume :32 EBU.	Aangenaam volmondig. Fruitige volle smaak gevolgd door een complexe, harmonieuze en kruidige afdronk. Bitterheid: 32 EBU
Pour in a single, slow movement in degreased, dry glasses. The yeast can be poured.	Verser lentement en un seul mouvement dans des verres dégraissés secs. Verser la levure selon le goût.	Traag en in 1 beweging schenken in ontvette, droge glazen. De gist naar keuze mee uitschenken.
Store in a dark, cool room. Beer with taste evolution.	Conserver à l'abri de la chaleur et de la lumière. Bière avec saveur évolutive.	Donker en koel bewaren. Bier met smaakevolutie.

	top-fermentation natural re-fermentation in the bottle	fermentation haute refermentation naturelle en bouteille	hoge gisting natuurlijke hergisting in de fles
	5 malt types, hops, cherries, Morpheus yeast, water	5 variétés de malt, 1 variété de houblon, cerises, levure Morpheus, eau	5 moutsoorten, 1 hopsoort, krieken, Morpheusgist, water
	95 EBC	95 EBC	95 EBC
	5 EBU	5 EBU	5 EBU

Brouwerij Het Sas 6,40% 4 39

	bottom-fermentation	fermentation basse	lage gisting
	Dortmunder or export	Dortmunder ou export	Dortmunder of export
	2 malt types, 2 different hops, yeast, water	2 variétés de malt, 2 variétés de houblon, levure, eau	2 moutsoorten, 2 hopsoorten, gist, water
	clear with a white foam head filtered	limpide avec faux col blanc filtrée	helder met witte schuim kraag gefilterd
	Malty scent and flavour with a fine hop touch in the aftertaste.	Parfum et goût maltés, avec une jolie touche de houblon en arrière-bouche.	Moutige geur en smaak met een mooie hoptoets in de afdronk.
	Serve in a bulb glass in a single movement.	Verser d' un seul mouvement fluide dans un verre ballon.	In 1 vlotte beweging uitschenken in een bolglas.
i			

Kerkomse Tripel

Brouwerij Kerkom by Brouwerij Sint-Jozef or Proefbrouwerij 9%

	top-fermentation re-fermented in the bottle	fermentation haute refermentation en bouteille	hoge gisting hergisting op de fles
	regional beer tripel	bière régionale triple	streekbier tripel
	2 Belgian hop varieties, barley malt, yeast, water	2 sortes de houblon belge, malt d'orge, levure, eau	2 Belgische hopsoorten, gerstemout, gist, water
	Beer with taste evolution.	Bière avec saveur évolutive.	Bier met smaakevolutie.
	100% Haspengouwen regional boutique beer.	Bière régionale 100% artisanale de Haspengouw.	100% ambachtelijk Haspengouws streekbier.

Kerstbie

Brouwerij De Bie

8% 6 43

	top-fermentation	fermentation haute	hoge gisting
	winter beer	bière hivernale	winterbier
	malt, hops, yeast, candy sugar, honey, herbs, water	malt, houblon, levure, sucre candi, miel, herbes, eau	mout, hop, gist, kandijsuiker, honing, kruiden, water
	dark	foncée	donker
	Spicy with a smooth honey taste.	Goût relevé avec une saveur moelleuse de miel.	Kruidig met een zachte honingsmaak.

crobrouwerij Achilles

7%

	top-fermentation	fermentation haute	hoge gisting
	winter beer	bière hivernale	winterbier
	pale amber with firm foam head	légèrement ambré avec faux col robuste	lichtamber met stoere schuimkraag
	Aroma of barley, mel-low-bitter taste that slips off the edge of the tongue. Full-bodied, typical Münich taste.	Arôme d'orge, goût doux-amer qui s'écoule sur le côté de la langue. Goût de Münich franc, typique.	Aroma van gerst, zacht-bittere smaak die weg-vloeit aan de zijkant van de tong.Volmondig, ty-pische Münichsmaak.
	Available from 1 October.	En vente à partir du 1er octobre.	Verkrijgbaar vanaf 1 ok-tober.

Kerstpater

Brouwerij Van den Bossche

9% 6 - 8 / 43 - 46

top-fermentation re-fermentation in the bottle	fermentation haute refermentation en bouteille	hoge gisting hergisting in de fles
herbal beer Christmas beer	bière aromatisée bière de Noël	kruidenbier kerstbier
pilsner, roasted and caramel malt, hops, fermentable sugar, yeast, water	malt de pils, malt caramélisé et torréfié, houblon, sucre refermentable, eau, levure	pils-, roost- en caramel mout, hop, vergistbare suiker, gist, water
deep dark brown with a red line and a beige foam head. Filtered, not pasteurised	brun foncé profond avec un trait rouge et un faux col beige. Filtrée, non pasteurisée	diep donkerbruin met een streepje rood en een beige schuimkraag. Gefilterd, niet gepasteuriseerd
Aroma: especially chocolate with panaché filling (in the style of Pater Lieven), supplemented with sweet (candy sugar and caramel) flavours and warmth (alcohol). Candy-sweet taste but not sticky owing to bitterness (like chocolate). Long aftertaste.	Arôme :surtout du chocolat fourré panaché (cf. Pater Lieven), complété par du sucré (sucre candi et caramel) et du chaud (alcool). Goût sucré candi mais pas collant, grâce à l'amertume (cf. chocolat). Longue arrière-bouche.	Aroma: vooral chocolade met panachévulling (cfr Pater Lieven), aangevuld met zoet (kandij en karamel) en warmte (alcohol). Kandijzoete smaak maar niet plakkerig door de bitterheid (cfr. chocolade). Lange afdronk.
Pour slowly, and avoid sloshing the beer, to achieve a nice foam head. Leave the yeast sediment in the bottle or add later.	Verser lentement sans clapotage de la bière pour former un faux col solide. Laisser le dépôt de levure dans la bouteille et le verser éventuellement par après.	Langzaam uitschenken zonder dat het bier klokt en een mooie schuimkraag vormen. Het gistdepot in de fles laten en eventueel achteraf bijschenken.

ouwerij 't Smiske

10% 10 °C 50 °F

	top-fermentation re-fermented in the bottle	fermentation haute refermentation en bouteille	hoge gisting hergisting op de fles
	dark Christmas beer	bière de Noël foncée	kerstbier donker
	4 malt varieties (crystal, cara, pilsner, wheat), Hallertau and Challenger hops, candy, two sorts of herbs, yeast, water	4 sortes de malt (cristal, cara, pils, froment), houblon Hallertau et Challenger, sucre candi, 2 sortes d'herbes, levure, eau	4 moutsoorten (kristal, cara, pils, tarwe), Hallertau en Challenger hop, kandij, 2 soorten kruiden, gist, water
	dark unfiltered	foncée non filtrée	donker niet gefilterd
	Fruity, malty and sweet aroma. Taste: caramel, sweet, spicy with a very long-lasting, bitter after-taste. Full-bodied beer.	Arôme fruité, houblonné et doux. Goût :caramel, doux, herbes avec une fin de bouche très longue, amère. Bière franche.	Fruitig, moutig en zoetig aroma. Smaak: karamel, zoet, kruidig met zeer lange, bittere afdronk. Volmondig bier.
	Boutique beer that can be kept up to 5 years after the bottling date. The label was designed by the American comic artist Bill Coleman.	Bière artisanale qui se conserve jusqu'à 5 ans après la date de la mise en bouteilles. L'étiquette est conçue par le cartooniste Américain Bill Coleman.	Artisanaal bier, 5 jaar houdbaar na botteldatum. Het etiket is ontworpen door de Amerikaanse striptekenaar Bill Coleman.

Kerstvuur

Bieren Pirlot by De Proefbrouwerij (soon at own brewery) 9% 8 - 10 / 46 - 50

	top-fermentation re-fermented in the bottle not centrifuged	fermentation haute refermentation en bouteille non centrifugée	hoge gisting hergisting in de fles niet gecentrifugeerd
	city or local beer winter or Christmas beer	bière citadine ou régionale bière hivernale ou de Noël	stads- of streekbier winter- of kerstbier
	malt (pilsner, Münich, wheat, oat, corn), hops (Brewers Gold, Styrian), herbs, yeast, spring water	malt (pils, Münich, froment, avoine, maïs), houblon (Brewers Gold, Styrian), herbes, levure, eau de source	mout (pils, Münich, tarwe, haver, mais), hop (Brewers Gold, Styrian), kruiden, gist, bronwater
	not filtered or pasteurised. The wheat malt proteins provide a firm, stable foam head. 16 EBC	non filtrée non pasteurisée Les protéines du malt de froment assurent un faux col solide stable. 16 EBC.	ongefilterd, niet gepasteuriseerd De tarwemouteiwitten zorgen voor een stevige, stabiele schuimkraag. 16 EBC.
	Pleasantly full-bodied. Extra malty owing to the Münich, which does not allow an alcohol flavour. Harmonious, spicy aftertaste. Bitterness: 32 EBU	Franche et agréable. Extra maltée (le malt Münich ne permet pas de goût alcoolisé). Fin de bouche harmonieuse, relevée. Amertume de 32 EBU.	Aangenaam volmondig. Extra moutigheid door de Münich die geen alcoholsmaak toelaat. Harmonieuze, kruidige afdronk. Bitterheid van 32 EBU.
	Pour in a single, slow movement in degreased, dry glasses. The yeast can be poured.	Verser lentement en un seul mouvement dans des verres dégraissés secs. Verser la levure selon le goût.	Traag en in 1 beweging uitschenken in ontvette, droge glazen. De gist naar keuze mee uitschenken.
i	Store in a dark, cool room. Beer with taste evolution.	Conserver à l'abri de la chaleur et de la lumière. Bière avec saveur évolutive.	Donker en koel bewaren. Bier met smaakevolutie.

Kessel 69

uwerij De Vlier

6,90% | 4 - 6 °C / 39 - 43 °F

bottom-yeast fermented on a high temperature re-fermentation in the bottle not centrifuged	levure basse fermentée à haute température refermentation en bouteille non centrifugée	lage gist vergist op hoge temperatuur hergisting in de fles niet gecentrifugeerd
amber	ambrée	amber
Münich and wheat malt, hops (Saaz), yeast, water	malt de Münich et de froment, houblon Saaz, levure, eau	Münich- en tarwemout, Saazhop, gist, water
clear to slightly cloudy amber with white, dense foam head not filtered or pasteurised	limpide à légèrement trouble ambré avec faux col compact blanc non filtrée, non pasteurisée	helder tot licht troebel amber met witte, dichte schuimkraag ongefilterd, niet gepasteuriseerd
Grainy and hoppy aroma, full-bodied and hoppy taste, slightly bitter aftertaste.	Arôme de céréales et de houblon, goût franc et arrière-bouche houblonnée, légèrement amère.	Granig en hoppig aroma, volmondige smaak en hoppige, licht bittere afdronk.
Pour into a tulip glass and leave the yeast sediment in the bottle or pour along.	Verser dans un verre tulipe et laisser le dépôt de levure dans la bouteille où le verser également.	Uitschenken in een tulpvormig glas en de gistbodem in de fles laten of meeschenken.

Kessel Blond

Brouwerij De Vlier 7,50% 4 - 6 / 39 - 43

	top-fermentation re-fermentation in the bottle not centrifuged	fermentation haute refermentation en bouteille non centrifugée	hoge gisting hergisting in de fles niet gecentrifugeerd
	strong blond	blonde forte	sterk blond
	pilsner and wheat malt, hops (Saaz and Perle), yeast, water	malt de pils et de froment, houblon (Saaz et Perle), levure, eau	pils- en tarwemout, hop (Saaz en Perle), gist, water
	clear to slightly cloudy gold-coloured blond with white, dense foam head not filtered or pasteurised	limpide à légèrement trouble blond doré avec faux col compact blanc non filtrée, non pasteurisée	helder tot licht troebel blond goudkleurig met witte, dichte schuimkraag ongefilterd, niet gepasteuriseerd
	Fresh, fruity and hoppy aroma. Mellow and refreshing flavour. Slightly hoppy aftertaste.	Arôme frais, fruité et houblonné, goût doux et rafraîchissant, arrière-bouche légèrement houblonnée.	Fris, fruitig en hoppig aroma. Zachte en verfrissende smaak. Licht hoppige afdronk.
	see Kessel 69.	voir Kessel 69.	zie Kessel 69.
	Brewery's first beer. The recipe is a remnant of one of brewer Marc's previous jobs when he carried out research into continuous fermentation systems at Meura-Delta. Kessel refers to Kessel-Lo where the brewery was located initially.	Première bière de la brasserie. La recette est une survivance d'un emploi antérieur du brasseur Marc, quand il réalisa une recherche sur les systèmes de fermentation continue chez Meura-Delta. Kessel vient de Kessel-Lo, où la brasserie était initialement établie.	Eerste bier van de brouwerij. Het recept is een overblijfsel van een vroegere job van brouwer Marc toen hij onderzoek deed naar continue gistingssystemen bij Meura-Delta. Kessel komt van Kessel-Lo waar de brouwerij initieel gevestigd was.

uwerij Strubbe

7,70% 8 °C 46 °F

	top-fermentation re-fermented in the bottle	fermentation haute refermentation en bouteille	hoge gisting nagisting op de fles
	tripel blond	triple blonde	tripel blond
	pilsner malt, Münich malt, clear candy sugar, hops, fresh yeast, spring water	malt de pils, malt Münich, sucre candi clair, houblon, levure fraîche, eau de source	pilsmout, Münichmout, lichte kandijsuiker, hopsoorten, verse gist, bronwater
	Full, bittersweet.	Pleine, doux-amère.	Vol, bitterzoet.
	Beer with taste evolution, made by order of the Ostend Bierjutters in 2004.	Bière avec saveur évolutive, fabriquée à la demande des 'Oostendse Bierjutters' en 2004.	Bier met smaakevolutie, gemaakt in opdracht van de Oostendse Bierjutters in 2004.

Keyte

Keyte Oostendse Dobbel-Tripel

Brouwerij Strubbe

9,20% 7-
45 - 4

	top-fermentation re-fermentation in the bottle	fermentation haute refermentation en bouteille	hoge gisting hergisting in de fles
	double	double	dubbel
	barley malt, roasted malt, candy sugar, different hops, yeast, water	malt d'orge, malt torréfié, sucre candi, variétés de houblon, levure, eau	gerstemout, geroosterde mout, kandijsuiker, hopsoorten, gist, wate
	shining ruby	rubis brillant	glanzend robijn
	Brewed in tandem with 'De Oostendse Bierjutters'. The beachcomber's beer which the brewer produces for Den Haene forms the basis of this beer.	Brassée en collaboration avec 'De Oostendse Bierjutters'. La Strandjuttersbier, que le brasseur réalise pour Den Haene, se trouve à la base de cette bière.	Gebrouwen in samenwerking met 'De Oostendse Bierjutters'. Het Strandjuttersbier dat de brouwer maakt voor Den Haene ligt aan de basis van dit bier.

Nest by De Scheldebrouwerij

10% 10 °C 50 °F

top-fermentation re-fermentation in the bottle not centrifuged	fermentation haute refermentation en bouteille non centrifugée	hoge gisting hergisting in de fles niet gecentrifugeerd
city or regional beer strong dubbel winter beer	bière citadine ou régionale double forte bière hivernale	stads- of streekbier sterk donker winterbier
malt, herbs, hops, yeast, sugar, water	malt, herbes, houblon, levure, sucre, eau	mout, kruiden, hop, gist, suiker, water
black-coloured with a beige foam head not filtered or pasteurised	noire avec un faux col beige non filtrée, non pasteurisée	zwartkleurig met een beige schuimkraag ongefilterd, niet gepasteuriseerd
Spicy and fruity aroma. Complex taste pallet of anise (dominant when serving temperature is too low), chocolate, coffee, dark fruit. Spicy aftertaste.	Arôme épicé et fruité. Palette de goûts complexe d'anis (dominant à une température de service trop basse), de chocolat, de café, de fruits noirs. Arrière-bouche épicée.	Kruidig en fruitig aroma. Complex smaakpalet van anijs (overheersend bij te lage schenktemperatuur), chocolade, koffie, donker fruit. Kruidige afdronk.
Serve in a goblet with or without yeast sediment.	Verser avec ou sans levure dans un verre calice.	Met of zonder gist uitschenken in een kelkglas.
The name refers to Turnhout, capital of the game card, where the brewery is based.	Le nom fait référence à Turnhout, capitale du jeu de cartes, où la brasserie est aussi installée.	De naam verwijst naar Turnhout, hoofdstad van de speelkaart, waar ook de brouwerij is gevestigd.

Kloeke Blonde

De Struise Brouwers at Brouwerij Deca 6% 4 - 39 - 4

	top-fermentation re-fermented in the bottle not centrifuged	fermentation haute refermentation en bouteille non centrifugée	hoge gisting hergisting in de fles niet gecentrifugeerd
	old-style blond	blonde style ancien	oude stijl blond
	pilsner malt, Münich malt, yeast, water, hops: Challenger, Hallertauer Mittelfrueh, herbs: sweet orange rind, thyme	malt de pils, malt Mü-nich, levure, eau, houblon: Challenger, Hallertauer Mittelfrueh, herbes: écorces d'orange doux, thym	pilsmout, Münichmout, gist, water, hop: Challenger, Haller-tauer Mittelfrueh, kruiden: zoete sinaas-schillen, tijm
	slightly hazy, gold-blond (11 EBC) with a white foam head not filtered or pasteur-ised	légèrement floue, blond doré (11 EBC) avec un faux col blanc non filtrée, non pasteu-risée	licht wazig, goudblond (11 EBC) met een witte schuimkraag ongefilterd, niet gepas-teuriseerd
	Intense, nice dry-malty flavour with light hints of caramel, grains, nuts and fruit. Refreshing bitter aftertaste owing to the hops. 24 EBU.	Joli goût malté sec, pi-quant, avec de légères touches de caramel, de céréales, de noix et d'un peu de fruits. Fin de bouche avec un peu d'amertume rafraîchis-sante du houblon. 24 EBU.	Pittige, mooie droog-moutige smaak met lich-te toetsen van karamel, granen, noten en ietwat fruit. Nasmaak met ver-frissend bittertje van de hop. 24 EBU.
	Pour out in a single movement.	Verser agilement.	Vlot uitschenken.
	The name referes to one of the Struise Brouwers' wife.	Le nom renvoie à l'épouse d'un des Struise Brouwers.	Genoemd naar Leentje, de vrouw van één van de brouwers.

as by De Proefbrouwerij

7% | 6 °C / 43 °F

top-fermentation re-fermentation in the bottle	fermentation haute refermentation en bouteille	hoge gisting hergisting in de fles
strong blond	blonde forte	sterk blond
barley malt, hops, yeast, water	malt d'orge, houblon, levure, eau	gerstemout, hop, gist, water
amber-coloured	ambrée	amberkleurig
Brewed for De Bierloods in Adegem.	Brassée pour De Bierloods à Adegem.	Gebrouwen voor De Bierloods in Adegem.

Koekelaring

Hoevebrouwers by Brouwerij De Graal

6,50% 6 - 43 -

	top-fermentation re-fermented in the bottle	fermentation haute refermentation en bouteille	hoge gisting hergisting op de fles
	specialty beer	bière spéciale	speciaalbier
	malt (pilsner, wheat, cara red, cara aroma, chocolate without bitter), hops (EK Goldings, Hallertau), yeast (T58), water	malt (pils, froment, cara red, arôme cara, chocolat pas amer), houblon (EK Goldings, Hallertau), levure (T58), eau	mout (pils, tarwe, cara red, cara aroma, ontbit terde chocolade), hop (EK Goldings, Hallertau gist (T58), water
	red-brown clear	brun rouge claire	roodbruin helder
	Full-bodied and rich. Sweet malty onset with a hoppy aftertaste.	Franche et riche. Début doux malté avec une fin de bouche houblonnée.	Volmondig en rijk. Zoet moutige aanhef met ee hoppige afdronk.
	Pour into a degreased goblet in a single movement, avoiding contact with glass or foam. Leave approx. 1 cm of beer in the bottle.	Verser en un seul mouvement dans un verre calice dégraissé sans toucher le verre et l'écume. Laisser environ 1 cm de bière dans la bouteille.	In 1 beweging in een ve vrij kelkglas gieten zon der het glas en het schuim te raken. Ongeveer 1 cm bier in de fles laten.
	Koekelaring is a bakery product from Zottegem, available from November to February.	Koekelaring est une spécialité pâtissière de Zottegem disponible de novembre à février.	Koekelaring is een Zotte gems kaneelbroodje da verkrijgbaar is tussen november en februari.

uwerij Maenhout 8,50% 9°C 48 °F

	top-fermentation re-fermentation in the bottle not centrifuged	fermentation haute refermentation en bouteille non centrifugée	hoge gisting hergisting in de fles niet gecentrifugeerd
	tripel	triple	tripel
	malt, hops, coriander, yeast, water	malt, houblon, coriandre, levure, eau	mout, hop, koriander, gist, water
	blond, slightly cloudy with a firm white foam head not filtered	blonde, légèrement trouble avec faux col solide blanc non filtrée	blond, licht troebel met stevige witte schuimkraag ongefilterd
	The brewer calls it a tripel abbey beer. Sweet, fruity aroma. Slightly tart owing to citrus and apricot. Slightly bitter aftertaste.	Le brasseur la qualifie de bière d'abbaye triple. Arôme sucré, fruité. Goût légèrement acidulé de citrus et d'abricot. Arrière-bouche légèrement amère.	De brouwer noemt het een tripel abdijbier. Zoet, fruitig aroma. Lichtzurige smaak van citrus en abrikoos. Licht bitterige afdronk.
	Pour slowly in a tall glass.	Verser lentement dans un verre oblong.	Traag inschenken in een langwerpig glas.
i	Koeketiene means '10 diamond' (card game) in the West-Flemish dialect. It is also the West-Flemish corruption of the French word 'concubine'.	Koeketiene signifie '10 de carreau' (jeu de cartes) en dialecte de Flandre Occidentale. C'est aussi la déformation dans ce dialecte du mot français 'concubine'.	Koeketiene betekent 'ruiten 10' (kaartspel) in het Westvlaamse dialect. Het is ook de Westvlaamse verbastering voor het Franse woord 'concubine'.

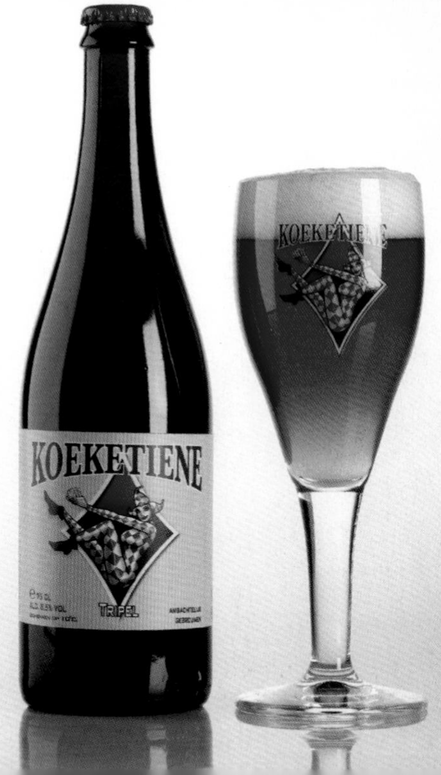

Brouwerij Kortrijk-d'Utsel

8,50% 4

	top-fermentation natural re-fermentation in the bottle not centrifuged	fermentation haute refermentation naturelle en bouteille non centrifugée	hoge gisting natuurlijke hergisting i de fles niet gecentrifugeerd
	brut beer	bière brute	brutbier
	barley malt, unmalted grain varieties, sugar, yeast, water	malt d'orge, grains non maltés, sucre, houblon, levure, eau	gerstemout, ongemoute granen, suiker, gist, wa ter
	champagne-coloured with creamy, white foam head not filtered or pasteurised	champagne avec faux col crémeux, blanc non filtrée, non pasteurisée	champagnekleurig met romige, witte schuimkraag ongefilterd, niet gepasteuriseerd
	Balanced aperitif beer with a refreshing, fruity aroma and long, dry aftertaste.	Bière d'apéritif équilibrée, avec un arôme fruité rafraîchissant et une arrière-bouche longue et sèche.	Uitgebalanceerd aperitiefbier met een verfris send, fruitig aroma en lange, droge afdronk.
	Serve in a champagne glass. Using a good stopper, the bottle can be kept in the fridge for a few days.	Verser dans un verre champagne. Par un bouchon bien étanche la bouteille se conserve dans le frigo quelques jours après ouverture.	Uitschenken in een champagneglas. Met ee goed afsluitende stop is de fles enkele dagen na opening houdbaar in de koelkast.
	Kortrijk-Dutsel is the age-old name of a Hageland village with a beer tradition. Since the 16th century, beer is brewed that is suitable to drink before a meal.	Kortrijk-Dutsel est le nom séculaire d'un village du Hageland qui possède une tradition de la bière. Depuis le 16e siècle, l'on y brasse de la bière qui convient parfaitement à une consommation avant le repas.	Kortrijk-Dutsel is de eeuwenoude naam van een Hagelands dorp met een biertraditie. Sinds de 16e eeuw wordt er bie gebrouwen dat geschikt is om te drinken voor de maaltijd.

sendonk by Brasserie du Bocq 3,50%

	barley malt, unmalted grain varieties, sugar, hops, yeast, water	malt d'orge, grains non maltés, sucre, houblon, levure, eau	gerstemout, ongemoute granen, suiker, hop, gist, water

Kriek Boon

Brouwerij Boon 4,50%

spontaneous fermentation	fermentation spontanée	spontane gisting
fruit beer	bière fruitée	fruitbier
Blend of young and old lambic, matured in oak barrels. Real cherries (25%).	Mélange de jeune et vieux lambic mûri en fûts en bois de chêne. Vraies cerises (25%).	Versnijding van jonge e oude lambiek gerijpt op eikenhouten vaten. Echte krieken (25%).
red	rouge	rood
Refreshing, non-foaming. Sweet-and-sour cherry taste.	Fraîche, sans écume. Saveur de cerise aigre-douce.	Fris, niet schuimend. Zuurzoete kriekensmaak.
Originally created with Schaarbeek cherries, now especially with Noord cherries and lambic that is at least six months old. Many taverns that had lambic, used to make their own kriek, tapping it from the typical stone bottles.	A l'origine fabriquée avec des cerises de Schaerbeek, maintenant principalement avec des cerises du nord et du lambic de minimum 6 mois. Beaucoup de brasseries qui avaient le lambic en stock fabriquaient autrefois leur propre kriek et la servaient dans des cruches en pierre typiques.	Oorspronkelijk gemaak met Schaarbeekse krieken, nu vooral met Noordkrieken, en lambiek van minimum 6 maanden oud. Vroeger maakten veel herbergen die lambiek hadden liggen zelf hun kriek. Ze tapten hem in de typische stenen kruiken.

sserie Cantillon 5,50% 12 - 16 °C / 54 - 61 °F

spontaneous fermentation naturally re-fermented in the bottle	fermentation spontanée refermentation naturelle en bouteille	spontane gisting natuurlijke hergisting op de fles
fruit beer lambic	bière fruitée lambic	fruitbier lambiek
barley malt, wheat, more than one year old hops, fresh cherries	malt d'orge, froment, houblon suranné, cerises fraîches	gerstemout, tarwe, overjaarse hop, verse kersen
ruby-red	rouge rubis	robijnrood
Intensely fruity, sourish taste and pronounced cherry aroma with a touch of kirsch.	Goût fruité intense, saveur acidulée et arôme de cerises prononcé, pointe de kirsch.	Intense fruitigheid, zurige smaak en uitgesproken kersenaroma, vleugje kirsch.
The use of a wine basket is recommended if the bottle was stored horizontally. Place the bottle in an upright position 48 hours before serving.	Un panier verseur est recommandé si la bouteille a été conservée en position horizontale. Mettre la bouteille 48 heures avant de servir dans une position verticale pour faire descendre la levure.	Een schenkmandje is aangewezen wanneer de fles horizontaal bewaard werd. De fles 48 uur voor het uitschenken verticaal plaasten om het bezinksel te decanteren.

Kriek Cantillon 100% Lambic

K

Kriek De Ranke

Brouwerij De Ranke 7% Modera co

	mixed fermentation	fermentation mixte	gemengde gisting
	fruit beer	bière fruitée	fruitbier
	malt, wheat, hop flowers, wild yeasts, cherries blended with lambic	malt, froment, fleurs de houblon, levures sauvages, cerises, coupée avec le lambic	mout, tarwe, hopbloemen, wilde gisten, krieken, versneden met lambiek
	red slightly cloudy	rouge légèrement trouble	rood licht troebel
	Sourish cherry taste and aroma.	Acidulée, saveur et arôme de cerises.	Zurig, kriekensmaak e -aroma.

Kriek de Silenrieux

sserie de Silenrieux **4,50%** 5 - 6 °C / 41 - 43 °F

top-fermentation	fermentation haute	hoge gisting
fruit beer	bière fruitée	fruitbier
malt, hops, cherries, water	malt, houblon, cerises, eau	mout, hop, kersen, water
cherry-red	rouge cerise	kersenrood
Quite sweet with distinct cherry flavour.	Assez sucrée, avec un goût de cerises prononcé.	Vrij gesuikerd met uitgesproken kersensmaak.
Pour out gently.	Verser lentement.	Langzaam uitschenken.

Kriek Fantastiek

Brouwerij De Ryck 4,90% 4 - 39 - 4

	top-fermentation re-fermented in the bottle	fermentation haute refermentation en bouteille	hoge gisting nagisting op de fles
	bitter-and-sour kriek based on ale	kriek amère-acidulée à base d'ale	zuurbittere kriek op basis van ale
	malt, hops, yeast, sucrose, cherry extract, water. Based on Arend winter.	malt, houblon, levure, sucrose, extrait de cerises, eau. A base de Arend winter.	mout, hop, gist, sucros kriekenextract, water. Op basis van Arend winter.
	brown-red	brun rouge	bruinrood
	Refreshing and summery, bitter-and-sour. Unusual combination of fruit flavours and aromas with typical malt and hop bitterness.	Rafraîchissante et estivale, amer-acidulée. Combinaison obstinée de goûts et de parfums fruités, amertume typique de malt et de houblon.	Verfrissend en zomers zuurbitter. Eigenzinni combinatie van fruitsmaken en -geuren me typische mout en hopbitterheid.
	Rinse the glass with cold water, take it by the stem and hold it slightly tilted. Slowly pour in a single movement, avoiding contact between bottle and glass or foam. Leave 1 cm yeast sediment in the bottle or pour it along.	Rincer le verre à l'eau froide, le tenir légèrement en oblique par le pied. Verser la bière lentement et en un seul mouvement sans que la bouteille touche le verre ou l'écume. Laisser 1 cm de levure dans la bouteille ou la verser.	Het glas koud spoelen, bij de voet vastnemen licht schuin houden. H bier traag en in 1 beweging uitschenken zonc dat de fles het glas of schuim raakt. Het gist depot van 1 cm in de fl laten ofwel uitschenke
i			

5% cool

spontaneous fermentation	fermentation spontanée	spontane gisting
fruit beer lambic beer	bière fruitée bière lambic	fruitbier lambiekbier
wheat, barley malt, more than 1 year old hops, cherries, water	froment, malt d'orge, houblon suranné, cerises, eau	tarwe, gerstemout, overjaarse hop, krieken, water
clear ruby-red	rouge rubis clair	helder robijnrood
Fruity, cherry, sourish.	Fruitée, cerise, acidulée.	Fruitig, krieken, zurig.
Like champagne. In a flute-glass.	Comme le champagne. Dans des flûtes.	Zoals champagne. In fluitglazen.
Made with real cherries still containing their stone (instead of with cherry juice).	Fabriquée à partir de vraies cerises avec noyau (au lieu de jus de cerises).	Gemaakt met echte krieken die nog hun pit bevatten (in plaats van kriekensap).

Kriek Girardin

Kriek Jacobins

Brouwerij Bockor (Vander Ghinste) 4,50% 5 - 5 -

	spontaneous fermentation	fermentation spontanée	spontane gisting
	fruit beer lambic beer	bière fruitée bière lambic	fruitbier lambiekbier
	barley malt, wheat, hops, yeast, cherry juices, natural flavours, water	malt d'orge, froment, houblon, levure, jus de cerises, arômes naturels, eau	gerstemout, tarwe, ho gist, kriekensap, natuurlijke aroma's, wate
	helderrood	rouge clair	helderrood
	Fresh fruity character. Sweet-and-sour taste.	Caractère fruité et frais. Saveur aigre-douce.	Zoetzure smaak. Frisfruitig karakter.
	Rinse the glass with cold water, tilt it a little and pour carefully half of the bottle. Next keep the glass upright and pour the rest of the bottle in a single movement.	Rincer le verre à l'eau froide, le tenir légèrement incliné et le remplir à moitié. Puis relever le verre et verser la bière qui reste d'un seul trait.	Het glas koud spoelen, licht schuin houden en voorzichtig half insche ken. Daarna het glas rechthouden en de res in 1 beweging uitschen ken.
i			

4% | 5 °C 41 °F

spontaneous fermentation	fermentation spontanée	spontane gisting
fruit beer based on lambic	bière fruitée à base de gueuze lambic	fruitbier op basis van geuze lambiek
malt, wheat, sugar, hops, cherries, flavouring, water. The sour cherries are immersed in Geuze Lambic during 6 monts.	malt, froment, sucre, houblon, cerises, arôme, eau. Les cérises acidulées restent au minimum 6 mois dans la gueuze lambic.	mout, tarwe, suiker, hop, krieken, aroma, water. De zure krieken liggen minimum 6 maanden in geuze lambiek.
deep red clear	rouge intense claire	dieprood helder
Refreshing and fruity. Cherry taste and aroma with discrete pip touch.	Fraîche et fruitée. Saveur et arôme de cerises avec une touche discrète de noyaux.	Fris en fruitig. Kriekensmaak en -aroma met discrete pittentoets.
Pour into a newly rinsed glass. Keep it tilted first, in a vertical position next.	Verser dans un verre rincé tenu d'abord en oblique et à la fin en position verticale.	Uitschenken in een vers gespoeld glas dat eerst schuin en op het einde verticaal gehouden wordt.

Kriek Lambic St Louis

K Kriek Lindemans

Brouwerij Lindemans 3,50% 3 - 37 - 3

	spontaneous fermentation	fermentation spontanée	spontane gisting
	fruit beer based on lambic	bière fruitée à base de lambic	fruitbier op basis van lambiek
	malt, wheat, hops, cherry juice (25%), fructose, water	malt, froment, houblon, jus de cerises (25%), fructose, eau	mout, tarwe, hop, kriekensap (25%), fructose water
	red slightly hazy	rouge légèrement voilée	rood licht gesluierd
	Fruity character. Lively and strong onset turning into a balance of sweet (fruit) and smooth sour (lambic).	Caractère fruité. Début vif et corsé passant à un équilibre de douceur (fruits) et d'acidité légère (lambic).	Fruitig karakter. Levendige en sterke aanzet die overgaat in een evenwicht van zoet (fruit) en zacht zuur (lambiek).
	Pour into a flute-glass or beer snifter.	Verser dans une flûte ou un verre ballon.	In een fluitglas of bolglas uitschenken.
	Suitable as an aperitif and as a thirst-quencher.	Convient comme apéritif et comme boisson désaltérante.	Geschikt als aperitief e als dorstlesser.

ouwerij Boon

8%

Kriek Mariage Parfait

	spontaneous fermentation refermentation in the bottle	fermentation spontanée refermentation en bouteille	spontane gisting nagisting in de fles
	Old Kriek	Vieille Kriek	Oude Kriek
	barley malt, wheat, fresh cherries (400 g/l), hops, water. Produced using 18-month old lambic. Matures in oak barrels.	malt d'orge, froment, cerises fraîches (400 g/l) houblon, eau. Brassée à base de lambic de 18 mois. Mûrie en foudres de chêne.	gerstemout, tarwe, verse krieken (400 g/l), hop, water. Gemaakt op basis van lambiek van 18 maanden. Rijpt op eikenhouten foeders.

Kriek Max Jacobins

Brouwerij Bockor (Vander Ghinste) 3,20% 5 - 8 / 41 - 46

	spontaneous fermentation	fermentation spontanée	spontane gisting
	fruit beer	bière fruitée	fruitbier
	barley malt, wheat, hops, yeast, cherry juices, natural flavouring, water	malt d'orge, froment, houblon, levure, jus de cerises, eau	gerstemout, tarwe, hop, gist, natuurlijk kriekensap, water
	clear red	rouge clair	helderrood
	Fresh fruity character. Sweet-and-sour taste.	Caractère fruité et frais. Saveur aigre-douce.	Zoetzure smaak. Frisfruitig karakter.
	Rinse the glass with cold water, tilt it a little and pour carefully half of the bottle. Next keep the glass upright and pour the rest of the bottle in a single movement.	Rincer le verre à l'eau froide, le tenir légèrement incliné et le remplir prudemment à moitié. Puis relever le verre et verser le reste de la bière d'un seul trait.	Het glas koud spoelen, licht schuin houden en voorzichtig half inschenken. Daarna het glas rechthouden en de rest in 1 beweging uitschenken.
i			

Kriekedebie

ouwerij De Bie

6% — 6 °C / 43 °F

top-fermentation	fermentation haute	hoge gisting
fruit beer	bière fruitée	fruitbier
malt, hops, yeast, cherry extract, water	malt, houblon, levure, extrait de cerises, eau	mout, hop, gist, kriekenextract, water
ruby red	rouge rubis	robijnrood
Slightly sour.	Légèrement acidulée.	Zachtzuur.

Kriekenbier

Brouwerij Sint-Jozef

3,50% 2 - 4 36 - 39

	bottom-fermentation	fermentation basse	lage gisting
	Witbier with fruit juice	bière blanche avec jus de fruits	witbier met vruchtensap
	malt, hops, wheat, oat, herbs, sugar, juice, water	malt, houblon, froment, avoine, herbes, sucre, jus, eau	mout, hop, tarwe, haver, kruiden, suiker, sap, water
	red	rouge	rood
	Sweet, fruity and refreshing. Overwhelming cherry taste.	Doux, fruité et rafraîchissant. Goût dominant de cerises.	Zoet fruitig en verfrissend. Overweldigende kriekensmaak.
	Pour into a clean, degreased glass, avoiding contact between bottle and foam.	Verser dans un verre propre et dégraissé sans que la bouteille touche l'écume.	Uitschenken in een zuiver, ontvet glas zonder dat de fles het schuim raakt.
i			

4,50% 4 °C 39 °F

	mixed and top-fermentation	fermentation mixte et haute	gemengde en hoge gisting
	West-Flemish red-brown with fruit	Flandre Occidentale bière brune rouge fruitée	Westvlaams roodbruin met fruit
	hops, malt, Morello cherries, water	houblon, malt, cerises, eau	hop, mout, krieken, water
	Cherry juice is macerated in the beer for a few weeks and is subsequently separated by centrifugation.	Jus de cerises macère pendant quelques semaines dans la bière et est séparé par la suite par centrifugation.	Kriekensap macereert enkele weken in het bier en wordt dan door centrifugatie gescheiden.

Kwaremont

Brouwerij Bavik

6,60% — 6 - 10 / 43 - 50

top-fermentation centrifuged	fermentation haute centrifugée	hoge gisting gecentrifugeerd
blond	blonde	blond
barley malt, hops, yeast, pure spring water	malt d'orge, houblon, levure, eau minérale pure	gerstemout, hop, gist, zuiver bronwater
clear, nice tanned colour with fixed foam head filtered, pasteurised	limpide, bronze joli avec faux col stable filtrée, pasteurisée	helder, mooie bronskleur met vaste schuimkraag gefilterd, gepasteuriseerd
Soft, full-bodied taste with a light, pleasant bitterness and spicy touch. Hoppy flavour.	Goût doux, franc, avec une légère amertume agréable et une touche épicée. Caractère houblonné.	Zachte, volle smaak met een lichte, aangename bitterheid en een kruidige toets. Hoppig karakter.
Pour into a clean, degreased glass, avoiding contact with the foam.	Verser dans un verre dégraissé rincé sans que la bouteille touche l'écume.	Uitschenken in een ontvet gespoeld glas zonder dat de fles het schuim raakt.
Brewed at the request of the municipality of Kluisbergen. The Kwaremont is one of the mythical slopes from the Flemish cycling classics.	Brassée pour le compte de la commune de Kluisbergen. Le Kwaremont est l'une des côtes mythiques des classiques cyclistes flamandes.	Gebrouwen in opdracht van de gemeente Kluisbergen. De Kwaremont is een van de mythische hellingen uit de Vlaamse wielerklassiekers.

'ouwerij Danny

6,40% 6 - 10 °C 43 - 50 °F

	top-fermentation re-fermentation in the bottle	fermentation haute refermentation en bouteille	hoge gisting hergisting in de fles
	blond	blonde	blond
	malt, hops, herbs, yeast, water	malt, houblon, herbes, levure, eau	mout, hop, kruiden, gist, water
	blond with slight amber touch fine pearly and stable foam head not filtered	blonde avec un ton légèrement ambré faux col fin pétillant et stable non filtrée	blond met lichte ambertoets fijne parelende en stabiele schuimkraag ongefilterd
	Fresh and balanced beer with an excellent bouquet, a mellow malt taste and hoppy aftertaste.	Bière fraîche et équilibrée, avec un excellent bouquet, un goût malté doux et une arrière-bouche houblonnée.	Fris en evenwichtig bier met een uitstekend boeket, een zachte moutsmaak en een gehopte afdronk.
	Pour gently into a tilted glass. Add the yeast sediment or leave it in the bottle.	Verser lentement dans un verre légèrement incliné. Ajouter le dépôt de levure ou le laisser dans la bouteille.	Traag uitschenken in een licht schuingehouden glas. De gistbodem toevoegen of in de fles laten.
i	Traditionally brewed regional beer from Erpe-Mere.	Bière régionale d'Erpe-Mere brassée de manière artisanale.	Ambachtelijk gebrouwen streekbier uit Erpe-Mere.

K

Kwibus Donker

Brouwerij Danny 6,40% 6 - 10 / 43 - 50

	top-fermentation re-fermentation in the bottle	fermentation haute refermentation en bouteille	hoge gisting hergisting in de fles
	double	double	dubbel
	malt, hops, yeast, water	malt, houblon, levure, eau	mout, hop, gist, water
	dark owing to the roasted malt varieties nice, fine, sparkling foam head. Not filtered	foncé par les variétés de malt torréfié faux col joli fin, pétillant. Non filtrée	donker door de gebrande moutsoorten mooie, fijne, parelende schuimkraag. Ongefilterd
	Slight caramel and coffee touch and a balanced bouquet. Pleasant, slightly bitter aftertaste setting off the hop aromas well. Not sweet.	Légère touche de caramel et de café et un bouquet équilibré. Arrière-bouche agréable, légèrement amère, en équilibre avec les arômes de houblon. Non sucrée.	Lichte karamel- en koffietoets en een evenwichtig boeket. Aangename, licht bittere afdronk in balans met de hoparoma's. Niet zoet.
	Pour gently into a tilted glass. Add the yeast sediment or leave it in the bottle.	Verser lentement dans un verre légèrement incliné. Ajouter le dépôt de levure ou le laisser dans la bouteille.	Traag uitschenken in een licht schuingehouden glas. De gistbodem toevoegen of in de fles laten.
i	Traditionally brewed regional beer from Erpe-Mere.	Bière régionale d'Erpe-Mere brassée de manière artisanale.	Ambachtelijk gebrouwen streekbier uit Erpe-Mere.

rasserie La Barbiot

9,50% 10 - 15 °C / 50 - 59 °F

	top-fermentation	fermentation haute	hoge gisting
	amber	ambrée	amber
	barley malt, wild hops, yeast, water	malt d'orge, houblon sauvage, levure, eau	gerstemout, wilde hop, gist, water
	amber	ambrée	amber
	Serve in a balloon glass.	Verser dans un verre ballon.	Uitschenken in een ballonglas.

La Barbiot Ambrée

La Barbiot Blonde

Brasserie La Barbiot 8% Cell temperatur

	top-fermentation	fermentation haute	hoge gisting
	blond	blonde	blond
	barley malt, wild hops, yeast, water	malt d'orge, houblon sauvage, levure, eau	gerstemout, wilde hop, gist, water
	blond	blonde	blond
	Serve in a balloon glass.	Verser dans un verre bal-lon.	Uitschenken in een bal-longlas.

La Bière de Beloeil

rasserie Dupont 8,50% 12 °C 54 °F

	top-fermentation re-fermented in the bottle	fermentation haute refermentation en bouteille	hoge gisting nagisting in de fles
	amber	ambrée	amber
	based on 5 different malt varieties and fine hop varieties	À base de 5 sortes différentes de malt et de variétés de houblon fines	op basis van 5 verschillende moutsoorten en fijne hopsoorten
	amber-coloured	ambrée	amberkleurig
	Fairly complex with malt and hop flavours.	Assez complexe avec des arômes de malt et de houblon.	Vrij complex met aroma's van mout en hop.
	Brewed since 1988 by order of the municipality of Beloeil, famous for its castle.	Brassée depuis 1988 à la demande de la commune de Beloeil, fameuse pour son château.	Gebrouwen sinds 1988 op aanvraag van de gemeente Beloeil, vermaard om zijn kasteel.

La Binchoise Blonde

Brasserie Artisanale La Binchoise 6,20%

	top-fermentation re-fermented in the bottle	fermentation haute refermentation en bouteille	hoge gisting hergisting in de fles
	blond	blonde	blond
	aromatic hop varieties, coriander, orange rind, malt	variétés de houblon aromatiques, coriandre, écorce d'orange, malt	aromatische hopsoorten, koriander, sinaasschil, mout
	gold-yellow slightly cloudy, unfiltered and unpasteurised. White, fine and creamy foam head.	jaune doré légèrement trouble, non filtrée ni pasteurisée. Avec un faux col fin et crémeux.	goudgeel licht troebel, niet gefilterd of gepasteuriseerd. Witte, fijne en romige schuimkraag.
	Fine bitterness and round mouthfeel.	Goût amer raffiné et rond en bouche.	Fijne bitterheid en rond in de mond.

asserie Artisanale La Binchoise 7,70%

La Binchoise Brune

	top-fermentation re-fermented in the bottle	fermentation haute refermentation en bouteille	hoge gisting hergisting in de fles
	dubbel	double	dubbel
	Based on 3 malt varieties of which 1 roasted, aromatic hop varieties.	Brassée à base de 3 sortes de malt dont 1 torréfié, variétés de houblon aromatiques.	Gebrouwen op basis van 3 moutsoorten waarvan 1 gebrand, aromatische hopsoorten.
	Very dark brown. Exuberant, light amber-coloured foam head. Unpasteurised	Brun très foncé. Faux col excessif, écume légèrement ambrée. Non pasteurisée	Zeer donkerbruin. Uitbundige, licht amberkleurige schuimkraag. Niet gepasteuriseerd
	Easily digestible with a malty character. Long-lasting and dry aftertaste influenced by the aromatic hop species.	Facile à digérer avec un caractère malté. Arrière-bouche longue et fin de bouche sèche renvoyant aux diverses sortes de houblon aromatisé.	Licht verteerbaar met een moutig karakter. Lange nasmaak en droge afdronk die verwijst naar de aromatische hopsoorten.
i			

La Binchoise Organic' Brune

Brasserie Artisanale La Binchoise 7%

	top-fermentation re-fermentation in the bottle	fermentation haute refermentation en bouteille	hoge gisting hergisting in de fles
	double	double	dubbel
	water, barley malt, sugar, hops, herbs, yeast	eau, malt d'orge, sucre, houblon, herbes, levure	water, gerstemout, suiker, hop, kruiden, gist
	not filtered or pasteurised	non filtrée, non pasteurisée	ongefilterd, niet gepasteuriseerd
	Eco guarantee.	Biogarantie.	Biogarantie.

rasserie Artisanale La Binchoise 8,50%

La Binchoise Organic' Miel

	top-fermentation re-fermentation in the bottle	fermentation haute refermentation en bouteille	hoge gisting hergisting in de fles
	herbal beer	bière aromatique	kruidenbier
	water, barley malt, sugar, hops, herbs, honey, yeast	eau, malt d'orge, sucre, houblon, herbes, miel, levure	water, gerstemout, suiker, hop, kruiden, honing, gist
	not filtered or pasteurised	non filtrée, non pasteurisée	ongefilterd, niet gepasteuriseerd
	Eco guarantee.	Biogarantie.	Biogarantie.

La Binchoise Organic' Triple

Brasserie Artisanale La Binchoise 8,50%

top-fermentation re-fermentation in the bottle	fermentation haute refermentation en bouteille	hoge gisting hergisting in de fles
tripel	triple	tripel
barley malt, hops, sugar, yeast, water	malt d'orge, houblon, sucre, levure, eau	gerstemout, hop, suiker, gist, water
not filtered or pasteurised	non filtrée, non pasteurisée	ongefilterd, niet gepasteuriseerd
Eco guarantee.	Biogarantie	Biogarantie.

·asserie Artisanale La Binchoise

9% — 4 - 6 °C / 39 - 43 °F

	top-fermentation re-fermented in the bottle	fermentation haute refermentation en bouteille	hoge gisting hergisting in de fles
	winter beer	bière hivernale	winterbier
	barley malt, sugar, hop, herbs, yeast, water	malt d'orge, sucre, houblon, épices, levure, eau	water, gerstemout, suiker, hop, kruiden, gist
	amber clear	ambrée brillante	amber helder
	Very aromatic with a complex taste and fine bitterness. Sipping beer, suitable as an aperitif.	Très aromatique avec un goût complexe et une amertume fine. Bière de dégustation qui se boit également comme apéritif.	Zeer aromatisch met complexe smaak en fijne bitterheid. Degustatiebier dat ook als aperitief geschikt is.

La Binchoise Spéciale Noël

La Binchoise Triple

Brasserie Artisanale La Binchoise 8,50%

	top-fermentation re-fermentation in the bottle	fermentation haute refermentation en bouteille	hoge gisting hergisting in de fles
	tripel	triple	tripel
	water, barley malt, sugar, hops, herbs, yeast	eau, malt d'orge, sucre, houblon, herbes, levure	water, gerstemout, suiker, hop, kruiden, gist
	not filtered or pasteurised	non filtrée, non pasteurisée	ongefilterd, niet gepasteuriseerd
	Traditional brewery that has been in existence since 1836.	Brasserie artisanale existant depuis 1836.	Artisanale brouwerij die bestaat sinds 1836.

rasserie Artisanale La Binchoise 12% 7 - 15 °C 45 - 59 °F

La Binchoise XO

	top-fermentation re-fermentation in the bottle	fermentation haute refermentation en bouteille	hoge gisting hergisting in de fles
	barley malt, hops, sugar, yeast, armagnac, water	malt d'orge, houblon, sucre, levure, armagnac, eau	gerstemout, hop, suiker, gist, armagnac, water
	not filtered or pasteur-ised	non filtrée, non pasteu-risée	ongefilterd, niet gepas-teuriseerd
	Suitable as an aperitif or desert beer. Matured in armagnac casks.	Convient comme boisson d'apéritif ou de dessert. Mûrie en fûts d'arma-gnac.	Geschikt als aperitief of dessertdrank. Gerijpt in armagnacvaten.

La Botteresse Ambrée

Brasserie Artisanale La Botteresse de Sur-les-bois 8,50% 10 50

	top-fermentation triple fermentation	fermentation haute triple fermentation	hoge gisting driedubbele gisting
	specialty beer boutique beer	bière spéciale artisanale	speciaalbier artisanaal
	aromatic malts and herbs	malts aromatiques et herbes	aromatische mouten en kruiden
	dark amber unfiltered	ambré foncé non filtrée	donker amber ongefilterd
	Sipping beer. Powerful, well-balanced taste of spices and aromatic hops and malt.	Bière de dégustation. Saveur corsée et équilibrée par les herbes, le houblon aromatique et le malt.	Degustatiebier. Krachtige en evenwichtige smaak door de kruiden en de aromatische hop en mout.
	Pour into a degreased, dry glass, leaving 1 cm of yeast sediment in the bottle.	Verser dans un verre dégraissé, sec et laisser un dépôt de levure de 1 cm dans la bouteille.	Uitschenken in een ontvet, droog glas en 1 cm gistdepot in de fles laten.
i			

La Botteresse Bière de Noël

rasserie Artisanale La Botteresse de Sur-les-bois 10,50% 8 °C 46 °F

	top-fermentation natural re-fermentation in the bottle not centrifuged	fermentation haute refermentation naturelle en bouteille non centrifugée	hoge gisting natuurlijke hergisting in de fles niet gecentrifugeerd
	Christmas beer	bière de Noël	kerstbier
	pale ale malt, crystal malt, chocolate malt, hers, hops, yeast, water	malt de pale ale, malt de cristal, malt de chocolat, herbes, houblon, levure, eau	pale ale mout, kristal-, chocolademout, kruiden, hop, gist, water
	black not filtered or pasteurised	noire non filtrée, non pasteurisée	zwart ongefilterd, niet gepasteuriseerd
	Strong beer with malty taste.	Bière forte d'un goût malté.	Sterk bier met moutige smaak.
	Serve in a balloon glass.	Verser dans un verre ballon.	Uitschenken in een ballonglas.

La Botteresse Blonde

Brasserie Artisanale La Botteresse de Sur-les-bois 7,50% 8 46

	top-fermentation triple fermentation	fermentation haute triple fermentation	hoge gisting driedubbele gisting
	specialty beer boutique beer	bière spéciale artisanale	speciaalbier artisanaal
	aromatic malts, malted grain varieties, unmalted wheat and oat	malts aromatiques, sortes de blé malté, froment non malté et avoine	aromatische mouten, gemoute graansoorten, ongemoute tarwe en haver
	blond hazy (unfiltered)	blonde voilée (non filtrée)	blond gesluierd (ongefilterd)
	Refreshing, round and well-balanced. Flower and fruit aromas, taste and aroma of wheat and oat.	Rafraîchissante, ronde et équilibrée. Arômes de fleurs et de fruits, saveur et arômes de froment et d'avoine.	Verfrissend, rond en evenwichtig. Aroma's van bloemen en fruit, smaak en aroma van tarwe en haver.
	Pour into a degreased, dry glass, with or without the yeast sediment.	Verser dans un verre dégraissé, sec avec ou sans dépôt de levure.	Uitschenken in een ontvet, droog glas met of zonder gistdepot.
i			

asserie Artisanale La Botteresse de Sur-les-bois

9,50% 10 °C 50 °F

	top-fermentation triple fermentation	fermentation haute triple fermentation	hoge gisting driedubbele gisting
	specialty beer boutique beer	bière spéciale artisanale	speciaalbier artisanaal
	aromatic and roasted malt varieties, herbs	malts aromatiques et brûlés, herbes	aromatische en gebrande moutsoorten, kruiden
	brown to black unfiltered	brune à noire non filtrée	bruin tot zwart ongefilterd
	Powerful but round and well-balanced sipping beer. Fruity, spicy taste with liquorice and roasty malt.	Bière de dégustation corsée mais ronde et équilibrée. Saveur fruitée et aromatisée de réglisse et de malt brûlé.	Krachtig maar rond en evenwichtig degustatiebier. De smaak is fruitig en kruidig met zoethout en gebrande mout.
	Pour into a degreased, dry glass, leaving 1 cm of yeast sediment in the bottle.	Verser dans un verre dégraissé, sec et laisser un dépôt de levure de 1 cm dans la bouteille.	Uitschenken in een ontvet, droog glas en 1 cm gistdepot in de fles laten.
i			

La Botteresse Brune

La Botteresse Cérise

Brasserie Artisanale La Botteresse de Sur-les-bois 5,50% 5 41

	top-fermentation natural re-fermentation in the bottle not centrifuged	fermentation haute refermentation naturelle en bouteille non centrifugée	hoge gisting natuurlijke hergisting in de fles niet gecentrifugeerd
	fruit beer	bière fruitée	fruitbier
	pilsner malt, hops, cherry juice (griottes), yeast, water	malt de pils, houblon, jus de cerises (griottes), levure, eau	pilsmout, hop, kersensap (griottes), gist, water
	red not filtered, pasteurised	rouge non filtrée, pasteurisée	rood ongefilterd, gepasteuriseerd
	Slightly tart cherry taste.	Goût de cerises légèrement acide.	Lichtzure kersensmaak.
	Serve in a balloon glass.	Verser dans un verre ballon.	Uitschenken in een ballonglas.
i			

La Botteresse Miel

asserie Artisanale La Botteresse de Sur-les-bois 8,50% 8 °C 46 °F

top-fermentation natural re-fermentation in the bottle not centrifuged	fermentation haute refermentation naturelle en bouteille non centrifugée	hoge gisting natuurlijke hergisting in de fles niet gecentrifugeerd
amber or speciale belge	ambrée ou spéciale belge	amber of speciale belge
pale ale malt, crystal cara malt, honey, herbs, hops, yeast, water	malt de pale ale, malt crystal cara, miel, épices, houblon, levure, eau	pale-ale mout, kristal caramout, honing, kruiden, hop, gist, water
amber not filtered or pasteurised	ambrée non filtrée, non pasteurisée	amber ongefilterd, niet gepasteuriseerd
Very spicy beer with a taste of honey.	Bière fort épicée avec un goût de miel.	Zeer kruidig bier met honingsmaak.
Serve in a balloon glass.	Verser dans un verre ballon.	Uitschenken in een ballonglas.

La Botteresse Pomme

Brasserie Artisanale La Botteresse de Sur-les-bois

5,40%

	top-fermentation natural re-fermentation in the bottle not centrifuged	fermentation haute refermentation naturelle en bouteille non centrifugée	hoge gisting natuurlijke hergisting in de fles niet gecentrifugeerd
	fruit beer	bière fruitée	fruitbier
	pilsner malt, hops, apple juice at the time of bottling, yeast, water	malt de pils, houblon, jus de pommes à l'embouteillage, levure, eau	pilsmout, hop, appelsap bij het bottelen, gist, water
	blond not filtered, pasteurised	blonde non filtrée, pasteurisée	blond ongefilterd, gepasteuriseerd
	Light fruit beer.	Bière de fruits légère.	Licht fruitbier.
	Serve in a balloon glass.	Verser dans un verre ballon.	Uitschenken in een ballonglas.
i			

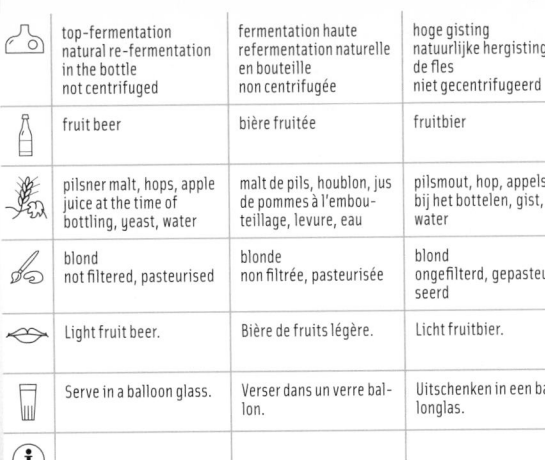

7%

La Bouillonnaise

	top-fermentation re-fermentation in the bottle	fermentation haute refermentation en bouteille	hoge gisting hergisting in de fles
	double	double	dubbel
	malt, hops, yeast, water	malt, houblon, levure, eau	mout, hop, gist, water
	not filtered	non filtrée	ongefilterd

La Chérie

Brasserie Val de Sambre 5 % (12° plato) 8 46

	top-fermentation	fermentation haute	hoge gisting
	fruit beer	bière fruitée	fruitbier
	witbier with barley and wheat, aromatised with sour cherries	bière blanche d'orge et froment aromatisée avec des cerises griottes	witbier van gerst en tarwe gearomatiseerd met griottekersen
	pink hazy	rose voilée	roze gesluierd
	Smooth and refreshing taste of sour cherries.	Saveur douce et rafraîchissante de cerises griottes.	Zachte en verfrissende smaak van griottekersen.

asserie de Bouillon

6% 8 - 12 °C 46 - 54 °F

La Chèvenis

top-fermentation re-fermented in the bottle	fermentation haute refermentation en bouteille	hoge gisting hergisting op de fles
specialty beer blond	bière spéciale blonde	speciaalbier blond
barley malt, hop varieties, Orval yeast, hemp grains, herbs, water	malt d'orge, variétés de houblon, levure Orval, graines de chanvre, herbes, eau	gerstemout, hopsoorten, Orvalgist, hennepkorrels, kruiden, water
blond unfiltered, unpasteurised	blonde non filtrée ni pasteurisée	blond niet gefilterd of gepasteuriseerd
Sipping beer with hemp flavour and aroma.	Bière de dégustation avec saveur et arômes de chanvre.	Degustatiebier met hennepsmaak en -aroma.
Hold the glass slightly tilted while pouring the beer.	Tenir le verre légèrement incliné et verser.	Het glas licht schuin houden en inschenken.

La Chouffe

Duvel Moortgat Corporation 8% 8 - 12 / 46 - 54

	top-fermentation re-fermented in the bottle	fermentation haute refermentation en bouteille	hoge gisting hergisting op de fles
	regional beer	bière régionale	streekbier
	malt, hops, coriander, sugar, yeast, water	malt, houblon, coriandre, sucre, levure, eau	mout, hop, koriander, suiker, gist, water
	golden blond unfiltered	blond doré non filtrée	goudblond ongefilterd
	Effervescent, strong, fruity, spicy beer where flavours develop. Aroma of tropical and citrus fruit with touches of coriander and hops. Pleasant fruity taste with coriander and subtle hops.	Bière pétillante, forte, fruitée, épicée, avec une évolution du goût. Arôme de fruits tropicaux et d'agrumes, avec des touches de coriandre et de houblon. Goût agréablement fruité grâce à la coriandre et au houblon subtil.	Bruisend, sterk, fruitig, kruidig bier met smaakevolutie. Aroma van tropische en citrusvruchten met toetsen van koriander en hop. Aangenaam fruitige smaak met koriander en subtiele hop.
	Store upright in a dark, cool room. A layer of yeast sediment at the bottom of the bottle is normal.	A conserver verticalement à l'abri de la lumière et de la chaleur. Un dépôt de levure au fond de la bouteille est normal.	Verticaal bewaren in een donkere, koele ruimte. Een gistlaagje op de bodem van de fles is normaal.

asserie d'Ebly at Brasserie des Légendes,
on at their own brewery

5,90% 3 - 5 °C 37 - 41 °F

La Corne du Bois des Pendus Blonde

top-fermentation not centrifuged	fermentation haute non centrifugée	hoge gisting niet gecentrifugeerd
blond	blonde	blond
pilsner malt, wheat, 2 different hops, yeast, water	malt de pils,froment, 2 variétés de houblon, levure, eau	pilsmout, tarwe, 2 hopsoorten, gist, water
cloudy when young; gold-yellow with abundant, creamy foam head that lingers for a long time.	trouble pour bière jeune; jaune doré avec faux col crémeux abondant très stable.	troebel bij jong bier; goudgeel met overvloedige, romige schuimkraag die zeer lang houdt.
Distinctly bitter (hoppy) with aromas of citrus and roses. Mellow yet thirst-quenching.	Goût amer (houblon) marqué, avec des arômes de citrus et de roses. Douce et désaltérante à la fois.	Uitgesproken bitter (hop) met citrus- en rozenaroma's. Zacht en dorstlessend tegelijk.
Pour out half into a tilted glass (45°). Hold the glass upright and empty the bottle from approx. 7 cm. The foam should reach up to the neck of the hanged person. Hold the glass by the leather strap to drink.	Verser la moitié dans un verre incliné (à 45°). Tenir le verre en position verticale et verser le restant à une distance de ca. 7 cm. L' écume doit se fixer autour du cou du suspendu. En buvant tenir le verre par le cuir.	De helft uitschenken in het schuingehouden glas (45°). Het glas rechthouden en het restant vanop ca. 7 cm inschenken. Het schuim moet rond de nek van de opgehangene komen. Het glas bij het leder vasthouden om te drinken.
See La Triple Corne	voir La Triple Corne	zie La Triple Corne

La Cré Tonnerre

Brasserie de Silly **7% (14° plato)** 4 - 7 / 39 - 45

top-fermentation refermented with rum	fermentation haute refermentation au rhum	hoge gisting hergisting met rum
tripel	triple	tripel
pale barley malt, sugar, yeast, Kent and Hallertau hops, brown Mayarum, water	malt d'orge pâle, sucre, levure, houblon Kent et Hallertau, rhum Maya brun, eau	bleke gerstemout, suiker, gist, Kent en Hallertauhop, bruine Mayarum, water
blond (9,8 EBC) shiny, clear	blonde (9,8 EBC) brillante, claire	blond (9,8 EBC) briljant, helder
Smooth and round with a Caribbean touch.	Moelleuse et ronde avec des touches caraïbes.	Zacht en rond met Caribische toets.
The name refers to a French music band.	Le nom renvoie à un groupe de musiciens français.	De naam verwijst naar een Franse muziekgroep

La Divine

asserie de Silly **9,50% (19° plato)** 7 - 10 °C / 45 - 50 °F

top-fermentation	fermentation haute	hoge gisting
abbey beer	bière d'abbaye	abdijbier
pale malt, caramelized malt, aromatic malt, sugar, Kent and Hallertau hops, yeast, water	malt pâle, malt caramélisé, malt aromatique, sucre, houblon Kent et Hallertau, levure, eau	bleke mout, gekaramelliseerde mout, aromatische mout, suiker, Kent- en Hallertauhop, gist, water
amber (35 EBC)	ambrée (35 EBC)	amber (35 EBC)
Extra strong beer with a velvety smooth flavour and a pleasant hop and wood taste. Very fine, bitter, smoky aftertaste with alcohol flavour.	Bière extra forte avec un arôme velouté et un goût agréable de houblon et de bois. Fin de bouche très raffinée, amère, fumée avec un goût d'alcool.	Extra sterk bier met een fluweelzacht aroma en een aangename hop- en houtsmaak. Heel fijne, bittere, gerookte afdronk met alcoholsmaak.
Pour carefully into a goblet.	Verser tranquillement dans un verre calice large.	Rustig uitschenken in een breed kelkglas.
Boutique beer.	Brassée de façon artisanale.	Artisanaal gebrouwen.

La Douce Vertus

Brasserie Artisanale Millevertus 7% 12° 54°

top-fermentation	fermentation haute	hoge gisting
ale	ale	ale
different malt, hop and yeast varieties, water	différentes variétés de malt, de houblon et de levure, eau	verschillende mout-, hop- en gistsoorten, water
amber, gold-coloured	ambrée, dorée	amber, goudkleurig
Smooth malty character beer. Bitter background taste.	Bière de caractère douce, maltée. Amertume en retrait.	Zacht, moutig karakterbier. Bitter op de achtergrond.

top-fermentation re-fermented in the bottle	fermentation haute refermentation en bouteille	hoge gisting natuurlijke hergisting in de fles
ale Rauch beer	ale bière Rauch	ale Rauchbier
peaty malt and other malt varieties, different hop and yeast varieties, water	malt tourbeux et d'autres sortes de malt, différentes sortes de houblon et de levures, eau	turfachtige mout en andere moutsoorten, verschillende hop- en gistsoorten, water
shiny amber creamy foam head unfiltered, unpasteurised	ambreé brillante, mousse crémeuse non filtreé, non pasteuriseé	helder amber romige schuimkraag ongefilterd, niet gepasteuriseerd
Malty, smoked, smooth.	Maltée, fumée, douce.	Moutig, gerookt, zacht.
Serve at cellar temperature. Pour in a fluent movement.	Server à température de cave. Verser franchement, puis relever doucement.	Serveren aan keldertemperatuur. Stevig doorschenken.
Smoked beer (by analogy with the Rauchbier from the Bamberg region) is difficult to brew. The first attempts of smoked beer on the basis of Belgian peat malt were too smoky in taste. Nowadays an appropriate amount of smoked malt from Bamberg is used.	Cette bière au goût fumé ('rookbier', par analogie avec la Rauchbier de la région de Bamberg, en Allemagne) est difficile à brasser. Les premiers brassins à base de malt de tourbe belge avaient un goût fumé trop prononcé. L'on utilise à présent du malt fumé parfaitement dosé originaire de Bamberg.	Rookbier (naar analogie met het Rauchbier uit de regio Bamberg) is moeilijk te brouwen. De eerste brouwsels op basis van Belgische turfmout hadden een te sterke rooksmaak. Nu wordt goed gedoseerde gerookte mout uit Bamberg gebruikt.

La Grognarde

Brasserie Sainte-Hélène 5,50% 10 - 12 / 50 - 54

	top-fermentation re-fermented in the bottle	fermentation haute refermentation en bouteille	hoge gisting hergisting op de fles
	blond	blonde	blond
	malt, hops, yeast, sugar, water	malt, houblon, levure, sucre, eau	mout, hop, gist, suiker, water
	blond unfiltered	blonde non filtrée	blond ongefilterd
	Smooth and bitter.	Moelleuse et amère.	Zacht en bitter.
	Boutique beer. The label was designed by the artist Palix.	Brassée de façon artisanale. L'étiquette est conçue par le dessinateur Palix.	Artisanaal gebrouwen. Het etiket is ontworpen door tekenaar Palix.

Brouwerij Huyghe

8,50% 5 °C 41 °F

	top-fermentation re-fermented in the bottle	fermentation haute refermentation en bouteille	hoge gisting hergisting op de fles
	strong blond	blonde forte	sterk blond
	brewed with 3 different hops (Saaz, Brewers Gold, Amarillo) dry hopping	brassée avec 3 variétés de houblon (Saaz, Brewers Gold, Amarillo) dry hopping	gebrouwen met 3 soorten hop (Saaz, Brewers Gold, Amarillo) dry hopping
	golden blond with very persistent foam head that sticks to the sides of the glass. Not filtered or pasteurised	blond doré avec un faux col solide collant au bord. Non filtrée, non pasteurisée	goudblond met zeer persistente wandklevende schuimkraag. Ongefilterd, niet gepasteuriseerd
	Complex scent with citrus aromas followed by hop aromas. Sweet onset owing to the alcohol. Intense bitterness is masked by full-bodied flavour. Very balanced beer with long, dry and bitter aftertaste.	Parfum complexe avec des arômes de citrus, suivis par des arômes houblonnés. Approche initiale douceâtre due à l'alcool. L'amertume élevée est masquée par le goût intense et franc. Bière fort équilibrée, avec une arrière-bouche longue, sèche et un peu amère.	Complexe geur met citrusaroma's gevolgd door hoparoma's. Zoetige aanzet door de alcohol. Hoge bitterheid wordt gemaskeerd door de intense smaak en volmondigheid. Zeer evenwichtig bier met lange, droge en bitterige afdronk.
	Gold medal in the category 'heavy beers' at the Brewing Industry International Awards in Londen, 2011.	Médaille d'or dans la catégorie 'bières fortes' aux Brewing Industry International Awards à Londres en 2011.	Gouden medaille in de categorie 'zware bieren' op de Brewing Industry International Awards in Londen, 2011.

La Guillotine

La Loubecoise

Brasserie d'Ecaussinnes 8% 8° 46°

	top-fermentation re-fermented in the bottle	fermentation haute refermentation en bouteille	hoge gisting hergisting in de fles
	regional beer	bière citadine ou régio-nale	stads- of streekbier
	malts, hops, candy sugar, maple syrup, yeast, spring water	malts, houblon, sucre candi, sirop d'érable, le-vure, eau de source	mouten, hop, kandijsui-ker, esdoornsiroop, gist, bronwater
	burgundy	bordeaux	bordeaux
	Flavour of brown sugar. Strong taste of Québec maple syrup.	Arôme de cassonade. Goût fort de sirop d'érable du Québec.	Aroma van bruine suiker. Sterke smaak van ahorn-siroop uit Québec.

rasserie Artisanale Millevertus 4,80% 6 - 12 °C 43 - 54 °F

La Mac Vertus

	top-fermentation	fermentation haute	hoge gisting
	stout Belgian British style stout	stout Belgian British style stout	stout Belgian British style stout
	malt, hops (English and American), yeast, water	malt, houblon (Anglais, et Américain), levure, eau	mout, hop (Engelse en Amerikaanse), gist, water
	brown-black with small beige foam head not filtered	brun noir avec petit faux col beige non filtrée	bruinzwart met kleine beige schuimkraag ongefilterd
	Light, balanced stout with a prevalent bitterness.	Stout légère, équilibrée, avec une amertume corsée.	Lichte, evenwichtige stout met een gecorseerde bitterheid.

La Médiévale Ambrée

Brasserie de Bouillon 6% 8 - 12 ° 46 - 54 °

	top-fermentation re-fermented in the bottle unpasteurised	fermentation haute refermentation en bouteille non pasteurisée	hoge gisting hergisting op de fles ongepasteuriseerd
	abbey beer amber	bière d'abbaye ambrée	abdijbier amber
	barley malt, cara malt, hops, Orval yeast, water	malt d'orge, malt cara, houblon, levure Orval, eau	gerstemout, caramout, hop, Orvalgist, water
	amber unfiltered	ambrée non filtrée	amber niet gefilterd
	Traditionally brewed, round sipping beer.	Bière de dégustation artisanale ronde.	Ambachtelijk rond degustatiebier.
	Hold the glass slightly tilted while pouring the beer.	Tenir le verre légèrement incliné et verser.	Het glas licht schuin houden en inschenken.
i			

6 - 12 °C
43 - 54 °F

	top-fermentation	fermentation haute	hoge gisting
	tripel	triple	tripel
	not filtered	non filtrée	ongefilterd
	Word play on the French word 'amer' which means bitter, while 'la mère' means the mother.	Jeu de mots 'La mère' / 'L'amère'.	Zinspeling op het Franse woord 'amer' wat bitter betekent.

La Moneuse

Brasserie de Blaugies 8% 6 - 8 / 43 - 46

	top-fermentation re-fermented in the bottle	fermentation haute refermentation en bouteille	hoge gisting hergisting in de fles
	specialty beer boutique beer	bière spéciale artisanale	speciaalbier artisanaal
	malt, hops, yeast, water Boutique beer without herbs or additives.	malt, houblon, levure, eau Produit artisanal sans herbes ou additifs.	mout, hop, gist, water Artisanaal product zonder kruiden of additieven.
	amber unfiltered	ambrée non filtrée	amber niet gefilterd
	Digestive and refreshing. Fine bitterness and long-lasting aftertaste.	Digestive et rafraîchissante. Saveur amère raffinée et arrière-bouche longue.	Digestief en verfrissend. Fijne bitterheid en lange nasmaak.
	The brewer is a descendant of Antoine Joseph Moneuse, the leader of the gang of thieves 'Chauffeurs du Nord', who put their victims with their feet in the furnace until they confessed where their money was hidden.	La femme brasseur est une descendante d'Antoine Joseph Moneuse, le chef de la bande de voleurs 'Chauffeurs du Nord' qui mettaient les pieds de leurs victimes dans le feu à jusqu'à ce qu'elles révèlent où elles avaient caché leur argent.	De vrouwelijke brouwer is een afstammeling van Antoine Joseph Moneuse, de leider van de dievenbende 'Chauffeurs du Nord' die hun slachtoffers met de voeten in de stookplaats staken tot ze vertelden waar ze hun geld verborgen.

asserie de Blaugies

8%

La Moneuse Spéciale Noël

	top-fermentation re-fermentation in the bottle	fermentation haute refermentation en bouteille	hoge gisting hergisting in de fles
	winter beer	bière hivernale	winterbier
	not filtered	non filtrée	ongefilterd

La Noire Fontaine

Brasserie de Bouillon 8%

	top-fermentation re-fermentation in the bottle	fermentation haute refermentation en bouteille	hoge gisting hergisting in de fles
	boutique malt beer: barley malt, hops, yeast, water	bière artisanale de malt : malt d'orge, houblon, levure, eau	artisanaal moutbier: gerstemout, hop, gist, water
	not filtered	non filtrée	niet gefilterd

rasserie d'Ecaussinnes

8% 4 - 6 °C 39 - 43 °F

La Penneffoise

	top-fermentation	fermentation haute	hoge gisting
	fruit beer	bière fruitée	fruitbier
	plum beer with 8% plums from Agen	bière de prunes avec 8% de prunes de Agen	pruimenbier met 8% pruimen uit Agen

La Poiluchette Blonde Cuvée du Château

Brouwerij Huyghe

7,50% 4 - 6 / 39 - 43

top-fermentation re-fermented in the bottle	fermentation haute refermentation en bouteille	hoge gisting hergisting in de fles
regional beer	bière régionale	streekbier
malt, hops, yeast, water	malt, houblon, levure, eau	mout, hop, gist, water
blonde clear	blonde claire	blond helder
Serve in a flute-glass.	Verser dans une flûte.	Uitschenken in een fluitglas.
Originally brewed for the carnival celebrations in the region of Charleroi. Today it is a best-seller on the international market.	Brassée à l'origine lors des fêtes de carnaval dans la région de Charleroi mais la bière s'est développée entre-temps et a obtenu un réel succès sur les marchés étrangers.	Werd origineel gebrouwen voor de carnavalsfeesten in de regio Charleroi maar is ondertussen uitgegroeid tot een commercieel succes op de buitenlandse markt.

7,50% 5 °C 41 °F

La Poiluchette Brune

	top-fermentation re-fermentation in the bottle	fermentation haute refermentation en bouteille	hoge gisting hergisting in de fles
	double	double	dubbel
	different malt varieties, hops, yeast, water	diverses variétés de malt, houblon, levure, eau	verschillende moutsoorten, hop, gist, water
	dark brown with thick foam head filtered, not pasteurised	brun foncé avec faux col collant au verre filtrée, non pasteurisée	donkerbruin met wandklevende schuimkraag gefilterd, niet gepasteuriseerd
	Balanced beer with hint of roasted malt and fruit. Somewhat chocolaty in the aftertaste.	Bière équilibrée, avec un peu de malt torréfié et de fruité. Un peu de chocolat en arrière-bouche.	Evenwichtig bier met wat gebrande mout en fruitigheid. Ietwat chocolade in de afdronk.
	Specially brewed for the Waterloo region. Poiluchette is a term which was known in Napoleon's day. It stands for a man with guts and courage.	Spécialement brassée pour la région de Waterloo. Poiluchette est un terme qui était déjà connu au temps de Napoléon. Il désigne un homme qui fait preuve de toupet et de courage.	Speciaal gebrouwen voor de regio van Waterloo. Poiluchette is een term die al bekend was ten tijde van Napoleon. Het staat voor een man met lef en moed.

La Prime

Brasserie Sainte-Hélène 8,50% 10 - 12 / 50 - 54

	top-fermentation re-fermentation in the bottle	fermentation haute refermentation en bouteille	hoge gisting hergisting in de fles
	boutique winter beer	bière hivernale artisanale	artisanaal winterbier
	barley malt, hops (Kent Goldings, Strisselpalt), yeast, water	malt d'orge, houblon (Kent Goldings, Strisselpalt), levure, eau	gerstemout, hop (Kent Goldings, Strisselpalt), gist, water
	shining red not filtered or pasteurised	rouge brillant non filtrée, non pasteurisée	glanzend rood ongefilterd, niet gepasteuriseerd
	Complex character beer. Roasted taste, subtle hops and touches of caramel. Slightly sour.	Bière de caractère complexe. Goût brûlé, houblon subtil et touches de caramel. Note légèrement acidulée.	Complex karakterbier. Gebrande smaak, subtiele hop en toetsen van karamel. Lichtzurige noot.

asserie Artisanale de Rulles

7%

La Rulles Blonde

	top-fermentation re-fermented in the bottle unpasteurised	fermentation haute refermentation en bouteille non pasteurisée	hoge gisting hergisting op de fles ongepasteuriseerd
	blond	blonde	blond
	pilsner and amber malt	malt de pils et malt ambré	pilsmout en ambermout
	golden blond unfiltered	blond doré non filtrée	goudblond niet gefilterd
	Light biscuit taste, both smooth and bitter.	Saveur légère de biscuit, douce et amère à la fois.	Lichte biscuitsmaak, zacht en bitter tegelijk.

La Rulles Brune

Brasserie Artisanale de Rulles 6,50% 8 - 1(
46 - 5(

	top-fermentation re-fermented in the bottle unpasteurised	fermentation haute refermentation en bouteille non pasteurisée	hoge gisting hergisting op de fles ongepasteuriseerd
	dubbel	double	dubbel
	pilsner malt, amber malt, caramel and roasted malt, hops, yeast, water	malt de pils et malt ambré, malt caramélisé et brûlé, houblon, levure, eau	pilsmout, ambermout, karamel- en gebrande mout, hop, gist, water
	brown unfiltered	brune non filtrée	bruin niet gefilterd
	Prominent malt flavour with a touch of fruit and bitterness.	Dominance de malt avec une touche de fruits et d'amertume.	Moutdominantie met een toets van fruit en bitterheid.

asserie Artisanale de Rulles 7,30% 8 -10 °C 46 - 50 °F

La Rulles Cuvée Meilleurs Vœux

	top-fermentation re-fermentation in the bottle	fermentation haute refermentation en bouteille	hoge gisting hergisting in de fles
	brown winter beer	bière hivernale brune	bruin winterbier
	not filtered	non filtrée	ongefilterd

La Rulles Estivale

Brasserie Artisanale de Rulles 5,20% 8 - 10 / 46 - 50

	top-fermentation re-fermented in the bottle	fermentation haute refermentation en bouteille	hoge gisting hergisting op de fles
	blond	blonde	blond
	pure malt	malt pur	pure mout
	blond unpasteurised	blonde non pasteurisée	blond niet gepasteuriseerd
	Refreshing and bitter.	Rafraîchissante et amère.	Verfrissend en bitter.
i			

sserie Artisanale de Rulles

10% 8 - 10 °C / 46 - 50 °F

La Rulles La Grande 10

top-fermentation re-fermentation in the bottle	fermentation haute refermentation en bouteille	hoge gisting hergisting in de fles
Belgian strong pale ale	Belgian strong pale ale	Belgian strong pale ale
barley malt, sugar, hops, yeast, water	malt d'orge, sucre, hou-blon, levure, eau	gerstemout, suiker, hop, gist, water

La Rulles Triple

Brasserie Artisanale de Rulles 8,40% 8 - 1 46 - 5

top-fermentation re-fermented in the bottle	fermentation haute refermentation en bouteille	hoge gisting hergisting op de fles
tripel	triple	tripel
unfiltered, unpasteurised	non filtrée ni pasteurisée	niet gefilterd of gepasteuriseerd
Sipping beer, full and bitter.	Bière de dégustation pleine et amère.	Degustatiebier, vol en bitter.

La Safranaise

sserie Artisanale Millevertus 7%

top-fermentation	fermentation haute	hoge gisting
herbal beer	bière aromatisée	kruidenbier
barley malt, hops, yeast, saffron, water	malt d'orge, houblon, levure, safran, eau	gerstemout, hop, gist, saffraan, water
yellow-gold, veiled with a rich foam head not filtered	jaune doré, voilée avec un faux col riche non filtrée	geelgoud, gesluierd met een rijke schuimkraag ongefilterd
Aroma of saffron.	Arôme de safran.	Aroma van saffraan.
Brewed in tandem with a saffron producer from Virton.	Brassée en collaboration avec un producteur de safran de Virton.	Gebrouwen in samenwerking met een saffraanproducent uit Virton.

La Sambresse Blonde

Brasserie Brootcoorens

8% 4 °C / 1
39 °F / 5

	top-fermentation	fermentation haute	hoge gisting
	blond	blonde	blond
	pilsner and amber malt, aromatic hops, orange rind, juniper-berry, coriander, yeast, water	malt de pils et malt ambré, houblon aromatique, écorce d'orange, baie de genièvre, coriandre, levure, eau	pils- en ambermout, aromatische hop, sinaasschil, jeneverbes, koriander, gist, water
	blond unfiltered yet transparent	blonde non filtrée mais transparente	blond ongefilterd maar transparant
	Pleasant, round and original but very accessible natural beer. Well-balanced taste evolution and an aroma with hoppy and spicy touch.	Bière naturelle agréable, ronde et originale mais très abordable. Saveur évolutive équilibrée et arôme avec touche de houblon et d'herbes.	Aangenaam, rond en origineel maar toch zeer toegankelijk natuurbier Evenwichtige evoluerende smaak en aroma met hoptoets en kruidentoets.
	Do not shake the bottle and pour carefully.	Prendre soin que la bouteille n'a pas été secouée et verser prudemment.	Zorgen dat de fles niet geschud is en voorzichtig uitschenken.
i			

sserie de Bouillon

8,50%

La Spéciale Fêtes

top-fermentation re-fermentation in the bottle	fermentation haute refermentation en bouteille	hoge gisting hergisting in de fles
boutique winter beer	bière hivernale artisa-nale	artisanaal winterbier
barley malt, hops, yeast, water	malt d'orge, houblon, le-vure, eau	gerstemout, hop, gist, water
not filtered or pasteur-ised	non filtrée, non pasteu-risée	ongefilterd, niet gepas-teuriseerd

La Triple Corne

Brasserie d'Ebly at Brasserie des Légendes, soon at their own brewery **10%** 7 - 1 45 - 5

top-fermentation not centrifuged	fermentation haute non centrifugée	hoge gisting niet gecentrifugeerd
tripel strong blond	triple blonde forte	tripel sterk blond
barley malt, hops, yeast, water	malt d'orge, houblon, levure, eau	gerstemout, hop, gist, water
copper-blond with lingering foam head; not filtered or pasteurised	blond cuivre avec faux col très stable; non filtrée, non pasteurisée	koperblond met lang aanhoudende schuimkraag; ongefilterd, nie gepasteuriseerd
Sipping bear with a surprising taste. Aroma of flowers. Rich flavour pallet with touches of fruit from the onset. Balanced bitterness in the aftertaste.	Bière de dégustation d'un goût surprenant. Arôme de fleurs. Riche palette de goûts dès le début avec des touches de fruits, une amertume équilibrée en arrière-bouche.	Degustatiebier met eer verrassende smaak. Ar ma van bloemen. Rijk smakenpalet vanaf het begin met toetsen van fruit. Evenwichtige bitterheid in de afdronk.
see La Corne du Bois des Pendus Blonde.	voir La Corne du Bois des Pendus Blonde.	zie La Corne du Bois de Pendus Blonde.
Refers to the legend of Cornelius and the tragic event during the 30-year war (17th century) whereby Eastern European troops hanged some 100 people in the horn-shaped wooded area (corne) of Anlier (in the south of Luxembourg) in the assumption that they were French enemies.	Fait référence à la légende de Cornelius et à un tragique événement pendant la Guerre de Trente Ans (17e siècle), où des soldats d'Europe de l'Est pendirent au lieu-dit 'La Corne du Bois des Pendus' dans la forêt d'Anlier (Sud Luxembourg) une centaine de personnes en supposant qu'il s'agissait d'adversaires français.	Verwijst naar de legend van Cornelius en naar een tragische gebeurte nis tijdens de 30-jarige oorlog (17e eeuw) waa bij Oosteuropese solda ten in het hoornvormig stuk (corne) bos van Ar lier (Z-Luxemburg) ee 100-tal mensen ophingen in de veronderstel ling dat het Franse tegenstanders waren.

asserie Jean Tout Seul

6,90% 8 °C 46 °F

	top-fermentation re-fermentation in the bottle	fermentation haute refermentation en bouteille	hoge gisting hergisting in de fles
	barley and wheat malt, hops, yeast, water	malt d'orge et de froment, houblon, levure, eau	gerste- en tarwemout, hop, gist, water
	Pour out slowly and leave the yeast sediment (approx. 1 cm) in the bottle or drink it.	Verser prudemment et laisser le dépôt de levure (ca 1 cm) dans la bouteille selon les souhaits.	Voorzichtig uitschenken en het gistdepot (ca. 1 cm) desgewenst in de fles laten.

La Trompeuse

La Trouffette Belle d'Eté

Brasserie de Bastogne 6%

	top-fermentation re-fermentation in the bottle	fermentation haute refermentation en bouteille	hoge gisting hergisting in de fles
	not filtered	non filtrée	ongefilterd

asserie de Bastogne 6,80%

La Trouffette Brune

top-fermentation re-fermentation in the bottle	fermentation haute refermentation en bouteille	hoge gisting hergisting in de fles
winter beer	bière hivernale	winterbier
not filtered	non filtrée	ongefilterd

La Trouffette Givrée

Brasserie de Bastogne 8%

	top-fermentation re-fermentation in the bottle	fermentation haute refermentation en bouteille	hoge gisting hergisting in de fles
	not filtered	non filtrée	ongefilterd

La Trouffette Rousse

asserie de Bastogne 7,80%

	top-fermentation re-fermentation in the bottle	fermentation haute refermentation en bouteille	hoge gisting hergisting in de fles
	not filtered	non filtrée	ongefilterd

La Vauban

Brasserie de Bouillon 6% 8 - 12 / 46 - 54

	top-fermentation re-fermented in the bottle	fermentation haute refermentation en bouteille	hoge gisting hergisting op de fles
	abbey beer	bière d'abbaye	abdijbier
	barley malt, hops, Orval yeast, herbs, water	malt d'orge, houblon, levure Orval, herbes, eau	gerstemout, hop, Orval-gist, kruiden, water
	blond unfiltered, unpasteurised	blonde non filtrée ni pasteurisée	blond niet gefilterd of gepasteuriseerd
	Light and slightly bitter sipping beer.	Bière de dégustation légère et légèrement amère.	Licht en lichtbitter degustatiebier.
	Hold the glass slightly tilted while pouring.	Tenir le verre légèrement incliné et verser.	Het glas licht schuin houden en inschenken.
	Brewed for the 300th anniversary of Maréchal Vauban's death. The label features the Castle of Bouillon on the background.	Brassée à l'occasion du 300ième anniversaire du décès du Maréchal Vauban. L'étiquette représente le Château de Bouillon.	Gebrouwen n.a.v. de 300e verjaardag van het overlijden van Maréchal Vauban. Op het etiket staat op de achtergrond Het Kasteel van Bouillon.

‹leman by Brouwerij Van Steenberge 6,20%

	top-fermentation re-fermented in the bottle	fermentation haute refermentation en bouteille	hoge gisting met nagisting in de fles
	dubbel	double	dubbel
	dark unfiltered	foncée non filtrée	donker ongefilterd
	Traditional, soft beer with a touch of star anise and caramelized malt.	Bière artisanale moelleuse avec une pointe d'anis et une touche maltée caramélisée.	Ambachtelijk zacht bier met een vleugje steranijs en gekaramelliseerde mouttoets.
i	Sipping beer with taste evolution. Store in a cool, dark room.	Bière de dégustation avec évolution de saveur. Conserver à l'abri de la chaleur et de la lumière.	Degustatiebier met smaakevolutie. Bewaren op een koele donkere plaats.

L'Amarante - Bière aux Poivres

Brasserie Artisanale Millevertus 7,50%

	top-fermentation	fermentation haute	hoge gisting
	herbal beer	bière aromatisée	kruidenbier
	beer with 2 exotic peppers	bière avec 2 piments exotiques	bier met 2 exotische pepers
	Very aromatic, both sweet and strong. Perfect balance between hop and pepper aromas.	Très aromatique, sucré et fort à la fois. Parfait équilibre d'arômes de houblon et de poivre.	Zeer aromatisch, zoet en sterk tegelijk. Perfect evenwicht van hop- en peperaroma's.
	Brewed at the request of Amarante, a herbal shop, in Virton.	Brassée pour le compte de la boutique d'épices fines Amarante à Virton.	Gebrouwen in opdracht van kruidenwinkel Amarante in Virton.

sage by De Proefbrouwerij

7,50% 6 - 9 °C 43 - 48 °F

top-fermentation re-fermentation in the bottle	fermentation haute refermentation en bouteille	hoge gisting hergisting in de fles
strong blond	blonde forte	sterk blond
malt, hops, honey, curaçao, coriander, yeast, water	malt d'orge, miel, curaçao, coriandre, houblon, levure, eau	mout, hop, honing, curaçao, koriander, gist, water
blond with solid and full white foam head not filtered	blond doré avec faux col stable et plein blanc non filtrée	hoogblond met vaste en volle, witte schuimkraag ongefilterd
A hint of honey and an unexpected bitter aftertaste.	Une pointe de miel et une arrière-bouche amère inattendue.	Een vleugje honing en een onverwachts bittere afdronk.
Pour out carefully and give sufficient oxygen. Revolve the last half in the bottle, to loosen up the yeast.	Verser prudemment et donner assez d'oxygène. Eventuellement secouer la seconde moitié pour détacher la levure.	Voorzichtig uitschenken en voldoende zuurstof geven. De laatste helft eventueel rondwalsen om de gist los te maken.

Lamme Goedzak

De Scheldebrouwerij

7% 8 - 1(46 - 5

	top-fermentation re-fermentation in the bottle	fermentation haute refermentation en bouteille	hoge gisting hergisting in de fles
	blond	blonde	blond
	barley malt, cara 20, hops, yeast, water	mat d'orge, cara 20, houblon, levure, eau	gerstemout, cara 20, hop, gist, water
	Clear, pale copper colour with orange glow (24 EBC). White foam that leaves a lace pattern on the glass. Not filtered or pasteurised.	Limpide, cuivre clair avec reflet orange (24 EBC). Faux col blanc laissant de belles dentelles au verre. Non filtrée, non pasteurisée	Helder, licht koperkleurig met oranje schijn (24 EBC). Wit schuim dat mooi kantwerk op het glas laat. Ongefilterd, niet gepasteuriseerd
	Rather aromatic with fruity undertones. Mellow, full-bodied taste with balanced sweet, caramel-like, fine-bitter components. Pleasantly prickly on the tongue. Pour out gently. 25 EBU.	Assez aromatique, avec un peu de fruité. Goût doux, franc, avec des composants sucrés, caramélisés, finement amers équilibrés. Picotement agréable sur la langue. Écoulement lent. 25 EBU.	Vrij aromatisch met iets fruitigs. Zachte, volle smaak met evenwichtig zoete, karamelachtige, fijnbittere componenten. Gezellige prikkelin op de tong. Langzaam uitvloeiend. 25 EBU.
	Lamme Goedzak is the jolly and gullible sidekick of Tijl Uilenspiegel. His aim in life: eat, drink and be merry.	Lamme Goedzak est le joyeux, rieur et naïf compagnon de Tijl Uilenspiegel. Son but dans la vie : bien manger, bien boire et s'amuser.	Lamme Goedzak is de jolige, goedlachse en goedgelovige compagnon van Tijl Uilenspiege Zijn levensdoel: lekker eten, drinken en plezier maken.

8% 6 - 8 °C 43 - 46 °F

	top-fermentation re-fermented in the bottle	fermentation haute refermentation en bouteille	hoge gisting hergisting op de fles
	regional beer	bière régionale	streekbier tripel
	hops, yeast, fermentable sugar, water. Malt varieties: pilsner, caramel, pale ale.	malt, houblon, sucre de fermentation, eau. Variétés de malt : pils, caramélisé, pale ale.	hop, gist, vergistbare suiker, water. Moutsoorten: pils, karamel, pale ale.
	amber blond nice, white foam head	blond ambré faux col solide, blanc	amberblond mooie, witte schuimkraag
	Aroma: mainly fruit and spices. Flavour: first spicy touches, then a fast evolution toward an intense, bitter aftertaste.	Parfum :dominance de fruits et d'herbes. Saveur :touches relevées aboutissant très rapidement à une fin de bouche amère intense.	Geur: overheersend fruitig en kruidig. Smaak: eerst kruidige toetsen die vrij snel evolueren naar een intens bittere afdronk.
	Pour slowly for a nice foam head with hat. Leave a small amount in the bottle (it can be served afterwards) and present the bottle with the glass.	Verser lentement pour obtenir un faux col solide avec chapeau. Laisser un peu de bière dans la bouteille (peut être versé par la suite) et offrir aussi la bouteille.	Langzaam uitschenken voor een mooie schuimkraag en schuimhoed. Een restje in de fles laten (kan achteraf bijgeschonken worden) en de fles mee aanbieden.
i			

Le Pavé de l'Ours

Brasserie de Silenrieux 7,50% 7 - 10 / 45 - 50

	top-fermentation natural re-fermentation in the bottle	fermentation haute refermentation naturelle en bouteille	hoge gisting natuurlijke hergisting in de fles
	amber or speciale belge	ambrée ou spéciale belge	amber of speciale belge
	barley malt, hop pellets, white candy sugar, honey, yeast, water	malt d'orge, pellets de houblon, sucre candi blanc, miel, levure, eau	gerstemout, hoppellets, witte kandijsuiker, honing, gist, water
	pale amber	légèrement ambré	licht amber
	Light honey taste.	Léger goût de miel.	Lichte honingsmaak.
	Pour out gently.	Verser lentement.	Langzaam uitschenken.

-Inbev (Abbaye Notre-Dame de Leffe) 9% 6 - 8 °C 43 - 46 °F

Leffe 9°

	top-fermentation	fermentation haute	hoge gisting
	Recognised Belgian abbey beer	Bière d'abbaye belge reconnue	Erkend Belgisch abdijbier
	barley malt, corn, hops, yeast, water	malt d'orge, maïs, houblon, levure, eau	gerstemout, maïs, hop, gist, water
	Powerful full taste. Strong fruity and spicy flavour (cloves, vanilla) with a slightly roasty touch, that reminds of cognac or whisky. Long aromatic and warm aftertaste.	Saveur pleine, corsée. Arôme très fruité et relevé (girofle, vanille) avec une touche légèrement fumée qui fait penser au cognac ou au whisky. Fin de bouche aromatique, longue et chaude.	Krachtige volle smaak. Sterk fruitig en kruidig (kruidnagel, vanille) aroma met licht gerookte toets die aan cognac of whisky doet denken. Lange aromatische en warme afdronk.
	Rinse the glass in cold water, tilt it and carefully pour the beer. Skim off if desired.	Rincer le verre à l'eau froide, le tenir incliné et verser la bière doucement. Ecumer selon le goût.	Het glas in koud water spoelen, schuin houden en het bier zacht uitschenken. Desgewenst afschuimen.
i	Delicious with cold meats, cheese or tapas.	Délicieuse avec de la charcuterie, du fromage et des tapas.	Heerlijk met charcuterie, kaas en tapas.

Leffe Blond

AB-Inbev (Abbaye Notre-Dame de Leffe)

6,60% 5 - 6 / 41 - 43

	top-fermentation	fermentation haute	hoge gisting
	Recognised Belgian abbey beer blond	Bière d'abbaye belge reconnue blonde	Erkend Belgisch abdijbier blond
	pale malt, corn, hops, yeast, water	malt pâle, maïs, houblon, levure, eau	bleekmout, maïs, hop, gist, water
	nice golden colour	joli doré	fraai goud
	Orange-like palette with a nut-like and creamy structure. Smooth, full and spicy taste, powerful aftertaste and spicy undertone.	Palette d'orange avec une structure crémeuse de noix. Saveur moelleuse, pleine et relevée, fin de bouche solide et arrière-fond corsé.	Sinaasachtig palet met een nootachtige en romige structuur. Zachte, volle en kruidige smaak, krachtige afdronk en pittige ondertoon.
	Rinse the glass in cold water, tilt it and carefully pour the beer. Skim off if desired.	Rincer le verre à l'eau froide, le tenir incliné et verser la bière doucement. Ecumer selon le goût.	Het glas in koud water spoelen, schuin houden en het bier zacht uitschenken. Desgewenst afschuimen.
	Goes well with red meat, smoked ham, sweet-and-sour dishes, brie and blue cheeses.	Savoureuse avec de la viande rouge, du jambon fumé, des mets aigres-doux, du brie et des fromages bleus.	Lekker bij rood vlees, gerookte ham, zoetzure gerechten, brie en blauwe kazen.

B-Inbev (Abbaye Notre-Dame de Leffe) 6,50% 5 - 6 °C 41 - 43 °F

Leffe Bruin

	top-fermentation	fermentation haute	hoge gisting
	Recognised Belgian abbey beer brown	Bière d'abbaye belge reconnue brune	Erkend Belgisch abdijbier bruin
	dark roasted malt, corn, hops, yeast, water	malt brûlé, maïs, houblon, levure, eau	donkergebrande mout, maïs, hop, gist, water
	deep autumn-brown	brun d'automne intense	diep herfstbruin
	Full taste. A trace of dessert apple in the bouquet. Fruity sweet and brown sugar with caramel and toffee. Dry, spicy aftertaste.	Saveur pleine. Touche de pomme de dessert dans le bouquet. Douce et fruitée, cassonade et caramel. Fin de bouche sèche et relevée.	Volle smaak. Zweem van dessertappel in het boeket. Fruitig zoet tot bruine suiker met karamel en toffee. Droge en kruidige afdronk.
	Rinse the glass in cold water, tilt it and carefully pour the beer. Skim off if desired.	Rincer le verre à l'eau froide, le tenir incliné et verser la bière doucement. Ecumer selon le goût.	Het glas in koud water spoelen, schuin houden en het bier zacht uitschenken. Desgewenst afschuimen.
	Store at cellar temperature.	Conserver à température de cave.	Bewaren op keldertemperatuur.

Leffe Kerst

AB-Inbev (Abbaye Notre-Dame de Leffe) 6,60%

	top-fermentation	fermentation haute	hoge gisting
	Recognised Belgian abbey beer dark	Bière d'abbaye belge reconnue foncée	Erkend Belgisch abdijbier donker
	amber-coloured with smooth foam head	ambrée avec faux col savoureux	amberkleurig met smeuige schuimkraag
	Sipping bear with a rich, fruity, spicy aroma and flavour.	Bière de dégustation d'un arôme et d'un goût riches, fruités, épicés.	Degustatiebier met een rijk, fruitig, kruidig aroma en smaak.
	Christmas beer was originally brewed with the new hop and barley harvest.	La bière de Noël était à l'origine brassée avec la nouvelle récolte de houblon et d'orge.	Kerstbier werd in origine gebrouwen met de nieuwe hop- en gerstoogst.

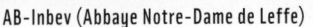

Leffe Lente

AB-Inbev (Abbaye Notre-Dame de Leffe) 6,60%

	top-fermentation	fermentation haute	hoge gisting
	Recognised Belgian abbey beer	Bière d'abbaye belge reconnue	Erkend Belgisch abdijbier
	orange-red to pale brown, shining with a fine, thick and lingering foam head	rouge orange à brun clair, brillante avec un faux col fin, stable collant au verre	oranjerood tot lichtbruin, glanzend met een fijne, wandklevende, lang blijvende schuimkraag
	Fruity bouquet with delicate impressions of clove and vanilla and phenol-like, smoky aromas (caramel, toffee, roasted). Soft and sweet with a nicely balanced bitter touch that is not too dry.	Bouquet fruité, avec de délicates sensations de clou de girofle et de vanille, et des arômes de phénol, fumeux (caramel, caramel mou, grillé). Douce et sucrée, avec une petite amertume joliment équilibrée, qui n'a pas d'effet desséchant.	Fruitig boeket met delicate impressies van kruidnagel en vanille en fenolachtige, rokerige aroma's (karamel, toffee, geroosterd). Zacht en zoet met een mooi evenwichtig bittertje dat niet uitdrogend werkt.
	Leffe is one of the oldest abbeys, founded in the 12th century by the Norbertines of Floreffe.	Leffe est l'une des plus anciennes abbayes, elle a été fondée au 12e siècle par les Prémontrés de Floreffe.	Leffe is één van de oudste abdijen, gesticht in de 12e eeuw door de Norbertijnen van Floreffe.

Leffe Radieuse

AB-Inbev (Abbaye Notre-Dame de Leffe) 8,20% 5 - 6° 41 - 43°

	top-fermentation	fermentation haute	hoge gisting
	Recognised Belgian abbey beer dark	Bière d'abbaye belge reconnue foncée	Erkend Belgisch abdijbier donker
	dark malt, corn, hops, herbs (incl. coriander), yeast, water	malt foncé, maïs, houblon, herbes (e.a. coriandre), levure, eau	donkere mout, mais, hop, kruiden (o.a. koriander), gist, water
	yellow-brown	jaune brun	geelbruin
	Most hopped of all Leffe beers. Rich, earthly bouquet with creamy crown. Powerful and full-bodied, fruity undertones, sweet with roasted flavours and the dryness of hops. A well-balanced sipping beer.	La plus houblonnée de toutes les bières de Leffe. Bouquet riche, terreux, avec un col crémeux. Puissante et franche en bouche, fruitée en profondeur, sucrée, avec une pointe de brûlé et la sécheresse du houblon. Une bière à savourer, parfaitement équilibrée.	Het meest gehopte van alle Leffebieren. Rijk, aards boeket met romige kroon. Krachtig en vol in de mond, fruitig in de diepte, zoet, met een vleugje gebrand en de droogte van hop. Een uitgebalanceerd genietbier.
	Rinse the glass in cold water, tilt and pour out the beer gently. Skim off excess if necessary.	Rincer le verre à l'eau froide, le tenir incliné et verser la bière doucement. Eventuellement écumer.	Het glas in koud water spoelen, schuin houden en het bier zacht uitschenken. Desgewenst afschuimen.
i	Goes well with foie gras, white mold cheeses and blue cheeses.	Délicieuse en accompagnement du foie gras, des fromages à moisissure blanche et des fromages bleus.	Lekker bij foie gras, witschimmelkazen en blauwe kazen.

Leffe Ruby

AB-Inbev (Abbaye Notre-Dame de Leffe) 5% 5 - 6 °C / 41 - 43 °F

	top-fermentation	fermentation haute	hoge gisting
	Recognised Belgian abbey fruit beer	Bière d'abbaye belge reconnue bière fruitée	Erkend Belgisch abdijbier fruitbier
	mixture of herbs and red fruits (strawberry, raspberry, bilberry)	mélange d'herbes et de fruits rouges (fraises, framboises, myrtilles)	mengeling van kruiden en rode vruchten (aardbei, framboos, bosbes)
	ruby-red	rouge rubis	robijnrood
	Mellow, refreshing, subtly spiced. Fruity taste set off nicely by a fine touch of wood.	Douce, rafraîchissante, subtilement épicée. Goût fruité avec une fine touche de bois qui assure l'équilibre de la balance du goût.	Zacht, verfrissend, subtiel gekruid. Fruitige smaak met een fijne toets van hout die de smaakbalans in evenwicht brengt.
	Rinse the glass in cold water, tilt and pour out the beer gently.	Rincer le verre dans de l'eau froide, le tenir incliné et verser la bière doucement. Eventuellement écumer.	Het glas in koud water spoelen, schuin houden en het bier zacht uitschenken.

Leffe Tripel

AB-Inbev (Abbaye Notre-Dame de Leffe)

8,40% 5 - 6° 41 - 43°

	top-fermentation re-fermentation in the bottle	fermentation haute refermentation en bouteille	hoge gisting hergisting in de fles
	Recognised Belgian abbey beer tripel	Bière d'abbaye belge reconnue triple	Erkend Belgisch abdijbier tripel
	malt, corn, hops, yeast, water	malt, maïs, houblon, levure, eau	mout, mais, hop, gist, water
	gold-brown	brun doré	goudbruin
	Firm and refined.	Vigoureuse et raffinée.	Stevig en verfijnd.
	Rinse the glass in cold water, tilt and pour out the beer gently.	Rincer le verre à l'eau froide, le tenir incliné et verser la bière doucement.	Het glas in koud water spoelen, schuin houden en het bier zacht uitschenken.
i	Goes well with game, grilled chicken, abbey cheeses and fish.	Délicieuse avec du gibier, du poulet rôti, des fromages d'abbaye et du poisson.	Lekker bij wild, gegrilde kip, abdijkazen en vis.

...uldenboot by Brouwerij Strubbe

6% | 3 °C 37 °F

	top-fermentation	fermentation haute	hoge gisting
	amber	ambrée	amber
	organic barley malt, organic buckwheat, biosucrose, hops, yeast, water	malt d'orge bio, sarrasin bio, sucrose bio, houblon, levure, eau	biogerstemout, bioboekweit, biosucrose, hop, gist, water
	7 EBC cloudy	7 EBC trouble	7 EBC troebel
	Full-bodied refreshening, round fruity.	Franche et fraîche, ronde et fruitée.	Volmondig fris, rond fruitig.
	Hold the glass tilted (45°) whilst pouring.	Tenir le verre incliné (45°) au moment de verser.	Het glas schuin houden (45 °) bij het inschenken.

Leireken Boekweit Blond

Leireken Boekweit Bruin

Guldenboot by Brouwerij Strubbe 6% 3° 37°

	top-fermentation	fermentation haute	hoge gisting
	dubbel	double	dubbel
	organic barley malt, organic buckwheat, organic cane sugar, hops, yeast, water	malt d'orge biologique, sarrasin biologique, sucre de canne biologique, houblon, levure, eau	biogerstemout, bioboekweit, biorietsuiker, hop, gist, water
	40 EBC cloudy	40 EBC trouble	40 EBC troebel
	Full-bodied with caramel taste.	Franche avec saveur caramélisée.	Volmondig met karamelsmaak.
	Hold the glass tilted (45°) whilst pouring.	Tenir le verre incliné (45°) au moment de verser.	Het glas schuin houden (45°) bij het inschenken.

uldenboot by Brouwerij Strubbe

5,20% (12° plato) 5 °C 41 °F

	bottom-fermentation	fermentation basse	lage gisting
	bio pilsner	biopils	biopils
	Belgian hops and barley malt, yeast, cane sugar, spring water	houblon Belge et malt d'orge, levure, sucre de canne, eau de source	Belgische hop en gerste-mout, gist, rietsuiker, bronwater
	Fresh, pure, very drinkable hoppy lager. Hoppy aroma with spicy touch in the nose. Malty sense in the mouth with a pleasant hint of lemon and sweet aftertaste.	Bière blonde houblonnée fraîche, pure, fort facile à boire. Arôme de houblon avec une touche épicée dans le bouquet. Sensation maltée en bouche, avec une agréable touche de citron et une fin de bouche sucrée.	Frisse, zuivere, zeer drinkbare hoppy lager. Hoparoma met kruidige toets in de neus. Moutachtig mondgevoel met aangename citroenhint en zoete nasmaak.
	Gluten-free organic beer.	Bière biologique sans gluten.	Glutenvrij biologisch bier.

Leireken Lager

Leireken Wilde Vruchten

Guldenboot by Brouwerij Strubbe

5,20% (12° plato) 5 41

	top-fermentation re-fermentation in the bottle centrifuged	fermentation haute refermentation en bouteille centrifugée	hoge gisting hergisting in de fles gecentrifugeerd
	organic fruit beer based on spelt	bière fruitée biologique à base d'épeautre	biologisch fruitbier op basis van spelt
	barley malt, white spelt, German hops, yeast, pomegranate, cherry, raspberry, bilberry, red elderberry, natural strawberry aroma, water	malt d'orge, épeautre blanc, houblon Allemand, levure, grenades, cerises, framboises, myrtilles bleues, baies de sureau rouges, arôme naturel de fraises, eau	gerstemout, witte spelt, Duitse hop, gist, granaatappel, kers, framboos, blauwe bosbes, rode vlierbes, natuurlijk aardbeienaroma, water
	cherry-red, cloudy with a full, lingering foam head not filtered	rouge cerise, trouble avec un faux col plein stable non filtrée	kersenrood, troebelig met een volle, lang blijvende schuimkraag ongefilterd
	Bitter hoppy aroma with a hint of fruit (especially raspberry) and strong spicy touch after revolving it. Dry, full, intense and bitter with fine, refreshing sour touch Long, bitter and peppery aftertaste which makes the mouth dry.	Arôme de houblon amer, avec une pointe de fruits (surtout framboise) et une touche fortement épicée après le remuage. Seche, franche, intense et amère, avec un peu d'acidité fine, rafraîchissante. Arrière-bouche longue, amère et poivrée, qui dessèche la bouche.	Bitter hoparoma met een vleugje fruit (vooral framboos) en een sterk kruidige toets na het walsen. Droog, vol, intens en bitter met fijn, verfrissend zuurtje. Lange, bittere en peperachtige afdronk die de mond droog maakt.

5% 5 °C 37 °F

Leireken Witte Spelt

	top-fermentation re-fermented in the bottle	fermentation haute refermentation en bouteille	hoge gisting hergisting op de fles
	spelt beer	bière d'épeautre	biologisch speltbier
	organic barley malt, organic spelt, organic sucrose, hops, yeast, water	malt d'orge bio, épeautre bio, sucrose bio, houblon, levure, eau	biogerstemout, biospelt, biosucrose, hop, gist, water
	5 EBC turbid and straw-yellow	5EBC trouble et jaune paille	5 EBC troebel en strogeel
	Fresh and fruity. Reminiscent of dessert apples.	Frais et fruité. Fait penser à des pommes de dessert.	Fris en fruitig. Doet denken aan dessertappels.
	Keep the glass tilted (45°) whilst pouring.	Tenir le verre incliné (45°) au moment de verser.	Het glas schuin houden (45°) bij het inschenken.
	Leireken is the nickname for Valère, the last train driver on the former Antwerp-Douai trainline.	Leireken est l'abréviation et le prénom usuel de Valère, le tout dernier machiniste sur l'ancienne ligne de chemin de fer Anvers-Douai.	Leireken is de afkorting en roepnaam van Valère, de laatste machinist op de vroegere spoorlijn Antwerpen-Douai.

L'Enfant Terrible

De Dochter van de Korenaar

7% 5 41

	mixed fermentation re-fermentation in the bottle not centrifuged	fermentation mixte refermentation en bouteille non centrifugée	gemengde gisting hergisting in de fles niet gecentrifugeerd
	The initial fermentation is followed by lactic acid fermentation in wine casks.	Après une première fermentation suit une fermentation en fût par acide lactique.	Na een eerste vergisting volgt een melkzure gisting op wijnvaten.
	barley malt, wheat malt, yeast, hops water	malt d'orge, malt de froment, levure, houblon, eau	gerstemout, tarwemout, gist, hop, water
	not filtered or pasteurised	non filtrée, non pasteurisée	ongefilterd, niet gepasteuriseerd
	Very limited availability.	Disponibilité fort limitée.	Zeer beperkt beschikbaar.

sage by De Proefbrouwerij

7% 8 - 12 °C / 46 - 54 °F

Lesage Blond

top-fermentation re-fermentation in the bottle not centrifuged	fermentation haute refermentation en bouteille non centrifugée	hoge gisting hergisting in de fles niet gecentrifugeerd
blond tripel	triple blonde	blonde tripel
barley malt, wheat, oat, hops, yeast, water	malt d'orge, froment, avoine, houblon, levure, eau	gerstemout, tarwe, haver, hop, gist, water
blond, slightly cloudy (yeast sediment) not filtered	blonde et légèrement trouble (dépôt de levure) non filtrée	blond en licht troebel (gistdepot) ongefilterd
Predominant wheat aroma supplemented with a full malt taste. Slightly bitter aftertaste.	Principalement un arôme de froment, complété par un goût malté franc. Arrière-bouche légèrement amère.	Overwegend tarwearoma aangevuld met een volle moutsmaak. Licht bittere afdronk.
Pour out carefully and give sufficient oxygen. Revolve the last half in the bottle, to loosen up the yeast.	Verser prudemment et donner assez d'oxygène. Eventuellement secouer la seconde moitié pour détacher la levure.	Voorzichtig uitschenken en voldoende zuurstof geven. De laatste helft eventueel rondwalsen om de gist los te maken.
Lesage is a popular name in Western Flanders. In French, it means 'the wise one' and hence an appropriate name for a beer!	Lesage est un nom fréquent en Flandre occidentale, qui vient du français 'Le sage' : Voilà une jolie appellation pour une bière !	Lesage is een frequent voorkomende naam in West-Vlaanderen. In het Frans betekent het 'de wijze' en vandaar is het ook een mooie naam voor een bier!

Lesage Dubbel

Lesage by De Proefbrouwerij

7,50% 7 - 11 / 45 - 52

	top-fermentation re-fermentation in the bottle	fermentation haute refermentation en bouteille	hoge gisting hergisting in de fles
	double	double	dubbel
	3 different malts (special B, Münich and pale ale)	3 variétés de malt (spécial B, Münich et pale ale)	3 moutsoorten (special B, Münich en pale ale)
	brown-red not filtered	brun rouge non filtrée	bruinrood ongefilterd
	Unique beer with a roasted and subtly bitter aftertaste owing to the roasted barley malt.	Bière unique avec une arrière-bouche brûlée et subtilement amère du fait du malt d'orge grillé.	Uniek bier met een gebrande en subtiel bittere afdronk door de geroosterde gerstemout.
	Pour out carefully and give sufficient oxygen. Revolve the last half in the bottle, if necessary, to loosen up the yeast.	Verser prudemment et donner assez d'oxygène. Eventuellement secouer la seconde moitié pour détacher la levure.	Voorzichtig uitschenken en voldoende zuurstof geven. De laatste helft eventueel rondwalsen om de gist los te maken.
	Brewed since January 2011.	Brassée depuis janvier 2011.	Gebrouwen sinds januari 2011.

Leute Bokbier

ouwerij Van Steenberge — 7,50% (16° plato) — 10 - 12 °C / 50 - 54 °F

top-fermentation re-fermented in the bottle	fermentation haute refermentation en bouteille	hoge gisting hergisting in de fles
regional beer dark	bière régionale foncée	streekbier donker
barley malt, hops, yeast, water	malt d'orge, houblon, levure, eau	gerstemout, hop, gist, water
dark red	rouge foncé	donkerrood
Aromatic, not too pronounced, but full and with a mild mouthfeel.	Aromatique, pas trop prononcé, mais pleine et douce dans la bouche.	Aromatisch, niet te uitgesproken, maar vol en mild in de mond.
Pour in a single, fluent and careful movement, leaving 1 cm of yeast sediment in the bottle. Typical tumbler in a wooden holder.	Verser en un seul mouvement fluide et doux et laisser 1 cm de dépôt de levure dans la bouteille. Verre typique inversable avec support en bois.	Uitschenken in 1 vloeiende, zachte beweging en 1 cm gistdepot in de fles laten. Heeft een typisch tuimelglas met houten voet.
'Leute' means 'fun' in Flemish. The goat and the hops in the logo refer to the brewery and the neighbouring hop fields when the production of the bok beer started in 1927.	'Leute' est flamand pour 'plaisir'. Le bouc et le vrille de houblon renvoient aux activités agricoles dans la brasserie et aux champs de houblon adjacents lors de la création de la bokbier en 1927.	'Leute' is Vlaams voor 'plezier'. De bok en hopperank in het logo verwijzen naar de agrarische activiteiten op de brouwerij en de aanpalende hoppevelden bij de opstart van het bokbier in 1927.

Liefmans Cuvée-Brut

Duvel Moortgat Corporation 6%

	mixed fermentation	fermentation mixte	gemengde gisting
	mixed beer	bière de coupage	versnijbier
	Kriek based on brown beer in which cherries have been macerated.	Kriek à base de bière brune où ont macéré des cerises.	Kriek op basis van bruin bier waarin krieken macereerden.
	deep red with firm, pale pink foam head	rouge profond avec faux col solide rose clair	dieprood met stevige, lichtroze schuimkraag
	Generous cherry aroma with touches of wood and almond. Sweet-sour onset, initially fruity in taste and eventually a complex full-bodied flavour. Complex Kriek with a fine sweet-and-sour balance.	Généreux arôme de griottes, avec des touches de bois et d'amande. Approche initiale aigre-douce, goût fruité qui se termine en une plénitude complexe. Kriek complexe, avec un équilibre d'acide et de sucré.	Royaal kriekenaroma met toetsen van hout en amandel. Zuurzoete aanzet, fruitige smaak die eindigt in een complexe volmondigheid. Complexe kriek met een evenwicht van zuur en zoet.
	After maturing for 1 year, the beer is mixed with Oud Bruin and Gouden Band.	Au bout d'1 an de mûrissement, la bière est coupée avec de l'Oud Bruin et de la Gouden Band.	Na 1 jaar rijping wordt het bier versneden met Oud Bruin en Gouden Band.

vel Moortgat Corporation 4,20%

	mixed fermentation	fermentation mixte	gemengde gisting
	mixed beer	bière de coupage	versnijbier
	Kriek with natural fruit juices (strawberry, raspberry, cherry, bilberry and elderberry)	kriek avec des jus de fruits naturels (fraises, framboises, cerises, myrtilles et baies de sureau)	kriekenbier met natuurlijke vruchtensappen (aardbei, framboos, krieken, bos- en vlierbessen)
	red, gently sparkling	rouge, légèrement mousseux	rood, zacht mousserend
	Fruity, pleasantly sweet and refreshing.	Fruitée, agréablement sucrée et rafraîchissante.	Fruitig, aangenaam zoet en verfrissend
i			

Liefmans Fruitesse Rood

Liefmans 'Goudenband' Provision Beer

Duvel Moortgat Corporation

8% 8 - 12 / 46 - 54

	top-fermentation	fermentation haute	hoge gisting
	soury dark-brown ale	ale brun foncé acidulé	zurige donkerbruine ale
	special malts, sugar, corn, hops, yeast, water Matures four to eight months in lager cellars.	malts spéciaux, sucre, maïs, houblon, levure, eau Mûrit 4 à 8 mois dans des caves.	speciale mouten, suiker, mais, hop, gist, water Rijpt 4 à 8 maanden in lagerkelders.
	dark brown slightly cloudy	brun foncé légèrement trouble	donkerbruin licht troebel
	Malty, spicy ester aroma. Soft body with a dry, complex, caramel-malty and nutty touch.	Arôme d'ester malté, épicé. Corps doux, avec une touche sèche, complexe, maltée de caramel et de noix.	Moutig, kruidig, esteraroma. Zachte body met een droge, complexe, karamelmoutige en notentoets.
	Can be kept for a long time. Positive taste evolution when stored horizontally at cellar temperature.	Se conserve longtemps, évolution de la saveur positive en position horizontale à température de cave.	Lang houdbaar en positieve smaakevolutie bij horizontale bewaring op keldertemperatuur.

uvel Moortgat Corporation

5% 6 - 10 °C / 43 - 50 °F

	mixed fermentation	fermentation mixte	gemengde gisting
	dark brown soury ale	brun foncé ale acidulé	donkerbruine zurige ale
	barley malt, sugar, hops, yeast, water Matures four to eight months in lagering.	malt d'orge, sucre, houblon, levure, eau Mûrit 4 à 8 mois.	gerstemout, suiker, hop, gist, water Rijpt 4 à 8 maanden in lagering.
	slightly turbid brown with clear white foam head	brun légèrment trouble avec un faux col clair blanc	licht troebel bruin met heldere witte schuimkraag
	Aromas of cherries, wood, almond and cherry icecream. Roasted flavour, caramel-like with a tart, refreshing aftertaste.	Arômes de cerises, de bois, d'amande et de glace aux cerises. Goût grillé, caramélisé, avec une arrière-bouche acidulée, rafraîchissante.	Aroma's van kersen, hout, amandel en kersenijs. Geroosterde smaak, karamelachtig met een zurige, verfrissende afdronk.

Liefmans Oud Bruin

Lily Blue

Brasserie Sainte-Hélène 7,50% 8 - 12° 46 - 54°

	top-fermentation re-fermented in the bottle	fermentation haute refermentation en bouteille	hoge gisting hergisting in de fles
	amber	ambrée	amber
	malt, hops (Perle, Brewers Gold), yeast, sugar, water	malt, houblon (Perle, Brewers Gold), levure, sucre, eau	op basis van 2 soorten hop (Perle en Brewers Gold), mout, gist, suiker, water
	copperbrown unfiltered	brun-cuivre non filtrée	koperbruin ongefilterd
	Smooth and full with taste evolution, caramel and fruit flavour. Balanced, slightly grilled aftertaste. 36 EBU.	Moelleuse et pleine avec évolution de la saveur. Saveur de caramel et de fruits. Equilibrée, fin de bouche légèrement grilleé. 36 EBU	Zacht en rond. Moutig en licht fruitig in de neus, harmoniërende smaak van karamel. Evenwichtig met licht geroosterde toets in de afdronk. 36 EBU.
	Boutique beer.	Brassée de façon artisanale.	Artisanaal gebrouwen.

Limburgse Witte

ouwerij Sint-Jozef

5% — 2 °C / 36 °F

top-fermentation unfiltered	fermentation haute non filtrée	hoge gisting ongefilterd
witbier	bière blanche	witbier
wheat, hops, yeast, lemon pulp, water	froment, houblon, levure, pulpe de citron, eau	tarwe, hop, gist, citroenpulp, water
cloudy nice, solid foam head	trouble faux col beau et solide	troebel mooie, vaste schuim-kraag
Full and well-rounded.	Pleine et ronde.	Vol en afgerond.
Pour half of the bottle, stop, revolve the bottle in your hand, then pour the rest.	Verser la bouteille à moitié, faire une pause, tourner la bouteille dans la main et puis continuer à verser.	De fles half uitschenken, eventjes stoppen, de fles draaien in de hand en daarna verder schenken.
Joint product from the Martens and Sint-Jozef breweries.	Produit commun des brasseries Martens et Sint-Jozef.	Gezamenlijk product van de brouwerijen Martens en Sint-Jozef.

Liter van Pallieter

Microbrouwerij Achilles 8%

	top-fermentation re-fermentation in the bottle	fermentation haute refermentation en bouteille	hoge gisting hergisting op de fles
	tripel regional beer	triple bière régionale	tripel streekbier
	barley malt, hops, yeast, re-fermentation sugar, water	malt d'orge, houblon, levure, sucre de refermentation, eau	gerstemout, hop, gist, hergistingssuiker, water
	Sweet-spicy flower aroma with a slightly bitter touch. Full of character with a full, pleasant body.	Arôme de fleurs sucré-épicé, avec une touche légèrement amère. Très caractéristique, avec un corps franc, agréable.	Zoet-kruidig bloemenaroma met een lichtbittere toets. Karaktervol met een gevulde, aangename body.

rouwerij Van den Bossche

5,20% 3 - 6 °C 37 - 43 °F

Livinus

	top-fermentation	fermentation haute	hoge gisting
	regional beer	bière régionale	streekbier
	pilsner malt, cara malt, fermentable sugar, yeast, hops, water	malt de pils, malt cara, sucre fermentable, levure, houblon, eau	pilsmout, caramout, vergistbare suiker, gist, hop, water
	golden blond	blond doré	goudblond
	Full taste with a slightly bitter aftertaste.	Goût plein avec une fin de bouche légèrement amère.	Volle smaak met een lichtbittere afdronk.
	Pour the beer slowly without sloshing. Make a nice foam head and hat.	Verser la bière lentement sans la laisser glouglouter. Former un beau faux col avec chapeau.	Het bier langzaam uitschenken zonder het te laten klokken. Een mooie schuimkraag en schuimhoed vormen.
	The beer was brewed for the first time for the Saint-Livinus celebrations in Sint-Lievens-Esse in 2007.	La bière a été brassée pour la première fois en 2007 à l'occasion des fêtes St Livinus à Sint-Lievens-Esse.	Het bier werd voor het eerst gebrouwen ter gelegenheid van de Sint-Livinusfeesten in Sint-Lievens-Esse in 2007.

Loterbol Blond

Brouwerij Loterbol 8%

	top-fermentation re-fermented in the bottle	fermentation haute refermentation en bouteille	hoge gisting hergisting op de fles
	blond	blonde	blond
	malt, hops, yeast, water. Dry-hopping.	malt, houblon, levure, eau. Dry hopping.	mout, hop, gist, water. Dry hopping.
	blond unfiltered	blonde non filtrée	blond niet gefilterd
	Bitter, fruity flavour, with a dry aftertaste.	Amère, arôme fruitée, arrière-bouche sèche.	Bitter, fruitig aroma, droge afdronk.
	From the same brewery: Tuverbol (11%) is a mixture of blond with 3 Fonteinen Lambik. Rodebol is made from Loterbol and cherries. Tuverbol and Roodebol are not readily available and do not have their own label.	De la même brasserie : Tuverbol (11%) est un mélange de blonde avec du 3 Fonteinen Lambik. Rodebol est faite de Loterbol et de griottes. Tuverbol et Roodebol ne sont pas couramment en vente et n'ont pas d'étiquette propre.	Van dezelfde brouwerij: Tuverbol (11%) is een mengeling van blond me 3 Fonteinen Lambik. Rodebol is gemaakt van Loterbol en krieken. Tuverbol en Roodebol zijn niet courant verkrijgbaar en hebben geen eigen etiket.

rouwerij Loterbol 8%

Loterbol Bruin

	top-fermentation re-fermentation in the bottle	fermentation haute refermentation en bouteille	hoge gisting hergisting op de fles
	strong double	double forte	sterk dubbel
	brown unfiltered	foncée non filtrée	bruin niet gefilterd
i	From the same brewery: Tuverbol (11%) is a mixture of blond with 3 Fonteinen Lambik. Rodebol is made from Loterbol and cherries. Tuverbol and Roodebol are not readily available and do not have their own label.	De la même brasserie : Tuverbol (11%) est un mélange de blonde avec du 3 Fonteinen Lambik. Rodebol est faite de Loterbol et de griottes. Tuverbol et Roodebol ne sont pas couramment en vente et n'ont pas d'étiquette propre.	Van dezelfde brouwerij: Tuverbol (11%) is een mengeling van blond met 3 Fonteinen Lambik. Rodebol is gemaakt van Loterbol en krieken. Tuverbol en Roodebol zijn niet courant verkrijgbaar en hebben geen eigen etiket.

Lou Pepe

Brasserie Cantillon 5% 15° 59°

	spontaneous fermentation	fermentation spontanée	spontane gisting
	gueuze	gueuze	geuze
	barley malt (65%), wheat (35%), more than one-year old hops, water	malt d'orge (65%), froment (35%), houblon de plus d'un an, eau	gerstemout (65%), tarwe (35%), overjaarse hop, water
	gold-coloured not filtered or pasteurised	dorée non filtrée, non pasteurisée	goudkleurig ongefilterd, niet gepasteuriseerd
	Dry and tart.	Sèche et acidulée.	Droog en zurig.
	Serve in a wine glass. Hold the glass reasonably upright.	Verser dans un verre de vin. Tenir le verre en position plus ou moins verticale.	Uitschenken in een wijnglas. Het glas tamelijk recht houden.
i			

Lucifer

rouwerij Het Anker 8% 5 - 7 °C / 41 - 45 °F

	top-fermentation re-fermentation in the bottle centrifuged	fermentation haute refermentation en bouteille centrifugée	hoge gisting hergisting in de fles gecentrifugeerd
	strong blond	blonde forte	sterk blond
	barley malt, hops, yeast, water	malt d'orge, houblon, levure, eau	gerstemout, hop, gist, water
	clear gold-yellow with creamy foam head filtered, pasteurised	limpide jaune doré avec faux col crémeux non filtrée, non pasteurisée	helder goudgeel met romige schuimkraag gefilterd, gepasteuriseerd
	Soft bitterness with a balanced aftertaste.	Douce amertume avec une arrière-bouche équilibrée.	Zachte bitterheid met een evenwichtige afdronk.
	Tilt the glass slightly and pour out beer gently.	Tenir le verre incliné et verser prudemment la bière.	Het glas licht schuin houden en het bier voorzichtig uitschenken.
	Launched in the 80s by the then Riva brewery.	Elle a été lancée sur le marché dans les années '80 par la brasserie de l'époque Riva.	Werd in de jaren '80 door de toenmailge brouwerij Riva op de markt gebracht.

Lupulus Blonde

Brasserie les 3 Fourquets 8,50%

	top-fermentation re-fermentation in the bottle	fermentation haute refermentation en bouteille	hoge gisting hergisting in de fles
	tripel	triple	tripel
	Lupulus brown was not ready in time for this book.	Lupulus brune n'était de justesse pas prête à temps pour ce livre.	Lupulus bruin was net niet op tijd klaar voor di boek.

	top-fermentation natural re-fermentation in the bottle not centrifuged	fermentation haute refermentation naturelle en bouteille non centrifugée	hoge gisting natuurlijke hergisting in de fles niet gecentrifugeerd
	(dark) wheat beer	bière de froment (foncée)	(donker) tarwebier
	lager malt, wheat malt, amber malt, chocolate malt, 3 different hops (Styrian, Saaz, East Kent Gold), coriander, dried orange peel, Irish moss	malt de lager, malt de froment, malt d'ambre, malt de chocolat, 3 variétés de cônes de houblon, (Styrian, Saaz, East Kent Gold), coriandre, écorce d'orange séchée, muscinées Irlandaises	lagermout, tarwemout, ambermout, chocolademout, 3 soorten hopbellen (Styrian, Saaz, East Kent Gold), koriander, gedroogde sinaasschil, Iers mos
	42 EBC not filtered or pasteurised	42 EBC non filtrée, non pasteurisée	42 EBC ongefilterd, niet gepasteuriseerd
	47 EBU (decreases when stored in a cool, dark place) Fresh citrus and lemon scent, full-bodied with a bitter aftertaste.	47 EBU (diminue en cas de conservation dans un endroit frais, sombre). Parfum frais de citrus et de citron, corps franc avec une arrière-bouche amère.	47 EBU (vermindert bij bewaring op een koele, donkere plaats) Frisse geur van citrus en citroen, volmondige body met een bittere afdronk.
	Serve in a goblet in a single movement. The yeast sediment can be poured in a small separate glass.	Verser d'un seul mouvement dans un verre calice. Déguster éventuellement le dépôt de levure séparément dans un petit verre.	In 1 beweging uitschenken in een kelkglas. De gistbodem eventueel degusteren in een klein afzonderlijk glaasje.
i			

Ma Mère Spéciale

Brouwerij De Leite

6% 4 - 10 / 39 - 50

	top-fermentation re-fermentation in the bottle not centrifuged	fermentation haute refermentation en bouteille non centrifugée	hoge gisting hergisting in de fles niet gecentrifugeerd
	blond	blonde	blond
	3 barley malt types, 4 different hops, yeast, water	3 variétés de malt, 4 variétés de houblon, levure, eau	3 soorten gerstemout, 4 soorten hop, gist, water
	clear blond with creamy foam head not filtered, pasteurised	limpide blond avec faux col crémeux non filtrée, pasteurisée	helder blond met romige schuimkraag ongefilterd, gepasteurise
	Bitter beer with a mellow malty fullness. Bitter hop taste is balanced out by a soft, fine citrus touch. Refined hoppy aftertaste that lingers.	Bière amère d'une plénitude doucement maltée. Goût amer houblonné équilibré, arrondi par une touche de citrus douce et fine. Arrière-bouche houblonnée raffinée qui persiste longtemps.	Bitter bier met een zachtmoutige volheid. Uitgebalanceerde hopbittere smaak afgerond met een zachte, fijne citrustoets. Geraffineerde hoppige afdronk die lang blijft.
	Serve in a Münich glass	Verser dans un verre Münich.	Uitschenken in een Münichglas
i	Ma Mère refers to both 'amère' (bitter) and brewer Luc's mother. The beer was brewed to mark her 80th birthday. According to the brewer, the gold-bitter 'mother' is incorrigible... Leite is a corruption of the word 'low level'.	Ma Mère fait référence à 'amère' et à la mère du brasseur Luc. La bière a été brassée à l'occasion de son 80e anniversaire. La 'mère' amère dorée est selon le brasseur 'impossible à rendre plus amère'... Leite est une altération du mot 'laagte'.	Ma Mère verwijst naar 'am re' (bitter) en de moeder van brouwer Luc. Het bier werd gebrouwen ter gelegenheid van haar 80e verjaardag. De goudbittere 'moeder' is volgens de br wer 'onverbitterbaar'... Leite is een verbastering van het woord 'laagte'.

6,50% 8 - 10 °C 46 - 50 °F

Maeght van Gottem

	top-fermentation re-fermentation in the bottle; not centrifuged	fermentation haute refermentation en bouteille; non centrifugée	hoge gisting hergisting in de fles; niet gecentrifugeerd
	city or regional beer	bière citadine ou régionale	stads- of streekbier
	pilsner and pale ale malt, Vlamertinge hops, yeast, water. With dry-hopping in the bottle (every bottle contains a hop bubble from Vlamertinge).	malt de pils et de pale ale, houblon de Vlamertinge, levure, eau. Avec dry-hopping en bouteille (chaque bouteille contient un cône de houblon de Vlamertinge).	pils- en pale ale mout, Vlamertingse hop, gist, water. Met dry-hopping in de fles (iedere fles bevat een hopbelletje uit Vlamertinge).
	gold blond not filtered or pasteurised	blond doré non filtrée, non pasteurisée	goudblond ongefilterd, niet gepasteuriseerd
	Unique hoppy aroma due to dry-hopping prior to bottling.	Arôme de houblon unique grâce au houblonnage à cru.	Uniek hoparoma door de dry-hopping voor het bottelen.
	When opening the bottle, the hop bubble is pushed out owing to the carbon dioxide present. Pour out gently.	Au moment de déboucher la bouteille la bulle de houblon est évacuée par le gaz carbonique. Ensuite verser tranquillement.	Bij het openen van de fles wordt de hoppebel door het koolzuurgas uit de fles gestuwd. Daarna rustig uitschenken.
	En extremely rare boutique beer, much like a 'Gottem maiden' is rare ...	Une bière artisanale extrêmement rare, comme l'est aussi une 'maagd van Gottem' ('vierge de Gottem')...	Een uiterst zeldzaam artisanaal bier, zoals ook een 'maagd van Gottem' zeldzaam is...

Brouwerij Alken-Maes

5,20% 3 37

bottom-fermentation	fermentation basse	lage gisting
pilsner	pils	pils
barley malt, Saaz hops, yeast, water	malt d'orge, houblon Saaz, levure, eau	gerstemout, Saaz hop, gist, water
gold-yellow	jaune doré	goudgeel
Refreshing and thirst-quenching. Fruity, pure, light flavour with a pleasant bitterness.	Rafraîchissante et désaltérante. Fruitée, pure, légère avec un goût amer agréable.	Verfrissend en dorstlessend. Fruitig, zuiver, licht van smaak met een aangename bitterheid.
Empty in a degreased, rinsed and wet glass. Let overflow and skim off the foam.	Verser complètement dans un verre dégraissé, rincé et mouillé. Laisser déborder et écumer.	Helemaal uitschenken in een ontvet, gespoeld en nat glas. Laten overlopen en afschuimen.

Malheur 6

rouwerij Malheur 6% 8 - 10 °C / 46 - 50 °F

	top-fermentation re-fermented in the bottle	fermentation haute refermentation en bouteille	hoge gisting hergisting op de fles
	blond	blonde	blond
	malt, hops, sugar, yeast, water	malt, houblon, sucre, levure, eau	mout, hop, suiker, gist, water
	golden blond	blond doré	goudblond
	Session beer with the powerful taste of a specialty beer. Accessible bitterness.	Facilement buvable avec la saveur corsée d'une bière spéciale. Goût amer accessible.	Doordrinkbier met de smaakkracht van een speciaalbier. Toegankelijke bitterheid.

M

Malheur 10

Brouwerij Malheur

10% 8 - 10 46 - 50

	top-fermentation re-fermented in the bottle	fermentation haute refermentation en bouteille	hoge gisting hergisting op de fles
	special blond	blonde spéciale	speciaal blond
	malt, hops, sugar, yeast, water	malt, houblon, sucre, levure, eau	mout, hop, suiker, gist, water
	sunny yellow	jaune soleil	zonnegeel
	Rose-like peach flavour with a touch of lemon and orange rind. A touch of bitter-sour and a warm aftertaste.	Arômes de pêches et de roses avec une touche d'écorce de citron et d'orange. Une pointe amère-acidulée et une fin de bouche chaleureuse.	Rozenachtig perzikaroma met toets van citroen- en sinaasappelschil. Een vleugje bitterzuur en een warme afdronk.

12% 8 - 10 °C 46 - 50 °F

	top-fermentation re-fermented in the bottle	fermentation haute refermentation en bouteille	hoge gisting hergisting in de fles
	strong brown	brune forte	sterk donker
	malt, hops, sugar, yeast, water	malt, houblon, sucre, levure, eau	mout, hop, suiker, gist, water
	red-brown	brun rouge	roodbruin
	Bouquet of hop flowers. Round, full taste, very drinkable.	Bouquet de fleurs de houblon. Goût rond et plein, se boit facilement.	Boeket van hopbloemen. Ronde en volle smaak, vlot drinkbaar.

Malheur 12

Malheur Bière Brut

Brouwerij Malheur

11% 4 - 6 / 39 - 43

top-fermentation re-fermented in the bottle	fermentation haute refermentation en bouteille	hoge gisting hergisting op de fles
brut beer	bière brute	brutbier
malt, barley, hops, yeast, water. The yeast is removed from the bottle by special procedures (riddling and disgorging).	malt, orge, houblon, levure, eau. La levure est enlevée de la bouteille par des procédés spéciaux (remuage et dégorgement).	mout, gerst, hop, gist, water. Via speciale procédés (remuage en dégorgement) wordt de gist uit de fles verwijderd.
blond	blonde	blond
Refined and sparkling with a lively foam head and an elegant aftertaste.	Raffinée et pétillante avec un faux col corsé et une arrière-bouche élégante.	Verfijnd en sprankelend met een pittige schuimkraag en een elegante nasmaak.
Can be drunk as an aperitif or as a dessert beer.	Convient comme apéritif et digestif ou en accompagnement du dessert.	Geschikt als aperitief en digestief of dessertbier.

ouwerij Malheur

9% 4 - 6 °C / 39 - 43 °F

Malheur Cuvée Royale 'à la Méthode Originale'

top-fermentation re-fermentation in the bottle	fermentation haute refermentation en bouteille	hoge gisting hergisting op de fles
brut beer sparkling strong blond à la méthode originale	bière brute pétillante blonde forte à la méthode originale	brut bier sprankelend sterk blond à la méthode originale
malt, sugar, different hops, yeast, water	malt, sucre, variétés de houblon, levure, eau	mout, suiker, hopsoorten, gist, water
blond filtered: the yeast is removed by means of remuage and dégorgement.	blond filtrée: la levure est enlevée par remuage et dégorgement.	blond gefilterd: de gist wordt verwijderd via remuage en dégorgement.
Keep the bottle flat in a wide ice bucket and pour into tilted glasses (holding 2). Pour like champagne.	Garder la bouteille dans un large seau de glaçons et remplir les verres en position oblique (2 sous la main). Verser comme le champagne.	De fles liggend in een brede ijsemmer houden en de glazen (2 bij de hand) schuin inschenken. Schenken zoals champagne.
Brewed to mark Belgium's 175th anniversary.	Brassée à l'occasion du 175e anniversaire de la Belgique.	Gebrouwen n.a.v. het 175-jarig bestaan van België.

Malheur Dark Brut 'à la Méthode Originale'

Brouwerij Malheur 12% 4 - 6 / 39 - 43

	top-fermentation re-fermented in the bottle	fermentation haute refermentation en bouteille	hoge gisting hergisting op de fles
	brut beer very effervescent brown à la méthode originale	bière brute forte brune pétillante à la méthode originale	brut bier sprankelend sterk bruin à la méthode originale
	malt, barley, hops, yeast, water. The yeast is removed from the bottle by special procedures (riddling and disgorging).	malt, orge, houblon, levure, eau. La levure est enlevée de la bouteille par des procédés spéciaux (remuage et dégorgement).	mout, gerst, hop, gist, water. Via speciale procédés (remuage en dégorgement) wordt de gist uit de fles verwijderd.
	dark brown with a brown, creamy and generous foam	brun foncé avec écume brune, crémeuse et abondante	donkerbruin met bruin, romig schuim.
	Aroma: bitterness brought into balance by the tannin of the wood and a touch of sugar owing to the alcohol. Flavour: oak-dry with a complex scent of sherry, madeira, vanilla and wood. Coffee-flavoured boiled sweets (roasted malt). Aftertaste: extremely dry.	Arôme : amertume en équilibre, avec le tanin du bois et une pointe de sucré de l'alcool. Goût : sec du chêne, avec un parfum complexe de xérès, de madère, de vanille et de bois. Caramels durs au goût de café (malt grillé). Arrière-bouche :archisèche.	Aroma: bitterheid in evenwicht met de tannine van het hout en een zweem zoet van de alcohol Smaak: eikdroog met complexe geur van sherry, madeira, vanille en hout. Haagse hopjes met koffiesmaak (geroosterde mout). Afdronk: kurkdroog.
	see Malheur Cuvée Royale	voir Malheur Cuvée Royale.	zie Malheur Cuvée Royale
	The first dark brut beer in the world.	La première bière brute foncée au monde.	Het eerste donkere brut bier ter wereld.

5% 15 °C 59 °F

	spontaneous fermentation	fermentation spontanée	spontane gisting
	lambic	lambic	lambiek
	barley malt (65%), wheat (35%), more than one-year old hops, elder-flower, water	malt d'orge (65%), froment (35%), houblon de plus d'un an, fleur de sureau, eau	gerstemout (65%), tarwe (35%), overjaarse hop, vlierbloesem, water
	gold-coloured not filtered or pasteurised	dorée non filtrée, non pasteurisée	goudkleurig ongefilterd, niet gepasteuriseerd
	Dry, sour and floral.	Sèche, acidulée et fleurie.	Droog, zurig en bloemig.
	Serve in a wine glass. Hold the glass reasonably upright.	Verser dans un verre de vin. Tenir le verre en position plus ou moins verticale.	Uitschenken in een wijnglas. Het glas tamelijk recht houden.
i	The elderflower is grown in 2-year old Lambic. Beer that changes in taste with time, can be kept up to 10 years following bottling.	On fait macérer les fleurs de sureau dans du lambic de 2 ans d'âge. Une bière dont le goût évolue et qui peut se conserver jusqu'à 10 ans après la mise en bouteille.	De vlierbloesem wordt geweekt in 2 jaar oude lambiek. Bier met smaakevolutie, houdbaar tot 10 jaar na botteling.

Maneblusser

Brouwerij Het Anker

6% 5 - 7 / 41 - 45

top-fermentation re-fermentation in the bottle centrifuged	fermentation haute refermentation en bouteille centrifugée	hoge gisting hergisting in de fles gecentrifugeerd
blond	blonde	blond
barley malt, hops, yeast, herbs, water	malt d'orge, houblon, levure, herbes, eau	gerstemout, hop, gist, kruiden, water
blond with solid foam head filtered, pasteurised	blonde avec un faux col solide filtrée, pasteurisée	blond met een stevige schuimkraag gefilterd, gepasteuriseerd
Very drinkable sipping beer with a light citrus aroma and a fine aftertaste.	Bière de dégustation facile à boire, avec un léger arôme de citrus et une fine arrière-bouche.	Vlot drinkbaar degustatiebier met een licht citrusaroma en een fijne afdronk.
Tilt the glass slightly and pour out the beer gently.	Tenir le verre incliné et verser prudemment la bière.	Het glas licht schuin houden en het bier voorzichtig uitschenken.
Beer brewed in tribute of the people from Malines: 'Maneblusser' is a nickname for someone from Malines.	Une bière brassée en l'honneur des Malinois :'Maneblusser' est un sobriquet du Malinois.	Bier gebrouwen ter ere van de Mechelaars: 'Maneblusser' is een spotnaam voor de Mechelaar

asserie Lefebvre 5,20% 3 - 6 °C 39 - 43 °F

	bottom-fermentation centrifuged	fermentation basse centrifugé	lage gisting gecentrifugeerd
	pilsner	pils	pils
	barley malt, corn, hops, yeast, water	malt d'orge, maïs, houblon, levure, eau	gerstemout, mais, hop, gist, water
	blond clear pasteurised	blonde claire pasteurisée	helderblond gepasteuriseerd
	Pure, savoury pilsner based on pure ingredients.	Pils franche et goûteuse à base de bons ingrédents.	Echte, pure pils die zeer smaakvol is op basis van pure ingrediënten.
	Pour out or drink from the bottle.	Verser dans un verre ou boire à la bouteille.	Uit de fles drinken of in een pilsglas uitschenken.
i			

Manneken Pils

Mano Negra

Picobrouwerij Alvinne

10% 8 - 10 / 46 - 50

	top-fermentation re-fermentation in the bottle	fermentation haute refermentation en bouteille	hoge gisting hergisting op de fles
	6 different malts, hops (Magnum, EK Goldings), Morpheus yeast, water	6 variétés de malt, houblon (Magnum, EK Goldings), levure Morpheus, eau	6 moutsoorten, hop (Magnum, EK Goldings), Morpheusgist, water
	69 EBU.	69 EBU.	69 EBU.

)uwerij Gulden Spoor

6% 8 - 10 °C 46 - 50 °F

top-fermentation re-fermentation in the bottle not centrifuged	fermentation haute refermentation en bouteille non centrifugée	hoge gisting hergisting in de fles niet gecentrifugeerd
double/dark	double/foncée	dubbel/donker
barley malt, hops, yeast, water	malt d'orge, houblon, levure, eau	gerstemout, hop, gist, water
red, almost dark with fixed foam head not filtered or pasteurised	rouge, presque foncé avec faux col stable non filtrée, non pasteurisée	rood, bijna donker met vaste schuimkraag ongefilterd, niet gepasteuriseerd
The taste turns from caramel to roasted chocolate.	Le goût évolue dans la bouche du caramel à du chocolat torréfié.	De smaak evolueert in de mond van karamel naar gebrande chocolade.
Degrease the glass, tilt it slightly and carefully pour the beer in a single movement.	Dégraisser le verre, tenir légèrement incliné et verser prudemment la bière d'un seul mouvement.	Het glas vetvrij maken, licht schuin houden en het bier voorzichtig in 1 beweging uitschenken.
Manten and his wife Kalle are the bell ringers or 'jacquemarts' of the Courtrai Belfry.	Manten et sa femme Kalle sont les frappeurs de cloche ou 'jacquemarts' du Beffroi de Courtrai.	Manten en zijn vrouw Kalle zijn de uurslagers of 'jacquemarts' van het Belfort in Kortrijk.

Brasserie La Ferme au Chêne 6,50% 8 -12 / 46 - 54

	top-fermentation	fermentation haute	hoge gisting
	amber	ambrée	amber
	malt, hops (Styrian Golding), sugar, herbs, yeast, water	malt, houblon (Styrian Golding), sucre, herbes, levure, eau	mout, hop (Styrian Golding), kandijsuiker, kruiden, gist, water
	amber slightly cloudy unfiltered	ambrée légèrement trouble non filtreé	amberkleurig licht troebel niet gefilterd
	Smooth and slightly bitter.	Douce et légèrement amère.	Zacht en licht bitter.
	Pour carefully so as to leave the yeast sediment in the bottle.	Verser prudemment de sorte que le dépôt de levure reste dans la bouteille.	Voorzichtig uitschenken zodat het gistbezinksel in de fles blijft.
	Available at the Microbrewery only.	Microbrasserie. Les bières y sont mises en bouteilles et vendues sur place.	Enkel verkrijgbaar bij Microbrouwerij La Ferme au Chêne.

6% 6 - 10 °C 43 - 50 °F

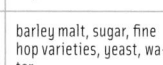

top-fermentation re-fermented in the bottle	fermentation haute refermentation en bouteille	hoge gisting hergisting in de fles
Recognised Belgian abbey beer blond	Bière belge d'abbaye reconnue blonde	Erkend Belgisch abdijbier blond
barley malt, sugar, fine hop varieties, yeast, water	malt d'orge, sucre, sortes fines de houblon, levure, eau	gerstemout, suiker, fijne hopsoorten, gist, water
blond	blonde	blond
The ideal thirst-quencher. Chiefly refreshing, slightly bitter aftertaste with a touch of fruit flavours.	Désaltérant idéal. Fin de bouche principalement fraîche, légèrement amère avec une touche fruitée.	Ideale dorstlesser. Overwegend frisse, lichtbittere afdronk met een toets fruitigheid.
Pour carefully into a dry tulip-shaped glass. Leave 1 cm of beer (the yeast sediment) in the bottle, as it makes the beer cloudy.	Verser prudemment dans un verre tulipe sec. Laisser un 1 cm de bière (fond de levure) dans la bouteille; il rend la bière trouble.	Voorzichtig uitschenken in een droog tulpvormig glas. 1 cm bier (gistfond) in de fles laten (maakt het bier troebel).
The draught version (without re-fermenting) is served in a wet glass.	Pour la version au fût (sans refermentation), on utilise un verre mouillé.	Voor de versie op vat (zonder hergisting) wordt een nat glas gebruikt.

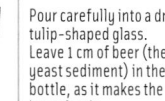

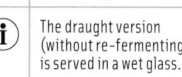

Maredsous Dark

Duvel Moortgat Corporation

8% 8 - 1 / 46 - 5

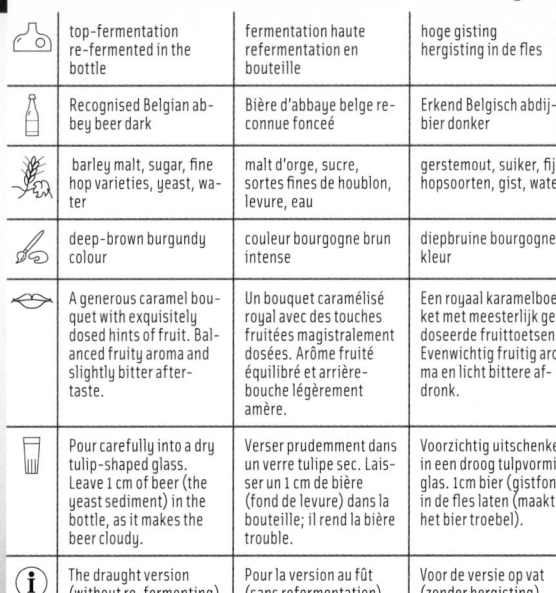

	top-fermentation re-fermented in the bottle	fermentation haute refermentation en bouteille	hoge gisting hergisting in de fles
	Recognised Belgian abbey beer dark	Bière d'abbaye belge reconnue foncée	Erkend Belgisch abdijbier donker
	barley malt, sugar, fine hop varieties, yeast, water	malt d'orge, sucre, sortes fines de houblon, levure, eau	gerstemout, suiker, fijn hopsoorten, gist, water
	deep-brown burgundy colour	couleur bourgogne brun intense	diepbruine bourgognekleur
	A generous caramel bouquet with exquisitely dosed hints of fruit. Balanced fruity aroma and slightly bitter aftertaste.	Un bouquet caramélisé royal avec des touches fruitées magistralement dosées. Arôme fruité équilibré et arrière-bouche légèrement amère.	Een royaal karamelboeket met meesterlijk gedoseerde fruittoetsen. Evenwichtig fruitig aroma en licht bittere afdronk.
	Pour carefully into a dry tulip-shaped glass. Leave 1 cm of beer (the yeast sediment) in the bottle, as it makes the beer cloudy.	Verser prudemment dans un verre tulipe sec. Laisser un 1 cm de bière (fond de levure) dans la bouteille; il rend la bière trouble.	Voorzichtig uitschenken in een droog tulpvormig glas. 1cm bier (gistfond) in de fles laten (maakt het bier troebel).
i	The draught version (without re-fermenting) is served in a wet glass.	Pour la version au fût (sans refermentation), on utilise un verre mouillé.	Voor de versie op vat (zonder hergisting) wordt een nat glas gebruikt.

Maredsous Tripel

vel Moortgat Corporation

10% 6 - 10 °C 43 - 50 °F

top-fermentation re-fermented in the bottle	fermentation haute refermentation en bouteille	hoge gisting hergisting in de fles
Recognised Belgian abbey beer tripel	Bière d'abbaye belge reconnue triple	Erkend Belgisch abdijbier tripel
barley malt, sugar, fine hop varieties, yeast, water	malt d'orge, sucre, sortes fines de houblon, levure, eau	gerstemout, suiker, fijne hopsoorten, gist, water
deep-blond tripel with very fine bubbles	triple blond intense avec des bulles très fines	diepblonde tripel met zeer fijne pareling
Harmonious, full taste of sour, sweet and bitter. Heartwarming aftertaste.	Saveur pleine harmonieuse acidulée, douce et amère. Fin de bouche chaleureuse.	Harmonieuze volle smaak van zuur, zoet en bitter. Hartverwarmende afdronk.
Pour carefully into a dry tulip-shaped glass. Leave 1 cm of beer (the yeast sediment) in the bottle, as it makes the beer cloudy.	Verser prudemment dans un verre tulipe sec. Laisser un 1 cm de bière (fond de levure) dans la bouteille; il rend la bière trouble.	Voorzichtig uitschenken in een droog tulpvormig glas. 1 cm bier (gistfond) in de fles laten (maakt het bier troebel).
The draught version (without re-fermenting) is served in a wet glass.	Pour la version au fût (sans refermentation), on utilise un verre mouillé.	Voor de versie op vat (zonder hergisting) wordt een nat glas gebruikt.

Martens Pils

Brouwerij Martens 5%

	bottom-fermentation	fermentation basse	lage gisting
	pilsner	pils	pils
	blond clear	blonde claire	blond helder
	Refreshing and full-bodied.	Fraîche et relevée.	Fris en pittig.
	cfr. pilsner	voir pils	cfr. pils

Martin's Blond

roep John Martin by various breweries 6%

	top-fermentation	fermentation haute	hoge gisting
	blond ale	ale blonde	blonde ale
	Slightly bitter and refreshing.	Légèrement amère et rafraîchissante.	Licht bitter en verfrissend.

M

Martin's Pale Ale

Groep John Martin by Palm Breweries 5,50% 6 - 8 / 43 - 46

	top-fermentation	fermentation haute	hoge gisting
	pale ale	pale ale	pale ale
	barley malt, sugar, corn, roasted barley, hops, water	malt d'orge, sucre, maïs, orge brûlé, houblon, eau	gerstemout, suiker, mais, gebrande gerst, hop, water
	amber	ambrée	amber
	The typical malt and aromatised hop give a dry bitterness from the onset.	Malt typique et houblon aromatisé se traduisant en un goût amer dès le début.	Typische mout en gearomatiseerde hop vertalen zich in een droge bitterheid vanaf het begin.

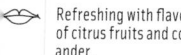

rouwerij Roman

5% 3 °C / 37 °F

Mater Wit Bier

	top-fermentation re-fermented in the bottle	fermentation haute refermentation en bouteille	hoge gisting hergisting in de fles
	witbier	bière blanche	witbier
	barley malt, wheat, hops, herbs, yeast, spring water	malt d'orge, froment, houblon, herbes, levure, eau de source	gerstemout, tarwe, hop, kruiden, gist, bronwater
	light-yellow cloudy, unfiltered	jaune clair trouble, non filtrée	lichtgeel troebel, niet gefilterd
	Refreshing with flavours of citrus fruits and coriander. Well-balanced sweet-and-sour taste.	Rafraîchissante avec des arômes d'agrumes et de coriandre. Saveur aigre-douce équilibrée.	Verfrissend met aroma's van citrusvruchten en koriander. Uitgebalanceerde zoet-zure smaak.
	Swiftly pour into a degreased, chilled and rinsed beer glass. Pour the sediment along with the beer.	Verser rapidement dans un verre de bière dégraissé, rafraîchi et rincé. Verser également le dépôt de levure.	Vlot uitschenken in een ontvet, gekoeld en gespoeld bierglas. De fond mee uitschenken.
	Store in a dark, cool room.	Conserver à l'abri de la lumière et de la chaleur.	Donker en koel bewaren.

M Mc Chouffe

Duvel Moortgat Corporation

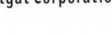

8% 8 - 12 / 46 - 54

	top-fermentation	fermentation haute	hoge gisting
	regional beer	bière régionale	streekbier
	malt, hops, sugar, yeast, water	malt, houblon, sucre, levure, eau	mout, hop, suiker, gist, water
	dark unfiltered	foncée non filtrée	donker ongefilterd
	Aroma of black fruit with touches of floral hops. Complex malt flavour with bitter twist. A Scotch from the Ardennes.	Arôme de fruits noirs, avec des touches de houblon floral. Goût malté complexe, avec un peu d'amertume. Une 'Scotch' ardennaise.	Aroma van zwarte vruchten met toetsen van florale hop. Complexe moutsmaak met bittertje. Een Ardense 'Scotch'.
	Store upright in a dark, cool room. A layer of yeast sediment at the bottom of the bottle is normal.	A conserver verticalement à l'abri de la lumière et de la chaleur. Un dépôt de levure au fond de la bouteille est normal.	Verticaal bewaren in een donkere, koele ruimte. Een gistlaagje op de bodem van de fles is normaal.

icobrouwerij Alvinne

11% 8 - 10 °C / 46 - 50 °F

	top-fermentation	fermentation haute	hoge gisting
	barley wine regional beer winter beer	vin d'orge bière régionale bière hivernale	gerstewijn streekbier winterbier
	malt (pilsner, wheat, amber), granulated sugar, hops, yeast, musterd seeds, water	malt (pils, froment, ambré), sucre cristallisé, houblon, levure, graines de moutarde, eau	mout (pils, tarwe, amber), kristalsuiker, hop, gist, mosterdzaden, water
	amber 33 EBC	ambrée 33 EBC	amber 33 EBC
	Spicy and alcoholic taste and aroma. Strong alcoholic 'barley wine'. 53 EBU.	Saveur et arôme relevés et alcoolisés. 'Barley wine' fortement alcoolisé. 53 EBU.	Kruidige en alcoholische smaak en aroma. Sterk alcoholische 'barley wine'. 53 EBU.
	Pour into a tulip-shaped glass or goblet. Leave the yeast (approx. 1 cm) at the bottom of the bottle. Pour slowly to obtain a nice foam head.	Verser dans un verre tulipe ou calice. Laisser la levure (environ 1 cm) au fond de la bouteille. Verser lentement de sorte qu'un beau faux col se forme.	Uitschenken in een tulp- of kelkvormig glas. De gist (ca. 1 cm) op de bodem van de fles laten. Langzaam schenken zodat er een mooie schuimkraag ontstaat.
i			

Métisse Saison

Du Lion à Plume at Brasserie Sainte-Hélène

5,70% — 10 - 12° / 50 - 54°

	top-fermentation natural re-fermentation in the bottle not centrifuged	fermentation haute refermentation naturelle en bouteille non centrifugée	hoge gisting natuurlijke hergisting in de fles niet gecentrifugeerd
	saison	saison	saison
	barley and wheat malt, hops (E.K. Goldings and Cascade), yeast, water	malt d'orge et de froment, houblon (E.K. Goldings et Cascade), levure, eau	gerste- en tarwemout, hop (E.K. Goldings en Cascade), gist, water
	copper-blond not filtered or pasteurised	blond cuivre non filtrée, non pasteurisée	koperblond ongefilterd, niet gepasteuriseerd
	Dry beer with a slightly tangy flavour (grapefruit) and a distinct bitterness which also dominates the aftertaste.	Bière sèche, avec un léger goût de citrus (pamplemousse) et une amertume marquée qui domine aussi l'arrière-bouche.	Droog bier met lichte citrussmaak (pompelmoes) en een uitgesproken bitterheid die ook de afdronk beheerst.
	Pour out carefully in a slightly tilted glass at eye level. Then lift the bottle for a nice foam head.	Verser prudemment dans un verre légèrement tenu incliné à hauteur des yeux. Lever par la suite la bouteille plus haut pour former un faux col solide.	Voorzichtig uitschenken in een licht schuingehouden glas op ooghoogte. De fles daarna hoger tillen voor een mooie schuimkraag.
i	Métisse' means 'mixture' and refers to the combination of English and American hops which afford this beer a unique flavour.	'Métisse' signifie 'mélange' et fait référence à la combinaison de houblon anglais et américain qui confère à cette bière un goût unique.	Métisse' betekent 'mengeling' en verwijst naar de combinatie van Engelse en Amerikaans hop die dit bier een unieke smaak geven.

Mistinguett

Brasserie Sainte-Hélène 6,50% 10 - 12 °C / 50 - 54 °F

	top-fermentation re-fermented in the bottle	fermentation haute refermentation en bouteille	hoge gisting hergisting in de fles
	blond	blonde	blond
	English and German hops	houblon anglais et allemand	Engelse en Duitse hop
	dark blond	blond foncé	donkerblond
	Smooth bitter provision beer with a hoppy flavour.	Bière de conservation amère-moelleuse avec un arôme houblonné.	Zacht, bitter bewaarbier met een hoppig aroma.
	Pour carefully in a tulip-shaped glass and leave the sediment in the bottle.	Verser prudemment dans un verre tulipe et laisser la lie dans la bouteille.	Voorzichtig uitschenken in een tulpglas en de droesem op de bodem van de fles laten.
	Boutique beer.	Brassée de façon artisanale.	Artisanaal gebrouwen.

Moeder Overste

Brasserie Lefebvre 7,50% 3 - 6 / 37 - 43

top-fermentation naturally re-fermented in the bottle centrifuged	fermentation haute refermentation naturelle en bouteille centrifugée	hoge gisting natuurlijke hergisting in de fles gecentrifugeerd
Recognised Belgian Abbey beer tripel	Bière d'abbaye belge reconnue triple	Erkend Belgisch Abdijbier tripel
barley malt, hops, candy sugar, yeast, water	malt d'orge, houblon, sucre candi, levure, eau	gerstemout, hop, kandijsuiker, gist, water
slightly hazed if served cold amber	légèrement voilée si servie froide ambrée	licht gesluierd indien koud geschonken amber
Full spirit flavour with harmonious bitterness and a light touch of caramel.	Goût franc et spiritueux, avec une amertume harmonieuse et une légère touche de caramel.	Volle en spiritueuze smaak met harmonieuze bitterheid en een licht kara meltoets.
Pour into a glass with a stem and leave the yeast sediment in the bottle.	Verser dans un verre à pied et laisser le dépôt de levure dans la bouteille.	Uitschenken in een glas met voet en het gistbezinksel in de fles laten.
Store the bottles upright.	Conserver les bouteilles en position verticale.	De flessen verticaal bewaren.

Moinette Biologique

rasserie Dupont 7,50% 12 °C 54 °F

top-fermentation re-fermented in the bottle	fermentation haute refermentation en bouteille	hoge gisting nagisting in de fles
blond	blonde	blond
blond unfiltered	blonde non filtrée	blond ongefilterd
Flavours of malt, fruit and fine hop. Thirst-quenching owing to the combination of smoothness, bitterness and fruitiness.	Arômes de malt, de fruits et de houblon fin. Désaltérant par la combinaison des goûts moelleux, amers et fruités.	Aroma's van mout, fruit en fijne hop. Dorstlessend door de combinatie van zachtheid, bitterheid en fruitigheid.
The production is supervised by Ecocert®. The beer carries the label of Biogarantie®.	La production est contrôlée par Ecocert®. Avec le label Biogarantie®.	De productie wordt gecontroleerd door Ecocert®. Met label Biogarantie®.

Moinette Blonde

Brasserie Dupont 8,50% 12° 54°

	top-fermentation re-fermented in the bottle	fermentation haute refermentation en bouteille	hoge gisting nagisting in de fles
	blond	blonde	blond
	copper-coloured	couleur cuivre	koperkleurig
	Fine hop and yeast flavours. Refreshing owing to the balance between sweet, bitter and fruity. Complex and harmonious owing to re-fermentation in the bottle.	Arômes raffinés de houblon et de levure. Rafraîchissante par l'équilibre de goûts doux, amers et fruités. Complexe et harmonieuse par la refermentation en bouteille.	Fijne hop- en gistaroma's. Verfrissend door evenwicht van zoet, bitter en fruitig. Complex en harmonieus door hergisting in de fles.
	The original name was 'Abbaye de la Moinette'. Moinette refers to the word 'moëne', meaning 'swamp'. The beer has the same name because the area around the brewery is rather swampy.	Le nom d'origine était 'Abbaye de la Moinette'. Moinette renvoie au vocable 'moëne' qui signifie marais; le nom de la bière y est relié parce que la région autour de la brasserie est assez marécageuse.	De oorspronkelijke naam was 'Abbaye de la Moinette'. Moinette verwijst naar het woord 'moëne' wat moeras betekent. De naam van het bier is hieraan gelinkt omdat de streek rond de brouwerij vrij moerassig is.

8,50% 12 °C 54 °F

Moinette Brune

top-fermentation re-fermented in the bottle	fermentation haute refermentation en bouteille	hoge gisting nagisting in de fles
dubbel	double	dubbel
Based on a blend of 4 special malts.	A base d'un mélange de 4 malts spéciaux.	Op basis van een mengeling van 4 speciale mouten.
Light dark-brown to rusty with scarlet hues	Brun foncé clair à roux avec des teintes rouges vives.	Licht donkerbruin tot rossig met vuurrode tinten.
Dominating hop and malt aroma and taste. Smoothly bitter and slightly fruity. Complex and harmonious taste evolution owing to re-fermentation in the bottle.	Saveur dominante, arômes de houblon et de malt. Légèrement amère en combinaison avec le goût légèrement fruité. Evolution de la saveur complexe et harmonieuse par la refermentation en bouteille.	Dominerende smaak en aroma's van hop en mout. Zacht bitter in combinatie met licht fruitig. Complexe en harmonieuse smaakevolutie door nagisting in de fles.
Store at cellar temperature for an optimal taste evolution.	Conserver à température de cave pour une évolution optimale de la saveur.	Bewaren op keldertemperatuur voor een optimale smaakevolutie.

Mongozo Banana

Brouwerij Huyghe 4,50% 4 39

top-fermentation	fermentation haute	hoge gisting
white beer with exotic fruit	bière blanche avec fruits exotiques	witbier met exotisch fruit
barley malt, fair trade organic bananas and quinoa, yeast, hops, sugar, water. Made with mangozo quinoa and banana.	malt d'orge, bananes biologiques fairtrade, quinoa, levure, houblon, sucre, eau. Faite à base de mangozo quinoa et de bananes.	gerstemout, fairtrade biologische bananen en quinoa, gist, hop, suiker, water. Gemaakt op basis van mangozo quinoa waaraan banaan is toegevoegd.
dark-yellow cloudy	jaune foncée trouble	donkergeel troebel
Banana flavour and aroma.	Saveur et arômes de banane.	Smaak en aroma van banaan.
Serve in an exotic coconut glass.	Verser dans le verre exotique noix de coco.	Uitschenken in het exotische kokosnootglas.

Mongozo Coconut

rouwerij Huyghe

3,50% 4 °C 39 °F

	top-fermentation	fermentation haute	hoge gisting
	white beer with exotic fruit	bière blanche avec fruits exotiques	witbier met exotisch fruit
	barley malt, fair trade organic quinoa (African grain species), coconut, yeast, hops, flavouring, water. Made with mangozo quinoa and natural coconut juice.	malt d'orge, quinoa biologique fairtrade (type de blé africain), noix de coco, levure, houblon, arômes, eau. Faite à base de mangozo quinoa et de jus naturel de noix de coco.	gerstemout, fairtrade biologische quinoa (Afrikaanse graansoort), kokosnoot, gist, hop, aroma's, water. Gemaakt op basis van mangozo quinoa waaraan natuurlijk kokosvruchtvleessap is toegevoegd.
	yellow-white cloudy	blanc jaune trouble	geelwit troebel
	Coconut flavour and aroma.	Saveur et arôme de noix de coco.	Smaak en aroma van kokosnoot.
	Serve in an exotic coconut glass.	Verser dans le verre exotique noix de coco.	Uitschenken in het exotische kokosnootglas.
i			

Mongozo Mango

Brouwerij Huyghe 3,60% 5 41

	top-fermentation	fermentation haute	hoge gisting
	white beer with exotic fruit	bière blanche aux fruits exotiques	witbier met exotisch fruit
	malt, wheat, fairtrade mango, yeast, different hops, sugar, water	malt, froment, mangue fairtrade, levure, variétés de houblon, sucre, eau	mout, tarwe, fairtrade mango, gist, hopsoorten, suiker, water
	dark yellow with solid foam head not filtered, pasteurised	jaune foncé avec faux col solide non filtrée, pasteurisée	donkergeel met stevige schuimkraag ongefilterd, gepasteuriseerd
	Fresh, exotic mango taste.	Goût de mangue frais, exotique.	Frisse, exotische mangosmaak.
	Serve in an exotic coconut glass.	Verser dans le verre exotique noix de coco.	Uitschenken in het exotische kokosnootglas.
i	Exotic beer with fairtrade mango. Brewed under licence on behalf of Mongozo BV in the Netherlands.	Une bière exotique avec de la mangue du commerce équitable. Brassée sous licence pour Mongozo BV aux Pays-Bas.	Exotisch bier met fairtrade mango. Onder licentie gebrouwen voor Mongozo BV in Nederland.

7% 4 °C 39 °F

	top-fermentation	fermentation haute	hoge gisting
	white beer with exotic fruit	bière blanche avec fruits exotiques	witbier met exotisch fruit
	barley malt, fair trade organic palm nuts and quinoa, yeast, hops, sugar, water. Made with mangozo quinoa and palm nut.	malt d'orge, noix de palmier biologiques fair-trade, quinoa, levure, houblon, sucre, eau. Faite à base de mangozo quinoa et de noix de palmier.	gerstemout, fairtrade biologische palmnoten en quinoa, gist, hop, suiker, water. Gemaakt op basis van mangozo quinoa waaraan palmnut is toegevoegd.
	amber-coloured	ambrée	amberkleurig
	Palm nut flavour and aroma.	Saveur et arôme de noix de palmier.	Smaak en aroma van palmnut.
	Serve in an exotic coconut glass.	Verser dans le verre exotique noix de coco.	Uitschenken in het exotische kokosnootglas.
i			

Mongozo Premium Pilsener

Brouwerij Huyghe

5% 5 41

bottom-fermentation centrifuged	fermentation basse centrifugée	lage gisting gecentrifugeerd
pilsner or lager beer	pils ou lager	pils- of lagerbier
barley malt, rice, yeast, hops water	malt d'orge, riz, levure, houblon, eau	gerstemout, rijst, gist, hop, water
pale blond with solid foam head filtered, pasteurised	blond clair avec faux col solide filtrée, pasteurisée	lichtblond met stevige schuimkraag gefilterd, gepasteuri-seerd
Full-bodied, slightly bitter pilsner.	Pils franche, légèrement amère.	Volmondig, licht bittere pils.
Serve in a flute glass.	Verser dans une flûte.	Uitschenken in een fluit-glas.
Organic, gluten-free fairtrade pilsner. Brewed under licence on behalf of Mongozo BV in the Netherlands. First and only pilsner with 3 logos: gluten-free, organic and fairtrade.	Pils biologique du com-merce équitable sans gluten. Brassée sous li-cence pour Mongozo BV aux Pays-Bas. Première et unique pils dotée de 3 logos :sans gluten, bio et commerce équitable.	Biologische, glutenvrije fairtrade pils. Onder li-centie gebrouwen voor Mongozo BV in Neder-land. Eerste en enige pils met 3 logo's: glutenvrij, bio en fairtrade.

rouwerij Huyghe

5,90% | 4 °C 39 °F

Mongozo Quinua

top-fermentation	fermentation haute	hoge gisting
white beer with exotic fruit	bière blanche avec fruits exotiques	witbier met exotisch fruit
malt, fair trade organic quinoa, yeast, hops, sugar, water	malt, quinoa biologique fairtrade, levure, houblon, sucre, eau	mout, fairtrade biologische quinoa, gist, hop, suiker, water
pilsner colour clear	pils claire	pilskleur helder
Serve in an exotic coconut glass.	Verser dans le verre exotique noix de coco.	Uitschenken in het exotische kokosnootglas.

M Monk's Stout

Brasserie Dupont 5,20%

	top-fermentation re-fermentation in the bottle	fermentation haute refermentation en bouteille	hoge gisting hergisting in de fles
	stout	stout	stout
	barley and wheat malt, sugar, hops, yeast, water	malt d'orge et de fro-ment, sucre, houblon, levure, eau	gerste- en tarwemout, suiker, hop, gist, water
	Dry and light stout with a distinct presence of roasted malt and English hops.	Stout sèche et légère, avec une présence claire de malt torréfié et de houblon anglais.	Droge en lichte stout met duidelijke aanwezigheid van gebrande mout en Engelse hop.
	A stout from the 50s which was very popular and which has recently been revived.	Une stout des années '50 qui était fort populaire et qui s'est vu insuffler récemment une nouvelle vie.	Een stout uit de jaren '50 die zeer populair was en die recent nieuw leven ingeblazen kreeg.

Montagnarde

rasserie de l'Abbaye des Rocs — 9% (20° plato) — 12 °C / 54 °F

	top-fermentation	fermentation haute	hoge gisting
	tripel	triple	tripel
	malt (pale, Münich), hops (Hallertau, Brewers Gold), well water from a rocky subsoil	malt (pâle, Münich), houblon (Hallertau, Bre-wers Gold), eau de puits d'un sous-sol rocailleux	mout (bleek, Münich), hop (Hallertau, Brewers Gold), boorputwater uit een rotsrijke ondergrond
	light amber	ambré clair	licht amber
	A touch of hops.	Touche de houblon.	Toets van hop.
	Savour in a bulb jar.	Déguster dans un verre ballon.	Degusteren uit een bal-lonvormig glas.
i	The abbey 'L'Abbaye des Rocs' dates back from the 12th century. The beer keeps for about a year in a dark room. Montagnard is the name given to the inhabitants of the region.	'L'Abbaye des Rocs' date du 12ième siècle. La bière se conserve en-viron un an à l'abri de la lumière. Montagnard est le nom donné aux habitants de la région.	De abdij 'L'Abbaye des Rocs' dateert uit de 12e eeuw. Het bier is ongeveer een jaar houdbaar in een donkere ruimte. Montagnard is de naam die gegeven wordt aan de inwoners uit de regio.

Morpheus Dark

Picobrouwerij Alvinne 10,20% 10 - 12 50 - 54

	top-fermentation re-fermentation in the bottle	fermentation haute refermentation en bouteille	hoge gisting hergisting in de fles
	7 different malts, 2 different hops (Magnum and EK Goldings), yeast, candy sugar, water	7 variétés de malt, 2 variétés de houblon, (Magnum et EK Goldings), levure, sucre candi, eau	7 moutsoorten, 2 hopsoorten (Magnum en EK Goldings), gist, kandijsuiker, water
	165 EBC	165 EBC	165 EBC
	47 EBU	47 EBU.	47 EBU

cobrouwerij Alvinne 7,10% 8 - 10 °C / 46 - 50 °F

Morpheus Extra

	top-fermentation re-fermentation in the bottle	fermentation haute refermentation en bouteille	hoge gisting hergisting in de fles
	3 malt types, 2 different hops (Chinook and Cascade), yeast, water	3 variétés de malt, 2 variétés de houblon (Chinook et Cascade), levure, eau	3 moutsoorten, 2 hopsoorten (Chinook en Cascade), gist, water
	8 EBC	8 EBC	8 EBC
	68 EBU	68 EBU.	68 EBU

Morpheus Tripel

Picobrouwerij Alvinne 8,70% 10 - 1 50 - 5

	top-fermentation re-fermentation in the bottle	fermentation haute refermentation en bouteille	hoge gisting hergisting in de fles
	tripel	triple	tripel
	4 different malts, 2 different hops (Magnum and EK Goldings), yeast, granulated sugar, water	4 variétés de malt, 2 variétés de houblon, (Magnum et EK Goldings), levure, sucre cristallisé, eau	4 moutsoorten, 2 hopsoorten (Magnum en EK Goldings), gist, kristalsuiker, water
	19 EBC	19 EBC	19 EBC
	35 EBU	35 EBU.	35 EBU

Morpheus Wild

:cobrouwerij Alvinne 5,90% 8 - 10 °C / 46 - 50 °F

	top-fermentation re-fermentation in the bottle	fermentation haute refermentation en bouteille	hoge gisting hergisting in de fles
	Flemish old brown	bière Flamande vieille brune	Vlaams oud bruin
	malt, hops, yeast, water	malt, levure, houblon, eau	mout, gist, hop, water
	99 EBC	99 EBC	99 EBC

Mort Subite Gueuze

Brouwerij Alken-Maes

4,50% 2 - 4 / 36 - 39

	spontaneous fermentation re-fermented in the bottle	fermentation spontanée refermentation en bouteille	spontane gisting nagisting op de fles
	gueuze	gueuze	geuze
	gold-yellow clear, filtered	jaune doré claire, filtrée	goudgeel helder, gefilterd
	Spicy, sweet-and-sour and thirst-quenching.	Désaltérant corsé, aigre-doux.	Pittige, zuurzoete dorst-lesser.
	Empty in a degreased, rinsed and wet glass. Let overflow and skim off the foam.	Verser complètement dans un verre dégraissé, rincé et mouillé. Laisser déborder et écumer.	Helemaal uitschenken in een ontvet, gespoeld en nat glas. Laten overlo-pen en afschuimen.
	Matured in oak barrels.	Mûrit en fûts de chêne.	Gerijpt op eiken vaten.

Mort Subite Kriek

ouwerij Alken-Maes — 4,50% — 2 - 4 °C / 36 - 39 °F

	spontaneous fermentation	fermentation spontanée	spontane gisting
	fruit beer	bière fruitée	fruitbier
	bright-red	rouge vif	helrood
	Refreshing, sweet-and-sour with the taste of fresh cherries.	Fraîche et aigre-douce avec une saveur de cerises fraîches.	Fris zuurzoet met de smaak van verse krieken.
	Empty in a degreased, rinsed and wet glass. Let overflow and skim off the foam.	Verser complètement dans un verre dégraissé, rincé et mouillé. Laisser déborder et écumer.	Helemaal uitschenken in een ontvet, gespoeld en nat glas. Laten overlopen en afschuimen.
	Authentic blend of old and young lambic with Belgian cherries added.	Mélange authentique de vieux et de jeune lambic auxquels sont ajoutées des cerises belges.	Authentieke mengeling van oude en jonge lambiek waaraan Belgische krieken zijn toegevoegd.

Mort Subite Oude Gueuze

Brouwerij Alken-Maes 7% 10 - 16 / 50 - 61

	spontaneous fermentation re-fermented in the bottle	fermentation spontanée refermentation en bouteille	spontane gisting nagisting op de fles
	gueuze	gueuze	geuze
	blend of old and young Lambic	mélange de vieux et de jeune lambic	mengeling van oude en jonge lambiek
	unfiltered, 100% re-fermented in the bottle	non filtrée avec 100% de refermentation en bouteille	ongefilterd met 100% hergisting op de fles
	Fresh and spicy citric character, no sweetening.	Caractère d'agrumes frais et corsé. Pas sucrée.	Fris en pittig citruskarakter zonder zoet.
	Empty carefully and leave a small amount in the bottle.	Verser prudemment et laisser un peu de fond dans la bouteille.	Voorzichtig uitschenken en een kleine bodem in de fles laten.
i			

Mort Subite Oude Kriek

ɔuwerij Alken-Maes 6,50%

spontaneous fermentation	fermentation spontanée	spontane gisting
fruit beer	bière fruitée	fruitbier
lambic (barley malt, wheat, hops, water) with 25% fresh Belgian cherries	lambic (malt d'orge, froment, houblon, eau) avec 25% de cerises belges fraîches	lambiek (gerstemout, tarwe, hop, water) met 25% verse Belgische krieken
bright red	rouge vif	helrood
Fresh-tart thirst-quencher with full cherry flavour.	Bière désaltérante fraîchement acidulée, avec un goût franc de griottes.	Friszurige dorstlesser met volle kriekensmaak.
Empty carefully and leave a small amount in the bottle.	Verser prudemment et laisser un peu de fond dans la bouteille.	Voorzichtig uitschenken en een kleine bodem in de fles laten.
The name Mort Subitet refers to the last throw in the dice game 'mort subite' that was played at the Brussels Café 'La Cour Royale'.	Le nom Mort Subite renvoie au dernier coup dans le jeu de dés 'mort subite' joué dans le café bruxellois 'La Cour Royale'.	De naam Mort Subite verwijst naar de laatste worp in het teerlingspel 'mort subite' dat gespeeld werd in het Brussels Café 'La Cour Royale'.

Mort Subite Xtreme Framboise

Brouwerij Alken-Maes 4,20% 2 - 4 / 36 - 39

	spontaneous fermentation	fermentation spontanée	spontane gisting
	fruit beer	bière fruitée	fruitbier
	pink champagne	champagne rose	roze champagne
	Extra fruity. Full-bodied sweet and fruity raspberry taste.	Extra fruitée. Saveur de framboises franche, douce et fruitée.	Extra fruitig. Volmondig zoete en fruitige frambozensmaak.
	Empty in a degreased, rinsed and wet glass. Let overflow and skim off the foam.	Verser complètement dans un verre dégraissé, rincé et mouillé. Laisser déborder et écumer.	Helemaal uitschenken in een ontvet, gespoeld en nat glas. Laten overlopen en afschuimen.
i			

Mort Subite Xtreme Kriek

uwerij Alken-Maes

4,30% 2 - 4 °C 36 - 39 °F

	spontaneous fermentation	fermentation spontanée	spontane gisting
	fruit beer	bière fruitée	fruitbier
	bright-red	rouge vif	felrood
	Extra fruity. Full-bodied sweet and fruity cherry taste.	Extra fruitée. Saveur de cerises franche, sucrée et fruitée.	Extra fruitig. Volmondig zoete en fruitige kriekensmaak.
	Empty in a degreased, rinsed and wet glass. Let overflow and skim off the foam.	Verser complètement dans un verre dégraissé, rincé et mouillé. Laisser déborder et écumer.	Helemaal uitschenken in een ontvet, gespoeld en nat glas. Laten overlopen en afschuimen.

Moulin de Hollange - Blonde d’Epeautre

Brasserie Artisanale Millevertus 6%

	top-fermentation	fermentation haute	hoge gisting
	blond spelt beer	bière blonde épeautre	blond speltbier
	malt, spelt, hops, yeast, water	malt, épeautre, houblon, levure, eau	mout, spelt, hop, gist, water

Scheldebrouwerij 5% 6 - 8 °C / 43 - 46 °F

	top-fermentation re-fermentation in the bottle	fermentation haute refermentation en bouteille	hoge gisting hergisting inde fles
	blond specialty beer	blonde spéciale	blond speciaalbier
	barley malt, Münchner malt, hops, yeast, water. Beer with dry-hopping.	malt d'orge, malt Mü-nich, houblon, levure, eau. Bière avec dry-hopping.	gerstemout, Münche-nermout, hop, gist, wa-ter. Bier met dry-hopping
	blond (18 EBC), slightly cloudy with generous, white foam head not filtered or pasteur-ised	blonde (18 EBC), légère-ment trouble avec faux col large blanc non filtrée, non pasteu-risée	blond (18 EBC), licht troebel met ruime, witte schuimkraag ongefilterd, niet gepas-teuriseerd
	Pronounced hoppy nose. Soft bitter taste with a long, tangy aftertaste. 30 EBU.	Bouquet houblonné pro-noncé. Goût doux-amer, avec une longue fin de bouche qui s'écoule avec un peu d'amertume. 30 EBU.	Uitgesproken hoppige neus. Zachtbittere smaak met een lange na-smaak die bitterig uit-vloeit. 30 EBU
	Was developed in 1988 by 'Barend van de Mug' from Milddelburg. De Mug is a well-known café-hotel-restaurant.	Elle a été développée en 1988 par 'Barend van de Mug' de Milddelburg. Le Mug est un célèbre café-hôtel-restaurant.	Werd in 1988 ontwikkeld door 'Barend van de Mug' uit Milddelburg. De Mug is een beroemd café-ho-tel-restaurant.

M

Mystic Krieken

Brouwerij Haacht 3,50% 3

	top-fermentation	fermentation haute	hoge gisting
	witbier with fruit	bière blanche fruitée	witbier met fruit
	barley malt, wheat malt, unmalted wheat, sugar, hops, herbs, yeast, fructose, cherry juice (25 %) water, acesulfame K (sweetener), natural flavouring	malt d'orge, froment, houblon, levure, jus de cerises (25 %) concentré, fructose, édulcorant (acesulfamide K), arômes, eau	gerstemout, tarwe, hop, gist, kriekensap (25%) uit concentraat, fructose, zoetstof (acesulfaam K), aroma's, water
	clear red filtered	rouge vif filtrée	helder rood gefilterd
	Powerful taste of cherries, combined with the freshness of a witbier. Fruity-sour onset, turning smoothly into a slightly sweet, non-sticky aftertaste.	Goût corsé de cerises avec la fraîcheur d'une bière blanche. Goût initial fruité, acidulé passant doucement à une fin de bouche légèrement douce, non collante.	Krachtige smaak van krieken gecombineerd met de frisheid van een witbier. Fruitzure aanzet die zachtjes overvloeit in een licht zoete, niet kleverige afdronk.
	Pour carefully into a rinsed, wet Mystic glass, avoiding contact between bottle and foam.	Verser prudemment dans un verre Mystic rincé et mouillé sans que la bouteille touche l'écume.	Voorzichtig uitschenken in een gespoeld, nat Mysticglas zonder dat de fles het schuim raakt.
i			

Mystic Limoen

rouwerij Haacht

3,80% 3 °C / 37 °F

	top-fermentation	fermentation haute	hoge gisting
	witbier with fruit	bière blanche fruitée	witbier met fruit
	barley malt, wheat, hops, yeast, apply juice, lemon and lime aromas, water, citric acid, sweeteners (acesulfaam K), water	malt d'orge, froment, houblon, levure, fructose, jus de pommes, arômes de citron et de citron vert, eau, acide alimentaire (acide citrique), édulcorant (acésulfamide K), eau	gerstemout, tarwe, hop, gist, fructose, appelsap, citroen- en limoenaroma's, water, voedingszuur (citroenzuur), zoetstof (acesulfaam K), water
	slightly cloudy foam head with fine bubbles unfiltered	légèrement trouble faux col avec des bulles fines non filtrée	licht troebel schuimkraag met fijne bellen ongefilterd
	Intense, spicy thirst-quencer. The citrus fruits provide a soft tingling sensation, with pleasant sweet touch and a refreshing aftertaste.	Bière désaltérante corsée, épicée. Les agrumes engendrent un doux picotement, avec une agréable touche sucrée et une arrière-bouche rafraîchissante.	Pittige, kruidige dorstlesser. De citrusvruchten zorgen voor een zachte prikkeling, met aangename zoete toets en een verfrissende afdronk.
	Pour 3/4 into a rinsed, wet glass. Revolve the remainder of the beer in the bottle to loosen up the yeast sediment and pour out.	Verser 3/4 dans un verre rincé, humide. Remuer le restant de la bière dans la bouteille pour dégager le fond de levure et verser.	3/4 uitschenken in een gespoeld, nat glas. Het resterende bier walsen in de fles om de gistbodem los te maken en uitschenken.
i			

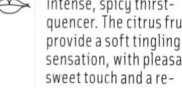

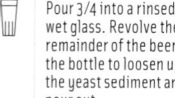

Mystic Witbier met Perzik

Brouwerij Haacht 3,70% 3 37

	top-fermentation	fermentation haute	hoge gisting
	white beer with fruit	bière blanche fruitée	witbier met fruit
	barley malt, wheat, hops, yeast, peach juice (26%) from concentrate, fructose, natural peach aroma, sweetener (acesulfame K), water	malt d'orge, froment, houblon, levure, jus de pêches (26%) concentré, fructose, arôme de pêches naturel, édulcorant (acésulfate K), eau	gerstemout, tarwe, hop, gist, perzikensap (26%) uit concentraat, fructose, natuurlijk perzikenaroma, zoetstof (acesulfaam K), water
	slightly cloudy, foam head with fine bubbles not filtered	légèrement trouble, faux col à bulles fines non filtrée	licht troebel, schuimkraag met fijne bellen ongefilterd
	Refreshing with subtle sweetness. Sunripened peaches and white beer as a counterbalance.	Rafraîchissante, avec une saveur sucrée subtile. Pêches mûries au soleil et bière blanche en compensation.	Verfrissend met subtiele zoetigheid. Zongerijpte perziken en witbier als tegengewicht.
	Pour 3/4 into a rinsed, wet glass. Swish the remaining beer in the bottle to release the yeast sediment and pour out.	Verser 3/4 dans un verre rincé mouillé. Remuer le restant de la bière pour détacher le résidu de levure et verser.	3/4 uitschenken in een gespoeld, nat glas. Het resterende bier walsen in de fles om de gistbodem los te maken en uitschenken.
i			

9,50% 10 °C 50 °F

	top-fermentation re-fermentation in the bottle	fermentation haute refermentation en bouteille	hoge gisting hergisting inde fles
	quattro (quadruple)	quattro (quadruple)	quattro (quadruple)
	barley malt, cara 20, hops, yeast, water	malt de pils, cara 20, houblon, levure, eau	pilsmout, cara 20, hop, gist, water
	blond gold-yellow (24 EBC), clear with white tufty foam head	jaune doré blond (24 EBC), claire avec faux col blanc, rocailleux	blond goudgeel (24 EBC), helder met wit, rotsachtig schuim
	Fruit-malty aroma and soft, sweet-fruity flavour with a modest bitter touch. Slightly bitter lingering aftertaste. 30 EBU.	Arôme malté fruité et goût doux, douceâtre et fruité, avec une petite amertume discrète. Fin de bouche s'écoulant en légère amertume. 30 EBU.	Fruitmoutig aroma en zachte, zoetigfruitige smaak met een bescheiden bittertje. Lichtbitter uitvloeiende nasmaak. 30 EBU.
i	Refers to the legend where one of the madmen, after drinking a Toeback, makes off with St Catherine's church in Hoogstraten. That 'Toeback' is therefore a magic potion ...	Fait référence à la légende où, après avoir bu une Toeback, un des Ogres s'en va se promener avec l'église Sainte-Catherine d'Hoogstraten. Une boisson miraculeuse donc que cette 'n Toeback...	Verwijst naar de legende waarbij een van de Wildemannen na het drinken van 'n Toeback met de Sint-Katarinakerk uit Hoogstraten op wandel gaat. Een wonderdrank dus die 'n Toeback...

Naked Ladies

Picobrouwerij Alvinne 4,40% 8 - 10 / 46 - 50

top-fermentation natural re-fermentation in the bottle	fermentation haute refermentation naturelle en bouteille	hoge gisting natuurlijke hergisting in de fles
15 EBC	15 EBC	15 EBC
46 EBU	46 EBU.	46 EBU
Partnership between Alvinne and Twickenham Fine Ales' main brewers	Collaboration entre Alvinne et les brasseurs en chef de Twickenham Fine Ales.	Samenwerking tussen Alvinne en de hoofdbrouwers van Twickenham Fine Ales

Ne Snoeper

Hofbrouwerijke 10%

	top-fermentation	fermentation haute	hoge gisting
	tripel	triple	tripel
	malt, hops, yeast, sugar, water	malt, houblon, levure, sucre, eau	mout, hop, gist, suiker, water
	Brewed for the card-playing club De Snoepers.	Brassée pour le club de joueurs de cartes De Snoepers.	Gebrouwen voor kaart-club De Snoepers.

Nen Bangelijke

Brouwerij 't Pakhuis

8 - 8,50% 2 - 3 36 - 37

	top-fermentation not centrifuged	fermentation haute non centrifugée	hoge gisting niet gecentrifugeerd
	strong blond	blonde forte	sterk blond
	malt, barley, hop, water	malt, orge, houblon, eau	mout, gerst, hop, water
	light blond and cloudy; filtered, not pasteurised	blonde clair, très voilée; filtrée, non pasteurisée	licht blond met zeer duidelijke troebele schijn e mooie schuimkraag; gefilterd, niet gepasteu riseerd
	Strong, hoppy beer; full-bodied with a wonderfully hopped mellow aftertaste.	Bière forte, lourdement houblonnée, avec une riche plénitude et une arrière-bouche d'une douceur exquise.	Sterk, zwaar gehopt bier met een rijke volmondigheid en een heerlijke zachte afdronk.
	Pour into a bulb glass with a short stem.	Verser dans un verre ballon à pied bas.	Uitschenken in een bol glas op lage voet.
	Only available at the brewery. When tasting the first beer, a beer conoisseur is known to have exclaimed: 'Da's een bangelijke goei pint!' ('That's a frightfully good beer!'). And that is how the beer acquired its name...	Seulement en vente à la brasserie. En goûtant le premier brassin, un fin connaisseur de la bière a eu la réaction suivante : 'Da's een bangelijke goei pint' ('Voilà un bon demi peureux!'). Le nom de la bière était trouvé...	Enkel verkrijgbaar in de brouwerij. Bij het proeven van het eerste brouwsel, gaf ee bierkenner volgende reactie: 'da's een bangelij ke goei pint!'. En metee was de naam van het bie gekozen...

acas at a nearby brewery

8% 6 °C 43 °F

	top-fermentation re-fermentation in the bottle	fermentation haute refermentation en bouteille	hoge gisting hergisting in de fles
	barley malt, hops, yeast, herbs, water	malt d'orge, houblon, levure, herbes, eau	gerstemout, hop, gist, kruiden, water
	Pour slowly into a degreased glass without sloshing the beer.	Verser lentement dans un verre dégraissé sans clapotage de la bière.	Traag inschenken in een ontvet glas zonder dat het bier klokt.
	Only available from De Bierloods.	Seulement en vente chez De Bierloods.	Enkel verkrijgbaar bij De Bierloods.

Nen Uts

Hoevebrouwers by Brouwerij De Graal 7% 6 - 10 / 43 - 50

	top-fermentation re-fermentation in the bottle	fermentation haute refermentation en bouteille	hoge gisting hergisting inde fles
	amber or speciale belge	ambrée ou spéciale belge	amber of speciale belge
	malt (pilsner, wheat, cara red), hops (East Kent Goldings, Hallertau Mittelfrüh), yeast (T58), water	malt (pils, froment, cara red), houblon (East Kent Goldings, Hallertau Mittelfrüh), levure (T58), eau	mout (pils,tarwe, cara red), hop (East Kent Goldings, Hallertau Mittelfrüh), gist (T58), water
	amber, slightly pearly with creamy foam head	ambrée, légèrement pétillante avec faux col crémeux	amber, lichtparelend met romige schuimkraag
	Sipping beer with a malty onset that turns into a bitter aftertaste with distinct hoppy touches in the nose.	Bière de dégustation d'une approche initiale maltée, qui se transforme en une arrière-bouche amère, avec des touches houblonnées claires dans le bouquet.	Degustatiebier met een moutige aanzet die overgaat in een bittere afdronk met duidelijke hoptoetsen in de neus.
	Pour in a single movement into a degreased goblet. Leave approx. 1 cm of the yeast sediment in the bottle.	Verser d'un seul mouvement dans un verre calice dégraissé. Laisser ca. 1 cm de dépôt de levure dans la bouteille.	In 1 beweging uitschenken in een vetvrij kelkglas. Ca. 1 cm gistdepot in de fles laten.
i	Nen Uts' means 'a hedgehog' in the local dialect.	'Nen Uts' veut dire 'un hérisson' en dialecte local.	Nen Uts' betekent 'een egel' in het plaatselijke dialect.

ꞌrouwerij Gulden Spoor

6,50% | 8 - 10 °C / 46 - 50 °F

	top-fermentation re-fermented in the bottle	fermentation haute refermentation en bouteille	hoge gisting hergisting in de fles
	strong blond to amber	blonde à ambrée forte	sterk blond tot amber
	barley malt, wheat, hops, sugar, yeast, water	malt d'orge, froment, houblon, sucre, levure, eau	gerstemout, tarwe, hop, suiker, gist, water
	golden blond slightly cloudy unpasteurised	blond doré légèrement trouble non pasteurisée	goudblond licht troebel niet gepasteuriseerd
	Full-bodied thrist-quencher. Full and mild mouthfeel with a lively hoppy touch and refreshing bitter-ness.	Désaltérant franc. Pleine et tendre dans la bouche avec une touche de houblon corsée et un goût amer rafraîchis-sant.	Volmondige dorstlesser. Vol en mild in de mond met een pittige toets van hop die de bitterheid fris laat uitvloeien.
	Degrease the glass and hold it slightly tilted whilst pouring. Pour the beer carefully in one single movement.	Dégraisser le verre et le tenir légèrement incliné au moment de verser. Verser la bière prudem-ment en un seul mouve-ment.	Het glas vetvrij maken en licht schuin houden tij-dens het inschenken. Het bier voorzichtig in 1 beweging uitschenken.
i			

Newton

Brasserie Lefebvre 3,50% 1 - 4° 34 - 39°

	top-fermentation centrifuged	fermentation haute centrifugée	hoge gisting gecentrifugeerd
	witbier with fruit	bière blanche fruitée	witbier met fruit
	barley malt, wheat, hops, apple juice, sugar, yeast, flavouring, water	malt d'orge, froment, houblon, jus de pommes, sucre, levure, arômes, eau	gerstemout, tarwe, hop, appelsap, suiker, gist, aroma's, water
	very pale slightly hazy pasteurised	très pâle légèrement voilée pasteurisée	zeer bleek licht gesluierd gepasteuriseerd
	Aroma and taste of green apples, slichtly tart. A marriage of white beer and apple.	Arôme et goût de pommes vertes, légèrement acidulées. Un mariage de bière blanche et de pomme.	Aroma en smaak van groene appels, licht aangezuurd. Een huwelijk van witbier met appel.
	Pour into a conic glass or drink straight from the bottle.	Verser dans un verre conique ou boire à la bouteille.	Uitschenken in een konisch glas of uit de fles drinken.
i			

uvel Moortgat Corporation

10% — 12 °C / 54 °F

	top-fermentation	fermentation haute	hoge gisting
	regional beer winter beer	bière régionale bière hivernale	streekbier winterbier
	malt, hops, sugar, thyme, curaçao rind, yeast, water	malt, houblon, sucre, thym, écorce de curaçao, levure, eau	mout, hop, suiker, tijm, curaçaoschil, gist, water
	dark unfiltered	foncée non filtrée	donker ongefilterd
	Warm character.	Caractère réchauffant.	Verwarmend karaker.

N'ice Chouffe

De dochter van de Korenaar

5,50% 8° 46°

	top-fermentation re-fermented in the bottle not centrifuged	fermentation haute refermentation en bouteille non centrifugée	hoge gisting hergisting in de fles niet gecentrifugeerd
	cross between Köllsch and Pale Ale	mélange de Köllsch et de pale ale	kruising van Köllsch en pale ale
	barley malt, wheat malt, 3 hop varieties, brewer's yeast, water	malt d'orge, malt de froment, 3 sortes de houblon, levure de bière, eau	gerstemout, tarwemout, 3 soorten hop, biergist, water
	blond clear but unfiltered	blonde claire mais non filtrée	blond helder maar ongefilterd
	Firmly hopped beer with a good combination of spicy, bitter and sweet touches. A solid session beer as well as a sipping beer to be enjoyed at ease.	Bière fort houblonnée avec une bonne combinaison de nuances relevées, amères et légèrement douces. A la fois une bière facilement buvable que de dégustation dont on profite lentement.	Stevig gehopt bier met een goede combinatie van kruidige/bittere en zachtzoete nuances. Zowel een stevig doordrinkbier als een degustatiebier waar je langzaam van geniet.
	Leave the yeast sediment in the bottle.	Laisser le dépôt de levure dans la bouteille.	Het gistdepot in de fles laten.
i			

e Dochter van de Korenaar

7% 5 - 6 °C 41 - 43 °F

	top-fermentation re-fermentation in the bottle not centrifuged	fermentation haute refermentation en bouteille non centrifugée	hoge gisting hergisting in de fles niet gecentrifugeerd
	mild IPA	IPA douce	milde IPA
	barley malt, wheat malt, yeast, hops water. With dry-hopping.	malt d'orge, malt de froment, levure, houblon, eau. Avec dry hopping.	gerstemout, tarwemout, gist, hop, water. Met dry-hopping.
	not filtered or pasteurised	non filtrée, non pasteurisée	ongefilterd, niet gepasteuriseerd
	Distinct hoppy flavour due to dry-hopping.	Bière d'un caractère houblonné prononcé, du fait du houblonnage à cru.	Bier met uitgesproken hopkarakter door de dry-hopping.

Noël de Silenrieux

Brasserie de Silenrieux 9% 7 - 9 ° 45 - 48 °

	top-fermentation natural re-fermentation in the bottle	fermentation haute refermentation naturelle en bouteille	hoge gisting natuurlijke hergisting in de fles
	tripel strong dubbel	triple double forte	tripel sterk bruin
	barley malt, hops, brown candy sugar, yeast, water	malt d'orge, houblon, sucre de candi brun, levure, eau	gerstemout, hop, bruine kandijsuiker, gist, water
	very dark with red glow filtered, not pasteurised	très foncé à reflet rouge filtrée, non pasteurisée	zeer donker met rode schijn gefilterd, niet gepasteuriseerd
	Prevalent and mild. Typical winter beer	Corsée et généreuse. Bière hivernale typique.	Gecorseerd en mild. Typisch winterbier.
	Tilt the glass slightly and pour out the beer gently. Leave a little in the bottle and pour out afterwards for a fine foam head.	Tenir le verre en position verticale et verser la bière prudemment. Garder un restant dans la bouteille et puis le verser pour former un faux col solide.	Het glas recht houden en het bier voorzichtig uitschenken. Een restje in de fles houden en dan uitschenken voor een mooie schuimkraag.
i			

rouwerij De Ranke

9%

Noir de Dottignies

top-fermentation re-fermentation in the bottle not centrifuged	fermentation haute refermentation en bouteille non centrifugée	hoge gisting hergisting in de fles niet gecentrifugeerd
strong dubbel	foncée forte	sterk donker
7 different malts (pilsner, pale ale, Münich, cara, crystal, chocolate, roasted), hops (Challenger and Styrian Goldings)	7 variétés de malt (pils, pale ale, Münich, cara, crystal, chocolat, torréfié), houblon (Challenger en Styrian Goldings)	7 moutsoorten (pils, pale ale, Münich, cara, chrystal, chocolat, gebrand), hop (Challenger en Styrian Goldings)
very dark not filtered or pasteurised	très foncé non filtrée, non pasteurisée	zeer donker ongefilterd, niet gepasteuriseerd
Very complex malt flavours with touches of chocolate, coffee and chicory.	Goûts de malt fort complexes, avec des touches de chocolat, de café et de chicorée.	Zeer complexe moutsmaken met toetsen van chocolade, koffie en cichorei.

Montaigu by 't Hofbrouwerijke

10,70% 8 - 10 ° 46 - 50 °

(fermentation)	top-fermentation re-fermentation in the bottle	fermentation haute refermentation en bouteille	hoge gisting hergisting in de fles
(type)	Belgian tripel	triple belge	Belgische tripel
(ingredients)	barley malt, sugar, hops, yeast, water	malt d'orge, sucre, houblon, levure, eau	gerstemout, suiker, hop, gist, water
(appearance)			
(taste)			
(glass)			
(info)			

rouwerij Donum Ignis 8,10% 6 - 8 °C / 43 - 46 °F

	top-fermentation re-fermentation in the bottle; not centrifuged	fermentation haute refermentation en bouteille; non centrifugée	hoge gisting hergisting in de fles; niet gecentrifugeerd
	boutique strong blond city or regional beer	artisanale blonde forte bière citadine ou régionale	artisanaal sterk blond stads- of streekbier
	4 different malts, 4 different hops (quadruple hops), beer yeast, candy sugar, water. Dry-hopping with aromatic hops during storage.	4 variétés de malt, 4 variétés de houblon (houblon quattro), levure de bière, sucre candi, eau. Dry-hopping avec houblon aromatique lors du lagering.	4 moutsoorten, 4 hopsoorten (quattro-hop), biergist, kandijsuiker, water. Dry-hopping met aromahop tijdens het lageren.
	amber blond, naturally cloudy with a creamy foam head; not filtered or pasteurised	blond ambré, trouble naturel avec un faux col crémeux; non filtrée ni pasteurisée	amberblond, natuurtroebel met een romige schuimkraag; ongefilterd, ongepasteuriseerd
	Aroma: Refreshing, hoppy and fruity Taste: full-bodied, citrus-sweet hops, hoppy aroma in the mouth (dry-hopping) Aftertaste: pleasant bitter flavour full of character	Arôme : rafraîchissant, houblonné et fruité. Goût : franc, citrus doux, sensation en bouche de houblon aromatique (houblonnage à cru). Arrière-bouche : très caractéristique, amertume agréable.	Aroma: verfrissend, hoppig en fruitig Smaak: volmondig, cituszoete hoppigheid, aromahoppig mondgevoel (dry-hopping) Afdronk: karaktervolle, aangename bitterheid
	Pour out slowly against the edge of a tilted goblet. To increase the foam head, pour the beer in the centre (of the glass).	Verser lentement contre le bord d'un verre calice tenu incliné. Verser plus au milieu (dans la bière) donne un faux col plus prononcé.	Traag uitschenken tegen de rand van een schuingehouden kelkglas. Meer in het midden schenken (in het bier) geeft meer schuimkraag.
i	Achieved 5th place at the Zythos Festival 2011.	Elle a obtenu la 5e place au Zythosfestival 2011.	Behaalde de 5e plaats op het Zythosfestival 2011.

N Nostradamus

Brasserie Caracole 9% Cell temperatu

	top-fermentation	fermentation haute	hoge gisting
	strong dubbel	double forte	sterk dubbel
	5 malt varieties, Hallertau hops, yeast, water	5 sortes de malt, houblon Hallertau, levure, eau	5 moutsoorten, Hallertau hop, gist, water
	brown	brune	bruin
	Powerful, full-bodied sipping beer for cold winter nights. Pear and chocolate flavours.	Bière de dégustation relevée et corsée pour les soirées hivernales. Arômes de poires et de chocolat.	Hartig en gecorseerd degustatiebier voor koude winteravonden. Aroma's van peren en chocolade.

ontaigu by 't Hofbrouwerijke

8,00% 8 - 10 °C / 46 - 50 °F

	top-fermentation re-fermentation in the bottle	fermentation haute refermentation en bouteille	hoge gisting hergisting in de fles
	Belgian Porter	Belgian Porter	Belgian Porter
	barley and wheat malt, hops, yeast, water	malt d'orge et de froment, houblon, levure, eau de brassage	gerste- en tarwemout, hop, gist, brouwwater
	Pour in a single, smooth movement into a rinsed tulip glass. Pour yeast sediment along, if necessary.	Verser d'un seul mouvement souple dans un verre tulipe rincé. Selon les souhaits également verser le dépôt de levure.	In 1 vloeiende, zachte beweging uitschenken in een gespoeld tulpglas. Het gistdepot desgewenst mee uitschenken.

Odlo Blond

Odlo by Brouwerij De Graal

6,70% 7 - 10 45 - 50

	top-fermentation re-fermentation in the bottle	fermentation haute refermentation en bouteille	hoge gisting hergisting in de fles
	blond	blonde	blond
	barley and wheat malt, hops, yeast, brewing water	malt d'orge et de froment, houblon, levure, eau de brassage	gerste- en tarwemout, hop, gist, brouwwater
	gold-blond with fine foam head not filtered or pasteurised	blond doré avec faux col blanche non filtreé ni pasteuriseé	goudblond met witte schuimkraag ongefilterd, niet gepasteuriseerd
	Fresh hoppy and malty aroma. Slightly malty onset with hint of sweetness that develops into a pleasant feeling in the mouth. Subtle, fine and distinctly bitter aftertaste that lingers.	Arôme houblonné et malté frais. Approche initiale légèrement maltée, avec une touche douceâtre qui évolue en une agréable sensation en bouche. Arrière-bouche subtile, fine et nettement amère, qui persiste longtemps.	Fris hoppig en moutig aroma. Licht moutige aanzet met zoetige toets die evolueert in een aangenaam mondgevoel. Subtiele, fijne en uitgesproken bittere afdronk die lang blijft.
	Pour in a single, smooth movement into a rinsed tulip glass. Pour yeast sediment along, if necessary.	Verser d'un seul mouvement souple dans un verre tulipe rincé. Le dépôt peut être versé.	In 1 vloeiende, zachte beweging uitschenken in een gespoeld tulpglas. Het gistdepot desgewenst mee uitschenken.
i	Original name of the municipality of Olen (994). 'Od' is wild and 'Lo' is wood.	Nom d'origine de la commune d'Olen (994). 'Od' veut dire sauvage et 'Lo', bois.	Originele naam van de gemeente Olen (994). Od is woest en Lo is bos.

9% 12 °C 54 °F

	top-fermentation re-fermented in the bottle uncentrifuged	fermentation haute refermentation en bouteille non centrifugée	hoge gisting nagisting op de fles niet gecentrifugeerd
	strong dubbel	double forte	sterk dubbel
	4 malt varieties, aromatic hops from Poperinge, no additives	4 sortes de malt, cônes de houblon aromatiques de Poperinge, aucun additif	4 moutsoorten, aromatische hopbellen uit Poperinge, geen additieven
	dark unfiltered	foncée non filtrée	donker ongefilterd
	Very full-bodied, touches of hop and malt bitter, sweet and slightly sourish. Great character and long aftertaste.	Très franche, touches houblonnées et maltées amères et un peu acidulées. Beaucoup de caractère et une fin de bouche longue.	Zeer volmondig, toetsen van hopbitter, moutbitter, zoet en een beetje zurig. Veel karakter en lange afdronk.
	The yeast sediment of approx. 2 cl is rich in vitamin B and can be drunk. Connoisseurs drink it separately. Serve in the typical 'Charente' glass.	Le dépôt de levure de 2 cl riche en vitamines B peut être bu. Les connaisseurs le boivent séparément. Verser dans un verre typique de vin de Charente.	Het vitaminerijke (vit. B) gistdepot van ca. 2 cl mag gedronken worden. Kenners drinken dit apart uit. Uitschenken in het typische 'Charenteglas'.
i	When the glass is half-empty, the text 'wet and stiff' appears. Oerbier is the brewery's flagship.	Quand le verre est à moitié vide, le texte 'humide et forte' apparaît. Oerbier est le navire-amiral de la brasserie.	Wanneer het glas halfleeg is, lees je de bedrukking 'nat en straf'. Oerbier is het vlaggeschip van de brouwerij.

Oesterstout

De Scheldebrouwerij

8,50% 9 - 11 48 - 52

	top-fermentation re-fermentation in the bottle	fermentation haute refermentation en bouteille	hoge gisting hergisting in de fles
	dark stout	stout foncée	stout donker
	barley malt, aroma 150, cara 120, roasted 900, hops, yeast, water	malt d'orge, arôme 150, cara 120, Roost 900, houblon, levure, eau	gerstemout, aroma 150, cara 120, Roost 900, hop, gist, water
	dark to black (90 EBC) with generous beige foam head. Not filtered or pasteurised	foncée, presque noire (90 EBC) avec faux col solide beige. Non filtrée, non pasteurisée	donker tot zwart (90 EBC) met ruime beige schuimkraag. Ongefilterd, niet gepasteuriseerd
	Fruity nose. Taste: in perfect harmony: mellow owing to cara malt, bitter owing to roasted malt, hoppy bitter and a hint of oyster. Long aftertaste of all components. 25 EBU.	Bouquet fruité. Goût :doux de caramalt, amer de malt torréfié, lupuline et une pointe d'huître. Un goût d'une harmonie parfaite. Longue fin de bouche avec tous les composants. 25 EBU.	Fruitige neus. Smaak: zacht van caramout, bitter van gebrande mout, hopbitter en een vleugje oester, perfect in harmonie. Lange nasmaak met alle componenten. 25 EBU.
	During the brewing process, the beer is poured over oyster shells, which adds an extra flavour.	Pendant le brassage, la bière est pompée à travers des écailles d'huître, ce qui lui procure un petit goût supplémentaire.	Tijdens het brouwen wordt het bier over oesterschelpen gepompt, wat zorgt voor een extra smaakje.

5% 2 - 4 °C 36 - 39 °F

	top-fermentation	fermentation haute	hoge gisting
	between pilsner and witbier	entre pils et bière blanche	tussen pils en witbier
	barley malt, wheat malt, wheat, spelt, oat	malt d'orge, malt de froment, froment, épeautre, avoine	gerstemout, tarwemout, tarwe, spelt, haver
	light-yellow	doré clair	lichtgoud
	Hoppy nose with citric touches. Bitter, mineral taste with a touch of roses, slightly malty with some bitterness near the end.	Parfum houblonné avec des touches d'agrumes. Goût amer, minéral avec des touches de roses, légèrement maltée avec une arrière-bouche un peu amère.	Hoppige neus met toetsen van citrus. Bittere, mineralige smaak met rozentoets, licht moutig met iets bitterheid op het einde.
	Preferably draught, poured into the appropriate glass.	De préférence du fût dans le verre approprié.	Bij voorkeur uit het vat in het corresponderende glas.
i			

O Omer

Brouwerij Bockor (Vander Ghinste) 8% 6 43

	top-fermentation re-fermentation in the bottle	fermentation haute refermentation en bouteille	hoge gisting hergisting in de fles
	strong blond	blonde forte	sterk blond
	barley malt, hops, yeast, water	malt d'orge, houblon, levure, eau	gerstemout, hop, gist, water
	gold blond	blond doré	goudblond
	Full taste owing to fruitiness and hops. Added character thanks to fresh bitterness.	Goût franc grâce au fruité et au houblon. Caractère supplémentaire apporté par la fraîche amertume.	Volle smaak door fruitigheid en hop. Extra karakter door de frisse bitterheid.
	Rinse the glass with cold water, dry, tilt slightly and pour the beer gently.	Rincer le verre à l'eau froide, essuyer, le tenir légèrement incliné et verser prudemment.	Glas koud spoelen, afdrogen, licht schuin houden en voorzichtig schenken.
i	Founder Omer Vander Ghinste (1892) promoted his beer by incorporating his name in the stained glass windows of the cafés. Since replacing these windows for the next generation was too expensive, it was decided to name every firstborn son 'Omer'. The current manager, Omer-Jean, is fourth-generation.	Le fondateur, Omer Vander Ghinste (1892), faisait sa promotion en mettant son nom dans les vitraux des cafés. Comme le remplacement de ces vitraux s'avérait trop coûteux pour la génération suivante, l'on choisit désormais d'appeler chaque aîné des fils 'Omer'. L'actuel chef d'entreprise, Omer-Jean, est le 4e de la série.	Stichter Omer Vander Ghinste (1892) voerde promotie door zijn naam in de brandglasramen van de cafés te zetten. Omdat het vervangen van die ramen voor de volgende generatie te duur was, werd ervoor gekozen om elke eerstgeboren zoon voortaan 'Omer' te noemen. De huidige zaakvoerder, Omer-Jean, is de 4e in de reeks.

rouwerij De Glazen Toren

8,50% 7 °C 45 °F

top-fermentation re-fermented in the bottle	fermentation haute refermentation en bouteille	hoge gisting hergisting op de fles
tripel	triple	tripel
barley malt, candy sugar, hops, yeast, water	malt d'orge, sucre candi, houblon, levure, eau	gerstemout, kandijsuiker, hop, gist, water
golden blond and slightly hazy, very sparkling with tiny bubbles, solid foam head	blond doré et légèrement voilée, pétillante fortement avec de petites bulles faux col solide	goudblond en lichtgesluierd, sterk en fijn parelend, stevige schuimkraag
Slightly bitter with hazy alcohol. Fruity, smoothly bitter with caramel malt in the aftertaste.	Légèrement amère avec de l'alcool voilé. Fruitée, moelleuse, amère avec une fin de bouche de malt caramélisé.	Licht bitter met gesluierde alcohol. Fruitig, zacht bitter met karamelmout in de afdronk.
Pour carefully into a dry, tall (e.g. a tulip-shaped) glass.	Verser prudemment dans un verre sec, oblong (p. ex. tulipe).	Voorzichtig uitschenken in een droog, langwerpig (bv. tulpvormig) glas.

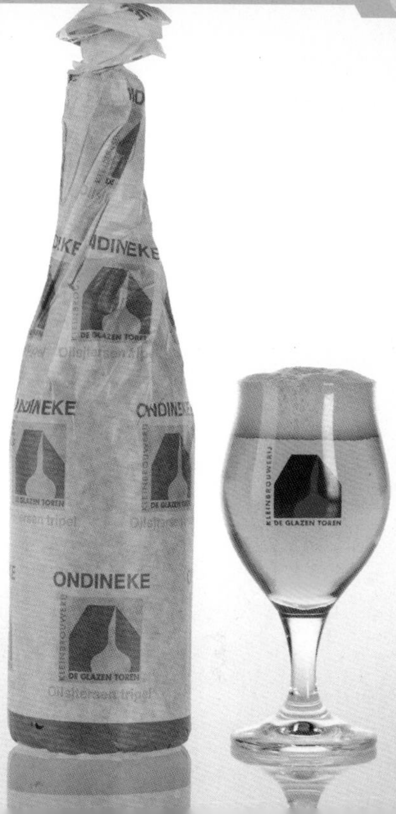

Ops-Ale

Brouwerij Sint-Jozef **5,50%** 2 - 4 / 36 - 39

bottom-fermentation	fermentation basse	lage gisting
premium pilsner	pils de luxe	luxepils
malt, hops, starch, water	malt, houblon, fécule, eau	mout, hop, zetmeel, water
slightly yellowish	légèrement jaunâtre	licht gelig
Refreshing thirst-quencher. Smooth pilsner taste with bitter background.	Désaltérant rafraîchissant. Saveur moelleuse de pils avec un arrière-fond amer.	Verfrissende dorstlesser. Zachte pilssmaak met bittere achtergrond.
Pour into a clean, degreased glass, avoiding contact between bottle and foam.	Verser dans un verre propre, dégraissé sans que la bouteille touche l'écume.	Uitschenken in een zuiver, ontvet glas zonder dat de fles het schuim raakt.
First regional product from the Limburg Kempen (2005).	Premier produit régional des Limburgse Kempen (2005).	Eerste streekproduct van de Limburgse Kempen (2005).

	top-fermentation re-fermented in the bottle	fermentation haute refermentation en bouteille	hoge gisting hergisting op de fles
	trappist	trappiste	trappist
	barley malt, pale malt, caramel malt, white candy sugar, hops (Hallertau, Styrie), top yeast, Orval yeast (re-fermentation in the barrel), water from the Mathild well	malt d'orge, malt pâle, malt caramélisé, sucre candi blanc, houblon (Hallertau, Styrie), levure haute, levure d'Orval (refermentation au réservoir), eau de la source de Mathilde	gerstemout, bleekmout, karamelmout, witte kandijsuiker, hop (Hallertau, Styrie), hoge gist, Orvalgist (nagisting op tank), water van de Mathildebron
	creamy foam head	faux col crémeux	romige schuimkraag
	Specific taste of Orval yeast and hoppy aroma.	Saveur spécifique de la levure d'Orval, et d'arôme houblonné.	Specifieke smaak van de Orvalgist en hoppig aroma.
	Pour the sediment separately.	Verser le dépôt séparément.	Het bezinksel afzonderlijk uitschenken.
	Store in a dark room at 10 to 15 °C. The label refers to the legend of Orval.	Conserver à l'abri de la lumière à 10 à 15 °C. L'étiquette renvoie à la légende d'Orval.	Donker bewaren bij 10 à 15 °C. Het etiket verwijst naar de legende van Orval.

Orvélo Tripel

Half Zeven by De Proefbrouwerij

7,50% 6 - 10 43 - 50

	top-fermentation re-fermentation in the bottle; centrifuged	fermentation haute refermentation en bouteille; centrifugée	hoge gisting hergisting op de fles; gecentrifugeerd
	barley malt, wheat, oat, floral and bitter hops, green herbs, yeast, sugar, water	malt d'orge, froment, avoine, houblon floral et amer, herbes vertes, levure, sucre, eau	gerstemout, tarwe, haver, florale en bitterhop, groene kruiden, gist, suiker, water
	slightly cloudy (wheat) with firm foam head (11 EBC) not filtered or pasteurised	légèrement trouble (froment) avec faux col solide (11 EBC) non filtrée, non pasteurisée	licht troebel (tarwe) met stevige schuimkraag (11 EBC) ongefilterd, niet gepasteuriseerd
	Full malt tripel with an EBU of 30/32. Aroma of floral hops and herbs. A fresh and spicy flavour is followed by a 'southern' aroma. Bitterness that lingers.	Triple pleinement maltée, avec un EBU de 30/32. Arôme de houblon floral et d'épices. D'abord un goût frais et épicé, suivi d'un arôme 'du sud'. Arrière-bouche amère, qui persiste longtemps.	Volmout tripel met een EBU van 30/32. Aroma van florale hop en kruiden. Eerst een frisse en kruidige smaak gevolgd door een 'Zuiders' aroma. Bittere afdronk die lang blijft.
i	Hobby that got out of hand of 3 former students from the Ghent Brewers' School. The clock in their brewery moved for the last time during a successful beer tasting session and has been indicating half past six ever since. The name of the beer is based on the brewers Jan and Dag's second passion, namely that of cycling.	C'est un hobby de 3 anciens étudiants de la Gentse Brouwerijschool. L'horloge de leur brasserie a produit son dernier tic-tac lors d'une dégustation de bières réussie et elle indique depuis invariablement six heures et demie ('half zeven'). Le nom de la bière a trouvé son inspiration dans l'amour du vélo, la deuxième passion des brasseurs Jan et Dag.	Uit de hand gelopen hobby van 3 voormalige studenten van de Gentse Brouwerijschool. De klok in hun brouwerij deed haar laatste tik tijdens een succesvolle bierdegustatie en duidt sindsdien altijd half zeven aan. De naam van het bier is geïnspireerd op de liefde voor de fiets, de tweede passie van brouwers Jan en Dag.

Oud Beitje

uzestekerij Hanssens Artisanaal 4% 10 - 15 °C / 50 - 59 °F

spontaneous fermentation	fermentation spontanée	spontane gisting
lambic	lambic	lambiek
lambic (70%) and strawberries (30%)	lambic (70%) et fraises (30%)	lambiek (70%) en aardbeien (30%)
not filtered or pasteurised	non filtrée, non pasteurisée	ongefilterd, niet gepasteuriseerd
Only brewed for exports.	Uniquement brassée pour l'exportation.	Enkel voor export gebrouwen.

Oud Kriekenbier

Crombé by Brouwerij Strubbe

6%

	top-fermentation	fermentation haute	hoge gisting
	fruit beer	bière fruitée	fruitbier
	Old Zottegem beer in which the cherries are steeped.	Vieille Zottegem lagerée aux cerises.	Oud Zottegems bier waarop krieken zijn gelagerd.
	Fresh and slightly tart.	Fraîche et légèrement acidulée.	Fris en licht zurig.

mbé by Brouwerij Strubbe 6,50%

	top-fermentation	fermentation haute	hoge gisting
	amber	ambrée	amber
	amber	ambrée	amber
	Bittersweet beer with taste evolution.	Bière douce-amère avec évolution de la saveur.	Bitterzoet bier met smaakevolutie.

Oude Geuze 3 Fonteinen

Geuzestekerij 3 Fonteinen 6%

	spontaneous fermentation spontaneous fermentation in the bottle	fermentation spontanée fermentation spontanée en bouteille	spontane gisting spontane gisting op de fles
	gueuze	gueuze	geuze
	60% barley malt, 40% wheat, more than one year old hops, water. A blend of 1, 2 and 3-year old lambic, matured in oak barrels.	60% malt d'orge, 40% froment, houblon suranné, eau. Mélange de lambic de 1, 2 et 3 ans d'âge, mûrit en fûts en bois de chêne.	60% gerstemout, 40% tarwe, overjaarse hop, water. Mengeling van 1, 2 en 3 jaar oude lambiek gerijp op eikenhouten vaten.
	unfiltered	non filtrée	ongefilterd
	Open the bottle carefully.	Ouvrir la bouteille prudemment.	De fles voorzichtig openen.
	Can be kept for at least 10 years after the bottling date. Old Gueuze is a protected brand (E.U.). 3 Fonteinen is a traditional gueuze blender.	Peut se conserver au moins 10 ans après la date de la mise en bouteille. Vieille Gueuze est une appellation protégée (U.E.). 3 Fonteinen est un coupeur artisanal de gueuze.	Kan minstens tot 10 jaar na botteldatum worden bewaard. Oude Geuze is een beschermde benaming (E.G.). De 3 Fonteinen is een ambachtelijke geuzestekerij.

rouwerij Boon 6,50% 10 - 16 °C 50 - 61 °F

	spontaneous fermentation. Re-fermented in the bottle by the young lambic which contains fermentable sugars.	fermentation spontanée. Refermentation en bouteille par le lambic jeune contentant des sucres commutables en levure.	spontane gisting. Nagisting op de fles door de jonge lambiek die vergistbare suikers bevat.
	gueuze	gueuze	geuze
	Selected blend of 90% mellow lambic (at least 18 months), 5% of 3-year old beer full of character, 5% very young lambic.	Mélange sélectionné de 90% de lambic doux (au moins 18 mois), 5% de bière de caractère de 3 ans, 5% de lambic très jeune.	Geselecteerde menge-ling van 90% malse lam-biek (minstens 18 maand), 5% karaktervol bier van 3 jaar, 5% heel jonge lambiek.
	Only champagne bottles are suitable for gueuze because of the high pressure. If stored under good conditions and at cellar temperature, this beer can keep for more than 20 years.	Seules les bouteilles de champagne résistent à la haute pression de la gueuze. Se conserve plus de 20 ans dans de bonnes conditions et à tempéra-ture de cave.	Enkel champagneflessen kunnen weerstaan aan de hoge druk van de geu-ze. Kan in goede omstandig-heden meer dan 20 jaar bewaard worden op kel-dertemperatuur.

Oude Geuze Boon

O

Oude Geuze De Cam

Geuzestokerij De Cam 6% 12 - 14 / 54 - 57

	spontaneous fermentation	fermentation spontanée	spontane gisting
	gueuze lambic	gueuze lambic	geuze lambiek
	65% wheat, 35% barley malt, water. 1, 3 and 5-year old lambic. Brewed in 4 different breweries.	65% froment, 35% malt d'orge, eau. Lambic de 1, 3 et 5 ans d'âge. Brassé en 4 brasseries différentes.	65% tarwe, 35% gerstemout, water. Lambiek van 1, 3 en 5 jaa oud, gebrouwen in 4 verschillende brouwerijen.
	Golden blond. Sparkling like champagne if served following the rules.	Blond doré. Perlant comme le champagne si versée selon les règles de l'art.	Goudblond. Parelend als champagne i dien uitgeschonken volge de regels van de kunst.
	Velvety soft with a winelike bouquet, sourish.	Veloutée avec un bouquet de vin, fraîche et acidulée.	Fluweelzacht met een wijnachtig boeket, friszurig.
	Remove the cork slantwise and do not let the bottle pop. Fill the glasses in one fluent movement. Let the foam overflow and leave the sediment in the bottle or serve it in a shot glass.	Enlever le bouchon en position oblique sans le faire exploser. Remplir les verres en un seul mouvement fluide, laisser la bière déborder et laisser le dépôt dans la bouteille ou le servir dans un petit verre.	Het kurk schuin verwijderen en niet laten ploffen. De glazen in 1 vloeiende beweging inschenken, het bier laten overschuimen en het be zinksel in de fles laten c in een borrelglaasje me serveren.
	Old Gueuze can be kept up to 20 years. Van De Cam has meanwhile become Oude Faro and Pajottenland, but they were not available during the production of this book.	L'Oude Geuze peut se conserver jusqu'à 20 ans. Van De Cam est aussi entre-temps une Oude Faro et Pajottenland, mais celles-ci n'étaient pas disponibles pendant la composition de ce livre.	Oude geuze kan tot 20 jaar bewaard worden. Van De Cam is er ondertussen ook een Oude Fa ro en Pajottenland, maa die waren niet beschikbaar tijdens de samenstelling van dit boek.

ıeuzerie Tilquin 6% 10 °C 50 °F

	spontaneous fermentation natural re-fermentation in the bottle	fermentation haute refermentation naturelle en bouteille	spontane gisting natuurlijke hergisting in de fles
	Old Gueuze	Vieille Gueuze	OudeGeuze
	malt, wheat, hops, water	malt, froment houblon, eau	mout, tarwe, hop, water
	pale orange, slightly cloudy; broken white foam head which, for a Gueuze, lasts a very long time; not pasteurised	orange clair, légèrement trouble; faux col blanc cassé, d'excellente tenue pour une gueuze; non pasteurisée	lichtoranje, licht troebel; gebrokken witte schuimkraag die zeer lang houdt voor een geuze; niet gepasteuriseerd
	Fresh and woody citrus aroma. Slightly tart (lemon and grapefruit), yet very accessible.	Arôme de citrus frais et au parfum boisé. Goût légèrement acide (citron et pamplemousse), mais fort accessible.	Fris en bosgeurend citrusaroma. Lichtzure smaak (citroen en pompelmoes) maar zeer toegankelijk.
	Tilt bottle and glass and pour out gently. Leave yeast sediment (approx. 1 cm) in the bottle.	Tenir la bouteille et le verre légèrement inclinés et verser prudemment. Laisser le dépôt de levure (ca. 1 cm) dans la bouteille.	Fles en glas schuinhouden en voorzichtig uitschenken. Het gistbezinksel (ca. 1 cm) in de fles laten.
i	Gueuze based on lambic that is 1, 2 and 3 years old, brewed by Boon, Lindemans, Girardin and Cantillon.	Gueuze à base de lambic d'1, 2 et 3 ans d'âge qui a été brassé par Boon, Lindemans, Girardin et Cantillon.	Geuze op basis van 1, 2 en 3 jaar oude lambiek die werden gebrouwen door Boon, Lindemans, Girardin en Cantillon.

Oude Geuze Tilquin à l'ancienne

Oude Geuze Vintage 3 Fonteinen

Geuzestekerij 3 Fonteinen

6%

spontaneous fermentation spontaneous fermentation in the bottle	fermentation spontanée fermentation spontanée sauvage en bouteille	spontane gisting spontane wilde gisting op fles
gueuze	gueuze	geuze
60% barley malt, 40% wheat, more than one year old hops, water. A blend of 1, 2 and 3-year old lambic, matured in oak barrels.	60% malt d'orge, 40% froment, houblon suranné, eau. Mélange de lambic de 1, 2 et 3 ans d'âge mûri en fûts en bois de chêne.	60% gerstemout, 40% tarwe, overjaarse hop, water. Mengeling van 1, 2 en 3 jaar oude lambiek gerijp op eikenhouten vaten.
unfiltered	non filtrée	ongefilterd
Can be kept for at least ten years after the bottling date. Old Gueuze is a protected brand (E.U.). De 3 Fonteinen is a traditional gueuze blender.	Peut se conserver au moins dix ans après la date de la mise en bouteilles. Vieille Gueuze est une appellation protégée (U.E.). 3 Fonteinen est un coupeur artisanal de gueuze.	Kan minstens tot 10 jaar na botteldatum worden bewaard. Oude Geuze is een beschermde benaming (E.G.). De 3 Fonteinen is een ambachtelijke geuzestekerij.

Oude Gueuze Hanssens

	spontaneous fermentation re-fermented in the bottle	fermentation spontanée refermentation en bouteille	spontane gisting hergisting in de fles
	gueuze	gueuze	geuze
	hops, barley malt, wheat, water. A blend of the finest lambic varieties. 100% matured in oak barrels.	houblon, malt d'orge, froment, eau. Mélange des lambics les plus fins. Mûri 100% en fûts de chêne.	hop, gerstemout, tarwe, water. Mengeling van de fijnste lambiek. 100% gerijpt op eiken vaten.
	Hanssens boutique Gueuze blender since 1896.	Hanssens Artisanal depuis 1896.	Hanssens Artisanaal sinds 1896.

O

Oude Gueuze Oud Beersel

Brouwerij Oud Beersel

6% 8 - 12° 46 - 54°

	spontaneous fermentation	fermentation spontanée	spontane gisting
	gueuze lambic	gueuze lambic	geuze lambiek
	wheat, barley malt, hops, water	froment, malt d'orge, houblon, eau	tarwe, gerstemout, hop, water
	gold-yellow	jaune doré	goudgeel
	Rich, refreshing, complex and intriguing. Hoppy flavour with the typical smell of wild yeasts. A taste of pleasant bitterness with a sourish and smooth character.	Riche, fraîche, complexe et intrigante. Arôme houblonné avec un parfum typique de levures sauvages. Saveur amère agréable avec un caractère acidulé et doux.	Rijk, fris, complex en intrigerend. Hoppig aroma met typische geur van wilde gisten. Een smaak van aangename bitterheid met een zurig en zacht karakter.
	Pour carefully into a degreased, dry glass. Keep the glass tilted and revolve it in your hand to obtain a nice foam head. Leave the yeast sediment in the bottle.	Verser prudemment dans un verre dégraissé et sec. Tenir le verre en oblique et le tourner dans la paume au moment de verser la bière pour obtenir un beau faux col. Laisser le dépôt de levure dans la bouteille.	Voorzichtig uitschenken in een ontvet droog glas. Het glas schuin houden en in de handpalm draaien tijdens het schenken voor een mooie schuimkraag. De gistfond in de fles laten.
i	Matured in chestnut barrels.	Mûrit en fûts de châtaignier.	Gerijpt op kastanjehouten vaten.

5%

spontaneous fermentation spontaneous re-fermen-tation in the bottle	fermentation spontanée fermentation spontanée en bouteille	spontane gisting spontane hergisting op fles
fruit beer	bière fruitée	fruitbier
60% barley malt, 40% wheat, more than one year old hops, full cher-ries (35%), water. A blend of young lambic and Schaarbeek cher-ries.	60% malt d'orge, 40% froment, houblon suran-né, cerises entières (35%), eau. Un assemblage de jeune lambic et de cerises de Schaerbeek.	60% gerstemout, 40% tarwe, overjaarse hop, volle krieken (35%), wa-ter. Een assemblage van jon-ge lambiek met Schaar-beekse krieken.
red unfiltered	rouge non filtrée	rood ongefilterd
Open the bottle careful-ly.	Ouvrir la bouteille pru-demment.	De fles voorzichtig ope-nen.
Can be kept for at least ten years after the bot-tling date. Oude Kriek is a protected brand (E.U.). De 3 Fonteinen is a bou-tique Gueuze blender.	Peut se conserver au moins 10 ans après la date de la mise en bou-teilles. Oude Kriek est une ap-pellation protégée (U.E.). 3 Fonteinen est un cou-peur artisanal de gueuze.	Kan minstens tot 10 jaar na botteldatum worden bewaard. Oude Kriek is een be-schermde benaming (E.G.). De 3 Fonteinen is een ambachtelijke geuzeste-kerij.

Oude Kriek Boon

Brouwerij Boon 6,50%

	spontaneous fermentation re-fermented in the bottle	fermentation spontanée refermentation en bouteille	spontane gisting hergisting op de fles
	fruit beer	bière fruitée	fruitbier
	A blend of young and old lambic, matured in oak barrels. Real cherries (300 g per litre), bottled with yeast.	Mélange de jeune et vieux lambic mûri en fûts de chêne. De vraies cerises (300 g par litre), mises en bouteilles avec de la levure.	Versnijding van jonge en oude lambiek gerijpt op eikenhouten vaten. Echte krieken (300 g per liter), gebotteld op gist.
	red	rouge	rood
	Refreshing, non-foaming. Sweet-and-sour cherry taste, pure and unsweetened.	Fraîche, sans écume. Saveur de cerises aigre-douce, pure et non sucrée.	Fris, niet schuimend. Zuurzoete kriekensmaak, puur en ongezoet.
	Originally created with Schaarbeek cherries, now mainly with North cherries, and lambic that is at least 6 months old.	A l'origine fabriquée avec des cerises de Schaerbeek, aujourd'hui surtout avec des cerises du Nord et du lambic d'au minimum 6 mois.	Oorspronkelijk gemaakt met Schaarbeekse krieken, nu vooral met Noordkrieken, en lambiek van minimum 6 maanden oud.

6,50% 10 °C 50 °F

	spontaneous fermentation	fermentation spontanée	spontane gisting
	lambic beer	bière lambic	lambiekbier
	65% wheat, 35% barley malt, more than one year old hops, min. 35% cherries with pip. No artificial sweetening, juices, other fruits or colouring agents.	65% froment, 35% malt d'orge, houblon suranné, min. 35% de cerises avec noyau. Pas de sucres artificiels, jus, autres fruits ou colorants.	65% tarwe, 35% gerstemout, overjaarse hop, min. 35% krieken met pit. Geen kunstmatige suikers, sappen, andere vruchten of kleurstoffen.
	ruby red	rouge rubis	robijnrood
	Complex character, vanilla and almond flavour.	Caractère complexe, touches de vanille et d'amande.	Complex karakter, toetsen van vanille en amandel.
	Remove the cork slantwise and do not let the bottle pop. Fill the glasses in one fluent movement. Let the foam overflow and leave the sediment in the bottle or serve it in a shot glass.	Enlever le bouchon en position oblique sans le faire exploser. Remplir les verres en un seul mouvement fluide, laisser la bière déborder et laisser le dépôt dans la bouteille ou le servir dans un petit verre.	Het kurk schuin verwijderen en niet laten ploffen. De glazen in 1 vloeiende beweging inschenken, het bier laten overschuimen en het bezinksel in de fles laten of in een borrelglaasje mee serveren.
i			

Oude Kriek Hanssens

Geuzestekerij Hanssens Artisanaal 6%

spontaneous fermentation re-fermented in the bottle	fermentation spontanée refermentation en bouteille	spontane gisting hergisting in de fles
fruit beer	bière fruitée	fruitbier
Hops, barley malt, wheat, fresh cherries, water. A blend of the finest lambic varieties. 100% matured in oak barrels.	Houblon, malt d'orge, froment, cerises fraîches, eau. Mélange des lambics les plus fins. Mûri 100% en fûts de chêne.	Hop, gerstemout, tarwe, verse krieken, water. Mengeling van de fijnste lambieksoorten. 100% gerijpt op eiken vaten.
red	rouge	rood
Hanssens boutique Gueuze blender since 1896.	Hanssens Artisanal depuis 1896.	Hanssens Artisanaal sinds 1896.

Brouwerij Oud Beersel 6,50% 8 - 12 °C / 46 - 54 °F

Oude Kriek Oud Beersel

	spontaneous fermentation	fermentation spontanée	spontane gisting
	gueuze lambic	gueuze lambic	geuze lambiek
	wheat, barley malt, hops, 400 g cherries/litre, water	froment, malt d'orge, houblon, 400 g de cerises/litre, eau	tarwe, gerstemout, hop, 400 g krieken/liter, water
	deep red	rouge intense	dieprood
	Rich, fresh, fruity and intriguing. An overwhelming fruitiness of cherry with a touch of almond from the cherry stones.	Riche, fraîche, fruitée et intrigante. Goût fruité éblouissant de cerises avec une touche d'amande du noyau.	Rijk, fris, fruitig en intrigerend. Overweldigende fruitigheid van krieken met amandeltoets van de pit.
	Pour carefully into a degreased, dry glass. Keep the glass tilted and revolve it in your hand to obtain a nice foam head. Leave the yeast sediment in the bottle.	Verser prudemment dans un verre dégraissé et sec.Tenir le verre en oblique et le tourner dans la paume au moment de verser la bière pour obtenir un beau faux col. Laisser le dépôt de levure dans la bouteille.	Voorzichtig uitschenken in een ontvet droog glas. Het glas schuin houden en in de handpalm draaien tijdens het schenken voor een mooie schuimkraag. De gistfond in de fles laten.
i			

Oude Lambiek De Cam

Geuzestokerij De Cam

5% 6-8° 43-46°

	spontaneous fermentation	fermentation spontanée	spontane gisting
	lambic	lambic	lambiek
	5-year old lambic. 65% wheat, 35% barley malt, more than 1 year old hops, water.	Lambic de 5 ans. 65% froment, 35% malt d'orge, houblon suranné, eau.	Lambiek van 5 jaar oud. 65% tarwe, 35% gerste-mout, overjaarse hop, water.
	straw-yellow beer without carbon di-oxide	jaune paille bière sans acide carbo-nique	strogeel plat bier zonder kool-zuurgas
	Very smooth with a wine bouquet. Evolution of apple to calvados or sherry. Surprising due to the lack of carbon diox-ide.	Veloutée avec un bou-quet de vin. Saveur de pomme passant au cal-vados ou au xéres. Sur-prenante par le manque de gaz carbonique.	Fluweelzacht met een wijnachtig boeket. Evo-lueert van appel naar calvados of sherry. Ver-rassend door het gebrek aan koolzuurgas.
	Leave the bottle for 3 weeks in an upright po-sition and put it in a bas-ket before serving. First rinse the glass with hot water, then cold, to remove all the deter-gent. Next, dry it.	Laisser reposer la bou-teille 3 semaines en po-sition verticale. Utiliser un panier verseur pour servir. Rincer le verre d'abord à l'eau chaude et puis à l'eau froide pour enlever le détergent et sécher.	De fles 3 weken rechtop-staand laten rusten. Voor het schenken in een mandje leggen. Het glas eerst met warm en dan met koud water spoelen om alle deter-gentresten te verwijde-ren en daarna afdrogen.
i	Lambic is called the missing link between beer and wine.	Le lambic est souvent appelé 'le missing link' entre la bière et le vin.	Lambiek wordt wel eens the missing link tussen bier en wijn genoemd.

Outblack

e Struise Brouwers at Brouwerij Deca 10% 12 °C 54 °F

	top-fermentation re-fermentation in the bottle not centrifuged	fermentation haute refermentation en bouteille non centrifugée	hoge gisting hergisting in de fles niet gecentrifugeerd
	Belgian strong ale strong dubbel	Belgian strong ale forte foncée	Belgian strong ale sterk donker
	slightly cloudy, ebony with red glow, firm beige foam head not filtered or pasteurised	légèrement fade, ébène avec éclat rouge, faux col solide beige non filtrée, non pasteurisée	licht wazig, ebbenhout met rode gloed, stevige beige schuimkraag ongefilterd, niet gepasteuriseerd
	Refined sipping beer with distinct silky aroma of grains, bread, milk chocolate, fruit, mint and a hint of coffee. Soft, full of character with touches of cigar box, milk chocolate, port, currant loaf, refreshing hops and a hint of eucalyptus.	Bière de dégustation raffinée, avec un arôme soyeux prononcé de céréales, de pain, de chocolat au lait, de fruits, de menthe et d'un peu de café. Goût doux, très caractéristique, avec des touches de boîte à cigares, de chocolat au lait, de porto, de pain aux raisins, de houblon rafraîchissant et d'un peu d'eucalyptus.	Verfijnd degustatiebier met uitgesproken zijdezacht aroma van granen, brood, melkchocolade, fruit, munt en ietwat koffie. Zachte, karaktervolle smaak met toetsen van sigarenkist, melkchocolade, port, krentenbrood, verfrissende hop en wat eucalyptus.
	Pour out in a single movement.	Verser agilement.	Vlot uitschenken.
	Came into being in tandem with Brian Strumke, brewer at the Stillwater Brewing Company (USA).	Elle a été réalisée en collaboration avec Brian Strumke, brasseur à la Stillwater Brewing Company (États-Unis).	Kwam tot stand in samenwerking met Brian Strumke, brouwer bij de Stillwater Brewing Company (USA).

Paasei

Vacas at a nearby brewery 7,80% 6° 43°

	top-fermentation re-fermentation in the bottle	fermentation haute refermentation en bouteille	hoge gisting hergisting in de fles
	strong dubbel	double forte	sterk bruin
	barley malt, hops, yeast, herbs, water	malt d'orge, houblon, levure, herbes, eau	gerstemout, hop, gist, kruiden, water
	Pour slowly into a degreased glass without sloshing the beer.	Verser lentement dans un verre dégraissé sans clapotage de la bière.	Traag inschenken in een ontvet glas zonder dat het bier klokt.
	Only available from De Bierloods.	Seulement en vente chez De Bierloods.	Enkel verkrijgbaar bij De Bierloods.

rasserie Caulier — 10%

Paix-Dieu

	top-fermentation re-fermentation in the bottle	fermentation haute refermentation en bouteille	hoge gisting hergisting in de fles
	strong blond Cistercienser abbey beer	blonde forte Bière d'abbaye de l'Abbaye des Cisterciens	sterk blond abdijbier Cisterciënzer-abdij
	malt, candy sugar, hops, yeast, water	malt, sucre candi, houblon, levure, eau	mout, kandijsuiker, hop, gist, water
	gold blond	blond doré	goudblond
	Very lively, thirst-quenching and balanced beer with much body.		Zeer levendig, dorstlessend en evenwichtig bier met veel body.
	Full-moon beer: only brewed during full moon.	Bière de pleine lune : elle est uniquement brassée pendant la pleine lune.	Vollemaanbier: wordt enkel gebrouwen tijdens volle maan.

Palm Breweries

5,40% 5 - 10 ° 41 - 50 °

	top-fermentation	fermentation haute	hoge gisting
	spéciale Belge amber	spéciale belge ambrée	speciale belge amber
	special Palm malts, fine, aromatic hops (e.g. from Kent), Palm yeasts, water	malts Palm spéciaux, houblons aromatiques fins (e.a. de Kent), levures Palm, eau	speciale Palmmouten, fijne aromahoppen (o.a. uit Kent), Palmgisten, water
	amber-coloured	couleur ambrée	amberkleurig
	Easy to drink and harmonious. Honey-like tenderness (Palm mouts) and fruity fermentation aroma (Palm yeasts).	Facilement buvable et harmonieuse. Caractère doux de miel (malts Palm) et arôme de fermentation fruité (levures Palm).	Laat zich vlot drinken en is harmonieus. Honingachtige malsheid (Palmmouten) en fruitig gistingsaroma (Palmgisten).
	Serve in a typical Palm snifter with a thick foam head.	Servir dans un verre ballon Palm typique avec un bon faux col.	Serveren in een typisch Palm bolglas met een flinke schuimkraag.
i			

6% 5 - 10 °C
41 - 50 °F

Palm Dobbel

top-fermentation	fermentation haute	hoge gisting
amber Christmas beer	bière de Noël ambrée	amber kerstbier
special Palm malts, fine aromatic hops, Palm yeasts, water	malts Palm spéciaux, houblons aromatiques fins, levures Palm, eau	speciale Palmmouten, fijne aromahoppen, Palmgisten, water
amber	ambrée	amber
Pronounced malty and hoppy character. A stronger version of Palm Spéciale.	Caractère malté et houblonné prononcé. Version plus forte de la Palm Spéciale.	Uitgesproken mout- en hopkarakter. Zwaardere versie van Palm Spéciale.
Serve in a typical Palm snifter with a fine foam head.	Servir dans un verre ballon Palm typique avec un faux col fin.	Serveren in een typisch Palm bolglas met een fijne schuimkraag.
Created in 1947 for the 200th anniversary of Brouwerij Palm.	Créée en 1947 à l'occasion du bicentenaire de la Brasserie Palm.	Gecreëerd in 1947 ter gelegenheid van het 200-jarig bestaan van Brouwerij Palm.

Palm Green

Palm Breweries

< 0,25% 5° 41°

	top-fermentation	fermentation haute	hoge gisting
	spéciale Belge amber	spéciale belge ambrée	speciale belge amber
	special Palm malts, fine, aromatic hops (among other places from Kent), Palm yeasts, water	malts Palm spéciaux, houblons aromatiques fins (e.a. de Kent), levures Palm, eau	speciale Palmmouten, fijne aromahoppen (o.a. uit Kent), Palmgisten, water
	amber-coloured	couleur ambrée	amberkleurig
	Smooth like honey.	Doux comme du miel.	Honingzacht.
	Serve in a typical Palm snifter with a thick foam head. The bottle can be emptied.	Servir dans un verre ballon Palm typique avec un bon faux col. Peut être complètement versée.	Serveren in een typisch Palm bolglas met een flinke schuimkraag. Mag volledig uitgeschonken worden.
	Non-alcoholic version.	Version sans alcool.	Alcoholvrije versie.

Palm Royale

alm Breweries 7,50% 5 - 10 °C 41 - 50 °F

top-fermentation re-fermented in the bottle	fermentation haute refermentation en bouteille	hoge gisting nagisting op de fles
amber	ambrée	amber
special Palm malts, fine, aromatic hops, Palm yeasts, water	malts Palm spéciaux, houblons aromatiques fins, levures Palm, eau	speciale Palmmouten, fijne aromahoppen, Palmgisten, water
copper-blond	blond cuivre	koperblond
Pronounced fruitiness due to fermentation.	Caractère fruité prononcé dû à la fermentation.	Nadrukkelijke gistingsfruitigheid.
Serve in a typical Palm snifter with a thick foam head.	Servir dans un verre calice Palm typique avec un bon faux col.	Serveren in een typisch Palm kelkglas met een flinke schuimkraag.
Created for brewer Alfred Van Roy's 90th birthday. Brewed with Palm yeasts, selected by him.	Créée à l'occasion du quatre-vingt-dixième anniversaire du brasseur Alfred Van Roy et brassée à base de levures Palm sélectionnées par lui-même.	Gecreëerd ter gelegenheid van de 90e verjaardag van brouwer Alfred Van Roy en gebrouwen op basis van zijn zelf geselecteerde Palmgisten.

Pannepeut (Old Monk's Ale)

De Struise Brouwers at Brouwerij Deca 10% 12 54

	top-fermentation re-fermented in the bottle non centrifuged	fermentation haute refermenation en bouteille non centrifugée	hoge gisting hergisting in de fles niet gecentrifugeerd
	Belgian strong ale strong dark	Belgian strong ale forte foncée	Belgian strong ale sterk donker
	pilsner malt, special B, carafa, cane sugar, yeast, water, hops (Bramling Cross, Hallertauer Mittelfrueh), herbs (cinnamon, sweet orange peel, thyme, coriander, vanilla, massis banda)	malt de pils, B spécial, carafa, sucre de canne, levure, eau, houblon (Bramling Cross, Hallertauer Mittelfrueh), herbes (cannelle, écorce d'orange, thym, coriandre, vanille, massis banda)	pilsmout, special B, carafa, rietsuiker, gist, water, hop (Bramling Cross, Hallertauer Mittelfrueh), kruiden (kaneel, zoete sinaasschil, tijm, koriander, vanille, massis banda)
	intense Sienna brown (84 EBC) with firm warm-beige foam head	brun intense Sienna (84 EBC) avec un faux col solide beige chaud	intens Siennabruin (84 EBC) met stevige warm-beige schuimkraag
	Flavour and aroma similar to Trappist. Slightly malty with touches of caramel, candy sugar, currant loaf, barley malt, shortbread, bread crust and mild hops.	Goût et arôme comparables à la trappiste. Malté doux, avec des touches de caramel, de sucre candi, de pain aux raisins, de malt d'orge, de petits sablés, de croûte de pain et de houblon doux.	Smaak en aroma vergelijkbaar met trappist. Zachtmoutig met toetsen van karamel, kandijsuiker, krentenbrood, gerstemout, zandkoekjes, broodkorst en milde hop.
	Pour out slowly into a Struise or Trappist glass.	Verser doucement dans un verre Struise ou trappiste.	Zacht uitschenken in een Struise of trappistenglas.
i	A twist on Pannepot's recipe. Created as a tribute to the Danish public which launched Pannepot internationally.	Une dérivation de la recette de la Pannepot. Créée comme hommage au public danois, qui a lancé la Pannepot au niveau international.	Een twist op het recept van Pannepot. Ontstaan als tribute aan het Deense publiek dat Pannepot internationaal heeft gelanceerd.

Pannepot (Old Fisherman's Ale)

e Struise Brouwers at Brouwerij Deca — 10% — 10 - 12 °C / 50 - 54 °F

	see Pannepeut	voir Pannepeut	zie Pannepeut
	Belgian strong ale strong dark	Belgian strong ale forte foncée	Belgian strong ale sterk donker
	intense dark brown (99 EBC) with firm brown-beige foam head not filtered or pasteurised	brun intense (99 EBC) avec un faux col solide brun beige non filtrée, non pasteurisée	intens donkerbruin (99 EBC) met stevige bruin-beige schuimkraag ongefilterd, niet gepasteuriseerd
	Very complex sipping beer with rich aroma of grains, roasted malts, currant loaf, chocolate, berries, candied fruit, nuts and spices. Very full flavour with hints of mocca, barley malt, caramel, bread, candied cherries, cedar wood and mild hops.	Riche arôme de céréales, de malts grillés, de pain aux raisins, de chocolat, de groseilles, de fruits confits, de noix et d'épices. Goût très franc, avec des touches de moka, de malt d'orge, de caramel, de pain, de cerises confites, de bois de cèdre et de houblon doux.	Zeer complex degustatiebier met rijk aroma van granen, geroosterde mouten, krentenbrood, chocolade, bessen, gekonfijt fruit, noten en kruiden. Zeer volle smaak met toetsen van mokka, gerstemout, karamel, brood, gekonfijte kersen, cederhout en milde hop.
	Pour out in a single movement	Verser agilement	Vlot uitschenken
	Named after the coastal boats which were used in De Panne around 1900. The label depicts the P50 of Cornelius Legein, brewer Carlos's great-grandfather. The beer is a remake of the winter beer which the fishing women brewed for own consumption during that period.	Désignée d'après les caboteurs qui étaient en service autour de 1900 à La Panne. Sur l'étiquette, figure le P50 de Cornelius Legein, l'arrière-grand-père du brasseur Carlo. La bière est un remake de la bière hivernale que les femmes de pêcheur brassaient dans cette période pour leur propre usage.	Vernoemd naar de kustboten die rond 1900 in De Panne dienst deden. Op het etiket staat de P50 van Cornelius Legein, overgrootvader van brouwer Carlo. Het bier is een remake van het winterbier dat de vissersvrouwen in die periode voor eigen gebruik brouwden.

Pannepot Grand Reserva Vintage 2005

De Struise Brouwers at Brouwerij Deca

10% 12 54

	top-fermentation re-fermentation in the bottle not centrifuged	fermentation haute refermentation en bouteille non centrifugée	hoge gisting hergisting in de fles niet gecentrifugeerd
	Belgian strong ale (oak aged); strong dubbel	Belgian strong ale (oak aged); foncée forte	Belgian strong ale (oak aged); sterk donker
	intense dark-brown with firm brown-beige foam head not filtered or pasteurised	brun foncé intense avec faux col solide brun beige non filtrée, non pasteurisée	intens donkerbruin met stevige bruinbeige schuimkraag ongefilterd, niet gepasteuriseerd
	Very complex sipping beer. Rich aroma of grains, roasted malts, currant loaf, pastries, apple, port, PX, candied fruit, nuts, herbs, tobacco and cedar wood. Full taste with touches of earl grey, barley malt, caramelised apple, bread, candied apricot, cedar wood and mild hops.	Riche arôme de céréales, de malts grillés, de pain aux raisins, de gâteaux secs, de pomme, de porto, de PX, de fruits confits, de noix, d'épices, de tabac et de bois de cèdre. Goût franc, avec des touches d'earl grey, de malt d'orge, de pomme caramélisée, de pain, d'abricot confit, de bois de cèdre et de houblon doux.	Zeer complex degustatiebier. Rijk aroma van granen, geroosterde mouten, krentenbrood, koffiekoeken, appel, porto, PX, gekonfijt fruit, noten, kruiden, tabak en cederhout. Volle smaak met toetsen van earl grey gerstemout, gekaramelliseerde appel, brood, gekonfijte abrikoos, cederhout en milde hop.
	Pour out gently into a Struise or Trappist glass	Verser doucement dans un verre Struise ou Trappiste.	Zacht uitschenken in een Struise of trappistenglas
	Pannepot which has matured in wine casks for 14 months and another 8 months in calvados casks.	Bière Pannepot qui a mûri 14 mois dans des fûts à vin et puis 8 mois dans des fûts à calvados.	Pannepot die 14 maanden op wijnvaten en daarna 8 maanden op calvadosvaten gerijpt is.

Pannepot Reserva

Struise Brouwers at Brouwerij Deca 10% 12 °C / 54 °F

top-fermentation re-fermentation in the bottle	fermentation haute refermentation en bouteille	hoge gisting hergisting in de fles
Belgian strong ale (oak aged); strong dubbel	Belgian strong ale (oak aged); foncée forte	Belgian strong ale (oak aged); sterk donker
intense dark-brown with firm brown-beige foam head not filtered or pasteurised	brun foncé intense avec faux col solide brun beige non filtrée, non pasteurisée	intens donkerbruin met stevige bruinbeige schuimkraag ongefilterd, niet gepasteuriseerd
Very complex sipping beer. Rich aroma of grains, roasted malts, currant loaf, chocolate, port, PX, candied fruit, nuts, herbs, tobacco and cedar wood. Full taste with touches of earl grey, barley malt, caramel, bread, candied cherry, cedar wood and mild hops.	Riche arôme de céréales, de malts grillés, de pain aux raisins, de chocolat, de porto, de PX, de fruits confits, de noix, d'épices, de tabac et de bois de cèdre. Goût franc, avec des touches d'earl grey, de malt d'orge, de caramel, de pain, de cerise confite, de bois de cèdre et de houblon doux.	Zeer complex degustatiebier. Rijk aroma van granen, geroosterde mouten, krentenbrood, chocolade, porto, PX, gekonfijt fruit, noten, kruiden, tabak en cederhout. Volle smaak met toetsen van earl grey, gerstemout, karamel, brood, gekonfijte kers, cederhout en milde hop.
Pour out gently into a Struise or Trappist glass	Verser doucement dans un verre Struise ou Trappiste	Zacht uitschenken in een Struise of trappistenglas
Pannepot which has matured in wine casks for 14 months.	Bière Pannepot qui a mûri 14 mois dans des fûts à vin.	Pannepot die 14 maanden op wijnvaten is gerijpt.

Papegaei

Verstraete by Brouwerij Deca

8% 5 - 7 / 41 - 45

	top-fermentation re-fermentation in the bottle	fermentation haute refermentation en bouteille	hoge gisting hergisting op de fles
	blond	blonde	blond
	malt, hops, sugar, herbs, yeast, water	malt, houblon, sucre, herbes, levure, eau	mout, hop, suiker, kruiden, gist, water
	not filtered or pasteurised	non filtrée, non pasteurisée	ongefilterd, niet gepasteuriseerd
	Pour out the beer chilled (4 hours) in a single movement. Store the bottles upright in a cool, dark place.	Verser la bière mise au frigo (4 heures) d'un seul mouvement. Conserver les bouteilles en position verticale dans un endroit frais, obscur.	Het bier gekoeld (4 uren) in 1 beweging uitschenken. De flessen rechtop bewaren op een koele, donkere plaats.
i	Papegaei is the name of a café in Diksmuide.	Papegaei est le nom d'un café à Dixmude.	Papegaei is de naam van een café in Diksmuide.

3% | 5 - 8 °C | 41 - 46 °F

	spontaneous fermentation	fermentation spontanée	spontane gisting
	fruit beer	bière fruitée	fruitbier
	barley malt, hops, wheat, fruit juices, nature-identical flavouring, yeast, water	malt d'orge, froment, houblon, levure, jus de fruits, arômes naturels, eau	gerstemout, tarwe, hop, vruchtensappen, aroma's, gist, water
	cloudy orange	orange trouble	troebel oranje
	Refreshingly fruity character. Fruity sweetness with a clearly recognisable citric taste.	Caractère frais et fruité. Fruitée et douce avec une saveur reconnaissable d'agrumes.	Fruitzoetig met herkenbare citrusvruchtensmaak. Frisfruitig karakter.
	Rinse the glass with cold water, tilt it a little and pour carefully half of the bottle. Next keep the glass upright and pour the rest of the bottle in one single movement.	Rincer le verre à l'eau froide, le tenir légèrement incliné et le remplir prudemment à moitié. Relever le verre et vider la bouteille en un seul mouvement.	Het glas koud spoelen, licht schuin houden en voorzichtig half inschenken. Daarna het glas rechthouden en de rest in 1 beweging uitschenken.
i			

Passion Max Jacobins

De Lelie by Scheldebrouwerij

6% 8 - 12 / 46 - 54

	top-fermentation re-fermentation in the bottle	fermentation haute refermentation en bouteille	hoge gisting hergisting in de fles
	double city or regional beer	double bière citadine ou régionale	dubbel stads- of streekbier
	malt, roasted caramel malt, aromatic hops, candy sugar, yeast, water	malt, malt caramélisé torréfié, houblon aromatique, sucre candi, levure, eau	mout, geroosterde karamelmout, aromatische hop, kandijsuiker, gist, water
	dark brown and clear, with a nice, creamy foam head not filtered or pasteurised	brun foncé et claire, avec un faux col joli crémeux non filtrée, non pasteurisée	donkerbruin en helder, met een mooie, romige schuimkraag ongefilterd, niet gepasteuriseerd
	Soft-sweet malty flavour and slightly hoppy aftertaste.	Goût malté franc doucement sucré et arrière-bouche légèrement houblonnée.	Zachtzoete volmondige moutsmaak en licht hopperige afdronk.
	Pour out gently (so that the yeast stays in the bottle) in a chalice-shaped glass.	Verser lentement (de sorte que la levure reste dans la bouteille) dans un verre calice.	Langzaam uitschenken (zodat de gist in de fles blijft) in een kelkvormig glas.
	Re-brewed since early 2009 for the local market. The original recipe of Brewery De Lelie (1907-1952) is followed as closely as possible. See also Papal beer.	Depuis le début de 2009, elle est à nouveau brassée pour le marché local. La recette originale de la Brouwerij De Lelie (1907-1952) est suivie aussi précisément que possible. Voir aussi Pausbier.	Sedert begin 2009 opnieuw gebrouwen voor de lokale markt. Het originele recept van Brouwerij De Lelie (1907-1952) wordt zo nauw mogelijk gevolgd. Zie ook Pausbier.

6,50% 6 - 8 °C 43 - 46 °F

Pater Lieven Blond

top-fermentation re-fermented in the bottle	fermentation haute refermentation en bouteille	hoge gisting hergisting op de fles
abbey beer blond	bière d'abbaye blonde	abdijbier blond
hops, yeast, fermentable sugar, water, malt varieties (pilsner, caramel, pale ale)	malt, houblon, sucre fermentescible, eau, sortes de malt (pils, caramélisé, pale ale)	hop, gist, vergistbare suiker, water, moutsoorten (pils, karamel, pale ale)
Pale yellow. Gentle carbon dioxide sparkling, creating a fine, white foam.	Jaune pâle. Léger pétillement d'acide carbonique créant une écume fine blanche.	Bleekgeel. Rustige koolzuurgaspareling die fijn, wit schuim geeft.
Pleasant aroma of malt and flowers with a touch of spicy bitterness. Tastes sweet and bitter at the same time. Dry and bitter aftertaste that reminds of grapefruit.	Parfum agréable de malt et de fleurs avec une touche amère relevée. Saveur à la fois douce et amère. Fin de bouche sèche et amère rappelant la pamplemousse.	Aangename geur van mout en bloemen met een vleugje kruidige bitterheid. Smaakt tegelijk zoet en bitter. Droge en bittere afdronk die aan pompelmoes doet denken.
Pour slowly for a nice foam head with hat. Leave a small amount in the bottle and present it with the glass.	Verser lentement pour obtenir un beau faux col avec chapeau. Laisser un peu de bière dans la bouteille et l'offrir également.	Langzaam inschenken voor een mooie schuimkraag met -hoed. Een restje in de fles laten en de fles mee aanbieden.
Brewed for the first time in 1957 for the Saint Livinus festivities.	Brassée pour la première fois en 1957 à l'occasion des fêtes de St-Livinus.	Voor de eerste keer gebrouwen in 1957 ter gelegenheid van de St-Livinusfeesten.

P

Pater Lieven Bruin

Brouwerij Van den Bossche

6,50% 6 - 8 43 - 46

top-fermentation re-fermented in the bottle	fermentation haute refermentation en bouteille	hoge gisting hergisting op de fles
abbey beer brown	bière d'abbaye brune	abdijbier bruin
hops, yeast, fermentable sugar, water, malt varieties (pilsner, caramel, roast).	malt, houblon, sucre fermentescible, eau, sortes de malt (pils, caramélisé, grillé).	hop, gist, vergistbare suiker, water, moutsoorten (pils, karamel, roost).
dark brown fine, stable, beige foam	brun foncé écume fine, beige, stable	donkerbruin fijn, stabiel beige schuim
Smell of black chocolate with nuts, rolled oats, raisins and cacao powder. Intense taste of bitter chocolate and cacao, complemented by liquorice. Aftertaste: cacao.	Parfum de chocolat noir avec noisettes, flocons d'avoine, raisins secs et poudre de cacao. Saveur intense de chocolat amer, de cacao et de réglisse. Fin de bouche avec goût de cacao.	Geur van zwarte chocolade met nootjes, havermout, rozijntjes en cacaopoeder. Intense smaak van bittere chocolade en cacao aangevuld met drop. Afdronk met nasmaak van cacao.
Pour slowly for a nice foam head. Leave a small amount in the bottle and present the bottle with the glass.	Verser lentement pour obtenir un beau faux col. Laisser un peu de bière dans la bouteille et l'offrir également.	Langzaam inschenken voor een mooie schuimkraag. Een restje in de fles laten en de fles mee aanbieden.
Brewed for the first time in 1957 for the Saint Livinus festivities.	Brassée pour la première fois en 1957 à l'occasion des fêtes de St-Livinus.	Voor de eerste keer gebrouwen in 1957 ter gelegenheid van de St-Livinusfeesten.

8% 6 - 8 °C 43 - 46 °F

	top-fermentation re-fermented in the bottle	fermentation haute refermentation en bouteille	hoge gisting hergisting op de fles
	abbey beer tripel	bière d'abbaye triple	abdijbier tripel
	hops, yeast, fermentable sugar, water, malt varieties (pilsner, pale ale, caramel, wheat)	malt, houblon, sucre fermentescible, eau, sortes de malt (pils, pale ale, caramel, froment)	hop, gist, vergistbare suiker, water, moutsoorten (pils, pale ale, karamel, tarwe)
	pale amber nice foam head, between white and off-white	ambré pâle beau faux col entre blanc et blanc cassé	bleekamber mooie schuimkraag tussen wit en gebroken wit
	The aroma is dominated by a spicy bitterness, complemented by floral touches. Slightly sweet malt and alcohol accents. Long-lasting, intensly bitter aftertaste.	Goût et parfum amers et relevés, complétés par des touches fleuries. Accents légèrement doux de malt et d'alcool. Fin de bouche longue, intense et amère.	Kruidige, bittere geur en aroma, aangevuld met florale toetsen. Lichtzoete accenten van mout en alcohol. Lange afdronk met intense bitterheid.
	Pour slowly for a nice foam head. Leave a small amount in the bottle and present it with the glass.	Verser lentement pour obtenir un beau faux col. Laisser un peu de bière dans la bouteille et l'offrir aussi.	Langzaam inschenken voor een mooie schuimkraag. Een restje in de fles laten en de fles mee aanbieden.
i	Brewed for the first time in 1957 for the Saint Livinus festivities.	Brassée pour la première fois en 1957 à l'occasion des fêtes de St-Livinus.	Voor de eerste keer gebrouwen in 1957 ter gelegenheid van de St-Livinusfeesten.

Pater Lieven Wit

Brouwerij Van den Bossche 4,50% 3 - 6 / 37 - 43

top-fermentation	fermentation haute	hoge gisting
witbier	blanche	witbier
pilsner malt, wheat, oat, hops, herbs, yeast, fermentable sugar, water Aromatised with orange rind and coriander.	malt de pils, froment, avoine, houblon, herbes, levure, sucre fermentescible, eau Aromatisé avec écorce d'orange et coriandre.	pilsmout, tarwe, haver, hop, kruiden, gist, vergistbare suiker, water Gearomatiseerd met sinaasschil en koriander.
yellow-white cloudy (wheat and oat) unfiltered	jaune blanc trouble (froment et avoine) non filtrée	geelwit troebel (tarwe en haver) niet gefilterd
Pleasant fruity taste and thirst-quenching character obtained by the orange and the coriander.	Caractère agréable fruité et désaltérant par l'orange et le coriandre.	Aangenaam fruitig en dorstlessend karakter door de sinaas en koriander.
Pour the beer slowly and avoid sloshing. Shake the bottle to loosen the yeast and pour it along with the beer. Form a nice foam head.	Verser la bière lentement sans la laisser glouglouter. Secouer pour dégager le fond de levure et le verser également. Former un beau faux col.	Het bier langzaam uitschenken zonder het te laten klokken. De gistbodem losschudden en mee in het glas gieten. Een mooie schuimkraag vormen.
As the beer is unfiltered, it contains living yeast cells.	Contient des cellules de levure vivantes parce que la bière n'est pas filtrée.	Het bier bevat levende gistcellen omdat het niet gefilterd is.

	top-fermentation	fermentation haute	hoge gisting
	blond abbey beer winter beer	bière d'abbaye blonde bière hivernale	blond abdijbier winterbier
	hopped twice	doublement houblonné	dubbel gehopt
	blond with creamy, white, thick foam head	blonde avec faux col cré-meux, blanc, collant au verre	blond met romige, witte, wandklevende schuim-kraag
	Hoppy aroma with spices and touches of fruit. Malty onset and tart in taste. Long aftertaste with a hint of alcohol.	Arôme houblonné avec des épices et des touches de fruits. Approche initiale et goût maltés, amers. Longue arrière-bouche, avec une pointe d'alcool.	Hoppig aroma met krui-den en fruittoetsen. Moutige aanzet en smaak, bitter. Lange afdronk met een vleugje alcohol.

P Paulus

Brouwerij Het Sas

6% 5 -
41 - 4

top-fermentation	fermentation haute	hoge gisting
old brown	vieille brune	oud bruin
malt, sweetener, hops, caramel, water	malt, édulcorant, houblon, caramel, eau	mout, zoetstof, hop, karamel, water
dark brown	brun foncé	donkerbruin
Summery session beer. Sweet-and-sour with a full character.	Bière d'été facilement buvable. Aigre-douce avec un caractère plein.	Zomers doordrinkbier. Zuurzoet met een vol karakter.
Pour slowly in a single, smooth movement, in a degreased glass. Keep the glass tilted and avoid sloshing. Skim off the foam	Verser lentement en un seul mouvement fluide dans un verre dégraissé tenu en oblique. Ne pas laisser la bière glouglouter. Ecumer le verre.	Traag en in 1 vloeiende beweging uitschenken i een vetvrij glas dat word schuingehouden. Het bier niet laten klotsen. Het glas afschuimen.
Named after Paul Priem, one of the salesmen of the brewery.	Son nom provient de Paul Priem, un des vendeurs de la brasserie.	Genoemd naar Paul Priem, een van de verkopers bij de brouwerij.

e Lelie by Scheldebrouwerij

8,50% — 8 - 12 °C / 46 - 54 °F

top-fermentation re-fermentation in the bottle	fermentation haute refermentation en bouteille	hoge gisting hergisting in de fles
strong blond city or regional beer	blonde forte bière citadine ou régionale	sterk blond stads- of streekbier
barley malt, wheat, hops, yeast, water	malt d'orge, froment, houblon, levure, eau	gerstemout, tarwe, hop, gist, water
blond, straw-yellow hazy with an attractive, creamy foam head not filtered or pasteurised	blonde, jaune paille fade avec un faux col joli, crémeux non filtrée, non pasteurisée	blond, strogeel wazig met een mooie, romige schuimkraag ongefilterd, niet gepasteuriseerd
Predominantly bitter sipping beer where the hops prevail in terms of scent and flavour. Set off nicely by malty fruitiness. Very long, hoppy aftertaste.	Bière amère corsée où prédomine le houblon dans le parfum et le goût. Le fruité malté assure l'équilibre. Arrière-bouche fort longue, houblonnée.	Gecorseerd bitter. Hop overheerst in geur en smaak.Mouterige fruitigheid zorgt voor evenwicht. Zeer lange, hopperige afdronk.
see Pater	voir Pater	zie Pater
Founded in 2008 as a tribute to the brewery of the same name that flourished in the early 20th century. The original brewery was very well-known locally but was forced to close its doors shortly after the 2nd World War. Pausbier (according to the original recipe) was the first beer. This was followed up in 2009 by best beer.	Fondé en 2008 en hommage à la brasserie du même nom qui était florissante au début du 20e siècle. La brasserie d'origine était fort connue dans la région mais elle a dû fermer ses portes peu de temps après la 2ième Guerre mondiale. La Pausbier (selon la recette originale) fut la 1re bière. En 2009, suivit la Patersbier.	In 2008 opgericht als hommage aan de gelijknamige brouwerij die floreerde begin 20e eeuw. De oorspronkelijke brouwerij (1907-1952) was zeer bekend in de regio maar moest kort na WOII de deuren sluiten. Pausbier gebrouwen naar het originele recept was het 1e bier. In 2009 volgde het Patersbier.

P Pauwel Kwak

Brouwerij Bosteels 8,10% 5 - 6 / 41 - 43

	top-fermentation	fermentation haute	hoge gisting
	specialty beer	bière spéciale	speciaalbier
	barley malts, candy sugar, hops, water	malts d'orge, sucre candi, houblon, eau	gerstemouten, kandijsuiker, hop, water
	deep, clear amber colour consistent, creamcoloured foam head	couleur ambrée intense faux col cohérant, couleur crème	diepe, heldere amberkleur consistente, crèmekleurige schuimkraag
	Smooth, fruity initial nougat flavour, light spicy character with a touch of liquorice turning into a warm and bitter aftertaste that reminds of caramelized bananas.	Saveur initiale douce et fruitée de nougat, caractère légèrement relevé avec une touche de réglisse aboutissant à une fin de bouche chaleureuse et amère qui fait penser à des bananes caramélisées.	Zachte, fruitige, nogaachtige smaakaanzet, licht kruidig karakter met zoethouttoets die overgaat in een warme en bittere afdronk die aan gekaramelliseerde banaan doet denken.
	Slightly tilt the glass and fill it. When the foam head reaches the edge of the glass, there must be 2 cm of foam left in the globe of the glass. After 15 seconds the foam head will have pulled up to approx. 7 cm from the edge.	Tenir le verre légèrement incliné et le remplir. Quand le faux col atteint le bord du verre, il doit rester encore 2 cm d'écume dans le ballon du verre. Après 15 secondes, le faux col se stabilise à ca. 7 cm du bord supérieur du verre kwak.	Het glas licht schuin houden en volschenken. Wanneer de schuimkraag de rand van het glas bereikt, moet er nog 2 cm schuim in de bol van het glas zitten. Na 15 seconden stabiliseert de schuimkraag zich op ca. 7 cm van de bovenkant van het kwakglas.
i			

Pax Pils

rouwerij Sint-Jozef 5,10% 2 - 4 °C / 36 - 39 °F

	bottom-fermentation	fermentation basse	lage gisting
	pilsner	pils	pils
	malt, hops, starch, water	malt, houblon, fécule, eau	mout, hop, zetmeel, water
	light-yellowish	légèrement jaunâtre	licht gelig
	Refreshing thristquencher. Smooth pilsner taste.	Désaltérant rafraîchissant. Saveur moelleuse de pils.	Verfrissende dorstlesser. Zachte pilssmaak.
	Pour into a clean, degreased glass, avoiding contact between the bottle and the foam.	Verser dans un verre propre, dégraissé sans que la bouteille touche l'écume.	Uitschenken in een zuiver, ontvet glas zonder dat de fles het schuim raakt.
i			

Pecheresse Lindemans

Brouwerij Lindemans 2,50% 3 - 4 / 37 - 39

	spontaneous fermentation	fermentation spontanée	spontane gisting
	fruit beer based on lambic	bière fruitée à base de lambic	fruitbier op basis van lambiek
	malt, wheat, hops, peach juice (30%), fructose, water	malt, froment, houblon, jus de pêches (30%), fructose, eau	mout, tarwe, hop, perzikensap (30%), fructose, water
	golden blond slightly hazy	blond doré légèrement voilée	goudblond licht gesluierd
	Fruity character. Lively and strong onset turning into a balance of sweet (fruit) and smooth sour (lambic).	Caractère fruité. Début vif et corsé passant à un équilibre de douceur (fruits) et d'acidulité légère (lambic).	Fruitig karakter. Levendige en sterke aanzet die overgaat in een evenwicht van zoet (fruit) en zacht zuur (lambiek).
	Pour into a flute-glass.	Verser dans une flûte.	In een fluitglas uitschenken.
i	Suitable as an aperitif and as a thirst-quencher.	Convient comme apéritif et boisson désaltérante.	Geschikt als aperitief en als dorstlesser.

Père Noël

rouwerij De Ranke — 7% — Medium cooled.

top-fermentation	fermentation haute	hoge gisting
Christmas beer amber	bière de Noël ambrée	kerstbier amber
3 malts, hop flowers, industrial yeast, liquorice	3 malts, fleurs de houblon, levure de culture, réglisse	3 mouten, hopbloemen, cultuurgist, zoethout
amber slightly cloudy	ambrée légèrement trouble	amber licht troebel
Bittersweet, hoppy and spicy.	Doux-amère, houblonnée et relevée.	Bitterzoet, hoppig en kruidig.

Petrus Aged Pale

Brouwerij Bavik 7,30% 46 - 54

	top-fermentation, mixed	fermentation haute mixte	hoge gisting gemengd
	unblended base beer for red-brown	bière de base non coupée pour brune-rouge	onversneden basisbier voor roodbruin
	barley malt (only pale malt), hops, yeast, pure spring water	malt d'orge (seulement malt pâle), houblon, levure, eau de source pure	gerstemout (enkel bleke mout), hop, gist, zuiver bronwater
	bronze, old yellow	bronze, vieux jaune	brons, oud geel
	Oak aroma with a touch of sherry and fruit (mainly pears). Classical, slightly sour but complex taste. Low carbon dioxide content.	Arôme de chêne avec une pointe de xéres et de fruits (surtout des poires). Goût classique légèrement acidulé mais complexe. Teneur basse en gaz carbonique.	Eikachtig aroma met een vleugje sherry en fruit (vooral peren). Klassieke lichtzurige maar complexe smaak. Laag koolzuurgehalte.
	Pour into a dry glass avoiding contact between bottle and foam.	Verser dans un verre sec sans que la bouteille touche le faux col.	Uitschenken in een droog glas zonder dat de fles het schuim raakt.
	An unblended beer that has matured 24 to 30 months in oak barrels. It is bottled straight from the barrel, which is why the brewer describes it as Lambic.	Une bière de base non coupée mûrie pendant 24 à 30 mois en fûts de chêne. Vu qu'elle est mise directement en bouteilles à partir des fûts en bois, le brasseur la décrit comme une bière lambic.	Een onversneden basisbier dat 24 à 30 maanden gerijpt heeft op eiken vaten. Het wordt rechtstreeks gebotteld vanuit de houten foeders. Vanuit die context wordt het door de brouwer omschreven als 'lambiek'.

rouwerij Bavik **6,60%** 8 - 12 °C / 46 - 54 °F

	top-fermentation	fermentation haute	hoge gisting
	blond	blonde	blond
	barley malt, hops, yeast, pure spring water	malt d'orge, houblon, levure, eau de source pure	gerstemout, hop, gist, zuiver bronwater
	Beautiful bronze colour with a solid foam head. Clear blond.	Jolie couleur de bronze avec un faux col solide. Blond clair.	Mooie bronskleur met een vaste schuimkraag. Helder blond.
	Smooth, full taste with a light, pleasant bitterness. Hoppy character.	Saveur douce et pleine avec un goût amer léger et agréable. Caractère houblonné.	Zachte volle smaak met een lichte, aangename bitterheid. Hoppig karakter.
	Pour into a degreased, rinsed and wet glass, avoiding contact between bottle and foam.	Verser dans un verre dégraissé, rincé et mouillé sans que la bouteille touche le faux col.	Uitschenken in een ontvet, gespoeld en nat glas zonder dat de fles het schuim raakt.
i			

P Petrus Dubbel Bruin

Brouwerij Bavik

6,50% 8 - 12 46 - 54

	top-fermentation	fermentation haute	hoge gisting
	dubbel brown	double brune	dubbel bruin
	barley malt, hops, yeast, pure spring water	malt d'orge, houblon, levure, eau de source pure	gerstemout, hop, gist, zuiver bronwater
	dark, mahogany	foncée, couleur acajoue	donker, mahoniekleur
	Bittersweet caramel and black chocolate. Full and creamy character.	Caramel amer-sucré et chocolat foncé. Caractère plein et crémeux.	Bitterzoete karamel en donkere chocolade. Vol en romig karakter.
	Pour into a degreased, rinsed and wet glass, avoiding contact between bottle and foam.	Verser dans un verre dégraissé, rincé et mouillé sans que la bouteille touche le faux col.	Uitschenken in een ontvet, gespoeld en nat glas zonder dat de fles het schuim raakt.

Petrus Gouden Tripel

rouwerij Bavik 7,50% 8 - 12 °C / 46 - 54 °F

	top-fermentation traditionally re-fermented in the bottle	fermentation haute refermentation traditionnelle en bouteille	hoge gisting tradionele hergisting in de fles
	triple ale	triple ale	triple ale
	barley malt, hops, yeast, pure spring water	malt d'orge, houblon, levure, eau de source pure	gerstemout, hop, gist, zuiver bronwater
	pale yellow	jaune pâle	bleekgeel
	Full, round taste of green apples and ripe pears, with a spicy, fresh and strong aroma.	Saveur pleine et ronde de pommes vertes et de poires mûres avec un arôme relevé, frais et corsé.	Volle, ronde smaak van groene appels en rijpe peren met een kruidig, fris en krachtig aroma.
	Pour into a dry glass and leave the sediment in the bottle.	Verser dans un verre sec. Laisser le dépôt de levure dans la bouteille.	Uitschenken in een droog glas. Het bezinksel in de fles laten.
i			

P

Petrus Oud Bruin

Brouwerij Bavik 5,50% 8 - 12 / 46 - 54

	top-fermentation, mixed	fermentation haute mixte	hoge gisting gemengd
	red old brown	vieille brune-rouge	rood oud bruin
	barley malt, hops, yeast, pure spring water	malt d'orge, houblon, levure, eau de source pure	gerstemout, hop, gist, zuiver bronwater
	dark, mahogany	foncée, couleur acajoue	donker, mahoniekleur
	Perfect balance between sour and sweet, with chocolate touches and a light, delicate vanilla flavour. Full and rich character with a refreshing sourness.	Equilibre parfait entre acidité et douceur, touches de chocolat et pointe de vanille. Caractère plein et riche avec un goût acidulé frais.	Perfecte balans tussen zuur en zoet, chocoladetoetsen en een snufje vanille. Vol en rijk karakter met een frisse zurigheid.
	Pour into a degreased, rinsed and wet glass.	Verser dans un verre dégraissé, rincé et mouillé.	Uitschenken in een ontvet, gespoeld en nat glas.
i	The mature, amber-coloured, lactic acidulous base beer is blended with a young beer.	Coupage de la bière de base mûre, lactique et de couleur ambrée avec une bière jeune.	Versnijding van het belegen, amberkleurig, melkzurig basisbier met een jong gebrouwen bier.

rouwerij Bavik 5,50% 6 - 10 °C 43 - 50 °F

Petrus Speciale

	top-fermentation	fermentation haute	hoge gisting
	amber	ambrée	amber
	barley malt, hops (Vienna hop varieties), yeast, pure spring water, coriander	malt d'orge, houblon (variétés de houblon viennois), levure, eau de source pure, coriandre	gerstemout, hop (Weense hopvariëteiten), gist, zuiver bronwater, koriander
	amber-coloured with a solid foam head	couleur ambrée avec un faux col solide	amberkleurig met een vaste schuimkraag
	Fruity, creamy flavour with a dry, malty background. Spicy with a slightly bitter aftertaste.	Arôme fruité et crémeux avec un arrière-fond sec et malté. Corsée avec une fin de bouche légèrement amère.	Fruitig en romig aroma met een droge moutachtige achtergrond. Pittig met een licht bittere afdronk.
	Pour into a degreased, rinsed and wet glass, avoiding contact between bottle and foam.	Verser dans un verre dégraissé, rincé et mouillé sans que la bouteille touche le faux col.	Uitschenken in een ontvet, gespoeld en nat glas zonder dat de fles het schuim raakt.
i			

Het Alternatief by Brouwerij De Graal

9% 8 - 10° 46 - 50°

	top-fermentation re-fermented in the bottle	fermentation haute refermentation en bouteille	hoge gisting hergisting in de fles
	specialty beer unpasteurised light amber	bière spéciale non pasteurisée légèrement ambrée	speciaalbier niet gepasteuriseerd licht amber
	5 malt varieties, 3 hop varieties, wheat, yeast, granulated sugar, brewing water, no additives	5 sortes de malt, 3 sortes de houblon, froment, levure, sucre cristallisé, eau de brassage, pas d'additifs	5 soorten mout, 3 hopsoorten, tarwe, gist, kristalsuiker, brouwwater, geen additieven
	dark blond (15 EBC) unfiltered	blond foncé (15 EBC) non filtrée	donkerblond (15 EBC) niet gefilterd
	Warming beer with malty and hoppy character. Taste and aroma: spices, pepper, caramel, alcohol.	Bière réchauffante avec un caractère malté et houblonné. Saveur et arômes : herbes, poivre, caramel, alcool.	Verwarmend bier met moutig en hoppig karakter. Smaak en aroma: kruidig, peper, karamel, alcohol.
	Pour carefully in the Alternatief glass.	Verser prudemment dans le verre Alternatief.	Voorzichtig uitschenken in het Alternatiefglas.
i			

rouwerij Bavik 8% 8 - 12 °C 46 - 54 °F

Pilaarbijter Blond

	top-fermentation re-fermented in the bottle centrifuged	fermentation haute refermentation en bouteille centrifugée	hoge gisting hergisting in de fles gecentrifugeerd
	strong blond	bière blonde forte	sterk blond
	barley malt, hops, yeast, pure spring water	malt d'orge, houblon, levure, eau de source pure	gerstemout, tarwe, hop, gist, zuiver bronwater
	golden yellow filtered, pasteurised	jaune très clair filtrée, pasteurisée	goudgeel gefilterd, gepasteuriseerd
	Full, fruity taste with a well-balanced hoppy bitterness. Slightly spicy. Malty, strong and creamy, full character.	Saveur pleine et fruitée avec un goût houblonné équilibré et légèrement relevé. Maltée, prononcée et crémeuse, pleine de caractère.	Vol en fruitig, evenwichtige hoppige bitterheid, licht gekruid. Moutig, sterk en romig, vol karakter
	Pour into a dry glass avoiding contact between bottle and foam. Leave the sediment in the bottle.	Verser dans un verre sec sans que la bouteille touche le faux col. Laisser le dépôt de levure dans la bouteille.	Uitschenken in een droog glas zonder dat de fles het schuim raakt. Gistfond in de fles laten.
i	Gebrouwen onder licentie van het bisdom Brugge.	Brassée sous licence de l'Evêché de Bruges.	Gebrouwen onder licentie van het bisdom Brugge.

P

Pilaarbijter Bruin

Brouwerij Bavik 6,50% 8 - 12° 46 - 54°

	top-fermentation re-fermented in the bottle centrifuged	fermentation haute refermentation en bouteille centrifugée	hoge gisting hergisting in de fles gecentrifugeerd
	dubbel	double	dubbel
	barley malt, wheat, hops, yeast, pure spring water	malt d'orge, froment, houblon, levure, eau de source pure	gerstemout, tarwe, hop, gist, zuiver bronwater
	burgundy slightly cloudy	bordeaux légèrement trouble	bordeaux licht troebel
	Oak-like, juicy, roasted, Armagnac-like taste. Solid and full.	Goût de chêne savoureux et grillé renvoyant à l'Armagnac. Solide et pleine.	Eikachtige, sappige, getoaste smaak die doet denken aan Armagnac. Stevig en vol.
	Pour into a dry glass avoiding contact between bottle and foam.	Verser dans un verre sec sans que la bouteille touche le faux col.	Uitschenken in een droog glas zonder dat de fles het schuim raakt.
	Pilaarbijter' [pillar biter] means hypocrite. The label depicts the painting Pieter Breughel senior's 'Flemish sayings'.	Pilaarbijter signifie 'Schijnheilige' (hypocrite). Sur l'étiquette, se trouve représenté le tableau 'Vlaamse Gezegden' (Expressions flamandes) de Pieter Breugel l'Ancien.	Pilaarbijter betekent 'Schijnheilige'. Op het etiket staat het schilderij 'Vlaamse gezegden' van Pieter Breughel de oude afgebeeld.

bottom-fermentation	fermentation basse	lage gisting
pilsner natural beer	pils bière naturelle	pilsbier natuurbier
barley malt, yeast, sugar, hops, water	malt d'orge, houblon, sucre, levure, eau	gerstemout, gist, suiker, hop, water
clear	claire	helder
Refreshing and thirst-quenching. Aroma of hop and typical taste of unpasteurised beer.	Fraîche et désaltérante. Arômes de houblon et goût typique de bière non pasteurisée.	Fris en dorstlessend. Aroma van hop en typische smaak van ongepasteuriseerd bier.
Pour into a degreased, rinsed and wet glass, avoiding contact between bottle and foam.	Verser complètement dans un verre dégraissé, rincé et mouillé sans que la bouteille touche l'écume.	Helemaal uitschenken in een ontvet, gespoeld, nat glas zonder dat de fles het schuim raakt.
This beer does not contain any preservatives and is not pasteurised. Therefore, it can only be kept for about four weeks in the refrigerator.	La bière ne contient pas de produits conservateurs et n'est pas pasteurisée; elle se conserve seulement 4 semaines au réfrigérateur.	Het bier bevat geen bewaarmiddelen en wordt niet gepasteuriseerd waardoor het maar een 4-tal weken houdbaar is op koelkasttemperatuur.

Pimpernelle

Jessenhofke by De Proefbrouwerij

8% 9 - 11 ° 48 - 52 °

	top-fermentation re-fermentation in the bottle centrifuged	fermentation haute refermentation en bouteille centrifugée	hoge gisting hergisting in de fles gecentrifugeerd
	tripel herbal beer	triple kruidenbier	tripel kruidenbier
	barley malt, wheat malt, unrefined cane sugar, bitter hops (Challenger), aromatic hops (Goldings and Fuggles), herbs (garlic, burnet, hyssop, thyme, summer savory, myrtle), water	malt d'orge, malt de froment, sucre de canne non raffiné, malt amer (Challenger), malt aromatique (Goldings et Fuggles), herbes (ail, pimprenelle, hysope, thym, sarriette, myrte), eau	gerstemout, tarwemout, ongeraffineerde rietsuiker, bitterhop (Challenger), aromahop (Goldings en Fuggles), kruiden (knoflook, pimpernelle, hyssop, tijm, bonenkruid, mirthe), water
	blond with solid foam head not filtered or pasteurised	blonde avec faux col solide non filtrée, non pasteurisée	blond met stevige schuimkraag ongefilterd, niet gepasteuriseerd
	Spicy taste and aftertaste.	Épicée de goût et d'arrière-bouche.	Kruidig van smaak en afdronk.
	see Jessenhofke Maya	voir Jessenhofke Maya	zie Jessenhofke Maya
	Partnership between demo brewery Jessenhofke and herb grower Sanguisorba. It is the tripel to which 5 different herbs have been added.	Collaboration entre la brasserie de test Jessenhofke et l'herboriste Sanguisorba. Il s'agit de la triple, à laquelle 5 sortes d'herbes ont été ajoutées.	Samenwerking tussen demobrouwerij Jessenhofke en kruidenkweker Sanguisorba. Het is de tripel waaraan 5 soorten kruiden zijn toegevoegd.

Pink killer

rasserie de Silly | **4,70% (11° plato)** | 4 - 7 °C / 39 - 45 °F

	top-fermentation	fermentation haute	hoge gisting
	fruity witbier	bière blanche fruitée	fruitig witbier
	malt, wheat, pink grape-fruit juice, flavouring, sugar, yeast, coriander, orange rind, Hallertau hops, water	malt, froment, jus de pamplemousse rose, arômes, sucre, levure, coriandre, écorce d'orange, houblon Hal-lertau, eau	mout, tarwe, roze-pom-pelmoessap, aroma's, suiker, gist, koriander, sinaasschil, Hallertau-hop, water
	pink (25 EBC) cloudy	rose (25 EBC) trouble	roze (25 EBC) troebel
	Fruity and thirst-quenching, sugared but not excessively sweet. Bitter grapefruit touch.	Fruitée et désaltérante, sucrée mais pas excessi-vement douce. Touche amère de pample-mousse.	Fruitig en dorstlessend, gesuikerd maar niet overdreven zoet. Bittere toets van pompelmoes.
i			

Pipedream

Brouwerij Alvinne

7,80%

top-fermentation re-fermentation in the bottle	fermentation haute refermentation en bouteille	hoge gisting hergisting in de fles
IPA	IPA	IPA
barley malt, wheat malt, 5 different hops, yeast, water	malt d'orge, malt de froment, 5 variétés de houblon, levure, eau	gerstemout, tarwemout, 5 hopsoorten, gist, water
19 EBC	19 EBC	19 EBC
56 EBU	56 EBU.	56 EBU
Joint venture between Alvinne, De Struise Brouwers and Pipeworks Brewing Co (USA)	Joint venture entre Alvinne, De Struise Brouwers et Pipeworks Brewing Co (États-Unis).	Joint venture tussen Alvinne, De Struise Brouwers en Pipeworks Brewing Co (USA)

rouwerij Van Steenberge 10,50% (23° plato) 10 - 12 °C 50 - 54 °F

	top-fermentation re-fermented in the bottle	fermentation haute refermentation en bouteille	hoge gisting hergisting in de fles
	strong blond	blonde forte	sterk blond
	barley malt, hops, yeast, water	malt d'orge, houblon, levure, eau	gerstemout, hop, gist, water
	light amber	ambré clair	licht amber
	Complex, rich taste. Spicy, light sweetness, richly balanced by a solid hoppy bitterness.	Saveur complexe et riche. Goût relevé, légèrement sucré et richement équilibré par un goût amer houblonné solide.	Complexe en rijke smaak. Kruidige, lichte zoetigheid die rijkelijk gebalanceerd wordt met een stevige hopbitterheid.
	Pour in one fluent movement, leaving 1 cm of yeast sediment in the bottle. The sediment can be poured, making the beer cloudy.	Verser en un seul mouvement fluide et doux et laisser 1 cm de dépôt de levure dans la bouteille. Le depôt de levure peut être versé et rend la bière trouble.	Uitschenken in 1 vloeiende, zachte beweging en 1 cm gistdepot in de fles laten. De gistfond kan worden uitgeschonken en maakt het bier troebel.
i	A lively beer with a powerful nutritional value, like the beers the Vikings used to drink whilst sailing. Also has a 9% version. Very much appreciated by American connoisseurs.	Une bière vive avec forte valeur nutritive comme les bières que buvaient les Vikings en mer. Existe aussi dans une version 9%. Cotée très haut par les connaisseurs américains.	Een levendig bier met hoge voedingswaarde zoals de bieren die de Vikings op zee dronken. Bestaat ook in een versie van 9%. Superhoog gekwoteerd bij Amerikaanse bierkenners.

Pissenlit

Brasserie Fantôme 8%

	top-fermentation	fermentation haute	hoge gisting
	saisons boutique beer	bière de saison artisanale	saison, artisanaal bier
	dandelions, barley malt, hops, yeast, water	pissenlits, malt d'orge, houblon, levure, eau	paardenbloemen, gerstemout, hop, gist, water
	amber yellow	jaune ambré	ambergeel
	Strong, savoury beer with a pronounced hoppy touch.	Bière forte et pleine de goût avec une touche houblonnée forte.	Sterk en smaakvol bier met een sterke hoptoets
	Serve in a tulip-shaped glass (cfr. Duvel).	Verser dans un verre tulipe (voir Duvel).	Uitschenken in een tulpglas (cfr. Duvel).
	Fantôme beers are very hard to find in Belgium. Even the brewer only has a small stock.	Les bières de Fantôme sont difficiles à trouver en Belgique, même le brasseur a peu de stock.	De bieren van Fantôme zijn in België heel moeilijk te vinden, zelfs de brouwer heeft weinig op voorraad.

7% 6 °C 43 °F

Plokkersbier

	top-fermentation	fermentation haute	hoge gisting
	amber	ambrée	amber
	malt, hops, wheat, candy sugar, yeast, herbs, water	malt, houblon, froment, sucre candi, levure, herbes, eau	mout, hop, tarwe, kandijsuiker, gist, kruiden, water
	amber	ambrée	amber
	Spicy.	Goût relevé.	Kruidig.
	Very suitable for cooking. 'Plokker' refers to the Plokkers route in Watou. 'Plokken' means to pluck, a reference to the hop harvesting.	Convient particulièrement pour la cuisine à la bière. 'Plokker' se réfère à la route des Plokkers à Watou. 'Plokken' signifie cueillir et renvoie au houblon.	Heel geschikt voor de bierkeuken. De naam Plokker refereert aan de de Plokkersroute in Watou. Plokken betekent plukken. Een verwijzing naar de hop.

P Poorter

Sterkens by Brasserie du Bocq

6,50% 6 - 10 43 - 50

	top-fermentation re-fermented in the bottle	fermentation haute refermentation en bouteille	hoge gisting hergisting in de fles
	dubbel abbey beer	bière d'abbaye double	dubbel abdijbier
	malt, hops, yeast, water	malt, houblon, levure, eau	mout, hop, gist, water
	dark brown, filtered	brun foncé, filtrée	donkerbruin, gefilterd
	Solid and powerful. Slightly sweet with caramel touches. Taste: alcohol and hops with a touch of chocolate and roasted malt. Dry aftertaste.	Solide et forte. Légèrement douce avec des touches caramélisées. Saveur :alcool et houblon avec une touche de chocolat et de malt brûlée. Fin de bouche sèche.	Stevig en krachtig. Lichtzoetig met toetsen van karamel. Smaak: alcohol en hop met een vleugje chocolade en gebrande mout. Droge afdronk.
	Carefully serve in the sipping glass, with a generous foam head.	Verser prudemment dans un verre de dégustation avec un faux col solide.	Voorzichtig uitschenken in het degustatieglas met een ruime schuimkraag.
i	More than 90% is destined for export.	Plus de 90% de la production est exporté.	Meer dan 90% is bestemd voor export.

Poperings Hommelbier

rouwerij Van Eecke 7,50% 6 - 8 °C 43 - 46 °F

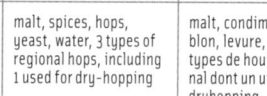

top-fermentation re-fermented in the bottle	fermentation haute refermentation en bouteille	hoge gisting nagisting op de fles
regional beer	bière régionale	streekbier
malt, spices, hops, yeast, water, 3 types of regional hops, including 1 used for dry-hopping	malt, condiments, houblon, levure, eau, 3 types de houblon régional dont un utilisé pour dryhopping	mout, specerijen, hop, gist, water, 3 types regionale hop waarvan 1 gebruikt voor dryhopping
light bronze	couleur bronze claire	licht bronskleurig
Very refreshing hop character. Very bitter with flowery hop flavours.	Caractère houblonné très rafraîchissant. Goût amer prononcé et arômes houblonnés fleuris.	Zeer verfrissend hopkarakter. Hoge bitterheid en bloemige hoparoma's.
Hold the glass by the stem and tilt it. Pour slowly in a single movement. Either pour the yeast sediment or leave it in the bottle.	Tenir le verre en oblique par le pied et verser la bière lentement en un seul mouvement. Verser le dépôt de levure selon le goût.	Het glas bij de voet schuin houden en het bier traag in 1 beweging uitschenken. Het gistdepot kan naar keuze al dan niet worden uitgeschonken.

Postel Blond

Brouwerij Alken-Maes 7% 8 - 10 ° 46 - 50 °

top-fermentation re-fermented in the bottle	fermentation haute refermentation en bouteille	hoge gisting hergisting op de fles
Recognised Belgian abbey beer blond	Bière d'abbaye belge reconnue blonde	Erkend Belgisch abdijbier blond
barley malt, hops, yeast, water	malt d'orge, houblon, levure, eau	gerstemout, hop, gist, water
golden blond	blond doré	goudblond
Hoppy nose, smoothly bitter, balance between malt and hops.	Parfum houblonné, doux-amère, équilibre entre malt et houblon.	Hoppige neus, zacht bitter, evenwicht tussen mout en hop.
Pour slowly, leaving the yeast in the bottle.	Verser lentement et laisser la levure dans la bouteille.	Langzaam uitschenken en de gist in de fles laten.
The abbey of Postel is located on the Belgian-Dutch border.	L'abbaye de Postel est située à la frontière entre la Belgique et les Pays-Bas.	De abdij van Postel ligt op de Belgisch-Nederlandse grens.

ouwerij Alken-Maes 7% 8 - 10 °C 46 - 50 °F

Postel Dubbel

	top-fermentation re-fermented in the bottle	fermentation haute refermentation en bouteille	hoge gisting hergisting op de fles
	Recognised Belgian abbey beer dubbel	Bière d'abbaye belge reconnue double	Erkend Belgisch abdijbier dubbel
	barley malt, hops, yeast, water	malt d'orge, houblon, levure, eau	gerstemout, hop, gist, water
	red-brown	brun rouge	roodbruin
	Spicy with a sweet touch, smooth mouthfeel with full aftertaste.	Goût relevé avec une touche douce, sensation moelleuse dans la bouche avec une fin de bouche pleine.	Kruidig met een zoete toets, zacht in de mond met volle afdronk.
	Slowly pour, leaving the yeast in the bottle.	Verser lentement et laisser la levure dans la bouteille.	Langzaam uitschenken en de gist in de fles laten.
	The abbey of Postel is located on the Belgian-Dutch border.	L'abbaye de Postel est située à la frontière entre la Belgique et les Pays-Bas.	De abdij van Postel ligt op de Belgisch-Nederlandse grens.

P

Postel Tripel

Brouwerij Alken-Maes 9% 8 - 10 / 46 - 50

	top-fermentation re-fermented in the bottle	fermentation haute refermentation en bouteille	hoge gisting hergisting op de fles
	Recognised Belgian abbey beer tripel	bière d'abbaye belge reconnue triple	Erkend Belgisch abdijbier tripel
	barley malt, hops, yeast, water	malt d'orge, houblon, levure, eau	gerstemout, hop, gist, water
	deep gold	doré intense	diepgoud
	Typical bitterness and full round aftertaste. Spicy character with flavours of malt and spices.	Goût amer typique et fin de bouche ronde pleine. Caractère corsé avec des arômes de malt et d'herbes.	Typische bitterheid en volronde afdronk. Pittig karakter met aroma van mout en kruiden.
	Pour slowly, leaving the yeast in the bottle.	Verser lentement et laisser la levure dans la bouteille.	Langzaam uitschenken en de gist in de fles laten.
i	The abbey of Postel is located on the Belgian-Dutch border.	L'abbaye de Postel est située à la frontière entre la Belgique et les Pays-Bas.	De abdij van Postel ligt op de Belgisch-Nederlandse grens.

8% 10 - 14 °C 50 - 57 °F

top-fermentation	fermentation haute	hoge gisting
dark ale	ale foncée	donkere ale
pilsner malt, cara and Münich malts, Vlamertinge hops, brown candy sugar, yeast, water	malt de pils, cara et Münich, houblon de Vlamertinge, sucre candi brun, levure, eau	pilsmout, cara en Münich mouten, Vlamertingse hop, bruine kandijsuiker, gist, water
deep brown, clear	brun intense, claire	diepbruin, helder
Intense, heart-warming and pleasantly sweet.	Intense, réchauffante et agréablement douce.	Intens, hartverwarmend en aangenaam zoet.
Leave the bottle for some days in an upright position. Pour carefully into a goblet, leaving the yeast sediment in the bottle. Pour out the yeast sediment separately.	Laisser reposer la bière quelques jours avant la dégustation. Verser prudemment dans un verre calice et laisser le dépôt de levure dans la bouteille. Le dépôt de levure peut être bu séparément.	Het bier voor het degusteren een paar dagen laten rusten. Voorzichtig uitschenken in een kelkglas en de gistbodem in de fles laten. De gistbodem kan afzonderlijk worden uitgedronken.
Brewed by order of the pottery 't Hoveke from Deinze. Therefore, it is served in a specific, hand-made stone jug.	Brassée à la demande de la poterie 't Hoveke de Deinze et pour cette raison bue dans un pot en pierre fait à la main.	Gebrouwen op vraag van Pottenbakkerij 't Hoveke uit Deinze en daarom gedronken uit een handgedraaide stenen pot.

Premium Cassis St Louis

Brouwerij Van Honsebrouck

3,20% 5 41

	spontaneous fermentation	fermentation spontanée	spontane gisting
	fruit beer based on gueuze lambic	bière fruitée à base de gueuze lambic	fruitbier op basis van geuze lambiek
	malt, wheat, sugar, hops, black currant juice, flavour, water	malt, froment, sucre, houblon, jus de cassis, arômes, eau	mout, tarwe, suiker, hop, zwartebessensap, aroma, water
	intense red-blue clear	rouge-bleu intense claire	intens roodblauw helder
	Refreshing. Pronounced black currant.	Rafraîchissante. Cassis prononcé.	Verfrissend. Uitgesproken cassis.
	Pour into a newly rinsed glass, keeping it tilted first and in a vertical position at the end.	Verser dans un verre rincé tenu d'abord en oblique et à la fin en position verticale.	Uitschenken in een vers gespoeld glas dat eerst schuin gehouden wordt en op het einde verticaal gehouden wordt.
i			

ouwerij Van Honsebrouck

3,20% — 5 °C / 41 °F

spontaneous fermentation	fermentation spontanée	spontane gisting
faro	faro	faro
malt, wheat, candy sugar, hops, water	malt, froment, sucre candi, houblon, eau	mout, tarwe, kandijsuiker, hop, water
amber clear	ambrée claire	amber helder
Refreshing. Sweet-and-sour with the taste of candy sugar.	Fraîche. Aigre-douce avec la saveur de sucre de candi.	Fris. Zuur en zoet met de smaak van kandijsuiker.
Pour into a newly rinsed glass, keeping it tilted first and in a vertical position at the end.	Verser dans un verre rincé tenu d'abord en oblique et à la fin en position verticale.	Uitschenken in een vers gespoeld glas dat eerst schuin gehouden wordt en op het einde verticaal gehouden wordt.

Premium Faro St Louis

P

Premium Framboise St Louis

Brouwerij Van Honsebrouck **2,80%** 5 41

	spontaneous fermentation	fermentation spontanée	spontane gisting
	fruit beer based on gueuze lambic	bière fruitée à base de gueuze lambic	fruitbier op basis van geuze lambiek
	malt, wheat, sugar, hops, raspberry juice, water	malt, froment, sucre, houblon, jus de framboises, eau	mout, tarwe, suiker, hop, frambozensap, water
	dark red clear	rouge foncé claire	donkerrood helder
	Refreshing and fruity. Strong raspberry flavour and aroma with a fruity aftertaste.	Rafraîchissante et fruitée. Saveur et arômes de framboises et arrière-bouche fruitée.	Verfrissend en fruitig. Sterke frambozensmaak en -aroma met fruitige nasmaak.
	Pour into a newly rinsed glass, keeping it tilted first and in a vertical position at the end.	Verser dans un verre rincé tenu d'abord en oblique et à la fin en position verticale.	Uitschenken in een vers gespoeld glas dat eerst schuin gehouden wordt en op het einde verticaal gehouden wordt.
i			

Premium Kriek St Louis

ouwerij Van Honsebrouck 3,20% 5 °C 41 °F

	spontaneous fermentation	fermentation spontanée	spontane gisting
	fruit beer based on gueuze lambic	bière fruitée à base de gueuze lambic	fruitbier op basis van geuze lambiek
	malt, wheat, sugar, hops, cherries, water	malt, froment, sucre, houblon, cerises, eau	mout, tarwe, suiker, hop, krieken, water
	dark red clear	rouge foncé claire	donkerrood helder
	Fresh and very fruity. Sweet-and-sour with a deep cherry taste and strong, refreshing aftertaste.	Fraîche et fruitée. Aigre-douce avec une saveur profonde de cerises et une arrière-bouche très rafraîchissante.	Fris en fruitig. Zuurzoet met diepe kriekensmaak en sterk verfrissende nasmaak.
	Pour into a newly rinsed glass, keeping it tilted first and in a vertical position at the end.	Verser dans un verre rincé tenu d'abord en oblique et à la fin en position verticale.	Uitschenken in een vers gespoeld glas dat eerst schuin gehouden wordt en op het einde verticaal gehouden wordt.
i			

P Premium Pêche St Louis

Brouwerij Van Honsebrouck 2,60% 5 41

	spontaneous fermentation	fermentation spontanée	spontane gisting
	fruit beer based on gueuze lambic	bière fruitée à base de gueuze lambic	fruitbier op basis van geuze lambiek
	malt, wheat, sugar, hops, peach juice, water	malt, froment, sucre, houblon, jus de pêches, eau	mout, tarwe, suiker, hop perzikensap, water
	amber clear	ambrée claire	amber helder
	Refreshing and fruity. Full flavour and aroma of peach, with a slightly sourish aftertaste.	Fraîche et fruitée. Saveur et arôme pleins de pêche avec une fin de bouche légèrement acidulée.	Verfrissend en fruitig. Volle smaak en aroma van perzik met lichte zurigheid in de nasmaak.
	Pour into a newly rinsed glass, keeping it tilted first and in a vertical position at the end.	Verser dans un verre rincé tenu d'abord en oblique et à la fin en position verticale.	Uitschenken in een vers gespoeld glas dat eerst schuin gehouden wordt en op het einde verticaal gehouden wordt.
i			

ouwerij Het Sas

3,25% 3 °C 37 °F

bottom-fermentation	fermentation basse	lage gisting
table beer tripel	bière de table triple	tafelbier tripel
malt, rice, hops, water	malt, riz, houblon, eau	mout, rijst, hop, water
blond clear	blonde claire	blond helder
Distinctive. Malt flavour and slightly bitter aftertaste.	Plein de caractère. Arôme malté et fin de bouche légèrement amère.	Karaktervol. Moutig aroma en licht bittere afdronk.
Pour slowly in a single, smooth movement in a degreased glass. Keep the glass tilted and avoid sloshing. Skim off the foam.	Verser lentement en un seul mouvement fluide dans un verre dégraissé tenu en oblique. Ne pas laisser la bière glouglou-ter. Ecumer le verre.	Traag en in 1 vloeiende beweging uitschenken in een vetvrij glas dat wordt schuingehouden. Het bier niet laten klotsen. Het glas afschuimen.

Primus

Brouwerij Haacht 5,20% 3 37

	bottom-fermentation centrifuged	fermentation basse centrifugée	lage gisting gecentrifugeerd
	pils or lagerbier	pils ou lagerbier	pils of lagerbier
	water, barley malt, hops, corn, yeast	eau, malt d'orge, houblon, maïs, levure	water, gerstemout, hop, mais, gist
	clear light blond foam head with fine bubbles filtered	blond clair faux col avec des bulles fines filtrée	helder lichtblond fijnbellige schuimkraag gefilterd
	Typical bitterness and hoppy flavour. Taste: sweet and slightly bitter, turning into a dry, thirst-quenching aftertaste.	Goût amer typique et arômes de houblon. Saveur initiale légèrement douce avec un goût amer retenu évoluant vers une fin de bouche sèche, désaltérante.	Typische bitterheid en hoparoma's. Lichtzoete aanzet met ingetoomde bitterheid die evolueert naar een droge, dorstlessende afdronk.
	Pour carefully into a rinsed, wet Primus glass, avoiding contact between bottle and foam.	Verser prudemment dans un verre Primus rincé et mouillé sans que la bouteille touche l'écume.	Voorzichtig uitschenken in een gespoeld, nat Primusglas zonder dat de fles het glas of schuim raakt.
i	The name refers to Jan Primus, duke of Brabant, who brought welfare in the 13th century and who loved a good party with delicious beer. Before 1975, this beer was brewed under the name Super 8.	Le nom fait référence à Jean Ier, duc de Brabant, qui apporta de la prospérité au 13e siècle et raffolait des grandes fêtes, avec de la bière délicieuse. Avant 1975, cette bière était brassée sous le nom Super 8.	De naam verwijst naar Jan Primus, hertog van Brabant, die in de 13e eeuw welvaart bracht en hield van een stevig feest met heerlijk bier. Voor 1975 werd dit bier gebrouwen onder de naam Super 8.

'ouwerij Boelens 5,50% 4 - 6 °C 39 - 43 °F

Prinsesken - Meilses Eiërebezenbier

top-fermentation re-fermented in the bottle	fermentation haute refermentation en bouteille	hoge gisting hergisting op de fles
fruit beer	bière fruitée	fruitbier
strawberry pink clear	rose fraises claire	aardbeiroze helder
Light, sour and non-sweet strawberry taste.	Saveur légère, acidulée et non sucrée de fraises.	Licht, zuur, niet zoete aardbeiensmaak.
Pour carefully so that the yeast sediment stays at the bottom of the bottle.	Verser prudemment pour garder le dépôt de levure au fond de la bouteille.	Voorzichtig uitschenken om het gistbezinksel op de bodem te houden.
Season's beer brewed by order of the Melsele Strawberry Committee.	Bière de saison brassée à la demande du comité des fraises de Melsele.	Seizoensbier gebrouwen in opdracht van het aard-beiencomité van Melse-le.

P

Prior Tongerlo

Brouwerij Haacht 9% 7° 45°

	top-fermentation re-fermentation in the bottle; centrifuged	fermentation haute refermentation en bouteille; centrifugée	hoge gisting hergisting in de fles gecentrifugeerd
	Recognised Belgian abbey beer tripel blond	Bière d'abbaye belge reconnue blonde triple	Erkend Belgisch Abdijbier tripel blond
	barley malt, wheat malt, hops (Saaz), sugar, yeast, water. After bottling, sugar and pure culture yeast are added to develop taste.	malt d'orge, malt de froment, houblon (Saaz), sucre, levure, eau. Après la mise en bouteille le sucre et la levure de culture microbienne sont ajoutés pour assurer l'évolution du goût.	gerstemout, tarwemout, hop (Saaz), suiker, gist, water. Na het bottelen worden suiker en reincultuurgist toegevoegd die zorgen voor smaakevolutie.
	gold-yellow with creamy foam head filtered, pasteurised	jaune doré avec faux col crémeux filtrée, pasteurisée	goudgeel met romige schuimkraag gefilterd, gepasteuriseerd
	Full-bodied onset with hints of fruit that develop into a spicy and slightly floral hoppy bitterness.	Approche initiale franche, avec des touches fruitées qui s'écoulent en une amertume houblonnée épicée et légèrement fleurie.	Volmondige aanzet met fruitige toetsen die uitvloeien in een kruidige en licht bloemige hopbitterheid.
	see Tongerlo Blond	voir Tongerlo Blond	zie Tongerlo Blond
	The Norbertines of Tongerlo have been brewing beer since the establishment of the abbey (1130). The beer was crowned in 2010 by 120 chefs and sommeliers with the Superior Taste Award.	Dès la fondation de l'abbaye (1130) déjà, les Prémontrés de Tongerlo brassent de la bière. La bière a été couronnée en 2010 du Superior Taste Award par 120 chefs et sommeliers.	Al sinds de oprichting van de abdij (1130) brouwen de Norbertijnen van Tongerlo bier. Het bier werd in 2010 door 120 chefs en sommeliers bekroond met de Superior Taste Award.

ontaigu by 't Hofbrouwerijke

5,60% — 8 - 10 °C / 46 - 50 °F

	top-fermentation re-fermented in the bottle	fermentation haute refermentation en bouteille	hoge gisting nagisting in de fles
	blond	blonde	blond
	barley malt, sugar, hops, yeast, water	malt d'orge, sucre, houblon, levure, eau	gerstemout, suiker, hop, gist, water

Q

Quintine Ambrée

Brasserie des Légendes 8,50% 8 - 12 / 46 - 54

	top-fermentation re-fermented in the bottle	fermentation haute refermentation en bouteille	hoge gisting nagisting in de fles
	specialty beer	bière spéciale	speciaalbier
	pale malt, caramel malt, hops, yeast, water	malt pâle, malt caramélisé, houblon, levure, eau	bleke mout, karamelmout, hop, gist, water
	amber hazy	ambrée voilée	amber gesluierd
	Very smooth character. Dry malt and caramel flavour.	Caractère très doux. Arômes de malt sec et de caramel.	Zeer zacht karakter. Droge mout en karamelaroma.

5,90% | 8 - 12 °C / 46 - 54 °F

	top-fermentation natural re-fermentation in the bottle	fermentation haute refermentation naturelle en bouteille	hoge gisting natuurlijke hergisting in de fles
	regional beer	bière régionale	streekbier
	organic pale malt, organic wheat, organic hops, yeast, water	malt pâle biologique, froment biologique, levure, eau	biologische bleke mout, biologische tarwe, biologische hop, gist, water
	blond, veiled not filtered or pasteurised	blonde, voilée non filtrée, non pasteurisée	blond, gesluierd ongefilterd, niet gepasteuriseerd
	Dry and thirst-quenching. Very fruity, yet distinctly hoppy. Dry and refreshing aftertaste.	Sèche et désaltérante. Fort fruitée, avec un caractère houblonné prononcé. Arrière-bouche sèche et vive.	Droog en dorstlessend. Zeer fruitig met een uitgesproken hoppig karakter. Droge en levendige afdronk.
i	Quintine is the name of a witch who died at the stake in 1610.	Quintine est le nom d'une sorcière qui mourut en 1610 sur le bûcher.	Quintine is de naam van een heks die in 1610 stierf op de brandstapel.

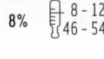

Quintine Blonde

Brasserie des Légendes

8% 8 - 12° 46 - 54

	top-fermentation; uncentrifuged re-fermented in the bottle	fermentation haute; non centrifugée refermentation en bouteille	hoge gisting niet gecentrifugeerd hergisting in de fles
	specialty beer	bière spéciale	speciaalbier
	malt, hops, yeast, water	malt, houblon, levure, eau	mout, hop, gist, water
	blond hazy unfiltered, unpasteurised	blonde voilée non filtrée ni pasteurisée	blond gesluierd niet gefilterd of gepasteuriseerd
	Smooth, robust and hoppy. Earthy, creamy flavour, dry malt and hoppy aftertaste.	Douce et robuste avec un goût de houblon prononcé. Arôme terreux et crémeux, malt sec et arrière-bouche houblonnée.	Zacht en robuust met duidelijke hop. Gronderig en romig aroma, droge mout en hoppige afdronk.
	The name refers to the folklore from Ellezelles: Quintine is a witch who was burnt at the stake in 1610.	Le nom renvoie au folkore d'Ellezelles : Quintine est une sorcière qui est morte sur le bûcher en 1610.	De naam verwijst naar de folklore van Ellezelles: Quintine is een heks die in 1610 op de brandstapel stierf.

Rebel Local

rouwers Verzet at Brouwerij Het Gulden Spoor 8,50% 5 - 7 °C 41 - 45 °F

	top-fermentation re-fermentation in the bottl; not centrifuged	fermentation haute refermentation en bouteille; non centrifugée	hoge gisting hergisting in de fles; niet gecentrifugeerd
	IPA city or regional beer	IPA bière régionale	IPA stads- of streekbier
	barley malt, hops, sugar, yeast, water	malt d'orge, houblon, sucre, levure, eau	gerstemout, hop, suiker, gist, water
	gold-blond, slightly hazy with a white, creamy foam head that lingers. Not filtered or pasteurised	blond doré, légèrement fade avec un faux col crémeux stable blanc. Non filtrée, non pasteurisée	goudblond, licht wazig met een witte, romige schuimkraag die lang blijft. Ongefilterd, niet gepasteuriseerd
	Light fruity, flowery and hoppy aroma. Sweet with slightly bitter aftertaste. Balanced, obstinate beer full of character.	Arôme légèrement fruité, fleuri et houblonné. Goût sucré, avec une arrière-bouche légèrement amère. Bière équilibrée, volontaire et très caractéristique.	Licht fruitig, bloemig en hoppig aroma. Zoete smaak met licht bittere afdronk. Evenwichtig, eigenzinnig en karaktervol bier.
	Pour slowly into a tall glass that narrows towards the top. Pour out yeast sediment separately.	Verser lentement dans un verre oblong se rétrécissant vers le haut. Verser séparément le dépôt de levure.	Traag uitschenken in een langwerpig glas dat naar boven toe versmalt. Het gistdepot apart uitschenken.
i	Fledgling brewery, founded by 3 friends active in the world of brewing. Their passion for brewing can be tasted in this wayward 'weekend' concoction.	Toute jeune brasserie, fondée par 3 amis qui sont actifs dans le monde des brasseurs. Leur passion pour le brassage se laisse déguster dans cet obstiné brassin de 'week-end'.	Piepjonge brouwerij, opgericht door 3 vrienden die in de brouwerswereld actief zijn. Hun passie voor het brouwen laat zich proeven in dit eigenzinnig 'weekend'-brouwsel.

Redbocq

Brasserie du Bocq 3,10% 4 - 6° / 39 - 43

	top-fermentation	fermentation haute	hoge gisting
	white beer with fruit/ fruit (juice)	bière blanche fruitée	witbier met fruit/fruit-sap
	barley malt, wheat, natural aromas of red fruits, sugar, sweeteners, hops, yeast, water	malt d'orge, froment, arômes naturels de fruits rouges, sucre, édulcorant, houblon, levure, eau	gerstemout, tarwe, natuurlijke aroma's van rode vruchten, suiker, zoetstof, hop, gist, water
	clear red, naturally pink foam head, fine bubbles	rouge vif, faux col rose naturel, pétillement fin	helder rood, natuurlijk roze schuimkraag, fijne pareling
	Aroma: mixture of wheat and natural fruit aromas of cherry, strawberry, plum and blackcurrant. A sugary-tart base in harmony with the 4 fruits.	Arôme : mélange de froment et d'arômes naturels de cerise, de fraise, de prune et de cassis. Une base sucrée-acide en harmonie avec les 4 fruits.	Aroma: mengeling van tarwe en natuurlijke fruitaroma's van kers, aardbei, pruim en cassis. Een suikerig-aangezuurde basis in harmonie met de 4 vruchten.
i			

Rédor Pils

rasserie Dupont 5% Cooled

bottom-fermentation	fermentation basse	lage gisting
pilsner	pils	pils
pure beer, brewed with barley malt	brassée seulement avec du malt d'orge	puur met gerstemout gebrouwen
blond filtered, unpasteurised	blonde filtrée, non pasteurisée	blond gefilterd, niet gepasteuriseerd
Pleasantly bitter.	Goût amer agréable.	Aangenaam bitter.
Can be kept for approximately three months.	Possibilité de conserver pendant 3 mois environ.	Beperkt houdbaar (circa 3 maanden).

Reinaert Blond

De Proefbrouwerij

7%

	top-fermentation re-fermented in the bottle	fermentation haute refermentation en bouteille	hoge gisting hergisting in de fles
	amber Belgian ale	ambrée Belgian ale	amber Belgian ale

9,50%

Reinaert Grand Cru

	top-fermentation re-fermented in the bottle	fermentation haute refermentation en bouteille	hoge gisting hergisting in de fles
	Belgian strong ale	Belgian strong ale	Belgian strong ale
	full-malt	pur malt	volmout
	dark red	rouge foncé	donkerrood
	Serve in a Trappist or tulip-shaped glass.	Verser dans un verre trappiste ou tulipe.	Uitschenken in een trappist- of tulpglas.

Reinaert Tripel

De Proefbrouwerij 9%

	top-fermentation re-fermented in the bottle	fermentation haute refermentation en bouteille	hoge gisting hergisting in de fles
	tripel	triple	tripel
	full-malt	pur malt	volmout
	blond	blonde	blond

Revolución Mexicana '10

roep John Martin by various breweries

5%

3 - 6 °C
37 - 43 °F

bottom-fermentation	fermentation basse	lage gisting
aromatised specialty beer	bière spéciale aromatisée	gearomatiseerd speciaalbier
barley malt, corn, sugar, hops, flavouring, water	malt d'orge, maïs, sucre, houblon, arômes, eau	gerstemout, maïs, suiker, hop, aroma's, water
blond	blonde	blond
Tequila and lime in the background. Touch of sugar in the aftertaste.	Arrière-fond de tequila et de citron vert. Touche sucrée dans la fin de bouche.	Tequila en limoen op de achtergrond. Toets van suiker in de afdronk.

Ridder

Brouwerij Het Sas 2,25% 3° 37°

	bottom-fermentation	fermentation basse	lage gisting
	low alcohol content	pauvre en alcool	alcoholarm
	malt, rice, hops, water	malt, riz, houblon, eau	mout, rijst, hop, water
	blond clear	blonde claire	blond helder
	Thirst-quencher with low alcohol content. Fresh, aromatic and slightly bitter.	Désaltérant légèrement alcoolisé. Fraîche, parfumée et légèrement amère.	Licht alcoholische dorstlesser. Fris, geurig en licht bitter.
	Pour slowly in a single, smooth movement into a degreased glass. Keep the glass tilted and avoid sloshing. Skim off the foam.	Verser lentement et en un seul mouvement fluide dans un verre dégraissé tenu en oblique. Ne pas laisser la bière glouglouter. Ecumer le verre.	Traag en in 1 vloeiende beweging uitschenken in een vetvrij glas dat wordt schuingehouden. Het bier niet laten klotsen. Het glas afschuimen.
i			

Riebedebie

rouwerij De Bie 9%

	top-fermentation	fermentation haute	hoge gisting
	tripel	triple	tripel
	malt, hops, sugar, yeast, herbs, water	malt, houblon, sucre, levure, herbes, eau	mout, hop, suiker, gist, kruiden, water
	blond clear	blonde claire	blond helder

Robustus

Brouwerij Gulden Spoor

10% 8 - 10° 46 - 50°

	top-fermentation re-fermentation in the bottle not centrifuged	fermentation haute refermentation en bouteille non centrifugée	hoge gisting hergisting in de fles niet gecentrifugeerd
	quadruple	quadruple	quadrupel
	barley malt, hops, yeast, water	malt d'orge, houblon, levure, eau	gerstemout, hop, gist, water
	pale brown and clear with small foam head not filtered or pasteurised	brun clair et limpide avec petit faux col non filtrée, non pasteurisée	lichtbruin en helder met kleine schuimkraag ongefilterd, niet gepasteuriseerd
	Full, caramel taste, rich taste pallet.	Goût franc de caramel, riche palette de goûts.	Vol, karamelsmaak, rijk smaakpallet.
	Degrease the glass, tilt it slightly and carefully pour the beer in a single movement.	Dégraisser le verre, tenir légèrement incliné et verser la bière prudemment d'un seul mouvement.	Het glas vetvrij maken, licht schuin houden en het bier voorzichtig in 1 beweging uitschenken.
	Is brewed once a year. Matures for 6 months in a storage tank.	Elle est brassée 1 fois par an et mûrit 6 mois dans une cuve de vieillissement.	Wordt 1 maal per jaar gebrouwen. Rijpt 6 maanden in een lagertank.

Rochefort 6

rasserie de l'Abbaye N.D. de Saint-Rémy 7,50% 12 - 14 °C 54 - 57 °F

top-fermentation	fermentation haute	hoge gisting
dark trappist	trappiste foncée	trappist donker
barley malt, grain starch, sugar, yeast, hops, spring water	malt d'orge, fécule de blé, sucre, levure, houblon, eau de source	gerstemout, zetmeel van graan, suiker, gist, hop, bronwater
red-brown	brun rouge	roodbruin
Smooth, full-bodied taste, evolving against the palate. Fruity touch.	Goût doux, plein dans la bouche évoluant au palais. Touche fruitée.	Zachte, volmondige smaak die evolueert tegen het gehemelte. Fruitige toets.
Pour slowly into a slightly tilted glass at eye level. Move the bottle away from the glass to obtain a nice foam head. Pour the last part (1/10th), which contains the yeast, separately.	Verser lentement dans un verre tenu légèrement incliné à hauteur d'yeux. Séparer la bouteille du verre pour obtenir un beau faux col. Verser séparément la dernière portion riche en vitamines (1/10e) qui contient la levure.	Traag uitschenken in een licht schuingehouden glas op ooghoogte. De fles van het glas verwijderen voor een mooie schuimkraag. Het laatste, vitaminerijke deel (1/10e) met gist afzonderlijk uitschenken.
The figure 6 does not indicate the alcohol content but is the value of the malt density before the fermentation process.	Le chiffre 6 n'indique pas la teneur en alcool, mais correspond à la valeur indiquant la densité des malts avant la fermentation.	Het cijfer 6 verwijst niet naar het alcoholpercentage maar stemt overeen met de waarde die de dichtheid van de mouten aanduidt vòòr het gistingsproces.

Rochefort 8

Brasserie de l'Abbaye N.D. de Saint-Rémy 9,20% 12 - 14° 54 - 57°

top-fermentation	fermentation haute	hoge gisting
dark trappist	trappiste foncée	trappist donker
barley malt, grain starch, sugar, yeast, hops, spring water	malt d'orge, fécule de blé, sucre, levure, houblon, eau de source	gerstemout, zetmeel van graan, suiker, gist, hop, bronwater
brown, tawny	brune, fauve	bruin, fauve
Pronounced taste, richer fruitiness, a touch of fig, strong aftertaste.	Saveur plus prononcée, fruitée avec une touche de figue. Bonne fin de bouche.	Meer uitgesproken smaak, fruitiger, een vleugje vijg. Goede afdronk.
Slowly pour into a slightly tilted glass at eye level. Move the bottle away from the glass to obtain a nice foam head. Pour the last part (1/10th), which contains the yeast, separately.	Verser lentement dans un verre tenu légèrement incliné à hauteur d'yeux. Séparer la bouteille du verre pour obtenir un beau faux col. Verser séparément la dernière portion riche en vitamines (1/10e) qui contient la levure.	Traag uitschenken in een licht schuingehouden glas op ooghoogte. De fles van het glas verwijderen voor een mooie schuimkraag. Het laatste, vitaminerijke deel (1/10e) met gist afzonderlijk uitschenken.
The figure 8 does not indicate the alcohol content but is the value of the malt density before the fermentation process.	Le chiffre 8 n'indique pas la teneur en alcool, mais correspond à la valeur indiquant la densité des malts avant la fermentation.	Het cijfer 8 verwijst niet naar het alcoholvolume maar stemt overeen met de waarde die de dichtheid van de mouten aanduidt vòòr het gistingsproces.

Rochefort 10

R

Brasserie de l'Abbaye N.D. de Saint-Rémy — 10,30% — 12 - 14 °C / 54 - 57 °F

	top-fermentation	fermentation haute	hoge gisting
	dark trappist	trappiste foncée	trappist donker
	barley malt, grain starch, sugar, yeast, hops, well water	malt d'orge, fécule de blé, sucre, levure, houblon, eau de source	gerstemout, zetmeel van graan, suiker, gist, hop, bronwater
	deep red-brown	brun rouge intense	diep roodbruin
	Honey evolving to very fruity (pears, bananas, raisins) with touches of fondant chocolate. Long-lasting aftertaste.	Saveur de miel évoluant à très fruitée (poire, bananes, raisins secs) et une touche de chocolat noir. Fin de bouche longue.	Honingsmaak evoluerend naar heel fruitig (peer, banaan, rozijn) en een toets van zwarte chocolade. Lange afdronk.
	Slowly pour into a slightly tilted glass at eye level. Move the bottle away from the glass to obtain a nice foam head. Pour the last part (1/10th) which contains the yeast, separately.	Verser lentement dans un verre tenu légèrement incliné à hauteur d'yeux. Séparer la bouteille du verre pour obtenir un beau faux col. Verser séparément la dernière portion (1/10e) qui contient la levure.	Traag uitschenken in een licht schuingehouden glas op ooghoogte. De fles van het glas verwijderen voor een mooie schuimkraag. Het laatste deel (1/10de) met gist afzonderlijk uitschenken.
i	The figure 10 does not indicate the alcohol content but is the value of the malt density before the fermentation process.	Le chiffre 10 n'indique pas la teneur en alcool, mais correspond à la densité des malts avant la fermentation.	Het cijfer 10 verwijst niet naar het alcoholvolume maar stemt overeen met de dichtheid van de mouten vòòr het gistingsproces.

Rodenbach

Palm Breweries 5,20% 6° 43°

	mixed fermentation	fermentation mixte	gemengde gisting
	Flemish red-brown	brune-rouge flamande	Vlaams roodbruin
	special malts, fine aromatic hops, mixed yeasts, water. A blend of 3/4 young beer and 1/4 beer that has matured in oak barrels for 24 months.	malts spéciaux, houblons aromatiques fins, levures mélangées, eau. Mélange de 3/4 bière jeune et 1/4 bière mûrie en fûts de chêne pendant 24 mois.	speciale mouten, fijne aromahoppen, gemengde gisten, water. Blend van 3/4 jong bier en 1/4 bier dat 24 maand gerijpt is op eik.
	red-brown	brun rouge	roodbruin
	Very refreshing. Acidity and complex volatile fruitiness of wine (due to the symbiosis of top yeasts and lactic acid flora and to the fermentation on oak).	Très rafraîchissante. Degré d'acidité et goût fruité, complexe et volatile de vin (résultat de la symbiose de levures mixtes et de la flore d'acide lactique d'une part et de la maturation en fûts de chêne d'autre part).	Zeer verfrissend. Zuurtegraad en complexe, vluchtige fruitigheid van wijn (als gevolg van de symbiose van hoge gisten en melkzuurflora enerzijds en de rijping op eik anderzijds).
	Serve in a tall goblet with stem.	Servir dans un verre calice haut à pied.	Serveren in een hoog kelkglas op voet.
i	Recognised regional product.	Produit régional reconnu.	Erkend streekproduct.

6% 6 °C 43 °F

mixed fermentation	fermentation mixte	gemengde gisting
Flemish red-brown	brune-rouge flamande	Vlaams roodbruin
special malts, fine, aromatic hops, mixed yeasts, water. Blend of 3/4 young beer and 1/4 beer that has matured in oak barrels for 24 months	malts spéciaux, houblons aromatiques fins, levures mixtes, eau. Mélange de 3/4 bière jeune et 1/4 bière mûrie en fûts de chêne pendant 24 mois.	speciale mouten, fijne aromahoppen, gemengde gisten, water. Blend van 3/4 jong bier en 1/4 bier dat 24 maand gerijpt is op eik.
red-brown	brun rouge	roodbruin
Very refreshing. Acidity and complex volatile fruitiness of wine (due to the symbiosis of top yeasts and lactic acid flora and to the fermentation on oak).	Très rafraîchissante. Degré d'acidité et goût fruité, complexe et volatile de vin (résultat de la symbiose de levures hautes et de la flore d'acide lactique d'une part et de la maturation en fûts de chêne d'autre part).	Zeer verfrissend. Zuurtegraad en complexe vluchtige fruitigheid van wijn (als gevolg van de symbiose van hoge gisten en melkzuurflora enerzijds en de rijping op eik anderzijds).
Serve in the typical Grand Cru goblet.	Servir dans un verre calice typique 'Grand Cru'.	Serveren in de typische 'Grand Cru' kelk.
Recognised regional product.	Produit régional reconnu.	Erkend streekproduct.

R

Rodenbach Vintage

Palm Breweries

7% 6 - 12 ° / 43 - 54 °

mixed fermentation centrifuged	fermentation mixte centrifugée	gemengde gisting gecentrifugeerd
(Western Flemish) red-brown beer	brune-rouge flamande	(Westvlaams) roodbruin bier
Matures on hand-made oak barrels, some of which are over 150 years old.	Mûrit en fûts de chêne fabriqués à la main dont certains datent de plus de 150 ans.	Rijpt op handgemaakte eikenhouten foeders waarvan sommige ouder zijn dan 150 jaar.
red-copper; filtered, not pasteurised	cuivre rouge; filtrée, non pasteurisée	roodkoper; gefilterd, niet gepasteuriseerd
Complex and full taste, also intense and refreshing. Tart fruitiness (apple) in combination with caramel, wild honey and oak which, when revolved in the mouth, is reminiscent of Calvados. Aroma with touches of caramel, green apples and oak. Long and balanced mildly tart, fruity aftertaste.	Goût complexe et franc, aussi piquant et rafraîchissant. Fruité acidulé de pomme avec du caramel, du miel sauvage et du chêne qui fait penser à du Calvados. Arôme avec des touches de caramel, de pommes vertes et de bois de chêne. Longue et équilibrée arrière-bouche légèrement acide, fruitée.	Complexe en volle smaak, ook pittig en verfrissend. Appelzurige fruitigheid in combinatie met karamel, wilde honing en eik die bij het walsen in de mond aan Calvados doet denken. Aroma met toetsen van karamel, groene appels en eikenhout. Lange en evenwichtige zachtzure, fruitige afdronk.
Every year, 35,000 bottles are corked up, the lion's share of which is exported to the USA. Vintage 2007 received a silver medal at the World Beer Cup 2010.	Chaque année, 35.000 bouteilles sont embouteillées :une bonne partie d'entre elles partent pour les États-Unis. Vintage 2007 a obtenu une médaille d'argent à la World Beer Cup 2010.	Jaarlijks worden er 35.000 flessen gebotteld waarvan een groot deel naar USA gaat. Vintage 2007 behaalde een zilveren medaille op de World Beer Cup 2010.

raagwater by Brouwerij De Graal

6,50% 5 - 9 °C 41 - 48 °F

top-fermentation re-fermentation in the bottle; centrifuged	fermentation haute refermentation en bouteille; centrifugée	hoge gisting hergisting in de fles; gencentrifugeerd
amber or speciale belge	ambrée ou spéciale belge	amber of speciale belge
barley malt, hops, yeast, water	malt, herbes, houblon, levure, eau	gerstemout, hop, gist, water
dark amber with white foam head not filtered or pasteur-ised	ambré foncé avec faux col blanc non filtrée, non pasteu-risée	donker amberkleurig met witte schuimkraag ongefilterd, niet gepas-teuriseerd
Dry (no residual sugar) with much hoppy bitter-ness and roasted malt. Smoky touch and fresh, slightly tart undertones.	Sèche (pas de sucre rési-duel), avec beaucoup de lu-puline et de malt torréfié. Touche fumeuse et accent légèrement acidulé, frais.	Droog (geen restsuiker) met veel hopbitter en gebrande mout. Rokerige toets en frisse, lichtzurige ondertoon.
Pour into a regular beer or tulip-shaped glass. Leave the yeast sedi-ment in the bottle, if necessary.	Verser dans un verre de bière ordinaire ou un verre tulipe. Laisser le dépôt dans la bouteille selon les souhaits.	Uitschenken in een ge-woon bier- of tulpvormig glas. Het bezinksel des-gewenst in de fles laten.
Louvain's official city beer (brewed at the re-quest of NV Apman, Lou-vain). Was brewed for the first time to mark the opening of M, Museum Louvain, on 20 Septem-ber 2009, in the frame-work of the 'Rogier van der Weyden' opening ex-hibition. 'The Passion of the Master'.	Bière officielle de la ville de Louvain (brassée pour le compte de NV Apman, Leuven). Elle a été bras-sée pour la première fois à l'occasion de l'inaugura-tion du M-Museum Leuven, le 20 septembre 2009, dans le cadre de l'exposition d'ouverture 'Rogier van der Weyden. De Passie van de Meester'.	Officieel stadsbier van Leuven (gebrouwen in opdracht van NV Apman, Leuven). Het werd voor het eerst gebrouwen n.a.v. de opening van M, Museum Leuven, op 20 september 2009 in het kader van de openings-tentoonstelling 'Rogier van der Weyden. De Pas-sie van de Meester'.

Romy Pils

Brouwerij Roman

5,10% 3 37

	bottom-fermentation	fermentation basse	lage gisting
	pilsner	pils	pilsbier
	barley malt, hops, corn, yeast, spring water	malt d'orge, houblon, maïs, levure, eau de source	gerstemout, hop, mais, gist, bronwater
	light yellow clear and shiny	jaune clair claire et brillante	lichtgeel helder en blinkend
	Spicy thirst-quencher with a fruity flavour. Pleasant malty onset turning into a bitterish taste.	Désaltérant corsé avec un arôme fruité. Début malté agréable passant à une saveur plutôt amère.	Pittige dorstlesser met een fruitig aroma. Aangenaam moutige aanzet die overgaat in een bitterige smaak.
	Pour slowly into a de-greased, rinsed beer glass.	Verser lentement dans un verre de bière dé-graissé et rincé.	Langzaam uitschenken in een ontvet en gespoeld bierglas.
i	Store in a dark, cool room.	Conserver à l'abri de la lumière et de la chaleur.	Donker en koel bewaren.

aapmutske by De Proefbrouwerij

7,40% — 9 - 10 °C / 48 - 50 °F

	top-fermentation re-fermentation in the bottle not centrifuged	fermentation haute refermentation en bouteille non centrifugée	hoge gisting hergisting in de fles niet gecentrifugeerd
	double winter beer	bière hivernale double	dubbel winterbier
	coloured malts, aromatic hops, yeast, water	malts colorés, houblon aromatique, levure, eau	kleurmouten, aromatische hop, gist, water
	deep red and slightly sparkling with a compact, creamy foam head not pasteurised	rouge profond et légèrement pétillante avec un faux col compact, crémeux non pasteurisée	dieprood en licht parelend met een compacte, romige schuimkraag niet gepasteuriseerd
	Full-bodied and slightly malty with a very mellow aftertaste. Spicy to fruity aroma.	Franche et légèrement maltée, avec une arrière-bouche fort douce. Arôme épicé à fruité.	Volmondig en licht moutig met een zeer zachte afdronk. Kruidig tot fruitig aroma.
	Pour out in a single movement and avoid sloshing the beer. Leave yeast sediment (approx. 2 cm) in the bottle and add later, if necessary.	Verser agilement d'un seul mouvement fluide sans clapotage de la bière. Laisser le dépôt de levure (ca. 2 cm) dans la bouteille et éventuellement verser par après.	In 1 vlotte beweging uitschenken zonder dat het bier klokt. Het gistdepot (ca. 2 cm) in de fles laten en eventueel achteraf bijschenken.
	Beer designed by beer architect Dany De Smet at the request of the city of Ronse.	Bière conçue par l'architecte de la bière Dany De Smet pour le compte de la ville de Renaix.	Bier ontworpen door bierarchitect Dany De Smet in opdracht van de stad Ronse.

Slaapmutske by De Proefbrouwerij

8% 8° 46°

	top-fermentation re-fermentation in the bottle	fermentation haute refermentation en bouteille	hoge gisting hergisting in de fles
	tripel	triple	tripel
	pilsner malt, coloured malt, hops, yeast, water	malt de pils, malt coloré, houblon, levure, eau	pilsmout, kleurmout, hop, gist, water
	blond with fine carbon dioxide bubbles and compact, thick foam head filtered, not pasteurised	blond avec pétillement carbonique fin et un faux col compact collant parfaitement au verre filtrée, non pasteurisée	blond met fijne koolzuurpareling en een compacte, wandklevende schuimkraag gefilterd, niet gepasteuriseerd
	Malty with a bitter aftertaste. Slightly hoppy aroma with a touch of esters.	Maltée, avec une arrière-bouche amère. Arôme légèrement houblonné, avec une touche d'esters.	Moutig met een bittere afdronk. Lichthoppig aroma met een toets van esters.
	Pour out in a single movement and avoid sloshing the beer. Leave yeast sediment (approx. 2 cm) in the bottle and add later, if necessary.	Verser agilement d'un seul mouvement fluide sans clapotage de la bière. Laisser le dépôt de levure (ca. 2 cm) dans la bouteille et éventuellement le verser par après.	In 1 vlotte beweging uitschenken zonder dat het bier klokt. Het gistdepot (ca. 2 cm) in de fles laten en eventueel achteraf bijschenken.
	Beer designed by beer architect Dany De Smet at the request of the city of Ronse.	Bière conçue par l'architecte de la bière Dany De Smet pour le compte de la ville de Renaix.	Bier ontworpen door bierarchitect Dany De Smet in opdracht van de stad Ronse.

ouwerij Nieuwhuys 5,80% (14° plato)

	top-fermentation	fermentation haute	hoge gisting
	amber	ambrée	amber
	barley malt, Poperinge hops, herbs, yeast, water	malt d'orge, houblon de Poperinge, herbes, levure, eau	gerstemout, Poperingse hop, kruiden, gist, water
	Rosdel is a nature reserve in Hoegaarden.	Rosdel est une réserve naturelle à Hoegaarden.	Rosdel is een natuurgebied in Hoegaarden.

Rosé de Gambrinus

Brasserie Cantillon 5,50% 12 - 16 / 54 - 61

	spontaneous fermentation naturally re-fermented in the bottle	fermentation haute refermentation naturelle en bouteille	spontane gisting natuurlijke hergisting op de fles
	fruit beer, lambic	bière fruitée, lambic	fruitbier, lambiek
	barley malt, wheat, more than one year old hops, fresh raspberries	malt d'orge, froment, houblon suranné, framboises fraîches	gerstemout, tarwe, overjaarse hop, verse frambozen
	dark pink	rose foncé	donkerroze
	Intensely fruity, sourish flavour and pronounced raspberry aroma.	Goût fruité intense, saveur acidulée et arôme de framboises prononcé.	Intense fruitigheid, zurige smaak en uitgesproken frambozenaroma.
	The use of a wine basket is recommended if the bottle was stored horizontally. Place the bottle in an upright position 48 hours before serving.	Un panier verseur est recommandé si la bouteille a été conservée en position horizontale. Mettre la bouteille 48 heures avant de servir dans une position verticale pour faire descendre le dépôt de levure.	Een schenkmandje is aangewezen wanneer de fles horizontaal bewaard werd. De fles 48 uur voor het uitschenken verticaal plaasten om het bezinksel te decanteren.
i			

'asserie Artisanale La Binchoise 4,50%

Rose des Remparts

	top-fermentation re-fermented in the bottle	fermentation haute refermentation en bouteille	hoge gisting hergisting in de fles
	fruit beer	bière fruitée	fruitbier
	perfumed with raspberry	parfumé aux framboises	geparfumeerd met frambos
	pink-red unpasteurised	rouge rose non pasteurisée	rozerood niet gepasteuriseerd
	Smooth, light and refreshing.	Douce, légère et rafraîchissante.	Zacht, licht en verfrissend.

Rosé Max

Brouwerij Bockor (Vander Ghinste) 4,50% 4 - 6 / 39 - 43

	spontaneous fermentation	fermentation spontanée	spontane gisting
	fruit beer	bière fruitée	fruitbier
	barley malt, wheat, hops, yeast, fruit juices, aromas, water	malt d'orge, froment, houblon, levure, jus de fruits, arômes, eau	gerstemout, tarwe, hop, gist, vruchtensappen, aroma's, water
	soft red	rouge tendre	zachtrood
	Fruity sweet and refreshing taste. Pleasant raspberry scent.	Goût fruité sucré et rafraîchissant. Agréable parfum de framboises.	Fruitig zoete en verfrissende smaak. Aangename frambozengeur.
	Rinse the glass cold, tilt it slightly and gently pour half of the bottle. Then hold the glass upright and pour the rest in a single movement.	Rincer le verre à l'eau froide, le tenir légèrement incliné et remplir prudemment pour moitié. Tenir ensuite le verre en position verticale et verser le restant d'un seul mouvement.	Het glas koud spoelen, licht schuin houden en voorzichtig half inschenken. Daarna het glas rechthouden en de rest in 1 beweging uitschenken.
i			

7% 6 - 8 °C 43 - 46 °F

top-fermentation re-fermentation in the bottle not centrifuged	fermentation haute refermentation en bouteille non centrifugée	hoge gisting hergisting in de fles niet gecentrifugeerd
city beer Belgian ale old-style dark	bière citadine Belgian ale style ancienne foncée	stadsbier Belgian ale oude stijl donker
slightly hazy, dark amber with an attractive ivory-coloured foam head not filtered or pasteurised	légèrement fade, ambré foncé avec faux col joli ivoire non filtrée, non pasteurisée	licht wazig, donker amber met mooie ivoorkleurige schuimkraag ongefilterd, niet gepasteuriseerd
Medium-dry malty beer with unique flavour pattern (grains, bread, nuts, dry caramel and a hint of fruit). Finely hopped and full of character. Scent and flavour of nuts and stone-baked bread.	Bière à caractère malté demi-sec, avec un modèle de goût unique (céréales, pain, noix, caramel sec et un peu de fruité). Finement houblonnée et très caractéristique. Parfum et goût de noix et de pain cuit sur pierre.	Medium droog moutachtig bier met uniek smaakpatroon (granen, brood, noten, droge karamel en iets fruitigs). Fijn gehopt en karaktervol. Geur en smaak van noten en op steen gebakken brood.
Pour out in a single movement.	Verser agilement.	Vlot uitschenken.
Brewed at the request of the city of Nieuwpoort to mark the Witches' Parade.	Brassée pour le compte de la ville de Nieuport à l'occasion du Heksenstoet.	Gebrouwen in opdracht van de stad Nieuwpoort ter gelegenheid van de Heksenstoet.

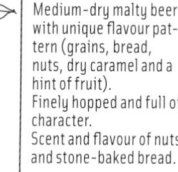

Saint-Lamvinus

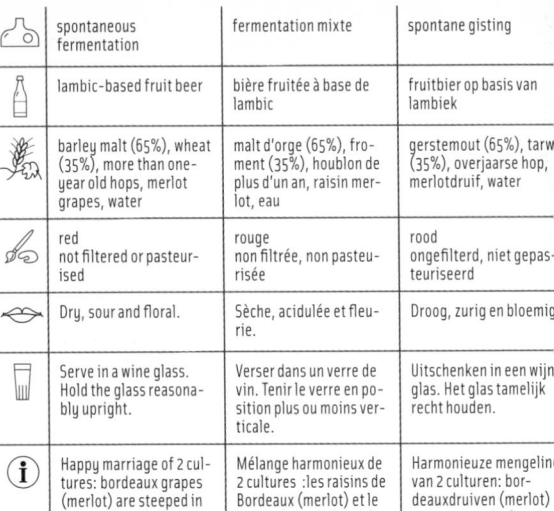

Brasserie Cantillon

6% 18 64

spontaneous fermentation	fermentation mixte	spontane gisting
lambic-based fruit beer	bière fruitée à base de lambic	fruitbier op basis van lambiek
barley malt (65%), wheat (35%), more than one-year old hops, merlot grapes, water	malt d'orge (65%), froment (35%), houblon de plus d'un an, raisin merlot, eau	gerstemout (65%), tarw (35%), overjaarse hop, merlotdruif, water
red not filtered or pasteurised	rouge non filtrée, non pasteurisée	rood ongefilterd, niet gepasteuriseerd
Dry, sour and floral.	Sèche, acidulée et fleurie.	Droog, zurig en bloemig
Serve in a wine glass. Hold the glass reasonably upright.	Verser dans un verre de vin. Tenir le verre en position plus ou moins verticale.	Uitschenken in een wijnglas. Het glas tamelijk recht houden.
Happy marriage of 2 cultures: bordeaux grapes (merlot) are steeped in Brussels lambic for months.	Mélange harmonieux de 2 cultures :les raisins de Bordeaux (merlot) et le lambic bruxellois macèrent des mois durant.	Harmonieuze mengelin van 2 culturen: bordeauxdruiven (merlot) weken maandenlang in Brusselse lambiek.

rasserie Saint-Monon

6,50% 6 - 10 °C / 43 - 50 °F

top-fermentation re-fermented in the bottle	fermentation haute refermentation en bouteille	hoge gisting nagisting op de fles
amber	ambrée	amber
special malts, pilsner malt, hop varieties, sugar, yeast, water	malts spéciaux, malt de pils, sortes de houblon, sucre, levure, eau	speciale mouten, pilsmout, hopsoorten, suiker, gist, water
amber clear with a white foam head	ambrée claire avec un faux col blanc	amber helder met witte schuimkraag
Bitter and thirstquenching with an aftertaste of caramelized malt. Hoppy flavour.	Amère et désaltérante avec une arrière-bouche de malt caramélisé. Arôme houblonné.	Bitter en dorstlessend met een nasmaak van gekarameliseerde mout. Hoparoma.
Pour slowly, leaving the yeast sediment in the bottle. Whilst pouring, move the bottle away from the glass to obtain a nice foam head.	Verser lentement et laisser le dépôt de levure dans la bouteille. Séparer la bouteille du verre au moment de verser pour obtenir un beau faux col.	Traag uitschenken en het gistdepot in de fles laten. Tijdens het schenken de fles van het glas verwijderen voor een mooie schuimkraag.

Saint-Monon Ambrée

Saint-Monon au Miel

Brasserie Saint-Monon 8% 6 - 10° 43 - 50°

	top-fermentation re-fermented in the bottle	fermentation haute refermentation en bouteille	hoge gisting nagisting op de fles
	tripel	triple	tripel
	malt varieties, hop varieties, yeast, local honey, sugar, water	sortes de malt, sortes de houblon, levure, miel de la région, sucre, eau	moutsoorten, hopsoorten, gist, honing van de streek, suiker, water
	honey-coloured	couleur miel	honingkleur
	Full and smooth taste, balanced by a fine bitterness. Flavours of yeast, hop and malt.	Saveur pleine et moelleuse équilibrée par un goût amer raffiné. Arômes de levure, de houblon et de malt.	Volle en zachte smaak gebalanceerd door een fijne bitterheid. Aroma van gist, hop en mout.
	Pour slowly, leaving the yeast sediment in the bottle. Keep the bottle upright near the end to obtain a nice foam head.	Verser lentement et laisser le dépôt de levure dans la bouteille. Tenir la bouteille à la fin en position verticale pour obtenir un beau faux col.	Traag uitschenken en het gistdepot in de fles laten. Op het einde van het schenken de fles rechthouden voor een mooie schuimkraag.
i			

7,50% 6 - 10 °C 43 - 50 °F

top-fermentation re-fermented in the bottle	fermentation haute refermentation en bouteille	hoge gisting nagisting op de fles
dubbel	double	dubbel
pilsner malt, roasted and caramelised malt, hop varieties, sugar, yeast, herbs, water	malt de pils, malt brûlé et caramélisé, sortes de houblon, sucre, levure, herbes, eau	pilsmout, gebrande en gekaramelliseerde mout, hopsoorten, suiker, gist, kruiden, water
dark brown white foam head	brun foncé faux col blanc	donkerbruin witte schuimkraag
Smooth and caramelized taste. Long and well-balanced aftertaste of roasty malt and bitterness.	Saveur moelleuse et caramélisée. Arrière-bouche longue et équilibrée de malt brûlé et de goût amer.	Zachte en gekaramelliseerde smaak. Lange en evenwichtige nasmaak van gebrande mout en bitterheid.
While pouring, keep the glass tilted first and in a vertical position at the end. The yeast sediment can be drunk afterwards.	Au moment de verser, tenir le verre d'abord en oblique et à la fin en position verticale. Le dépôt de levure peut être bu par la suite.	Tijdens het uitschenken het glas eerst schuin houden en tegen het einde recht houden. De gistfond kan achteraf worden uitgedronken.

Saint-Monon Brune

Saison 1900

Brasserie Lefebvre 5,20% 4 - 6 / 39 - 43

	top-fermentation centrifuged	fermentation haute centrifugée	hoge gisting gecentrifugeerd
	saisons	saison	saison
	barley malt, candy sugar, hops, yeast, water	malt d'orge, sucre candi, houblon, levure, eau	gerstemout, kandijsuiker, hop, gist, water
	copper blond filtered, not pasteurised	blond cuivre filtrée, non pasteurisée	koperblond gefilterd, niet gepasteuriseerd
	Well-dosed hops brewed according to the Henegouwen saison beer tradition.	Houblon bien dosé, bière brassée selon la tradition des bières saison hainuyères.	Goed gedoseerde hop gebrouwen volgens de traditie van Henegouwse saisonbieren.
	Pour into a conic glass, with a thick foam head.	Verser dans un verre conique et prévoir un large faux col.	Uitschenken in een konisch glas en een ruime schuimkraag laten.
i			

rasserie de Cazeau 5% 10 °C 50 °F

Saison Cazeau aux Fleurs de Sureau

top-fermentation re-fermentation in the bottle	fermentation haute refermentation en bouteille	hoge gisting hergisting in de fles
saison	saison	saison
pilsner malt, hops, elderflower, yeast, water	malt de pils, houblon, fleur de sureau, levure, eau	pilsmout, hop, vlier-bloesem, gist, water
blond	blonde	blond
Refreshing summery sipping beer with a hint of bitterness.	Bière de dégustation d'été légèrement rafraîchissante, avec une pointe d'amertume.	Licht verfrissend zomers degustatiebier met een vleugje bitterheid.
Store the bottles upright.	Conserver les bouteilles en position verticale.	De flessen rechtop-staand bewaren.

Saison de Dottignies

Brouwerij De Ranke 5,50%

	top-fermentation re-fermentation in the bottle not centrifuged	fermentation haute refermentation en bouteille non centrifugée	hoge gisting hergisting in de fles niet gecentrifugeerd
	saison	saison	saison
	pilsner and pale ale malt, different hops (Challenger, Brewers Gold, Hallertau, Styrian Goldings)	malt de pils et de pale ale, variétés de houblon (Challenger, Brewers Gold, Hallertau, Styrian Goldings)	pils- en pale ale mout, hopsoorten (Challenger, Brewers Gold, Hallertau, Styrian Goldings)
	amber, veiled not filtered or pasteurised	ambrée, voilée non filtrée, non pasteurisée	amber, gesluierd ongefilterd, niet gepasteuriseerd
	Balanced sponge-cake taste with thirst-quenching bitterness. Typical Henegouwen saison.	Goût de biscuit équilibré d'une amertume désaltérante. Typique Saison hainuyère.	Gebalanceerde biscuitsmaak met dorstlessende bitterheid. Typische Henegouwse saison.

rasserie Saint-Monon

8,30% 8 °C 46 °F

	top-fermentation	fermentation haute	hoge gisting
	saisons boutique beer	saison artisanale	saison artisanaal
	malt varieties, hop varieties, sweet woodruff, herbs, yeast, water	sortes de malt, sortes de houblon, aspérule odorante, herbes, levure, eau	moutsoorten, hopsoorten, lievevrouwbedstro, kruiden, gist, water
	amber slightly cloudy	ambrée légèrement trouble	amber licht troebel
	Bitter, flowery character. Taste of sweet woodruff with a touch of orange. Spring flavours.	Caractère amer, fleuri. Saveur d'aspérule odorante avec une touche d'orange. Arômes printaniers.	Bitter, bloemig karakter. Smaak van lievevrouwbedstro met een toets van sinaasappel. Lentearoma's.

Saison de Pipaix

Brasserie à Vapeur

6% 13° 55°

top-fermentation natural re-fermentation in the bottle not centrifuged	fermentation haute refermentation naturelle en bouteille non centrifugée	hoge gisting natuurlijke hergisting in de fles niet gecentrifugeerd
saison Belgian ale	saison Belgian ale	saison Belgian ale
3 different barley malts, 2 different hops, 2 different yeasts, herbs, sugar, water	3 variétés de malt d'orge, 2 variétés de houblon, 2 variétés de levure, herbes, sucres, eau	3 soorten gerstemout, 2 hopsoorten, 2 gistsoorten, kruiden, suikers, water
blond-amber unfiltered, not pasteurised	blond ambré non filtrée, non pasteurisée	blond-amber ongefilterd, niet gepasteuriseerd
Dry beer, neutral hops, slightly sour and very spicy (pepper, ginger, smooth orange rind, curaçao).	Bière sèche, houblon neutre, légèrement acidulé et très relevé (poivre, gingembre, écorce d'orange doux, curaçao).	Droog bier, neutrale hop, lichtzuur en zeer kruidig (peper, gember, curaçao, zachte sinaasschil).
Pour gently into a balloon-shaped glass	Verser prudemment dans un verre ballon.	Voorzichtig uitschenken in een ballonglas.
Brewed since the foundation of the brewery in 1785.	Brassée depuis 1785, au moment où la brasserie a été fondée.	Wordt gebrouwen sinds 1785 toen de brouwerij werd opgericht.

Saison d'Epeautre

Brasserie de Blaugies — 6% — 6 - 8 °C / 43 - 46 °F

	top-fermentation re-fermented in the bottle	fermentation haute refermentation en bouteille	hoge gisting hergisting in de fles
	specialty beer	bière spéciale	speciaalbier
	malt, spelt, hops, yeast, water. Boutique beer without herbs or additives.	malt, épeautre, houblon, levure, eau. Produit artisanal sans herbes ou additifs.	mout, spelt, hop, gist, water. Artisanaal product zonder kruiden of additieven.
	blond unfiltered	blonde non filtrée	blond niet gefilterd
	Digestive and refreshing. Fine bitterness and plenty of body, despite the medium alcohol content.	Digestive et rafraîchissante. Saveur amère raffinée et assez de corps malgré la basse teneur en alcool.	Digestief en verfrissend. Fijne bitterheid en voldoende body ondanks het middelmatige alcoholgehalte.

Saison d'Erpe-Mere

Brouwerij De Glazen Toren 6,90% 6°
43°

top-fermentation re-fermented in the bottle	fermentation haute refermentation en bouteille	hoge gisting hergisting in de fles
blond, saison	blonde, saison	blond, saison
pilsner malt, wheat malt, sugar, hops, yeast, water	malt de pils, malt de froment, sucre, houblon, levure, eau	pilsmout, tarwemout, suiker, hop, gist, water
straw-yellow and very effervescent with firm foam head (owing to wheat) which sticks to the glass; not filtered	jaune paille avec un faux col solide pétillant (grâce au froment) collant au verre; non filtrée	strogeel en sterk parelend met stevige schuimkraag (dank zij de tarwe) die aan het glas kleeft; ongefilterd
Very accessible (owing to the wheat, among others), dry and thirst-quenching. Citrusy with slightly bitter touch and pronounced hops aroma (late hopping during cooling). Long aftertaste.	Très accessible (e.a. grâce au froment), sèche et désaltérante. Citronnée, avec une touche douce amère et un arôme de houblon prononcé (houblonnage tardif lors du refroidissement). Longue arrière-bouche.	Zeer toegankelijk (o.a. door de tarwe), droog en dorstlessend. Citrusachtig met zachtbittere toets en geprononceerd hoparoma (late hopping bij de koeling). Lange afdronk.
Pour gently into a dry, tall glass. Hold the bottle horizontally and do not remove the foil.	Verser dans un verre oblong sec. Tenir la bouteille à l'horizontale et ne pas enlever l'emballage.	Uitschenken in een droog langwerpig glas. De fles horizontaal houden en de wikkel niet verwijderen.
Saison or season beer is a Henegouwen tradition. It was brewed on farms for the workers at harvest time.	Une tradition originaire du Hainaut. Ces bières étaient autrefois brassées dans les exploitations agricoles pour rafraîchir les travailleurs pendant la moisson.	Saison of seizoensbier is een traditie uit Henegouwen. Het werd vroeger op de boerderijen gebrouwen om de werklui te verfrissen tijdens de oogst.

Brasserie de Bouillon

6%

Saison des Chasses Blonde

	top-fermentation re-fermentation in the bottle	fermentation haute refermentation en bouteille	hoge gisting hergisting in de fles
	boutique blond	blonde artisanale	artisanaal blond
	barley malt, hops, yeast, herbs, water	malt d'orge, houblon, herbes, levure, eau	gerstemout, hop, kruiden, gist, water
	not filtered or pasteurised	non filtrée, non pasteurisée	ongefilterd, niet gepasteuriseerd

Saison Dupont

Brasserie Dupont

6,50% 12 ° 54 °

	top-fermentation re-fermented in the bottle	fermentation haute refermentation en bouteille	hoge gisting hergisting in de fles
	saisons	saison	saison
	barley and wheat malt, liquid sugar, hops (aroma and bitter hops), yeast, water	malt d'orge et de froment, sucre liquide, houblon (aromatique et houblon amer), levure, eau	gerste- en tarwemout, vloeibare suiker, hop (aroma en bitterhop), gist, water
	copper blond	blond cuivré	koperblond
	Thirst-quencher with dry bitterness and fine hoppy flavour.	Désaltérant avec un goût amer sec et des arômes de houblon raffinés.	Dorstlesser met droge bitterheid en fijne hoparoma's.
	This beer was originally brewed in the winter as a thirst-quencher for the seasonal workers at the farm during the summer.	A l'origine brassée en hiver comme désaltérant pour les ouvriers saisonniers à la ferme en été.	Werd oorspronkelijk gebrouwen in de winter als dorstlesser voor de seizoensarbeiders op de hoeve in de zomer.

Saison Dupont Biologique

Brasserie Dupont

5,50% 12 °C 54 °F

	top-fermentation re-fermented in the bottle	fermentation haute refermentation en bouteille	hoge gisting nagisting in de fles
	blond	blonde	blond
	blond	blonde	blond
	Thirst-quenching with an exceptional dryness and bitterness. Citric touches (mainly grapefruit).	Désaltérant avec une saveur sèche et amère exceptionnelle. Touches d'agrumes (principalement pamplemousse).	Dorstlessend met uitzonderlijke droogheid en bitterheid. Citrustoetsen (vooral pompelmoes).
	Beer with label of Biogarantie®. The production is supervised by Ecocert®.	La production est contrôlée par Ecocert®. Avec le label Biogarantie®.	De productie wordt gecontroleerd door Ecocert®. Met label Biogarantie®.

Saison Dupont Cuvée Dry Hoppping

Brasserie Dupont

6,50% 6 - 8 °C 43 - 46 °F

top-fermentation re-fermentation in the bottle centrifuged	fermentation haute refermentation en bouteille centrifugée	hoge gisting hergisting in de fles gecentrifugeerd
saison	saison	saison
barley malt, hops, sugar, yeast, water. Traditional saison with dry hopping.	malt d'orge, houblon, sucre, levure, eau. Saison classique avec dry-hopping.	gerstemout, hop, suiker, gist, water. Klassieke saison met dry hopping.
copper blond, slightly cloudy with superb foam head not filtered or pasteurised	blond cuivre, légèrement trouble avec faux col brillant non filtrée, non pasteurisée	koperblond, licht troebel met schitterende schuimkraag ongefilterd, niet gepasteuriseerd
Saison Dupont but with extra aromas owing to the dry hopping.	Saison Dupont, mais avec des arômes supplémentaires dus au houblonnage à cru.	Saison Dupont maar met extra aroma's van de dry hopping.

rasserie du Bocq

5,50% 5 - 12 °C 41 - 54 °F

top-fermentation re-fermented in the bottle	fermentation haute refermentation en bouteille	hoge gisting met hergisting in de fles
specialty amber beer saison	bière spéciale ambrée saison	speciaalbier amber saison
barley malt, wheat starch, hop varieties, yeast, herbs, water	malt d'orge, fécule de froment, sortes de houblon, levure, herbes, eau	gerstemout, tarwezetmeel, hoppesoorten, gist, kruiden, water
amber-coloured and clear (30 EBC) fine, compact foam head	couleur ambrée et claire (30 EBC) faux col fin et épais	amberkleurig en helder (30 EBC) fijne, dichte schuimkraag
Versatile nose, hoppy base with a fruity touch. Thirstquenching and light with a clearly bitter taste (30 EBU).	Bouquet varié à base de houblon avec une touche fruitée. Désaltérante et légère avec une saveur amère prononcée (30 EBU).	Veelzijdige neus, hopbasis met een fruitig tintje. Dorstlessend en licht met een duidelijke bitterheid in de smaak (30 EBU).
Gently pour into a perfectly degreased glass. Leave the yeast sediment (due to natural refermenting) in the bottle.	Verser doucement dans un verre parfaitement dégraissé. Laisser le dépôt de levure (refermentation naturelle) dans la bouteille.	Zacht uitschenken in een perfect ontvet glas. Het gistbezinksel (natuurlijke hergisting) in de fles laten.

Saison Regal

Saison Silly

Brasserie de Silly 5% (11,3° plato) 4 - 9° 39 - 48°

	top-fermentation	fermentation haute	hoge gisting
	saison	saison	saison
	aromatic malt, sugar, yeast, Kent and Hallertau hops, water	malt aromatique, sucre, levure, houblon Kent et Hallertau, eau	aromatische mout, suiker, gist, Kent en Hallertauhop, water
	brown (45 EBC)	brune (45 EBC)	bruin (45 EBC)
	Light, both fruity and slightly sugared, with a fresh aftertaste.	Légère, à la fois fruitée et légèrement sucrée avec une arrière-bouche fraîche.	Licht, tegelijk fruitig en licht gesuikerd met frisse nasmaak.

Saison St-Feuillien

S

rasserie St-Feuillien 6,50% 6 - 8 °C 43 - 46 °F

top-fermentation natural re-fermentation in the bottle	fermentation haute refermentation naturelle en bouteille	hoge gisting natuurlijke hergisting in de fles
saison	saison	saison
barley malt, sugar, hops, yeast, vitamin C, brewing water	malt d'orge, sucre, houblon, levure, vitamine C, eau de brassage	gerstemout, suiker, hop, gist, vitamine C, brouwwater
dark blond not filtered	blond foncé non filtrée	donkerblond ongefilterd
Distinct bitterness, full-bodied in the mouth.	Amertume claire, jolie plénitude en bouche.	Duidelijke bitterheid, mooie volheid in de mond.

Saison Voisin

Brasserie des Légendes

5% 5 - 8 / 41 - 46

top-fermentation re-fermented in the bottle	fermentation haute refermentation en bouteille	hoge gisting nagisting in de fles
saison	saison	saison
pale malt, caramel malt, hops, yeast, water	malt pâle, malt caramélisé, houblon, levure, eau	bleekmout, karamelmout, hop, gist, water
amber unfiltered	ambrée non filtrée	amber ongefilterd
Very dry beer with pronounced, long-lasting bitterness. Malt, hop and caramel flavours.	Bière très sèche avec un goût amer durable. Arômes de malt, de houblon et de caramel.	Zeer droog bier met uitgesproken bitterheid die lang blijft hangen. Aroma's van mout, hop en karamel.
Degrease the glass, rinse with hot water and dry. With yeast sediment: smoothly revolve the bottle before serving the last third. Without yeast sediment: pour carefully and leave the sediment in the bottle.	Dégraisser le verre, bien le rincer à l'eau chaude et sécher. Avec dépôt de levure :tourner le dernier tiers de bière avant de le verser. Sans dépôt de levure :verser prudemment et laisser le fond de levure dans la bouteille.	Het glas ontvetten, goed spoelen met warm water en drogen. Met gistbezinkel: het laatste derde in de fles walsen voor het uitschenken. Zonder gistbezinksel: voorzichtig schenken en de fond in de fles laten.
Brewed following an original recipe from 1884.	Brassée selon la recette originale de 1884.	Gebrouwen volgens een origineel recept van 1884.

rouwerij Urthel by Bierbrouwerij De Koningshoeven 6%

	top-fermentation re-fermented in the bottle centrifuged	fermentation haute refermation en bouteille centrifugeé	hoge gisting hergisting in de fles gecentrifugeerd
	blond specialty beer	blonde spéciale	blond speciaalbier
	barley malt, pilsner malt, wheat, hops, sugar, yeast, water	malt d'orge, malt de pils, froment, houblon, sucre, levure, eau	gerstemout, pilsmout, tarwe, hop, suiker, gist, water
	not filtered	non filtrée	ongefilterd
	Soft, tart thirst-quencher.	Bière désaltérante doucement amère.	Zacht bittere dorstlesser.
	The brewery makes samples in Ruiselede but the beers are brewed in the Netherlands.	La brasserie réalise les brassins d'essai à Ruiselede, mais les bières sont brassées aux Pays-Bas.	De brouwerij maakt de proefbrouwels in Ruiselede maar de bieren worden gebrouwen in Nederland.

Santa Bee

Brouwerij Boelens

8,70% 7 45

	top-fermentation re-fermented in the bottle	fermentation haute refermentation en bouteille	hoge gisting hergisting op de fles
	dark winter beer	bière hivernale foncée	donker winterbier
	dark clear	foncée claire	donker helder
	Spicy, caramel malt, winter spices. Deliciously creamy with a rich bouquet.	Goût relevé de malt caramélisé, herbes d'hiver. Délicieusement crémeuse avec un bouquet riche.	Kruidig, karamelmout, winterse specerijen. Heerlijk romig met een rijk boeket.
	Pour carefully so that the yeast sediment stays at the bottom of the bottle.	Verser prudemment pour garder le dépôt de levure au fond de la bouteille.	Voorzichtig uitschenken om het gistbezinksel op de bodem te houden.
i			

6% 7 - 10 °C 45 - 50 °F

Sara Blond (Bio)

	top-fermentation re-fermented in the bottle	fermentation haute refermentation en bouteille	hoge gisting nagisting op de fles
	specialty beer buckwheat beer	bière spéciale bière de sarrasin	speciaalbier boekweitbier
	barley, buckwheat (25%), hops, herbs, water	orge, sarrasin (25%), houblon, herbes, eau	gerst, boekweit (25%), hop, kruiden, water
	blond amber cloudy (unfiltered) compact foam head	blond ambré trouble (non filtrée) faux col dense	blond amber troebel (niet gefilterd) dichte schuimkraag
	Fruity, aromatic thirst-quencher. Full-bodied, slightly hopped, buckwheat taste and slightly bitter.	Désaltérant fruité aromatique. Franche, légèrement houblonnée, goût de sarrasin et légèrement amer.	Fruitige, aromatische dorstlesser. Volmondig, licht gehopt, boekweitsmaak en lichtbitter.
	Softly revolve or shake the bottle before opening to obtain a cloudy beer.	Tourner légèrement ou secouer la bouteille avant de l'ouvrir pour obtenir une bière trouble.	De fles licht draaien of schudden voor het openen om een troebel bier te bekomen.
	Organic beer. Buckwheat has a high nutritional value, stimulating digestion and lowering blood pressure.	Bière biologique. Le sarrasin a une valeur nutritive élevée, stimule la digestion et baisse la tension artérielle.	Biologisch bier. Boekweit heeft een hoge voedingswaarde, bevordert de spijsvertering en werkt bloeddrukverlagend.

Sara Bruin

Brasserie de Silenrieux

6% 7 - 10 / 45 - 50

	top-fermentation re-fermented in the bottle	fermentation haute refermentation en bouteille	hoge gisting nagisting op de fles
	specialty beer buckwheat beer	bière spéciale bière de sarrasin	speciaalbier boekweitbier
	barley, buckwheat, hops, herbs, water	orge, sarrasin, houblon, herbes, eau	gerst, boekweit, hop, kruiden, water
	brown cloudy (unfiltered)	brune trouble (non filtrée)	bruin troebel (niet gefilterd)
	Refreshing. Slight bitter, buckwheat taste.	Rafraîchissante. Légèrement amère, goût de sarrasin.	Verfrissend. Licht bitter, boekweitsmaak.
	Softly revolve or shake the bottle before opening to obtain a cloudy beer.	Tourner légèrement ou secouer la bouteille avant de l'ouvrir pour obtenir une bière trouble.	De fles licht draaien of schudden voor het openen om een troebel bier te bekomen.
i			

5,30% 4 °C 39 °F

	bottom-fermentation	fermentation basse	lage gisting
	dark	foncée	donker
	yeast, malt, hops, caramel, water	levure, malt, houblon, caramel, eau	gist, mout, hop, karamel, water
	deep red with beige foam head filtered, not pasteurised	rouge foncé avec faux col beige filtrée, non pasteurisée	donkerrood met beige schuimkraag gefilterd, niet gepasteuriseerd
	Caramel and toffee.	Caramel et caramel mou.	Karamel en toffee.
	Serve in a pilsner glass in a single movement.	Verser d'un seul mouvement fluide dans un verre de pils.	In 1 vlotte beweging uitschenken in een pilsglas.
	Brewed for exports.	Brassée pour l'exportation.	Gebrouwen voor export.

Sas Brune

Sas Export

Brouwerij Het Sas

5% 3 37

	bottom-fermentation	fermentation basse	lage gisting
	export	export	export
	malt, rice, hops, water	malt, riz, houblon, eau	mout, rijst, hop, water
	blond	blonde	blond
	Powerful and refreshing. Malt flavour with a bitter aftertaste.	Corsée et rafraîchis-sante. Arôme malté avec une fin de bouche amère.	Krachtig en verfrissend. Moutig aroma met bitte-re afdronk.
	Pour slowly in a single, smooth movement into a degreased glass. Keep the glass tilted and avoid sloshing. Skim off the foam.	Verser lentement en un seul mouvement fluide dans un verre dégraissé tenu en oblique. Ne pas laisser la bière clapoter. Ecumer le verre.	Traag en in 1 vloeiende beweging uitschenken in een vetvrij glas dat wordt schuingehouden. Het bier niet laten klotsen. Het glas afschuimen.
i			

rouwerij Het Sas

5% 3 °C 37 °F

bottom-fermentation	fermentation basse	lage gisting
pilsner	pils	pils
malt, rice, hops, water	malt, riz, houblon, eau	mout, rijst, hop, water
blond clear	blonde claire	blond helder
Powerful and refreshing. Malty flavour with bitter aftertaste.	Corsée et rafraîchissante. Arôme malté avec une fin de bouche amère.	Krachtig en verfrissend. Moutig aroma met bittere afdronk.
Pour slowly in a single, smooth movement into a degreased glass. Keep the glass tilted and avoid sloshing. Skim off the foam.	Verser lentement en un seul mouvement fluide dans un verre dégraissé tenu en oblique. Ne pas laisser la bière clapoter. Ecumer le verre.	Traag en in 1 vloeiende beweging uitschenken in een vetvrij glas dat wordt schuingehouden. Het bier niet laten klotsen. Het glas afschuimen.

Brouwerij Het Sas

6,30% 3° 37°

	bottom-fermentation	fermentation basse	lage gisting
	Dortmunder pilsner	pils Dortmunder	Dortmunder pils
	malt, hops, water	malt, houblon, eau	mout, hop, water
	blond clear	blonde claire	blond helder
	Solid and aromatic. Strong malty and hoppy flavour.	Corsée et parfumée. Arôme prononcé de malt et de houblon.	Stevig en geurig. Sterk mout- en hoparoma.
	Pour slowly in a single, smooth movement into a degreased glass. Keep the glass tilted and avoid sloshing. Skim off the foam.	Verser lentement en un seul mouvement fluide dans un verre dégraissé tenu en oblique. Ne pas laisser la bière clapoter. Ecumer le verre.	Traag en in 1 vloeiende beweging uitschenken in een vetvrij glas dat wordt schuingehouden. Het bier niet laten klotsen. Het glas afschuimen.
i	One of the few Dortmunders left in Belgium.	Une des peu Dortmunders subsistant encore en Belgique.	Een van de weinige Dortmunders die nog overblijven in België.

8% — 6 - 8 °C / 43 - 46 °F

	top-fermentation re-fermented in the bottle	fermentation haute refermentation en bouteille	hoge gisting hergisting op de fles
	strong blond	blonde forte	sterk blond
	wheat, malt, hops, yeast, water	froment, malt, houblon, levure, eau	tarwe, mout, hop, gist, water
	blond clear unpasteurised	blonde claire non pasteurisée	blond helder niet gepasteuriseerd
	Fresh and deep, full character. Rich palette of yeast with a considerable fruit and flower touch.	Caractère frais, profond et plein. Palette riche de levure et touche profonde fruitée et fleurie.	Fris en diep, vol karakter. Rijk palet van gist en diepe toets van fruit en bloemen.
	cfr Chimay	voir Chimay	cfr. Chimay
	Store the beer upright.	Conserver la bière en position verticale.	Het bier verticaal bewaren.

S Satan Red

Brouwerij De Block 8% 6 - 8 43 - 46

	top-fermentation re-fermented in the bottle	fermentation haute refermentation en bouteille	hoge gisting hergisting op de fles
	Flemish brown	brune flamande	Vlaams bruin
	wheat, malt, hops, yeast, water	froment, malt, houblon, levure, eau	tarwe, mout, hop, gist, water
	red, clear unpasteurised	rouge, clair non pasteurisée	rood, helder niet gepasteuriseerd
	Fresh, deep and full character. Rich palette of yeast with a considerable fruit and flower touch.	Caractère frais, profond et plein. Palette riche de levure et touche profonde fruitée et fleurie.	Fris, diep en vol karakter. Rijk palet van gist en diepe toets van fruit en bloemen.
	cfr Chimay	voir Chimay	cfr. Chimay
	Store the beer upright. This beer is described by the brewer as a strong red beer.	Conserver la bière en position verticale. Le brasseur décrit Satan Red comme une bière rouge forte.	Het bier verticaal bewaren. De brouwer omschrijft het als zwaar rood bier.

top-fermentation	fermentation haute	hoge gisting
strong blond	blonde forte	sterk blond
pilsner malt, wheat malt, barley malt, coriander, Saaz hops, yeast, water	malt de pils, malt de froment, malt d'orge, coriandre, houblon Saaz, levure, eau	pilsmout, tarwemout, gerstemout, koriander, Saazhop, gist, water
golden blond	blond doré	goudblond
Light, fruity and vegetable nose with green apple flavours. Flexible and refined, with a strong but delicate bitterness.	Parfum légèrement fruité et végétal avec des arômes de pommes vertes. Souple et raffinée avec une touche amère corsée mais délicate.	Licht fruitige en vegetale neus met aroma's van groene appels. Soepel en geraffineerd met een sterke maar delicate bitterheid.
Exists in an organic version.	Existe aussi dans une version bio.	Bestaat ook in een bioversie.

Schaarbeekse Oude Kriek

Geuzestekerij 3 Fonteinen 5%

	spontaneous fermentation	fermentation spontanée	spontane gisting
	fruity lambic	lambic fruitée	lambiek met fruit
	young Lambic (60% barley malt, 40% wheat, more than one-year old hops, water) and 35% Schaarbeek cherries.	jeune lambic (60% malt d'orge, 40% froment, houblon de plus d'un an, eau) et 35% cerises de Schaarbeek.	jonge lambiek (60% gerstemout, 40% tarwe, overjaarse hop, water) en 35% Schaarbeekse krieken.

et Nest by De Scheldebrouwerij

8,50% 6 °C 43 °F

top-fermentation re-fermentation in the bottle not centrifuged	fermentation haute refermentation en bouteille non centrifugée	hoge gisting hergisting in de fles niet gecentrifugeerd
city or regional beer tripel	bière citadine ou régionale triple	stads- of streekbier tripel
malt, herbs, hops, yeast, sugar, water	malt, herbes, houblon, levure, sucre, eau	mout, kruiden, hop, gist, suiker, water
blond, clear with a firm foam head with fine bubbles not filtered or pasteurised	blonde, limpide avec un faux col solide à bulles fines non filtrée, non pasteurisée	blond, helder met een stevige, fijncellige schuimkraag ongefilterd, niet gepasteuriseerd
Fruity aroma and flavour owing to the yeast and herbs, with a tart touch owing to the citrus.	Arôme et goût fruités du fait de la levure et des épices, avec une légère amertume de citrus.	Fruitig aroma en smaak door de gist en de kruiden, met een lichte citrusachtige bitterheid.
Serve in a goblet and leave the yeast sediment in the bottle.	Verser dans un verre calice et laisser le dépôt de levure dans la bouteille.	Uitschenken in een kelkglas en het gistdepot in de fles laten.
The name (jack of spades) refers to Turnhout, capital of the game card, where the brewery is based.	Le nom (valet de pique) fait référence à Turnhout, capitale du jeu de cartes, où la brasserie aussi est installée.	De naam verwijst naar Turnhout, hoofdstad van de speelkaart, waar ook de brouwerij is gevestigd.

Scotch Silly

Brasserie de Silly **7,80% (17,2° plato)** 6 - 9° 43 - 48°

	top-fermentation	fermentation haute	hoge gisting
	scottish style	scotch	scotch
	pale malt, caramelised malt, aromatic malt, sugar, Kent and Hallertau hops, yeast, water	malt pâle, malt caramélisé, malt aromatique, sucre, houblon Kent et Hallertau, levure, eau	bleke mout, gekaramelliseerde mout, aromatische mout, suiker, Kent en Hallertau hop, gist, water
	dark brown (62 EBC)	brun foncé (62 EBC)	donkerbruin (62 EBC)
	Woody aroma with a touch of hazelnut. Bitter and with a fuller taste than the traditional British Scottish style.	Parfum boisé renvoyant à la noisette. Saveur amère et plus pleine que celle de la Scotch anglaise traditionnelle.	Houtachtige geur die refereert aan hazelnoot. Bittere en vollere smaak dan de traditionele Britse scotch.
	Pour carefully in a wide goblet.	Verser tranquillement dans un verre calice large.	Rustig uitschenken in een breed kelkglas.
i			

icrobrouwerij Achilles 6,20%

	top-fermentation re-fermentation in the bottle	fermentation haute refermentation en bouteille	hoge gisting hergisting op de fles
	blond	blonde	blond
	barley malt, hops, yeast, re-fermentation sugar, clove, water	malt d'orge, houblon, levure, sucre de refermentation, girofle, eau	gerstemout, hop, gist, hergistingssuiker, kruidnagel, water
	blond with solid foam head	blonde avec faux col plein	blond met volle schuimkraag
	Proper session beer.	Agréable bière facilement buvable.	Vlotte doordrinker.

Serafijn Donker

Microbrouwerij Achilles 8%

	top-fermentation re-fermented in the bottle	fermentation haute refermentation en bouteille	hoge gisting hergisting op de fles
	dubbel	double	dubbel
	coloured malt, aromatic hops, yeast, water	malt coloré, houblon aromatique, levure, eau	kleurmout, aromatische hop, gist, water
	dark brown-purple	brun-violet foncé	donker paarsbruin
	Spicy with smooth bitterness. Distinctive taste owing to the roasted barley varieties, which give this beer its colour in a natural way.	Relevée avec un goût légèrement amer. Goût plein de caractère par les types d'orge brûlée donnant aussi de façon naturelle à la bière sa couleur.	Kruidig met zachte bitterheid. Karaktervolle smaak door de gebrande gerstsoorten die ook op natuurlijke wijze dit bier kleuren.

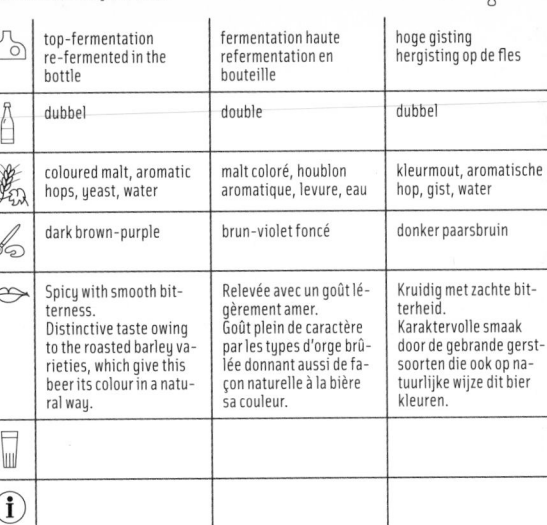

icrobrouwerij Achilles

9%

Serafijn Grand Cru

	top-fermentation re-fermentation in the bottle	fermentation haute refermentation en bouteille	hoge gisting hergisting op de fles
	specialty beer	bière spéciale	speciaalbier
	barley malt, hops, yeast, re-fermentation sugar, water	malt d'orge, houblon, levure, sucre de refermentation, eau	gerstemout, hop, gist, hergistingssuiker, water
	pale amber	légèrement ambré	lichtamber
	Richly filled body and a slightly bitter after-taste.	Corps parfaitement franc et une arrière-bouche légèrement amère.	Rijkelijk gevulde body en een lichtbittere afdronk.

Serafijn Tripel

Microbrouwerij Achilles 8%

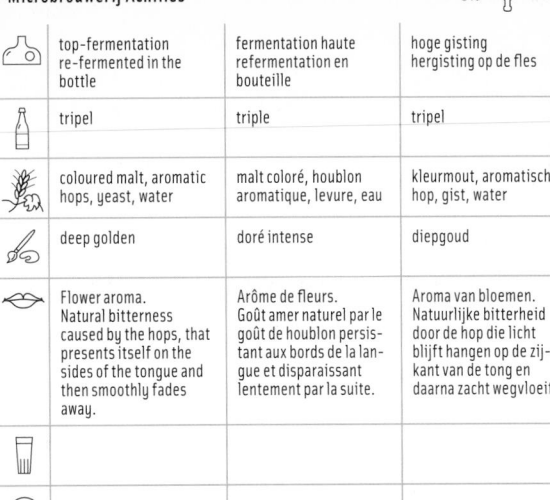

	top-fermentation re-fermented in the bottle	fermentation haute refermentation en bouteille	hoge gisting hergisting op de fles
	tripel	triple	tripel
	coloured malt, aromatic hops, yeast, water	malt coloré, houblon aromatique, levure, eau	kleurmout, aromatische hop, gist, water
	deep golden	doré intense	diepgoud
	Flower aroma. Natural bitterness caused by the hops, that presents itself on the sides of the tongue and then smoothly fades away.	Arôme de fleurs. Goût amer naturel par le goût de houblon persistant aux bords de la langue et disparaissant lentement par la suite.	Aroma van bloemen. Natuurlijke bitterheid door de hop die licht blijft hangen op de zijkant van de tong en daarna zacht wegvloeit.

rouwerij Martens

6% 2 °C 36 °F

Sezoens Blond

top-fermentation	fermentation haute	hoge gisting
specialty beer	bière spéciale	speciaalbier
malt, hops, water	malt, houblon, eau	mout, hop, water
gold-coloured clear	dorée claire	goudkleurig helder
Remarkable hoppy character obtained by dry-hopping.	Caractère houblonné remarquable par le dryhopping.	Opmerkelijk hopkarakter door dryhopping.
cfr. Abbey beer	voir bière d'Abbaye	cfr. Abdijbier

Sezoens Quattro

Brouwerij Martens

8%

top-fermentation	fermentation haute	hoge gisting
strong amber	ambrée forte	sterk amber
malt, hops, water	malt, houblon, eau	mout, hop, water
dark	foncée	donker
Coffee-like onset, then pure fruitiness and an intense finale. Well-bound hoppy dryness, not a thirst-quencher.	Goût café au début, puis fruité et pur, fin de bouche intense. Caractère sec, houblonné bien lié. Pas de désaltérant.	Koffie-achtige start, daarna een zuivere fruitigheid en een intense finale. Goed gebonden hoppige droogheid. Geen dorstlesser.
cfr. Abbey beer	voir bière d'Abbaye	cfr. Abdijbier

Silly Pils

rasserie de Silly

5% (11,2° plato) 3 - 6 °C 37 - 43 °F

bottom-fermentation	fermentation basse	lage gisting
pilsner	pils	pils
pale malt, yeast, Saaz and Hallertau hops, water	malt pâle, levure, houblon Saaz et Hallertau, eau	bleke mout, gist, Saaz en Hallertauhop, water
7 EBC clear	7 EBC claire	7 EBC helder
Malty thirst-quencher with a hoppy bitter touch.	Désaltérant malté avec une bouche amère houblonnée.	Moutige dorstlesser met hoppig bittere toets.
No provision beer.	Pas de bière de conservation.	Geen bewaarbier.

Silly Pils Bio

Brasserie de Silly 5% 3 - 6° 37 - 43°

	bottom-fermentation	fermentation basse	lage gisting
	pilsner or lager beer	pils ou lager	pils of lagerbier
	pale bio malt, yeast, bio hops, water	malt bio pâle, levure, houblon bio, eau	bleke biomout, gist, bio-hop, water
	blond and clear filtered	blonde et limpide filtrée	blond en helder gefilterd
	More mellow than the regular pilsner. Light onset, thirst-quenching with an intensely malty aftertaste.	Plus douce que la pils habituelle. Approche initiale légère, bière désaltérante, avec une arrière-bouche intensément maltée.	Zachter dan de gewone pils. Lichte aanzet, dorstlessend met een intens moutige afdronk.
i	Organic beer made organic with barley malt and hops.	Bière biologique avec du malt d'orge et du houblon de l'agriculture biologique.	Biologisch bier met gerstemout en hop van biologische landbouw.

Sinpalsken Blond

e Cock at Brouwerij Van Steenberge — 8,50% — 8 °C / 46 °F

	top-fermentation re-fermented in the bottle	fermentation haute refermentation en bouteille	hoge gisting hergisting op de fles
	regional beer	bière régionale	streekbier
	malt, hops, yeast, water. No preservatives added.	malt, houblon, levure, eau. Sans conservateurs.	mout, hop, gist, water. Zonder bewaarmiddelen.
	clear golden blond (12 EBC) nice, full foam head	claire blond doré (12 EBC) beau faux col plein	helder goudblond (12 EBC) mooie, volle schuim-kraag
	Soft beer with a typical hoppy flavour, fairly full-bodied.	Bière moelleuse avec un arôme houblonné typique et un caractère légèrement franc.	Zacht biertje met een typisch hoparoma en een beetje volmondigheid.

S Sinpalsken Donker

De Cock at Brouwerij Van Steenberge 8,50% 8° 46°

	top-fermentation re-fermented in the bottle	fermentation haute refermentation en bouteille	hoge gisting hergisting op de fles
	regional beer	bière régionale	streekbier
	malt, hops, yeast, roasted malt, water. No preservatives added.	malt, houblon, levure, malt grillé, eau. Sans conservateurs.	mout, hop, gist, geroosterde mout, water. Zonder bewaarmiddelen.
	clear red-brown nice, full foam head	claire brun rouge beau faux col plein	helder roodbruin mooie, volle schuimkraag
	Slightly roasted taste with a touch of sweetness and a light bitterness in the aftertaste.	Légèrement brûlée avec une touche sucrée et une fin de bouche légèrement amère.	Lichtgebrand met een vleugje zoetigheid en een lichte bitterheid in de nasmaak.

Huisbrouwerij Sint Canarus at De Proefbrouwerij

7,50% 8 - 12 °C / 46 - 54 °F

top-fermentation re-fermented in the bottle	fermentation haute refermentation en bouteille	hoge gisting hergisting op de fles
tripel	triple	tripel
pilsner malt, special malts, Vlamertinge hops, yeast, water	malt de pils, malts spéciaux, houblon de Vlamertinge, levure, eau	pilsmout, speciale mouten, Vlamertingse hop, gist, water
golden blond clear	blond doré claire	goudblond helder
Triple session beer. Well-balanced, smoothly bitter, fruity.	Triple facilement buvable. Equilibrée, moelleuse, amère, fruitée.	Doordrinktripel. Evenwichtig, zacht bitter, fruitig.
Pour carefully into a goblet and leave the yeast sediment in the bottle. The latter can be drunk separately. Let the beer rest for a few days before tasting.	Laisser reposer la bière quelques jours avant la dégustation. Verser prudemment dans un verre calice et laisser le dépôt de levure dans la bouteille. Le dépôt de levure peut être bu séparément.	Het bier voor het degusteren een paar dagen laten rusten. Voorzichtig uitschenken in een kelkglas en de gistbodem in de fles laten. De gistbodem kan afzonderlijk worden uitgedronken.
'Canarus' is dog Latin for 'canard', which means drunk in the local dialect.	En latin de cuisine, 'Canarus' veut dire 'canard', ce qui signifie 'ivre' dans le dialecte local.	'Canarus' is potjeslatijn voor canard, wat in het lokale dialect 'dronken' betekent.

Sint Canarus Tripel

S

Sint Gummarus Dubbel

Brouwerij Sint-Jozef 7% 2 - 4 ° 36 - 39 °

	top-fermentation re-fermented in the bottle	fermentation haute refermentation en bouteille	hoge gisting nagisting op de fles
	specialty beer	bière spéciale	speciaalbier
	malt, hops, sugar, herbs, water	malt, houblon, sucre, herbes, eau	mout, hop, suiker, kruiden, water
	dark	foncée	donker
	Full and spicy flavour with a strong aftertaste.	Saveur pleine et corsée avec une fin de bouche forte.	Volle en pittige smaak met sterke afdronk.
	Pour into a clean, degreased glass, avoiding contact between bottle and foam.	Verser dans un verre propre, dégraissé sans que la bouteille touche l'écume.	Uitschenken in een zuiver, ontvet glas zonder dat de fles het schuim raakt.
i			

Sint Gummarus Tripel

Brouwerij Sint-Jozef 8% 2 - 4 °C 36 - 39 °F

	top-fermentation re-fermented in the bottle	fermentation haute refermentation en bouteille	hoge gisting nagisting op de fles
	strong blond	blonde forte	zwaar blond
	malt, hops, sugar, herbs, water	malt, houblon, sucre, herbes, eau	mout, hop, suiker, kruiden, water
	yellowish and shiny	jaunâtre et brillante	gelig en blinkend
	Full-bodied and spicy flavour with strong aftertaste.	Saveur franche et corsée avec une fin de bouche forte.	Volle en pittige smaak met sterke afdronk.
	Pour carefully into a goblet, avoiding contact between bottle and foam.	Verser dans un verre propre, dégraissé sans que la bouteille touche l'écume.	Uitschenken in een zuiver, ontvet glas zonder dat de fles het schuim raakt.

Slaapmutske Bio Tripel

Slaapmutske by De Proefbrouwerij

8% (16 ° plato) — 8 °C / 46 °F

	top-fermentation re-fermentation in the bottle	fermentation haute refermentation en bouteille	hoge gisting hergisting in de fles
	tripel	triple	tripel
	organic malt, aromatic natural hops, yeast, water	malts biologiques, houblon naturel aromatique, levure, eau	biologische mouten, aromatische natuurhop, gist, water
	gold-blond with fine carbon dioxide bubbles (owing to re-fermentation) and a compact firm foam head. Filtered, not pasteurised	blond doré avec pétillement carbonique fin (par refermentation) et un faux col compact solide Filtrée, non pasteurisée	goudblond met fijne koolzuurpareling (door de hergisting) en een compacte stevige schuimkraag. Gefilterd, niet gepasteuriseerd
	Fresh aroma and an intense, bitter (after) taste. Malty aftertaste that develops into a pleasant, mellow bitter malty feeling in the mouth. 30 EBU.	Arôme frais et un (arrière-)goût piquant, amer. Arrière-bouche maltée qui s'écoule en une agréable sensation en bouche houblonnée, douce-amère. 30 EBU.	Fris aroma en een pittige, bittere (na)smaak. Moutige afdronk die uitvloeit in een aangenaam, zachtbitter hopmondgevoel. 30 EBU
	Pour out in a single movement and avoid sloshing the beer. Leave a yeast sediment of approx. 2 cm in the bottle and add later.	Verser dans un verre sec d' un seul mouvement fluide sans clapotage de la bière. Laisser un dépôt de levure de ca. 2 cm dans la bouteille et le verser éventuellement par après.	In een droog glas in 1 vlotte beweging uitschenken zonder dat het bier klokt. Een gistdepot van ca. 2 cm in de fles laten en eventueel achteraf bijschenken.
i			

laapmutske by De Proefbrouwerij

6,40% (14 ° plato) 6 °C 43 °F

	top-fermentation re-fermented in the bottle	fermentation haute refermentation en bouteille	hoge gisting hergisting op de fles
	regional beer, blond	bière régionale blonde	streekbier blond
	pilsner malt, wheat malt, aromatic hop varieties, yeast, water	malt de pils, malt de froment, sortes de houblon aromatiques, levure, eau	pilsmout, tarwemout, aromatische hopsoorten, gist, water
	blond with possibly a light cloudiness when served very cold	blonde, aspect légèrement trouble est possible si la bière est très froide	blond, lichte koudetroebelheid is mogelijk
	Refreshing and thirst-quenching smooth bitter character beer. Smooth, mild full-malt flavour with fine aromatic, slightly citric hoppy touch. 30 EBU	Bière de caractère rafraîchissante et légèrement amère. Saveur maltée moelleuse avec des arômes de houblon aromatiques et une touche légère d'agrumes.	Verfrissend en dorstlessend zachtbitter karakterbier. Zachte en malse volmoutsmaak met fijn aromatisch, licht citrusachtig hoparoma. 30 EBU
	Pour into a dry glass in a single, fluent movement, and avoid sloshing. Leave 2 cm in the bottle and serve it alongside the glass of beer. The yeast sediment can be added to the beer afterwards.	Verser en un seul mouvement fluide dans un verre sec sans que la bière clapote. Laisser 2 cm de bière dans la bouteille et la servir avec le verre rempli. Le dépôt de levure dans la bouteille peut être ajouté selon le goût.	In 1 vlotte beweging uitschenken in een droog glas zonder dat het bier klokt. 2 cm in de fles laten en dit samen met het ingeschonken glas serveren. Het gistresidu in de fles kan desgewenst achteraf worden bijgeschonken.
i			

S Slaapmutske Bruin

Slaapmutske by De Proefbrouwerij 6% (14 ° plato) 9° 48°

	top-fermentation re-fermented in the bottle	fermentation haute refermentation en bouteille	hoge gisting hergisting op de fles
	regional beer, dubbel	bière régionale double	streekbier dubbel
	different kinds of coloured malts, pilsner malt, hops, coriander, yeast, water	différentes sortes de malt coloré, malt de pils, houblon, coriandre, levure, eau	verschillende soorten kleurmouten, pilsmout, hop, koriander, gist, water
	red-brown clear and slightly sparkling compact, solid and creamy foam head	brun rouge, claire et legèrement perlante faux col dense, solide et crémeux	roodbruin, helder en licht parelend compacte, stevige en romige schuimkraag
	Spicy and full-bodied character beer. 30 EBU. Full-bodied, slighty sweetish with a spicy aftertaste (colour malt and coriander touch).	Bière de caractère relevée et franche avec une amertume de 30 EBU. Franche, légèrement douce avec une fin de bouche corsée et relevée (malts colorés et touche de coriandre).	Kruidig en volmondig karakterbier met een bitterheid van 30 EBU. Volmondig, licht zoetig met een pittige, kruidige afdronk (kleurmouten en koriandertoets).
	Pour into a dry glass in a single, fluent movement, and avoid sloshing. Leave 2 cm in the bottle and serve it along with the glass of beer.	Verser en un seul mouvement fluide dans un verre sec sans que la bière clapote. Laisser 2 cm de bière dans la bouteille et la servir avec le verre rempli.	In 1 vlotte beweging uitschenken in een droog glas zonder dat het bier klokt. 2 cm in de fles laten en dit samen met het ingeschonken glas serveren.
i			

Slaapmutske Christmas

laapmutske by De Proefbrouwerij 7,40% (16 ° plato) 9 °C 48 °F

	top-fermentation re-fermentation in the bottle not centrifuged	fermentation haute refermentation en bouteille non centrifugée	hoge gisting hergisting in de fles niet gecentrifugeerd
	winter or Christmas beer	bière hivernale ou bière de Noël	winter- of kerstbier
	coloured malts, aromatic hops, yeast, water	malts colorés, houblon aromatique, levure, eau	kleurmouten, aromatische hop, gist, water
	slightly sparking burgundy-coloured (owing to the coloured malts) beer with a compact, firm and creamy foam head. Not pasteurised.	légèrement pétillante bourgogne (par les malts colorés) bière avec un faux col compact, solide et crémeux. Non pasteurisée.	licht parelend bourgognekleurig (door de kleurmouten) met een compacte, stevige en romige schuimkraag. Niet gepasteuriseerd
	Soft-sweet, slightly spicy aroma pallet. Malty, mellow taste with nicely finished and warm feeling in the mouth. Pleasant, spicy aftertaste.	Palette d'arômes doucement sucrés, légèrement épicés. Goût malté, succulent, avec une jolie sensation ronde et chaude en bouche. Arrière-bouche agréable, épicée.	Zachtzoet, licht gekruid aromapalet. Moutige, malse smaak met mooi afgerond en warm mondgevoel. Aangename, kruidige afdronk.
	Pour out in a single movement and avoid sloshing the beer. Leave a yeast sediment of approx. 2 cm in the bottle and add later, if necessary.	Verser dans un verre sec d'un seul mouvement fluide sans clapotage de la bière. Laisser un dépôt de levure de ca. 2 cm dans la bouteille et le verser éventuellement par après.	In een droog glas in 1 vlotte beweging uitschenken zonder dat het bier klokt. Een gistdepot van ca. 2 cm in de fles laten en eventueel achteraf bijschenken.
	Gold medal 2009 for best international Christmas beer at Esbjerg beer festival in Denmark.	Médaille d'or 2009 comme meilleure bière de Noël internationale au festival de la bière à Esbjerg au Danemark.	Gouden medaille 2009 als beste internationale kerstbier op het Esbjerg bierfestival in Denemarken.

Slaapmutske Dry Hopped Lager

Slaapmutske by De Proefbrouwerij

5,30% (12 ° plato) 6 ° 43 °

	bottom-fermentation re-fermentation in the bottle	fermentation basse refermentation en bouteille	lage gisting hergisting in de fles
	Dortmunder with dry-hopping	Dortmunder avec dry-hopping	Dortmunder met dry-hopping
	pilsner malt, aromatic hops, yeast, water. Dry-hopped.	malt de pils, houblon aromatique, levure, eau. Dry-hopped.	pilsmout, aromatische hop, gist, water. Dry-hopped.
	blond, slightly veiled with a compact, firm foam head. Filtered, not pasteurised	blonde, légèrement voilée avec un faux col compact, solide. Filtrée, non pasteurisée.	blond, licht gesluierd met een compacte, stevige schuimkraag. Gefilterd, niet gepasteuriseerd.
	Very drinkable and very hoppy. Unique beer full of taste and character despite its low alcohol content. Reminiscent of an authentic 'export'. 35 EBU.	Facile à boire et fortement houblonnée. Bière unique, fort goûteuse et très caractéristique malgré sa faible teneur en alcool. Fait penser à une authentique 'export'. 35 EBU.	Vlot drinkbaar en stevig gehopt. Uniek, smaak- en karaktervol bier ondanks zijn lage alcoholgehalte. Het doet denken aan een authentieke 'export'. 35 EBU.
	see Slaapmutske Christmas	voir Slaapmutske Christmas	zie Slaapmuske Christmas
	Initially only brewed in casks for the Spanish market. These days, permanently available in casks or bottled both in Belgium and elsewhere.	À l'origine, uniquement brassée en fût pour le marché espagnol. Actuellement, aussi disponible en permanence en Belgique et dans d'autres pays, tant en fût qu'en bouteilles.	Aanvankelijk enkel op vat gebrouwen voor de Spaanse markt. Momenteel ook in België en andere landen permanent verkrijgbaar zowel op vat als gebotteld.

Slaapmutske by De Proefbrouwerij

8,10% (16 ° plato) — 8 °C 46 °F

	top-fermentation re-fermented in the bottle	fermentation haute refermentation en bouteille	hoge gisting hergisting op de fles
	regional beer tripel	bière régionale triple	streekbier tripel
	pilsner malt, coloured malt, two strong aromatic hop varieties, yeast, water	malt de pils, malt coloré, 2 sortes de houblon très aromatiques, levure, eau	pilsmout, kleurmout, 2 sterk aromatische hopsoorten, gist, water
	golden blond clear 40 EBC	blond doré claire 40 EBC	goudblond helder 40 EBC
	Fresh hoppy aroma and a spicy, bitter taste. Malty aftertaste with evolution toward a pleasantly bitter mouthfeel. 31 EBU	Arôme houblonné frais et saveur corsée, amère. Fin de bouche maltée aboutissant à une sensation amère agréable dans la bouche. 31 EBU	Fris hoparoma en een pittige, bittere smaak. Moutige afdronk die uitvloeit in een aangenaam bitter mondgevoel. 31 EBU
	see Slaapmutske Christmas	voir Slaapmutske Christmas	zie Slaapmuske Christmas
	In America, this beer is sold under the name Triple Nightcap. Was voted one of Belgium's best special beers in Norway in 2007 by the magazine Apéritiv.	Sur le marché américain, cette bière est vendue sous le nom Triple Nightcap. Elle a été élue en 2007 l'une des meilleures bières spéciales belges en Norvège par le magazine Apéritiv.	Op de Amerikaanse markt wordt dit bier verkocht onder de naam Triple Nightcap. Werd in 2007 verkozen tot een van de beste Belgische speciaalbieren in Noorwegen door het tijdschrift Apéritiv.

Slaefke - Aughems Fluytjesbier

De Verhuisbrouwerij by Brouwerij Sint-Canarus 7,50% 12° 54°

	top-fermentation natural re-fermentation in the bottle not centrifuged	fermentation haute refermentation naturelle en bouteille non centrifugée	hoge gisting natuurlijke hergisting in de fles niet gecentrifugeerd
	boutique blond tripel	triple blonde artisanale	artisanale blonde tripel
	pilsner malt, wheat malt, light malt extract, hops (Magnum and Hallertau Tradition), tap water	malt de pils, malt de froment, extrait de malt léger, houblon (Magnum et Hallertau Tradition), eau de conduite	pilsmout, tarwemout, licht moutextract, hop (Magnum en Hallertau Tradition), leidingwater
	12 EBC not filtered or pasteurised	12 EBC non filtrée, non pasteurisée	12 EBC ongefilterd, niet gepasteuriseerd
	Fruity scent with a slightly bitter body. Ends in a sweet aftertaste.	Parfum fruité, avec un corps légèrement amer. Se termine par une fin de bouche douceâtre.	Fruitige geur met een licht bittere body. Eindigt met een zoetige nasmaak.
	Serve in a goblet.	Verser dans un verre calice.	Uitschenken in een kelkglas.
	Brewed to mark the Ouwegem Fluitjes Festival. For this occasion, a red sweet has been developed that can be used as a whistle.	Brassée en l'honneur des Fluitjesfeesten d'Ouwegem. Pour cette occasion, il existe aussi déjà une friandise rouge qui peut être utilisée comme sifflet.	Gebrouwen ter ere van de Ouwegemse Fluitjesfeesten. Voor deze gelegenheid bestaat ook al een rood snoepje dat als fluitje kan worden gebruikt.

rouwerij Slaghmuylder 5,20% 6 - 10 °C / 43 - 50 °F

Slaghmuylder's Kerstbier

bottom-fermentation	fermentation basse	lage gisting
luxury/premium pilsner Christmas beer	pils de luxe/premium bière de Noël	luxe/premium pils kerstbier
barley malt, yeast, water, hop varieties (Belgian Hallertau, Czech Styrie). Heavy brewing technique, with extra local hops.	malt d'orge, levure, eau, sortes de houblon (Hallertau belge, Styrie tchèque). Brassage fort, extra houblonné avec du houblon de la propre région.	gerstemout, gist, water, hopsoorten (Belgische Hallertau, Tsjechische Styrie). Zwaar gebrouwen en extra gehopt met hop uit eigen streek.
Blond with a stable foam head. Crystal-clear with gentle bubbles. Unpasteurised. Also available in an unfiltered version.	Blonde avec faux col stable. Claire comme du cristal et perlant tranquillement. Non pasteurisée. Egalement disponible dans une version non filtrée.	Blond met stabiele schuimkraag. Kristalhelder en rustig parelend. Niet gepasteuriseerd. Ook ongefilterd verkrijgbaar.
Hop aroma in the bitter aftertaste.	Arômes houblonnés dans la fin de bouche amère.	Aroma's van hop in de bittere afdronk.
Pour in one single, smooth movement.	Verser en un seul mouvement fluide et doux.	Uitschenken in 1 vloeiende, zachte beweging.
Recognised regional product. An exceptional product: blond low-fermenting Christmas beer.	Reconnu comme produit régional. Produit exceptionnel : bière blonde de Noël à fermentation basse.	Erkend als streekproduct. Een uitzonderlijk product: blond van lage gisting als kerstbier.

Slaghmuylder's Paasbier

Brouwerij Slaghmuylder 5,20% 6 - 10 ° 43 - 50 °

	bottom-fermentation	fermentation basse	lage gisting
	premium pilsner	pils de luxe/premium	luxe/premium pilsner
	barley malt, yeast, water, hop varieties (Belgian Hallertau, Czech Styrie). Heavy brewing technique with extra local hops. Main fermentation and lagering take 3 months.	malt d'orge, levure, eau, sortes de houblon (Hallertau belge, Styrie tchèque). Brassage fort, extra houblonné avec du houblon de la propre région. La conservation et la fermentation principale durent 3 mois.	gerstemout, gist, water, hopsoorten (Belgische Hallertau, Tsjechische Styrie). Zwaar gebrouwen en extra gehopt met hop uit eigen streek. 3 maanden lagering en hoofdgisting.
	Blond with a stable foam head. Crystal-clear with fine bubbles. Also available in an unfiltered version.	Blonde avec un faux col stable. Claire comme du cristal et légèrement perlant. Egalement disponible dans une version non filtrée.	Blond met stabiele schuimkraag. Kristalhelder en fijn parelend. Ook ongefilterd verkrijgbaar.
	Hoppy luxury pilsner. Hop aroma in the bitter aftertaste.	Pils de luxe houblonnée. Arômes de houblon dans la fin de bouche amère.	Hoppige luxepils. Aroma's van hop in de bittere afdronk.
	Pour in 1 fluent, smooth movement.	Verser en un seul mouvement fluide et doux.	Uitschenken in 1 vloeiende, zachte beweging.
i			

Sloeber

rouwerij Roman 7,50% 6 °C 43 °F

top-fermentation re-fermented in the bottle	fermentation haute refermentation en bouteille	hoge gisting nagisting op de fles
strong blond	blonde forte	sterk blond
barley malt, hops, sugars, yeast, spring water	malt d'orge, houblon, sucres, levure, eau de source	gerstemout, hop, suikers, gist, bronwater
blond	blonde	blond
Sipping beer with a spicy, full-bodied taste and a powerful alcoholic aftertaste.	Bière de dégustation avec une saveur corsée, franche et une fin de bouche corsée, alcoolisée.	Degustatiebier met een pittige, volmondige smaak en een krachtige alcoholische afdronk.
Pour carefully in a single, smooth movement, avoiding contact between bottle and foam. Leave the yeast sediment in the bottle.	Verser prudemment en un seul mouvement fluide sans que la bouteille touche le faux col. Laisser le dépôt de levure dans la bouteille.	Voorzichtig uitschenken in 1 vlotte beweging zonder dat de fles de schuimkraag raakt. De gistfond in de fles laten.
Store in a dark, cool room.	Conserver à l'abri de la lumière et de la chaleur.	Donker en koel bewaren.

Brouwerij 't Smisje

7% 5 - 10 ° 41 - 50 °

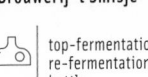

	top-fermentation re-fermentation in the bottle not centrifuged	fermentation haute refermentation en bouteille non centrifugée	hoge gisting hergisting in de fles niet gecentrifugeerd
	blond tripel	triple blonde	blond tripel
	barley malt, 4 different Belgian hops, candy sugar, beer yeast, spring and mineral water	malt d'orge, 4 variétés de houblon Belge, sucre candi, levure de bière, eau de source et eau minérale	gerstemout, 4 soorten Belgische hop, kandijsuiker, biergist, bron- en mineraalwater
	blond with solid creamy foam head not filtered or pasteurised	blonde avec un faux col solide, crémeux non filtrée, non pasteurisée	blond met een stevige, romige schuimkraag ongefilterd, niet gepasteuriseerd
	Fruity nose. Strong taste, hoppy bitter, full-bodied with a long, pleasant, bitter aftertaste.	Bouquet fruité. Goût fort, d'une amertume houblonnée, franc, avec une longue arrière-bouche agréablement amère.	Fruitige neus. Stevige smaak, hopbitter, volmondig met een lange, aangenaam bittere afdronk.

Brouwerij 't Smisje 7% 5 - 10 °C / 41 - 50 °F

Smiske Bruin

	top-fermentation re-fermentation in the bottle not centrifuged	fermentation haute refermentation en bouteille non centrifugée	hoge gisting hergisting in de fles niet gecentrifugeerd
	double	double	dubbel
	barley malt, 2 different Belgian hops, candy sugar, beer yeast, spring and mineral water	malt d'orge, 2 variétés de houblon Belge, sucre candi, levure de bière, eau de source et eau minérale	gerstemout, 2 soorten Belgische hop, kandijsuiker, biergist, bron- en mineraalwater
	brown with a red glow, creamy foam head not filtered or pasteurised	brune avec reflet rouge, faux col crémeux non filtrée, non pasteurisée	bruin met rode schijn, romige schuimkraag ongefilterd, niet gepasteuriseerd
	Dry beer with fruity nose. Strong taste, bitter (owing to malt) and full-bodied with a long, pleasant aftertaste.	Bière sèche d'un bouquet fruité. Goût fort, amer (amer malté) et franc, avec une arrière-bouche longue et agréable.	Droog bier met fruitige neus. Stevige smaak, bitter (moutbitter) en volmondig met een lange, aangename afdronk.

Special 6 Block

Brouwerij De Block 6% 6 - 8° 43 - 46°

	top-fermentation re-fermented in the bottle	fermentation haute refermentation en bouteille	hoge gisting hergisting op de fles
	amber brown-red blended beer	ambrée bière de coupage brune-rouge	amber bruinrood versnijbier
	wheat, malt, hops, yeast, water	froment, malt, houblon, levure, eau	tarwe, mout, hop, gist, water
	red, clear	rouge, claire	rood, helder
	Fruity and fresh. Full aroma, with pomegranate flavour.	Fruitée et fraîche. Plein d'arômes, goût de grenade.	Fruitig en fris. Vol aroma, smaak van granaatappel.
	Cfr. Chimay: in a goblet with a stem.	Voir Chimay, dans un verre calice à pied.	Zoals Chimay, in een kelkglas met voet.
	Store the beer in an upright position. According to the brewer, it is an Old Flemish red beer, blended with young beer. Beer connoisseurs however, claim that it would better belong in the 'amber' category.	Conserver la bière en position verticale. Selon le brasseur, Special 6 est une Vieille bière rouge flamande coupée avec une bière jeune. Des amateurs de bière réagissent en disant qu'elle appartient mieux à la catégorie des bières ambrées.	Het bier verticaal bewaren. Volgens de brouwer is het een Oud Vlaams rood bier, versneden met jong bier. Vanuit kringen van bierfanaten komt de reactie dat het bier beter past in de categorie 'amber'.

ouwerij De Ryck

5,50% 4 - 6 °C / 39 - 43 °F

top-fermentation re-fermented in the bottle	fermentation haute refermentation en bouteille	hoge gisting hergisting in de fles
ale amber beer	ale bière ambrée	ale amberbier
malt, hops, yeast, sucrose, water	malt, houblon, levure, sucrose, eau	mout, hop, gist, sucrose, water
light amber slightly hazy	ambré clair légèrement voilée	licht amber licht gesluierd
Rich, fresh and slightly alcoholic character. Fruity, hoppy aroma. A typical combination of a malty, full-bodied flavour and a smoothly bitter aftertaste.	Caractère riche, frais et légèrement alcoolisé. Arôme houblonné fruité. Combinaison typique d'un goût houblonné franc et d'une fin de bouche légèrement amère.	Rijk, fris en licht alcoholisch karakter. Fruithoppig aroma. Typische combinatie van moutige volmondigheid en zachtbittere afdronk.
Rinse the glass with cold water, take it by the handle and tilt it slightly. Pour slowly in a single movement, avoiding contact between bottle and glass or foam. Leave the 1 cm yeast sediment in the bottle or pour it.	Rincer le verre à l'eau froide et le tenir légèrement en oblique par l'anse. Verser la bière lentement et en un seul mouvement sans que la bouteille touche le verre ou l'écume. Laisser un dépôt de levure de 1 cm dans la bouteille ou la vider.	Het glas koud spoelen, bij het oor vastnemen en licht schuin houden. Het bier traag en in 1 beweging inschenken zonder dat de fles het glas of schuim raakt. Het gistdepot van 1 cm in de fles laten of uitschenken.
The draught version of this beer is clear (filtered).	La bière au fût est claire (filtrée).	Van het vat is het bier helder (gefilterd).

Special Extra Export Stout

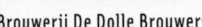

Brouwerij De Dolle Brouwers 9% 10 - 12 / 50 - 54

top-fermentation	fermentation haute	hoge gisting
stout	stout	stout
malt (roasted, pale, cara), Nugget hops, yeast, water	malt (grillé, pâle, cara), houblon Nugget, levure, eau	mout (geroosterd, bleek, cara), Nugget hop, gist, water
intense black with beige foam head	noir foncé avec faux col beige	pikzwart met beige schuimkraag
Appreciated among the Anglo-Saxon public. Heavy, bitter, slightly tart and very stout.	Appréciée auprès du public anglo-saxon. Forte, amère, un peu acidulée et très solide.	Geliefd bij een Angelsaksisch publiek. Zwaar, bitter, een beetje zuur en zeer kloek.
Serve in a robust glass, like a Guinness glass	Dans un verre solide et robuste tel que pour Guinness.	In een kloek en robuust glas zoals voor Guinness.
Has been brewed since 2004 at the request of the American importers. Stout used to be recommended for people who needed to convalesce as it increases the hematocrite levels in the blood.	Brassée depuis 2004 à la demande de l'importateur américain. Le stout était jadis recommandé pour la convalescence et augmente la valeur de l'hématocrite dans le sang.	Wordt sedert 2004 gebrouwen op aanvraag van de Amerikaanse invoerder. Stout werd vroeger aangeraden voor revalidatie. Het verhoogt het hematocriet-gehalte in het bloed.

ouwerij Roman

5,50% 8 °C 46 °F

	top-fermentation	fermentation haute	hoge gisting
	Flemish brown Oudenaards	brune flamande d'Audenarde	Vlaams bruin Oudenaards
	barley malt, corn, hops, candy sugar, yeast, spring water	malt d'orge, maïs, houblon, sucre candi, levure, eau de source	gerstemout, mais, hop, kandijsuiker, gist, bronwater
	red-brown clear	brun rouge claire	roodbruin helder
	Sipping beer with a full-bodied, bittersweet taste. Smoothly aromatic, slightly frivolous and yet very spicy.	Bière de dégustation avec un goût franc, doux-amer. Doucement aromatique, un peu frivole et quand même très corsé.	Degustatiebier met een volmondige, zoetbittere smaak. Zacht aromatisch, iets frivool en toch zeer pittig.
	Slowly pour into a degreased, rinsed beer glass, making a nice foam head.	Verser lentement dans un verre de bière dégraissé et rincé et former un beau faux col.	Langzaam uitschenken in een ontvet en gespoeld bierglas en een mooie schuimkraag vormen.
	Store in a dark, cool room.	Conserver à l'abri de la lumière et de la chaleur.	Donker en koel bewaren.

Speciale 1900

Brouwerij Haacht

5% 5 - 6 / 41 - 43

top-fermentation centrifuged	fermentation haute centrifugée	hoge gisting gecentrifugeerd
Spéciale Belge amber	spéciale belge ambrée	spéciale belge amber
barley malt, wheat malt, corn, sugar, hops, herbs, water	malt d'orge, malt de froment, maïs, sucre, houblon, herbes, eau	gerstemout, tarwemout, mais, suiker, hop, kruiden, water
amber to copper colour filtered, pasteurised	ambré cuivre filtrée, pasteurisée	amber tot koperkleur gefilterd, gepasteuriseerd
Session beer with a full-bodied, balanced taste, a fresh slightly fruity touch and a pleasant bitter (hops) aftertaste.	Facilement buvable, d'un goût franc, équilibré, une touche légèrement fruitée fraîche et une agréable arrière-bouche amère houblonnée.	Doordrinkbier met een volmondige, evenwichtige smaak, een frisse lichtfruitige toets en een aangename hopbittere afdronk.
Pour carefully into a rinsed, wet Speciale glass, avoiding contact between bottle and foam.	Verser prudemment dans un verre Speciale rincé et mouillé sans que la bouteille touche l'écume.	Voorzichtig uitschenken in een gespoeld, nat Speciale-glas zonder dat de fles het schuim raakt.
Brewed again since 2007 as a tribute to the 'spéciale belge' an authentic beer style that was started at the beginning of the 20th century. Between 1930 to 1960 Brewery Haacht brewed the 'Belge Double Speciale' (formerly Bavaro Belge). Between 1960 and 1980, it distributed the 'Speciale Aerts', Brewery Aerts's amber beer.	Brassée de nouveau depuis 2007 en hommage à la 'spéciale belge', un authentique style de bière apparu au début du 20e siècle. Des années '30 aux années '60, la Brouwerij Haacht brassait la 'Belge Double Spéciale' (auparavant de Bavaro Belge). De '60 à '80, elle distribua la 'Speciale Aerts', la bière ambrée de la Brouwerij Aerts.	Sinds 2007 opnieuw gebrouwen als eerbetoon aan de 'spéciale belge' een authentieke bierstijl ontstaan begin 20e eeuw. Van de jaren '30 tot '60 brouwde Brouwerij Haacht de 'Belge Double Speciale' (vroeger van Bavaro Belge). Van '60 tot '80 verdeelde ze de 'Speciale Aerts' het amberbier van Brouwerij Aerts.

5% 7 °C 45 °F

top-fermentation	fermentation haute	hoge gisting
amber	ambrée	amber
barley malt, yeast, water	malt d'orge, levure, eau	gerstemout, gist, water
copper colour fine foam head	couleur cuivre faux col fin	koperkleur fijne schuimkraag
Spicy, hoppy and slightly fruity with a dry after-taste.	Corsée, houblonnée et légèrement fruitée avec une fin de bouche sèche.	Pittig, hoppig en licht fruitig met droge af-dronk.
Produced for the local market.	Destinée au marché lo-cal.	Bestemd voor de lokale markt.

Brasserie Artisanale Millevertus

4,50% 4 39

	top-fermentation	fermentation haute	hoge gisting
	ale	ale	ale
	different malt, hop and yeast varieties, water	différentes sortes de malt, de houblon et de levure, eau	verschillende mout-, hop- en gistsoorten, water
	blond	blonde	blond
	Light but round spelt beer with austere bitterness and hop flavours.	Bière d'épeautre légère mais ronde avec une amertume sobre et des arômes houblonnés.	Licht maar rond speltbier met sobere bitterheid en hoparoma's.

en Haene by Brouwerij Strubbe

5,70% 4 - 5 °C / 39 - 41 °F

Spioenkopje Wit Kriekenbier

	top-fermentation re-fermentation in the bottle	fermentation haute refermentation en bouteille	hoge gisting hergisting op de fles
	witbier with fruit	bière blanche fruitée	witbier met fruit
	malt, barley, wheat, oat, hops, cherry, yeast, water	malt, orge, froment, avoine, houblon, cerises, levure, eau	mout, gerst, tarwe, haver, hop, krieken, gist, water
	not filtered	non filtrée	ongefilterd
	Summery thirst-quencher, neither sweet nor sour.	Bière désaltérante d'été, pas sucrée, ni acide.	Zomerse dorstlesser, niet zoet en niet zuur.

St Benoît Blonde

Brasserie du Bocq

6,30% 5 - 12° 41 - 54°

	top-fermentation re-fermented in the bottle	fermentation haute refermentation en bouteille	hoge gisting hergisting in de fles
	blond abbey beer	bière d'abbaye blonde	abdijbier blond
	barley malt, hop varieties, yeast, herbs, water	malt d'orge, sortes de houblon, levure, herbes, eau	gerstemout, hoppesoorten, gist, kruiden, water
	nice straw-yellow colour (10,5 EBC) with a fine, white foam head.	jolie couleur jaune paille (10,5 EBC) avec un faux col fin blanc	mooie strogele kleur (10,5 EBC) met fijne witte kraag
	Fruity flavour with a light hoppy aroma. Smooth, pleasant and fine beer, slightly bitter (22 EBU).	Arôme fruité avec un parfum légèrement houblonné. Bière douce, agréable et fine avec une légère amertume (22 EBU).	Fruitig aroma met een lichte hopgeur. Zacht bier, aangenaam en fijn met een lichte bitterheid (22 EBU).
	Gently pour into a perfectly degreased glass. Leave the yeast sediment (due to natural refermenting) in the bottle.	Verser doucement dans un verre parfaitement dégraissé. Laisser le dépôt de levure (refermentation naturelle) dans la bouteille.	Zacht uitschenken in een perfect ontvet glas. Het gistbezinksel (natuurlijke hergisting) in de fles laten.
i			

top-fermentation re-fermented in the bottle	fermentation haute refermentation en bouteille	hoge gisting hergisting in de fles
dark abbey beer	bière d'abbaye foncée	abdijbier donker
barley malt, wheat starch, hop varieties, yeast, herbs, water	malt d'orge, fécule de froment, sortes de houblon, levure, herbes, eau	gerstemout, tarwezetmeel, hoppesoorten, gist, kruiden, water
dark brown (70 EBC) clear fine, nice, solid foam head	brune foncée (70 EBC) claire faux col fin, joli, solide	donkerbruin (70 EBC) helder fijne, mooie, vaste kraag
Pleasant flavour of dark malt. Slightly fruity. Bitterness: 28 EBU.	Arôme agréable de malt foncé. Amertume 28 EBU. Légèrement fruitée.	Aangenaam aroma van donkere mout. Licht fruitig. Bitterheid 28 EBU.
Gently pour into a perfectly degreased glass. Leave the yeast sediment (due to natural refermenting) in the bottle.	Verser doucement dans un verre parfaitement dégraissé. Laisser le dépôt de levure (refermentation naturelle) dans la bouteille.	Zacht uitschenken in een perfect ontvet glas. Het gistbezinksel (natuurlijke hergisting) in de fles laten.
Beer in memory of St-Benoît/St. Benedict (480 - 547), founder of the Benedictine order which has a tradition of rich and intense beers.	Bière en mémoire de saint Benoît (480 - 547), fondateur de l'ordre des Bénédictins, qui jouit d'une tradition de bières riches et intenses.	Bier ter nagedachtenis van Saint-Benoît/Sint-Benedictus (480-547) stichter van de Benediktijnenorde die een traditie heeft van rijke en intense bieren.

St. Amatus (Oostvleteren 12)

De Struise Brouwers at Brouwerij Deca 10,50% 12° 54°

	top-fermentation re-fermentation in the bottle not centrifuged	fermentation haute refermentation en bouteille non centrifugée	hoge gisting hergisting in de fles niet gecentrifugeerd
	quadruple	quadruple	quadrupel
	Slightly hazy, dark chestnut with brown-red glow. Firm, old-ivory-coloured foam head. Not filtered or pasteurised	Légèrement fade, marron foncé avec éclat brun rouge. Faux col solide vieux ivoire. Non filtrée, non pasteurisée	Licht wazig, donker kastanje met bruinrode gloed. Stevige schuimkraag met kleur van oud ivoor. Ongefilterd, niet gepasteuriseerd
	Complex sipping beer with distinct, refined aroma of cedar wood, milk bread, caramel, nuts, grin, black tea and a hint of port. Rich, mellow flavour. Long aftertaste which flavours that are reminiscent of malt, bread, caramel, tobacco, tea and wine. The fine hoppy touch adds freshness at the very end.	Bière de dégustation complexe, avec un arôme raffiné prononcé de cèdre, de pain au lait, de caramel, de noix, de céréales, de thé noir et une pointe de porto. Goût riche et doux. Longue arrière-bouche, avec des goûts faisant penser à du malt, du pain, du caramel, du tabac, du thé et du vin. La touche houblonnée fine apporte un peu de fraîcheur dans la finale.	Complex degustatiebier met uitgesproken, verfijnd aroma van cederhout, melkbrood, karamel, noten, granen, zwarte thee en een vleugje port. Rijke, zachte smaak. Lange afdronk met smaken die doen denken aan mout, brood, karamel, tabak, thee en wijn.De fijne hoptoets brengt wat fraicheur in de finale.
	Pour out in a single movement.	Verser agilement.	Vlot uitschenken.
	St Amatus is Oostvleteren's patron saint.	Saint Aimé est le saint patron d'Oostvleteren.	Sint-Amatus is de patroonheilige van Oostvleteren.

top-fermentation re-fermented in the bottle	fermentation haute refermentation en bouteille	hoge gisting hergisting op de fles
Belgian abbey beer	Bière d'abbaye belge	Belgisch abdijbier
malt varieties, hops, sugar, yeast and 'historical' water (rain water fallen in Jeanne d'Arc's time, pumped in Watou)	sortes de malt, houblon, sucre, levure et eau 'historique' (pompée à Watou et provenant de la pluie de l'époque de Jeanne d'Arc)	moutsoorten, hop, suiker, gist en 'historisch' water (opgepompt in Watou en afkomstig van de regenval uit de tijd van Jeanne d'Arc)
dark ivory, unfiltered	ivoire foncé, non filtrée	donker ivoor, ongefilterd
Fruity aroma and smooth full-bodied taste.	Arôme fruité et goût doux et franc.	Fruitig aroma en zachte volmondige smaak.
Pour into a glass, rinsed with cold water. Leave the glass upright and pour the beer carefully in a single, fluent movement. The yeast sediment can be left in the bottle and drunk separately.	Verser la bière prudemment et en un seul mouvement dans un verre rincé à l'eau froide et tenu en position verticale. Laisser le dépôt de levure (peut être bu séparément) dans la bouteille.	Het bier voorzichting in 1 vloeiende beweging uitschenken in een met koud water gespoeld glas dat rechtop staat. Het gistdepot in de fles laten (kan apart worden gedronken).
The name of the brewery refers to the shelter, erected in Watou in the 1900s, by the abbey community of Catsberg who had been elbowed out of France.	Le nom de la brasserie renvoie au refuge établi à Watou au début du 20ième siècle par la communauté abbatiale de Catsberg refoulée de France.	De naam van de brouwerij verwijst naar de refuge die begin 20e eeuw in Watou werd opgericht door de abdijgemeenschap van Catsberg die in Frankrijk werd verdrongen.

St. Bernardus Christmas Ale

Brouwerij Sint-Bernardus 10% 6 - 10° / 43 - 50°

	top-fermentation re-fermented in the bottle	fermentation haute refermentation en bouteille	hoge gisting hergisting op de fles
	dark Christmas beer	bière de Noël foncée	donker kerstbier
	malt varieties, hops, sugar, yeast and historical' water (rain water fallen in Jeanne d'Arc's time, pumped in Watou)	sortes de malt, houblon, sucre, levure et eau 'historique' (pompée à Watou et provenant de la pluie de l'époque de Jeanne d'Arc)	moutsoorten, hop, suiker, gist en 'historisch' water (opgepompt in Watou en afkomstig van de regenval uit de tijd van Jeanne d'Arc)
	deep brown	brun foncé	diepbruin
	Malty, fruity, full taste, with an aftertaste that is more sweet than bitter.	Houblonné-fruitée, saveur pleine, fin de bouche plutôt douce qu'amère.	Moutfruitig, volle smaak, eerder zoete dan bittere afdronk.
	Empty in a glass rinsed with cold water. Leave the glass upright and pour the beer carefully in one single movement. Leave the yeast sediment in the bottle or serve it separately.	Verser la bière prudemment et en un seul mouvement dans un verre rincé à l'eau froide et tenu verticalement. Laisser le dépôt de levure (peut être bu séparément) dans la bouteille.	Het bier voorzichting in 1 vloeiende beweging uitschenken in een met koud water gespoeld glas dat rechtop staat. Het gistdepot in de fles laten (kan apart worden gedronken).
i	The name of the brewery refers to the shelter, erected in Watou in the 1900s, by the abbey community of Catsberg.	Le nom de la brasserie renvoie au refuge établi à Watou au début du 20ième siècle par la communauté abbatiale de Catsberg.	De naam van de brouwerij verwijst naar de refuge die begin 20e eeuw in Watou werd opgericht door de abdijgemeenschap van Catsberg.

St. Bernardus Pater 6

Brouwerij Sint-Bernardus — 6,70% — 6 - 10 °C / 43 - 50 °F

	top-fermentation re-fermented in the bottle	fermentation haute refermentation en bouteille	hoge gisting hergisting op de fles
	Belgian abbey beer	Bière d'abbaye belge	Belgisch abdijbier
	malt varieties, hops, sugar, yeast and 'historical' water (rain fallen in Jeanne d'Arc's time, pumped in Watou)	sortes de malt, houblon, sucre, levure et eau 'historique' (pompée à Watou, provenant de la pluie de l'époque de Jeanne d'Arc)	moutsoorten, hop, suiker, gist en 'historisch' water (opgepompt in Watou en afkomstig van de regenval uit de tijd van Jeanne d'Arc)
	chestnut	marrone	kastanjekleur
	Full taste.	Goût plein.	Volle smaak.
	Pour into a glass, rinsed with cold water. Leave the glass upright and pour the beer carefully in a single, fluent movement. The yeast sediment can be left in the bottle or drunk separately.	Verser la bière prudemment et en un seul mouvement dans un verre rincé à l'eau froide et tenu en position verticale. Laisser le dépôt de levure (peut être bu séparément) dans la bouteille.	Het bier voorzichting in 1 vloeiende beweging uitschenken in een met koud water gespoeld glas dat rechtop staat. Het gistdepot in de fles laten (kan apart worden gedronken).
	The name of the brewery refers to the shelter, erected in Watou in the 1900s, by the abbey community of Catsberg who had been elbowed out of France.	Le nom de la brasserie renvoie au refuge établi à Watou au début du 20ième siècle par la communauté abbatiale de Catsberg refoulée de France.	De naam van de brouwerij verwijst naar de refuge die begin 20e eeuw in Watou werd opgericht door de abdijgemeenschap van Catsberg die in Frankrijk werd verdrongen.

St. Bernardus Prior 8

Brouwerij Sint-Bernardus 8% 6 - 10 °C / 43 - 50 °F

top-fermentation re-fermented in the bottle	fermentation haute refermentation en bouteille	hoge gisting hergisting op de fles
Belgian abbey beer	Bière d'abbaye belge	Belgisch abdijbier
malt varieties, hops, sugar, yeast and 'historical' water (rain water fallen in Jeanne d'Arc's time, pumped in Watou)	sortes de malt, houblon, sucre, levure et eau 'historique' (pompée à Watou, provenant de la pluie de l'époque de Jeanne d'Arc)	moutsoorten, hop, suiker, gist en 'historisch' water (opgepompt in Watou en afkomstig van de regenval uit de tijd van Jeanne d'Arc)
ruby purple unfiltered, nice round foam head	violet rubis non filtrée joli faux col rond	robijnpaars ongefilterd, mooie ronde schuimkraag
Malty, fruity, full taste and bittersweet aftertaste.	Goût de houblon fruité, plein et fin de bouche douce-amère.	Moutfruitige, volle smaak en zoetbittere nasmaak.
Pour into a glass, rinsed with cold water. Leave the glass upright and pour the beer carefully. The yeast sediment can be drunk separately.	Verser la bière prudemment dans un verre rincé à l'eau froide et tenu en position verticale. Le dépôt de levure peut être bu séparément.	Het bier voorzichtig uitschenken in een met koud water gespoeld glas dat rechtop staat. Het gistdepot kan apart worden gedronken.
The name of the brewery refers to the shelter, erected in Watou in the 1900s, by the abbey community of Catsberg who had been elbowed out of France.	Le nom de la brasserie renvoie au refuge établi à Watou au début du 20ième siècle par la communauté abbatiale de Catsberg refoulée de France.	De naam van de brouwerij verwijst naar de refuge die begin 20e eeuw in Watou werd opgericht door de abdijgemeenschap van Catsberg die in Frankrijk werd verdrongen.

St. Bernardus Tripel

Brouwerij Sint-Bernardus — 8% — 4 - 8 °C / 39 - 46 °F

	top-fermentation re-fermented in the bottle	fermentation haute refermentation en bouteille	hoge gisting hergisting op de fles
	Belgian abbey beer	Bière d'abbaye belge	Belgisch abdijbier
	malt varieties, hops, sugar, yeast and 'historical' water (rain water fallen in Jeanne d'Arc's time, pumped in Watou)	sortes de malt, houblon, sucre, levure et eau 'historique' (pompée à Watou, provenant de la pluie de l'époque de Jeanne d'Arc)	moutsoorten, hop, suiker, gist en 'historisch' water (opgepompt in Watou en afkomstig van de regenval uit de tijd van Jeanne d'Arc)
	amber/blonde unfiltered thick, smooth foam head	ambrée/blonde non filtrée faux col crémeux	amber/blond ongefilterd smeuïge schuimkraag
	Flowery, fruity aroma, bittersweet balance, well-balanced aftertaste	Arôme fleuri et fruité, équilibre doux-amer, fin de bouche équilibrée.	Bloemig, fruitig aroma, zoetbitter evenwicht, uitgebalanceerde nasmaak.
	Leave the glass upright and pour the beer carefully in a single movement. The sediment can be left in the bottle or drunk separately	Laisser le verre en position verticale et verser la bière prudemment. Laisser le dépôt (peut être bu séparément) dans la bouteille.	Het glas rechtop laten staan en het bier in voorzichtig uitschenken. Het gistdepot (kan apart worden uitgedronken) in de fles laten.
	The name of the brewery refers to the shelter, erected in Watou in the 1900s, by the abbey community of Catsberg.	Le nom de la brasserie renvoie au refuge établi à Watou au début du 20ième siècle par la communauté abbatiale de Catsberg.	De naam van de brouwerij verwijst naar de refuge die begin 20e eeuw in Watou werd opgericht door de abdijgemeenschap van Catsberg.

St. Bernardus Witbier

Brouwerij Sint-Bernardus

5,50% 2 - 6 °C / 36 - 43 °F

top-fermentation re-fermented in the bottle	fermentation haute refermentation en bouteille	hoge gisting hergisting op de fles
witbier	bière blanche	witbier
malt, wheat, hops, yeast, water	malt, froment, houblon, levure, eau	mout, tarwe, hop, gist, water
Clear yellow and slightly cloudy, produced by the wheat. Off-white foam head.	Couleur jaune clair, quelque peu trouble due au froment. Le faux col est blanc cassé.	Heldergele, ietwat troebele kleur door de tarwe. De schuimkraag is gebroken wit.
Light and refreshing.	Légère et rafraîchissante.	Licht en verfrissend.
Pour into a tall glass, rinsed with cold water. Leave the glass upright and pour the beer carefully in a single, fluent movement.	Verser dans un verre haut rincé à l'eau froide. Laisser le verre en position verticale et verser la bière prudemment en un seul mouvement fluide.	Uitschenken in een met koud water gespoeld hoog glas. Het glas rechtop laten staan en het bier in 1 vloeiende beweging voorzichtig uitschenken.
Developed in collaboration with Pierre Celis, the father of the Hoegaarden Witbier and Celis White.	Développée en collaboration avec Pierre Celis, le 'père' de la bière blanche Hoegaarden et Celis White.	Ontwikkeld in samenwerking met Pierre Celis, de 'vader' van Hoegaarden witbier en Celis White.

St. Paul Blond

Sterkens by Brasserie du Bocq

5,30% 6 - 10 °C 43 - 50 °F

top-fermentation re-fermented in the bottle	fermentation haute refermentation en bouteille	hoge gisting hergisting in de fles
blond abbey beer	bière d'abbaye blonde	blond abdijbier
malt, hops, yeast, water	malt, houblon, levure, eau	mout, hop, gist, water
light blond unfiltered, cloudy	blond clair non filtrée, trouble	lichtblond ongefilterd, troebel
Fairly high saturation, mild and soft. Flavours of coriander, lime and green apple. Refreshing taste with a dry aftertaste.	Saturation assez haute, moelleuse et douce. Arômes de coriandre, de citron vert et de pomme verte. Saveur rafraîchissante avec une fin de bouche sèche.	Vrij hoog gesatureerd, mild en zacht. Aroma's van koriander, limoen en groene appel. Verfrissende smaak met droge afdronk.
Pour carefully with a generous foam head.	Verser prudemment avec un faux col large.	Voorzichtig uitschenken met ruime schuimkraag.
More than 90 % is destined for export.	Plus de 90% est destiné à l'exportation.	Meer dan 90% is bestemd voor export.

St. Paul Double

Sterkens by Brasserie du Bocq 6,90% 6 - 10 °C / 43 - 50 °F

	top-fermentation re-fermented in the bottle	fermentation haute refermentation en bouteille	hoge gisting hergisting in de fles
	dubbel abbey beer	bière d'abbaye double	dubbel abdijbier
	malt, hops, yeast, water	malt, houblon, levure, eau	mout, hop, gist, water
	brown, filtered	brune, filtrée	bruin, gefilterd
	Sweet and bitter. Caramel malt perfume with light fruit aromas. Hops and herbs touches. Full malt taste. Touches of chocolate, nuts, fruit and wood.	Douce et amère. Parfum de malt caramélisé avec des arômes fruités légers. Touches de houblon et d'herbes. Goût malté plein, touches de chocolat, de noix, de fruits et de bois.	Zoet en bitter. Parfum van karamelmout met lichte fruitaroma's. Toetsen van hop en kruiden. Volle moutsmaak, toetsen van chocolade, noten, fruit en hout.
	Pour carefully with a generous foam head.	Verser prudemment avec un faux col large.	Voorzichtig uitschenken met ruime schuimkraag.
i	More than 90 % is destined for export.	Plus de 90% est destiné à l'exportation.	Meer dan 90% is bestemd voor export.

St. Paul Speciale

Sterkens by Brasserie du Bocq

5,50% 6 - 10 °C / 43 - 50 °F

top-fermentation re-fermented in the bottle	fermentation haute refermentation en bouteille	hoge gisting hergisting in de fles
amber abbey beer	bière d'abbaye ambrée	amber abdijbier
malt, hops, yeast, water	malt, houblon, levure, eau	mout, hop, gist, water
filtered	filtrée	gefilterd
Pour carefully with a generous foam head.	Verser prudemment avec un faux col large.	Voorzichtig uitschenken met ruime schuimkraag.
More than 90 % is destined for export.	Plus de 90% est destiné à l'exportation.	Meer dan 90% is bestemd voor export.

St. Paul Tripel

Sterkens by Brasserie du Bocq 7,60% 6 - 10 °C 43 - 50 °F

	top-fermentation re-fermented in the bottle	fermentation haute refermentation en bouteille	hoge gisting hergisting in de fles
	tripel abbey beer	bière d'abbaye triple	tripel abdijbier
	malt, hops, yeast, water	malt, houblon, levure, eau	mout, hop, gist, water
	light blonde, filtered	blond clair, filtrée	lichtblond, gefilterd
	Refreshing, very drinkable Tripel. Aroma of flowers, malt, herbs and citrus. Full malty, creamy taste.	Triple rafraîchissante qui se boit facilement. Arômes de fleurs, de malt, d'herbes et d'agrumes. Goût houblonné plein, crémeux.	Verfrissende tripel die zich gemakkelijk laat drinken. Aroma's van bloemen, mout, kruiden en citrus. Volmoutige, romige smaak.
	Pour carefully with a generous foam head.	Verser prudemment avec faux col large.	Voorzichtig uitschenken met een ruime schuimkraag.
i	More than 90 % is destined for export.	Plus de 90% est destiné à l'exportation.	Meer dan 90% is bestemd voor export.

terkens by Brasserie du Bocq

6,90% — 6 - 10 °C / 43 - 50 °F

top-fermentation re-fermented in the bottle	fermentation haute refermentation en bouteille	hoge gisting hergisting in de fles
dubbel abbey beer	bière d'abbaye double	dubbel abdijbier
malt, hops, yeast, water	malt, houblon, levure, eau	mout, hop, gist, water
dark brown, filtered	brun foncé, filtrée	donkerbruin, gefilterd
Well-balanced and very drinkable. Aroma of caramel and nuts. Light bitter nose. Taste of caramel, chocolate and dark malt.	Bien équilibré, se boit facilement. Arômes de caramel et de noix, parfum légèrement amer. Goût de caramel, chocolat et malt foncé.	Goed gebalanceerd, laat zich makkelijk drinken. Aroma van karamel en noten, lichtbittere neus. Smaak van karamel, chocolade en donkere mout.
Pour carefully with a generous foam head.	Verser prudemment avec un faux col large.	Voorzichtig uitschenken met ruime schuimkraag.
More than 90 % is destined for export.	Plus de 90% est destiné à l'exportation.	Meer dan 90% is bestemd voor export.

St. Sebastiaan Dark

St. Sebastiaan Grand Cru

Sterkens by Brasserie du Bocq 7,60% 6 - 10 ° 43 - 50 °

	top-fermentation re-fermented in the bottle	fermentation haute refermentation en bouteille	hoge gisting hergisting in de fles
	strong blond, abbey beer	blonde forte, bière d'abbaye	sterk blond, abdijbier
	malt, hops, yeast, water	malt, houblon, levure, eau	mout, hop, gist, water
	golden blond, filtered	blond doré, filtrée	goudblond, gefilterd
	Heavy sipping beer. Sweet flavour with apricot and grapefruit touches. Softly malty but fullbodied with a touch of honey and sweet fruit.	Bière de dégustation forte. Arôme doux avec des touches d'abricot et de pamplemousse. Légèrement houblonné mais franc avec une touche de miel et de fruits doux.	Zwaar degustatiebier. Zoet aroma met toetsen van abrikoos en pompelmoes. Zachtmoutig maar toch volmondig met een vleugje honing en zoet fruit.
	Pour carefully with a generous foam head.	Verser prudemment avec un faux col large.	Voorzichtig uitschenken met ruime schuimkraag.
i	More than 90 % is destined for export.	Plus de 90% est destiné à l'exportation.	Meer dan 90% is bestemd voor export.

6,50% 3 - 6 °C 37 - 43 °F

top-fermentation re-fermentation in the bottle	fermentation haute refermentation en bouteille	hoge gisting hergisting in de fles
Recognised Belgian abbey beer blond	Bbière d'abbaye belge reconnue blonde	Erkend Belgisch Abdijbier blond
made on the basis of 'gruit' (herbal mixture)	fabriquée à base de gruit (mélange d'herbes)	gemaakt op basis van gruut (kruidenmengsel)
blond filtered	blonde filtrée	blond gefilterd
Warm, full flavour and a slightly smoked fermentation aroma, in combination with the subtle herbal mixture.	Goût chaud, franc et un léger arôme de fermentation fumé, en combinaison avec le subtil mélange d'épices.	Warme, volle smaak en een licht gerookt gistingsaroma, in combinatie met het subtiele kruidenmengsel.
Serve in a goblet.	Verser dans un verre calice.	Uitschenken in een kelkglas.
In the olden days, every town had its own beer with its own character that was determined by the 'gruit' (herbal mixture). In Bruges, the brewers were required to buy the 'gruit' from the herbal shop 'Gruuthuse'.	Chaque ville avait autrefois une bière, avec un caractère propre qui était déterminé par le gruit (mélange d'épices). À Bruges, les brasseurs devaient obligatoirement acheter le gruit à la maison des épices 'Gruuthuse'.	Elke stad had vroeger een bier met eigen karakter dat bepaald werd door de gruut (kruidenmengsel). In Brugge moesten de brouwers de gruut verplicht aankopen in het kruidenhuis 'Gruuthuse'.

Steenbrugge Dubbel Bruin

Palm Breweries 6,50% 8 - 12° 46 - 54°

	top-fermentation re-fermented in the bottle	fermentation haute refermentation en bouteille	hoge gisting hergisting op de fles
	dubbel abbey beer	bière d'abbaye double	dubbel abdijbier
	ruby	rubis	robijnkleur
	Frank, full taste. Malty.	Saveur franche, pleine. Maltée.	Rondborstige, volle smaak. Moutig.
	Leave 1 cm of yeast sediment in the bottle.	Laisser 1 cm de dépôt de levure dans la bouteille.	1 cm gistdepot in de fles laten.
	The founder of the abbey of Steenbrugge, Saint Arnoldus, is the patron saint of the brewers.	Le fondateur de l'abbaye de Steenbrugge, le Saint Arnould, est le patron des brasseurs.	De stichter van de abdij van Steenbrugge, de heilige Arnoldus, is de patroonheilige van de brouwers.

alm Breweries 8,50%

top-fermentation re-fermented in the bottle	fermentation haute refermentation en bouteille	hoge gisting hergisting op de fles
blond abbey beer	bière d'abbaye blonde	blond abdijbier
golden blond	blond doré	goudblond
Spicy flavour with a noble aftertaste	Arôme relevé et fin de bouche noble.	Kruidig aroma en nobele afdronk.
Leave 1 cm of yeast sediment in the bottle.	Laisser 1 cm de dépôt de levure dans la bouteille.	1 cm gistdepot in de fles laten.

Steenbrugge Tripel

Steenbrugge Wit/Blanche

Palm Breweries 5% 3 - 6° 37 - 43

	top-fermentation re-fermentation in the bottle	fermentation haute refermentation en bouteille	hoge gisting hergisting in de fles
	Recognised Belgian abbey beer white	Bière d'abbaye belge reconnue blanche	Erkend Belgisch Abdijbier witbier
	40% unmalted wheat, 60 % malt, 'gruit', coriander, curaçao	40% froment non malté, 60 % malt, gruit, coriandre, curaçao	40% ongemoute tarwe, 60 % mout, gruut, koriander, curaçao
	not filtered	non filtrée	ongefilterd
	Refreshing taste and a slightly smoked fermentation aroma. Subtle herbal mixture ('gruit'), but mainly coriander and curaçao.	Goût désaltérant et un léger arôme de fermentation fumé. Subtil mélange d'épices (gruit), avec l'accent sur la coriandre et le curaçao.	Verfrissende smaak en een licht gerookt gistingsaroma. Subtiel kruidenmengsel (gruut) met de nadruk op koriander en curaçao.
	Serve in a goblet.	Verser dans un verre calice.	Uitschenken in een kelkglas.
	St Arnold of Tiegem founded the St Peter's Abbey in 1084. He would brew beer and heal the sick with it, or so the legend goes. He is the brewers' patron saint.	Saint Arnould de Tiegem a fondé en 1084 l'abbaye Saint-Pierre. La légende raconte qu'il brassait de la bière et s'en servait pour guérir des malades. Il est le saint patron des brasseurs.	St-Arnoldus van Tiegem stichtte in 1084 de Sint-Pietersabdij. De legende vertelt dat hij bier brouwde en er zieken mee genas. Hij is de patroonheilige van de brouwers.

6,50% 6 °C 43 °F

	top-fermentation re-fermentation in the bottle; centrifuged	fermentation haute refermentation en bouteille; centrifugée	hoge gisting hergisting in de fles gecentrifugeerd
	strong blond	blonde forte	sterk blond
	malt, corn, hops, yeast, sweet-scented woodruff, blackthorn, angelica, water	malt, maïs, houblon, levure, aspérule odorante, épine noire, angélique, eau	mout, maïs, hop, gist, lievevrouwbedstro, sleedoorn, engelwortel, water
	filtered, not pasteurised	filtrée, non pasteurisée	gefilterd, niet gepasteuriseerd
	Different, full-bodied aroma and a hoppy bitter taste that is supported by the herbs. Distinct flavour development resulting in bitter aftertaste.	Arôme particulier, franc et une amertume houblonnée qui est soutenue par les épices. Évolution claire du goût, avec une amertume qui s'écoule.	Apart, volmondig aroma en een hopbitterheid die ondersteund wordt door de kruiden. Duidelijke smaakevolutie met uitvloeiende bitterheid.
	Rinse the glass, take it by the stem and tilt. Slowly pour the beer in a single movement, avoiding contact with the foam or glass.	Rincer le verre, le tenir incliné par le pied. Verser la bière lentement et d'un seul mouvement sans que la bouteille touche l'écume ou le verre.	Het glas spoelen, bij de voet vastnemen en schuin houden. Het bier traag en in 1 beweging uitschenken zonder dat de fles het schuim of glas raakt.
	Brewed at the request of the Regional Landscape Flemish Ardennes to mark the Little Owl Project. This is why it is a hoppy beer with 3 herbs from the Flemish Ardennes.	Brassée pour le compte du Regionaal Landschap Vlaamse Ardennen à l'occasion du projet Steenuil. Voilà pourquoi c'est aussi une petite bière houblonnée avec 3 herbes des Ardennes flamandes.	Gebrouwen in opdracht van het Regionaal Landschap Vlaamse Ardennen n.a.v. het Steenuilproject. Daarom is het ook een hoppig biertje met 3 kruiden uit de Vlaamse Ardennen.

Stella Artois

AB-Inbev Leuven

5,20% 3 37

	bottom-fermentation	fermentation basse	lage gisting
	pilsner	pils	pilsbier
	pale malt, corn, hops, yeast, water	malt pâle, maïs, houblon, levure, eau	bleekmout, maïs, hop, gist, water
	blond	blonde	blond
	The character of Czech hop and a vague impression of recently mowed hay. Fresh, full taste with a fine bitterness.	Caractère de houblon tchèque et vague impression de foin coupé. Goût frais, plein avec une amertume fine.	Karakter van Tsjechische hop en vage impressie van pas gemaaid hooi. Frisse, volle smaak met fijne bitterheid.
	Rinse the glass in cold water, tilt it and smoothly pour the beer. Skim off if desired.	Rincer le verre à l'eau froide, le tenir incliné et verser la bière doucement. Ecumer selon le goût.	Het glas onder koud water spoelen, schuin houden en het bier zacht uitschenken. Desgewenst afschuimen.
i			

rasserie Saint-Feuillien

7,50% — 6 °C / 12 °C — 43 °F / 54 °F

St-Feuillien Blonde

	top-fermentation naturally re-fermented in the bottle	fermentation haute refermentation naturelle en bouteille	hoge gisting natuurlijke hergisting in de fles
	Recognised Belgian abbey beer blond	Bière d'abbaye belge reconnue blonde	Erkend Belgisch abdijbier blond
	barley malt, sugar, hops, yeast, vitamin C, brewing water	malt d'orge, sucre, houblon, levure, vitamine C, eau de brassage	gerstemout, suiker, hop, gist, vitamine C, brouwwater
	deep golden colour filtered	doré intense filtrée	diepe goudkleur gefilterd
	Digestive with a very perfumed aroma. Intense, distinctive bitterness and prominent malt flavour with a full mouthfeel. Dry and hoppy aftertaste.	Digestive, avec un arôme très parfumé. Amertume intense, très caractéristique et pleine. Le goût malté dominant laisse une impression pleine dans la bouche. Arrière-bouche sèche et houblonnée.	Digestief met zeer geparfumeerd aroma. Intense, zeer karakteristieke volle bitterheid. De dominante moutsmaak laat een volle indruk na in de mond. Droge en hoppige afdronk.
	Dry goblet.	Verre ballon sec.	Droog ballonglas.
i			

St-Feuillien Brune Réserve

Brasserie Saint-Feuillien 8,50% 6 °C / 12 43 °F / 54

	top-fermentation naturally re-fermented in the bottle	fermentation haute refermentation naturelle en bouteille	hoge gisting natuurlijke hergisting in de fles
	Recognised Belgian abbey beer strong brown	Bière d'abbaye belge reconnue bière brune forte	Erkend Belgisch abdijbier sterk bruin
	barley malt, sugar, hops, yeast, vitamin C, brewing water	malt d'orge, sucre, houblon, levure, vitamine C, eau de brassage	gerstemout, suiker, hop, gist, vitamine C, brouwwater
	ruby-brown filtered	brun rubis filtrée	robijnbruin gefilterd
	Exceptional sensual palette with a hoppy taste and powerful flavour. Touches of fruit in harmony with the prominent liquorice and caramel.	Palette exceptionnellement sensorielle avec une saveur houblonnée et un arôme fort. Touches fruitées en harmonie avec la dominance de réglisse et de caramel.	Uitzonderlijk zintuiglijk palet met een hoppige smaak en een krachtig aroma. Toetsen van fruit in harmonie met de dominantie van zoethout en karamel.
	Dry goblet.	Verre ballon sec.	Droog ballonglas.

9% 6 °C / 12 °C 43 °F / 54 °F

	top-fermentation naturally re-fermented in the bottle	fermentation haute refermentation naturelle en bouteille	hoge gisting natuurlijke hergisting in de fles
	Recognised Belgian abbey beer tripel	Bière d'abbaye belge reconnue triple	Erkend Belgisch abdijbier tripel
	barley malt, sugar, hops, yeast, vitamin C, brewing water, roasted and caramelised malt	malt d'orge, sucre, houblon, levure, vitamine C, eau de brassage, malt brûlé et caramélisé	gerstemout, suiker, hop, gist, vitamine C, brouwwater, gebrande en gekaramelliseerde mout
	Deep ruby-brown colour, brownish due to the roasted malt.	Couleur rubis profonde, brunâtre de malt brûlé.	Diep robijnrode, bruinachtige kleur van gebrande mout.
	Round and smooth. Intense, perfumed aroma. Harmonious taste, with some bitterness in the background.	Ronde et moelleuse. Arôme intensément parfumé. Saveur harmonieuse avec une amertume à l'arrière-plan.	Rond en zacht. Intens geparfumeerd aroma. Harmonieuze smaak waar de bitterheid op de achtergrond blijft.
	Dry goblet.	Verre ballon sec.	Droog ballonglas.
i			

St-Feuillien Cuvée de Noël

St-Feuillien Triple

Brasserie Saint-Feuillien 8,50% 6 °C / 12 43 °F / 54

	top-fermentation naturally re-fermented in the bottle	fermentation haute refermentation naturelle en bouteille	hoge gisting natuurlijke hergisting in de fles
	Recognised Belgian abbey beer winter beer	Bière d'abbaye belge reconnue bière hivernale	Erkend Belgisch abdijbier winterbier
	barley malt, sugar, hops, yeast, vitamin C, brewing water	malt d'orge, sucre, houblon, levure, vitamine C, eau de brassage	gerstemout, suiker, hop, gist, vitamine C, brouwwater
	light amber	ambré clair	licht amber
	Sipping beer with a very perfumed and fruity aroma of hop, spices and yeast. Powerful taste, exceptional mouthfeel.	Bière de dégustation avec des arômes très parfumés et fruités de houblon, herbes et levure. Saveur forte et fin de bouche exceptionnelle.	Degustatiebier met zeer geparfumeerd en fruitig aroma van hop, kruiden en gist. Krachtige smaak en uitzonderlijke afdronk.
	Dry goblet.	Ballon sec.	Droog ballonglas.

rouwerij Huyghe 6,50%

top-fermentation re-fermented in the bottle	fermentation haute refermentation en bouteille	hoge gisting hergisting in de fles
Belgian abbey beer blond	Bière d'abbaye belge blonde	Belgisch abdijbier blond
malt, hops, yeast, water	malt, houblon, levure, eau	mout, hop, gist, water
blond clear	blonde claire	blond helder
Fairly light, malty and bitter. A thirst-quencher.	Assez légère, maltée et amère. Désaltérant.	Tamelijk licht, moutig en bitter. Dorstlessend.
Serve in a goblet.	Verser dans un verre calice.	Uitschenken in een kelkglas.
Brewed following an ancient tradition based on a recipe of Saint Idesbald, the third abbot of the Duinen Abbey (ca. 1130).	Brassée selon une tradition séculaire d'après une recette de St-Idesbald, 3ième abbé de l'Abbaye des Dunes (vers 1130).	Gebrouwen volgens eeuwenoude traditie naar een recept van St-Idesbald, 3e abt van de Duinenabdij (ca 1130).

St-Idesbald Réserve Ten Duinen Blond

S

St-Idesbald Réserve Ten Duinen Dubbel

Brouwerij Huyghe 8%

	top-fermentation re-fermented in the bottle	fermentation haute refermentation en bouteille	hoge gisting hergisting in de fles
	Belgian abbey beer dubbel	Bière d'abbaye belge double	Belgisch abdijbier dubbel
	malt, hops, yeast, water	malt, houblon, levure, eau	mout, hop, gist, water
	brown	brune	bruin
	Character and taste are similar to Flemish oud-bruin with a discrete, pleasant sourness. Bitter caramel and fine bitterness.	Caractère et goût semblables aux Vieilles brunes flamandes, avec une acidulité discrète et agréable. Caramel amer et amertume fine.	Neigt qua karakter en smaak naar Vlaams oud-bruin met discrete aangename zurigheid. Bittere karamel en fijne bitterheid.
	Serve in a goblet.	Verser dans un verre calice.	Uitschenken in een kelkglas.
	Brewed following an ancient tradition based on a recipe of Saint Idesbald, the third abbot of the Duinen Abbey (ca. 1130).	Brassée selon une tradition séculaire d'après une recette de St-Idesbald, 3ième abbé de l'Abbaye des Dunes (vers 1130).	Gebrouwen volgens eeuwenoude traditie naar een recept van St-Idesbald, 3e abt van de Duinenabdij (ca 1130).

rouwerij Huyghe

7%

St-Idesbald Réserve Ten Duinen Rousse

S

	top-fermentation re-fermented in the bottle	fermentation haute refermentation en bouteille	hoge gisting hergisting in de fles
	Belgian abbey beer rousse	Bière d'abbaye belge rousse	Belgisch abdijbier rousse
	malt, hops, yeast, water	malt, houblon, levure, eau	mout, hop, gist, water
	red-brown	brun rouge	roodbruin
	Serve in a goblet.	Verser dans un verre calice.	Uitschenken in een kelkglas.
	Brewed following an ancient tradition based on a recipe of Saint Idesbald, the third abbot of the Duinen Abbey (around 1130).	Brassée selon une tradition séculaire d'après une recette de St-Idesbald, 3ième abbé de l'Abbaye des Dunes (vers 1130).	Gebrouwen volgens eeuwenoude traditie naar een recept van St-Idesbald, 3e abt van de Duinenabdij (ca 1130).

St-Idesbald Réserve Ten Duinen Tripel

Brouwerij Huyghe 9%

	top-fermentation re-fermented in the bottle	fermentation haute refermentation en bouteille	hoge gisting hergisting in de fles
	Belgian abbey beer tripel	Bière d'abbaye belge triple	Belgisch abdijbier tripel
	malt, hops, yeast, water	malt, houblon, levure, eau	mout, hop, gist, water
	blond cloudy	blonde trouble	blond troebel
	Velvety soft with a light bitterness.	Veloutée avec une amertume légère.	Fluweelzacht met lichte bitterheid.
	Serve in a goblet.	Verser dans un verre calice.	Uitschenken in een kelkglas.
	Brewed following an ancient tradition based on a recipe of Saint Idesbald, the third abbot of the Duinen Abbey (ca. 1130).	Brassée selon une tradition séculaire d'après une recette de St-Idesbald, 3ième abbé de l'Abbaye des Dunes (vers 1130).	Gebrouwen volgens eeuwenoude traditie naar een recept van St-Idesbald, 3e abt van de Duinenabdij (ca 1130).

12% 10 - 12 °C / 50 - 54 °F

	top-fermentation re-fermented in the bottle uncentrifuged	fermentation haute refermentation en bouteille non centrifugée	hoge gisting nagisting op de fles, niet gecentrifugeerd
	specialty beer winter beer	bière spéciale bière hivernale	speciaalbier winterbier
	pale malt, white candy sugar, Golding hops	malt pâle, sucre candi blanc, houblon Golding	bleke mout, witte kandijsuiker, Golding hop
	amber unfiltered	ambrée non filtrée	amber ongefilterd
	Flavour of alcohol, malt and hops. Smooth and strong.	Arôme d'alcool, de malt et de houblon. Douce et forte.	Aroma van alcohol, mout en hop. Zacht en straf.
	Serve in an Oerbeer glass or wine glass.	Servir dans un verre oerbier ou un verre de vin.	Serveren in een oerbierglas of wijnglas.
	Can be kept for 20 years or longer.	Se conserve jusqu'à 20 ans et plus.	Houdbaar tot 20 jaar en meer.

Stout Leroy

Brouwerij Het Sas

5% 5 - 6° 41 - 43°

	bottom-fermentation	fermentation basse	lage gisting
	sweet stout	stout douce	zoete stout
	malt, rice, hops, caramel, water	malt, riz, houblon, caramel, eau	mout, rijst, hop, karamel, water
	dark brown	brun foncé	donkerbruin
	Sweet session beer. Sweet toffee taste with a hint of liquorice.	Bière douce facilement buvable. Goût de caramel doux avec une touche de réglisse.	Zoet doordrinkbier. Zoete toffeesmaak met een hint van zoethout.
	Pour slowly in a single, smooth movement, into a degreased glass. Keep the glass tilted to avoid sloshing. Skim off the foam.	Verser lentement en un seul mouvement fluide dans un verre dégraissé tenu en oblique. Ne pas laisser la bière clapoter. Ecumer le verre.	Traag en in 1 vloeiende beweging uitschenken in een vetvrij glas dat wordt schuingehouden. Het bier niet laten klotsen. Het glas afschuimen.
i	During storage, the beer goes through an evolution similar to wine, developing a nut-like flavour.	Pendant la conservation, la bière 'vinifie' et développe un goût de noix.	Tijdens het bewaren 'verwijnt' het bier en ontwikkelt het een notensmaak.

rouwerij De Bie

5,50%

Stoute Bie

	top-fermentation	fermentation haute	hoge gisting
	sweet stout	stout douce	zoete stout

Stouterik - The Brussels Stout

Brasserie de la Senne 4,50% 8° 46°

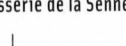

	top-fermentation natural re-fermentation in the bottle not centrifuged	fermentation haute refermentation naturelle en bouteille non centrifugée	hoge gisting natuurlijke hergisting in de fles niet gecentrifugeerd
	stout	stout	stout
	malt varieties, roasted barley, different hops, yeast, water	variétés de malt, orge torréfiée, variétés de houblon, levure, eau	moutsoorten, gebrande gerst, hopsoorten, gist, water
	black with dense and fine foam head not filtered or pasteurised	noire avec un faux col épais non filtrée, non pasteurisée	zwart met dichte en fijne schuimkraag ongefilterd, niet gepasteuriseerd
	Fresh-bitter, light, dry stout. Roasted flavour. Aromatic English hops in the nose, appreciated among connoisseurs.	Stout fraîchement amère, légère, sèche. Une pointe de brûlé. Houblon anglais aromatique dans le bouquet, apprécié des connaisseurs.	Frisbittere, lichte, droge stout. Een vleugje gebrand. Aromatische Engelse hop in de neus, geapprecieerd door de kenners.
	Pour out slowly and leave 1 cm (yeast) in the bottle. Drink yeast separately.	Verser prudemment et laisser 1 cm (levure) dans la bouteille. Eventuellement boire la levure séparément.	Voorzichtig uitschenken en 1 cm (gist) in de fles laten. De gist eventueel afzonderlijk uitdrinken.
i	Old-fashioned stout according to the Irish tradition.	Stout à l'ancienne selon la tradition irlandaise.	Ouderwetse stout volgens de Ierse traditie.

Brouwerij De Halve Maan   11%   10 - 12 °C / 50 - 54 °F

top-fermentation re-fermentation in the bottle not centrifuged	fermentation haute refermentation en bouteille non centrifugée	hoge gisting hergisting in de fles niet gecentrifugeerd
strong dubbel	foncée forte	sterk donker
5 different malts, hops, yeast, water	5 variétés de malt, houblon, levure, eau	5 moutsoorten, hop, gist, water
dark with solid foam head filtered, pasteurised	foncée avec faux col solide filtrée, pasteurisée	donker met stevige schuimkraag gefilterd, gepasteuriseerd
Sipping beer with spicy, punchy taste, bitter aftertaste.	Bière de dégustation d'un goût franc épicé, puissant, une arrière-bouche amère.	Degustatiebier met kruidige, machtige v olle smaak, bittere afdronk.
Serve in a goblet.	Verser dans un verre calice.	Uitschenken in een kelkglas.

Straffe Hendrik Brugs Quadrupel Ale

S

Straffe Hendrik Tripel

Brouwerij De Halve Maan 9% 8 - 10 °C 46 - 50 °F

	top-fermentation re-fermentation in the bottle not centrifuged	fermentation haute refermentation en bouteille non centrifugée	hoge gisting hergisting in de fles niet gecentrifugeerd
	tripel city beer	triple citadine	tripel stadsbier
	malt, different aromatic hops, yeast, water	malt, variétés de houblon aromatiques, levure, eau	mout, aromahopsoorten, gist, water
	dark blond with fine, carbon dioxide foam head filtered, pasteurised	blond foncé avec faux col fin pétillant filtrée, pasteurisée	donkerblond met fijne, parelende schuimkraag gefilterd, gepasteuriseerd
	Fruity nose full of aroma and fine, bitter aftertaste.	Bouquet fruité plein d'arôme et une arrière-bouche fine, amère.	Fruitige neus vol aroma en fijne, bittere afdronk.
	Serve in a goblet.	Verser dans un verre calice.	Uitschenken in een kelkglas.
i	De Halve Maan, a unique family brewery, has been in the historical part of Bruges since 1856	De Halve Maan est depuis 1856 une brasserie familiale unique dans le centre-ville historique de Bruges.	De Halve Maan is sedert 1856 een unieke familiebrouwerij in het historische stadscentrum van Brugge

Strandgaper

De Scheldebrouwerij 6,20% 6 - 8 °C / 43 - 46 °F

	top-fermentation re-fermentation in the bottle	fermentation haute refermentation en bouteille	hoge gisting hergisting in de fles
	blond	blonde	blond
	barley malt, hops, yeast, water	malt d'orge, houblon, levure, eau	gerstemout, hop, gist, water
	yellow-gold-blond (21 EBC) with white, thick foam that leaves a lace pattern on the glass. Not filtered or pasteurised	jaune blond doré (21 EBC) avec faux col blanc collant au verre laissant des dentelles. Non filtrée, non pasteurisée	geel goudblond (21 EBC) met wit, wandklevend schuim dat kantwerk op het glas laat. Ongefilterd, niet gepasteuriseerd
	Tasty thirst-quencher with modest, sweet aroma with a hint of hops. Pleasant, fresh, mellow taste. Fine sweet-and-sour balance. Modest bitter aftertaste that lingers. 25 EBU.	Bière désaltérante fort goûteuse, d'un arôme douceâtre discret, avec une pointe de houblon. Goût fondant agréable, frais. Joli équilibre d'amer et de sucré. Fin de bouche s'écoulant dans un peu d'amertume discrète. 25 EBU.	Smaakvolle dorstlesser met bescheiden, zoetig aroma met een vleugje hop. Aangename, frisse, malse smaak. Mooie balans van bitter en zoet. Bescheiden bitterig uitvloeiende nasmaak. 25 EBU
	'Strandgaper' (mollusk) is a clam that buries himself into muddy and sandy soils up to 40 cm deep and is also prevalent, therefore, in the Scheldt region.	La Mye commune (Mya arenaria) est un mollusque qui s'enfouit à une profondeur de 40 cm dans des sols vaseux et sablonneux, et qui se rencontre donc aussi dans le domaine de l'Escaut.	Strandgaper is een weekdier dat zich 40 cm diep ingraaft in modderige en zandige bodems en dus ook in het Scheldegebied voorkomt.

Strandjuttersbier Mong de Vos

Den Haene by Brouwerij Strubbe — 9,20%

	top-fermentation re-fermentation in the bottle	fermentation haute refermentation en bouteille	hoge gisting hergisting in de fles
	quadruple, brown tripel	quadruple, triple brune	quadruppel, bruine tripel
	malt, barley, hops, sugar, herbs, yeast, water	malt, orge, houblon, sucre, herbes, levure, eau	mout, gerst, hop, suiker, kruiden, gist, water
	not filtered	non filtrée	ongefilterd
	Punchy brown beer with fine malt and hoppy taste, not sweet.	Une petite brune forte d'un goût malté et houblonné fin, pas sucré.	Krachtig bruintje met fijne mout- en hopsmaak, niet zoet.
	Named after the legendary beachcomber from Vossenslag who died at the stake and is remembered at the annual Vossenslag Festival (De Haan). The sculpture depicted on the label is by Martine Labbeke.	Désignée d'après un légendaire pilleur d'épaves de Vosseslag qui mourut sur le bûcher et dont la mémoire est célébrée lors des Vosseslagfeesten (De Haan) annuelles. La sculpture représentée sur l'étiquette est de Martine Labbeke.	Genoemd naar een legendarische strandjutter uit Vossenslag die stierf op de brandstapel en herdacht wordt op de jaarlijkse Vossenslagfeesten (De Haan). De sculptuur afgebeeld op het etiket is van Martine Labbeke.

Brouwerij Strubbe

5,20% — 4 °C / 39 °F

Strubbe Pils

	bottom-fermentation	fermentation basse	lage gisting
	pilsner	pils	pilsbier
	pilsner malt, corn, sugar, hops, water	malt de pils, maïs, sucre, houblon, eau	pilsmout, mais, suiker, hop, water
	blond clear (filtered)	blonde claire (filtrée)	blond helder (gefilterd)
	Malty, pure, slightly bitter, thirst-quenching.	Maltée, pure, légèrement amère, désaltérante.	Moutig, zuiver, lichtbitter, dorstlessend.

De Struise Brouwers at Brouwerij Deca

6% — 4 - 6 °C / 39 - 43 °F

top-fermentation re-fermented in the bottle; not centrifuged	fermentation haute refermentation en bouteille; non centrifugée	hoge gisting hergisting in de fles niet gecentrifugeerd
old-style amber	ambrée style ancien	amber oude stijl
pilsner malt, Vienna malt, Münich malt, cara Münich, corn flocks, yeast, water. Hops: Brewers gold, Challenger. Herbs: sweet orange rind, coriander, cloves.	malt de pils, malt Vienna, malt Münich, cara Münich, flocons de maïs, levure, eau. Houblon: Brewers gold, Challenger. Herbes: écorce d'orange doux, coriandre, girofle.	Pilsmout, Viennamout, Münichmout, caramünich, maisvlokken, gist, water. Hop: Brewers gold, Challenger. Kruiden: zoete sinaasschil, koriander, kruidnagel.
slightly hazy amber (29 EBC) with nice white foam head unfiltered	légèrement flou ambré (29 EBC) avec un joli faux col blanc non filtrée	licht wazig amber (29 EBC) met mooie witte schuimkraag ongefilterd
Intense, fine dry-malty taste with light touches of caramel, grain, nuts, fruit. Refreshing bitter of mild hops in aftertaste. 20 EBU	Goût piquant, joliment malté sec, avec de légères touches de caramel, de blé, de noix, d'un peu de fruits. Légère amertume rafraîchissante du houblon doux dans la fin de bouche. 20 EBU.	Pittig, mooi droogmoutige smaak met lichte toetsen van karamel, graan, noten, ietwat fruit. Verfrissend bittertje van de milde hop in de nasmaak. 20 EBU.
Pour out in a single movement	Verser agilement	Vlot uitschenken
De Rosse is the result of a mistake made by the brewer... with positive consequences.	La Rosse est le résultat d'une erreur du brasseur; la suite a été une réussite.	Ontstaan door een brouwersfoutje, gelukkig met goede afloop...

Struise Witte

De Struise Brouwers at Brouwerij Deca 5% 4 - 6 °C / 39 - 43 °F

	top-fermentation re-fermented in the bottle not centrifuged	fermentation haute refermentation en bouteille non centrifugée	hoge gisting hergisting in de fles niet gecentrifugeerd
	wheat beer	bière de froment	witbier
	pilsner malt, wheat malt, corn flocks, yeast, water. Hops: Bramling Cross, Hallertauer Mittelfrueh. Herbs: bitter orange rind, coriander.	malt de pils et de froment, flocons de maïs, levure, eau. Houblon: Bramling Cross, Hallertauer Mittelfrueh. Herbes: écorce d'orange amer, coriandre.	pilsmout, tarwemout, maisvlokken, gist, water. Hop: Bramling Cross, Hallertauer Mittelfrueh. Kruiden: bittere sinaasschil, koriander.
	hazy, citrus yellow (6 EBC) with nice white foam head; not filtered, not pasteurised	floue, jaune citron (6 EBC) avec un faux col blanc; non filtrée, non pasteurisée	wazig, citrusgeel (6 EBC) met mooie wittte schuimkraag; ongefilterd, niet gepasteuriseerd
	Fresh scent. Fine balance between the citrus-like character and the intense hoppy touch in scent and flavour. 15 EBU	Fraîchement odorant. Joli équilibre entre le caractère légèrement citronné et la touche houblonnée corsée dans le parfum et le goût. 15 EBU.	Fris geurend. Mooie balans tussen het licht citrusachtige karakter en de pittig gehopte toets in geur en smaak. 15 EBU.
	Pour out in a single movement	Verser agilement	Vlot uitschenken
	The first beer of De Struise Brouwers; brewed on the ostrich farm in Lo in 2001.	La première bière de De Struise Brouwers brassée en 2001 à l'autrucherie à Lo.	Het eerste bier van De Struise Brouwers in 2001 gebrouwen op de struisvogelfarm in Lo.

Struiselensis

De Struise Brouwers at Brouwerij Deca

6% 6 °C 43 °F

	spontaneous fermentation re-fermentation in the bottle; not centrifuged	fermentation spontanée refermentation en bouteille; non centrifugée	spontane gisting hergisting in de fles niet gecentrifugeerd
	lambic winter beer	lambic bière hivernale	lambiek winterbier
	Brewed according to the lambic tradition, fermented using Brettanomyces Bruxellensis and Pediococus Cerivisae, the natural yeasts of the Zenne region.	Brassée suivant la tradition lambic, fermentée sur Brettanomyces Bruxellensis et Pediococus Cerivisae, les levures naturelles de la région de la de Zenne.	Gebrouwen volgens de lambiektraditie, vergist op Brettanomyces Bruxellensis en Pediococus Cerivisae, de natuurlijke gisten uit de Zennestreek.
	slightly hazy, citrus yellow with fine white foam head; not filtered or pasteurised	légèrement fade, jaune citron avec faux col fin blanc; non filtrée, non pasteurisée	licht wazig, citrusgeel met fijne witte schuimkraag; ongefilterd, niet gepasteuriseerd
	Fresh citrus-like aroma with hints of grapefruit, ripe lemon, horse blanket and blond malt. Slightly tart flavour with a dry malty taste and hints of grass, fern and unripe rhubarb.	Arôme frais au caractère de citrus, avec des touches de pamplemousse, de citron mûr, de couverture de cheval et de malt blond. Goût légèrement acidulé, avec un caractère malté sec et des touches d'herbe, de fougères et de rhubarbe pas mûre.	Fris citrusachtig aroma met toetsen van pompelmoes, rijpe citroen, paardendeken en blonde mout. Licht zurige smaak met een droog moutig karakter en toetsen van gras, varens en onrijpe rabarber.
	Pour out in a single movement.	Verser agilement.	Vlot uitschenken.
	A reference to the Lambic brewers from Pajottenland.	Un clin d'œil aux brasseurs de lambic du Pajottenland.	Een knipoog naar de lambiekbrouwers uit het Pajottenland.

Super 64

Brasserie de Silly — 5% (11,3° plato) — 4 - 9 °C / 39 - 48 °F

	top-fermentation	fermentation haute	hoge gisting
	amber	ambrée	amber
	aromatic malt, sugar, yeast, Kent and Hallertau hops, water	malt aromatique, sucre, levure, houblon Kent et Hallertau, eau	aromatische mout, suiker, gist, Kent en Hallertauhop, water
	amber (8 EBC)	ambrée (8 EBC)	amber (8 EBC)
	Subtle malt and hop flavour and aroma, slightly bitter with grain and caramel touches.	Saveur et arômes subtiles de malt et de houblon, légèrement amers avec des touches de blé et de caramel.	Subtiele smaak en aroma's van mout en hop, licht bitter met toetsen van graan en karamel.
	Provision beer.	Bière de conservation	Bewaarbier.

Super des Fagnes Blonde

Brasserie des Fagnes 7,50% 6 - 10 °C 43 - 50 °F

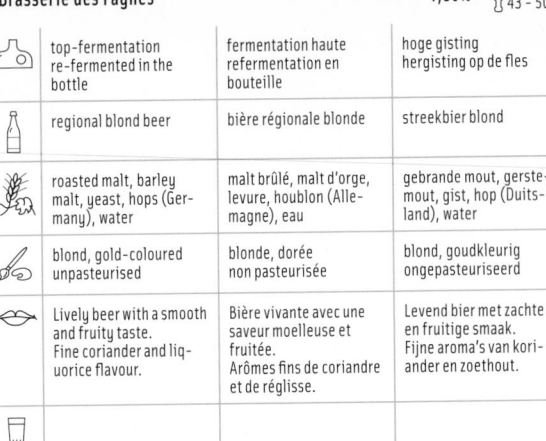

	top-fermentation re-fermented in the bottle	fermentation haute refermentation en bouteille	hoge gisting hergisting op de fles
	regional blond beer	bière régionale blonde	streekbier blond
	roasted malt, barley malt, yeast, hops (Germany), water	malt brûlé, malt d'orge, levure, houblon (Allemagne), eau	gebrande mout, gerstemout, gist, hop (Duitsland), water
	blond, gold-coloured unpasteurised	blonde, dorée non pasteurisée	blond, goudkleurig ongepasteuriseerd
	Lively beer with a smooth and fruity taste. Fine coriander and liquorice flavour.	Bière vivante avec une saveur moelleuse et fruitée. Arômes fins de coriandre et de réglisse.	Levend bier met zachte en fruitige smaak. Fijne aroma's van koriander en zoethout.
	Boutique beer.	Brassée de façon artisanale.	Ambachtelijk gebrouwen.

Super des Fagnes Brune

Brasserie des Fagnes 7,50% 6 - 10 °C 43 - 50 °F

	top-fermentation re-fermented in the bottle	fermentation haute refermentation en bouteille	hoge gisting hergisting op de fles
	regional beer	bière régionale	streekbier
	roasted malt, barley malt, yeast, hops (Germany), water	malt brûlé, malt d'orge, levure, houblon (Allemagne), eau	gebrande mout, gerstemout, gist, hop (Duitsland), water
	brown, ruby red unpasteurised	brune, rouge rubis non pasteurisée	bruin, robijnrood niet gepasteuriseerd
	Boutique beer.	Brassée de façon artisanale.	Ambachtelijk gebrouwen.

Super des Fagnes Griottes

Brasserie des Fagnes 4,80% 4 - 8 °C 39 - 46 °F

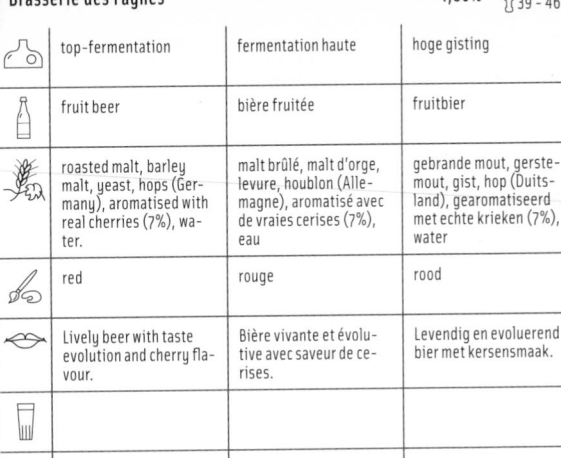

top-fermentation	fermentation haute	hoge gisting
fruit beer	bière fruitée	fruitbier
roasted malt, barley malt, yeast, hops (Germany), aromatised with real cherries (7%), water.	malt brûlé, malt d'orge, levure, houblon (Allemagne), aromatisé avec de vraies cerises (7%), eau	gebrande mout, gerstemout, gist, hop (Duitsland), gearomatiseerd met echte krieken (7%), water
red	rouge	rood
Lively beer with taste evolution and cherry flavour.	Bière vivante et évolutive avec saveur de cerises.	Levendig en evoluerend bier met kersensmaak.
Boutique beer.	Brassée de façon artisanale.	Ambachtelijk gebrouwen.

rasserie Artisanale La Botteresse de Sur-les-bois

8% — 6 - 7 °C / 43 - 45 °F

Sur-les-Bois Ambrée

top-fermentation natural re-fermentation in the bottle not centrifuged	fermentation haute refermentation naturelle en bouteille non centrifugée	hoge gisting natuurlijke hergisting in de fles niet gecentrifugeerd
specialty beer boutique beer	bière spéciale artisanale	speciaalbier artisanaal
traditional and roasted malt varieties, herbs	malts traditionnels et brûlés, herbes	traditionele en gebrande moutsoorten, kruiden
amber unfiltered	ambrée non filtrée	amber ongefilterd
Refreshing, digestive, smooth and slightly hopped. Slightly fruity and spicy taste and aroma.	Rafraîchissante, digestive, douce et légèrement houblonnée. Saveur et arômes légèrement fruités et relevés.	Verfrissend, digestief, zacht en licht gehopt. Licht fruitige en kruidige smaak en aroma.
Pour into a degreased, dry glass, leaving 1 cm of yeast sediment in the bottle.	Verser dans un verre dégraissé, sec et laisser un dépôt de levure de 1 cm dans la bouteille.	Uitschenken in een ontvet, droog glas en 1 cm gistdepot in de fles laten.

Sur-les-Bois Blonde

Brasserie Artisanale La Botteresse de Sur-les-bois 7% 6 - 7° 43 - 45°

	top-fermentation natural re-fermentation in the bottle not centrifuged	fermentation haute refermentation naturelle en bouteille non centrifugée	hoge gisting natuurlijke hergisting in de fles niet gecentrifugeerd
	specialty beer boutique beer	bière spéciale artisanale	speciaalbier artisanaal
	traditional malt varieties and orange rind	variétés traditionnelles de malt et écorce d'orange	traditionele moutsoorten en sinaasappelschil
	blond unfiltered	blonde non filtrée	blond ongefilterd
	Refreshing and fruity with a fine hoppy taste and aroma.	Rafraîchissante et fruitée avec saveur et arômes houblonnés raffinés.	Verfrissend en fruitig met fijne hopsmaak en -aroma.
	Pour into a degreased, dry glass, leaving 1 cm of yeast sediment in the bottle.	Verser dans un verre dégraissé, sec et laisser un dépôt de levure de 1 cm dans la bouteille.	Uitschenken in een ontvet, droog glas en 1 cm gistdepot in de fles laten.
i			

rasserie Artisanale La Botteresse de Sur-les-bois 9% 10 °C 50 °F

	top-fermentation natural re-fermentation in the bottle not centrifuged	fermentation haute refermentation naturelle en bouteille non centrifugée	hoge gisting natuurlijke hergisting in de fles niet gecentrifugeerd
	specialty beer boutique beer	bière spéciale artisanale	speciaalbier artisanaal
	traditional malt varieties, aromatic malt varieties, chocolate malt	variétés traditionnelles et aromatiques de malt, malt chocolat	traditionele moutsoorten, aromatische moutsoorten, chocolademout
	brown unfiltered	brune non filtrée	bruin ongefilterd
	Round and well-balanced sipping beer. Fruity with a taste of roasty malt, liquorice and coffee.	Bière de dégustation ronde et équilibrée. Goût fruité avec des touches de malt brûlé, réglisse et café.	Rond en evenwichtig degustatiebier. Fruitig met smaaktoetsen van gebrande mout, zoethout en koffie.
	Pour into a degreased, dry glass and leave 1 cm yeast sediment in the bottle.	Verser dans un verre dégraissé, sec et laisser un dépôt de levure de 1 cm dans la bouteille.	Uitschenken in een ontvet, droog glas en 1 cm gistdepot in de fles laten.

Svea IPA

De Struise Brouwers at Brouwerij Deca

7% 4 - 6° 39 - 43°

	top-fermentation re-fermentation in the bottle not centrifuged	fermentation haute refermentation en bouteille non centrifugée	hoge gisting hergisting in de fles niet gecentrifugeerd
	IPA	IPA	IPA
	slightly hazy, orange-copper with ivory-coloured foam head; not filtered or pasteurised	légèrement fade, cuivre orange avec faux col ivoire; non filtrée, non pasteurisée	licht wazig, oranjekoper met ivoorkleurige schuimkraag; ongefilterd, niet gepasteuriseerd
	Bridging course for an IPA (Indian Pale Ale): fresh, aromatic and fine-hoppy in character. The flavour is malty and relatively dry with light hints of nuts, brown bread and refined bitter hops.	Version de base pour une IPA (Indian Pale Ale) : caractère frais, aromatique et finement houblonné. Le goût est malté et assez sec, avec des touches légères de noix, de pain brun et de lupulines raffinées.	Instapversie voor een IPA (Indian Pale Ale): fris, aromatisch en fijnhoppig karakter. De smaak is moutig en vrij droog met luchtige toetsen van noten, bruin brood en verfijnde hopbitters.
	Pour out in a single movement to obtain a fine foam head	Verser agilement pour un faux col solide.	Vlot uitschenken voor een mooie schuimkraag.
	Brewed at the request of Monk's Café in Stockholm.	Brassée pour le compte du Monk's Café à Stockholm.	Gebrouwen in opdracht van Monk's Café in Stockholm.

Hofbrouwerijke 6,50%

t Baronneke

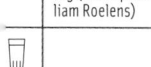

top-fermentation	fermentation haute	hoge gisting
regional beer, stout	bière régionale, stout	streekbier, stout
dark with full beige foam head	foncée avec faux col plein beige	donker met volle beige schuimkraag
Aroma: slightly fruity (dark plums) initially, then fresh bread and a touch of roasted malt. Taste: initially malty, slightly bitter, touches of coffee, slightly smoked. Aftertaste: bitter and dry (description by William Roelens)	Arôme :d'abord légèrement fruité (prunes noires), puis pain frais et un peu de malt grillé. Goût :approche initiale maltée, légèrement amer, picotements de café, légèrement fumé. Arrière-bouche :amère et sèche (description par William Roelens).	Aroma: eerst licht fruitig (donkere pruimen), daarna vers brood en ietwat geroosterde mout. Smaak: moutige aanzet, licht bitter, koffieprikkels, licht gerookt. Adronk: bitter en droog (beschrijving door William Roelens)
Village beer of the village of Vorselaar, tribute to Baron De Borrekens. The label shows the castle of Vorselaar.	Bière du village de Vorselaar, hommage au Baron De Borrekens. L'étiquette montre le château de Vorselaar.	Dorpsbier van Vorselaar, hommage aan Baron De Borrekens. Het etiket toont het kasteel van Vorselaar.

t Gaverhopke Blondje

Brouwerij 't Gaverhopke

6,80% 12 54

top-fermentation re-fermentation in the bottle	fermentation haute refermentation en bouteille	hoge gisting hergisting in de fles
blond boutique specialty beer	bière spéciale artisanale blonde	blond artisanaal speci-aalbier
barley malt, Belgian hops, yeast, water	malt d'orge, houblon Belge, levure, eau	gerstemout, Belgische hop, gist, water
blond	blonde	blond
Specialty beer with a sweet-bitter, fruity and bitter (hops) aroma. No herbs added.	Bière spéciale avec un arôme doux-amer, fruité et une amertume hou-blonnée. Pas d'addition d'épices.	Speciaalbier met een zoetbitter, fruitig en hopbitter aroma. Geen kruiden toege-voegd.
Mother beer for Easter Beer and Kriek.	Bière mère pour la Paas-bier et la Kriek.	Moederbier voor Paas-bier en Kriek.

t Gaverhopke Bruintje

ouwerij 't Gaverhopke — 6,80% — 12 °C / 54 °F

	top-fermentation re-fermentation in the bottle	fermentation haute refermentation en bouteille	hoge gisting hergisting in de fles
	brown boutique specialty beer	bière spéciale artisanale brune	bruin artisanaal speciaalbier
	barley malt, Belgian hops, yeast, water	malt d'orge, houblon Belge, levure, eau	gerstemout, Belgische hop, gist, water
	brown, semi-sparkling	brune, demi pétillante	bruin, half parelend
	Specialty beer with a sweet and very light, spicy flavour. No herbs added.	Bière spéciale d'un goût douceâtre et très légèrement relevé. Pas d'addition d'épices.	Speciaalbier met een zoetige en zeer licht kruidige smaak. Geen kruiden toegevoegd.
	Mother beer for Gaverhopke Christmas Beer.	Bière mère pour la Gaverhopke Kerstbier.	Moederbier voor Gaverhopke Kerstbier.

t Gaverhopke Extra - den Twaalf

Brouwerij 't Gaverhopke

12% 12 54

	top-fermentation re-fermentation in the bottle	fermentation haute refermentation en bouteille	hoge gisting hergisting in de fles
	brown boutique specialty beer	bière spéciale artisanale brune	bruin artisanaal speciaalbier
	barley malt, Belgian hops, yeast, water	malt d'orge, houblon Belge, levure, eau	gerstemout, Belgische hop, gist, water
	brown	brune	bruin
	Full-bodied specialty beer with a sweet and malty taste and hints of chocolate.	Bière spéciale franche d'un goût douceâtre et malté, avec des touches de chocolat.	Volmondig speciaalbier met een zoetige en moutige smaak met chocoladetoetsen.

ouwerij 't Gaverhopke

6,80% 12 °C 54 °F

	top-fermentation re-fermentation in the bottle	fermentation haute refermentation en bouteille	hoge gisting hergisting in de fles
	brown boutique specialty beer	bière spéciale artisanale brune	bruin artisanaal speciaalbier
	barley malt, Belgian hops, yeast, water	malt d'orge, houblon Belge, levure, eau	gerstemout, Belgische hop, gist, water
	brown	brune	bruin
	Sweet, exotic, spicy specialty beer. Based on Bruintje, but finished off with a mild seasoning.	Bière spéciale douceâtre, exotique, épicée. À base de la Bruintje, mais finition avec des épices légères.	Zoetig, exotisch, kruidig speciaalbier. Op basis van het Bruintje, maar afgewerkt met een lichte kruiding.

t Gaverhopke Kerstbier

t Gaverhopke Koerseklakske

Brouwerij 't Gaverhopke

5,50% 12 54

	top-fermentation re-fermentation in the bottle	fermentation haute refermentation en bouteille	hoge gisting hergisting op de fles
	blond boutique specialty beer	bière spéciale blonde artisanale	blond artisanaal speciaalbier
	barley malt, Belgian hops, yeast, water	malt d'orge, houblon Belge, levure, eau	gerstemout, Belgische hop, gist, water
	blond	blonde	blond
	Fresh and light specialty beer. Summer beer full of aroma.	Bière spéciale fraîche et légère. Petite bière d'été pleine d'arôme.	Fris en licht speciaalbier. Zomerbiertje vol aroma.
	Desselgem beer of which Briek (Schotte) would never leave any (klakske) in his glass. Initially brewed to mark the 67th Memorial Briek Schotte.	La bière de Desselgem, dont Briek (Schotte) ne renoncerait jamais à une casquette (Klakske). Initialement brassée à l'occasion du 67e Mémorial Briek Schotte.	Desselgems bier waarvan Briek (Schotte) nooit een 'klakske' zou laten staan. Initieel gebrouwen naar aanleiding van de 67e Memorial Briek Schotte.

ouwerij 't Gaverhopke 6,80% 12 °C 54 °F

t Gaverhopke Kriek

	top-fermentation re-fermentation in the bottle	fermentation haute refermentation en bouteille	hoge gisting hergisting in de fles
	boutique fruit beer	bière fruitée artisanale	artisanaal fruitbier
	blond with tart cherries without added colouring agents or sweeteners	blonde avec cerises acides sans colorants ni édulcorants	blondje met zurige krieken zonder kleur- of zoetstoffen
	pale red	rouge clair	licht rood

't Gaverhopke Paasbier

Brouwerij 't Gaverhopke

8%

top-fermentation re-fermentation in the bottle	fermentation haute refermentation en bouteille	hoge gisting hergisting in de fles
blond boutique specialty beer	bière spéciale artisanale blonde	blond artisanaal speci-aalbier
barley malt, Belgian hops, yeast, water	malt d'orge, houblon Belge, levure, eau	gerstemout, Belgische hop, gist, water
blond	blonde	blond
Slightly tart and bitter (hops) specialty beer. Based on Bruintje, but finished off with a mild seasoning.	Bière spéciale légère-ment acidulée et avec une amertume houblon-née. À base de la Blondje, mais finition avec des épices légères.	Lichtzurig en hopbitter speciaalbier. Op basis van het Blondje, maar afgewerkt met een lichte kruiding.

rouwerij 't Gaverhopke

9,80% — 12 °C / 54 °F

top-fermentation post-fermentation in the bottle	fermentation haute refermentation en bouteille	hoge gisting nagisting op de fles
blond boutique	blonde artisanale	blond artisanaal
barley malt, hops, yeast, water	malt d'orge, houblon, levure, eau	gerstemout, hop, gist, water
blond	blond doré	hoogblond
Full-bodied specialty beer with a sweet onset and a slightly bitter aftertaste.	Bière spéciale franche avec un départ sucré et une arrière-bouche légèrement amère.	Volmondig speciaalbier met een zoete start en een licht bittere afdronk.

t Gaverhopke Zingende Blondine

Taras Boulba

Brasserie de la Senne 4,50% 5 - 7 / 41 - 45

	top-fermentation natural re-fermentation in the bottle not centrifuged	fermentation haute refermentation naturelle en bouteille non centrifugée	hoge gisting natuurlijke hergisting in de fles niet gecentrifugeerd
	bitter blond	blonde amère	bitter blond
	malt, hops, yeast, water	malt, houblon, levure, eau	mout, hop, gist, water
	blond, slightly veiled with dense and fine foam head not filtered or pasteurised	blonde, légèrement voilée avec un faux col épais et fin non filtrée, non pasteurisée	blond, licht gesluierd met dichte en fijne schuimkraag ongefilterd, niet gepasteuriseerd
	Light, dry and convincing bitter. Generous, refined, aromatic hops make for a very refreshing character and an aroma with floral touches and a hint of citrus	Léger, sec et une amertume convaincante. Le généreux houblon aromatique raffiné procure un caractère fort rafraîchissant et un arôme avec des touches florales et une pointe de citrus.	Licht, droog en overtuigend bitter. Genereuze verfijnde aromatische hop zorgt voor een zeer verfrissend karakter en een aroma met florale toetsen en een vleugje citrus.
	Pour out slowly and leave 1 cm (yeast) in the bottle. The yeast can be drunk separately.	Verser prudemment et laisser 1 cm (levure) dans la bouteille. Eventuellement boire la levure séparément.	Voorzichtig uitschenken en 1 cm (gist) in de fles laten. Gist eventueel afzonderlijk uitdrinken.
	The name refers to a character from the novel Gogol.	Le nom fait référence à un personnage d'un roman de Gogol.	De naam verwijst naar een personage uit een roman van Gogol.

t Alternatief at Alvinne

6% | 6 °C 43 °F

top-fermentation natural re-fermentation in the bottle not centrifuged	fermentation haute refermentation spontanée en bouteille non centrifugée	hoge gisting natuurlijke hergisting in de fles niet gecentrifugeerd
amber or speciale belge	ambrée ou spéciale belge	amber of speciale belge
English hop varieties, pale ale, cara malts	variétés Anglaises de houblon, pale ale, malt cara	Engelse hopsoorten, pale ale, caramouten
amber-coloured with solid foam head not filtered or pasteurised	ambrée avec faux col solide non filtrée et non pasteurisée	amberkleurig met stevige schuimkraag ongefilterd en niet gepasteuriseerd
Very malty, slightly bitter, with hints of caramel, dry aftertaste.	Fort goût malté, légèrement amère, touches de caramel, sèche en arrière-bouche.	Stevige moutigheid, licht bitter, karameltoetsen, droog in de afdronk.
Serve in a tulip glass.	Verser dans un verre tulipe.	Uitschenken in een tulpglas.
Local delicatessen in Izegem. The name refers to the cobbler's anvil.	Spécialité locale à Izegem. Le nom fait référence à l'enclume du cordonnier.	Lokale specialiteit in Izegem. De naam verwijst naar het aambeeld van de schoenmaker.

Tempelier

Corsendonk by Brasserie du Bocq

6% 5 41

	top-fermentation	fermentation haute	hoge gisting
	slightly cloudy, gold-copper	légèrement trouble, cuivre doré	licht troebel, goudkoper
	The Templars fought for their convictions, with 2 on 1 horse.	Les Templiers allaient au combat pour leur foi à 2 sur 1 cheval.	De Tempeliers gingen ten strijde voor hun geloof, met z'n 2 op 1 paard.

Ter Dolen Blond

rouwerij De Dool — 6,10% — 4 - 5 °C / 39 - 41 °F

	top-fermentation	fermentation haute	hoge gisting
	abbey beer blond	bière d'abbaye blonde	abdijbier blond
	2 malt varieties, 2 noble hop varieties, water	2 sortes de malt, 2 variétés précieuses de houblon, eau	2 moutsoorten, 2 edele hopsoorten, water
	clear blond	blond clair	helder blond
	Full-bodied, velvety soft and incomparably blond. Slightly bitter and fruity sipping beer.	Franche, veloutée et incomparablement blonde. Bière de dégustation légèrement amère et fruitée.	Volmondig, fluweelzacht en onvergelijkbaar blond. Lichtbitter en fruitig degustatiebier.
	Lift the bottle and pour in a single, smooth movement to obtain a nice foam head.	Verser de haut et en un seul mouvement fluide de façon à obtenir un beau faux col.	Hoog en vloeiend uitschenken om een mooie schuimkraag te bekomen.

Ter Dolen Donker

Brouwerij De Dool 7,10% 5 - 10 / 41 - 50

	top-fermentation re-fermented in the bottle	fermentation haute refermentation en bouteille	hoge gisting nagisting op de fles
	abbey beer dark	bière d'abbaye foncée	abdijbier donker
	3 malt varieties, 2 hop varieties, light and dark candy sugar, water	3 sortes de malt, 2 sortes de houblon, sucre candi clair et foncé, eau	3 moutsoorten, 2 hop-soorten, lichte en don-kere kandijsuiker, water
	clear dark	foncé clair	helder donker
	Neutral, fruity, slightly sweet and soft dark ab-bey beer with a sponge-cakelike touch.	Bière d'abbaye neutre, fruitée, légèrement douceâtre et doucement foncée, avec une touche biscuitée.	Neutraal, fruitig, licht-zoetig en zacht donker abdijbier met een bis-cuitachtige toets.
	Lift the bottle and pour in a single, smooth movement to obtain a nice foam head.	Verser de haut et en un seul mouvement fluide de façon à obtenir un beau faux col.	Hoog en vloeiend uit-schenken om een mooie schuimkraag te beko-men.
i			

rouwerij De Dool

4,50% 4 - 5 °C / 39 - 41 °F

Ter Dolen Kriek

	top-fermentation	fermentation haute	hoge gisting
	abbey beer kriek	bière d'abbaye kriek	abdijbier kriek
	1 malt variety, wheat, 2 hop varieties, coriander, orange rind, fresh cherry juice, water	1 sorte de malt, froment, 2 sortes de houblon, coriandre, écorce d'orange, jus de cerises frais, eau	1 moutsoort, tarwe, 2 hopsoorten, koriander, sinaasappelschil, vers kriekensap, water
	unfiltered red	rouge non filtrée	ongefilterd rood
	Sweet and deliciously refreshing. Fruit beer with citric acid touch that does not overpower the beer taste.	Douce et agréablement rafraîchissante. Bière fruitée avec une touche acidulée de citron ne reniant pas la saveur de bière.	Zoet en lekker verfrissend. Fruitbier met citroenzurige toets die de biersmaak niet verloochent.
	Lift the bottle and pour in a single, smooth movement to obtain a nice foam head.	Verser de haut et en un seul mouvement fluide de façon à obtenir un beau faux col.	Hoog en vloeiend uitschenken om een mooie schuimkraag te vormen.
i	The only kriek abbey beer in the world.	La seule bière d'abbaye kriek au monde.	Het enige kriek-abdijbier ter wereld.

Ter Dolen Tripel

Brouwerij De Dool 8,10%

	top-fermentation re-fermented in the bottle	fermentation haute refermentation en bouteille	hoge gisting nagisting op de fles
	abbey beer tripel	bière d'abbaye triple	abdijbier tripel
	full malt tripel brewed according to the Rheinheitsgebot with 2 different malts, 2 types of natural 100% Belgian hops, yeast, water	triple malt plein brassé suivant le Rheinheitsgebot avec 2 variétés de malt, 2 variétés de houblon naturel 100% belge, levure,eau	volmout tripel gebrouwen volgens Rheinheitsgebot met 2 soorten mout, 2 soorten natuurlijke 100% Belgische hop, gist, water
	clear copper-blond	blond cuivre clair	helder koperblond
	Typical Ter Dolen mellowness is reinforced by using single wheat (no sugar). Rich taste in the mouth. Soft tones initially with much body and no sweetness. Full hops (only natural hops) provides a pleasant bitter aftertaste. 30 EBU bitterness.	La tendresse Ter Dolen typique est renforcée par l'usage uniquement de froment (pas de sucre). Riche sensation en bouche. Des notes d'abord douces, avec beaucoup de corps sans caractère sucré. Le 'houblon franc' (uniquement houblon naturel) procure une fin de bouche agréablement amère. 30 EBU d'amertume.	Typische Ter Dolen malsheid wordt versterkt door enkel tarwe (geen suiker) te gebruiken. Rijk mondgevoel. Eerst zachte tonen met veel body zonder zoet. 'Vol hop' (enkel natuurlijke hop) zorgt voor een aangenaam bittere nasmaak. 30 EBU bitterheid.
	Lift the bottle and pour in a single, smooth movement to obtain a nice foam head.	Verser de haut et en un seul mouvement fluide de façon à obtenir un beau faux col.	Hoog en vloeiend uitschenken om een mooie schuimkraag te bekomen.
i			

rouwerij Timmermans (Groep John Martin) 4%

Timmermans Framboise Lambic

	spontaneous fermentation	fermentation spontanée	spontane gisting
	fruit beer	bière fruitée	fruitbier
	raspberry-coloured	framboise	frambozenkleur
	Raspberry flavour dominates the tart lambic flavours. Fresh aftertaste.	La framboise domine le caractère acidulé du lambic. Fraîche arrière-bouche.	Framboos overheerst het zurige lambiekkarakter. Frisse afdronk.

Timmermans Kriek Lambic

Brouwerij Timmermans (Groep John Martin) **4%** 3 - 6 ° / 37 - 43 °

	spontaneous fermentation	fermentation spontanée	spontane gisting
	fruit beer	bière fruitée	fruitbier
	barley malt, sugar, wheat, hops, fruit juices, water	malt d'orge, sucre, froment, houblon, jus de fruits, eau	gerstemout, suiker, tarwe, hop, fruitsappen, water
	red	rouge	rood
	Sweet and velvety.	Douce et veloutée.	Zoet en fluwelig.
i			

rouwerij Timmermans (Groep John Martin)

5,50%

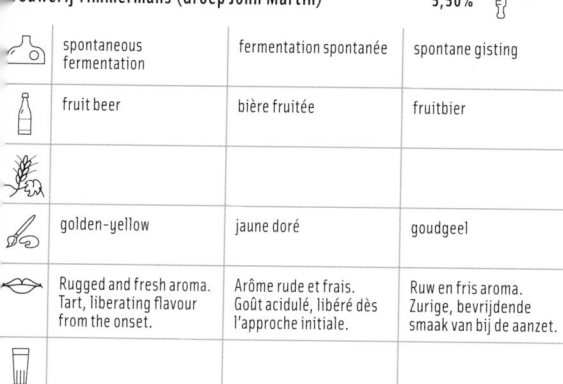

	spontaneous fermentation	fermentation spontanée	spontane gisting
	fruit beer	bière fruitée	fruitbier
	golden-yellow	jaune doré	goudgeel
	Rugged and fresh aroma. Tart, liberating flavour from the onset.	Arôme rude et frais. Goût acidulé, libéré dès l'approche initiale.	Ruw en fris aroma. Zurige, bevrijdende smaak van bij de aanzet.

Timmermans Oude Kriek

Brouwerij Timmermans (Groep John Martin) 5,50%

	spontaneous fermentation	fermentation spontanée	spontane gisting
	fruit beer	bière fruitée	fruitbier
	3/4 old Lambic and 1/4 young lambic	3/4 vieille lambic et 1/4 jeune lambic	3/4 oude lambiek en 1/4 jonge lambiek
	Naturally tart with cherry flavour.	Naturellement acidulée, avec un goût de cerise.	Natuurlijk zurig met kerssmaak.

rouwerij Timmermans (Groep John Martin)

4% 3 - 6 °C / 37 - 43 °F

Timmermans Pêche

	spontaneous fermentation	fermentation spontanée	spontane gisting
	fruit beer	bière fruitée	fruitbier
	barley malt, sugar, wheat, hops, fruit juices, water	malt d'orge, sucre, froment, houblon, jus de fruits, eau	gerstemout, suiker, tarwe, hop, fruitsappen, water
	blond	blonde	blond
	Very fruity aroma. Taste of fruit and sugar with a touch of bitterness owing to peach skin and stone.	Arôme très fruité. Saveur de fruits et de sucre avec une pointe d'amertume de l'écorce et du noyau de la pêche.	Zeer fruitig aroma. Smaak van fruit en suiker met een vleugje bitterheid van de schil en pit van de perzik.
i			

Timmermans Strawberry Lambic

Brouwerij Timmermans (Groep John Martin) **4%**

	spontaneous fermentation	fermentation spontanée	spontane gisting
	fruit beer	bière fruitée	fruitbier
	Strawberry in aroma and flavour with fresh touch. Not too sweet, steady flavour that spreads rapidly in the mouth. Fruity aftertaste.	De la fraise dans l'arôme et le goût, avec une touche fraîche. Goût persistant pas trop sucré, qui se répand très vite dans la bouche. Arrière-bouche fruitée.	Aardbei in aroma en smaak met frisse toets. Niet te zoete, bestendige smaak die zich zeer snel verspreidt in de mond. Fruitige afdronk.

Timmermans Tradition Faro

rouwerij Timmermans (Groep John Martin) 4% 3 - 6 °C / 37 - 43 °F

	spontaneous fermentation	fermentation spontanée	spontane gisting
	faro lambic	faro lambic	faro lambiek
	barley malt, sugar, wheat, hops, fruit juice, water	malt d'orge, sucre, froment, houblon, jus de fruits, eau	gerstemout, suiker, tarwe, hop, fruitsap, water
	amber	ambrée	amber
	Smooth beer, perfect thirst-quencher.	Bière moelleuse, désaltérant idéal.	Zacht bier, perfecte dorstlesser.

Timmermans Tradition Gueuze Lambic

Brouwerij Timmermans (Groep John Martin) 5,50% 3 - 6 / 37 - 43

	spontaneous fermentation	fermentation spontanée	spontane gisting
	gueuze	gueuze	geuze
	barley malt, wheat, hop extract, water	malt d'orge, froment, extraits de houblon, eau	gerstemout, tarwe, hop-extract, water
	amber	ambrée	amber
	Pronounced sourness without being sharp. Discrete touch of bitterness and full mouthfeel.	Goût acidulé prononcé sans être trop aigu. Touche amère discrète en pleine bouche.	Uitgesproken zuurheid zonder te scherp te zijn. Discrete toets van bitterheid in volle mond.

Timmermans Tradition Kriek Retro

Brouwerij Timmermans (Groep John Martin) 5%

	spontaneous fermentation	fermentation spontanée	spontane gisting
	fruit beer	bière fruitée	fruitbier
	Tart aroma. Prevalence of old lambic on the palate, harldy mellowed by the fruity touch.	Arôme acidulé. Prépondérance de vieux lambic dans le palais, à peine arrondi par le fruité. Rafraîchissante, arrière-bouche franchement acide.	Zurig aroma. Overwicht van oude lambiek in het gehemelte, nauwelijks afgerond door het fruitige. Verfrissend, oprecht zure afdronk.

Timmermans Tradition Lambicus blanche

Brouwerij Timmermans (Groep John Martin) 4,40% 3 - 6 ° 37 - 43 °

	spontaneous fermentation	fermentation spontanée	spontane gisting
	lambic witbier	lambic bière blanche	lambiek witbier
	barley malt, sugar, wheat, hops, flavouring, water	malt d'orge, sucre, froment, houblon, arômes, eau	gerstemout, suiker, tarwe, hop, aroma's, water
	white cloudy	blanche trouble	wit troebel
	Slightly sour but round taste. Sugary touch. A thirst-quencher.	Saveur légèrement acidulée mais arrondie. Touche sucrée. Désaltérant.	Lichtzure maar ronde smaak. Toets van suiker. Dorstlesser.

Timmermans Warme Kriek

Brouwerij Timmermans (Groep John Martin) 4%

	spontaneous fermentation	fermentation spontanée	spontane gisting
	fruit beer	bière fruitée	fruitbier
	red	rouge	rood
	Heart-warming mulled Kriek has a spicy cinnamon flavour as well as a sweet, fruity Kriek flavour.	Glühkriek réchauffante, avec un goût piquant de cannelle et un goût de griotte sucré, fruité.	Verwarmende glühkriek met pittige kaneelsmaak en zoete, fruitige krieksmaak.

Tineke van Heule

Brouwerij Gulden Spoor

8% 8 - 10 ° / 46 - 50 °

	top-fermentation re-fermentation in the bottle not centrifuged	fermentation haute refermentation en bouteille non centrifugée	hoge gisting hergisting in de fles niet gecentrifugeerd
	strong blond	blonde forte	sterk blond
	barley malt, hops, yeast, water	malt d'orge, houblon, levure, eau	gerstemout, hop, gist, water
	blond and clear with big foam head owing to high level of saturation not filtered or pasteurised	blonde et limpide avec faux col ample par une forte saturation non filtrée, non pasteurisée	blond en helder met grote schuimkraag door een sterke saturatie ongefilterd, niet gepasteuriseerd
	Soft-malty onset with bitter aftertaste full of character.	Approche initiale légèrement maltée, avec une arrière-bouche amère fort caractéristique.	Zachtmoutige aanzet met karaktervolle, bittere afdronk.
	Degrease the tulip glass, tilt it slightly and carefully pour the beer in a single movement.	Dégraisser le verre tulipe, le tenir légèrement incliné et verser prudemment la bière d'un seul mouvement.	Het tulpglas vetvrij maken, licht schuin houden en het bier voorzichtig in 1 beweging uitschenken.
i	Brewed in tandem with Pauwels drinks manufacturer to mark the Tineke Festival in Heule.	Brassée en collaboration avec Dranken Pauwels à l'occasion des Tinekesfeesten à Heule.	Gebrouwen in samenwerking met dranken Pauwels ter gelegenheid van de Tinekesfeesten in Heule.

Brasserie de Silly — **4,70% (11° plato)** — 4 - 7 °C / 39 - 45 °F

	top-fermentation	fermentation haute	hoge gisting
	witbier	bière blanche	witbier
	malt, wheat, sugar, yeast, coriander, dried orange rind, Hallertau hops, water	malt, froment, sucre, levure, coriandre, écorce d'orange séché, houblon Hallertau, eau	mout, tarwe, suiker, gist, koriander, gedroogde sinaasschil, Hallertauhop, water
	white (14 EBC) cloudy	blanche (14 EBC) trouble	wit (14 EBC) troebel
	Refreshening thirst-quencher with coriander effect. The orange rind gives a long-lasting, stimulating flavour.	Saveur extrêmement rafraîchissante. Le coriandre désaltère, l'écorce d'orange séché caresse la langue.	Uiterst verfrissende smaak. De koriander fungeert als dorstlesser, de gedroogde sinaasappelschil streelt de tong.

Tongerlo Blond

Brouwerij Haacht 6,50% 8 °C 48 °F

	top-fermentation re-fermentation in the bottle; centrifuged	fermentation haute refermentation en bouteille; centrifugée	hoge gisting hergisting in de fles gecentrifugeerd
	Recognised Belgian Abbey beer blond	bière d'abbaye belge reconnue blonde	Erkend Belgisch Abdijbier blond
	barley malt, corn, hops, sugar, yeast, water	malt d'orge, maïs, houblon, sucre, levure, eau	gerstemout, mais, hop, suiker, gist, water
	copper-coloured filtered, pasteurised	cuivre filtrée, pasteurisée	koperkleurig gefilterd, gepasteuriseerd
	Honey aroma and a full-bodied taste with a smooth aftertaste. Pronounced taste and aroma obtained by weeks of re-fermentation and fermentation in the bottle.	Arôme de miel et saveur franche. Saveur et arôme prononcés par la refermentation et le mûrissement de plusieurs semaines en bouteille.	Aroma van honing en een volmondige smaak die zacht uitvloeit. Uitgesproken smaak en aroma door wekenlange hergisting en rijping op de fles.
	Pour 4/5 into a tilted glass. Revolve the remainder of the beer in the bottle to loosen up the yeast sediment and pour out (into a separate glass, if necessary).	Verser 4/5 dans un verre incliné. Remuer le restant de la bière dans la bouteille pour dégager le fond de levure et verser (éventuellement dans un verre séparément).	4/5 uitschenken in een schuingehouden glas. Het resterende bier walsen in de fles om de gistbodem los te maken en uitschenken (evtl.in een apart glaasje).
i			

Brouwerij Haacht

7% | 10 °C 50 °F

Tongerlo Bruin

	top-fermentation re-fermentation in the bottle centrifuged	fermentation haute refermentation en bouteille centrifugée	hoge gisting hergisting in de fles gecentrifugeerd
	Recognised Belgian Abbey beer dark	Bière d'abbaye belge reconnue foncée	Erkend Belgisch Abdijbier donker
	barley malt, corn, hops, sugar, yeast, water	malt d'orge, maïs, houblon, sucre, levure, eau	gerstemout, mais, hop, suiker, gist, water
	red-brown filtered, pasteurised	brun rouge filtrée, pasteurisée	roodbruin gefilterd, gepasteuriseerd
	Sweetish aroma, full taste, slightly roasty aftertaste. Pronounced taste and aroma obtained by weeks of re-fermentation and fermentation in the bottle.	Arôme doux, saveur pleine, fin de bouche légèrement grillée. Saveur et arôme prononcés par la refermentation et le mûrissement de plusieurs semaines en bouteille.	Zoetig aroma, volle smaak, licht geroosterde afdronk. Uitgesproken smaak en aroma door wekenlange hergisting en rijping op de fles.
	see Tongerlo Blond	voir Tongerlo Blond	zie Tongerlo Blond
	Ever since the abbey's estabishment in 1130, the Norbertines have been brewing Tongerlo beer. They are active to this day and one of the largest communities still in existence The flavour development can be followed by keeping an eye on the bottling date on the label.	Dès la fondation de l'abbaye (1130) les Prémontrés de Tongerlo brassent de la bière. Ils se montrent jusqu'à aujourd'hui fort actifs et sont l'une des plus importantes communautés qui subsiste. L'évolution du goût peut être suivie en gardant à l'œil la date d'embouteillage.	Al sinds de oprichting van de abdij (1130) brouwen de Norbertijnen van Tongerlo bier. Tot op vandaag zijn zij zeer actief en 1 van de grootste resterende gemeenschappen. De smaakevolutie kan worden gevolgd door de botteldatum op het etiket in het oog te houden.

Tongerlo Winterbier

Brouwerij Haacht 7% 7 °C 45 °F

	top-fermentation re-fermentation in the bottle centrifuged	haute fermentation refermentation en bouteille centrifugée	hoge gisting hergisting in de fles gecentrifugeerd
	Recognised Belgian Abbey beer dark winter or Christmas beer	Bière d'abbaye belge reconnue foncée bière hivernale ou de Noël	Erkend Belgisch Abdijbier donker winter- of kerstbier
	barley malt, corn, hops, yeast, water	malt d'orge, maïs, houblon, sucre, levure, eau	gerstemout, mais, hop, gist, water
	amber-coloured with a full foam head filtered, pasteurised	ambré avec un faux col plein filtrée, pasteurisée	amberkleurig met een volle schuimkraag gefilterd, gepasteuriseerd
	Complex, fruity and spicy hops aroma. Balanced bitterness (hops) with a pleasant, slightly bitter aftertaste. Aroma and flavour are intensified by re-fermentation.	Arôme houblonné complexe, fruité et épicé. Amertume houblonnée équilibrée, avec une arrière-bouche agréable, légèrement amère. L'arôme et le goût sont accentués par la Wrefermentation.	Complex, fruitig en kruidig hoparoma. Evenwichtige hopbitterheid met een aangename, licht bittere afdronk. Aroma en smaak worden geaccentueerd door de hergisting.
	see Tongerlo Blond	voir Tongerlo Blond	zie Tongerlo Blond
(i)	All Tongerlo abbey beers re-ferment in the bottle: just before the bottle is sealed, sugar and pure-culture yeast are added to the beer.	Toutes les bières de l'abbaye de Tongerlo refermentent dans la bouteille :juste avant que la capsule soit mise sur la bouteille remplie, du sucre et de la levure de culture microbienne sont ajoutés à la bière.	Alle Tongerlo abdijbieren hergisten in de fles: vlak voor de kroonkurk op de gevulde fles gaat, worden suiker en reincultuurgist aan het bier toegevoegd.

Tonneke

Brouwerij Contreras 5% 4 - 6 °C / 39 - 43 °F

	top-fermentation	fermentation haute	hoge gisting
	typical Belgian ale	Belgian ale typique	typical Belgian ale
	barley malt, hop (Hallertau, Styrian, Brewers gold), top-fermenting yeast, water	malt d'orge, houblon (Hallertau, Styrian, Brewers gold), levure de fermentation haute, eau	gerstemout, hop (Hallertau, Styrian, Brewers gold), hogegistingsgist, water
	orange-amber clear	orange-ambrée claire	oranje-amber helder
	Malty, sweet, fruity.	Maltée, douce, fruitée.	Moutig, zoet, fruitig.
	Empty in a degreased, rinsed and dry glass. Tilt the glass about 45° and pour the beer, avoiding contact between the bottle and the foam. Provide a foam head of approx. 5 cm.	Verser complètement dans un verre dégraissé, rincé et sec. Tenir le verre incliné à 45° et verser la bière sans que la bouteille touche l'écume. Prévoir un faux col de 5 cm environ.	Helemaal uitschenken in een ontvet, gespoeld en droog glas. Het glas 45° schuinhouden, het bier uitschenken zonder dat de fles het schuim raakt. Een schuimkraag van ca. 5 cm voorzien
	Also available in 30 litre oak barrels. Since 1918. Recognised as a regional product since 2008.	Egalement disponible en fûts de chêne de 30 litres. Depuis 1818. Reconnu comme produit régional depuis 2008.	Ook verkrijgbaar op eikenhouten vaatjes van 30 liter. Sinds 1818. Sinds 2008 erkend als streekproduct.

Toria Blond

Hoevebrouwers by Brouwerij De Graal 6,50% 6 - 10 °C 43 - 50 °F

	top-fermentation re-fermented in the bottle	fermentation haute refermentation en bouteille	hoge gisting hergisting inde fles
	specialty beer	bière spéciale	speciaalbier
	malt (pilsner, wheat), hops (EK Goldings, Hallertau), yeast (T58), water	malt (pils, froment), houblon (EK Goldings, Hallertau), levure (T58), eau	mout (pils, tarwe), hop (EK Goldings, Hallertau), gist (T58), water
	blond clear	blonde claire	blond helder
	Light and refreshing. Dry with a bitter aftertaste.	Légère et rafraîchissante. Sèche avec une fin de bouche amère.	Licht en verfrissend. Droog, met een bittere afdronk.
	Pour into a degreased goblet in a single movement, avoiding contact between bottle and foam. Leave approx. 1 cm of beer in the bottle.	Verser en un seul mouvement dans un verre calice dégraissé sans toucher le verre et l'écume. Laisser environ 1 cm de bière dans la bouteille.	In 1 beweging in een vetvrij kelkglas gieten zonder het glas en het schuim te raken. Ongeveer 1 cm bier in de fles laten.
i	Toria was a popular character from Zottegem, who forecasted the weather.	Toria était une figure populaire et un monsieur météo de Zottegem.	Toria was een Zottegems volksfiguur en weervoorspeller.

Toria Tripel

Hoevebrouwers by Brouwerij De Graal 8,70% 6 - 10 °C / 43 - 50 °F

	top-fermentation re-fermentation in the bottle	fermentation haute refermentation en bouteille	hoge gisting hergisting inde fles
	blond tripel	triple blonde	blonde tripel
	pilsner and wheat malt, hops (Tomahawk, Hallertau Mittelfrüh), yeast (T58), water	malt de pils et de froment, houblon (Tomahaws, Hallertau Mittelfrüh), levure (T58), eau	pils- en tarwemout, hop (Tomahawk, Hallertau Mittelfrüh), gist (T58), water
	blond with creamy foam head	blonde avec faux col crémeux	blond met romige schuimkraag
	Very hoppy sipping beer. The American hops provides a punchy bitter touch with hints of citrus and a bitter but robust aftertaste.	Bière de dégustation fortement houblonnée. Le houblon américain assure une touche amère puissante, avec des touches de citrus et une arrière-bouche amère mais stable.	Sterk gehopt degustatiebier. De Amerikaanse hop zorgt voor een krachtige bittertoets met een vleugje citrus en een bittere maar stabiele afdronk.
	Pour in a single movement into a degreased goblet. Leave approx. 1 cm of the yeast sediment in the bottle.	Verser d'un seul mouvement dans un verre calice dégraissé. Laisser ca. 1 cm de dépôt de levure dans la bouteille.	In 1 beweging uitschenken in een vetvrij kelkglas. Ca. 1 cm gistdepot in de fles laten.
	Toria is a Zottegem character.	Toria est une figure populaire de Zottegem.	Toria is een Zottegemse volksfiguur.

Totentrekker

Buitenlust door Proefbrouwerij 5% 6 - 10 °C / 4 °C 43 - 50 °F / 39 °F

	mixed fermentation re-fermentation in the bottle (top fermentation, wild yeasts)	fermentation mixte refermentation en bouteille (fermentation haute et levures sauvages)	gemengde gisting hergisting in de fles (hoge gisting en wilde gisten)
	old brown kriek	bière kriek vieille brune	oud bruin kriekbier
	malt (Münchner, cara, pilsner), Poperinge hops, water, yeasts, sour concentrated cherry juice, saccharin, naturally fermented lactic acid (0,5%)	malt (Münchner, cara, pils), houblon de Poperinge, eau, levures, jus de cerises concentré, saccharine et acide lactique fermenté de façon naturelle (0,5%)	mout (Münchner, cara, pils), Poperingse hop, water, gisten, zuur kriekensap in geconcentreerde vorm, sacharine en natuurlijk vergist melkzuur (0,5%)
	light to dark-red	rouge clair à foncé	licht- tot donkerrood
	Beer with taste evolution. Slightly hoppy. 15 EBU. Sweet-and-sour, the sour fruit slightly stronger than the malt sugar.	Bière avec saveur évolutive. Légèrement houblonné. 15 EBU. Aigre-douce où l'acide (fruits) dépasse légèrement la douceur (sucre de malt).	Bier met smaakevolutie. Lichte hopsmaak. 15 EBU. Zuurzoet waarbij het zuur (fruit) net boven het zoet (moutsuiker) uitkomt.
	Smoothly pour in a single movement. The sediment can be served separately.	Verser doucement en un seul mouvement. Le dépôt de levure peut être servi séparément.	Zacht uitschenken in 1 beweging. Het gistdepot kan afzonderlijk geserveerd worden.
	Store in a dark place, with constant temperature and vibration-free.	Conserver à l'abri de la lumière et des tremblements à une température constante.	Donker en trillingsvrij bewaren op een constante temperatuur.

Brasserie de Cazeau **6,70%** 8 - 10 °C / 46 - 50 °F

	top-fermentation re-fermented in the bottle	fermentation haute refermentation en bouteille	hoge gisting hergisting op de fles
	regional beer	bière régionale	streekbier
	malt: blond and caramel 4 hop varieties	malt: blond et caraméli-sé 4 sortes de houblon	mout: blond en karamel 4 hopsoorten
	gold-coloured slightly cloudy at the bottom of the bottle	dorée légèrement trouble au fond de la bouteille	goudkleurig licht troebel onderaan in de fles
	Well-balanced. Fruity nose, well-bal-anced aromas, hoppy and fairly dry aftertaste.	Equilibrée. Parfum fruité, arômes de goût équilibrés, fin de bouche houblonnée et assez sèche.	Evenwichtig. Fruitige neus, evenwich-tige smaakaroma's, hop-pige en vrij droge afdronk.
	Keep the glass upright and pour the beer. Hold the glass tilted at the end.	Tenir le verre d'abord en position verticale, ver-ser la bière et incliner le verre à la fin.	Het glas eerst verticaal houden, het bier uit-schenken en het glas schuin houden op het einde.
ⓘ			

Tournay de Noël

Brasserie de Cazeau 8,20% 10 - 12 °C 50 - 54 °F

	top-fermentation re-fermented in the bottle	fermentation haute refermentation en bouteille	hoge gisting hergisting in de fles
	stout	stout	stout
	malt varieties: blond, light caramel, strong caramel, roasted 2 hop varieties	sortes de malt: blond, caramélisé clair, caramélisé prononcé, brûlé 2 sortes de houblon	moutsoorten: blond, lichte karamel, uitgesproken karamel, gebrand 2 hopsoorten
	black	noire	zwart
	Powerful character. Pronounced bitterness (hop and roasty malt) with chocolate and malt perfumes in the mouth. Very clear roasty aftertaste.	Caractère corsé. Goût amer prononcé (houblon et malt brûlé) avec parfums de chocolat et de houblon dans la bouche. Arrière-bouche brûlée très prononcée.	Krachtig karakter. Uitgesproken bitterheid (hop en gebrande mout) met parfums van chocolade en hop in de mond. Zeer duidelijke gebrande nasmaak.
	Keep the glass upright and pour the beer. Hold it tilted at the end.	Tenir le verre d'abord en position verticale, verser la bière et incliner le verre à la fin.	Het glas eerst verticaal houden, het bier uitschenken en het glas schuin houden op het einde.

	top-fermentation re-fermentation in the bottle	fermentation haute refermentation en bouteille	hoge gisting hergisting in de fles
	Belgian stout	Belgian stout	Belgian stout
	malt, hops, candy sugar, yeast, water	malt, houblon, sucre candi, levure, eau	mout, hop, kandijsuiker, gist, water
	Store the bottles upright.	Conserver la bouteille en position droite.	De flessen rechtopstaand bewaren.

Tournée Générale Tripel Hop

Palm Breweries 7,50% 10° 50°

	top-fermentation re-fermentation in the bottle; centrifuged	fermentation haute refermentation en bouteille; centrifugée	hoge gisting hergisting op de fles gecentrifugeerd
	strong blond tripel	blonde forte triple	sterk blond tripel
	Hoppy Tripel: early hopping (in the brew kettle) with Magnum, late hopping (just prior to cooking and fermentation) with Amarillo, dry hopping (during storage, not included in cooking process) with Cascade.	Triple hopping: early hopping (dans le brassin) avec Magnum, late hopping (juste avant le refroidissement et la fermentation) avec Amarillo, dry hopping (lors du lagering, sans cuisson) avec Cascade.	Tripel hopping: early hopping (in de brouwketel) met Magnum, late hopping (net voor koeling en gisting) met Amarillo, dry hopping (tijdens de lagering, niet meegekookt) met Cascade.
	filtered	filtrée	gefilterd
	Very hoppy with a fine sweet-and-sour balance and with a fresh fruity and spicy flavour. Basic bitterness (Magnum), citrus (late hopping with Amarillo), very hoppy scent and flavour with extra subtle citrus and grapefruit aroma (Cascade).	Fort houblonné, avec un bon équilibre entre amère et sucrée et avec un fruité et un goût épicé frais. Amertume de base (Magnum), citrus (l'Amarillo), parfum et goût fort houblonnés, avec un arôme subtil de citrus et de pamplemousse supplémentaire (Cascade).	Zeer hoppig met een goed evenwicht tussen bitter en zoet en met een frisse fruitig- en kruidigheid. Basisbitterheid (Magnum), citrus (late hopping met Amarillo), zeer hoppige geur en smaak met extra subtiel citrus- en pompelmoesaroma (Cascade).
	Pour into the 18 cl Master Beer glass.	Verser dans le verre Master Beer de 18 cl.	Uitschenken in het Master Beerglas van 18 cl.
	Brewed to mark the second series (2011) of the TV programme Tournée Générale.	Brassée à l'occasion de la 2e saison (2011) du programme TV Tournée Générale.	Gebrouwen n.a.v. de 2e reeks (2011) van het TV-programma Tournée Générale.

Toverhekske

Brouwerij Walrave

5,90% — 5 °C / 41 °F

	top-fermentation centrifuged	fermentation haute centrifugée	hoge gisting gecentrifugeerd
	Belgian ale	Belgian ale	Belgian ale
	filtered, pasteurised	filtrée, pasteurisée	gefilterd, gepasteuri-seerd

Den Haene by Brouwerij Strubbe 6,50% 6 - 8 °C 43 - 46 °F

	top-fermentation re-fermentation in the bottle	fermentation haute refermentation en bouteille	hoge gisting hergisting op de fles
	amber	ambrée	amber
	malt, barley, wheat, Poperinge hops, sugar, yeast, water	malt, orge, froment, houblon de Poperinge, sucre, levure, eau	mout, gerst, tarwe, Poperingse hop, suiker, gist, water
	not filtered	non filtrée	ongefilterd
	Tastes like and old-fashioned pale ale, spicy with bitter-sweet aftertaste.	A le goût d'une pale ale du passé, épicé avec une arrière-bouche douce-amère.	Smaakt als een ouderwetse pale ale, kruidig met bitterzoete afdronk.

rappieter at Proefbrouwerij 6,50%

	top-fermentation re-fermentation in the bottle	fermentation haute refermentation en bouteille	hoge gisting nagisting op fles
	amber unfiltered	ambrée non filtrée	amber ongefilterd
	2 malt varieties (pils and amber), different hops	2 variétés de malt (pils et amber), différentes variétés de houblon	2 moutsoorten (pils- en ambermout), verschillende hopsoorten

Tremist

Brouwerij Van Eecke for Extremis

6% 6° 43°

	top-fermentation re-fermentation in the bottle	fermentation haute refermentation en bouteille	hoge gisting hergisting in de fles
	strong blond	blonde forte	sterk blond
	barley, hops, yeast, water	orge, houblon, levure, eau	gerst, hop, gist, water
	misty blond with white foam head not filtered or pasteurised	blond nébuleux avec faux col blanc non filtrée, non pasteurisée	mistig blond met witte schuimkraag ongefilterd, niet gepasteuriseerd
	Fresh and fruity beer full of character. Very hoppy and slightly bitter. Very hoppy aftertaste.	Bière épicée fraîche très caractéristique. Fortement houblonnée et légèrement amère. Arrière-bouche fort houblonnée.	Karaktervol fris kruidig bier. Sterk gehopt en licht bitter. Zeer hoppige afdronk.
	Pour carefully and leave yeast sediment in the bottle. The glass was designed by Nedda El-Asmar, Belgian Designer of the Year in 2007.	Verser lentement et laisser le dépôt de levure dans la bouteille. Le verre a été conçu par Nedda El-Asmar, le designer Belge de l'année 2007.	Langzaam uitschenken en het gistdepot in de fles laten. Het glas werd ontworpen door Nedda El-Asmar, Belgische Designer van het Jaar in 2007.
i	Brewed by designer Dirk Wynants (Extremis) with his own hops. The beer is served to customers at events and trade fairs. Extremis stands for Belgian, Burgundy and not least homely design. The beer is not available in the shops.	Brassée par le designer Dirk Wynants (Extremis) avec du houblon de son propre champ. La bière est servie aux clients lors d'événements et de foires. Extremis veut dire design belge, bourguignon et surtout design agréable. La bière ne se vend pas dans le commerce.	Gebrouwen door designer Dirk Wynants (Extremis) met hop van eigen veld. Het bier wordt op events en beurzen geserveerd aan de klanten. Extremis staat voor Belgisch, Boergondisch en vooral gezellig design. Het bier is niet verkrijgbaar in de handel.

Triest Blond

Brouwerij Den Triest 6% 8 - 12 °C / 46 - 54 °F

	top-fermentation re-fermentation in the bottle not centrifuged	fermentation haute refermentation en bouteille non centrifugée	hoge gisting hergisting in de fles niet gecentrifugeerd
	blond city or regional beer	bière citadine ou régionale blonde	blond stads- of streekbier
	3 different malts and 2 different hops	3 variétés de malt et 2 variétés de houblon	3 mout- en 2 hopsoorten
	yellow-blond, clear not filtered or pasteurised	blond jaune, claire non filtrée, non pasteurisée	geelblond, helder ongefilterd, niet gepasteuriseerd
	Hoppy with fresh citrus aroma.	Houblonnée, avec un frais arôme de citrus.	Hoppig met fris citrusaroma.

Triest Dubbel

Brouwerij Den Triest

8% 8 - 12 ° 46 - 54 °

	top-fermentation re-fermentation in the bottle not centrifuged	fermentation haute refermentation en bouteille non centrifugée	hoge gisting hergisting in de fles niet gecentrifugeerd
	double city or regional beer	bière citadine ou régio-nale double	dubbel stads- of streek-bier
	4 different malts and 2 different hops	4 variétés de malt et 2 variétés de houblon	4 mout- en 2 hopsoorten
	brown, clear with a pale brown foam head	brune, claire avec un faux col brun clair	bruin, helder met een lichtbruine schuimkraag
	Mellow malt scent.	Doux parfum de malt.	Zachte moutgeur.

Triest Kriek

Brouwerij Den Triest 5,20% 8 - 12 °C / 46 - 54 °F

	top-fermentation re-fermentation in the bottle not centrifuged	fermentation haute refermentation en bouteille non centrifugée	hoge gisting hergisting in de fles niet gecentrifugeerd
	white beer with fruit city or regional beer	bière blanche fruitée bière citadine ou régionale	witbier met fruit stads- of streekbier
	4 different malts, American hops (bitter and aromatic hops). With dry-hopping	4 variétés de malt, houblon Américain (houblon amer et aromatique). Avec dry-hopping.	4 moutsoorten, Amerikaanse hop (bitter- en aromahop). Met dry-hopping
	nice red with red foam head not filtered or pasteurised	joli rouge avec faux col rouge non filtrée, non pasteurisée	mooi rood met rode schuimkraag ongefilterd, niet gepasteuriseerd
	Fresh fruity taste, not sweet or tart.	Un frais goût de fruits, pas sucré, peu acide.	Frisse fruitsmaak, niet zoet, weinig zuur.

Triest Speciale

Brouwerij Den Triest 7,50% 8 - 12 ° / 46 - 54 °

	top-fermentation re-fermentation in the bottle not centrifuged	fermentation haute refermentation en bouteille non centrifugée	hoge gisting hergisting in de fles niet gecentrifugeerd
	tripel city or regional beer Belgian ale	triple bière citadine ou régionale Belgian ale	tripel stads- of streek-bier Belgian ale
	3 different malts, 1 Bel-gian hop variety, aro-matic hops from New Zealand	3 variétés de malt, 1 va-riété de houblon Belge, houblon aromatique de Nouvelle Zélande	3 moutsoorten, 1 Belgi-sche hopsoort, aroma-hop uit Nieuw-Zeeland
	gold-coloured, clear not filtered or pasteur-ised	dorée, claire non filtrée, non pasteu-risée	goudachtig, helder ongefilterd, niet gepas-teuriseerd
	Fruity aroma, mellow hoppy taste, fresh after-taste.	Arôme fruité, doux goût de houblon, arrière-bouche fraîche.	Fruitig aroma, zachte hopsmaak, frisse af-dronk.

Triest Tripel

Brouwerij Den Triest 7,50% 8 - 12 °C / 46 - 54 °F

	top-fermentation re-fermentation in the bottle not centrifuged	fermentation haute refermentation en bouteille non centrifugée	hoge gisting hergisting in de fles niet gecentrifugeerd
	tripel city or regional beer Belgian ale	triple bière citadine ou régionale Belgian ale	tripel stads- of streek-bier Belgian ale
	3 different malts, 3 Belgian hop varieties	3 variétés de malt, 3 variétés de houblon Belge	3 moutsoorten, 3 Belgische hopsoorten
	gold-coloured, clear not filtered or pasteurised	dorée, claire non filtrée, non pasteurisée	goudachtig, helder ongefilterd, niet gepasteuriseerd
	Mellow hoppy taste and fresh aftertaste.	Doux goût de houblon et fraîche arrière-bouche.	Zachte hopsmaak en frisse afdronk.

Triest X-mas

Brouwerij Den Triest 8,50% 8 - 12 °C 46 - 54 °F

	top-fermentation re-fermentation in the bottle not centrifuged	fermentation haute refermentation en bouteille non centrifugée	hoge gisting hergisting in de fles niet gecentrifugeerd
	dubbel	double	dubbel
	natural beer based on 4 malt varieties, 2 hops, spices, yeast, water	bière naturelle à base de 4 variétés de malt, 2 variétés de houblon, épices, levure, eau	natuurbier op basis van 4 moutsoorten, 2 hopsoorten, kruiden, gist, water
	brown, clear with a pale brown foam head not filtered or pasteurised	brune, claire avec un faux col brun clair non filtrée ni pasteurisée	bruin, helder met een lichtbruine schuimkraag ongefilterd, niet gepasteuriseerd
	Mellow hoppy and oak aroma.	Doux arôme de houblon et de chêne.	Zachte moutgeur en eikaroma.
i	Den Triest is a hamlet along the Willebroekse Canal, straddling the provinces Brabant and Antwerp. Ethymologically, 'Triest' means farmland.	Den Triest est un hameau sur le Willebroekse Vaart (Canal de Willebroek), à la frontière entre les provinces de Brabant et d'Anvers. Le sens mythologique de Triest est 'terres cultivables'.	Den Triest is een gehucht aan de Willebroekse Vaart op de grens tussen de provincies Brabant en Antwerpen. De ethymologische betekenis van Triest is akkerland.

Brouwerij Bosteels

8,10% 5 - 6 °C 41 - 43 °F

Tripel Karmeliet

	top-fermentation re-fermented in the bottle	fermentation haute refermentation en bouteille	hoge gisting hergisting op de fles
	tripel 3-grains	triple 3-grains	tripel 3-granen
	wheat, haver, barley, hops, water	froment, avoine, orge, houblon, eau	tarwe, haver, gerst, hop, water
	complex gold- to bronze- coloured nice, creamy foam head	couleur bronze-dorée complexe beau faux col crémeux	complex goud- tot bronskleurig mooie, romige kraag
	Light freshness of wheat, creamy oat, citric dryness. Complex, refined flavour (grains and yeast, hops). Touches of vanilla mixed with citric flavours.	Goût légèrement frais de froment, crémeux d'avoine et sec de citron. Arôme raffiné et complexe (grains et levure, houblon). Touches de vanille et de citron.	Lichte frisheid van tarwe, romigheid van haver, citroenachtige droogheid. Verfijnd en complex aroma (granen en huisgist, hop). Toetsen van vanille en citrusachtige aroma's.
	Slightly tilt the glass and fill carefully. Leave a yeast sediment of approx. 1/2 cm at the bottom of the bottle. The yeast sediment can be drunk separately.	Tenir le verre légèrement incliné et le remplir prudemment. Laisser dans la bouteille un fond de levure de 1/2 cm environ. Ce dépôt peut être bu.	Het glas licht schuinhouden en voorzichtig volschenken. 1/2 cm gistbodem in de fles laten. Het gistdepot mag uitgedronken worden.
	Historical 3-grain beer brewed following a Carmelite recipe from 1679.	Bière 3-grains historique brassée selon une recette des Carmélites de 1679.	Historisch 3-granenbier gebrouwen volgens een Karmelietenrecept uit 1679.

Tripel Klok

Brouwerij Boelens 8,50%

	top-fermentation	fermentation haute	hoge gisting
	tripel blond	triple blonde	tripel blond
	blond	blonde	blond
	Malty beer with intense aroma (fine hops) and a hint of fruit.	Bière maltée avec un arôme corsé (houblon fin) et une touche fruitée.	Moutig bier met pittig aroma (fijne hop) en een fruitige toets.

Brasserie du Bocq

7,30% | 5 - 12 °C | 41 - 54 °F

Triple Moine

	top-fermentation re-fermented in the bottle	fermentation haute refermentation en bouteille	hoge gisting met hergisting in de fles
	specialty beer tripel	bière spéciale triple	speciaalbier tripel
	barley malt, wheat starch, hop varieties, yeast, herbs, water	malt d'orge, fécule de froment, sortes de houblon, levure, herbes, eau	gerstemout, tarwezetmeel, hoppesoorten, gist, kruiden, water
	blond, lively beer (9EBC) fine, full foam head	blonde (9 EBC), vivante mousse fine et généreuse	blond, levendig bier (9 EBC) fijne, volle kraag
	Well-balanced mixture of green apple and fine hops. Smooth character beer, low bitterness (25 EBU).	Mélange équilibré de pommes vertes et de houblon fin. Bière pleine de caractère avec une saveur peu amère (25 EBU).	Evenwichtige mengeling van groene appel en fijne hop. Zacht bier vol karakter met weinig bitterheid (25 EBU).
	Gently pour into a perfectly degreased glass. Leave the yeast sediment (natural re-fermenting) in the bottle	Verser doucement dans un verre parfaitement dégraissé. Laisser le dépôt de levure (refermentation naturelle) dans la bouteille.	Zacht uitschenken in een perfect ontvet glas. Het gistbezinksel (natuurlijke hergisting) in de fles laten.
i			

Trisser (XIV)

De Verhuisbrouwerij by de Proefbrouwerij 7,70% 12 °C / 54 °F

	top-fermentation natural re-fermentation in the bottle not centrifuged	fermentation haute refermentation spontanée en bouteille non centrifugée	hoge gisting natuurlijke hergisting in de fles niet gecentrifugeerd
	blond tripel	triple blonde	blonde tripel
	pilsner and Münich malt, hops (Saaz, East Kent Gold, Tomahawk), well water	malt de pils et de Münich, houblon (Saaz, East Kent Gold, Tomahawk), eau de puits	pils- en Münichmout, hop (Saaz, East Kent Gold, Tomahawk), putwater
	12 EBC not filtered or pasteurised	12 EBC non filtrée, non pasteurisée	12 EBC ongefilterd, niet gepasteuriseerd
	Fruity flavour develops into a slightly bitter taste. Beer mellows with age in terms of bitter aftertaste.	Goût fruité qui se transforme en légèrement amer. Plus vieille est la bière, moins amère est la fin de bouche.	Fruitige smaak die overgaat naar lichtbitter. Hoe ouder het bier, hoe minder bitter de nasmaak.
	Serve in a goblet.	Verser dans un verre calice.	Uitschenken in een kelkglas.
	A 'trisser' is a student who resits the same year three times. The association with the number 3 is also in the world tripel. This beer was brewed in tribute to someone who was a 'trisser' once. No names are mentioned to protect the privacy of the chairperson ...	Un trisseur est un étudiant qui fait trois fois une même année. L'association avec le chiffre 3 se retrouve aussi dans le mot 'triple'. Cette bière a été brassée en l'honneur de quelqu'un qui a été un jour un trisseur. On ne citera aucun nom, afin de ne pas violer la vie privée du président...	Een trisser is een student die driemaal eenzelfde jaar overdoet. De associatie met het cijfer 3 zit ook in het woord tripel. Dit bier werd gebrouwen ter ere van iemand die ooit een trisser is geweest. Er worden geen namen genoemd om de privacy van de voorzitter niet te schenden...

The Musketeers by De Proefbrouwerij

6,50% 5 - 8°C 41 - 46 °F

	top-fermentation re-fermentation in the bottle centrifuged	fermentation haute refermentation en bouteille centrifugée	hoge gisting hergisting in de fles gecentrifugeerd
	blond Belgian ale	blonde Belgian ale	blond Belgian ale
	barley malt, hops, sugar, yeast, water	malt d'orge, houblon, sucre, levure, eau	gerstemout, hop, gist, water
	clear gold-blond with nice, full white foam head; filtered	blond doré clair avec un joli faux col plein blanc; filtrée	helder goudblond met mooie, volle witte schuimkraag; gefilterd
	Mild bitterness, spicy, fresh and slightly dry in aftertaste.	Amertume douce, goût épicé, frais et plutôt sec en arrière-bouche.	Milde bitterheid, kruidig, fris en eerder droog in de afdronk.
	Pour out slowly into a slightly tilted glass and leave the yeast sediment (approx. 1/2 cm) in the bottle, if necessary.	Verser lentement dans un verre légèrement incliné et laisser le dépôt de levure (ca 1/2 cm) dans la bouteille selon les souhaits.	Langzaam uitschenken in een licht schuingehouden glas en het gistdepot (ca. 1/2 cm) desgewenst in de fles laten.
	Gold Medal World Beer Cup 2010.	Médaille d'or World Beer Cup 2010.	Gold Medal World Beer Cup 2010.

Troubadour Blond

Troubadour Magma

The Musketeers by De Proefbrouwerij 9% 5 - 8 °C 41 - 46 °F

top-fermentation re-fermentation in the bottle centrifuged	fermentation haute refermentation en bouteille centrifugée	hoge gisting hergisting in de fles gecentrifugeerd
Belgian tripel IPA Belgian ale	triple belge IPA Belgian ale	Belgische tripel IPA Belgian ale
barley malt, hops, yeast, water. Dry hopping	malt d'orge, houblon, levure, eau. Dry-hopping	gerstemout, hop, gist, water. Dry-hopping
orange-amber with clear, white foam head filtered	orange ambré avec faux col clair, blanc filtrée	oranje-amber met heldere, witte schuimkraag gefilterd
Explosion of scents with a fruity onset. Perfect marriage between a Belgian tripel and IPA (Indian Pale Ale). Harmonious balance between bitter hops and fruitiness.	Explosion de parfums qui démarre en fruité. Mariage parfait entre une triple belge et une IPA (Indian Pale Ale). Équilibre harmonieux d'amertume houblonnée et de fruité.	Geurexplosie die fruitig start. Perfect huwelijk tussen een Belgische tripel en IPA (Indian Pale Ale). Harmonieus evenwicht van hopbitterheid en fruitigheid.
Pour out slowly in a slightly tilted glass and leave the yeast sediment (approx. 1/2 cm) in the bottle, if necessary.	Verser lentement dans un verre tenu légèrement incliné et laisser selon les souhaits le dépôt de levure (ca. 1/2 cm) dans la bouteille.	Langzaam uitschenken in een licht schuingehouden glas en het gistdepot (ca. 1/2 cm) desgewenst in de fles laten.
Zythos Consumer Trophy 2010. Silver in the Denver International Beer Competition 2011.	Zythos Tropheé du consommateur 2010. Argent à la Denver International Beer Competition 2011.	Zythos Consumententrofee 2010. Zilver in de Denver International Beer Competition 2011.

Troubadour Obscura

The Musketeers by De Proefbrouwerij — 8,20% — 8 - 10 °C / 43 - 50 °F

top-fermentation re-fermentation in the bottle centrifuged	fermentation haute refermentation en bouteille centrifugée	hoge gisting hergisting in de fles gecentrifugeerd
strong dark Belgian ale	foncée forte Belgian ale	sterk donker Belgian ale
barley malt and other malts, hops, yeast, water	malt d'orge et autres malts, houblon, levure, eau	gerstemout en andere mouten, hop, gist, water
dark red-brown with full, creamy, beige foam head; filtered	foncé brun rouge avec un faux col plein, crémeux, beige; filtrée	donker roodbruin met volle, romige, beige schuimkraag; gefilterd
Mild stout which, in terms of flavour, is somewhere between a Belgian brown and English stout. Touches of roasted malt, chocolate and coffee.	Stout douce qui se situe pour le goût entre une brune belge et une stout anglaise. Touches de malt torréfié, de chocolat, de café.	Milde stout die zich qua smaak situeert tussen een Belgisch bruin en Engelse stout. Toetsen van gebrande mout, chocolade, koffie.
Pour out slowly into a slightly tilted glass and leave the yeast sediment (approx. 1/2 cm) in the bottle, if necessary.	Verser lentement dans un verre légèrement incliné et laisser le dépôt de levure (ca 1/2 cm) dans la bouteille selon les souhaits.	Langzaam uitschenken in een licht schuingehouden glas en het gistdepot (ca. 1/2 cm) desgewenst in de fles laten.

Troubadour Spéciale

The Musketeers by De Proefbrouwerij

5,70% 5 - 8 °C / 41 - 46 °F

	top-fermentation re-fermentation in the bottle centrifuged	fermentation haute refermentation en bouteille centrifugée	hoge gisting hergisting in de fles gecentrifugeerd
	amber or speciale belge	ambrée ou spéciale belge	amber of speciale belge
	barley malt, hops, yeast, water	malt d'orge, houblon, levure, eau	gerstemout, hop, gist, water
	amber with a distinctly white foam head filtered	ambré avec faux col blanc clair filtrée	amber met helder witte schuimkraag gefilterd
	An original 'spéciale belge' with a mellow, nice bitterness. Refreshing thirst-quencher.	Une 'spéciale Belge' originale, avec une douce jolie amertume. Bière rafraîchissante, désaltérante.	Een originele 'spéciale belge' met een zachte, mooie bitterheid. Verfrissende dorstlesser.
	Pour out slowly in a slightly tilted glass and leave the yeast sediment (approx. 1/2 cm) in the bottle, if necessary.	Verser lentement dans un verre tenu légèrement incliné et laisser selon les souhaits le dépôt de levure (ca. 1/2 cm) dans la bouteille.	Langzaam uitschenken in een licht schuingehouden glas en het gistdepot (ca. 1/2 cm) desgewenst in de fles laten.
i			

Brasserie Caracole

5,50% Refrigerated

	top-fermentation	fermentation haute	hoge gisting
	witbier	bière blanche	witbier
	barley malt, wheat, pilsner malt, aromatic hops, lemon rind, yeast, water	malt d'orge, froment, malt de pils, houblon aromatique, écorce de citron, levure, eau	gerstemout, tarwe, pilsmout, aromatische hop, citroenschil, gist, water
	light blond	blond clair	lichtblond
	Light and refreshing with a lemon touch. A real thirst-quencher.	Légère et rafraîchissante avec une touche de citron, désaltérant.	Licht en verfrissend met citroentoets, dorstlesser.
	Also has an organic version.	Existe également dans une version bio.	Bestaat ook in een bioversie.

Tsjeeses

De Struise Brouwers at Brouwerij Deca

10% 6 - 8 °C 43 - 46 °F

	top-fermentation re-fermented in the bottle	fermentation haute refermentation en bouteille	hoge gisting hergisting in de fles
	blond Christmas beer	bière de Noël blonde	blond winterbier
	pilsner, cara Münich, and wheat malt, cane sugar, yeast, water. Hops: Brewers Gold, Marynka, Bramling Cross. Sweet orange rind, massis banda, mint.	malt de pils et de froment, cara Münich, sucre de canne, levure, eau, houblon (Brewers Gold, Marynka, Bramling Cross), herbes (écorce d'orange doux, massis banda, menthe).	pilsmout, caramünich, tarwemout, rietsuiker, gist, water, hop (Brewers Gold, Marynka, Bramling Cross), kruiden (zoete sinaasschil, massis banda, munt).
	slightly hazy, deep orange (114 EBC) with an ivory-coloured foam head; not filtered	légèrement floue, orange profond (114 EBC) avec un faux col crémeux ivoire; non filtrée	licht wazig, dieporanje (114 EBC) met een ivoorkleurige schuimkraag; ongefilterd
	A range of refined aromas and flavours. Fruity, strong and malty in a refined way. Touches of Mandarine Napoléon, cake, breakfast cereals, marmalade, milk bread, cherry pips, stone fruit and mild floral hops. 32 EBU.	Un éventail d'arômes et de goûts raffinés. Fruitée, forte et finement maltée. Touches de Mandarine Napoléon, de cake, de céréales de petit-déjeuner, de marmelade, de pain au lait, de noyau de cerise, de fruits à noyau et de houblon floral doux. 32 EBU.	Een waaier aan verfijnde aroma's en smaken. Fruitig, sterk en verfijnd moutig. Toetsen van Mandarine Napoléon, cake, ontbijtgranen, marmelade, melkbrood, kersenpit, steenvruchten en milde florale hop. 32 EBU.
i	When the brewer tasted the beer, he exclaimed: 'Tsjeeses wat een lekker biertje!' (Gee, what a nice little beer!').	En dégustant la bière le maître brasseur s'est écrié 'Tsjeeses quelle bière agréable!'.	De naam is ontstaan toen meesterbrouwer Urbain bij het proeven van het jonge bier uitriep: 'Tsjeeses, moar is da goe bier'.

Tsjeeses Reserva

T

De Struise Brouwers at Brouwerij Deca

10% 6 - 8 °C 43 - 46 °F

top-fermentation re-fermentation in the bottle not centrifuged	fermentation haute refermentation en bouteille non centrifugée	hoge gisting hergisting in de fles niet gecentrifugeerd
oak aged winter beer	oak aged bière hivernale	oak aged winterbier
slightly hazy, deep orange with ivory-coloured foam head not filtered or pasteurised	légèrement fade, orange profond avec un faux col ivoire non filtrée, non pasteurisée	licht wazig, dieporanje met een ivoorkleurige schuimkraag ongefilterd, niet gepasteuriseerd
A whole gamut of refined aromas and flavours. Fruity, punchy, full of character and malty in a refined way. Hints of Mandarine Napoléon, cake, breakfast cereals, oak, chardonnay, milk bread, cherry pip, stone fruit and mild floral hops.	Un éventail d'arômes et de goûts raffinés. Bière fruitée, forte, très caractéristique et délicatement maltée. Touches de Mandarine Napoléon, de cake, de céréales de petit-déjeuner, de chêne, de chardonnay, de pain au lait, de noyau de cerises, de fruits à noyau et de houblon floral doux.	Een waaier aan verfijnde aroma's en smaken. Fruitig, sterk, karaktervol en verfijnd moutig. Toetsen van Mandarine Napoléon, cake, ontbijtgranen, eik, chardonnay, melkbrood, kersenpit, steenvruchten en milde florale hop.
Pour out in a single movement.	Verser agilement.	Vlot uitschenken.
Tsjeeses which has matured in oak casks for 6 months.	Tsjeeses qui a mûri 6 mois en fûts de chêne.	Tsjeeses die 6 maanden op eiken vaten is gerijpt.

Tumulus 800

De Kale Ridders by De Proefbrouwerij 6% 2 - 4 ° 36 - 39 °

	top-fermentation re-fermentation in the bottle centrifuged	fermentation haute refermentation en bouteille centrifugée	hoge gisting hergisting in de fles gecentrifugeerd
	Indian pale ale	Indian pale ale	Indian pale ale
	4 different malts, hops (Goldings from UK), yeast, water	4 variétés de malt, houblon (Goldings du UK), levure, eau	4 moutsoorten, hop (Goldings uit UK), gist, water
	pale blond, naturally cloudy (wheat) not filtered or pasteurised	blond clair, trouble naturel (froment) non filtrée, non pasteurisée	lichtblond, natuurlijk troebel (tarwe) ongefilterd, niet gepasteuriseerd
	Very dry beer with many fruity aromas and a distinct bitterness (50 EBU).	Bière très sèche, avec beaucoup d'arômes fruités et une amertume prononcée (50 EBU).	Zeer droog bier met veel fruitige aroma's en een uitgesproken bitterheid (50 EBU).
	Pour yeast sediment along or leave in the bottle.	Verser également le dépôt de levure ou laisser dans la bouteille.	Het gistdepot meeschenken of in de fles laten.
	Brewed as a festival beer to mark the 800th anniversary of the city of Landen.	Brassée comme bière de fête à l'occasion du 800e anniversaire de la ville de Landen.	Gebrouwen als feestbier t.g.v. de 800e verjaardag van de stad Landen.

De Kale Ridders by De Proefbrouwerij

9% 4 °C 39 °F

top-fermentation re-fermentation in the bottle; centrifuged	fermentation haute refermentation en bouteille; centrifugée	hoge gisting hergisting in de fles gecentrifugeerd
tripel Weizen beer strong wheat beer	triple Weizen bière de froment forte	tripel Weizenbier sterk tarwebier
4 different malts (esp. wheat malt), hops (Hallertau from Czech Republic), yeast, water	4 variétés de malt (surtout malt de froment), houblon (Hallertau de Tsjechie), levure, eau	4 moutsoorten (vooral tarwemout), hop (Hallertau uit Tsjechië), gist, water
pale amber, cloudy (wheat) with firm foam head; not filtered or pasteurised	ambré clair, trouble (froment) avec un faux col solide; non filtrée, non pasteurisée	lichtamber, troebel (tarwe) met een flinke schuimkraag; ongefilterd, niet gepasteuriseerd
Initially soft malt touches, fruity nose. Ends in a bitter taste (hops) (40 EBU).	Initialement, des touches maltées douces, un bouquet fruité. Se termine en arrière-bouche amère houblonnée (40 EBU).	Initieel zachte mouttoetsen, fruitige neus. Eindigt met een hopbittere afdronk (40 EBU).
Revolve the bottle and pour along sediment as is done with all wheat beers.	Remuer dépôt de la bouteille et le verser également comme pour toutes les bières de froment.	De bodem in het flesje walsen en meeschenken zoals bij alle tarwebieren.
Many centuries ago, important inhabitants of the rich Haspengouw were honoured with impressive memorial graves or tumuli. These are still present, strikingly so, in the landscape.	Il y a des siècles, pour honorer les habitants importants de la riche Hesbaye, on leur édifiait d'imposants monuments funéraires ou tumuli. Il est remarquable de constater que ceux-ci sont encore de nos jours présents dans le paysage.	Eeuwen geleden werden belangrijke inwoners in het rijke Haspengouw vereerd met indrukwekkende graftomben of tumuli. Die zijn vandaag nog opvallend aanwezig in het landschap.

Tumulus Magna

Uitzet 1730

Paeleman by Brouwerij Van Steenberge

6,80%

	top-fermentation re-fermented in the bottle	fermentation haute refermentation en bouteille	hoge gisting met nagisting in de fles
	tripel	triple	tripel
	malt, oat, hops, yeast, herbs, water	malt, avoine, houblon, levure, herbes, eau	mout, haver, hop, gist, kruiden, water
	unfiltered, generous fine foam head	non filtrée, faux col fin abondant	ongefilterd, overvloedige fijne schuimkraag
	Boutique beer, bitter with a fruity flavour and a touch of coriander.	Bière artisanale amère avec un arôme fruité et une pointe de coriandre.	Ambachtelijk bitter bier met een fruitig aroma en een vleugje koriander.
	Sipping beer with taste evolution. Store in a cool, dark room.	Bière de dégustation avec évolution de saveur. Conserver à l'abri de la chaleur et de la lumière.	Degustatiebier met smaakevolutie. Bewaren op een koele donkere plaats.

rouwerij Girardin 5% Cool

	bottom-fermentation	fermentation basse	lage gisting
	lager / pilsner	lager/pils	lager/pils
	barley malt, rice, hops, water	malt d'orge, riz, houblon, eau	gerstemout, rijst, hop, water
	gold-yellow, darker than common pilsner (slightly roasted, direct flame under the beerkettle). Clear.	jaune doré, plus foncé que la pils traditionnelle (légèrement brûlée, flamme directement sous la marmite). Claire.	goudgeel, donkerder dan gewone pils (licht gebrand, directe vlam onder de bierketel). Helder.
	Refreshing. Dry, malty, slightly bitter and roasty.	Rafraîchissante. Sèche, maltée, légèrement amère et légèrement brûlé.	Verfrissend. Droog, moutig, licht bitter. Licht gebrand.
	cfr pilsner	voir pils	cfr. pils
i			

Ulricher Extra

Ultra Ambrée

Brasserie d'Ecaussinnes

7% 3° 37°

	top-fermentation re-fermented in the bottle	fermentation haute refermentation en bouteille	hoge gisting hergisting in de fles
	amber - ale	ambrée - ale	amber - ale
	malts, hops, candy sugar, yeast, spring water	malts, houblon, sucre candi, levure, eau de source	mouten, hop, kandijsuiker, gist, bronwater
	yellow-copper unfiltered	cuivre jaune non filtrée	geelkoper niet gefilterd
	Pronounced malt and rind aroma. Taste: initially malty, turning into dry bitterness. No long-lasting aftertaste.	Arôme malté prononcé sur fond d'écorce. Introduction principalement maltée, rejointe en milieu de bouche par un amer sec, sans prolongation excessive.	Geprononceerd moutaroma, schil op de achtergrond. De smaak begint moutig en vloeit over in een droge bitterheid. Geen te lange afdronk.

rasserie d'Ecaussinnes 3,50% 2 - 3 °C 36 - 37 °F

	top-fermentation re-fermented in the bottle	fermentation haute refermentation en bouteille	hoge gisting hergisting in de fles
	blond	blonde	blond
	malts, hops, candy sugar, yeast, spring water	malts, houblon, sucre candi, levure, eau de source	mouten, hop, kandijsuiker, gist, bronwater
	blond	blonde	blond
	Pronounced taste despite the very low alcohol content.	Saveur prononcée malgré la faible teneur en alcool.	Uitgesproken smaak ondanks het minieme alcoholvolume.

Ultra Soif

Brasserie d'Ecaussinnes

5% 3° 37°

	top-fermentation re-fermented in the bottle	fermentation haute refermentation en bouteille	hoge gisting hergisting in de fles
	blond	blonde	blond
	malts, hops, candy sugar, yeast, spring water	malts, houblon, sucre candi, levure, eau de source	mouten, hop, kandijsuiker, gist, bronwater
	blond	blonde	blond
	A young beer with a pronounced taste that reminds of Witbier. Refreshing with a malty taste and a touch of hop.	Bière jeune avec une saveur prononcée renvoyant à la bière blanche. Rafraîchissante avec un goût malté et une pointe de houblon.	Jong bier met uitgesproken smaak die refereert aan witbier. Verfrissend met moutige smaak en een tikje hop.
i	Boutique beer.	Bière artisanale.	Artisanaal bier.

8% 3 °C 37 °F

	top-fermentation re-fermented in the bottle	fermentation haute refermentation en bouteille	hoge gisting hergisting in de fles
	strong blond	blonde forte	sterk blond
	selected pale malt varieties, hops, candy sugar, yeast, well water	sortes sélectionnées de malt pâle, houblon, sucre candi, levure, eau de source	geselecteerde bleke moutsoorten, hop, kandijsuiker, gist, bronwater
	gold-coloured	dorée	goudkleurig
	Subtle, fruity character. Pronounced malty character combined with a fine bitterness.	Caractère fruité subtile. Caractère malté prononcé combiné avec un goût amer raffiné.	Subtiel fruitig karakter. Geprononceerd moutkarakter gekoppeld aan een fijne bitterheid.

Ultrabrune

Brasserie d'Ecaussinnes 10% 10 - 12 °C / 50 - 54 °F

top-fermentation re-fermented in the bottle	fermentation haute refermentation en bouteille	hoge gisting hergisting in de fles
scottish style - strong brown	scotch - brune forte	scotch - sterk bruin
malts, hops, candy sugar, yeast, spring water. Based on hop varieties from Poperinge. Triple fermentation	malts, houblon, sucre candi, levure, eau de source. A base de sortes de houblon de Poperinge. Triple fermentation	mouten, hop, kandijsuiker, gist, bronwater. Op basis van hopsoorten uit Poperinge. Drievoudige fermentatie
brown, almost black filtered	brune, presque noire filtrée	bruin, bijna zwart gefilterd
Strong perfume of liquorice and alcohol. Taste of roasty malt varieties, coffee with liquorice and bitter orange rind.	Parfum fort de réglisse et d'alcool. Goût de sortes de malt brûlé, café avec réglisse et écorce d'orange amer.	Sterk parfum van zoethout en alcohol. Smaak van gebrande moutsoorten, koffie met zoethout en bittere sinaasschil.

Ultradélice

rasserie d'Ecaussinnes

8% 8 °C 46 °F

top-fermentation re-fermented in the bottle	fermentation haute refermentation en bouteille	hoge gisting hergisting in de fles
regional beer brown	bière citadine ou régionale, brune	stads- of streekbier bruin
malts, hops, candy sugar, yeast, spring water	malts, houblon, sucre candi, levure, eau de source	mouten, hop, kandijsuiker, gist, bronwater
dark brown	brun foncé	donkerbruin
Slightly sugared flavour. Light touch of sugar with special spices.	Arôme légèrement sucré. Touche légèrement sucrée avec un goût relevé spécial.	Licht gesuikerd aroma. Lichte suikertoets met speciale kruidensmaak.

Ultramour

Brasserie d'Ecaussinnes

5%

	top-fermentation	fermentation haute	hoge gisting
	blond fruit beer	blonde bière fruitée	blond fruitbier
	malts, hops, candy sugar, 3 kinds of red fruits, lemon juice, yeast, spring water	malts, houblon, sucre candi, 3 sortes de fruits rouges, jus de citron, levure, eau de source	mouten, hop, kandijsuiker, 3 soorten rode vruchten, citroensap, gist, bronwater
	hazy reddish unfiltered	rougeâtre, voilée non filtrée	gesluierd roodachtig niet gefilterd
	Very perfumed aroma. Light touch of white candy sugar, longlasting fruit taste, not bitter at all.	Arôme très parfumé. Touche légère de sucre candi blanc, goût fruité qui reste longtemps dans la bouche, pas du tout amer.	Zeer geparfumeerd aroma. Lichte toets van witte kandijsuiker, fruitsmaak die lang in de mond blijft, niets bitter.

rasserie des Légendes 7,50% 7 - 10 °C / 45 - 50 °F

Urchon

	top-fermentation re-fermented in the bottle	fermentation haute refermentation en bouteille	hoge gisting nagisting in de fles
	specialty beer	bière spéciale	speciaalbier
	pale malt, caramel malt, roasted malt, hops, yeast, water	malt pâle, malt caramélisé, malt brûlé, houblon, levure, eau	bleekmout, karamelmout, gebrande mout, hop, gist, water
	brown	brune	bruin
	Dry character: coffee and caramel. Aroma of roasty malt and pronounced bitterness.	Caractère sec :café et caramel. Arôme de malt brûlé et goût amer prononcé.	Droog karakter: koffie en karamel. Aroma van gebrande mout en duidelijke bitterheid.
	Degrease the glass with some detergent, rinse thoroughly with hot water and dry. With yeast sediment: smoothly revolve the bottle before serving. Without yeast sediment: pour carefully, leaving the sediment in the bottle.	Dégraisser les verres avec un peu de détergent, bien les rincer à l'eau chaude et sécher. Avec dépôt de levure : tourner le dernier tiers de bière avant de le verser. Sans dépôt : verser prudemment et laisser la levure dans la bouteille.	Het glas ontvetten (beetje detergent), goed spoelen met warm water en drogen. Met gistbezinkel: het laatste derde in de fles walsen voor het uitschenken. Zonder gistbezinksel: voorzichtig schenken en de fond in de fles laten.
i			

Urthel Hop-it

Brouwerij Urthel bу Bierbrouwerij de Koningshoeven 9,50% 6 - 8 / 43 - 46

	top-fermentation re-fermented in the bottle; centrifuged	fermentation haute refermentation en bouteille; centrifugée	hoge gisting nagisting op de fles; gecentrifugeerd
	strong blond	blonde forte	sterk blond
	pilsner malt, yeast, European hops, water	malt de pils, levure, houblon européen, eau	pilsmout, gist, Europese hop, water
	pale blond, slightly cloudy with a big creamy foam head not filtered	blond pâle, légèrement trouble avec riche faux col crémeux non filtrée	bleekblond, licht troebel met een rijkelijke, romige schuimkraag ongefilterd
	Urthel Hop-it is fruity like a strong tripel but also spicy owing to the generous amount of European fine hops used.	Urthel Hop-it a le fruité d'une triple forte, combiné au goût épicé du houblon, grâce à la grande quantité de houblons nobles européens.	Zeer hoppig en bitter. Urth Hop-it heeft het fruitige van een krachtige tripel ge combineerd met het kruidi ge van hop door de royale hoeveelheid Europese nobelhoppen.
	Slowly pour into a tilted Urthel glass and preferably leave the yeast sediment in the bottle. The rich foam head can take more or less half of the glass.	Verser lentement dans un verre Urthel tenu en oblique et laisser de préférence le fond de levure dans la bouteille. Le riche faux col peut prendre environ la moitié du verre.	Langzaam uitschenken in een schuingehouden Urthelglas en de gistfond bij voorkeur in de fles laten. De rijkelijke schuimkraag mag ongeveer de helft van het glas innemen.
i	The beer was developed in 1995 for the American market, but is now being distributed in Belgium too. The female brewer creates her trial beers in Ruiselede and has a great passion for hoppy beers.	La bière a été développée en 1995 pour le marché américain, mais est à présent également distribuée en Belgique. La brasseuse réalise ses brassins d'essai à Ruiselede et témoigne d'une grande passion pour les bières houblonnées.	Het bier werd in 1995 ontwikkeld voor de Amerikaanse markt maar wordt nu ook in België wordt verdeeld. De brouwster maakt haar proefbrouwsels in Ruiselede en heeft een grote passie voor hoppige bieren.

rouwerij Urthel by Bierbrouwerij de Koningshoeven

11,50% — 8 - 10 °C / 46 - 50 °F

Urthel Samaranth

	top-fermentation re-fermented in the bottle centrifuged	fermentation haute refermentation en bouteille centrifugée	hoge gisting nagisting op de fles gecentrifugeerd
	barley wine strong dubbel	vin d'orge double forte	gerstewijn sterk donker
	malts (pale, cara and chocolate), yeast, hops, water	malts (pâle, cara et chocolat), levure, houblon, eau	mout (bleek, cara en chocolade), gist, hop, water
	deep amber, clear	ambré intense, claire	diep amberkleurig, helder
	Aroma of malt chocolate and ripe summer fruits. Exceptionally round and full taste with a light sweet liqueur-like aftertaste.	Arôme de chocolat malté et de fruits mûrs d'été. La saveur est particulièrement ronde et pleine, avec une fin de bouche légèrement douce de liqueur.	Aroma van moutige chocolade en rijpe zomervruchten. De smaak is bijzonder rond en vol, met een lichtzoete likeurachtige afdronk.
	Slowly pour into a tilted Urthel glass and preferably leave the yeast sediment in the bottle. The rich foam head can take more or less half of the glass.	Verser lentement dans un verre Urthel tenu en oblique et laisser de préférence le fond de levure dans la bouteille. Le riche faux col peut prendre environ la moitié du verre.	Langzaam uitschenken in een schuingehouden Urthelglas en de gistfond bij voorkeur in de fles laten. De rijkelijke schuimkraag mag ongeveer de helft van het glas innemen.
	Samaranth is the language Erthels speak: tiny little men from a story, created and drawn by the brewer's husband.	Samaranth est la langue des Erthels :les petits personnages du récit crée et dessiné par l'époux du brasseur.	Samaranth is de taal van de Erthels: kleine mannetjes in een verhaal gecreëerd en getekend door de echtgenoot van de brouwer.

Val-Dieu Bière de Noël

Brasserie de l'Abbaye du Val-Dieu

7% 8 - 12 / 46 - 54

	top-fermentation re-fermented in the bottle	fermentation haute refermentation en bouteille	hoge gisting hergisting op de fles
	Recognised Belgian abbey beer	Bière d'abbaye belge reconnue	Erkend Belgisch abdijbier
	malt, hops, yeast, water	malt, houblon, levure, eau	mout, hop, gist, water
	warm amber-yellow gentle bubbles	jaune ambré chaud perle tranquillement	warm ambergeel rustige pareling
	Easily digestible. Captivatingly smooth with fine, well-balanced flavours. A pronounced aroma of yeast and malt varieties.	Facilement digestible. Douceur envoûtante comprenant de fines saveurs nuancées. Arôme prononcé de levure et de sortes de malt.	Licht verteerbaar. Onweerstaanbaar zacht met een genuanceerde smaak. Uitgesproken aroma van gist en moutsoorten.
	Whilst pouring, first keep the glass slightly tilted, then slowly straighten it to obtain a nice, white foam head.	D'abord tenir le verre légèrement en oblique et le redresser doucement par la suite pour obtenir un faux col blanc.	Tijdens het uitschenken het glas eerst licht schuin houden en zacht recht brengen voor een witte schuimkraag.
i			

6% 6 - 10 °C 43 - 50 °F

	top-fermentation re-fermented in the bottle	fermentation haute refermentation en bouteille	hoge gisting hergisting op de fles
	Recognised Belgian abbey beer, blond	Bière d'abbaye belge reconnue, blonde	Erkend Belgisch abdijbier, blond
	malt, two traditional hop varieties, yeast, water	malt, 2 sortes traditionnelles de houblon, levure, eau	mout, 2 traditionele hopsoorten, gist, water
	light yellow slightly hazy	jaune clair légèrement voilée	lichtgeel licht gesluierd
	Very refreshing digestive. Initial sugar taste which evolves into light bitterness and ends in a short, slightly bitter aftertaste. Perfumed and slightly stimulating aroma.	Très rafraîchissante et disgestive. Goût initial sucré évoluant à un goût légèrement amer et une arrière-bouche courte, légèrement amère. Arôme parfumé et légèrement stimulant.	Zeer verfrissend en digestief. Aanzet van suiker die evolueert naar lichte bitterheid en een korte, licht bittere nasmaak. Geparfumeerd en licht prikkelend aroma.
	Whilst pouring, first keep the glass slightly tilted, then slowly straighten it to obtain a white, smooth-edged foam head.	Tenir le verre d'abord légèrement en oblique et le redresser doucement par la suite pour obtenir un faux col blanc pas trop large.	Tijdens het uitschenken het glas eerst licht schuin houden en zacht recht brengen voor een witte maar niet te hoge schuimkraag.
i	A traditional recipe dating back from 1216, when the abbey was founded.	Une recette traditionnelle datant de 1216, quand l'abbaye a été fondée.	Een traditioneel recept dat dateert van 1216 toen de abdij gesticht werd.

Val-Dieu Brune

Brasserie de l'Abbaye du Val-Dieu 8% 10 - 12 ° / 50 - 54 °

	top-fermentation re-fermented in the bottle	fermentation haute refermentation en bouteille	hoge gisting hergisting op de fles
	Recognised Belgian abbey beer, brown	Bière d'abbaye belge reconnue, brune	Erkend Belgisch abdijbier, bruin
	malt, hops, yeast, water	malt, houblon, levure, eau	mout, hop, gist, water
	deep ruby, despite its name	rubis foncé malgré son nom	donker robijn ondanks zijn naam
	Rich and energetic. Slightly stimulating coffee flavour that seeps away without a trace of bitterness.	Riche et énergique. Arôme légèrement stimulant de café absorbé dans le goût sans laisser de goût amer.	Rijk en energiek. Licht prikkelend aroma van koffie dat wegebt in de smaak en geen bitterheid laat.
	Whilst pouring, first keep the glass slightly tilted, then slowly straighten it to obtain a brownish foam head.	D'abord tenir le verre légèrement en oblique et le redresser doucement par la suite pour obtenir un faux col brunâtre.	Tijdens het uitschenken het glas eerst licht schuin houden en zacht recht brengen voor een bruinachtige schuimkraag.
i	A traditional recipe dating back from 1216, when the abbey was founded.	Une recette traditionnelle datant de 1216, quand l'abbaye a été fondée.	Een traditioneel recept dat dateert van 1216 toen de abdij gesticht werd.

	top-fermentation re-fermentation in the bottle	fermentation haute refermentation en bouteille	hoge gisting hergisting in de fles
	dark quadruple abbey beer	bière d'abbaye foncée quadruple	donker abdijbier quadrupel
	pilsner and roasted malt, hops (Hallertau and Saaz)	malt de pils et malt torréfié, houblon (Hallertau et Saaz)	pils- en gebrande mout, hop (Hallertau en Saaz)
	dark-brown	brun foncé	donkerbruin
	Wine-like sweet beer with a touch of caramel. Bitter aftertaste with roasted flavours. Special aroma of earthly scents and spiced biscuits. Complex beer with much body and long aftertaste.	Bière sucrée vineuse, avec une touche de caramel. Arrière-bouche amère, avec une pointe de brûlé. Arôme spécial de parfums terreux et de spéculoos. Bière complexe, avec beaucoup de corps et une longue arrière-bouche.	Wijnachtig zoet bier met een toets van karamel. Bittere afdronk met een vleugje gebrand. Speciaal aroma van aardse geuren en speculoos. Complex bier met veel body en een lange afdronk.
i	Preferably leave to mature for a year in the cellar before tasting it.	La laisser de préférence mûrir un an dans la cave avant de la déguster.	Bij voorkeur een jaar in de kelder laten rijpen vooraleer te degusteren.

Val-Dieu Triple

Brasserie de l'Abbaye du Val-Dieu 9% 11 - 13 ° 52 - 55 °

	top-fermentation re-fermented in the bottle	fermentation haute refermentation en bouteille	hoge gisting hergisting op de fles
	Recognised Belgian abbey beer	Bière d'abbaye belge reconnue	Erkend Belgisch abdijbier
	malt, hops, yeast, water	malt, houblon, levure, eau	mout, hop, gist, water
	warm yellow slightly hazy	jaune chaud légèrement voilée	warmgeel licht gesluierd
	Easily digestible. Agreeably spicy. Light touch of sugar in the middle, sometimes with alcohol, bitter and soft.	Facilement digestible. Agréablement corsée. Légère touche sucrée au centre, parfois avec de l'alcool, goût amer et moelleux.	Licht verteerbaar. Aangenaam kruidig. Lichte toets van suiker in het midden soms met alcohol, bitter en zacht.
	Whilst pouring, first keep the glass slightly tilted, then slowly straighten it to obtain a nice, white but not too creamy foam head.	D'abord tenir le verre légèrement en oblique et le redresser doucement par la suite pour obtenir un faux col blanc mais pas trop onctueux.	Tijdens het uitschenken het glas eerst licht schuin houden en zacht recht brengen voor een mooie witte maar niet te smeuïge schuimkraag.
i	A traditional recipe dating back from 1216, when the abbey was founded.	Une recette traditionnelle datant de 1216, quand l'abbaye a été fondée.	Een traditioneel recept dat dateert van 1216 toen de abdij gesticht werd.

	top-fermentation re-fermented in the bottle (and the barrel)	fermentation haute refermentation en bouteille (et au fût)	hoge gisting nagisting op de fles (en op het vat)
	blond specialty beer	bière spéciale blonde	blond speciaalbier
	barley malt, hops (Sterling), top-fermentation yeast, sugar (for re-fermentation), water. Dry-hopped during storage.	malt d'orge, houblon (Sterling), levure de haute fermentation, sucre (pour refermentation), eau. Dry hopped lors du lagering.	gerstemout, hop (Sterling), hogegistingsgist, suiker (voor hergisting), water. Gedry-hopped tijdens de lagering.
	orange-blond, clear	blond orange, claire	oranjeblond, helder
	Spicy and hoppy. Pleasantly refreshing.	Relevée et houblonnée. Agréablement rafraîchissante.	Kruidig en hoppig. Aangenaam verfrissend.
	see Valeir Divers	voir Valeir Divers	zie Valeir Divers
	Store vertically to keep the yeast at the bottom. Since 2004. Beerhunter Michael Jackson described this beer as a hidden treasure	Conserver en position verticale pour garder la levure au fond. Depuis 2004. The Beerhunter Michael Jackson a défini cette bière comme l'un des joyaux cachés.	Verticaal bewaren om de gist op de bodem te houden. Sinds 2004. The Beerhunter Michael Jackson omschreef dit bier als een van de verborgen juweeltjes

Valeir Divers

Brouwerij Contreras 8,50% 6 °
43 °

	top-fermentation re-fermented in the bottle (and the barrel)	fermentation haute refermentation en bouteille (et au fût)	hoge gisting hergisting op de fles (en op het vat)
	tripel	triple	tripel
	gerstemout, hop (Sterling), hogegistingsgist, suiker (voor hergisting), water.	malt d'orge, houblon (Saaz), sucre (pour refermentation), levure de fermentation haute, eau	gerstemout, hop (Saaz), suiker (voor hergisting), hogegistingsgist, water
	light blond	blond clair	lichtblond
	Silky smooth. Dry and hoppy.	Soyeuse. Sèche et houblonnée.	Zijdezacht. Droog en hoppig.
	Pour into a degreased, rinsed and dry glass. Tilt the glass about 45° and gently pour the beer, avoiding contact between bottle and foam. Provide a foam head of about 2.5 cm and leave 1 cm of beer in the bottle. Present the bottle along with the glass.	Verser dans un verre dégraissé, rincé et sec. Tenir le verre incliné à 45° et verser la bière doucement sans que la bouteille touche l'écume. Prévoir un faux col de 2,5 cm et laisser 1 cm de bière dans la bouteille. Servir la bouteille avec le verre rempli.	Schenken in ontvet, gespoeld en droog glas. Het glas 45° schuin houden en het bier zacht inschenken zonder dat de fles het schuim raakt. Een schuimkraag van ca. 2,5 cm voorzien en 1 cm bier in de fles laten. De fles samen met het glas serveren.
	Store upright to ensure that the yeast settles on the bottom of the bottle. Since 2005.	Conserver en position verticale pour tenir la levure au fond. Depuis 2005.	Verticaal bewaren om de gist op de bodem te houden. Sinds 2005.

Valeir Donker

Brouwerij Contreras 6,50% 7 °C 45 °F

	top-fermentation re-fermented in the bottle	fermentation haute refermentation en bouteille	hoge gisting hergisting op de fles
	dark specialty beer	bière spéciale foncée	donker speciaalbier
	barley malt, hops (Hallertau, Styrian, Brewers gold), sugar, top-fermenting yeast, water	malt d'orge, houblon (Hallertau, Styrian, Brewers gold), sucre, levure de fermentation haute, eau	gerstemout, hop (Hallertau, Styrian, Brewers gold), suiker, hogegistingsgist, water
	chestnut	brun marron	kastanjebruin
	Caramel malt. Smooth and bitter.	Caramel maltée. Moelleuse et amère.	Karamelmoutig. Zacht en bitter.
	Pour into a degreased, rinsed and dry glass. Tilt the glass about 45° and gently pour the beer, avoiding contact between bottle and foam. Provide a foam head of about 2.5 cm and leave 1 cm of beer in the bottle. Present the bottle along with the glass.	Verser dans un verre dégraissé, rincé et sec. Tenir le verre incliné à 45° et verser la bière doucement sans que la bouteille touche l'écume. Prévoir un faux col de 2,5 cm et laisser 1 cm de bière dans la bouteille. Servir la bouteille avec le verre rempli.	Schenken in een ontvet, gespoeld en droog glas. Het glas 45° schuin houden en het bier zacht inschenken zonder dat de fles het schuim raakt. Een schuimkraag van ca. 2,5 cm voorzien en 1 cm bier in de fles laten. De fles samen met het glas serveren.
i	Store upright to ensure that the yeast settles on the bottom of the bottle. Since 2005.	Conserver en position verticale pour tenir la levure au fond. Depuis 2005.	Verticaal bewaren om de gist op de bodem te houden. Sinds 2005.

Valeir Extra

Brouwerij Contreras 6,50% 6 °C 43 °F

	top-fermentation post-fermentation in the bottle	fermentation haute refermentation en bouteille	hoge gisting nagisting op de fles
	blond specialty beer IPA style (Indian Pale Ale)	spéciale blonde IPA style (Indian Pale Ale)	blond speciaalbier IPA style (Indian Pale Ale)
	barley malt, hops (Sterling and Ammarillo), top-fermentation yeast, sugar (for re-fermentation), water	malt d'orge, houblon (Sterling et Ammarillo), levure de haute fermentation, sucre (pour re-fermentation), eau	gerstemout, hop (Sterling en Ammarillo), hogegistingsgist, suiker (voor hergisting), water
	gold blond	blond doré	goudblond
	Complex. Floral, spicy, well-balanced beer with an aromatic and bitter (hops) aftertaste.	Complexe. Bière fleurie épicée, équilibrée, avec une arrière-bouche aromatique et amère houblonnée.	Complex. Bloemig, kruidig, evenwichtig bier met een aromatische en hopbittere afdronk.
	see Valeir Donker	voir Valeir Donker	zie Valeir Donker
	Since 2008. In those days, the British would shop particularly hoppy beer to their colonies (incl. India). Hops provides bitterness but is also a natural preservative.	Depuis 2008. Les Anglais ont dans le temps transporté par bateau une bière extrêmement houblonnée vers leurs colonies (e.a. l'Inde). Le houblon non seulement procure de l'amertume, mais encore il garantit une conservation naturelle.	Sinds 2008. De Engelsen verscheepten destijds extra hoppig bier naar hun kolonies (o.a. India). Hop zorgt niet alleen voor bitterheid maar staat ook garant voor natuurlijke bewaring.

Brasserie à Vapeur

9% 13 - 18 °C / 55 - 64 °F

Vapeur Cochonne - Cochonnette

	top-fermentation natural re-fermentation in the bottle not centrifuged	fermentation haute refermentation naturelle en bouteille non centrifugée	hoge gisting natuurlijke hergisting op de fles niet gecentrifugeerd
	amber, strong brown Belgian ale	ambré, forte brune Belgian ale	amber, sterk bruin Belgian ale
	4 different types of barley malt, hops, yeast, herbs, water	4 variétés de malt d'orge, houblon, levure, herbes, eau	4 soorten gerstemout, hop, gist, kruiden, water
	intense amber not filtered or pasteurised	ambré intense non filtrée, non pasteurisée	intens amber niet gefilterd, niet gepasteuriseerd
	Very strong. Delicate and fruity nose. Soft and full-bodied, soft hops but seasoned in a balanced manner (roasted chicory, coriander, orange peel).	Très fort. Bouquet délicat et fruité. Douce et franche, houblon doux mais épicée de façon équilibrée (chicorée brûlée, coriandre, écorce d'orange).	Zeer sterk. Delicate en fruitige neus. Zacht en volmondig, zachte hop maar evenwichtig gekruid (gebrande cichorei, koriander, sinaasappelschil).
	Pour carefully into a dry balloon-shaped glass.	Verser prudemment dans un verre ballon sec.	Voorzichtig uitschenken in een droog ballonglas.
	Brewed since 1992, originally under the name Bissextile - bière cochonne. The label was designed by Louis-Michel Carpentier, author of the comic strip 'Chansons Cochonnes'. Cochonnette is 33 cl, Grosse Cochonne is 150 cl.	Brassée depuis 1992, à l'origine sous le nom Bissextile - bière cochonne. L'étiquette a été créée par Louis-Michel Carpentier, auteur de la bande dessinée 'Chansons Cochonnes'. Cochonnette est une 33 cl, Grosse Cochonne est une 150 cl.	Sinds 1992 gebrouwen, oorspronkelijk onder de naam Bissextile - bière cochonne. Het etiket is ontworpen door Louis-Michel Carpentier, auteur van de stripreeks 'Chansons Cochonnes'. Cochonnette is 33 cl, Grosse Cochonne is 150 cl.

Vapeur en Folie

Brasserie à Vapeur

8% — 13 °C / 55 - 64 °F

	top-fermentation natural re-fermentation in the bottle not centrifuged	fermentation haute refermentation naturelle en bouteille non centrifugée	hoge gisting natuurlijke hergisting op de fles niet gecentrifugeerd
	strong blond Belgian ale	blonde forte Belgian ale	sterk blond Belgian ale
	barley malt, hops, yeast varieties, herbs, sugar, water	malt d'orge, houblon, variétés de levure, herbes, sucre, eau	gerstemout, hop, gist-soorten, kruiden, suiker, water
	blond not filtered or pasteur-ised	blond non filtrée, non pasteu-risée	blond ongefilterd, niet gepas-teuriseerd
	Soft and dry with a mod-erate flavour of hops and spices (cummin, smooth orange rind).	Douce et sèche, modéré-ment houblonnée et lé-gèrement épicée (cumin et écorce d'orange douce).	Zacht en droog, matig gehopt en licht gekruid (komijn en zachte si-naasschil).
	Pour carefully into a bal-loon-shaped glass.	Verser prudemment dans un verre ballon.	Voorzichtig uitschenken in een ballonglas.
	The label was designed by Louis-Michel Carpen-tier, author of the comic strip 'Chansons Co-chonnes'.	L'étiquette a été créée par Louis-Michel Car-pentier, auteur de la bande dessinée 'Chan-sons Cochonnes'.	Het etiket is ontworpen door Louis-Michel Car-pentier, auteur van de stripreeks 'Chansons Co-chonnes'.

Duvel Moortgat Corporation 5,20% 0 - 5 °C 32 - 41 °F

Vedett Extra Blond

	bottom-fermentation	fermentation basse	lage gisting
	premium pilsner	premium pils	premium pils
	barley malt, rice grits, hops (Saaz), lager yeast, water	malt d'orge, semoule de riz, houblon (Saaz), levure de basse fermentation, eau	gerstemout, griesmeel van rijst, hop (Saaz), lagergist, water
	golden	doré	goudkleurig
	Sweet, fruity and hoppy background. Typical taste of Saaz hop and lager yeast.	Touche douce, fruitée et houblonnée sur le fond. Saveur typique de houblon Saaz et de levure de basse fermentation.	Zoete, fruitige en hoppige achtergrondtoets. Typische smaak van Saazhop en lagergist.
	Pour in a single movement in a cool glass, previously rinsed with pure, cold water. Let the foam run over the rim of the glass and skim off the excess foam and big bubbles with a spatula or knife (big carbon dioxide bubbles cause the foam head to disappear more quickly).	Verser d'un seul trait dans un verre refroidi rincé à l'avance à l'eau froide propre. Laisser déborder et enlever l'écume redondante ainsi que les grosses bulles avec une spatule ou un couteau (de grandes bulles de dioxyde de carbone font disparaître l'écume).	In 1 keer uitschenken in een koel glas dat vooraf gespoeld is met koud, zuiver water. Laten overschuimen en het overtollige schuim en grove bellen met een spatel of mes van de rand van het glas afhalen (grote koolzuurbellen doen het schuim verdwijnen).
i			

Vedett Extra White

Duvel Moortgat Corporation 4,70%

	top-fermentation re-fermentation in the bottle	fermentation haute refermentation en bouteille	hoge gisting hergisting op de fles
	white beer	bière blanche	witbier
	wheat, barley, different hops, coriander, dried orange peel	froment, orge, variétés de houblon, coriandre, écorce d'oranges séchée	tarwe, gerst, hopsoorten, koriander, gedroogde sinaasschil
	hazy yellow not filtered	jaune fade non filtrée	wazig geel ongefilterd
	Refreshing taste, with hint of citrus peel, mellowed by a mild-bitter flavour and a dry aftertaste.	Goût rafraîchissant, étonnamment croquant, avec une touche de zeste de citrus, arrondi par un goût doucement amer et une arrière-bouche sèche.	Verfrissende smaak, met toets van citrusschil, afgerond door een mildbittere smaak en een droge afdronk.

Brouwerij Verhaeghe

5,10% 3 °C 37 °F

	bottom-fermentation	fermentation basse	lage gisting
	pilsner	pils	pilsbier
	malt, hops, yeast, corn, water	malt, houblon, levure, maïs, eau	mout, hop, gist, maïs, water
	golden yellow filtered	jaune doré filtrée	goudgeel gefilterd
	Bitter and malty.	Amère et houblonnée.	Bitter en moutig.
	Pour carefully into a de-greased, rinsed, wet glass.	Verser prudemment en un seul mouvement dans un verre dégraissé et mouillé.	Voorzichtig uitschenken in 1 beweging in een nat, ontvet glas.
i			

Brouwerij Dilewyns 7,00% 6 - 9 °C / 43 - 48 °F

	top-fermentation re-fermented in the bottle	fermentation haute refermentation en bouteille	hoge gisting hergisting op de fles
	tripel gueuze	gueuze triple	tripel-geuze
	malt, barley, hops, yeast, sugar, Gueuze from Girardin brewery, water. No herbs or syrups added.	malt, orge, houblon, levure, sucre, gueuze de la brasserie Girardin, eau. Sans adjonction d'herbes, ni de sirops.	mout, gerst, hop, gist, suiker, geuze van brouwerij Girardin, water. Er worden geen kruiden of siropen toegevoegd.
	orange-yellow clear	jaune orange claire	oranjegeel helder
	Summer beer with added Gueuze. Fruity and refreshing with a smooth aftertaste.	Bière d'été avec une petite extra par l'adjonction de gueuze. Fruitée, fraîche avec une fin de bouche moelleuse.	Zomerbier met een extraatje door de toegevoegde geuze. Fruitig, fris met zachte afdronk.
	Keep the glass tilted and pour the beer slowly, with or without yeast sediment.	Tenir le verre en oblique et verser la bière lentement, avec ou sans dépôt de levure.	Het glas schuinhouden en het bier langzaam inschenken, met of zonder gistdepot.
i			

Vicaris Generaal

Brouwerij Dilewyns 8,80% 6 - 9 °C 43 - 48 °F

	top-fermentation re-fermented in the bottle	fermentation haute refermentation en bouteille	hoge gisting hergisting op de fles
	dark specialty beer	bière spéciale foncée	speciaalbier donker
	barley, malt, hops, sugar, water. No herbs or syrups added.	orge, malt, houblon, sucre, eau. Sans adjonction d'herbes, ni de sirops.	gerst, mout, hop, suiker, water. Er worden geen kruiden of siropen toegevoegd.
	red-brown clear	brun rouge claire	roodbruin helder
	Roasty malt flavour, suggesting a Christmas beer.	Arôme de malt brûlé, ce qui fait penser à une bière de Noël.	Aroma van gebrande mout, wat doet denken aan een kerstbier.
	Keep the glass tilted and pour the beer slowly, with or without yeast sediment.	Tenir le verre en oblique et verser la bière lentement, avec ou sans dépôt de levure.	Het glas schuinhouden en het bier langzaam inschenken, met of zonder gistdepot.
i			

Vicaris Kerst

Brouwerij Dilewyns

10% 6 - 9 °C 43 - 48 °F

	top-fermentation re-fermentation in the bottle not centrifuged	fermentation haute refermentation en bouteille non centrifugée	hoge gisting hergisting in de fles niet gecentrifugeerd
	very dark specialty beer winter beer	spéciale foncée forte bière hivernale	sterk donker speciaal-bier winterbier
	malt, hops, yeast, 1 herb, water	malt, houblon, levure, 1 sorte d' herbes, eau	mout, hop, gist, 1 kruidensoort, water
	dark red with a steady, creamy foam head and nice bubbles; not filtered or pasteurised	rouge foncé avec un faux col stable, crémeux et joli pétillement; non filtrée, non pasteurisée	donkerrood met een stabiele, romige schuimkraag en mooie pareling; ongefilterd, niet gepasteuriseerd
	Strong character, slightly spiced, strong aftertaste, full-bodied.	Caractère fort, légèrement épicée, forte arrière-bouche, franche.	Stevig karakter, licht gekruid, sterke afdronk, volmondig.
	Serve in a degreased, dry and tilted Trappist glass.	Verser dan un verre trappiste dégraissé, sec et incliné	Uitschenken in een ontvet, droog en schuingehouden trappistenglas.
i			

	top-fermentation re-fermented in the bottle	fermentation haute refermentation en bouteille	hoge gisting hergisting op de fles
	tripel	triple	tripel
	barley, malt, hops, sugar, water. No herbs or syrups added.	orge, malt, houblon, sucre, eau . Sans adjonction d'herbes ou de sirops.	gerst, mout, hop, suiker, water. Er worden geen kruiden of siropen toegevoegd.
	golden yellow clear	jaune doré claire	goudgeel helder
	A perfectly well-balanced beer with a fruity flavour, not too bitter or too sweet.	Bière parfaitement équilibrée avec un arôme fruité pas trop amer, ni trop doux.	Perfect uitgebalanceerd bier met een fruitig aroma, dat niet te bitter en niet te zoet is.
	Keep the glass tilted and pour the beer slowly, with or without yeast sediment.	Tenir le verre en oblique et verser la bière lentement, avec ou sans dépôt de levure.	Het glas schuinhouden en het bier langzaam inschenken, met of zonder gistdepot.
i			

Vichtenaar

Brouwerij Verhaeghe 5,10% 4 °C / 8 - 12 ° 39 °F / 46 - 54 °

	mixed fermentation	fermentation mixte	gemengde gisting
	West-Flanders red-brown Flemish ale	brune-rouge de la Flandre Occidentale Flemish ale	Westvlaams roodbruin Flemish ale
	malt, hops, wheat, water. Matured in oak barrels for an average of eight months.	malt, houblon, froment, eau. Mûrit en moyenne 8 mois en fûts de chêne.	mout, hop, tarwe, water. Gemiddeld 8 maanden gerijpt op eikenhouten vaten.
	red-brown filtered	brun rouge filtrée	roodbruin gefilterd
	Thirst-quencher. Refreshing taste with a slightly sweet and fruity aftertaste.	Désaltérant. Saveur fraîche avec une fin de bouche légèrement douce et fruitée.	Dorstlesser. Frisse smaak met een lichtzoete en fruitige afdronk.
	Pour carefully in a cold, rinsed glass.	Verser prudemment dans un verre refroidi et rincé.	Voorzichtig uitschenken in een koud, gespoeld glas.
i			

Vieux Temps

B-Inbev Leuven 4,50% 3 °C 37 °F

	top-fermentation	fermentation haute	hoge gisting
	Belgian ale amber or speciale belge	Belgian ale ambrée ou spéciale belge	Belgian ale amber of speciale belge
	barley malt, corn, hops, invert sugar, water, colouring agent	malt d'orge, maïs, houblon, sucre inversif, eau, pigment	gerstemout, mais, hop, invertsuiker, water, kleurstof
	amber-coloured	ambrée	amberkleurig
	Fruity with a slightly dry aftertaste.	Fruitée, avec un peu d'arrière-bouche sèche.	Fruitig met ietwat droge afdronk.

Vigneronne

Brasserie Cantillon 6% 15° 59°

	spontaneous fermentation	fermentation spontanée	spontane gisting
	lambic-based fruit beer	bière fruitée à base de lambic	fruitbier op basis van lambiek
	barley malt (65%), wheat (35%), more than one-year old hops, muscat grapes (300 g/l), water	malt d'orge (65%), froment (35%), houblon de plus d'un an, raisin muscadet (300 g/l), eau	gerstemout (65%), tarwe (35%), overjaarse hop, muscatdruif (300 g/l), water
	gold-coloured not filtered or pasteurised	dorée non filtrée, non pasteurisée	goudkleurig ongefilterd, niet gepasteuriseerd
	Full of character and taste. Compromise between wine and beer: fruity white grape in harmony with 2-year old Lambic that is full of character.	Bière très caractéristique et goûteuse. Compromis entre le vin et la bière :du raisin blanc fruité en harmonie avec du lambic typique de 2 ans.	Karakter- en smaakvol. Compromis tussen wijn en bier: fruitige witte druif in harmonie met karaktervolle lambiek van 2 jaar.
	Serve in a wine glass. Hold the glass reasonably upright.	Verser dans un verre de vin. Tenir le verre plus ou moins en position verticale.	Uitschenken in een wijnglas. Het glas tamelijk recht houden.
i			

Brouwerij Huyghe

8%

	top-fermentation re-fermented in the bottle	fermentation haute refermentation en bouteille	hoge gisting hergisting in de fles
	regional beer tripel abbey beer	bière régionale bière d'abbaye triple	streekbier abdijbier tripel
	barley malt, hops, yeast, re-fermentation sugar, water, coriander and orange rind	malt d'orge, houblon, levure, sucre de refermentation, eau, coriandre et écorce d'orange	gerstemout, hop, gist, hergistingssuiker, water, koriander en sinaasschil
	blond slightly cloudy with fine bubbly foam	blonde légèrement trouble avec faux col légèrement perlant	blond lichttroebel met fijn parelschuim
	Taste of hops, coriander and orange rind. Aftertaste: controlled bitterness, pleasant freshness, alcohol.	Goût de houblon, coriandre et écorce d'orange. Fin de bouche :goût amer contrôlé, fraîcheur agréable, alcool.	Smaak van hop, koriander en sinaasschil. Afdronk: gecontroleerde bitterheid, aangename frisheid, alcohol.
	Also available in a brown version 'Vieille Villers'.	Egalement disponible dans une version brune 'Vieille Villers'.	Bestaat ook in een bruine versie 'Vieille Villers'.

Villers Vieille

Brouwerij Huyghe 7% 6 ° 43 °

	top-fermentation re-fermentation in the bottle	fermentation haute refermentation en bouteille	hoge gisting hergisting in de fles
	double abbey beer	bière d'abbaye double	dubbel abdijbier
	dark malt and pilsner malt, hops, yeast, re-fermentation sugar, water	malts foncés et malt de pils, houblon, levure, sucre de refermentation, eau	donkere mouten en pilsmout, hop, gist, hergistingssuiker, water
	not filtered or pasteurised	non filtrée, non pasteurisée	ongefilterd, niet gepasteuriseerd
	Decidedly full-bodied and sweet with a bitter twist at the end.	Très franche et douceâtre, avec un petit rien d'amère dans l'arrière-bouche.	Zeer volmondig en zoetig met een klein bittertje in de afdronk.
	Serve in a typical goblet.	Verser dans un verre calice typique.	Uitschenken in de typische kelk.
i	Specially brewed for the region of Villers-la-Ville (well-known abbey).	Spécialement brassée pour la région de la célèbre abbaye de Villers-la-Ville.	Speciaal gebrouwen voor de streek van Villers-la-Ville (bekende abdij).

an Viven by De Proefbrouwerij

5% 5 - 8 °C 41 - 46 °F

	top-fermentation re-fermentation in the bottle centrifuged	fermentation haute refermentation en bouteille centrifugée	hoge gisting hergisting op de fles gecentrifugeerd
	amber or speciale belge	ambrée ou spéciale belge	amber of speciale belge
	malt, hops (Goldings), yeast, water	malt, houblon (Goldings), levure, eau	mout, hop (Goldings), gist, water
	amber-coloured with a full white foam head not filtered, pasteurised	ambrée avec un faux col plein blanc non filtrée, pasteurisée	amberkleurig met een volle witte schuimkraag ongefilterd, gepasteuriseerd
	Fruity aromas of citrus and pears. Hoppy and slightly bitter. Fruity accents of peach and apricot flavour.	Arômes fruités de citrus et de poires. Houblonné et légèrement amer. Accents fruités de pêche et d'abricot dans le goût.	Fruitige aroma's van citrus en peren. Hoppig en licht bitter. Fruitige accenten van perzik en abrikoos in de smaak.
	Pour gently into a tilted tulip glass. Hold the glass upright halfway through for a fine foam head.	Verser lentement dans un verre tulipe tenu incliné. Relever le verre en position verticale à mi-chemin pour former un faux col solide.	Langzaam uitschenken in een schuingehouden tulpglas. Het glas halverwege rechthouden voor een mooie schuimkraag.
	Declared Belgium's best speciale belge by a beer panel of Het Nieuwsblad (paper) in 2010.	Proclamée en 2010 meilleure spéciale belge de Belgique par les experts de la bière du journal Het Nieuwsblad.	In 2010 door het bierpanel van Het Nieuwsblad uitgeroepen tot beste speciale belge van België.

Viven Blond

van Viven by De Proefbrouwerij 6,10% 8 - 10 ° 46 - 50 °

top-fermentation	fermentation haute	hoge gisting
blond	blonde	blond
brewed with Poperinge hop varieties	brassée avec des variétés de houblon de Poperinge	gebrouwen met Poperingse hopsoorten
hazy gold with a nice, firm white foam head filtered, pasteurised	doré fade avec un faux col joli, stable blanc filtrée, pasteurisée	wazig goudachtig met een mooie, vaste witte schuimkraag gefilterd, gepasteuriseerd
Hay flavour with hints of green apple.	Caractère de foin, intentions de pommes vertes.	Hooiachtig, intenties van groene appels.
Pour slowly into a tulip glass. Very effervescent, so hold the bottle close to the glass.	Verser lentement dans un verre tulipe. La bière écumant facilement, tenir la bouteille près du verre.	Traag uitschenken in een tulpvormig glas. Het bier schuimt gemakkelijk, het flesje best dicht bij het glas houden.
Still brewed according to the original recipe of Willy de Lobel, founder of the brand Viven (then called Kapel van Viven).	Toujours brassée selon la recette d'origine de Willy de Lobel, fondateur de la marque Viven (appelée à l'époque Kapel van Viven).	Nog steeds gebrouwen volgens het originele recept van Willy de Lobel, stichter van het merk Viven (destijds Kapel van Viven genoemd).

an Viven by De Proefbrouwerij

6,10% 8 °C 46 °F

Viven Bruin

	top-fermentation	fermentation haute	hoge gisting
	double	double	dubbel
	brewed with Poperinge hop varieties	brassée avec des variétés de houblon de Poperinge	gebrouwen met Poperingse hopsoorten
	hazy red-brown with a full, white-beige foam head filtered, pasteurised	brun rou ge fade avec un faux col plein, blanc beige filtrée, pasteurisée	wazig roodbruin met een volle, witbeige schuimkraag gefilterd, gepasteuriseerd
	Roasted malt with tasty hints of chocolate. Nuances of caramel and mocha.	Malt torréfié, avec des nuances de délicieux chocolat. Nuances de caramel et de moka.	Gebrande mout met lekkere chocoladetinten. Nuances van karamel en mokka.
	Serve in a slightly tilted tulip glass. Lift the bottle at the halfway stage away from the glass to obtain a fine foam head.	Verser dans un verre tulipe tenu légèrement incliné. Eloigner la bouteille quelque peu du verre à mi chemin pour former un faux col solide.	Uitschenken in een licht schuingehouden tulpvormig glas. De fles halverwege wat van het glas verwijderen voor een mooie schuimkraag.
i			

Viven Imperial IPA

van Viven by De Proefbrouwerij 8% 10° 50°

	top-fermentation	fermentation haute	hoge gisting
	Imperial IPA	Imperial IPA	Imperial IPA
	brewed with Tomahawk and Simcoe hops	brassée avec houblon Tomahawk et Simcoe	gebrouwen met Tomahawk en Simcoe hop
	hazy yellow-green glow, firm white foam head not filtered, pasteurised	reflet fade jaune vert, faux col solide blanc non filtrée, pasteurisée	wazige geelgroenige schijn, stevige witte schuimkraag ongefilterd, gepasteuriseerd
	Definitely hoppy with accents of citrus. Fruity nose with floral touches. Extensive range of flavours with distinct hops. Pleasantly bitter, citrusy with touches of pink grapefruit and resin.	Fortement houblonné, avec des accents de citrus. Bouquet fruité, avec des touches florales. Large palette de goûts, avec clairement du houblon. Agréablement amer, caractère de citrus, avec des touches de pamplemousse rose et de résine.	Stevig hoppig met citrusaccenten. Fruitige neus met florale toetsen. Uitgebreid smakenpalet met duidelijke hop. Aangenaam bitter, citrusachtig met toetsen van roze pompelmoes en hars.
	Serve in a wine glass. Hold the glass reasonably upright.	Tenir le verre (de vin) plus ou moins en position verticale.	Uitschenken in een wijnglas. Het glas tamelijk recht houden.
	A unique recipe that is reminiscent of the original IPAs of the American west coast. Was voted the second best beer (after Westvleteren) at the BAB beer fair in 2009.	Une recette unique qui fait rêver des IPA originales de la côte ouest américaine. Elle a été élue 2e meilleure bière (après la Westvleteren) à la foire de la bière BAB de 2009.	Een uniek recept dat doet dromen van de originele IPA's van de Amerikaanse westkust. Het bier werd op de BAB bierbeurs van 2009 tot 2e beste bier (na Westvleteren) verkozen.

7% 5 - 12 °C 41 - 54 °F

	top-fermentation	fermentation haute	hoge gisting
	smoked Porter	smoked Porter	smoked Porter
	brewed with American bitter hops and smoked malts	brassée avec houblon amer Américain et malt fumé	gebrouwen met Amerikaanse bitterhop en gerookte mout
	deep black with pale brown, full foam head not filtered, pasteurised	noir foncé avec faux col plein brun clair non filtrée, pasteurisée	donkerzwart met lichtbruine, volle schuimkraag ongefilterd, gepasteuriseerd
	Smoky undertones with light liqueur aromas. Mocha scent with touches of peat and leather. Distinctly smoked malt, supplemented with American bitter hops and dark chocolate.	Notes fumées, avec de légers arômes de liqueur. Parfum de moka, avec des touches de tourbe et de cuir. Malt fumé prononcé, complété par du houblon amer américain et du chocolat fondant.	Gerookte noten met lichte likeuraroma's. Mokkageur met toetsen van turf en leder. Uitgesproken gerookte mout, aangevuld met Amerikaanse bitterhop en fondantchocolade.
	Serve in a tilted tulip or wine glass. Hold the glass upright halfway through for a fine foam head.	Verser lentement dans un verre tulipe ou verre de vin tenu incliné. Relever le verre en position verticale à mi-chemin pour former un faux col solide.	Uitschenken in een schuingehouden tulp- of wijnglas. Het glas halverwege rechthouden voor een mooie schuimkraag.
	Launched as a try-out at the BAB beer festival in Bruges in 2009.	A été lancée à titre d'essai en 2009 au festival de la bière BAB à Bruges.	Als try-out gelanceerd in 2009 op het BAB bierfestival te Brugge.

Vlaamsche Leeuw Blondje

van Vlaanderen by Brouwerij Van Steenberge **5,50%** 4 - 6° 39 - 43°

	top-fermentation post-fermentation in the bottle	fermentation haute refermentation en bouteille	hoge gisting nagisting op de fles
	blond	blonde	blond
	Session beer with a nice body.	Facilement buvable, au joli corps.	Doordrinkbier met mooie body.

top-fermentation post-fermentation in the bottle	fermentation haute refermentation en bouteille	hoge gisting nagisting op de fles
double	double	dubbel
deep brown	brun profond	diepbruin
Full-bodied with a slightly sweet taste owing to the dark malt, and a soft bitter, yet fruity aftertaste.	Franche, avec un goût légèrement sucrée du malt foncé, et une arrière-bouche doucement amère, fruitée.	Volmondig met een lichtzoete smaak van de donkere mout, en een zacht bittere, fruitige afdronk.

Vlaamsche Leeuw Donker

Vlaamsche Leeuw Tripel

van Vlaanderen by Brouwerij Van Steenberge 8,50%

	top-fermentation post-fermentation in the bottle	fermentation haute refermentation en bouteille	hoge gisting nagisting op de fles
	tripel	triple	tripel
	blond, clear	blonde, claire	blond, helder
	Aroma of Saaz hops, soft malt and scented fruitiness of pears and apples in the aftertaste.	Arôme de houblon Saaz, malt doux et fruité parfumé de poires et de pommes en arrière-bouche.	Aroma van Saaz hop, zachte mout en geparfumeerde fruitigheid van peren en appels in de afdronk.

6,50% 6 °C 43 °F

	top-fermentation re-fermentation in the bottle	fermentation haute refermentation en bouteille	hoge gisting hergisting in de fles
	blond	blonde	blond
	3 malt types, 3 different hops, sugar, yeast, water	3 variétés de malt, 3 variétés de houblon, sucre levure, eau	3 moutsoorten, 3 hopsoorten, suiker, gist, water
	blond pilsner colour with persistent white foam head (18 EBC) not filtered or pasteurised	blond pils avec un faux col stable blanc (18 EBC) non filtrée, non pasteurisée	blonde pilskleur met persistente witte schuimkraag (18 EBC) ongefilterd, niet gepasteuriseerd
	Malty, spicy taste with a soft, bitter aftertaste.	Goût malté, épicé, avec une arrière-bouche doucement amère.	Moutige, kruidige smaak met een zacht bittere afdronk.
	Pour out slowly and leave the yeast sediment (approx. 1 cm) in the bottle.	Verser lentement et laisser le dépôt de levure (ca. 1 cm) dans la bouteille.	Langzaam uitschenken en het gistdepot (ca. 1 cm) in de fles laten.
i	Brewed to accompany Vlaskaas.	Brassée pour être dégustée avec du fromage de lin (le vlaskaas).	Gebrouwen om te degusteren bij vlaskaas.

Vlaskapelle

Brouwerij Gulden Spoor

5% 8 - 10 ° 46 - 50 °

	top-fermentation re-fermentation in the bottle not centrifuged	fermentation haute refermentation en bouteille non centrifugée	hoge gisting hergisting in de fles niet gecentrifugeerd
	Flemish red-brown	bière Flamande brune rouge	Vlaams roodbruin
	barley malt, whisky malt, hops, yeast, water	malt d'orge, malt de whisky, houblon, levure, eau	gerstemout, whisky-mout, hop, gist, water
	red and clear with small foam head not filtered or pasteurised	rouge et limpide avec faux col petit non filtrée, non pasteurisée	rood en helder met kleine schuimkraag ongefilterd, niet gepasteuriseerd
	Pleasant session beer with caramel touches and aromas of roasted chocolate. Long, surprising aftertaste owing to the whisky malt.	Bière facilement buvable agréable, avec des touches de caramel et des arômes de chocolat brûlé. Arrière-bouche longue, surprenante du fait du malt de whisky.	Aangename doordrinker met karameltoetsen en aroma's van gebrande chocolade. Lange, verrassende afdronk door de whisky-mout.
	Degrease the glass, tilt it slightly and carefully pour the beer in a single movement.	Dégraisser le verre, le tenir légèrement incliné et verser la bière prudemment d'un seul mouvement.	Het glas vetvrij maken, licht schuin houden en het bier voorzichtig in 1 beweging uitschenken.
	Carnival beer of Gullegem.	Bière du carnaval de Gullegem.	Karnavalsbier van Gullegem.

Vlaskop Gerstebier

Brouwerij Strubbe

5,50% 6 °C 43 °F

	top-fermentation re-fermented in the bottle	fermentation haute refermentation en bouteille	hoge gisting nagisting op de fles
	witbier	bière blanche	witbier
	40% unmalted barley, wheat, oat, rye, herbs, hops, yeast, water	40 % orge non maltée, froment, avoine, orge, herbes, houblon, levure, eau	40 % ongemoute gerst, tarwe, haver, rogge, kruiden, hop, gist, water
	blond cloudy (unfiltered)	blonde trouble (non filtrée)	blond troebel (ongefilterd)
	Fruity. Refreshing, thirst-quenching session beer.	Fruitée. Bière facilement buvable fraîche et désaltérante.	Fruitig. Fris en dorstlessend doordrinkbier.
	Unlike most Witbier brands, this one is based on unmalted barley instead of wheat.	Contrairement à la plupart des bières blanches, cette bière est produite à base d'orge non maltée au lieu de froment.	In tegenstelling tot de meeste witbieren is Vlaskop gemaakt op basis van ongemoute gerst in plaats van tarwe.

Vleteren Alt

Brouwerij Deca

8% 6 - 10 ° 43 - 50 °

	top-fermentation re-fermented in the bottle	fermentation haute refermentation en bouteille	hoge gisting hergisting op de fles
	dark ale	ale foncée	ale donker
	barley malt, hops, candy sugar, yeast, water	malt d'orge, houblon, sucre candi, levure, eau	gerstemout, hop, kandijsuiker, gist, water
	dark brown	brun foncé	donkerbruin
	Bottle can be emptied.	Peut être versée complètement.	Mag helemaal uitgeschonken worden.
i			

Brouwerij DijkWaert

11% — 6 - 8 °C / 43 - 46 °F

Vurig Bierreke

	top-fermentation natural re-fermentation in the bottle	fermentation haute refermentation naturelle en bouteille	hoge gisting natuurlijke hergisting in de fles
	strong blond tripel	blonde forte triple	sterk blond tripel
	malt, hops, herbs, yeasts, water	malt, houblon, herbes, levures, eau	mout, hop, kruiden, gisten, water
	gold (7.75 EBC)	dorée (7,75 EBC)	gold (7,75 EBC)
	Spicy beer with a touch of citrus, subtly bitter (27 EBU).	Bière épicée, avec une touche de citrus, subtilement amère (27 EBU).	Kruidig bier met een citrustoets, subtiel bitter (27 EBU).
i			

Waaslander

Brouwerij Boelens

6,50% 7° 45°

	top-fermentation re-fermented in the bottle	fermentation haute refermentation en bouteille	hoge gisting hergisting in de fles
	witbier	bière blanche	witbier
	barley malt, wheat malt, citric herbs, hops, brewer's yeast, water	malt d'orge, malt de froment, herbes de citron, houblon, levure de bière, eau	gerstemout, tarwemout, citruskruiden, hop, biergist, water
	blond slightly cloudy	blonde légèrement trouble	blond licht troebel
	Very spicy summer beer, smooth and light, with a complex taste due to the use of citrus, coriander and curaçao. Typical wheat aftertaste.	Bière d'été tres relevée, douce et légère, goût complexe par l'utilisation d'agrumes, de coriandre et de curaçao. Arrière-bouche typique de froment.	Zeer kruidig zomerbier, zacht en licht, complexe smaak door het gebruik van citrus, koriander en curaçao. Typische tarweafdronk.
	Pour carefully, so the yeast sediment remains at the bottom of the bottle.	Verser prudemment pour tenir le dépôt de levure au fond de la bouteille.	Voorzichtig uitschenken om het gistbezinksel op de bodem te houden.
i			

Wase Wolf - Bier uit het Waasland

Brouwerij Boelens — 6,50% — 5 - 7 °C / 41 - 45 °F

	top-fermentation re-fermented in the bottle	fermentation haute refermentation en bouteille	hoge gisting hergisting op de fles
	witbier amber	bière blanche ambrée	witbier amber
	wheat, caramel malt, coriander, yeast, water	froment, malt de caramel, coriandre, levure, eau	tarwe, karamelmout, koriander, gist, water
	amber clear	ambrée claire	amber helder
	Very spicy amber beer with a touch of coriander. The added caramel is noticeable in the taste.	Bière ambrée très relevée avec une touche de coriandre. L'adjonction de caramel se traduit dans la saveur.	Sterk gekruid amberbier met een toets van koriander. De toevoeging van karamel vertaalt zich in de smaak.
	Pour carefully, so the yeast sediment remains at the bottom of the bottle.	Verser prudemment pour tenir le dépôt de levure au fond de la bouteille.	Voorzichtig uitschenken om het gistbezinksel op de bodem te houden.
i	Refers to the legend of 'The Wolf of the Waasland' anno 2000.	Renvoie à la légende du 'Loup du Waasland' anno 2000.	Verwijst naar de legende van 'De Wolf van het Waasland' anno 2000.

Waterloo Double 8 Dark

Brasserie du Bocq

8,50% 8 °C 46 °F

	top-fermentation	fermentation haute	hoge gisting
	strong double	double forte	sterk dubbel
	brown with a fine, rich foam head	brune avec un faux col fin, riche	bruin met een fijne, rijke schuimkraag
	Punchy but well-balanced aroma of fresh yeast and herbs. Touches of roasted malt and hops flavour. Slightly caramelised but mellow and harmonious with a fruity touch.	Arôme puissant mais équilibré de levure fraîche et d'épices. Touches de malt torréfié et de houblon dans le goût. Légèrement caramélisé, mais rond et harmonieux, avec une touche fruitée.	Krachtig maar evenwichtig aroma van verse gist en kruiden. Toetsen van gebrande mout en hop in de smaak. Licht gekaramelliseerd maar rond en harmonieus met een fruitige toets.
	Boutique beer that was brewed originally by 'La Brasserie du Marché' in Eigenbrakel (1456). This beer is said to give the troops courage and strength during the Battle of Waterloo.	Bière artisanale qui fut à l'origine brassée par 'La Brasserie du Marché' à Braine-l'Alleud (1456). Cette bière allait donner des forces et du courage aux combattants pendant la Bataille de Waterloo.	Ambachtelijk bier dat origineel werd gebrouwen door 'La Brasserie du Marché' in Eigenbrakel (1456). Dit bier zou kracht en moed geven aan de strijdkrachten tijdens de Slag bij Waterloo.

Brasserie du Bocq

7,50% 8 °C 46 °F

	top-fermentation	fermentation haute	hoge gisting
	tripel	triple	tripel
	blond with a fine, rich foam head	blonde avec un faux col fin, riche	blond met een fijne, rijke schuimkraag
	Harmonious aroma of green apple and fine hops. Smooth and mellow character beer. Not bitter, malty taste with a touch of fruit.	Arôme harmonieux de pomme verte et de houblon fin. Bière de caractère ronde et onctueuse. Peu amère, goût malté, avec un peu de fruité.	Harmonieus aroma van groene appel en fijne hop. Rond en smeuïg karakterbier. Weinig bitter, moutsmaak met iets fruitigs.
	Boutique beer that was brewed originally by 'La Brasserie du Marché' in Eigenbrakel (1456). This beer is said to give the troops courage and strength during the Battle of Waterloo.	Bière artisanale qui fut à l'origine brassée par 'La Brasserie du Marché' à Braine-l'Alleud (1456). Cette bière allait donner des forces et du courage aux combattants pendant la Bataille de Waterloo.	Ambachtelijk bier dat origineel werd gebrouwen door 'La Brasserie du Marché' in Eigenbrakel (1456). Dit bier zou kracht en moed geven aan de strijdkrachten tijdens de Slag bij Waterloo.

Watou Tripel

Brouwerij Sint-Bernardus 7,50% 4 - 8 °C 39 - 46 °F

	top-fermentation re-fermented in the bottle	fermentation haute refermentation en bouteille	hoge gisting hergisting op de fles
	Belgian abbey beer tripel	Bière d'abbaye belge triple	Belgisch abdijbier tripel
	malt varieties, hops, sugar, yeast and 'historical' water (rain water fallen in Jeanne d'Arc's time, pumped in Watou)	sortes de malt, houblon, sucre, levure et eau 'historique' (pompée à Watou et provenant de l'époque de Jeanne d'Arc)	moutsoorten, hop, suiker, gist en 'historisch' water (opgepompt in Watou en afkomstig uit de tijd dat Jeanne d'Arc leefde)
	amber/blond unfiltered	ambrée/blonde non filtrée	amber/blond ongefilterd
	Agreeably smooth flavour, slightly bitter and well-balanced, with a fruity orange touch and fresh aftertaste.	Arôme doux agréable, légèrement amer et équilibré avec une touche fruitée d'orange et une fin de bouche fraîche.	Aangenaam zacht aroma, licht bitter en evenwichtig met fruitige sinaastoets en frisse afdronk.
	Pour into a glass, rinsed with cold water. Keep the glass upright and pour the beer carefully in a single movement. The yeast sediment can be left in the bottle or drunk separately.	Verser dans un verre rincé à l'eau froide. Laisser le verre en position verticale et verser la bière prudemment en un seul mouvement. Laisser le dépôt de levure dans la bouteille ou le boire séparément.	Uitschenken in een met koud water gespoeld glas. Het glas rechtop laten staan en het bier in 1 vloeiende beweging voorzichtig uitschenken. Het gistdepot (kan desgewenst apart worden uitgedronken) in de fles laten.
i			

Brouwerij Van Eecke

Watou's Wit Bier

5% 3 °C 37 °F

	top-fermentation	fermentation haute	hoge gisting
	witbier	bière blanche	witbier
	malt, wheat, spices, yeast, water	malt, froment, condiments, levure, eau	mout, tarwe, specerijen, gist, water
	light yellow, cloudy	jaune clair, trouble	lichtgeel, troebel
	Refreshing thirst-quencher. Sourish taste with fruity coriander.	Désaltérant frais. Saveur légèrement acidulée avec une touche de coriandre fruitée.	Frisse dorstlesser. Lichtzure smaak met fruitige koriander.
	Pour slowly in a single, smooth movement in a degreased glass. Keep the glass tilted to avoid sloshing. Leave the last 4 cm in the bottle. Next, revolve the bottle to loosen the yeast sediment. Empty the bottle and skim off the foam.	Verser lentement et en un seul mouvement fluide dans un verre dégraissé tenu en oblique. Ne pas laisser la bière clapoter. Laisser les derniers 4 cm de bière dans la bouteille et secouer pour dégager le dépôt de levure. Vider la bouteille et écumer le verre.	Traag en in 1 vloeiende beweging uitschenken in een vetvrij glas dat wordt schuingehouden. Het bier niet laten klotsen. De laatste 4 cm in de fles laten en rondwalsen om de gistsluier los te maken. De fles leegschenken en het glas afschuimen.
i			

West Pils

Brouwerij Het Sas 5% 4 °C 39 °F

bottom-fermentation	fermentation basse	lage gisting
pilsner or lager beer	pils ou lager	pils- of lagerbier
barley malt, hops, yeast, water	malt d'orge, houblon, levure, eau	gerstemout, hop, gist, water
blond, clear with a fine-lace white foam head filtered, not pasteurised	blonde, limpide avec faux col compact blanc filtrée, non pasteurisée	blond, helder met fijnmazig wit schuim gefilterd, niet gepasteuriseerd
Malty onset, hoppy aftertaste.	Première approche maltée, arrière-bouche houblonnée.	Moutige aanzet, hoppige afdronk.
Pour in a single movement and skim off the excess.	Verser agilement et écumer.	Doorschenken en afschuimen.

Westmalle Trappist Dubbel

Brouwerij van de Abdij ter Trappisten 7% 10 - 14 °C / 46 - 54 °F

top-fermentation natural re-fermentation in the bottle centrifuged	fermentation haute refermentation naturelle en bouteille centrifugée	hoge gisting natuurlijke hergisting in de fles gecentrifugeerd
trappist beer	trappiste	trappistenbier
barley malt, sugar, hops, yeast, water	malt d'orge, sucre, houblon, levure, eau	gerstemout, suiker, hop, gist, water
dark red-brown with a cream-coloured foam head which leaves a nice lace pattern on the glass.	foncé brun rouge avec un faux col crème laissant une jolie dentelle au verre	donker roodbruin met crèmekleurige schuimkraag die een mooi 'kantwerk' in het glas achterlaat.
Special malt scent. Rich and complex flavour, spicy and fruity with a fresh-bitter finale. Well-balanced with soft feeling in the mouth and long, dry aftertaste.	Parfum de malt spécial. Goût riche et complexe, épicé et fruité, avec une finale fraîchement amère. Équilibré, avec une sensation douce en bouche et une longue arrière-bouche sèche.	Geur van speciale mout. Rijke en complexe smaak, kruidig en fruitig met een frisbittere finale. Evenwichtig met zacht mondgevoel en lange, droge afdronk.
see Westmalle tripel	cfr Triple Westmalle	cfr. Westmalle tripel
Brewed since 1856 by the monks who, alongside their table beer, also produced dark Trappist. In 1926, the recipe was adapted and the beer became heavier. This is at the basis of the current double.	Depuis 1856, les moines brassent, à côté de leur bière de repas, aussi une trappiste foncée. En 1926, la recette a été adaptée et la bière est devenue un peu plus forte. C'est la base de l'actuelle double.	Sinds 1856 brouwen de monniken naast hun maaltijdbier nog een donkere trappist. In 1926 werd het recept aangepast en werd het bier wat zwaarder. Daar ligt de basis voor de huidige dubbel.

Westmalle Trappist Tripel

Brouwerij van de Abdij ter Trappisten 9,50% 10 - 14 °C / 46 - 54 °F

	top-fermentation natural re-fermentation in the bottle; centrifuged	fermentation haute refermentation naturelle en bouteille; centrifugée	hoge gisting natuurlijke hergisting in de fles; gecentrifugeerd
	trappist beer	trappiste	trappistenbier
	barley malt, sugar, hops, yeast, water	malt d'orge, sucre, levure, houblon, eau	gerstemout, suiker, hop, gist, water
	Complex beer with a fruity scent and well-balanced hoppy nose. Soft and creamy in the mouth with bitter touch that is carried by the fruity aroma. Much finesse and elegance and a wonderfully long aftertatse.	Bière complexe, avec un parfum fruité et un bouquet de houblon nuancé. Douce et veloutée en bouche, avec une touche amère qui est soutenue par l'arôme de fruits. Beaucoup de finesse et d'élégance et une agréable longue arrière-bouche.	Complex bier met een fruitige geur en genuanceerde hopneus. Zacht en romig in de mond met bittere toets die gedragen wordt door het fruitaroma. Veel finesse en elegantie en een heerlijk lange afdronk.
	Pour slowly and in a single movement along the rim of a degreased, tilted chalice (for added aroma and thick foam head). Hold glass vertical at the end and pour beer into the middle. Drink yeast sediment of approx. 1 cm separately.	Verser lentement et d'un seul mouvement autour du bord d'un verre calice dégraissé, incliné (pour un arôme supplémentaire et un faux col riche). A la fin tenir le verre horizontalement et verser au milieu. Boire séparément Le fond de levure de ca 1 cm.	Langzaam en 1 beweging uitschenken langs de rand van een vetvrij, schuingehouden kelkglas (voor extra aroma en rijke schuimkraag). Op het einde het glas horizontaal houden en in het midden schenken. Gistbodem van ca. 1 cm apart uitdrinken.
i	Sometimes referred to as the 'mother of all tripels'. Brewed for the first time in the abbey in 1934 to mark the commissioning of the new brewing room. The yeast sediment is rich in vitamin B and has a blood-cleansing effect.	On l'appelle à l'occasion la 'mère de toutes les triples'. Elle a été brassée pour la première fois à l'abbaye en 1934, dans le cadre de la mise en service de la nouvelle salle de brassage. Le dépôt de levure est riche en vitamine B et a un effet dépuratif.	Wordt wel eens de 'moeder van alle tripels' genoemd. Werd in 1934 voor het eerst in de abdij gebrouwen n.a.v. de ingebruikname van de nieuwe brouwzaal. De gistbodem is rijk aan vitamine B en heeft een bloedzuiverend effect.

Brouwerij der Sint-Sixtusabdij

10% 12 - 16 °C / 54 - 61 °F

	top-fermentation re-fermented in the bottle	fermentation haute refermentation en bouteille	hoge gisting nagisting op de fles
	dark trappist	trappiste foncée	trappist donker
	malt, hops, sugar, yeast, water	malt, houblon, sucre, levure, eau	mout, hop, suiker, gist, water
	red-brown clear	brun rouge claire	roodbruin helder
	Full, creamy aroma. Rich, caramel-like and malt flavour palette.	Arôme plein et crémeux. Palette de saveurs riche, caramélisée et maltée.	Vol, romig aroma. Rijk, karamelachtig en moutig smaakpalet.
	Pour carefully into a goblet.	Verser prudemment dans un verre calice.	Voorzichtig uitschenken in een kelkglas.
i	Store the bottles upright in a dark room between 12 and 18 °C.	Conserver les bouteilles en position verticale à l'abri de la lumière entre 12 et 18 °C.	De flessen verticaal op een donkere plaats bewaren tussen 12 en 18 °C.

Westvleteren 8

Brouwerij der Sint-Sixtusabdij 8% 12 - 16 ° / 54 - 61 °

	top-fermentation re-fermented in the bottle	fermentation haute refermentation en bouteille	hoge gisting nagisting op de fles
	dark trappist	trappiste foncée	trappist donker
	malt, hops, sugar, yeast, water	malt, houblon, sucre, levure, eau	mout, hop, suiker, gist, water
	red-brown clear	brun rouge claire	roodbruin helder
	Sweetish, fruity aroma with a melon accent.	Arôme sucré, fruité avec accent de melon.	Zoetig, fruitig aroma met een meloenaccent.
	Pour carefully into a goblet.	Verser prudemment dans un verre calice.	Voorzichtig uitschenken in een kelkglas.
i	Store the bottles upright in a dark room between 12 and 18 °C.	Conserver les bouteilles en position verticale à l'abri de la lumière entre 12 et 18 °C.	De flessen verticaal op een donkere plaats bewaren tussen 12 en 18 °C.

Westvleteren Blond

Brouwerij der Sint-Sixtusabdij 5,80% 12 - 16 °C / 54 - 61 °F

	top-fermentation re-fermented in the bottle	fermentation haute refermentation en bouteille	hoge gisting nagisting op de fles
	blond trappist	trappiste blonde	trappist blond
	malt, hops, sugar, yeast, water	malt, houblon, sucre, levure, eau	mout, hop, suiker, gist, water
	blond clear	blonde claire	blond helder
	Hoppy, spicy aroma. Slightly smooth taste with pronounced bitter aftertaste.	Arôme houblonné, relevé. Saveur légèrement moelleuse avec une fin de bouche amère prononcée.	Hoppig, kruidig aroma. Lichtzacht van smaak met geaccentueerde bittere afdronk.
	Pour carefully into a goblet.	Verser prudemment dans un verre calice.	Voorzichtig uitschenken in een kelkglas.
	Store the bottles upright in a dark room between 12 and 18 °C.	Conserver les bouteilles en position verticale à l'abri de la lumière entre 12 et 18 °C.	De flessen verticaal op een donkere plaats bewaren tussen 12 en 18 °C.

Brouwerij Haacht

5,10% — 3 °C / 37 °F

	top-fermentation	fermentation haute	hoge gisting
	white beer	bière blanche	witbier
	barley and wheat malt (30%), wheat, sugar, hops, orange peel, coriander, anti-oxidant (ascorbic acid), yeast, water	malt d'orge et de froment (30%), froment, sucre, houblon, écorce d'oranges, coriandre, antioxydant (acide ascorbine), levure, eau	gerste- en tarwemout (30%), tarwe, suiker, hop, sinaasschil, koriander, antioxidant (ascorbinezuur), gist, water
	naturally slightly cloudy not filtered	légèrement trouble naturel non filtrée	natuurlijk licht troebel ongefilterd
	Thirst-quencher with a full, pleasant sense in the mouth. Refined and spicy aroma owing to the subtle touches of coriander and orange peel. Fleeting fruity touches.	Bière désaltérante, avec une sensation en bouche franche et agréable. Arôme raffiné et épicé, grâce aux subtiles touches de coriandre et d'écorce d'orange. Touches fruitées volatiles.	Dorstlessend met een vol, aangenaam mondgevoel. Verfijnd en kruidig aroma door de subtiele toetsen van koriander en sinaasschil. Vluchtige fruitige toetsen.
	Pour 3/4 into a rinsed, wet glass. Twist the bottle briskly to loosen up the yeast sediment and pour out the rest of the beer while turning the bottle vertically.	Verser 3/4 dans un verre rincé, humide. Tourner brièvement la bouteille pour dégager le dépôt de levure et verser le restant de la bière en relevant la bouteille en position verticale.	3/4 uitschenken in een gespoeld, nat glas. De fles kort draaien om de gistbodem los te maken en het resterende bier uitschenken terwijl je de fles recht brengt.
i	Basic beer for the Mystic fruit beers.	Bière de base pour les bières de fruits Mystic.	Basisbier voor de Mystic-fruitbieren.

Wieze Tripel Blond

Brouwerij Wieze

8% 9 °C 48 °F

top-fermentation re-fermentation in the bottle not centrifuged	fermentation haute refermentation en bouteille non centrifugée	hoge gisting hergisting in de fles niet gecentrifugeerd
tripel	triple	tripel
pilsner and ale malt, 2 different hops, herbs, yeast, well water	malt de pils et malt de ale, 2 variétés de houblon, herbes, levure, eau de puits	pils- en alemout, 2 hopsoorten, kruiden, gist, putwater
gold-blond, slightly cloudy (owing to the yeast cells in post-fermentation) not filtered or pasteurised	blond doré, légèrement trouble (à cause des cellules de levure de la refermentation) non filtrée, non pasteurisée	goudblond, licht troebel (door de gistcellen van de nagisting) ongefilterd, niet gepasteuriseerd
Aromatic with sweet touches and a slightly tart aftertaste.	Aromatique, avec des touches sucrées et une arrière-bouche légèrement amère.	Aromatisch met zoete toetsen en een licht bittere afdronk.
Pour 1/3 into a tripel glass, revolve the remainder in the bottle and pour out gently.	Verser un tiers dans un verre triple, remuer le restant dans la bouteille et verser prudemment.	Een derde inschenken in een tripelglas, het restant rondwalsen in de fles en voorzichtig uitschenken.
This tripel breathed new life into Wieze as beer village. The logo of the old brewery Wieze is brought back to life.	Avec cette triple, un nouveau départ fut donné à Wieze en tant que village de la bière. Le logo de l'ancienne brasserie Wieze renaît.	Met deze tripel werd een nieuwe start gegeven aan Wieze als bierdorp. Het logo van de vroegere brouwerij Wieze komt weer tot leven.

Wieze Tripel Zoet Bruin

Brouwerij Wieze

8% 9 °C 48 °F

	top-fermentation re-fermentation in the bottle not centrifuged	fermentation haute refermentation en bouteille non centrifugée	hoge gisting hergisting in de fles niet gecentrifugeerd
	sweet brown tripel desert beer	triple brune sucrée bière de dessert	zoete bruine tripel dessertbier
	pilsner, ale, cara, roasted malt, hops, herbs, yeast, well water	malt de pils, malt de ale, malt de cara et malt torréfié, houblon, herbes, levure, eau de puits	pils-, ale-, cara- en roostmout, hop, kruiden, gist, putwater
	brown, slightly cloudy (owing to the yeast cells in post-fermentation) not filtered or pasteurised	brune, légèrement trouble (à cause des cellules de levure de la refermentation) non filtrée, non pasteurisée	bruin, licht troebel (door de gistcellen van de nagisting) ongefilterd, niet gepasteuriseerd
	Sweet beer with caramelised flavour and very slight bitterness.	Bière sucrée d'un goût caramélisé et une très légère amertume.	Zoet bier met gekaramelliseerde smaak en zeer lichte bitterheid.
	Pour 1/3 into a tripel glass, revolve the remainder in the bottle and pour out gently.	Verser un tiers dans un verre triple, remuer le restant dans la bouteille et verser prudemment.	Een derde inschenken in een tripelglas, het restant rondwalsen in de fles en voorzichtig uitschenken.
i	This tripel breathed new life into Wieze as beer village. The logo of the old brewery Wieze is brought back to life.	Avec cette triple, un nouveau départ fut donné à Wieze en tant que village de la bière. Le logo de l'ancienne brasserie Wieze renaît.	Met deze tripel werd een nieuwe start gegeven aan Wieze als bierdorp. Het logo van de vroegere brouwerij Wieze komt weer tot leven.

De Scheldebrouwerij 6,50% 7 - 9 °C / 45 - 48 °F

Wildebok

	top-fermentation post-fermentation in the bottle	haute fermentation refermentation en bouteille	hoge gisting nagisting op de fles
	bock beer	bock	bockbier
	barley malt, aroma 150, cara 120, roasted 900, hops, yeast, water	malt d'orge, arôme 150, cara 120, Roost 900, houblon, levure, eau	gerstemout, aroma 150, cara 120, Roost 900, hop, gist, water
	dark brown (90 EBC), clear with high number of air bubbles and a beige-brown foam head. Not filtered or pasteurised	brun foncé (90 EBC), limpide avec beaucoup de petites bulles d'air et un faux col brun beige. Non filtrée, non pasteurisée	donkerbruin (90 EBC), helder met veel kleine luchtbelletjes en een beigebruine schuimkraag. Ongefilterd, niet gepasteuriseerd
	Slightly roasted malt in the nose that blends in well with the sweet malt flavours. Caramel-malty flavour. Soft-bitter aftertaste that lingers. 24 EBU.	Dans le bouquet, principalement du malt légèrement grillé, qui s'harmonise bien avec un goût malté douceâtre. Goût malté de caramel. Fin de bouche s'écoulant en doux-amer. 24 EBU.	In de neus overwegend lichtgeroosterde mout die goed harmonieert met een zoetige moutigheid. Karamelmoutige smaak. Zachtbitter uitvloeiende nasmaak. 24 EBU.
i	Bo(c)k beer came into being in the early 17th century in Einbeck (Lower Saxony), the name was corrupted to Ein Bock. It is particularly popular in the Netherlands and was voted 'Holland's tastiest bock beer' in 2008, when the brewery was still based there.	La Bo(c)kbier est née au début du 17e siècle à Einbeck (Nedersaksen), le nom a été déformé en Ein Bock. Elle est surtout populaire aux Pays-Bas et a été élue en 2008, quand la Scheldebrouwerij y était encore établie, 'plus délicieux bock des Pays-Bas'.	Bo(c)kbier ontstond begin 17e eeuw in Einbeck (Nedersaksen), de naam werd verbasterd tot Ein Bock. Het is vooral populair in Nederland en werd in 2008, toen de Scheldebrouwerij er nog was gevestigd, verkozen tot 'lekkerste bokbier van Nederland'.

Wilderen Goud

Brouwerij Wilderen 6,20% 8 - 10 °C / 46 - 50 °F

top-fermentation re-fermentation in the bottle	haute fermentation refermentation en bouteille	hoge gisting hergisting op de fles
city or regional beer ale	bière citadine ou régionale ale	stads- of streekbier ale
barley, hops, yeast, water	orge, houblon, levure, eau	gerst, hop, gist, water
deep gold-coloured glow with a nice, fine, white foam head filtered, not pasteurised	reflet profond doré avec joli faux col, fin, blanc filtrée, non pasteurisée	diep goudkleurige gloed met een mooie, fijne, witte schuimkraag gefilterd, niet gepasteuriseerd
Slightly fruity, blond thirst-quencher with a mellow bitterness (hops).	Bière blonde désaltérante légèrement fruitée, avec une douce amertume houblonnée.	Lichtfruitige, blonde dorstlesser met een zachte hopbitterheid.
Pour vigorously into the unique 'Wilderen pot'.	Verser agilement dans un 'Pot Wilderen'	Vlot uitschenken in de unieke 'Wilderen pot'.
Wilderen is a new brewery and alcohol distillery in the village of Wilderen (Sint-Truiden) based in a protected, Haspengouw, timber-framed 18th-century cottage.	Wilderen est une nouvelle brasserie et distillerie d'alcool établie dans le village de Wilderen (Saint-Trond), dans une ferme hesbignonne à colombage classée, datant du 18e siècle.	Wilderen is een nieuwe brouwerij en alcoholstokerij in het dorp Wilderen (Sint-Truiden) gevestigd in een beschermde Haspengouwse vakwerkhoeve uit de 18e eeuw.

Brouwerij Wilderen

8,20% 7 - 9 °C / 45 - 48 °F

Wilderen Tripel Kanunnik

	top-fermentation re-fermentation in the bottle not centrifuged	haute fermentation refermentation en bouteille non centrifugée	hoge gisting hergisting op de fles niet gecentrifugeerd
	tripel	triple	tripel
	barley, oat, wheat, rye, 3 herbs, 2 hop varieties, yeast, water	orge, avoine, froment, seigle, 3 herbes, 2 variétés de houblon, levure, eau	gerst, haver, tarwe, rogge, 3 kruiden, 2 hopsoorten, gist, water
	blond with a fine, white foam head filtered, not pasteurised	blonde avec faux col fin, blanc filtrée, non pasteurisée	blond met fijne, witte schuimkraag gefilterd, niet gepasteuriseerd
	Refined, complex and fruity multigrain tripel with a mild aftertaste owing to the herbs and fine hops. Full-bodied and mellow.	Triple 4 céréales raffinée, complexe et fruitée, avec une arrière-bouche généreuse due aux épices et au houblon noble. Franche et ronde de goût.	Verfijnde, complexe en fruitige 4-granentripel met een milde afdronk afkomstig van de kruiden en edele hop. Vol en rond van smaak.
	Pour slowly into a tulip glass.	Verser lentement dans un verre tulipe	Langzaam uitschenken in een tulpvormig glas.
	Wilderen is a new brewery and alcohol distillery in the village of Wilderen (Sint-Truiden) based in a protected, Haspengouw, timber-framed 18th-century cottage.	Wilderen est une nouvelle brasserie et distillerie d'alcool établie dans le village de Wilderen (Saint-Trond), dans une ferme hesbignonne à colombage classée, datant du 18e siècle.	Wilderen is een nieuwe brouwerij en alcoholstokerij in het dorp Wilderen (Sint-Truiden) gevestigd in een beschermde Haspengouwse vakwerkhoeve uit de 18e eeuw.

Winterkoninkske

Brouwerij Kerkom by Brouwerij Sint-Jozef or Proefbrouwerij 8,30%

	top-fermentation re-fermented in the bottle unpasteurised	fermentation haute refermentation en bouteillee non pasteurisée	hoge gisting nagisting op de fles niet gepasteuriseerd
	specialty beer winter beer	bière spéciale bière hivernale	speciaalbier winterbier
	7 malt varieties, including oat malt, 2 Belgian hop varieties, including Saaz	7 sortes de malt dont malt d'avoine, 2 sortes de houblon belge dont Saaz.	7 moutsoorten waaronder havermout, 2 Belgische hopsoorten waaronder Saaz.
	dark unfiltered	foncée non filtrée	donker ongefilterd
	Deep and full-bodied with a refreshing taste, obtained by the oats. Pleasant and smooth bitterness due to the different hop varieties. Full, pure, slightly sweetish taste and long, smoothly bitter aftertaste.	Saveur franche profonde et rafraîchissante par les flocons d'avoine. Goût amer agréable et moelleux par les sortes de houblon utilisées. Saveur pleine, pure et légèrement douce, fin de bouche longue et légèrement amère.	Diepe volmondigheid en verfrissende smaak door de havermout. Aangename en zachte bitterheid door de hopsoorten. Volle, zuivere, lichtzoetige smaak en lange zachtbittere afdronk.

Brouwerij Kerkom by Brouwerij Sint-Jozef or Proefbrouwerij 13%

Winterkoninkske Haspengouwse Grand Cru

	top-fermentation re-fermentation in the bottle centrifuged	fermentation haute refermentation en bouteille centrifugée	hoge gisting hergisting in de fles gecentrifugeerd
	Christmas beer	bière de Noël	kerstbier
	barley malt, Belgian hops, yeast, water	malt d'orge, houblon Belge, levure, eau	gerstemout, Belgische hop, gist, water
	not filtered or pasteurised	non filtrée, non pasteurisée	ongefilterd, niet gepasteuriseerd

Wintersnood 1

De Verhuisbrouwerij at 't Hofbrouwerijke

6,40% 12 °C 54 °F

	top-fermentation natural re-fermentation in the bottle not centrifuged	fermentation haute refermentation naturelle en bouteille non centrifugée	hoge gisting natuurlijke hergisting in de fles niet gecentrifugeerd
	winter beer	bière hivernale	winterbier
	barley and wheat malt, hops (Hallertau Spalt Select, Saaz and East Kent Golding), ground hazelnut, candy sugar, Irish moss, Wyeast 1762 Belgian Abbey II yeast, water	malt d'orge et malt de froment, houblon (Hallertau Spalt Select, Saaz et East Kent Golding), noisette moulue, sucre candi, muscinées Irlandaises, Wyeast 1762 Belgian Abbey II levure, eau	gerste- en tarwemout, hop (Hallertau Spalt Select, Saaz en East Kent Golding), gemalen hazelnoot, kandijsuiker, Iers mos, Wyeast 1762 Belgian Abbey II gist, water
	63 EBC; not filtered or pasteurised	63 EBC; non filtrée, non pasteurisée	63 EBC; ongefilterd, niet gepasteuriseerd
	Sweet honey scent with a touch of chocolate spread. The taste develops into a lovely, dry white wine with a slightly tart touch owing to the hazelnut peelings.	Parfum de miel douceâtre, avec une pointe de choco. Le goût se termine comme un vin blanc sec délicieux, avec une touche légèrement acidulée due aux enveloppes de noisettes.	Zoetige honinggeur met een vleugje choco. De smaak eindigt als een heerlijke, droge witte wijn met een lichtzurige toets door de hazelnotenpellen.
i	In their spare time, the 5 brewers drive around in a brewing caravan to give free brewing demonstrations of specialty beer. The heavy snowfall in 2010 created extreme weather conditions and complete chaos on the roads. The name also refers to the main ingredient (nut).	Les 5 brasseurs font bénévolement pendant leurs loisirs le tour avec une caravane de brassage pour donner des démonstrations de brassage de bière spéciale. La Wintersnood est née pendant les fortes chutes de neige en 2010, en plein chaos de la circulation. Le nom fait aussi référence à l'ingrédient principal (noisette).	De 5 brouwers rijden in hun vrije tijd belangeloos rond met een brouwcaravan om brouwdemonstraties van speciaalbier te geven. Wintersnood ontstond tijdens de hevige sneeuwval in 2010, in volle verkeerschaos. De naam verwijst ook naar het hoofdingrediënt (noot).

De Scheldebrouwerij 5% 5 - 7 °C 41 - 45 °F

	top-fermentation post-fermentation in the bottle	fermentation haute refermentation en bouteille	hoge gisting nagisting op de fles
	white beer	bière blanche	witbier
	barley malt, wheat malt, hops, coriander, yeast, water and curaçao	malt de froment, malt d'orge, houblon, coriandre, levure, eau et curaçao	tarwemout, gerstemout, hop, koriander, gist, water en curaçao
	pale blond (26 EBC) cloudy; fine, slowly rising bubbles and a thin, white foam head. Not filtered or pasteurised	blond pâle(26 EBC) trouble; bulles d'air doucement pétillantes et un faux col fin, blanc. Non filtrée, non pasteurisée	blondbleek (26 EBC) troebelig; fijne, traag opklimmende luchtbelletjes en een dunne, witte schuimkraag. Ongefilterd, niet gepasteuriseerd
	Slight wheat scent in the nose. Fresh spicy wheaty flavour, not too sweet, with a bitter twist in the background. Short, soft aftertaste. 16 EBU.	Léger parfum de froment dans le bouquet. Goût de froment épicé et frais, pas trop sucré, avec un peu d'amertume en arrière-plan. Fin de bouche douce s'écoulant brièvement. 16 EBU.	Lichte tarwegeur in de neus. Friskruidige, niet te zoete tarweachtige smaak met een bittertje op de achtergrond. Kort uitvloeiende, zachte nasmaak. 16 EBU.
	The name refers to the Norbertines or Premonstratensians who wear a white habit daily.	Le nom fait référence aux pères Norbertins ou Prémontrés, qui portent tous les jours un habit blanc.	De naam verwijst naar de paters Norbertijnen of Premonstratenzers die dagelijks een wit habijt dragen.

Witkap - Dubbele Pater

Brouwerij Slaghmuylder 7% 8 - 12 ° 46 - 54 °

	top-fermentation naturally re-fermented in the bottle	fermentation haute avec refermentation naturelle en bouteille	hoge gisting met natuurlijke hergisting op de fles
	dark abbey beer	bière d'abbaye foncée	abdijbier donker
	barley malt, yeast, water, hop varieties (Belgian Hallertau, Czech Styrie)	malt d'orge, levure, eau, sortes de houblon (Hallertau belge, Styrie tchèque)	gerstemout, gist, water, hopsoorten (Belgische Hallertau, Tsjechische Styrie)
	dark brown with cream-coloured foam head	brun foncé avec un faux col couleur crème	donkerbruin met crème-kleurige schuimkraag
	Lively beer with taste evolution, that matches bitter chocolate. Full-bodied with touches of caramel and fine bitter aftertaste.	Bière vivante avec évolution de la saveur qui se marie parfaitement avec le chocolat amer. Franche avec des touches caramélisées et une fin de bouche amère, raffinée.	Levend bier met smaakevolutie dat past bij bittere chocolade. Volmondig met toetsen van karamel en fijne bittere afdronk.
	Pour carefully in a single, fluent and smooth movement. Leave the yeast sediment in the bottle.	Verser prudemment en un seul mouvement fluide et doux. Laisser le dépôt de levure dans la bouteille.	Voorzichtig uitschenken in 1 vloeiende, zachte beweging. Het gistdepot in de fles laten.
i			

Brouwerij Slaghmuylder

5,50% 8 - 12 °C / 46 - 54 °F

Witkap - Pater Special

W

	top-fermentation naturally re-fermented in the bottle	fermentation haute refermentation naturelle en bouteille	hoge gisting natuurlijke hergisting op de fles
	spéciale Belge	spéciale belge	speciale belge
	barley malt, yeast, water, hop varieties: Belgian Hallertau, Czech Styrie	malt d'orge, levure, eau, variétés de houblon: Hallertau belge, Styrie tchèque	gerstemout, gist, water, hopsoorten: Belgische Hallertau, Tsjechische Styrie
	amber	ambrée	amber
	Lively beer with taste evolution. Nice session beer. Fruity esters (banana) of the yeast.	Bière vive facilement buvable avec saveur évolutive. Esters fruités (banane) de la levure.	Levend bier met smaakevolutie, vlot doordrinkbier. Fruitige esters (banaan) van de gist.
	Pour in a single, fluent and smooth movement. Leave the sediment in the bottle.	Verser prudemment en un seul mouvement fluide et laisser le dépôt de levure dans la bouteille.	Voorzichtig uitschenken in 1 vloeiende, zachte beweging. Het gistdepot in de fles laten.
	Brewed for the 2004 European Town Criers' Championship. The initial name of this beer is a dialect expression meaning "a lot of noise".	Brassée à l'occasion du Championnat Européen des 'Bellemannen' en 2004. Le nom initial 'Greut Lawaith' de la bière est l'expression dialectale de 'beaucoup de bruit'.	Gebrouwen t.g.v. van het Europees Kampioenschap van de Bellemannen in 2004. De originele naam van het bier 'Greut Lawaith' is een dialectuitdrukking voor 'veel lawaai'.

W Witkap - Pater Stimulo

Brouwerij Slaghmuylder

6% 8 - 12° 46 - 54°

	top-fermentation naturally re-fermented in the bottle	fermentation haute refermentation naturelle en bouteille	hoge gisting natuurlijke hergisting op de fles
	blond abbey beer	bière d'abbaye blonde	abdijbier blond
	barley malt, yeast, water, hop varieties (Belgian Hallertau, Czech Styrie)	malt d'orge, levure, eau, sortes de houblon (Hallertau belge, Styrie tchèque)	gerstemout, gist, water, hopsoorten (Belgische Hallertau, Tsjechische Styrie)
	Gold-coloured with a creamy foam head. Clear bubbles when served gently. Possibly cloudy when cold (due to the proteins).	Dorée avec un faux col crémeux. Clairement perlant si on verse doucement. Possiblement trouble si la bière est froide (par les protéines).	Goudkleurig met romige schuimkraag. Helder parelend indien zacht uitgeschonken. Koudetroebel is mogelijk (eiwitten).
	Lively beer with taste evolution, a unique thirst-quencher. Velvety smooth mouthfeel and pleasant hoppy bitter aftertaste.	Bière vivante avec évolution de la saveur, désaltérant unique. Sensation de bouche veloutée et fin de bouche houblonnée, amère.	Levend bier met smaakevolutie, unieke dorstlesser. Fluweelzacht mondgevoel en aangename hopbittere afdronk.
	Pour carefully in a single, fluent and smooth movement. Leave the yeast sediment in the bottle.	Verser prudemment en un seul mouvement fluide et doux. Laisser le dépôt de levure dans la bouteille.	Voorzichtig uitschenken in 1 vloeiende, zachte beweging. Het gistdepot in de fles laten.
	One of the few abbey beers that are not pasteurised and re-fermented in the barrel.	Une des rares bières d'abbaye non pasteurisées et sans refermentation au fût.	Een van de weinige abdijbieren dat niet gepasteuriseerd is en hergist is op vat.

Witkap - Pater Tripel

Brouwerij Slaghmuylder 7,50% 8 - 12 °C / 46 - 54 °F

	top-fermentation naturally re-fermented in the bottle	fermentation haute refermentation naturelle en bouteille	hoge gisting natuurlijke hergisting op de fles
	tripel blond	triple blonde	tripel blond
	barley malt, yeast, water, hop varieties (Belgian Hallertau, Czech Styrie)	malt d'orge, levure, eau, sortes de houblon (Hallertau belge, Styrie tchèque)	gerstemout, gist, water, hopsoorten (Belgische Hallertau, Tsjechische Styrie)
	gold-yellow with fine, white foam, clear and gentle CO_2 bubbles	jaune doré avec écume fine blanche, bulles CO_2 claires et tranquilles	goudgeel met fijn wit schuim, heldere en rustige CO_2 parels
	Lively beer with a fruity nose, a wide range of flowery and spicy aromas and a complex taste, due to the fermentation. Long, dry, bitter aftertaste due to the hops from Aalst.	Bière vivante avec un parfum fruité, une multitude d'arômes (fleuris et relevés) et une saveur complexe par la fermentation. Arrière-bouche longue, sèche et amère par les houblons d'Alost.	Levend bier met fruitige neus, een veelheid aan aroma's (bloemig en kruidig) en een complexe smaak door de gisting. Lange, droge, bittere afdronk door de Aalsterse hop.
	Pour carefully in one fluent movement. Leave the yeast sediment in the bottle.	Verser prudemment en un seul mouvement fluide. Laisser le dépôt de levure dans la bouteille.	Voorzichtig uitschenken in 1 vloeiende, zachte beweging. Het gistdepot in de fles laten.
i			

Witte Pol

Brouwerij Inter-Pol 5,60% 2° 36°

	top-fermentation re-fermentation in the bottle not centrifuged	fermentation haute refermentation en bouteille non centrifugée	hoge gisting hergisting in de fles niet gecentrifugeerd
	white beer	bière blanche	witbier
	barley malt, wheat malt, oat, rice, hops, coriander, orange and lemon, yeast, water	malt d'orge, malt de froment, avoine, riz, houblon, coriandre, oranges et citrons, levure, eau	gerstemout, tarwemout, haver, rijst, hop, koriander, sinaas en citroen, gist, water
	blond, cloudy with a large, white foam head not filtered or pasteurised	blond trouble avec faux col ample, blanc non filtrée, non pasteurisée	blond troebel met grote, witte schuimkraag ongefilterd, niet gepasteuriseerd
	Fruity, citrusy, dry slightly tart aftertaste, fizzing with a light body.	Fruitée, citrus, arrière-bouche sèche légèrement acidulée, pétillante, avec un corps léger.	Fruitig, citrus, droge lichtzurige afdronk, bruisend met lichte body.
	Swing the bottle gently before pouring and share out the sediment across the glasses.	Bouger doucement la bouteille avant de la verser et partager le dépôt parmi les verres.	De fles zachtjes swingen voor het uitschenken en het bezinksel over de glazen verdelen.
	Only available locally in 75 cl bottles. The brewery is linked to a Bed & Breakfast in the valley of Achouffe. See also Zwarte Pol.	Uniquement disponible sur place en bouteilles de 75 cl. La brasserie est liée à un Bed & Breakfast dans la vallée d'Achouffe. Voir aussi Zwarte Pol.	Enkel ter plaatse verkrijgbaar in flessen van 75 cl. De brouwerij is gelinkt aan een Bed & Breakfast in de vallei van Achouffe. Zie ook Zwarte Pol.

rouwerij Bavik

4,30% 4 - 6 °C / 39 - 43 °F

	top-fermentation centrifuged	fermentation haute centrifugée	hoge gisting gecentrifugeerd
	fruit beer	bière fruitée	fruitbier
	barley malt, wheat, hops, mango juice (12%), fructose, acesulfame K, yeast, pure spring water	malt d'orge, froment, houblon, jus de mangue(12%), fructose, acésulfate K, levure, eau de source pure	gerstemout, tarwe, hop, mangosap (12%), fructose, acesulfaam K, gist, zuiver bronwater
	orange with a nice, solid, white to pale orange foam head not filtered, pasteurised	orange avec un faux col joli, solide, blanc à blond orange non filtrée, pasteurisée	oranje met een mooie, stevige, witte tot lichtoranje schuimkraag ongefilterd, gepasteuriseerd
	Naturally refreshing, soft and full-bodied in character. Fresh-sweet aftertaste with soft mango taste and refreshing orange aroma.	Caractère naturellement rafraîchissant, doux et remplissant la bouche. Arrière-bouche fraîche et sucrée, avec un goût de mangue douce et un arôme d'orange rafraîchissant.	Natuurlijk verfrissend, zacht en mondvullend karakter. Friszoete afdronk met zachte mangosmaak en verfrissend sinaasaroma.
	Pour into a clean, degreased glass, avoiding contact with the foam. Revolve the bottle at the halfway stage to loosen up the sediment for a creamy foam head.	Verser dans un verre dégraissé rincé sans que la bouteille touche l'écume. Remuer à mi-chemin le dépôt pour former un faux col crémeux.	Uitschenken in een ontvet gespoeld glas zonder dat de fles het schuim raakt. Halverwege de bodem loswalsen voor een romige schuimkraag.
	Variation on Wittekerke Rosé beer.	Variante de la Wittekerke Rosébier.	Variant op het Wittekerke Rosébier.

Wittekerke Rosé

Brouwerij Bavik 4,30% 4 - 6° 39 - 43°

	top-fermentation centrifuged	fermentation haute centrifugée	hoge gisting gecentrifugeerd
	witbier with fruit	bière blanche fruitée	witbier met bier
	barley malt, wheat, hops, raspberry juice (10%), fructose, aspartame, yeast, pure spring water	malt d'orge, froment, houblon, jus de framboises (10 %), fructose, aspartame, levure, eau de source pure	gerstemout, tarwe, hop, frambozensap (10%), fructose, aspartaam, gist, zuiver bronwater
	rosé with a nice, firm, white to pale pink foam head not filtered, not pasteurised	rose avec un faux col solide, blanc à légèrement rose non filtrée, non pasteurisée	rosé met een mooie, stevige, witte tot lichtroze schuimkraag ongefilterd, niet gepasteuriseerd
	Naturally refreshing, soft and full-bodied character. Sweet-and-sour with distinct raspberry flavour.	Caractère naturellement rafraîchissant, doux et franc en bouche. Aigre-doux avec un goût de framboises nettement reconnaissable.	Natuurlijk verfrissend, zacht en mondvullend karakter. Zoetzuur met duidelijk herkenbare frambozensmaak.
	Pour out into a degreased rinsed glass, avoiding contact with the foam. At the halfway stage, revolve the bottle to loosen the sediment for a creamy foam head.	Verser dans un verre dégraissé rincé sans que la bouteille touche l'écume. A mi-chemin remuer et dégager le fond pour former un faux col crémeux.	Uitschenken in een ontvet gespoeld glas zonder dat de fles het schuim raakt. Halfweg de bodem loswalsen voor een romige schuimkraag.
	The first original Rosé beer based on white beer.	La première bière Rosé d'origine à base de bière blanche.	Het eerste originele Rosébier op basis van witbier.

Wittekerke Wit Bier

rouwerij Bavik

5% 4 - 6 °C 39 - 43 °F

top-fermentation	fermentation haute	hoge gisting
witbier - Wheat Ale	bière blanche	witbier
barley malt, hops, wheat, fructose, flavouring, pure spring water	malt d'orge, houblon, froment, fructose, arômes, eau de source pure	gerstemout, hop, tarwe, fructose, aroma's, zuiver bronwater
attractive, opalescent light golden green colour	couleur attractive opaline, vert doré clair	aantrekkelijke, opaalachtige, licht groengouden kleur
Very aromatic with a fragrant fruitiness, slightly spicy, with an underlying sweetness and a touch of citrus. Round and complex character.	Très aromatisée :arôme fruité, légèrement épicé avec une douceur sous-jacente, touche d'agrumes. Caractère complexe et rond.	Zeer aromatisch met geurige fruitigheid, lichtjes kruidig met onderliggende zoetigheid, toets van citrus. Rond en complex karakter.
Pour into a degreased, rinsed and wet glass, avoiding contact between bottle and foam.	Verser dans un verre dégraissé, rincé et mouillé sans que la bouteille touche le faux col.	Uitschenken in een ontvet, gespoeld en nat glas zonder dat de fles het schuim raakt.
Named after a successful TV soap.	Nommé après un feuilleton télévisé à succès.	Genoemd naar een succesvolle TV soap.

Wittoen

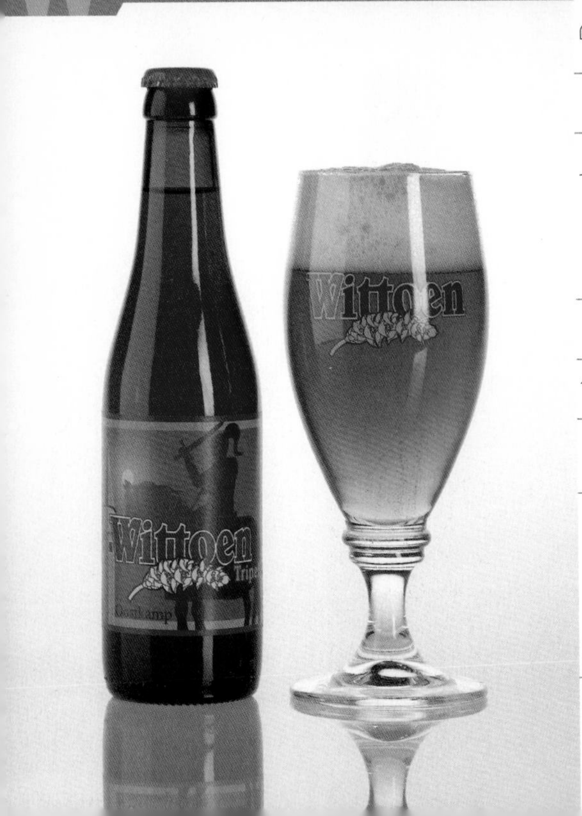

Brouwerij Strubbe

8,20% 8° 46°

	top-fermentation re-fermented in the bottle	fermentation haute refermentation en bouteille	hoge gisting nagisting op de fles
	tripel amber	triple ambrée	tripel amber
	pilsner malt, caramel malt, candy sugar, hops, gruit (mainly gale and rosemary) yeast, water. Gruit is a mixture of herbs, the predecessor of the hops.	malt de pils, malt caramélisé, sucre candi, houblon, gruit (surtout myrte bâtard et romarin), levure, eau. Gruit est un mélange d'herbes et est le précurseur du houblon.	pilsmout, karamelmout, kandijsuiker, hop, gruut (vooral gagel en rozemarijn), gist, water. Gruut is een kruidenmengsel, de voorloper van de hop.
	amber	ambrée	amber
	Spicy, full, bittersweet.	Relevée, pleine, doux-amère.	Kruidig, vol, zoetbitter.
	Pour into a glass suitable for abbey beers or into a Wittoen-glass.	Verser dans un verre pour bières d'abbaye ou un verre Wittoen.	Uitschenken in een glas voor abdijbieren of Wittoenglas.
i	Aromatised with herbs in the same way as the local beers of the Middle Ages. The name refers to the Oostkamp knight Jan Wittoen (or Jan Winteyn) who lived in the 15th century.	Aromatisé aux herbes comme les bières locales du Moyen-Age. Le nom renvoie au chevalier d'Oostkamp Jan Wittoen (ou Jan Winteyn) qui a vécu au 15ième siècle.	Gearomatiseerd met kruiden zoals de lokale bieren uit de Middeleeuwen. De naam verwijst naar de Oostkampse ridder Jan Wittoen (of Jan Winteyn) die leefde in de 15e eeuw.

Brouwerij Lupus 7,40%

	top-fermentation re-fermentation in the bottle	fermentation haute refermentation en bouteille	hoge gisting hergisting in de fles
	blond	blonde	blond
	gold-blond with firm, white foam head	blond doré avec faux col stable, blanc	goudblond met vaste, witte schuimkraag
	Aroma of vanilla, white pear and a hint of fruit. Soft sweet, full-bodied with moderate hint of al-cohol. Peach, nectarine and soft, fine bitterness in the aftertaste.	Arôme de vanille, de poivre blanc et d'un peu de fruits. Goût franc doucement sucré, avec une touche d'alcool mo-dérée. Pêche, nectarine et une amertume douce et fine en fin de bouche.	Aroma van vanille, witte peper en ietwat fruit. Zacht zoete, volmondige smaak met matige alcoholhint. Perzik, nectarine en zachte, fijne bitterheid in de nasmaak.

W Wolf 8

Brouwerij Lupus 8,50%

	top-fermentation re-fermentation in the bottle	fermentation haute refermentation en bouteille	hoge gisting hergisting in de fles
	strong double speciality beer	bière spéciale double forte	sterk dubbel speciaal-bier
	bordeaux with solid, broken, white foam head	bordeaux avec faux col solide blanc cassé	bordeaux met stevige, gebroken, witte schuim-kraag
	Nice aroma with touches of pear and roasted nuts. Nutty taste with touch of chocolate and subse-quently exotic fruit. Pleasant aftertaste with touches of bitterness (hops) and caramel.	Joli arôme, avec des touches de poire et de noix grillées. Goût de noix, avec une touche de chocolat et puis de fruit exotique. Jolie arrière-bouche, avec un peu de lupuline et de caramel.	Mooi aroma met toetsen van peer en geroosterde noten. Nootachtige smaak met toets van chocolade en daarna exotisch fruit. Mooie afdronk met wat hopbitter en karamel.

Brouwerij Lupus

9%

Wolf 9

top-fermentation re-fermentation in the bottle	fermentation haute refermentation en bouteille	hoge gisting hergisting in de fles
amber	ambrée	amber
dark amber with firm, tufty foam head	ambré foncé avec faux col solide rocailleux	donker amber met stevige, rotsachtige schuimkraag
Very fruity aroma (pear, banana..). Full-bodied, sweet-fruity onset with hints of apricot. Spicy, punchy aftertaste with sweet, warm impression of alcohol.	Arôme fort fruité (poire, banane,...). Approche initiale remplissant la bouche, sucrée et fruitée, avec un peu d'abricot. Fin de bouche épicée, forte, avec une impression d'alcool sucrée, chaude.	Zeer fruitig aroma (peer, banaan..). Mondvullende, zoet fruitige aanzet met wat abrikoos. Kruidige, krachtige nasmaak met zoete, warme alcoholimpressie.

X-mas Zinnebier

Brasserie de la Senne 8% 12 °C 54 °F

	top-fermentation re-fermentation in the bottle not centrifuged	fermentation haute refermentation en bouteille non centrifugée	hoge gisting hergisting in de fles niet gecentrifugeerd
	winter beer	bière hivernale	winterbier
	different malts, sugar (during boiling), different hops, yeast, water	variétés de malt, sucre (en chaudière), variétés de houblon, levure, eau	moutsoorten, suiker (tijdens het koken), hopsoorten, gist, water
	copper-brown with a compact, fine foam head not filtered or pasteurised	brun cuivre avec un faux col compact, fin non filtrée, non pasteurisée	koperbruin met een compacte, fijne schuimkraag ongefilterd, niet gepasteuriseerd
	Beer with character. Hoppy and malty aroma with touches of currant, black chocolate and orange marmalade. Mellow onset, but dry aftertaste with a powerful bitterness.	Bière de caractère. Arôme houblonné et malté, avec des touches de raisins de Corinthe, de chocolat noir et de marmelade d'orange. Approche initiale ronde, mais finale sèche où se développe une forte amertume.	Karakterbier. Hoppig en moutig aroma met toetsen van krenten, zwarte chocolade en sinaasmarmelade. Ronde aanzet, maar droge finale waarbij zich een krachtige bitterheid ontwikkelt.
	Pour carefully and leave 1 finger of yeast sediment in the bottle. Finish yeast separately, if necessary.	Verser prudemment et laisser un doigt de dépôt de levure dans la bouteille. Eventuellement boire séparément.	Voorzichtig uitschenken en een vinger gistdepot in de fles laten. Eventueel afzonderlijk uitdrinken.
i			

XX Bitter

Brouwerij De Ranke 6,20% Moderately cooled

	top-fermentation	fermentation haute	hoge gisting
	bitter blond	blonde amère	bitter blond
	pale malt, hop flowers, industrial yeast	malt pâle, fleurs de houblon, levure de culture	bleekmout, hopbloemen, cultuurgist
	blond slightly cloudy	blonde légèrement trouble	blond licht troebel
	Hoppy and extra bitter.	Houblonnée et extra amère.	Hoppig en extra bitter.

Yperman

Brouwerij Het Sas 5,50% 5 - 6 °C / 41 - 43 °F

	bottom-fermentation	fermentation basse	lage gisting
	ale	ale	ale
	malt, spices, sweetener, hops, water	malt, condiments, édulcorant, houblon, eau	mout, specerijen, zoetstof, hop, water
	brown	brune	bruin
	Full-bodied. Light roasty cereal taste.	Franche. Saveur de céréales légèrement fumée.	Volmondig. Licht gerookte graansmaak.
	Pour slowly in a single, smooth movement, into a degreased glass. Keep the glass tilted to avoid sloshing. Skim off the foam.	Verser lentement en un seul mouvement fluide dans un verre dégraissé tenu en oblique. Ne pas laisser la bière clapoter. Ecumer le verre.	Traag en in 1 vloeiende beweging uitschenken in een vetvrij glas dat wordt schuingehouden. Het bier niet laten klotsen. Het glas afschuimen.
i	Named after the medieval surgeon Jan Yperman from Ypres.	Porte le nom du chirurgien médiéval d'Ypres Jan Yperman.	Genoemd naar de middeleeuwse Ieperse chirurgijn Jan Yperman.

Zatte Bie

Brouwerij De Bie

9% 6 °C 43 °F

	top-fermentation	fermentation haute	hoge gisting
	dark	brune	donker
	malt, hops, candy sugar, yeast, herbs, water	malt, houblon, sucre candi, levure, herbes, eau	mout, hop, kandijsuiker, gist, kruiden, water
	brown	brune	bruin
	Spicy.	Epicée.	Kruidig.

Zeezuiper

De Scheldebrouwerij

8% 8 - 10 °C / 46 - 50 °F

	top-fermentation re-fermentation in the bottle	fermentation haute refermentation en bouteille	hoge gisting hergisting in de fles
	tripel	triple	tripel
	barley malt, coriander, hops, yeast, water	malt d'orge, coriandre, houblon, levure, eau	gerstemout, koriander, hop, gist, water
	gold-yellow (21 EBC) and slightly cloudy with collapsing, generous, white foam head. Not filtered or pasteurised	jaune doré (21 EBC) et légèrement trouble avec faux col, croulant, ample, blanc. Non filtrée, non pasteurisée	goudgeel (21 EBC) en licht troebel met inzakkende, ruime, witte schuimkraag. Ongefilterd, niet gepasteuriseerd
	Fruity, malty, spicy nose. The gentle bitterness of the hops is another flavour added to the mix. Long aftertaste that lingers for a long time. 30 EBU.	Fruitée, maltée, bouquet épicée. Dans le goût, il s'ajoute encore de l'amertume houblonnée bénéfique. Longue fin de bouche, qui s'écoule lentement. 30 EBU.	Fruitig, moutig, kruidige neus. In de smaak komt daarbij nog weldoende hopbitterheid. Lange nasmaak die langzaam uitvloeit. 30 EBU.
	Zeezuiper is a nature reserve where broads and woodland were created when the peat was dug up.	Une 'zeezuiper' est une région naturelle où les marais et les bois sont apparus du fait de l'enlèvement de la tourbe.	Een zeezuiper is een natuurgebied waar vennen en bossen zijn ontstaan door het afgraven van veen.

Zeven Zonden Gula

Brouwerij Gulden Spoor 9% 12 - 14 °C / 54 - 57 °F

	top-fermentation re-fermentation in the bottle not centrifuged	fermentation haute refermentation en bouteille non centrifugée	hoge gisting hergisting in de fles niet gecentrifugeerd
	city beer, spicy beer, winter beer	bière citadine, bière aromatisée, bière hivernale	stadsbier, kruidenbier, winterbier
	4 different malts (pilsner, amber, chocolate and special B), candy sugar, 3 different hops, 6 spices (incl. liquorice), 2 different yeasts, water	4 variétés de malt (pils, ambre, chocolat et spécial B), sucre candi, 3 variétés de houblon, 6 herbes (e.a. réglisse), 2 types de levure, eau	4 soorten mout (pils-, amber-, chocolade- en special B), kandijsuiker, 3 soorten hop, 6 kruiden (o.a. zoethout), 2 soorten gist, water
	ruby-red and clear with pale beige, very dense foam not filtered or pasteurised	rouge rubis et limpide avec faux col très dense, beige clair non filtrée, non pasteurisée	robijnrood en helder met lichtbeige, heel dens schuim ongefilterd, niet gepasteuriseerd
	Extremely full-bodied, overwhelming spices. Very long sweet aftertaste. Special sipping beer owing to extreme spiciness.	Extrêmement franche, énormément d'épices. Très longue arrière-bouche au goût sucré. Bière de dégustation spéciale du fait du goût épicé extrême.	Extreem volmondig, overweldigende kruiden. Zeer lange, zoetsmakende afdronk. Speciaal degustatiebier door de extreme kruidigheid.
	Pour carefully. Taste the yeast separately, if possible.	Verser prudemment. Goûter la levure de préférence séparément.	Voorzichtig uitschenken. De gist apart best proeven.
	Second in a series of 7 beers. Related to the lighter 'Luxuria'. Gula stands for 'gluttonous sin'.	La deuxième dans une série de 7 bières. Apparentée à son frère plus léger 'Luxuria', Gula désigne 'le péché de gloutonnerie'.	Tweede in een reeks van 7 bieren. Verwant aan zijn lichtere broer 'Luxuria'. Gula staat voor 'gulzige zonde'.

Zeven Zonden Luxuria

Brouwerij Gulden Spoor 8,50% 12 - 14 °C / 54 - 57 °F

	top-fermentation re-fermentation in the bottle not centrifuged	fermentation haute refermentation en bouteille non centrifugée	hoge gisting hergisting in de fles niet gecentrifugeerd
	city beer, spicy beer, winter beer	bière citadine, bière aromatisée, bière hivernale	stadsbier, kruidenbier, winterbier
	4 different malts (pilsner, amer, chocolate and special B), candy sugar, 3 different hops, 6 spices (incl. liquorice), 2 different yeasts, water	4 variétés de malt (malt de pils, malt d'ambré, malt de chocolat et spécial B), sucre candi, 3 variétés de houblon Belge, 6 herbes (e.a. réglisse), 2 types de levure, eau	4 soorten mout (pils-, amber-, chocolademout en special B), kandijsuiker, 3 soorten Belgische hop, 6 kruiden (o.a. zoethout), 2 soorten gist, water
	ruby-red and clear with pale beige, very dense foam not filtered or pasteurised	rouge rubis et limpide avec faux col très dense, beige clair non filtrée, non pasteurisée	robijnrood en helder met lichtbeige, heel dens schuim ongefilterd, niet gepasteuriseerd
	Very full-bodied sipping beer, hoppy, spicy flavours. Very long coffee-bitter aftertaste.	Bière de dégustation très franche, joliment houblonnée, épices piquantes. Très longue arrière-bouche avec une amertume de café.	Zeer volmondig degustatiebier, mooi hoppig, pittige kruiden. Zeer lange koffiebittere afdronk.
	Pour carefully. Taste the yeast separately, if possible.	Verser prudemment. Goûter la levure de préférence séparément.	Voorzichtig uitschenken. De gist apart best proeven.
i	First in a series of 7 beers. Luxuria stands for 'lust and impurity', the sweetest of the 7 capital sins.	La première dans une série de 7 bières. Luxuria désigne 'le désir et l'impureté', le plus doux des 7 péchés capitaux.	Eerste in een reeks van 7 bieren. Luxuria staat voor 'lust en onkuisheid', de zoetste van de 7 hoofdzonden.

Brasserie de la Senne

5,80% 6 - 8 °C 43 - 46 °F

	top-fermentation natural re-fermentation in the bottle not centrifuged	fermentation haute refermentation naturelle en bouteille non centrifugée	hoge gisting natuurlijke hergisting in de fles niet gecentrifugeerd
	Belgian ale local beer	Belgian ale bière régionale	Belgian ale streekbier
	malt, hops, yeast, water	malt, houblon, levure, eau	mout, hop, gist, water
	gold-amber, slightly veiled with dense and fine foam head. Not filtered or pasteurised	ambré doré, légèrement voilée avec un faux col fin. Non filtrée, non pasteurisée	goudamber, licht gesluierd met dichte en fijne schuimkraag. Oongefilterd, niet gepasteuriseerd
	Malty, soft, pleasantly bitter. Flavour that lingers in the mouth, dry and refreshing aftertaste. Complex aroma, intensely hoppy-fruity with touches of orange marmalade.	Maltée, douce, agréablement amère. Goût qui persiste longtemps en bouche, arrière-bouche sèche et rafraîchissante. Arôme complexe, intensément houblonné-fruité et touches de marmelade d'orange.	Moutig, zacht, aangenaam bitter. Smaak die lang in de mond blijft, droge en verfrissende afdronk. Complex aroma, intens hoppig-fruitig en toetsen van sinaasmarmelade.
	Pour carefully and leave 1 cm (yeast) in the bottle. Drink the yeast separately, if necessary.	Verser prudemment et laisser 1 cm (levure) dans la bouteille. Eventuellement boire la levure séparément.	Voorzichtig uitschenken en 1 cm (gist) in de fles laten. De gist eventueel afzonderlijk uitdrinken.
i	Tribute to the Brussels citizen or 'Zinneke' and to the river Zenne which lies at the city's origins.	Hommage au Bruxellois ou 'Zinneke' et à la Senne, la rivière à laquelle Bruxelles doit sa naissance.	Hommage aan de Brusselaar of 'Zinneke' en aan de rivier de Zenne waaraan Brussel zijn ontstaan dankt.

Zonderik Dubbel Donker

Zonderik Beer Company by De Proefbrouwerij 8% 7 - 11 °C / 45 - 52 °F

	top-fermentation re-fermentation in the bottle centrifuged	fermentation haute refermentation en bouteille centrifugée	hoge gisting hergisting in de fles gecentrifugeerd
	double	double	dubbel
	Münich and cara malt, hops (Golding and Saaz), coriander, cumin, caraway, candy sugar, honey and storage using heavy toasted oak	malt de Münich et malt cara, houblon (Golding et Saaz), coriandre, cumin, carvi, candi, miel et lagering avec heavy toasted oak	Münich- en caramout, hop (Golding en Saaz), koriander, komijn, karwij, kandij, honing en lagering met heavy toasted oak
	dark brown, red glow with thick, creamy foam head. Not filtered, pasteurised.	brun foncé, reflet rouge avec faux col épais, crémeux. Non filtrée, pasteurisée	donkerbruin, rode schijn met dikke, romige schuimkraag. Ongefilterd, gepasteuriseerd.
	Aroma: fresh, spicy, cumin. Taste: pleasant bitterness, caramel with a hint of alcohol, mellow, sponge cake. Aftertaste: bitter with touches of nut, honey and wood.	Arôme :frais, épicé, cumin. Goût :jolie amertume, caramel avec un soupçon d'alcool, fond dans la bouche, biscuit. Arrière-bouche :amère, avec des touches de noix, de miel et de bois.	Aroma: fris, kruidig, komijn. Smaak: mooie bitterheid, karamel met een tikkeltje alcohol, botermals, biscuit. Afdronk: bitter met toetsen van noot, honing en hout.
	see Zonderik Tripel	voir Zonderik Tripel	zie Zonderik Tripel
i	In partnership with the municipality of Zonhoven. The Zonderik creek straddles Zonhoven and Zolder.	Avec la collaboration de la commune de Zonhoven. Le Zonderikbeek se situe à la limite entre Zonhoven et Zolder.	Met medewerking van de gemeente Zonhoven. De Zonderikbeek ligt op de grens tussen Zonhoven en Zolder.

Zonderik Beer Company by De Proefbrouwerij 8% 7 - 11 °C / 45 - 52 °F

	top-fermentation re-fermentation in the bottle centrifuged	fermentation haute refermentation en bouteille centrifugée	hoge gisting hergisting in de fles gecentrifugeerd
	tripel	triple	tripel
	barley and cara malt, hops (Golding and Saaz), coriander, cumin, caraway, candy sugar, honey and storage using heavy toasted oak	malt d'orge et malt cara, houblon (Golding et Saaz), coriandre, cumin, carvi, candi, miel et lagering avec heavy toasted oak	gerste- en caramout, hop (Golding en Saaz), koriander, komijn, karwij, kandij, honing en lagering met heavy toasted oak
	gold-blond with thick, creamy foam head not filtered, pasteurised	blond doré avec faux col épais, crémeux non filtrée, pasteurisée	goudblond met dikke, romige schuimkraag ongefilterd, gepasteuriseerd
	Aroma: fruity (banana owing to the esters from the yeast) and spicy. Taste: full-bodied, yet drinkable tripel, herbs (candy sugar, cumin) and wood (oak-vanilla). Aftertaste: honey and wood, bitterness (hops).	Arôme : fruité (banane, grâce aux esters provenant de la levure) et épicé. Goût : triple franche mais facilement buvable, épices (sucre candi, cumin) et bois (chêne-vanille). Arrière-bouche : miel et bois, amertume houblonnée.	Aroma: fruitig (banaan, door de esters afkomstig van de gist) en kruidig. Smaak: volmondige maar doordrinkbare tripel, kruiden (kandij, komijn) en hout (eik-vanille). Afdronk: honing en hout, hopbitterheid.
	Pour out gently along the rim of a tilted glass to create a fine foam head. Leave the yeast sediment in the bottle.	Verser prudemment autour du bord d'un verre tenu incliné jusqu'à ce qu'un faux bord solide se forme. Laisser le dépôt de levure dans la bouteille.	Voorzichtig uitschenken langs de rand van een schuingehouden glas tot er zich een mooie schuimkraag vormt. De gistfond in de fles laten.
	see Zonderik Dubbel Donker	voir Zonderik Dubbel Donker	zie Zonderik Dubbel Donker

Zonderik Beer Company by De Proefbrouwerij

10% 7 - 11 °C 45 - 52 °F

	top-fermentation re-fermentation in the bottle; centrifuged	fermentation haute refermentation en bouteille; centrifugée	hoge gisting hergisting in de fles; gecentrifugeerd
	tripel	triple	tripel
	barley and cara malt, hops (Golding and Saaz), coriander, cumin, caraway, candy sugar, honey and storage using heavy toasted oak	malt d'orge et malt cara, houblon (Golding et Saaz), coriandre, cumin, carvi, candi, miel et lagering avec heavy toasted oak	gerste- en caramout, hop (Golding en Saaz), koriander, komijn, karwij, kandij, honing en houtlagering met heavy toasted oak
	gold-blond amber with thick, creamy foam head. Not filtered, pasteurised	blond doré ambré avec faux col épais crémeux. Non filtrée, pasteurisée	goudblond amber met dikke, romige schuimkraag. Ongefilterd, gepasteuriseerd
	Aroma: fruity (banana owing to the esters from the yeast) and spicy. Taste: full-bodied, yet drinkable tripel, herbs (candy sugar, cumin) and wood (oak-vanilla). Aftertaste: honey and wood, bitterness (hops).	Arôme : fruité (banane, grâce aux esters provenant de la levure) et épicé. Goût : triple franche mais facilement buvable, épices (sucre candi, cumin) et bois (chêne-vanille). Arrière-bouche : miel et bois, amertume houblonnée.	Aroma: fruitig (banaan, door de esters afkomstig van de gist) en kruidig. Smaak: volmondige maar doordrinkbare tripel, kruiden (kandij, komijn) en hout (eik-vanille). Afdronk: honing en hout, hopbitterheid.
	see Zonderik Tripel	voir Zonderik Tripel	zie Zonderik Tripel
i	In partnership with the municipality of Zonhoven. The Zonderik creek straddles Zonhoven and Zolder.	Avec la collaboration de la commune de Zonhoven. Le Zonderikbeek se situe à la limite entre Zonhoven et Zolder.	Met medewerking van de gemeente Zonhoven. De Zonderikbeek ligt op de grens tussen Zonhoven en Zolder.

Crombé by Brouwerij Strubbe

8,40%

	top-fermentation re-fermentation in the bottle	fermentation haute refermentation en bouteille	hoge gisting hergisting in de fles

Zottegemse Grand Cru

ZUIDerbierke

Brouwerij Donum Ignis 8,20% 6 - 8 °C / 43 - 46 °F

	top-fermentation re-fermentation in the bottle not centrifuged	fermentation haute refermentation en bouteille non centrifugée	hoge gisting hergisting in de fles niet gecentrifugeerd
	boutique beer, very dark city or regional beer	bière citadine ou régionale artisanale foncée	artisanaal sterk donker stads- of streekbier
	(dark) malt, hops, beer yeast, candy sugar, seasoning, water	malt (foncé), houblon, levure de bière, sucre candi, épices, eau	(donkere) mout, hop, biergist, kandijsuiker, specerijen, water
	dark brown-red, naturally cloudy with a full beige creamy foam head. Not filtered or pasteurised	brun rouge foncé, trouble naturel avec un faux col plein crémeux beige. Non filtrée, non pasteurisée	donker bruinrood, natuurtroebel met een volle beige romige schuimkraag. Ongefilterd, niet gepasteuriseerd
	Aroma: soft, refreshing, southern, well-balanced spiciness. Taste: full-bodied with a lovely, fruity hint of currant. Aftertaste: caramel malty, complex yet pleasantly fresh.	Arôme : doux, rafraîchissant, du sud, goût épicé équilibré. Goût : franc, avec une touche fruitée délicieuse de raisins secs. Arrière-bouche : malt de caramel, complexe mais agréablement fraîche.	Aroma: zachte, verfrissende, zuiderse, uitgebalanceerde kruidigheid. Smaak: volmondig met een heerlijk fruitige rozijnentoets. Afdronk: karamelmoutig, complex maar aangenaam fris.
	see NOORDerbierke	voir NOORDerbierke	zie NOORDerbierke
i	In the footsteps of the NOORderbierke. The more southern one travels, the darker the skin tones. And perhaps a little more spicy...	À l'instar de la NOORderbierke. Plus on va vers le sud, plus l'espèce humaine devient foncée. Et peut-être aussi un peu plus épicée...	In navolging van het NOORderbierke. Hoe zuidelijker men gaat, hoe donkerder het mensenras wordt. En misschien ook iets meer spicy...

Brouwerij Inter-Pol

6,50% | 8 °C 46 °F

Zwarte Pol

	top-fermentation re-fermentation in the bottle not centrifuged	fermentation haute refermentation en bouteille non centrifugée	hoge gisting hergisting in de fles niet gecentrifugeerd
	stout (milk stout)	stout (milk stout)	stout (milk stout)
	barley malt, roasted malt, hops, dark candy sugar, lactose, yeast, water	malt d'orge, malt torréfié, houblon, candi brun, lactose, levure, eau	gerstemout, gebrande mout, hop, donkere kandij, lactose, gist, water
	black-coloured with a solid, beige foam head not filtered or pasteurised	noire avec faux col stable, beige non filtrée, non pasteurisée	zwart met vaste, beige schuimkraag ongefilterd, niet gepasteuriseerd
	Taste: bitter (wood), roasted, chocolate. Aftertaste: sweet, chocolate, slightly bitter, yet dry. Aroma: dark malt, sweet.	Goût : un peu d'amertume de bois, grillé, chocolat. Arrière-bouche : douceâtre, chocolat, légèrement amère mais tout de même sèche. Arôme : malt foncé, douceâtre.	Smaak: houtbitterig, geroosterd, chocolade. Afdronk: zoetig, chocolade, licht bitter maar toch droog. Aroma: donkere mout, zoetig.
	Pour out slowly and leave the yeast sediment (approx. 1.5 cm) in the bottle.	Verser prudemment et laisser le dépôt (ca 1,5 cm) dans la bouteille.	Voorzichtig uitschenken en het bezinksel (ca. 1,5 cm) in de fles laten.
i	Inter-Pol is probably Belgium's smallest brewery. The beer is only available locally in 75 cl bottles. See also Witte Pol.	Inter-Pol est peut-être la plus petite brasserie de Belgique. La bière est uniquement disponible sur place en bouteilles de 75 cl. Voir aussi Witte Pol.	Inter-Pol is wellicht de kleinste brouwerij van België. Het bier is enkel ter plaatse verkrijgbaar in flessen van 75 cl. Zie ook Witte Pol.

Zwet.be

Geuzestekerij 3 Fonteinen

7%

	spontaneous fermentation	fermentation spontanée	spontane gisting
	black beer	bière noire	zwart bier
	Maris Otter malt, cara malt, hops, water. Fermentation using traditional culture yeast and 3 Fonteinen Brethanomyces.	malt Maris Otter, malt cara, houblon, eau. Fermentation avec levure de culture traditionnelle et 3 Fontaines Brethanomyces.	Maris Otter mout, caramout, hop, water. Gisting met traditionele cultuurgist en 3 Fonteinen Brethanomyces.
	not filtered	non filtrée	ongefilterd

6% 7 °C 45 °F

	top-fermentation	fermentation haute	hoge gisting
	regional beer	bière régionale	streekbier
	different malts, hops, herbs, yeast, water	variétés de malt, houblon, herbes, levure, eau	moutsoorten, hop, kruiden, gist, water
	dark brown with a nice, firm foam head filtered, not pasteurised	brun foncé avec un faux col compact beige filtrée, non pasteurisée	donkerbruin met een dichte, beige schuimkraag gefilterd, niet gepasteuriseerd
	Tasty thirst-quencher with a malty taste and a hint of bitterness.	Bière désaltérante fort goûteuse, avec un goût malté et une pointe d'amertume.	Smaakvolle dorstlesser met moutsmaak en een vleugje bitterheid.
	Pour out slowly to form a fine foam head. Leave the yeast sediment in the bottle.	Verser lentement et former un faux col solide. Laisser le dépôt de levure dans la bouteille.	Langzaam uitschenken en een mooie schuimkraag vormen. Het gistdepot in de fles laten.
i	The name '3 Schtèng' is dialect for '3 stones'. It refers to the border stones of the place where Holland, Belgium and Germany meet, a tourist attraction, in the municipality of Hombourg where the brewery is based.	Le nom '3 Schtèng' est du dialecte pour '3 stenen' ('3 pierres'). Il fait référence aux bornes du point limitrophe des trois pays, une attraction touristique dans la commune de Hombourg, où la brasserie est établie.	De naam '3 Schtèng' is dialect voor '3 stenen'. Hij verwijst naar de grensstenen van het drielandenpunt, toeristische trekpleister in de gemeente Hombourg waar de brouwerij gevestigd is.

IV Saison

Brasserie de Jandrain Jandrenouille 6,50% 4 - 11 ° 39 - 52 °

top-fermentation not centrifuged	fermentation haute non centrifugée	hoge gisting niet gecentrifugeerd
saison	saison	saison
malt, water, yeast, 4 different hops brewed according to the Reinheitsgebot	malt, eau, levure, 4 variétés de houblon brassée suivant le Reinheitsgebot	mout, water, gist, 4 hopsoorten gebrouwen volgens het Reinheitsgebot
blond, slightly cloudy not filtered or pasteurised	blonde, légèrement trouble non filtrée, non pasteurisée	blond, licht troebel ongefilterd, niet gepasteuriseerd
Lemony aroma owing to the hops, bitter and long aftertaste.	Arôme citronné du fait du houblon, amer et longue arrière-bouche.	Citroenig aroma door de hop, bitter en lange afdronk.
Serve in a tulip glass.	Verser dans un verre tulipe.	Uitschenken in een tulpglas.
The name refers to the 4 basic ingredients and the 4 different hops used to brew the beer. A saison was originally brewed on farms for the seasonal workers.	Le nom fait référence aux 4 ingrédients de base et aux 4 variétés de houblon avec laquelle elle est brassée. Une saison était à l'origine brassée dans les exploitations agricoles pour les saisonniers.	De naam verwijst naar de 4 basisingrediënten en de 4 hopsoorten waarmee het bier gebrouwen wordt. Een saison werd oorspronkelijk gebrouwen op de boerderijen voor de seizoensarbeiders.

Brasserie de Jandrain Jandrenouille 7,50% 4 - 11 °C / 39 - 52 °F

top-fermentation	fermentation haute	hoge gisting
amber or speciale belge	ambrée ou spéciale belge	amber of speciale belge
3 different malts, water, yeast, hops	3 variétés de malt, eau, levure, houblon	3 soorten mout, water, gist, hop
orange, slightly cloudy not filtered or pasteurised	ambrée, légèrement trouble non filtrée, non pasteurisée	amber, licht troebel ongefilterd, niet gepasteuriseerd
Aromas of tangerine. Distinct bitterness that is mellowed by the malt.	Arômes de mandarine. Amertume claire qui est arrondie par le malt.	Aroma's van mandarijn. Duidelijke bitterheid die afgerond wordt door de mout.
Pour into a closed tulip glass that accentuates the aromas.	Verser dans un verre tulipe fermé accentuant les arômes.	Uitschenken in een gesloten tulpglas dat de aroma's accentueert.
Second beer of this brewery (V follows IV). Stimulates all the senses (sens) owing to its complex flavour and aroma. 'Cense' means 'robust' in old-French.	Deuxième bière de cette brasserie (après IV, vient V). Stimule tous les sens grâce à son goût et son arôme complexes. 'Cense' signifiait 'ferme' en ancien français.	Tweede bier van deze brouwerij (na IV volgt V). Prikkelt alle zintuigen (sens) door zijn complexe smaak en aroma. 'Cense' betekende 'ferm' in het oud-Frans.

VI Wheat

Brasserie de Jandrain Jandrenouille 6% / 6,50% 4 - 11 ° 39 - 52 °

	top-fermentation	fermentation haute	hoge gisting
	wheat beer but not a typical white beer	bière de froment mais pas de bière blanche typique	tarwebier maar geen typisch witbier
	barley malt, wheat malt, water, yeast, hops	malt d'orge, malt de froment, eau, levure, houblon	gerstemout, tarwemout, water, gist, hop
	white-blond not filtered or pasteurised	blanc blond non filtrée, non pasteurisée	witblond ongefilterd, niet gepasteuriseerd
	Mellow beer with aromas of lychee and mango owing to the different hops used.	Bière douce, avec des arômes de litchi et de mangue, du fait des variétés de houblon utilisées.	Zacht bier met aroma's van lychee en mango door de gebruikte hopsoorten.
	Serve in a tulip glass.	Verser dans un verre tulipe.	Uitschenken in een tulpglas.
i	A typical wheat beer where the typical herbs have been replaced by specific hop varieties. The French expression sounds like 'Si sweet...'.	Une bière de froment typique où les épices typiques ont été remplacées par des variétés spécifiques de houblon. Prononcez en français 'Si sweet...'.	Een typisch tarwebier waarbij de typische kruiden vervangen zijn door specifieke hopsoorten. De Franse uitspraak klinkt als 'Si sweet...'.

Interesting websites
Des sites internet intéressantes
Enkele interesante websites

www.belgianbeerboard.com
www.ratebeer.com
www.beerparadise.be
www.zythos.be
www.bjcp.org
www.belgenbier.be
www.belgische-bieren.be
www.levenindebrouwerij.be
www.beeradvocate.com
blog.seniorennet.be/bierblog (bierblog William Roelens)

From the brewers' jargon

(Source: Basic Beer Course of the Belgische Brouwers – Brasseurs Belges)

Raw materials

Brewing water – water, one of the main materials in the brewing process, can be corrected to guarantee a constant quality and composition. The bacteriological purity and the chemical composition of the water are of crucial importance when brewing beer. Some beer types require a specific 'kind' of water. The English Pale Ale, for example, is known for its high mineral content, while the water used for Czech Pilsner contains a very low mineral percentage.

Barley – not all varieties are suitable for beer production. Only the two-row summer barley and the six-row winter barley qualify for malting. Belgian brewers mainly use imported barley. To produce one litre of 5 % alc. vol. beer (e.g. Pilsner) approximately 250 grams of barley are needed.

Malt / malting – barley grains germinate with water, warmth and air. After the grain is moistened, it begins to germinate. The germs produce enzymes that convert the starch in the grain into sugars during the brewing process. As soon as the enzymes appear, the germinating process slows down. At this moment the malter stops the germinating process by kilning (or drying) the grain. The higher the kilning temperature, the darker the malt: **light-coloured** malt dries at 85 °C, **caramel malt** at 105 °C and **black roasted** malt at approximately 130 °C.

Wheat – after barley the most commonly used grain species. The wheat is added to the **mash**. It gives Witbier and Gueuze their typical, fresh-sour flavour.

Corn – is used to give specialty beers a fuller-bodied taste. The corn is added to germination first because the germ contains a fat that alters the taste and the foaming of the beer. Corn and rice are added to the **mash** to guarantee a constant flavour and stability. They increase the starch content of the mash without increasing the protein level. Proteins are important for the growth of the yeast and the foaming of the beer.

Rice – broken rice is used to give blond Lager beers a drier, lighter feel in the mouth.

Spelt – a grain species, mainly used as cattle feed and also sporadically in the beer brewing process.

Hops – this 'green gold' is used very sparingly (100 to 300 grams per hectolitre of beer). It gives the beer its typical fine bitter taste and aroma. Hops are also meant to keep the beer better for a longer time. Hops (natural or dried in pellets) are added during the boil of the **wort**. Only female hop cones are used. They contain lupulone, a yellow, very strong bitter component. Hop varieties can be divided into two classes: **bittering hops**, of which only a small quantity is needed, and **aroma hops**, which are less bitter and contain a high level of aromatic, volatile oils. The aromatic Hallertau from Bavaria was introduced in Belgium by the priest of Affligem in 1907. The bitterness of the beer is expressed in EBUs.

EBU – abbreviation of European Bitter Unit. This is a measurement unit to express the bitterness of the beer. One EBU is equivalent to 1 mg iso-alpha acids per litre of beer. However, the overall bitterness of the beer is not only determined by the hops but also by tanning substances in malt or other grains and the presence or absence of herbs. Beers with a mild bitterness have an EBU value that ranges from 5 to 15. Very bitter beers have an EBU value of 40 or more. A Pilsner with a bitterness of 25 EBUs is already considered bitter.

Hop pellets – grains of ground hops.

Ageing hops – hop cones that are two to three years old and that are therefore less bitter. They are mainly used for the production of lambics.

Yeasting – the yeast culture or pure culture of every brewery determines the characteristics of the beer or beer style. Every style has its own, specific yeast. E.g. *Saccharomyces Carlsbergensis* is the most suitable yeast for lagers, *Saccharomyces Cerevisiae* is used for ales. The yeast converts the sugars in the **wort** into alcohol and carbon dioxide. Proteins are important for the growth of the yeast.

Lager yeasts – are pitched to the hopped wort by the brewer. They operate best at low temperatures (ranging from 6 to 12 °C) and settle to the bottom at the end of the fermentation process. They are often referred to as bottom-fermenting yeasts. As the chance that wild yeast strains develop is rather small, lagers have a stable flavour.

Ale yeasts – are pitched to the hopped wort by the brewer. They operate best at high temperatures (ranging from 15 to 25 °C) and rise to the surface at the end of the fermentation process. Therefore they are often called top-fermenting yeasts. As there is a higher chance that wild yeast strains develop, there are more differences in taste.

Spontaneous or wild yeasts – are not pitched to the wort by the brewer. The **wort** is impregnated with wild yeasts, such as *Brettanomyces Bruxellensis* and *Brettanomyces Lambicus*, when in touch with cool air. These yeasts are only found in certain regions, more precisely in regions where Lambics are made: the Zenne valley and southwestern Brabant (Payottenland).

Mixed yeasts – the basis of beers of mixed origin is usually a top-fermenting beer. After the main fermentation, part of the brew is pumped into oak barrels called 'foeders' for eighteen months or more. During fermentation a lactic acid yeast is produced, while the microorganisms and tannins in the wood also act on the beer, forming fruity esters. Then, the beer is filtered and blended with young beer. Examples are the Flemish red-brown beers.

The brewing process

Mashing – the first step in the brewing process, where the milled malt, mixed with brewing water, is heated. This way the enzymes in the malt convert the starch in the malt grains into fermentable sugars and the proteins are broken down. The tannins in the barley have an influence on the colour and flavour of the beer. It is possible to add raw grains to the mash, so the brewer can increase the quantity of starch without increasing the protein content. This is favourable to the beer's stability.

Wort – a sugary liquid, ready for fermentation, obtained by the infusion or decoction of farinaceous materials (malt, wheat or other raw grains), following the brewing procedure and by adding hop during the boil. The **density** and the colour of the beer are now determined. The colour is expressed in **EBC** colour units, the density in degrees Plato.

EBC Colour scale – colour scale to determine the colour of beer or wort, as established by the European Brewery Convention. 1 EBC corresponds to 1 ml iodine per 100 ml of water. In practice the colour of the beer is compared to a set of tubes that all represent a different colour gradation. The darker the beer, the higher the EBC colour value.

Density – the percentage of sucrose by the weight of the wort. It is expressed in degrees **Plato** or **Balling** (percentage of sucrose per 100 grams of unfermented wort at a temperature of 20 °C). Density is also referred to as specific gravity or weight of extract.

Whirlpooling – a centrifugal mechanism separates components of different density from each other. This way the trub (the hops and insoluble components or yeast rests) can be separated from the liquid wort. The mechanism can be compared to that of a juice extractor.

Primary fermentation – after the wort has been whirlpooled or filtered, it is chilled (the temperature depends on the yeast used) and passed through yeast cells in the fermentation tanks. The yeast converts the sugars into alcohol and carbon dioxide. The higher the sugar content, the higher the alcohol content and the more carbon dioxide. At the end of fermentation some 20 % of unfermentable residual sugars is left. The alcohol stays in the slightly alcoholised liquid. This is the first time in the brewing process that the product can be called **'beer'**. The carbon dioxide escapes and is collected to be added again afterwards, at the moment of bottling.

Lagering or secondary fermentation – after primary fermentation the beer is racked to big lager tanks for further maturation. Here it is allowed to sit for up to several months. Some breweries regularly tap the yeast, that little by little settles on the bottom of the tank. During this stage of the process the flavour, bouquet and character of the beer are refined. The remaining sugars are converted into alcohol and carbon dioxide to a previously determined percentage that varies for each beer, until the beer is saturated.

Alcohol by volume percentage – the number of centilitres of alcohol per 1 litre of beer.

Filtering – before the beer is bottled or kegged, the protein flocks are removed by filtering, although some breweries offer unfiltered beer.

Pasteurising – filtered beers are usually pasteurised to prevent the development of bacteria or possible re-fermentation. Although this has a certain impact on the taste, it makes the taste more constant and is necessary for a long storage life, especially where export beer is concerned.

Re-fermentation in the bottle – this is the third fermentation, after primary and secondary fermentation during lagering. Right before bottling or kegging some sugar and a minimal quantity of yeast are added in order for the beer to continue fermenting while it is stocked in warm storage rooms (20 to 22 °C). The taste of a beer that has been re-fermented in the bottle constantly evolves. After a year it may be totally different from the taste after the first month. By re-fermentation an additional quantity of carbon dioxide is formed, producing extra pressure in the bottle and a nice, full foam head.

Dry hopping – dry hopping means that hops are added after boiling the wort. Often hop extracts or oil are used, but also dried aroma hops. They are usually added between primary and secondary fermentation to enhance the hop aroma in the beer.

Bottling – the bottles or kegs must be filled carefully so as not to lose any carbon dioxide. Therefore, the bottles or kegs are first pressurized before they are filled with beer. Contact between the beer and air should be avoided as much as possible so that the air in the bottle does not cause the beer to oxidize. Right before bottling it is possible to add certain components to increase the foam head (e.g. carbon dioxide), adjust the colour (e.g. caramel) or improve the taste (e.g. saccharin).

Aperçu du jargon des brasseurs

(Source : Cours élémentaire bière des 'Belgische Brouwers – Brasseurs Belges')

Les matières premières

Eau de brassage – l'eau, l'une des plus importantes matières premières dans le brassage, peut être améliorée afin de garantir une qualité et une composition constantes. La pureté bactériologique et la composition chimique de l'eau sont primordiales pour le brassage d'une bière. Pour certains types de bière, une eau spécifique est exigée. Ainsi, la Pale Ale anglaise est connue pour son haut taux en sel tandis que l'eau de la pils tchèque n'en contient que très peu.

Orge – Toutes les variétés ne conviennent pas pour la production de bière. Seul l'orge d'été à deux rangs et l'orge d'hiver à six rangs entrent en considération pour être maltés. Les brasseurs belges utilisent surtout de l'orge provenant de l'étranger. Pour brasser 1 litre de bière à 5 % vol. d'alcool (telle la Pils), environ 250 grammes d'orge sont nécessaires.

Malt / malts – c'est sous l'influence de l'eau, de la chaleur et de l'air que les grains d'orge germent. Après humidification des grains, ils commencent à germer. Au cours du processus de brassage, ces germes produisent des enzymes qui transforment l'amidon des grains en sucres. Dès que ces enzymes sont présents, le processus de germination ralentit. Le malt arrêtera de germer grâce au touraillage du grain (ou séchage). Plus haute est la température de séchage, plus sombre est le malt : le malt clair est séché en l'occurrence à 85 °C, le malt caramel à 105 °C et le malt noir brûlé à environ 130 °C.

Froment – après l'orge, c'est la céréale la plus utilisée. Ajouté à la pâte, il apporte le goût frais caractéristique des bières blanches et de la gueuze.

Maïs – on l'utilise pour donner aux bières spéciales un goût plus enveloppant. Le maïs est dégermé car le germe contient de la graisse qui altère le goût et la formation de mousse. Du maïs et du riz sont ajoutés à la pâte, garantissant ainsi la stabilité des bières et un goût constant. Ils veillent à augmenter la teneur en amidon du brassin sans pour autant augmenter la quantité de protéines. Les protéines jouent un rôle important dans l'activation de la levure et la formation de la mousse.

Riz – le riz brisé est utilisé pour donner aux bières blondes à fermentation basse une saveur plus sèche et légère.

Epeautre – cette variété de froment est avant tout destinée au fourrage mais elle est occasionnellement utilisée pour le brassage.

Houblon – appelé 'l'or vert', il est utilisé avec parcimonie (100 à 300 grammes par hectolitre de bière). C'est lui qui donne à la bière son goût amer typique et son arôme raffiné. Grâce au houblon, on peut également mieux conserver la bière et plus longtemps. Le houblon (naturel, séché ou en pellets) est ajouté pendant l'ébullition du moût. Seules les cônes du houblon femelles sont utilisés. Ils contiennent de la lupuline, une substance jaune très corsée et amère. Deux grandes variétés sont utilisées : le houblon amer dont seule une petite quantité est nécessaire et les variétés aromatiques qui, elles, sont moins amères et contiennent un grand taux d'huiles essentielles. Le Hallertau aromatique de Beieren a été introduit pour la première fois en Belgique en 1907 par le pasteur d'Affligem. L'amertume de la bière est exprimée en EBU.

EBU – abréviation de 'European Bitter Unit'. Elle sert d'indication de mesure pour l'amertume de la bière. Une unité de mesure est égale à 1 mg d'acide iso-alpha par litre de bière. Le houblon à lui seul ne détermine pas toute l'amertume de la bière. Les tannins du malt et d'autres grains ainsi que l'ajout d'épices jouent également un rôle important à cet égard. Une bière faiblement amère a une valeur EBU de 5 à 15, une bière très amère une valeur EBU de 40 ou plus. Une pils avec une amertume de 25 EBU est déjà perçue comme amère.

Pellets de houblon – grains de houblon moulu.

Houblon suranné – des cônes de houblon âgés de deux à trois ans, qui ont une amertune réduite. Il est surtout utilisé dans la production de lambic.

Levures – la culture de levure et ses bouillons propres à chaque brasserie donnent à chaque type de bière sa particularité. Chaque type de bière a en effet sa levure spécifique : la Saccharomyces Carlsbergensis est la mieux adaptée aux bières à basse fermentation, la Saccharomyces Cerevisiaeaux aux bières à haute fermentation. La levure transforme les sucres du moût en alcool et gaz carbonique. Les protéines, quant à elles, sont importantes pour l'activation de la levure.

Fermentation basse – les levures sont placées par le brasseur sur le moût houblonné. Elles sont actives à basse température (6 - 12 °C) et descendent au fond à la fin de la fermentation. Les bières à fermentation basse ont un goût très stable car le risque que se développent des levures sauvages est faible.

Fermentation haute – les levures sont placées par le brasseur sur le moût houblonné. Elles sont actives à des températures plus hautes (15 - 25 °C) et flottent à la surface en fin de fermentation. C'est pourquoi on les appelle souvent bières 'fermentées en haut'. Dans les bières à fermentation haute, les différences de goût sont plus marquées car il y a davantage de risque que des levures sauvages se développent.

Fermentation spontanée – les levures ne sont pas placées par le brasseur sur le moût. Les levures sauvages comme Brettanomyces Bruxellensis et Brettanomyces Lambicus ensemencent le moût au contact de l'air froid. Ces levures ne sont présentes que dans certaines régions, notamment là où le lambic est fabriqué : la vallée de la Senne et le Brabant du Sud-Ouest (Pajottenland).

Fermentation mixte – une bière à fermentation haute sert souvent de base aux bières à fermentation mixte. Après la fermentation principale, une partie du brassin est transvasée pour dix-huit mois ou plus dans des fûts de chêne. Durant cette maturation naît une fermentation lactique. Les micro-organismes et tannins présents dans le bois vont influer sur la bière et former des esters fruités. Ensuite, après avoir été filtrée, la bière est coupée avec une bière jeune. Citons pour exemple les bières rouges-brunes flamandes.

Pâte ou saccharification – c'est la première étape du brassage. Le malt broyé est mélangé avec de l'eau de brassage puis chauffé. Les enzymes transforment l'amidon des grains de malt en sucres fermentescibles. Les protéines sont brisées. Les tannins de l'orge influencent la couleur et le goût de la bière. Des grains crus pourront être ensuite ajoutés à la pâte. Le brasseur peut ainsi augmenter la quantité d'amidon sans pour autant augmenter la quantité de protéines. Ceci détermine la stabilité d'une bière.

Moût – un liquide sucré (la pâte chauffée) servant à la fermentation. Il est obtenu par infusion ou décoction de matières premières contenant de l'amidon (malt, blé ou autres grains bruts) suite au procédé de brassage et à l'ajout de houblon lors de l'ébullition. Il détermine la densité et la couleur de la bière. La couleur est traduite en EBC, la densité en degrés Plato.

Echelle de couleurs EBC – l'échelle de la couleur de la bière / du moût déterminée par la Convention Européenne de Brasserie (European Brewery Convention). 1 EBC correspond à 1 ml d'iode par 100 ml d'eau. En pratique, on compare la couleur de la bière en la posant à côté de tubes ayant chacun une gradation différente. Plus une bière est foncée, plus la valeur EBC est élevée.

Densité primitive – correspond à la proportion de sucre dans le moût. La densité est exprimée en degrés Plato ou Balling (quantité de sucre par 100 grammes de moût non fermenté à une température ambiante de 20 °C). Notons d'autres qualificatifs de la densité : masse volumique, poids, teneur en extrait.

Centrifugation – en utilisant des forces centrifuges, les substances de densités différentes sont séparées les unes des autres. Ainsi, la drêche (le houblon et les composants non dissous) est séparée du moût liquide. Son fonctionnement est analogue à celui d'une centrifugeuse à jus.

Fermentation principale – il faut d'abord que le moût soit refroidi (à une température dépendant du type de fermentation) et centrifugé ou filtré. Puis, il est transféré dans des cuves à fermentation où il est ensemencé par des souches très pures de levure. Celle ci transforme les sucres du moût en alcool et gaz carbonique. Plus la teneur en sucre est élevée, plus la teneur en alcool sera élevée et davantage de gaz carbonique sera formé. A la fin de la fermentation, il reste environ 20% de sucres résiduels infermentescibles. L'alcool, par contre, reste dans le liquide à présent légèrement alcoolisé : l'on peut maintenant parler pour la première fois de 'bière'. Le gaz carbonique qui s'échappe est récupéré pour être rajouté ensuite lors de la mise en bouteille.

Conditionnement ou fermentation secondaire – après la fermentation principale, la bière entre en maturation pendant quelques mois dans de grandes cuves de garde. Certaines brasseries enlèvent régulièrement la levure amassée au fond de la cuve. Durant cette maturation, le goût, le bouquet et le caractère mûrissent et s'affinent. Les sucres résiduels sont transformés en alcool et en gaz carbonique, et ce jusqu'à un taux préétabli et que la bière soit saturée.

Pourcentage en volume / teneur en alcool – le rapport du nombre de centilitres d'alcool par litre de bière.

Filtrage – les protéines coagulées (flocon) sont éliminées par filtrage avant que la bière ne soit mise en bouteille ou en fût. Certaines brasseries proposent des bières non filtrées.

Pasteurisation – les bières filtrées sont la plupart du temps pasteurisées afin d'éviter le développement de bactéries et une nouvelle fermentation. Ceci se fait aux dépens du goût (qui reste néanmoins constant) mais est indispensable pour une conservation longue en cas d'exportation.

Nouvelle fermentation en bouteille – cette troisième fermentation fait suite à la fermentation principale et à la fermentation secondaire lors du conditionnement. Peu avant la mise en bouteille / le remplissage sont ajoutés un peu de sucre et une infime quantité de levure. La bière continue ainsi à mûrir lors du stockage en chambres chaudes (20 à 22 °C). Une bière qui a subi une nouvelle fermentation en bouteille verra son goût évoluer avec le temps. Après un an, son goût sera parfois totalement différent qu'après un mois. Avec cette fermentation, une quantité supplémentaire de dioxyde de carbone est formée. Cela génère une pression supplémentaire dans la bouteille et garantit un beau faux col plein.

Dry hopping – ou houblonnage à sec. On ajoute du houblon après l'ébullition du moût. Cela se fait souvent avec des extraits de houblon ou d'huile de houblon. De l'arôme de houblon séché est parfois aussi utilisé. Ceci se fait le plus souvent après la fermentation principale et avant la fermentation secondaire afin d'augmenter l'arôme du houblon de la bière.

Mise en bouteille – le remplissage des bouteilles / fûts doit se faire avec grand soin pour ne pas perdre le gaz carbonique. C'est pourquoi les bouteilles / fûts sont d'abord mis sous pression avant d'être remplis de bière. La bière est mise le moins possible en contact avec l'air pour éviter l'oxydation de la bière. Juste avant la mise en bouteille, certaines substances sont ajoutées pour améliorer le faux col (p. ex. du gaz carbonique), pour modifier la couleur (p. ex. du caramel), ou pour adapter le goût (p. ex. de la saccharine).

Uit het brouwersjargon

(Bron: Basiscursus Bier van 'Belgische Brouwers – Brasseurs Belges')

De grondstoffen

Brouwwater – water, een van de belangrijkste grondstoffen bij het brouwen, kan gecorrigeerd worden om een constante kwaliteit en samenstelling te garanderen. De bacteriologische zuiverheid en de scheikundige samenstelling van het water zijn van primordiaal belang voor het brouwen van bier. Voor bepaalde biertypen zijn er specifieke 'soorten' water vereist. Zo staat bv. de Engelse pale ale bekend om zijn hoog zoutgehalte, terwijl het water van Tsjechische pils heel weinig zout bevat.

Gerst – niet alle variëteiten zijn geschikt voor de bierproductie, enkel de tweerijige zomergerst en de zesrijige wintergerst komen in aanmerking om gemout te worden. Belgische brouwers gebruiken vooral gerst uit het buitenland. Om 1 liter bier van 5 % vol. alc. (vb. Pils) te brouwen is er circa 250 gram gerst nodig.

Mout/mouten – gerstkorrels kiemen onder invloed van water, warmte en lucht. Na bevochtiging van het graan begint het te kiemen. De kiemen produceren enzymen die het zetmeel uit de korrel tijdens het brouwproces omzetten in suikers. Zodra de enzymen aanwezig zijn, vertraagt het kiemingsproces. Dan stopt de mouter het kiemen door het graan te eesten (of te drogen). Hoe hoger de droogtemperatuur, hoe donkerder het mout: **bleke mout** droogt op 85 °C, **karamelmout** op 105 °C, **zwartgebrande mout** op ongeveer 130 °C.

Tarwe – na gerst de meest gebruikte graansoort. Tarwe wordt toegevoegd aan het **beslag**. Het geeft de typische friszurige smaak aan witbier en geuze.

Maïs – wordt gebruikt om speciaalbieren een vollere smaak te geven. De maïs wordt ontkiemd omdat de kiem vet bevat die de smaak en schuimvorming van het bier verstoort.

Maïs en rijst worden toegevoegd aan het **beslag** waardoor een constante smaak en stabiliteit van de bieren kan worden gewaarborgd. Ze zorgen ervoor dat het zetmeelgehalte van het brouwsel verhoogt zonder de hoeveelheid eiwitten erin te vergroten. Eiwitten zijn van belang voor de voeding van de gist en de schuimvorming van het bier.

Rijst – breukrijst wordt gebruikt om blonde bieren van lage gisting een droger en lichter mondgevoel te geven.

Spelt – een tarwesoort die hoofdzakelijk bestemd is als veevoer en sporadisch ook bij het brouwen gebruikt wordt.

Hop – dit 'groene goud' wordt zeer spaarzaam aangewend (100 tot 300 gram per hectoliter bier). Het geeft de typische, fijnbittere smaak en aroma aan het bier. Dankzij de hop kan men bier ook langer en beter bewaren. De hop (natuurlijk, gedroogd of in pellets) wordt toegevoegd tijdens het koken van het **wort**. Enkel vrouwelijke hopbellen worden gebruikt. Ze bevatten lupuline, een gele zeer pittig - bittere stof.
Er zijn twee rassen: **bitterhop** waarvan slechts een kleine hoeveelheid nodig is en **aromatische variëteiten** die minder bitter zijn en een hoog gehalte aan aromatische vluchtige oliën bevatten. De aromatische Hallertau uit Beieren werd in 1907 voor het eerst in België geïntroduceerd door de pastoor van Affligem. De bitterheid van het bier wordt uitgegedrukt in EBU.

EBU – afkorting van 'European Bitter Unit'. Het is een maataanduiding voor de bitterheid van bier. Eén maateenheid is gelijk aan 1 mg iso - alfazuur per liter bier. Maar niet alleen de hop bepaalt de totale bitterheid van het bier. Ook looistoffen uit de mout of andere granen en de eventuele toevoeging van kruiden spelen hierbij een rol. Een bier dat zwak bitter is, heeft een EBU - waarde van 5 tot 15. Een erg bitter bier heeft een EBU - waarde van 40 of meer. Een pils met een bitterheid van 25 EBU wordt al als bitter ervaren.

Hoppellets – korrels van gemalen hop

Overjaarse hop – hopbellen die twee tot drie jaar oud zijn waardoor hun bitterheid afgenomen is. Wordt vooral gebruikt bij de productie van lambiek.

Gisting – De gistcultuur van elke brouwerij, de reincultuur, is verantwoordelijk voor de eigenheid van de bieren en het biertype. Elk biertype heeft zijn specifieke gist: *Saccharomyces Carlsbergensis* is het meest geschikt voor lage-gistingsbieren, *Saccharomyces Cerevisiae* voor hoge-gistingsbieren. De gist zet de suikers in het **wort** om tot alcohol en koolzuurgas. Eiwitten zijn van belang voor de voeding van de gist.

Lage gisten – worden door de brouwer op het gehopte wort geplaatst. Ze zijn actief bij lage temperaturen (6 - 12 °C) en zakken op het einde van de gisting naar de bodem. Bij lage-gistingsbieren is de smaak van het bier stabiel omdat de kans klein is dat er zich wilde gisten ontwikkelen.

Hoge gisten – worden door de brouwer op het gehopte wort geplaatst. Ze zijn actief bij hogere temperaturen (15 - 25 °C) en drijven op het einde van het gistingsproces aan de oppervlakte. Daarom worden deze bieren ook vaak bovengegiste bieren genoemd. Bij hoge-gistingsbieren komen meer smaakverschillen voor omdat de kans groter is dat er zich wilde gisten ontwikkelen.

Spontane of wilde gisten – worden niet door de brouwer op het gehopte wort geplaatst. De wildgisten zoals de *Brettanomyces Bruxellensis* en *Brettanomyces Lambicus* enten zich op het **wort** door contact met de koele lucht. Deze gisten komen enkel in bepaalde regio's voor, namelijk in de regio's waar lambiek wordt gemaakt: de Zennevallei en Zuidwest-Brabant (Pajottenland).

Gemengde gisten – de basis van gemengde-gistingsbieren is meestal bier van hoge gisting; een gedeelte van het brouwsel wordt na de hoofdgisting overgepompt en gaat voor achttien maanden of langer in eiken vaten en foeders. Tijdens dit rijpingsproces ontstaat een melkzure gisting, terwijl de micro-organismen en tannines die in het hout zitten eveneens op het bier gaan inwerken en fruitige esters vormen. Daarna wordt het bier gefilterd en versneden met jong bier. Voorbeelden hiervan zijn de Vlaamse roodbruine bieren.

Het brouwproces

Beslag of versuikering – de eerste stap in het brouwproces waarbij het geplette mout, vermengd met brouwwater, wordt opgewarmd. De enzymen zetten het zetmeel in de moutkorrels om in vergistbare suikers en de eiwitten worden afgebroken. De looistoffen van de gerst beïnvloeden de kleur en de smaak van het bier. Aan het beslag kunnen nog ruwe granen worden toegevoegd, waardoor de brouwer de hoeveelheid zetmeel kan vergroten zonder dat de hoeveelheid eiwitten toeneemt. De stabiliteit van een bier wordt hierdoor gunstig beïnvloed.

Wort – een suikerhoudende vloeistof (het opgewarmde beslag) klaar voor de gisting. Het wordt verkregen door infusie of decoctie van zetmeelhoudende grondstoffen (mout, tarwe of andere ruwe granen) volgens het brouwprocédé en door toevoeging van hop bij het koken. De **densiteit** en de kleur van het bier zijn nu bepaald. De kleur wordt uitgedrukt in **EBC**, de densiteit in graden plato.

EBC-kleurenschaal – de schaal voor de bepaling van de kleur van bier/wort vastgesteld door de Europese Brouwerij Conventie (European Brewery Convention). 1 EBC komt overeen met 1 ml jodium per 100 ml water. In de praktijk vergelijkt men de kleur door het bier naast buisjes te leggen die elk een verschillende kleurgradatie weergeven. Naarmate een bier donkerder is, heeft het een hogere EBC-waarde.

Densiteit – de verhouding suiker tot het wort. De densiteit wordt uitgedrukt in graden **plato** of **balling** (hoeveelheid suikers per 100 gram ongegist wort bij een temperatuur van 20 °C). Synoniemen voor densiteit: dichtheid, zwaarte, extractgehalte.

Centrifugeren – door gebruik te maken van ronddraaiende krachten worden stoffen van verschillende dichtheid van elkaar gescheiden. Zo wordt draf (de hop en onopgeloste bestanddelen) gescheiden van het vloeibare wort. De werking kan worden vergeleken met die van een sapcentrifuge.

Hoofdgisting – het afgekoelde (de temperatuur is afhankelijk van de soort gisting) en gecentrifugeerde of gefilterde wort wordt in de gisttanks met gistcellen bezaaid. De gist zet de suikers om in alcohol en koolzuurgas. Hoe hoger het suikergehalte, hoe hoger het alcoholgehalte en hoe meer koolzuurgas er wordt gevormd. Bij het einde van de gisting blijft er ongeveer 20 % onvergistbare restsuiker over. De alcohol blijft in de vloeistof die nu licht gealcoholiseerd is en voor het eerst wordt er in het brouwproces van 'bier' gesproken . Het koolzuurgas ontsnapt en wordt opgevangen om later te worden toegevoegd bij het bottelen.

Lagering of nagisting – na de hoofdgisting ondergaat het bier een rijpingsproces in grote lagertanks waarin het enkele maanden kan verblijven. Sommige brouwerijen tappen de gist, die zich langzamerhand op de bodem van de tank verzamelt, geregeld af. Tijdens deze rijping verfijnen de smaak, het boeket en het karakter en worden de nog resterende suikers omgezet in alcohol en koolzuurgas, tot op een vooraf per bier vastgesteld percentage, tot het bier verzadigd is.

Volumeprocent / alcoholgehalte – de verhouding van het aantal centiliters alcohol op 1 liter bier.

Filteren – voor het bier gebotteld of op vat wordt afgevuld, worden de eiwitverbindingen (vlokken) verwijderd door filtering. Enkele brouwerijen bieden ongefilterd bier aan.

Pasteuriseren – gefilterde bieren worden meestal gepasteuriseerd om de ontwikkeling van bacteriën en eventuele hergisting tegen te gaan. Dit gaat ten koste van de smaak (die hiermee wel constant blijft) maar is noodzakelijk voor een lange houdbaarheid met het oog op de export.

Hergisting op de fles – dit is de derde gisting na de hoofdgisting en de nagisting tijdens het lageren. Vlak voor de botteling / afvulling wordt nog wat suiker en een minuscule hoeveelheid gist toegevoegd waardoor het bier verder rijpt bij stockage in warme kamers (20 à 22 °C). De smaak van een bier met hergisting op de fles ontwikkelt zich verder met de tijd. Na een jaar smaakt het soms totaal anders dan na een maand. Door de hergisting wordt nog een extra hoeveelheid koolzuur gevormd. Die brengt extra druk in het flesje en zorgt voor een mooie, volle schuimkraag.

Dry hopping – drooghoppen is het toevoegen van hop na het koken van het wort. Vaak gebeurt dit met hopextracten of hopolie, maar naar verluidt wordt ook wel gedroogde aromahop gebruikt. De hop wordt meestal na de hoofdgisting en voor de nagisting toegevoegd om het hoparoma van het bier te verhogen.

Bottelen – het vullen van de flessen/vaten moet zorgvuldig gebeuren om het aanwezige koolzuurgas niet te verliezen. Daarom worden de flessen/vaten eerst onder druk gebracht voor zij met bier worden gevuld. Het bier wordt zo weinig mogelijk met lucht in contact gebracht om te vermijden dat de lucht in het flesje het bier zou laten oxideren. Vlak voor het bottelen worden soms producten toegevoegd om de schuimkraag te verbeteren (bv. koolzuurgas), om de kleur bij te sturen (bv. karamel), of om de smaak aan te passen (bv. sacharine).

Definitions & Beer styles

Definitions

Beer – the drink obtained after alcoholic fermentation of a wort, composed mainly of farinaceous and sugary materials, of which at least 60 % barley or wheat malt, hop (whether or not processed) and brewing water. *(Definition according to the Belgian Royal Decree of 1993)*

Gueuze and Lambic (or a combination) – the name can only be used for sour beers obtained by spontaneous fermentation. The names **Old Gueuze** and **Old Lambic** are protected by European regulations and stand for the authentic, traditional specialty beers that are obtained by spontaneous fermentation only and that have matured for a long time in oak wood barrels.

Organic beer – beer that is exclusively made from certified organic materials, processed without any chemical additives. The norms are established in an EEC regulation of 1991 *(Council regulation No 2092 / 91 / EEC of 24 June 1991 on organic production of agricultural products and indications referring thereto on agricultural products and foodstuffs, amended by regulation 1991 / 2006 of 21 December 2006).*

Belgian beer styles

Different opinions exist about beer styles, their names, definitions and classifications. The classification of the 'Belgian Brewers' divides beer styles according to yeasting method.

Bottom-fermenting (lagers)

Pilsner or lager beer – pioneered in the Czech town of Pilsen in 1842. Pilsner is brewed with soft water and a light coloured malt (pale malt). It is richly hopped and has a solid, relatively long-lasting head. The original bitter taste has evolved to a refined, hop bitter flavour. The alcohol level ranges from 4.5 to 5.2 % alc. vol.

Table beer – beer with an extract content between 1 and 4 ° Plato and an alcohol level ranging from 0.8 to 2.5 % alc. vol. They contain mainly complex sugars. They exist in neutral to bitter versions, in blond and trippel. Sweet table beers usually receive the additional title of brown, faro, stout or bock.

Low-alcohol and non-alcoholic beer – these beers are brewed with a lower density and less yeast cells are added during fermentation. **Low-alcohol:** alcohol content between 0.5 and 1.2 % alc. vol. **Non-alcoholic:** alcohol content of maximum 0.5 % alc. vol.

Bock – especially popular in Germany and originally brewed during the months that it is not too hot (autumn, winter and spring) because it was difficult to conserve this beer in summer without cooling techniques. Less hopped than Pilsner but with a higher alcohol content: 6.4 to 7.6 alc. vol.

Dortmunder or export – beer style from the region of Dortmund. Lighter coloured, milder and less bitter than Pilsner. The density and the alcohol content (5.5 to 6 alc. vol.) are higher than in Pilsner beers. It is brewed with water that is rich in sulphate and minerals.

Rauchbier – typical low-fermenting beer from the German region of Nürnberg-Bamberg. The barley malt is dried above a beech wood fire, giving the beer its typical burned, smoked or roasted taste. Usually slightly sweet and amber-coloured to very dark. Not common in Belgium

Top-fermenting (ales)

Amber or Speciale Belge – launched after World War I as the 'English-style beer of victory'. The specific amber colour is produced by the use of colour or cara(mel) malts. The density and alcohol content can be compared to those of Pilsner, although a number of degustation beers with a higher alcohol content (from 6 to 12 % alc. vol.) have been developed over the past few years.

Witbier or White beer – Hoegaarden – and especially Pierre Celis, who started to brew this typical wheat beer again in 1966 – played a pioneer's role in the revival of White beers. The mash contains unmalted wheat (30%), sometimes blended with oat. During the boil, coriander and orange peels (curaçao) may be added to the wort, resulting in the typical, refreshing flavour. White beers are usually not filtered and slightly turbid. The alcohol content is, just like in Pilsner, 4.5 to 5 % alc. vol.

Trappist ale – beer brewed in abbeys following the traditions of the Trappist-Cistercian monks (hence the authenticity logo). Exists in three versions: blond, double / dark or trippel. Worldwide there are only seven Trappist abbeys left where beer is brewed, six of them in Belgium: Chimay, Orval, Rochefort, Westmalle, Westvleteren and Achel (on the Dutch border).

Abbey beer – collective name used for beers where the brand refers to an existing or no longer existing abbey. Like Trappist beer, Abbey beer exists in three versions, but blond and trippel are slightly more represented. In order to carry the label of 'Certified Belgian Abbey Beer', beer commercialised after 12 August 1999 must comply with the following conditions:

- **either** the beer is brewed at an existing non-Trappist abbey (or an existing abbey that commercialises a beer brewed under its responsibility and in license in a lay brewery);
- **or** the beer is brewed by a lay brewery that has a contractual, legal relationship with an existing abbey to use the abbey's name. Commercialisation is done by the lay brewery;
- **and** the abbey or order concerned is paid royalties to support charity projects;
- **and** it should be based on a historical background (the abbey must have brewed beer in the past);
- **and** the abbey has the right to monitor the publicity.

Blond – light blond to gold-coloured top-fermenting beer with a lightly malty, sweet aroma and a fairly neutral, slightly sweet taste. The aftertaste is rather bitter. Alcohol content ranges from 2.5 to 7 % alc. vol.

Dubbel (double) or dark – originally a beer produced with a double quantity of malt, but now evolved toward a light or dark brown beer with a sweet taste and a bitter aftertaste. Aroma of raisins, liquorice and candy with a roasted touch. Alcohol content approximately 6 % alc. vol.

Tripel (also Trippel) – originally a beer produced with more than twice the normal quantity of malt. Now it stands for a gold-coloured beer with a malty, alcoholic and sometimes slightly sweet taste. The alcohol content ranges between 7 and 9 % alc. vol. The primary fermentation is followed by a secondary fermentation at 8 to 10 °C lasting a fortnight. After that the beer is filtered and bottled, being re-fermented in the bottle at 21 °C for three weeks.

Strong blond – collective name referring to so-called virtuoso beers that excel in their clarity, voluminous head and high alcohol content (7 to 11 % and more). They distinguish themselves by the use of aromatic malt types, ester-like yeasts and high fermentation and maturation temperatures. After a cold maturation in lager tanks, the beer is filtered and bottled with additional dextrose and some yeast. The result is re-fermentation in the bottle during storage in a warm room. After this third fermentation it is stored in a cold room for several months allowing it to stabilise. Strong double also exists.

Saisons – orange-yellow to bronze-coloured summer beer, typically from the regions of Hainaut and Walloon-Brabant. It contains a high level of fermentable sugars and is submitted to warm maturation with dry hopping. The raw hop character is compensated by the unfermented sugars that can form the basis of a possible re-fermentation in the bottle, which contributes to the sparkling, fruity character of this typical summer beer.

Oud Bruin or Flanders brown – this beer style, originating from the region of Oudenaarde-Zottegem, is a slightly sweet-sour beer with a subtle, nut-like character. It is created by a blend of old and young beer, matured in lager tanks. In this sense, it is also a mixed fermenting beer. This blend guarantees a constant flavour and re-fermentation is possible. The alcohol content ranges from 4 to 8.5 % alc. vol.

City or regional beer, Barley Wine and specialty beer – beer with a creative touch given by the brewer, featuring special herbs, honey, chocolate, different raw or malted wheat types and unique yeasts. These beers usually have a fairly high alcohol content. They are deeply rooted in the different regions and hard to classify because they are unique and unequalled. Some beers are inspired by champagne, lagered in marl caves or matured following the champagne production method. The 'Brut'- beers or 'champagne beers', in which the yeast is eliminated from the bottle by 'remuage et dégorgement à la méthode originale' are a fine example of that.

Ale – originally an English / Scottish top-fermenting beer style that can be divided into two main varieties: Pale Ale and Mild Ale. Pale Ale is pale and strongly hopped. Mild Ale is a little darker and less hopped. Their alcohol content ranges from 4 to 6 % alc. vol. Belgium brews its own Ale beers, but they have a totally different character than the English ales: they have a higher density and carbon dioxide content because Belgians prefer a nice foam head, rather than the 'plain' English beers. British beers are either imported to Belgium in containers and bottled there, or brewed in Belgium under licence with an alcohol content and flavour, adapted to the Belgian market.

Scotch (ale) – hard to find in its country of origin, it has become a specialty of Walloon-Brabant and Hainaut. Scotch ale is a heavy, strong and dark beer, very malty, with a slightly burned character and a sweet taste, obtained by the addition of candy sugar.

Stout – originally an Irish beer. Dark, creamy, sweet-bitter with a strong burned or roasted aroma.

Fruit beers – top - fermentation beers with added fruit, fruit juice or fruit flavor. Some have been sweetened artificially, others are brewed according to traditional methods or organically.

Winter or Christmas beer – beers that are especially brewed for the end of year celebrations, with herbs added (honey, cinnamon, cloves and / or liquorice). Most of these beers are malty.

Spontaneous fermenting

Lambic – one of the oldest beers (early middle ages) with ageing hops. Micro-organisms that are present in the air between November and March start the spontaneous fermentation of the wort. The beer matures for months or years in oak wood barrels where the secondary fermentation with the *Brettanomyces Lambicus* and *Bruxellensis* begins, giving the Lambic its dry-sour character. Foamless beer.

Gueuze – a blend of old, not completely fermented out Lambic with young Lambic that undergoes an additional fermentation in the bottle (a champagne bottle that resists the increased carbon dioxide pressure). See also 'Definitions' p. 1164.

Fruit beer – during the lagering fruits (usually cherries) are added to the Lambic. As a result the fructose ferments and a fruity, non-sweet taste is created. Varieties with raspberry, peach, etc. are normally made with fruit juice.

Faro – sour Lambic with added candy sugar, syrup or caramel. Sometimes also a blend of sweetened Lambic and top-fermenting beer.

Mixed fermenting

Red-brown ale – beer from southwestern Flanders, based on reddish barley malts, spicy and less bitter hop varieties and a fresh, slightly sour yeast with lactic acid bacteria. It has a complex taste and is a blend of young beer and filtered beer* that has matured in oak wood barrels for 18 months or more. The tannin and micro-organisms in the barrels act upon the beer, creating fruity esters.

Doctored beer – mix of spontaneous, top- and bottom - fermentation beers.

* According to this definition, Flanders brown can also be considered as a mixed fermentation beer.

- The Beer Judge Certification Program (BJCP Styles) (Belgian) beer style definition is chiefly focused on the technical aspects of production, but takes also into account flavour, colour, look and feel (see: www.bjcp.org). Belgian beers are divided into two groups of Ales, each of which contain several subcategories. As a number of brewers mention these categories, we include them below:

Belgian & French Ale – (Witbier, Belgian Pale Ale, Saison, Bière de Garde, Belgian Specialty Ale).

Belgian Strong Ale – (Belgian Blond Ale, Belgian Dubbel, Belgian Tripel, Belgian Golden Strong Ale, Belgian Dark Strong Ale).

Other categories of BJCP Styles that are also applicable to Belgian beers are Lager Bock, Ale or Lager Fruit Beer, Lager Pilsner, Ale Stout, IPA (English, American or Imperial Pale Ale) and Sour Ale. To the latter belong Flanders Red Ale, Flanders Brown Ale/Oud Bruin, Straight Lambic, Gueuze and Fruit Lambic.

In this classification, Trappist ale and Abbey beer are not regarded as a beer style or category. Rather, they are considered an 'appellation contrôlée': an authenticity label.

Définitions & styles de bières belges

Quelques définitions

Bière – boisson obtenue après fermentation alcoolique d'un moût préparée essentiellement à partir de matières premières amylacées et sucrées dont au moins 60 % de malt d'orge ou de froment, ainsi qu'à partir de houblon, éventuellement sous une forme transformée, et d'eau de brassage. *(définition d'après un arrêté royal de 1993)*

Gueuze et Lambic (ou mélange) – la dénomination ne peut être utilisée que pour des bières acides dont la fermentation spontanée intervient dans le processus de fabrication. Les appellations **Vieille Gueuze** et **Vieux Lambic** sont protégées à un niveau européen et désignent les spécialités traditionnelles authentiques qui ont à 100 % fermenté spontanément et mûri longtemps en fût de chêne.

Bière biologique – bière pour laquelle on utilise exclusivement des ingrédients certifiés biologiques sans ajout chimique. Les directives sont reprises dans une réglementation des EEG de 1991. *(Arrêté nr. 2092 / 91 / EEG du Conseil du 24 juin 1991 concernant les méthodes de production biologiques et directives relatives aux produits agricoles et produits alimentaires, modifié depuis par l'arrêté 1991 / 2006 du 21 décembre 2006)*

Styles de bières belges

- Il existe une diversité de points de vue au sujet des styles de bières, de leur dénomination, leur définition et répartition en catégories. Le classement de 'Brasseurs Belges' répartit les bières en catégories en fonction de leur type de fermentation :

Fermentation basse

Pils ou bière blonde – créée en 1842 dans la ville tchèque Pilsen. Les pils sont brassées avec de l'eau douce et un pâle (malt pils). Cette bière est richement houblonnée et a un faux col solide et relativement constant. Son goût amer à l'origine a évolué vers une saveur amère et raffinée de houblon. La teneur en alcool varie entre 4,5 et 5,2 % vol.

Bière de table – bières avec une teneur en extraits située entre 1° et 4° Plato et une teneur en alcool entre 0,8 et 2,5 % vol qui contiennent surtout des sucres complexes. Ces bières blondes ou triples varient d'un goût neutre à un goût plus amer. Les versions sucrées s'accompagnent quant à elles des dénominations complémentaires de bière brune, faro, stout ou bock.

Bière pauvre en alcool et sans alcool – cette bière est brassée à une densité plus basse et lors de la fermentation, une quantité réduite de levure est ajoutée. **Pauvre en alcool / faiblement alcoolisée :** teneur en alcool entre 0,5 et 1,2 % vol. **Sans alcool :** teneur en alcool de maximum 0,5 % vol.

Bock – populaire surtout en Allemagne, elle était initialement brassée en dehors des mois d'été. La raison était que cette bière pouvait difficilement se conserver en été sans une technique de réfrigération. Moins houblonnée que la pils, mais sa teneur en alcool est plus élevée : de 6,4 à 7,6 % vol.

Dortmunder ou export – style de bière originaire de la région de Dortmund. Plus pâle, plus douce et moins amère que la pils. Sa densité et sa teneur en alcool (5,5 à 6 % vol) sont plus élevées que celles des pils. Elles sont brassées avec une eau riche en sulfate qui contient une quantité importante de sels.

Rauchbier – bière typique à fermentation basse provenant de la région de Nürnberg-Bamberg en Allemagne. Le malt d'orge est séché au-dessus d'un feu de bois d'hêtre. La bière obtient un goût particulier de brûlé, de fumé voire de grillé. En général, elle est un peu plus sucrée et de couleur ambrée à très foncée. Cette style de bière est peu courant en Belgique.

Fermentation haute

Ambrée ou Spéciale Belge – bière de style anglais, lancée après la Première Guerre mondiale en tant que 'bière de la victoire'. Sa couleur ambrée spécifique s'obtient par l'utilisation d'un malt coloré ou cara(mélisé). La densité et la teneur en alcool sont comparables à celle des pils, et ce malgré que ces dernières années, plusieurs bières de dégustation aient été fabriquées avec un taux d'alcool plus élevé (entre 6 et 12 % vol).

Bière blanche – Hoegaarden – et surtout Pierre Celis qui a recommencé en 1966 à brasser cette bière de froment typique – a joué un rôle pionnier dans la renaissance des bières blanches. La pâte est composée à 30 % de froment non malté auquel est parfois mélangé de l'avoine. Lors de l'ébullition, on ajoute de la coriandre et des écorces d'oranges (curaçao), ce qui donne à la bière son goût typique et rafraîchissant. Les bières blanches ne sont généralement pas filtrées et légèrement troubles. La teneur en alcool est la même que celle des pils : de 4,5 à 5 % vol.

Bière trappiste – bière brassée au sein de l'abbaye selon les traditions des trappistes cisterciens (logo d'authenticité). Existe en version blonde, double / foncée ou triple. Il n'existe à travers le monde plus que sept abbayes trappistes qui produisent de la bière et six se situent en Belgique : Chimay, Orval, Rochefort, Westmalle, Westvleteren et Achel (à la frontière avec les Pays-Bas).

Bière d'abbaye – dénomination commune pour les bières dont la marque déposée se réfère à une abbaye existante ou disparue. Dans ces bières d'abbaye, on retrouve les mêmes types de bières que chez les trappistes mais l'accent a été davantage porté sur la bière blonde et la triple. Pour qu'une bière mise sur le marché après le 12 août 1999 puisse avoir le label de licence 'Bière d'Abbaye belge reconnue', elle doit satisfaire aux conditions suivantes :

- **soit** la bière est brassée dans une abbaye non trappiste existante (ou une abbaye fait brasser la bière sous sa responsabilité et licence dans une brasserie laïque tout en commercialisant elle-même la bière),

- **soit** la bière est brassée par une brasserie laïque qui est juridiquement liée par un contrat avec une abbaye existante pour l'utilisation du nom. La commercialisation se fait par la brasserie laïque,
- **et** des royalties doivent être payées à l'abbaye concernée / à l'ordre qui soutient avec ces sommes des projets caritatifs,
- **et** doit reposer sur des antécédents historiques (l'abbaye en question doit avoir également brassé de la bière dans le passé),
- **et** il y a un droit de contrôle de l'abbaye sur la publicité.

Blonde – bière blonde pâle à dorée à fermentation haute. Son arôme doux est légèrement malté et son goût neutre ou légèrement sucré. L'arrière-goût est plutôt amer. Sa teneur en alcool se situe entre 5,5 et 7 % vol.

Double ou foncée – à l'origine, on utilisait pour cette bière une double quantité de malt. Elle a évolué vers une bière de couleur brun clair ou foncée avec un goût sucré et un arrière-goût amer. Arôme de raisin sec, de réglisse et de candi avec une touche de brûlé. Sa teneur en alcool se situe autour de 6 % vol.

Triple – à l'origine, on utilisait pour cette bière plus d'une double quantité de malt. Aujourd'hui, c'est une bière dorée avec un goût malté, alcoolisé et parfois légèrement sucré. Sa teneur en alcool se situe entre 7 à 9 % vol. Après la fermentation principale, commence la seconde fermentation de cinq semaines à une température entre 8 et 10 °C. La bière est ensuite filtrée et mise en bouteille avec une troisième fermentation pendant trois semaines (à 21 °C).

Blonde forte – une dénomination commune pour les bières 'virtuoses' qui excellent de par leur limpidité, leur faux col volumineux et leur haute teneur en alcool (7 à 11 % vol et plus). Elles se distinguent par l'utilisation de malts aromatiques, de levure estérifiée et de températures de fermentation et de maturation plus élevées. Après une maturation froide dans les cuves de garde, la bière est filtrée puis mise en bouteille avec du dextrose et un peu de levure. Ainsi une troisième fermentation s'effectue dans la bouteille lors du stockage en chambre chaude. Elle est entreposée ensuite pendant quelques mois dans un endroit froid afin qu'elle se stabilise. Il existe également des bières fortes doubles.

Bière de saison – bière d'été jaune orangée à bronze typique du Hainaut et du Brabant Wallon. Elle est brassée avec une haute teneur en sucres fermentescibles et subit une maturation chaude avec houblonnage à cru. Le caractère rugueux du houblon est compensé par les sucres non fermentescibles. Ces derniers peuvent permettre une nouvelle fermentation en bouteilles. Cette troisième fermentation apporte un caractère pétillant et fruité à cette bière d'été.

Bière brune flamande ou vieille brune – ce style de bière est originaire de la région d'Audenarde - Zottegem. Cette bière est légèrement sucrée voire lactique et a un goût subtil de noix. Elle provient d'un mélange de vieilles et jeunes bières qui arrivent ensemble à maturation dans les cuves de garde, et est dès lors le produit d'une fermentation mixte. Ce coupage garantit un goût constant et peut donner lieu à une fermentation secondaire. La teneur en alcool se situe entre 4 et 8,5 % vol.

Bières citadines ou régionales, vins d'orge et spécialités – bières portant la touche créative du brasseur : ajout d'épices spéciales, miel, chocolat, plusieurs grains crus ou moulus, de levures uniques. Elles ont souvent une teneur en alcool relativement élevée. Ce sont souvent des bières typiquement régionales et difficiles à cataloguer puisqu'elles sont tellement uniques et inégalées. Plusieurs bières sont fabriquées suivant le même procédé que le champagne : conditionnées en grotte de marne ou portées à maturation selon la méthode champenoise. Les bières brutes, également appelées bières de champagne, en sont un parfait exemple. Les levures de ces bières sont enlevées de la bouteille à l'aide de la méthode originale du remuage et du dégorgement.

Ale – à l'origine un type de bière anglaise / écossaise à fermentation haute. Il en existe deux variétés principales : Pale Ale et Mild Ale. Pale Ale est de couleur claire et fortement houblonnée ; Mild Ale a une couleur légèrement plus foncée et est moins houblonnée. La teneur en alcool des Ales se situe entre 4 et 6 % vol. En Belgique, diverses variétés de Ale sont également brassées. Elles possèdent toutefois un caractère totalement différent que les variétés anglaises (densité et teneur en gaz carbonique plus élevées vu que nous préférons les bières avec un joli faux col aux bières anglaises 'plate'). Les bières britanniques sont soit transportées en containers et mises en bouteilles en Belgique, soit brassées en Belgique sous licence avec un taux d'alcool et un goût adaptés au marché belge.

Scotch (ales) – sont devenues une spécialité du Brabant Wallon et du Hainaut (alors qu'on ne les retrouve presque plus dans leur pays d'origine). Des bières lourdes, fortes et foncées. Elles sont très maltées et possèdent un léger goût de brûlé. Leur saveur est sucrée grâce à l'ajout de sucre candi.

Stout – bière originale irlandaise. Foncée, crémeuse, sucrée et amère. Avec un goût corsé de brûlé ou grillé.

Bières fruitées – bières de fermentation haute auxquelles sont ajoutés des fruits, des jus ou des arômes de fruits. Certaines de ces bières sont sucrées artificiellement, d'autres sont artisanales ou biologiques à 100 %.

Bières hivernales ou de Noël – des bières qui sont brassées pour l'hiver ou pour les fêtes de fin d'année et qui contiennent des herbes (miel, cannelle, girofle et/ou réglisse). La plupart de ces bières sont des bières de dégustation maltées, de couleur ambrée ou foncée et ont un pourcentage d'alcool relativement élevé.

Fermentation spontanée

Lambic – une des plus vieilles bières (du début du Moyen-Âge) avec l'ajout de houblon suranné. Des micro-organismes dans l'air ambiant (entre novembre et mars) déclenchent la fermentation spontanée du moût. La bière mûrit des mois ou des années dans des fûts en chêne. C'est là que commence la fermentation secondaire avec *Brettanomyces Lambicus* et *Bruxellensis*. Elle donne au lambic son caractère sec et acide. Bière sans mousse.

Gueuze – un mélange de vieux lambic, non complètement fermenté avec du jeune lambic qui subit une nouvelle fermentation en bouteille (une bouteille de champagne qui résiste à la pression carbonique plus élevée). Voir également 'Définitions'.

Bière fruitée – des variétés de fruits (souvent des cerises) sont ajoutées au lambic lors du conditionnement. Leurs sucres vont entièrement fermenter et donner un goût fruité et non sucré. Pour les variétés aux framboises, pêches, etc. l'on utilise le plus souvent des jus de fruits.

Faro – lambic pur auquel on a ajouté du sucre candi, du sirop ou caramel. Parfois aussi, l'on coupe le lambic sucré avec une bière à fermentation haute.

Fermentation mixte

Bière brune-rouge – bière du Sud-Ouest des Flandres. A base de malts d'orge rougeâtre, de variétés de houblon relevées et moins amères et de levure rafraîchissante et acidulée avec des bactéries lactiques. Elle a un goût complexe et résulte du coupage d'une bière jeune avec une bière filtrée* qui a mûri en fûts de chêne (pendant 18 mois ou plus). Les tannins et micro-organismes présents dans le bois vont influer et former des esters fruités.

Bière de coupage – coupage / mélange de bières à fermentation spontanée, fermentation haute et fermentation basse.

L'approche du Beer Judge Certification Program (BJCP Styles) dans la catégorisation des styles de bières (belges) est avant tout technique et liée au produit, mais tient également compte de l'arôme, de la couleur, de l'aspect extérieur et de la sensation dans la bouche (voir www.bjcp.org). Les bières belges sont réparties en 2 catégories de bières ale qui contiennent à leur tour quelques sous-catégories. Comme certains brasseurs y reféfèrent, nous en donnons un bref inventaire :

Belgian & French Ale (bière blanche, Belgian Pale Ale, Saison, Bière de Garde, Belgian Specialty Ale).

Belgian Strong Ale (Belgian Blond Ale, Belgian Dubbel, Belgian Tripel, Belgian Golden Strong Ale, Belgian Dark Strong Ale).

D'autres catégories BJCP qui s'appliquent aux bières belges sont : Lager Bock, Ale ou Lager Fruit Beer, Lager Pilsner, Ale Stout, IPA (English, American ou Imperial Pale Ale) et Sour Ale. Dans cette dernière catégorie figurent les Flanders Red Ale, Flanders Brown Ale / Oud Bruin, Straight Lambic, Gueuze et Fruit Lambic.

Dans ce classement, les bières trappistes et les bières d'abbaye ne font pas fonction de style de bière, ni de catégorie. Elles sont plutôt considérées comme étant une espèce d''appellation contrôlée', une étiquette d'authenticité.

* Selon cette même définition, les bières brunes flamandes peuvent elles aussi être considérées comme étant des bières mixtes.

Definities & Belgische bierstijlen

Enkele definities

Bier – "de drank verkregen na alcoholische gisting van een wort hoofdzakelijk bereid uit zetmeel- en suikerhoudende grondstoffen, waarvan ten minste 60 % gerst- of tarwemout, alsmede hop, eventueel in verwerkte vorm en brouwwater." *(definitie volgens een Koninklijk Besluit van 1993)*

Geuze en lambiek (of combinatie) – de naam mag alleen worden gebruikt voor zure bieren waarin spontane gisting deel uitmaakt van het productieproces. De benamingen **'Oude Geuze'** en **'Oude Lambiek'** zijn Europees beschermd en staan voor de echte, traditionele specialiteiten die 100 % spontaan zijn gegist en langdurig gerijpt zijn op eikenhouten vaten.

Biologisch bier – bier waarbij exclusief gebruik wordt gemaakt van grondstoffen met biologisch certificaat die verwerkt worden zonder chemische toevoeging. De richtlijnen zijn vervat in een reglementering van de EEG van 1991. *(Verordening nr. 2092/91/EEG van de Raad van 24 juni 1991 inzake de biologische productiemethode en aanduidingen dienaangaande op landbouwproducten en levensmiddelen, laatst gewijzigd door verordening 1991/2006 van 21 december 2006)*

Belgische bierstijlen

Over bierstijlen, hun benaming, definiëring en indeling bestaan verschillende visies. 'Belgische Brouwers' hanteert een indeling waarbij de bierstijlen volgens gistingswijze worden onderverdeeld:

Lage gisting

Pils of lagerbier – ontstaan in 1842 in de Tsjechische stad Pilsen. Pils wordt gebrouwen met zacht water en een bleke mout (pilsmout). Het is rijk gehopt en het heeft een stevige en relatief lang blijvende schuimkraag. De originele bittere smaak is geëvolueerd naar een verfijnde hopbittere smaak. Het alcoholgehalte schommelt tussen de 4,5 en 5,2 vol %.

Tafelbier – bieren met een extractgehalte tussen 1 en 4 ° Plato en een alcoholgehalte tussen 0,8 en 2,5 vol % die vooral complexe suikers bevatten. Ze bestaan in neutrale tot bittere versies, in blond en tripel; zoete tafelbieren krijgen meestal de ondertitel bruin, faro, stout of bock mee.

Alcoholarm en alcoholvrij – dit bier wordt gebrouwen met een lagere densiteit en er worden minder gistcellen toegevoegd tijdens de gisting. **Alcoholarm / laag alcoholisch:** alcoholgehalte tussen 0,5 en 1,2 volumeprocent. **Alcoholvrij:** alcoholgehalte van maximum 0,5 volumeprocent.

Bock – vooral populair in Duitsland en aanvankelijk gebrouwen buiten de zomermaanden omdat het bier zonder koeltechniek moeilijk kon worden bewaard in de zomer. Minder gehopt dan pils maar wel hoger qua alcoholgehalte: 6,4 à 7,6 vol %.

Dortmunder of export – bierstijl afkomstig uit de regio Dortmund. Bleker, zachter en minder bitter dan pils. De densiteit en het alcoholgehalte (5,5 à 6 vol %) zijn hoger dan bij de pilsbieren. Ze worden gebrouwen met sulfaatrijk water dat veel zouten bevat.

Rauchbier – typisch lage-gistingsbier uit de regio Nürnberg-Bamberg in Duitsland. Het gerstemout wordt gedroogd boven een beukenhoutvuur waardoor het een typische verbrande en gerookte of geroosterde smaak krijgt. Meestal iets zoetig en amberkleurig tot zeer donker. Niet courant in België.

Hoge gisting

Amber of Speciale Belge – gelanceerd na de le Wereldoorlog als 'overwinningsbier in Engelse stijl'. De specifieke amberkleur ontstaat door het gebruik van kleur- of kara(mel)-mouten. De dichtheid en het alcoholgehalte zijn vergelijkbaar met die van pils hoewel de laatste jaren een aantal degustatiebieren zijn ontwikkeld die hogere alcoholgehaltes hebben (tussen 6 en 12 vol. %).

Witbier – Hoegaarden – en vooral Pierre Celis die in 1966 het typische tarwebier opnieuw is gaan brouwen – heeft een pioniersrol gespeeld bij de heropleving van de witbieren. Het beslag bestaat voor 30 % uit ongemoute tarwe waarbij soms haver wordt gemengd. Aan het wort worden tijdens het koken koriander en sinaasschillen (curaçao) toegevoegd, wat resulteert in de typische, verfrissende smaak. De witbieren worden doorgaans niet gefilterd en zijn licht troebel. Het alcoholgehalte is zoals bij pils, 4,5 à 5 vol %.

Trappistenbier – bier gebrouwen binnen de abdijmuren volgens de tradities van de trappisten – cisterciënzers (authenticiteitslogo). Bestaat in blond, dubbel / donker of tripelversie. Wereldwijd zijn er nog zeven brouwende trappistenabdijen, waarvan zes in België: Chimay, Orval, Rochefort, Westmalle, Westvleteren en Achel (op de grens met Nederland).

Abdijbier – verzamelnaam van bieren waarvan de merknaam verwijst naar een bestaande of verdwenen abdij. Abdijbier heeft dezelfde biertypes als de trappistbieren, hoewel de klemtoon iets meer op blond en tripel ligt.Om het licentielabel 'Erkend Belgisch Abdijbier' te dragen moet het bier dat na 12 augustus 1999 op de markt werd gebracht, voldoen aan volgende voorwaarden:

- **ofwel** wordt het bier gebrouwen in een bestaande niet – trappistenabdij (ofwel een bestaande abdij die onder haar verantwoordelijkheid en in licentie het bier laat brouwen in een lekenbrouwerij en het bier zelf mee commercialiseert),
- **ofwel** een bier dat gebrouwen wordt door een lekenbrouwerij die een juridische band heeft via contract met een bestaande abdij voor het gebruik van de naam. De commercialisatie gebeurt door de lekenbrouwerij,
- **en** er dienen royalties aan de betrokken abdij / orde betaald te worden waarmee de orde caritatieve doeleinden ondersteunt,
- **en** het bier moet gebaseerd zijn op historische achtergronden (de abdij in kwestie moet in het verleden ook bier gebrouwen hebben),
- **en** er is een controlerecht van de abdij op de publiciteit.

Blond – lichtblond tot goudkleurig bier van hoge gisting met een lichtmoutig en zoetig aroma en een vrij neutrale, lichtzoetige smaak. De nasmaak is eerder bitter. Alcoholpercentage tussen 5,5 en 7 vol %.

Dubbel of donker – oorspronkelijk een bier waarbij een dubbele hoeveelheid mout werd gebruikt, maar het is geëvolueerd naar een licht- of donkerbruin bier met zoetige smaak en bittere nasmaak. Aroma van rozijn, zoethout en kandij met een gebrande toets. Alcoholpercentage rond de 6 vol %.

Tripel – oorspronkelijk een bier waarbij meer dan een dubbele hoeveelheid mout werd gebruikt; nu staat het voor een goudkleurig bier met een moutige, alcoholische en soms lichtzoete smaak. Alcoholpercentage van 7 à 9 vol %. Na de hoofdgisting volgt een tweede gisting van 5 weken bij 8 à 10 °C. Daarna wordt het bier gefilterd en gebotteld met een hergisting op de fles van 3 weken (bij 21 °C).

Sterk blond – een verzamelnaam van zogenaamde virtuoze bieren die uitblinken door hun grote helderheid, hun volumineuze schuimkraag en hun hoger alcoholgehalte (7 à 11 vol % en meer). Ze onderscheiden zich door het gebruik van aromatische moutsoorten, esterachtige gisten, en hogere gistings- en rijpingstemperaturen. Na een koude rijping in lagertanks wordt het bier gefilterd en gebotteld met toevoeging van dextrose en een beetje gist. Daardoor ondergaat het een hergisting op de fles bij stockage in een warme kamer. Na deze derde gisting wordt het nog een aantal maanden opgeslagen in een koude ruimte om het te laten stabiliseren. Zoals sterk blond is er ook sterk dubbel.

Saisons – oranjegeel tot bronskleurig zomerbier dat typisch is voor Henegouwen en Waals-Brabant. Het wordt gebrouwen met een hoog gehalte aan vergistbare suikers en ondergaat een warme rijping met dry hopping. Het ruwe hopkarakter wordt gecompenseerd door de onvergiste suikers die de basis kunnen vormen voor een mogelijke hergisting op de fles. Deze hergisting draagt bij tot het sprankelende en fruitige karakter van dit typische zomerbier.

Vlaamse bruine bieren of oud bruin – deze bierstijl is afkomstig uit de regio Oudenaarde-Zottegem en staat voor licht zoetig-(melk)zurig bier met een subtiel nootachtig karakter. Het ontstaat door een vermenging van oud en jong bier gerijpt in lagertanks en is op die manier ook een soort 'gemengde gisting'. Deze versnijding garandeert een constante smaak en kan leiden tot een hergisting. Het alcoholgehalte ligt tussen de 4 en 8,5 vol %.

Stads - of streekbier, gerstewijnen en speciaalbier – bieren met een creatieve toets van de brouwer: toevoeging van aparte kruiden, honing, chocolade, verscheidene graansoorten in ruwe en gemoute vorm, unieke gisten. Zij hebben meestal een vrij hoog alcoholgehalte. Vaak zijn ze sterk regionaal verankerd en moeilijk catalogeerbaar omdat zij zo uniek en ongeëvenaard zijn.
Een aantal bieren zijn geïnspireerd op champagne: gelagerd in mergelgrotten of gerijpt volgens de champagnemethode. De Brutbieren, ook champagnebieren genoemd, waarbij de gist met 'remuage et dégorgement à la méthode originale' uit de fles wordt verwijderd, zijn hiervan een uitstekend voorbeeld.

Ale – van oorsprong een Engelse / Schotse biersoort van hoge gisting die zich onderscheidt in twee hoofdsoorten: Pale Ale en Mild Ale. Pale Ale is licht van kleur en sterk gehopt; Mild Ale is iets donkerder van kleur en minder gehopt. Het alcoholgehalte van Ales ligt tussen de 4 en 6 vol %. Ook in België worden diverse alesoorten gebrouwen maar die hebben een totaal ander karakter dan de Engelse soorten (hogere dichtheid en hoger koolzuurgehalte omdat wij nu eenmaal houden van bieren met een mooie schuimkraag in plaats van de 'platte' Engelse bieren). De Britse bieren worden ofwel in containers aangevoerd en daarna in België gebotteld, ofwel onder licentie in België gebrouwen met een alcoholgehalte en smaak die aangepast zijn aan de Belgische markt.

Scotch (ales) – uitgegroeid tot een specialiteit uit Waals - Brabant en Henegouwen (in hun vaderland zijn ze nog nauwelijks te vinden). Zware, sterke en donkere bieren die zeer moutig zijn, een licht gebrand karakter hebben en zoet smaken door de toevoeging van kandijsuiker.

Stout – origineel Iers bier. Donker, romig, zoetbitter met een sterk gebrand of geroosterd aroma.

Fruitbieren – bieren van hoge gisting waaraan fruit, fruitsappen en / of fruitaroma's worden toegevoegd. Sommige zijn artificieel aangezoet, andere zijn 100 % puur natuurlijk, artisanaal of biologisch.

Winter- of Kerstbier – bieren gemaakt voor de eindejaarsfeesten en de winter, met toevoeging van kruiden (honing, kaneel, kruidnagel, en/of zoethout). De meeste zijn moutige degustatiebieren, amber of donker gekleurd, met een relatief hoog alcoholgehalte. Er zijn ook winterbieren van lage gisting.

Spontane gisting

Lambiek – een van de oudste bieren (vroege middeleeuwen) met toevoeging van overjaarse hop. Micro-organismen uit de buitenlucht (tussen november en maart) starten de spontane gisting van het wort. Het bier rijpt maanden of jaren in eikenhouten tonnen waar de nagisting met de *Brettanomyces Lambicus* en *Bruxellensis* begint, waardoor de lambiek zijn droog-zurig karakter krijgt. Schuimloos bier.

Geuze – een mengeling van oude, nog niet volledig uitgegiste lambiek met jonge lambiek die een bijkomende gisting krijgt op de fles (een champagnefles die bestand is tegen verhoogde koolzuurdruk). Zie ook 'Definities' op p. 1178.

Fruitbier – fruitsoorten (meestal krieken) worden aan de lambiek toegevoegd tijdens de lagering, waardoor de vruchtensuikers vergisten en er een fruitige, niet-zoete smaak ontstaat. Voor variëteiten met framboos, perziken, enz. worden meestal vruchtensappen gebruikt.

Faro – zure lambiek met toevoeging van kandijsuiker, stroop of karamel. Soms ook versnijding van gezoete lambiek met hoge-gistingsbier.

Gemengde gisting

Roodbruin bier – bier uit Zuid-West-Vlaanderen, op basis van roodachtige gerstemouten, kruidige en minder bittere hopvariëteiten en frisse lichtzure gist met melkzuurbacteriën. Het heeft een complexe smaak en is een versnijding van jong bier met gefilterd bier * dat op eikenhouten vaten is gerijpt (18 maanden of langer). De tannine en micro-organismen in de vaten gaan inwerken op het bier waardoor fruitige esters ontstaan.

Versnijbier – versnijding/mengeling van bieren van spontane, hoge en lage gisting.

* Volgens deze definiëring kan ook Vlaams bruin als gemengd bier beschouwd worden.

- De invalshoek van The Beer Judge Certification Program (BJCP Styles) bij de definiëring van de (Belgische) bierstijlen is vooral product - technisch maar houdt ook rekening met het aroma, de kleur, het uitzicht en het mondgevoel (zie www.bjcp.org). De Belgische bieren worden hier ingedeeld in twee categorieën Ale-bieren die elk een aantal subcategorieën bevatten. Omdat een aantal brouwers eraan refereert, volgt hieronder een summiere opsomming:

  Belgian & French Ale – (met witbier, Belgian Pale Ale, Saison, Bière de Garde, Belgian Specialty Ale).

  Belgian Strong Ale – (met Belgian Blond Ale, Belgian Dubbel, Belgian Tripel, Belgian Golden Strong Ale, Belgian Dark Strong Ale).

  Andere categorieën bij BJCP styles die ook van toepassing zijn voor Belgische biersoorten zijn Lager Bock, Ale of Lager Fruit Beer, Lager Pilsner, Ale Stout, IPA (English, American of Imperial Pale Ale) en Sour Ale. Bij deze laatste groep horen de Flanders Red Ale, Flanders Brown Ale / Oud Bruin, Straight Lambic, Gueuze en Fruit Lambic.

Trappist en abdijbier zijn bij deze indeling niet aan de orde als bierstijl of categorie. Ze worden veeleer beschouwd als een soort 'appellation contrôlée' een authenticiteitslabel.

Belgian Breweries and their Beers
Les Brasseries belges et leurs Bières
De Belgische Brouwerijen en hun Bieren

A

Wittekerke Passion 1119
Wittekerke Rosé 1120
Wittekerke Wit Bier 1121

BELLEVAUX
Bellevaux (Brasserie de)
Bellevaux 5
4960 Malmedy
www.brasseriedebellevaux.be

Brasserie de Bellevaux Black 187
Brasserie de Bellevaux Blanche 188
Brasserie de Bellevaux Blonde 189
Brasserie de Bellevaux Brune 190

BINCHOISE
Brasserie La Binchoise
38, Faubourg Saint-Paul
7130 Binche
www.brasserielabinchoise.be

Bière des Ours 129
Bière Spéciale Belge 132
La Binchoise Blonde 596
La Binchoise Brune 597
La Binchoise Organic' Brune 598
La Binchoise Organic' Miel 599
La Binchoise Organic' Triple 600
La Binchoise Spéciale Noël 601
La Binchoise Triple 602
La Binchoise XO 603
Rose des Remparts 863

BLAUGIES
Brasserie de Blaugies
435, Rue de la Frontière
7370 Blaugies-Dour
www.brasseriedeblaugies.com

Bière Darbyste 123
La Moneuse 626
La Moneuse Spéciale Noël 627
Saison d'Epeautre 875

BOCKOR (VANDERGHINSTE)
Brouwerij Bockor
Kwabrugstraat 5
8510 Bellegem
www.bockor.be

Bellegems Bruin 111
Bellegems Wit 112
Bockor Blauw 163
Bockor Pils 164
Framboise Max Jacobins 402
Geuze Jacobins 419
Kriek Jacobins 582
Kriek Max Jacobins 586
Omer 760
Passion Max Jacobins 793
Rosé Max 864

BOELENS
Huisbrouwerij Boelens
Kerkstraat 7
9111 Belsele
www.brouwerijboelens.be

Bieken 122
Jezuwiet 528
Prinsesken - Meilses Eiërebezenbier 835
Santa Bee 886
Tripel Klok 1032
Waaslander 1092
Wase Wolf - Bier uit het Waasland 1093

BOON
Boon NV
Fonteinstraat 65
1502 Lembeek
www.boon.be

Duivels Bier 339
Faro Boon 369
Framboise Boon 399
Geuze Mariage Parfait 422
Kriek Boon 576
Kriek Mariage Parfait 585
Oude Geuze Boon 769
Oude Kriek Boon 776

BOSTEELS
Brouwerij Bosteels
Kerkstraat 92
9255 Buggenhout
www.bestbelgianspecialbeers.be

Deus, Brut des Flandres 325
Pauwel Kwak 802
Tripel Karmeliet 1031

BOTTERESSE
Brasserie Artisanale La Botteresse de Sur-les-Bois
Rue Fond Méan 6
4470 Saint-Georges

La Botteresse Ambrée 604
La Botteresse Bière de Noël 605
La Botteresse Blonde 606
La Botteresse Brune 607
La Botteresse Cérise 608

La Botteresse Miel 609
La Botteresse Pomme 610
Sur-les-Bois Ambrée 977
Sur-les-Bois Blonde 978
Sur-les-Bois Brune 979

BOUILLON
Brasserie de Bouillon
Rue de la Giraffe 76
6832 Sensenruth (Bouillon)
Grand'Rue 22
6830 Bouillon
www.brasseriedebouillon.be

Cuvée de Bouillon 278
Blanche de Bouillon 148
Jack'Ouille 521
La Bouillonnaise 611
La Chèvenis 613
La Médiévale Ambrée 624
La Noire Fontaine 628
La Spéciale Fête 642
La Vauban 648
Saison des Chasses Blonde 877

BROOTCOORENS-ERQUELINNES
Brasserie Brootcoorens
197, Rue de Maubeuge
6560 Erquelinnes
www.brasserie-brootcoorens-erquelinnes.be

Abbaye de la Thure 16
Angelus Blonde 48
Angelus Brune 49
Angelus Spéciale Noël 50
Belgian Angel Stout 99
La Sambresse Blonde 640

BRUNEHAUT
Brasserie de Brunehaut
17, Rue des Panneries
7623 Rongy-Brunehaut
www.brunehaut.com

Abbaye de Saint-Martin Blonde 17
Abbaye de Saint-Martin Brune 18
Abbaye de Saint-Martin Cuvée de Noël 19
Abbaye de Saint-Martin Triple 20
Bière du Mont Saint-Aubert 131
Brunehaut Bio Amber 201
Brunehaut Bio Blanche 202
Brunehaut Bio Blonde 203

C

CANTILLON
Brouwerij Cantillon
Rue Gheude straat 56
1070 Brussel
www.cantillon.be
Geuze Cantillon 100% Lambic 415
Grand Cru Bruocsella 449
Iris 518
Kriek Cantillon 100% Lambic 577
Lou Pepe 682
Mamouche 695
Rosé de Gambrinus 862
Saint-Lamvinus 866
Vigneronne 1076

CARACOLE
Brasserie Caracole
86, Côte Marie-Thérèse
5500 Falmignoul
www.brasserie-caracole.be

Caracole 229
Nostradamus 754
Saxo 895
Troublette 1039

CAULIER
Brasserie et Distillerie Caulier sprl
134, Rue Sondeville
7600 Peruwelz
www.brasseriecaulier.com

Bon Secours Ambrée 171
Bon Secours Blonde 172
Bon Secours Blonde de Noël 173
Bon Secours Brune 174
Bon Secours Framboise 175
Bon Secours Myrtille 176
Paix-dieu 783

CAZEAU
Brasserie de Cazeau
67, Rue de Cazeau
7520 Templeuve
www.brasseriedecazeau.be

Saison Cazeau aux Fleurs de Sureau 871
Tournay 1017
Tournay de Noël 1018
Tournay Noire 1019

CHIMAY
Brasserie de l'Abbaye N.D. de Scourmont
Route du Rond-Point 294
6464 Forges
www.chimay.be

G

GAVERHOPKE
Brouwerij 't Gaverhopke
Steenbrugstraat 187
8530 Stasegem-Harelbeke
www.tgaverhopke.be

Bitter Sweet Symphony 138
t Gaverhopke Blondje 982
t Gaverhopke Bruintje 983
t Gaverhopke den Twaalf 984
t Gaverhopke Kerstbier 985
t Gaverhopke Koerseklakske 986
t Gaverhopke Kriek 987
t Gaverhopke Paasbier 988
t Gaverhopke Zingende Blondine 989

GIGI
Brasserie Gigi
96, Grand'Rue
6769 Gérouville
www.brasseriegigi.eu

Gigi speciale 423

GIRARDIN
Brouwerij Girardin
Lindenbergstraat 10
1700 Sint-Ulriks-Kapelle
Faro Girardin 370
Framboise Girardin 400
Geuze Fond Girardin 416
Geuze gefilterd Girardin 418
Kriek Girardin 581
Ulricher Extra 1045

GRAIN D'ORGE
Brasserie Grain d'Orge
Rue Laschet 3
4852 Hombourg
www.grain-dorge.com

Brice 192
Canaille 224
Grelotte 452
Hervoise 488
Joup 530
3 Schténg 1141

GRUUT
Gruut Gentse Stadsbrouwerij bvba
Grote Huidevettershoek 10
9000 Gent
www.gruut.be

Gruut Amber 467
Gruut Blond 468
Gruut Bruin 469
Gruut Inferno 470
Gruut Wit 471

GULDEN SPOOR
Huisbrouwerij Het Gulden Spoor
Heulestraat 168
8560 Gullegem
www.brouwkot.be

Kalle 537
Manten 699
Netebuk 745
Robustus 850
Tineke van Heule 1008

Vlaskapelle 1088
Zeven Zonden Gula 1131
Zeven Zonden Luxuria 1132

H

HAACHT
Brouwerij Haacht
Provinciesteenweg 28
3190 Boortmeerbeek
www.primus.be

Adler 36
Eupener 360
Export 8 361
Gildenbier 424
Keizer Karel Goudblond 553
Keizer Karel Robijnrood 554
Mystic Krieken 736
Mystic Limoen 737
Mystic Perzik 738
Primus 834
Prior Tongerlo 836
Speciale 1900 928
Tongerlo Blond 1010
Tongerlo Bruin 1011
Tongerlo Winterbier 1012
White (by Mystic) 1104

HERBERG
Den Herberg
O. De Kerckhove d'Exaerdestraat 6
1501 Buizingen
www.denherberg.be

Den Herberg Amber 314
Den Herberg Blond 315
Den Herberg Bruin 316
Den Herberg Tarwe 317

HOFBROUWERIJKE
't Hofbrouwerijke
Hoogstraat 151
2580 Beerzel
www.thofbrouwerijke.be

t Baronneke	981
Bosprotter	184
Hof Korvatunturi	498
Hofblues	503
Hofdraak	504
Hofelf	505
Hofnar	506
Hoftrol	507
Ne Snoeper	741

HOF TEN DORMAAL
Caubergstraat 2
3150 Tildonk
www.hoftendormaal.com

Hof ten Dormaal Amber	499
Hof ten Dormaal Blond	500
Hof ten Dormaal Donker	501
Hof ten Dormaal Wit Goud, Witloofbier	502

HOPPERD
Brouwerij Den Hopperd
Netestraat 67
2235 Westmeerbeek

Kameleon Amber	538
Kameleon Donker	539
Kameleon Ginseng	540
Kameleon Tripel of Veller	541

HUYGHE
Brouwerij Huyghe
Geraardsbergsesteenweg 14B
9090 Melle
www.delirium.be

Artevelde	70
Artevelde Grand Cru	71
Bière du Corsaire Cuvée Spéciale	130
Blanche des Neiges	155
Campus	221
Campus Gold	222
Campus Premium	223
Delirium Christmas	306
Delirium Nocturnum	307
Delirium Red	308
Delirium Tremens	309
Floris Apple	384
Floris Chocolat	385
Floris Fraise	386
Floris Framboos	387
Floris Honey	388
Floris Kriek	389
Floris Mango	390
Floris Ninkeberry	391
Floris Passion	392
Floris Wit	393
La Guillotine	621
La Poiluchette Blonde Cuvée du Château	630
La Poiluchette Brune	631
Mongozo Banana	716
Mongozo Coconut	717
Mongozo Mango	718
Mongozo Palmnut	719
Mongozo Premium Pilsener	720
Mongozo Quinua	721
St-Idesbald Réserve Ten Duinen Blond	957
St-Idesbald Réserve Ten Duinen Dubbel	958
St-Idesbald Réserve Ten Duinen Rousse	959
St-Idesbald Réserve Ten Duinen Tripel	960
Villers Tripel	1077
Villers Vieille	1078

INBEV:ARTOIS/BELLE-VUE/HOEGAARDEN/JUPILER
SA Inbev Belgium NV
Vaartkom 31
3000 Leuven
www.inbev.com

Belle-Vue Extra Kriek	113
Belle-Vue Framboise	114
Belle-Vue Geuze	115
Belle-Vue Kriek	116
Hoegaarden Citron	492
Hoegaarden Grand Cru	493
Hoegaarden Rosée	494
Hoegaarden Speciale	495
Hoegaarden Verboden Vrucht	496
Hoegaarden Wit	497
Jupiler	534
Jupiler Blue	535
Jupiler Tauro	536
Leffe 9°	655
Leffe Blond	656
Leffe Bruin	657
Leffe Kerst	658
Leffe Lente	659
Leffe Radieuse	660
Leffe Ruby	661
Leffe Tripel	662
Stella Artois	952
Vieux Temps	1075

SAS
Brouwerij Het Sas (vroeger Leroy)
Diksmuidesesteenweg 406
8904 Boezinge

Blauwersbier 158
Bock Leroy 161
Bruin Leroy 200
Christmas Leroy 256
Crackpils 273
Katje Special 552
Kerelsbier 558
Paulus 800
Prima 833
Ridder 848
Sas Brune 889
Sas Export 890
Sas Pils 891
Sasbräu 892
Stout Leroy 962
Vlasbier 1087
West Pils 1098
Yperman 1128

SCHELDEBROUWERIJ
Scheldebrouwerij bvba
Wenenstraat 7
2321 Meer
www.scheldebrouwerij.be

Dulle Griet 340
Hop-ruiter 510
Lamme Goedzak 652
Mug 735
n Toeback 739
Oesterstout 758
Strandgaper 967
Wildebok 1107
Witheer 1113
Zeezuiper 1130

SENNE
Brasserie de la Senne/Zennebrouwerij
Steenweg op Gent 565
1080 Brussel
www.brasseriedelasenne.be

Crianza 274
Equinox 358
Jambe-de-Bois 523
Stouterik - The Brussels Stout 964
Taras Boulba 990
X-mas Zinnebier 1126
Zinnebir 1133

SILENRIEUX
Brasserie de Silenrieux
Rue Noupré 1
5630 Silenrieux

Autruche Bière des Gilles 83
Joseph 529
Kriek de Silenrieux 579
Le Pavé de l'Ours 654
Noël de Silenrieux 750
Sara Blond (Bio) 887
Sara Bruin 888

SILLY
Brasserie de Silly
2, Rue Ville Basse
7830 Silly
www.silly-beer.com

Abbaye de Forest 15
Double Enghien Blonde 332
Double Enghien Brune 333
Enghien Noël 357
La Cré Tonnerre 616
La Divine 617
Pink Killer 817
Saison Silly 882
Scotch Silly 898
Silly Pils 905
Silly Pils Bio 906
Super 64 973
Titje 1009

SINT-BERNARDUS
Brouwerij Sint-Bernardus
Trappistenweg 23
8978 Watou
www.sintbernardus.be

Grotten Flemish Ale 465
Grottenbier/Grotten Brown 466
St. Bernardus Abt 12 935
St. Bernardus Christmas Ale 936
St. Bernardus Pater 6 937
St. Bernardus Prior 8 938
St. Bernardus Tripel 939
St. Bernardus Witbier 940
Watou Tripel 1096

SINT CANARUS
Huisbrouwerij Sint Canarus
Polderweg 2
9800 Gottem
www.sintcanarus.be

Maeght van Gottem	687
Potteloereke	827
Sint Canarus Tripel	909

SINT-JOZEF

Brouwerij Sint-Jozef
Itterplein 19
3960 Opitter (Bree)
www.brouwerijsintjozef.be

Bokkereyer	168
Bosbier	182
Herkenrode Bruin	485
Herkenrode Tripel	486
Itters Bruin tafelbier	520
Kriekenbier	588
Limburgse Witte	677
Ops-Ale	762
Pax Pils	803
Sint Gummarus Dubbel	910
Sint Gummarus Tripel	911

SLAGHMUYLDER

Brouwerij Slaghmuylder
Denderhoutembaan 2
9400 Ninove
www.witkap.be

Slaghmuylder's Kerstbier	919
Slaghmuylder's Paasbier	920
Witkap - Dubbele Pater	1114
Witkap - Pater Special	1115
Witkap - Pater Stimulo	1116
Witkap - Pater Tripel	1117

SMISJE

Brouwerij 't Smisje (bvba Abron)
Driesleutelstraat 1
9700 Oudenaarde
www.smisje.be

Kerstsmiske	563
Smiske	922
Smiske Bruin	923

STRUBBE

Brouwerij Strubbe
Markt 1
8480 Ichtegem
www.brouwerij-strubbe.be

Couckelaerschen Doedel	271
Dikke Mathile	327
Houten kop	513
Ichtegem's Grand Cru	514
Ichtegem's Oud Bruin	515
IPA	517
Keyte	567
Keyte Oostendse Dobbel-Tripel	568
Kriekenbier	589
Strubbe Pils	969
Vlaskop Gerstebier	1089
Wittoen	1122

T

TIMMERMANS (GROUP JOHN MARTIN)

Brouwerij Timmermans
Kerkstraat 11
1701 Itterbeek
www.anthonymartin.be

Timmermans Framboise Lambic	997
Timmermans Kriek Lambic	998
Timmermans Oude Geuze	999
Timmermans Oude Kriek	1000
Timmermans Pêche	1001
Timmermans Strawberry Lambic	1002
Timmermans Tradition Faro	1003
Timmermans Tradition Gueuze Lambic	1004
Timmermans Tradition Kriek Retro	1005
Timmermans Tradition Lambicus Blanche	1006
Timmermans Warme Kriek	1007

TOETELER

Brouwerij Den Toetëlèr
Kleistraat 54
3730 Hoeselt
www.toeteler.be

Den Toetëlèr	319

TRIEST

Microbrouwerij Den Triest
Trieststraat 24
1880 Kapelle op den Bos
www.dentriest.be

Triest Blond	1025
Triest Dubbel	1026
Triest Kriek	1027
Triest Speciale	1028
Triest Tripel	1029
Triest X-mas	1030

TROIS FOURQUETS

Brasserie Les 3 Fourquets
Courtil 50
6670 Courtil-Gouvy
www.les3fourquets.be

Lupulus blonde 684

TUBIZE
Brasserie de Tubize
Rue de Bruxelles 109d
1480 Tubize
www.brasseriedetubize.com

Betchard Blonde 120
Betchard Brune 121
Blanche de Tubize 153
Boneffe 177

V

VAL DE SAMBRE
Brasserie Val de Sambre
273, Rue Emile Vandervelde
6534 Gozeé
www.valdesambre.be

Ada Blonde des Pères 6° 28
Ada Brune des Pères 6° 29
Ada Super Noël 9° 30
Ada Triple Blonde 8° 31
Ada Triple Brune 8° 32
Ada Val de Sambre 6° Ambrée 33
Blanche de Charleroi 151
La Chérie 612

VAL-DIEU
Brasserie de l'Abbaye du Val-Dieu
225, Val-Dieu
4880 Aubel
www.val-dieu.com

Val-Dieu Bière de Noël 1056
Val-Dieu Blonde 1057
Val-Dieu Brune 1058
Val-Dieu Grand Cru 1059
Val-Dieu Triple 1060

VAN DEN BOSSCHE
Brouwerij Van den Bossche
Sint-Lievensplein 16
9550 Sint-Lievens-Esse
www.brouwerijvandenbossche.be

Buffalo 1907 207
Buffalo Belgian Stout 208
Buffalo Bitter 209
Kerstpater 562
Lamoral degmont 653
Livinus 679
Pater Lieven Blond 795
Pater Lieven Bruin 796
Pater Lieven Tripel 797
Pater Lieven Wit 798

VAN EECKE
Brouwerij Van Eecke
Douvieweg 2
8978 Watou
www.brouwerijvaneecke.be

Kapittel Blond 542
Kapittel Dubbel 543
Kapittel Pater 544
Kapittel Prior 545
Kapittel Tripel Abt 546
Poperings Hommelbier 823
Tremist 1024
Watou's Wit Bier 1097

VAN HONSEBROUCK
Brouwerij Van Honsebrouck
Oostrozebekestraat 43
8770 Ingelmunster
www.vanhonsebrouck.be
www.kasteelbier.be

Bacchus 84
Bacchus Framboos 85
Bacchus Kriek 86
Brigand 193
Cuvée du Château 283
Geuze Fond Tradition 417
Geuze Lambic St Louis 420
Kasteel Blond 548
Kasteel Bruin 549
Kasteel Rouge 550
Kasteel Tripel 551
Kriek Lambic St Louis 583
Premium Cassis St Louis 828
Premium Faro St Louis 829
Premium Framboise St Louis 830
Premium Kriek St Louis 831
Premium Pêche St Louis 832

VAN STEENBERGE/BIOS
Brouwerij Van Steenberge/Bios
Lindenlaan 25
9940 Ertvelde
www.vansteenberge.be

Augustijn Blond 75
Augustijn Donker 76
Augustijn Grand Cru 77
Bornem Dubbel 179
Bornem Tripel 180

Celis White 237
Gulden Draak 473
Leute Bokbier 671
Piraat 817

VAPEUR
Brasserie à Vapeur
1, rue du Maréchal
7904 Pipaix-Leuze
www.vapeur.com

Saison de Pipaix 874
Vapeur Cochonne - Cochonnette 1065
Vapeur en Folie 1066

VERHAEGHE
Brouwerij Verhaeghe
Sint-Dierikserf 1
8570 Vichte
www.brouwerijverhaeghe.be

Barbe d'Or - Goudbaard 90
Barbe Rouge - Roodbaard 91
Cambrinus 220
Christmas Verhaeghe 257
Duchesse de Bourgogne 338
Echt Kriekenbier 345
Verhaeghe Pils 1069
Vichtenaar 1074

VISSENAKEN
Brouwerij Vissenaken
Metselstraat 74
3300 Vissenaken-Tienen
www.brouwerijvissenaken.net

De Nacht 304
Fasso Blond 372
Himelein 491

W

WALRAVE
Brouwerij Walrave
Lepelstraat 36
9270 Laarne

Pils Pick-up Natuurbier 815
Toverhekske 1021

WESTMALLE
Brouwerij van de Abdij der Trappisten
Antwerpsesteenweg 496
2390 Westmalle
www.trappistwestmalle.be

Westmalle Trappist Dubbel 1099
Westmalle Trappist Tripel 1100

WESTVLETEREN
Brouwerij der Sint-Sixtusabdij
Donkerstraat 12
8640 Westvleteren
www.sintsixtus.be

Westvleteren 12 1101
Westvleteren 8 1102
Westvleteren Blond 1103

WIEZE
Brouwerij Wieze
Schrovestraat 70
9080 Wieze
www.wiezebier.be

Wieze Tripel Blond 1105
Wieze Tripel Zoet Bruin 1106

WILDEREN
Brouwerij en Alcoholstokerij Wilderen
Wilderenlaan 8
3803 Wilderen
www.brouwerijwilderen.be

Wilderen Goud 1108
Wilderen Tripel Kanunnik 1109

Belgian Brew Firms and their Beers
Les Locataires de Brasserie et leurs Bières
De Brouwerijhuurders en hun Bieren

A

ALTERNATIEF

Brouwerij Het Alternatief
Meensesteenweg 65
8870 Izegem
www.brouwerijhetalternatief.be

Ambetanterik	47
Bittere Waarheid	139
Den Alternatief	310
Eerwaarde Pater	346
Hik Blond	489
Hik Bruin	490
Piet-Agoras	812
Tatsevoet	991

BELGO

Belgobeer
Faubourg Saint-Paul 38
7130 Binche
www.belgoobeer.com

Belgoo Arboo	103
Belgoo Luppoo	104
Belgoo Magus	105

B

BGV

B.G.V. sprl
Rue Stocus 64c
5351 Haillot
www.forestinne.be

Forestinne Ambrosia	394
Forestinne Gothika	395
Forestinne Mysteria	396
Forestinne Nordika	397
Forestinne Primoria	398

BROUWERS VERZET

Grote Leiestraat 117
8570 Anzegem
www.brouwersverzet.be

Rebel Local	841

D

DE COCK

De Cock Meesterbrouwers
Potterstraat 10
9170 Sint-Pauwels
www.brouwerijdecock.com

Sinpalsken Blond	907
Sinpalsken Donker	908

DE LEYERTH

De Leyerth bvba
Krommekeerstraat 21B
8755 Ruiselede
www.urthel.com

Saisonnière	885
Urthel Hop-it	1054
Urthel Samaranth	1055

DRUIDE

Brouwerij Druïde VOF
Pikkelstraat 37
8540 Deerlijk
www.druide.be

Druïde Blond	334
Druïde Bruin	335
Druide Grand Q	336

E

EBLY

Brasserie d'Ebly
Rue Champs Claire 70
6860 Ebly

Belgian Beer Firms and their Beers
Les Sociétés Brassicoles et leurs Bières
De Bierfirma's en hun Bieren

Carnavalsbier 231
Den Zytholoog 321
Irma 519
Koantjesbier 571
Nen Kerstbal 743
Paasei 782

VERSTRAETE
Grote Dijk 13
8600 Diksmuide

Papegaei 792

VIVEN
Beerdevelopment Viven
Stationsstraat 87A
8340 Sijsele
www.viven.be

Viven Ale 1079
Viven Blond 1080
Viven Bruin 1081
Viven Imperial IPA 1082
Viven Porter 1083

VLAANDEREN
Van Vlaanderen bvba
Elzendreef 19
2970 Schilde
www.vlaamscheleeuw.com

Vlaamsche Leeuw Blondje 1084
Vlaamsche Leeuw Donker 1085
Vlaamsche Leeuw Tripel 1086

Gueuze Blenders and their Beers
Les Coupeurs de Gueuze et leurs Bières
De Geuzestekerijen en hun Bieren

D

DE CAM
Dorpsstraat 67A
1755 Gooik
www.decam.be

DRIE FONTEINEN
Hoogstraat 2a
1650 Beersel
www.3fonteinen.be

H

HANSSENS
Vroenenbosstraat 15
1653 Dworp

O

OUD BEERSEL
Brouwerij-Geuzestekerij Oud Beersel bvba
Laarheidestraat 230
1650 Beersel
www.oudbeersel.com

T

TILQUIN
Gueuzerie Tilquin SA
Chaussée Maïeur Habils 110
1430 Bierghes
www.gueuzerietilquin.be

Index

C

D

E

F

G

H

I

J

K

P

Q

R

S

ONCEPT

ak Van Damme

XT AND EDITING

lde Deweer

IOTOGRAPHY

oup Van Damme, Oostkamp

IGLISH AND FRENCH TRANSLATION

AL-AD-VISIE, Brugge

YOUT

w.groupvandamme.eu

PRINTING

www.pureprint.be

PUBLISHED BY

Stichting Kunstboek

Legeweg 165

B – 8020 Oostkamp

T. +32 (0) 50 46 19 10

F. +32 (0) 50 49 19 18

info@stichtingkunstboek.com

www.stichtingkunstboek.com

THANKS TO

Filip Geerts, www.belgianbeerboard.com

for his interesting tips and for checking the information.

All Belgian brewers, Brew Firms, Beer Firms & Geuze Blenders.

3N 978-90-5856-377-4
R: 448
2011/6407/25

stichting kunstboek

Jupiler
HAPKIN
ANNO 1877
Corsendonk
Agnus
BIOS
BROUWERIJ
PETRUS
FORT
DES TRAPPISTES
8
Affligem
Dubbel-Double
Kwak
Anno 1791
BLONDE
Extra
KRIEK
1883
MARTENS
PILS
GROTTENBIER
BRUGGE
Blond
St. Bernardus
6
Urthel
SUPERIOR SPECIAL ALE
SINCE 2000
ABBAYE
Tripel
Affligem
GRIMBERGEN